Handbook of Research on Corporate Restructuring and Globalization

Antonio Carrizo Moreira
University of Aveiro, Portugal

Pedro Silva
University of Aveiro, Portugal

A volume in the Advances in Business Strategy and Competitive Advantage (ABSCA) Book Series

IGI Global
DISSEMINATOR OF KNOWLEDGE

Published in the United States of America by
IGI Global
Business Science Reference (an imprint of IGI Global)
701 E. Chocolate Avenue
Hershey PA, USA 17033
Tel: 717-533-8845
Fax: 717-533-8661
E-mail: cust@igi-global.com
Web site: http://www.igi-global.com

Library of Congress Cataloging-in-Publication Data

Names: Moreira, Antonio Carrizo, editor. | Silva, Pedro, 1982- editor.
Title: Handbook of research on corporate restructuring and globalization / Antonio Carrizo Moreira and Pedro Silva, editors.
Description: Hershey, PA : Business Science Reference, [2019]
Identifiers: LCCN 2018061674| ISBN 9781522589068 (hardcover) | ISBN 9781522589075 (ebook)
Subjects: LCSH: Corporate reorganizations. | Consolidation and merger of corporations. | International business enterprises.
Classification: LCC HD58.8 .H3615 2019 | DDC 658.1/6--dc23 LC record available at https://lccn.loc.gov/2018061674

This book is published in the IGI Global book series Advances in Business Strategy and Competitive Advantage (ABSCA) (ISSN: 2327-3429; eISSN: 2327-3437)

British Cataloguing in Publication Data
A Cataloguing in Publication record for this book is available from the British Library.

All work contributed to this book is new, previously-unpublished material. The views expressed in this book are those of the authors, but not necessarily of the publisher.

For electronic access to this publication, please contact: eresources@igi-global.com.

Advances in Business Strategy and Competitive Advantage (ABSCA) Book Series

Patricia Ordóñez de Pablos
Universidad de Oviedo, Spain

ISSN:2327-3429
EISSN:2327-3437

Mission

Business entities are constantly seeking new ways through which to gain advantage over their competitors and strengthen their position within the business environment. With competition at an all-time high due to technological advancements allowing for competition on a global scale, firms continue to seek new ways through which to improve and strengthen their business processes, procedures, and profitability.

The **Advances in Business Strategy and Competitive Advantage (ABSCA) Book Series** is a timely series responding to the high demand for state-of-the-art research on how business strategies are created, implemented and re-designed to meet the demands of globalized competitive markets. With a focus on local and global challenges, business opportunities and the needs of society, the **ABSCA** encourages scientific discourse on doing business and managing information technologies for the creation of sustainable competitive advantage.

Coverage

- Strategic alliances
- Customer-Orientation Strategy
- Business Models
- Cost Leadership Strategy
- Joint Ventures
- Innovation Strategy
- Outsourcing
- Core Competencies
- Foreign Investment Decision Process
- Tacit Knowledge

The Advances in Business Strategy and Competitive Advantage (ABSCA) Book Series (ISSN 2327-3429) is published by IGI Global, 701 E. Chocolate Avenue, Hershey, PA 17033-1240, USA, www.igi-global.com. This series is composed of titles available for purchase individually; each title is edited to be contextually exclusive from any other title within the series. For pricing and ordering information please visit http://www.igi-global.com/book-series/advances-business-strategy-competitive-advantage/73672. Postmaster: Send all address changes to above address.

Titles in this Series

For a list of additional titles in this series, please visit: www.igi-global.com/book-series

Innovation and Social Capital in Organizational Ecosystems
Brychan Celfyn Thomas (University of South Wales, UK) and Lyndon John Murphy (Cardiff Metropolitan University, UK)
Business Science Reference • copyright 2019 • 341pp • H/C (ISBN: 9781522577218) • US $225.00 (our price)

Cases on Corporate Social Responsibility and Contemporary Issues in Organizations
Alexandros Antonaras (University of Nicosia, Cyprus) and Paraskevi Dekoulou (University of Nicosia, Cyprus)
Business Science Reference • copyright 2019 • 402pp • H/C (ISBN: 9781522577157) • US $225.00 (our price)

Women Entrepreneurs and Strategic Decision Making in the Global Economy
Florica Tomos (University of South Wales, UK) Naresh Kumar (Universiti Malaysia Kelantan, Malaysia) Nick Clifton (Cardiff Metropolitan University, UK) and Denis Hyams-Ssekasi (University of Bolton, UK)
Business Science Reference • copyright 2019 • 411pp • H/C (ISBN: 9781522574798) • US $215.00 (our price)

Linking Cultural Dimensions and CSR Communication Emerging Research and Opportunities
Maria Palazzo (University of Salerno, Italy)
Business Science Reference • copyright 2019 • 169pp • H/C (ISBN: 9781522579465) • US $165.00 (our price)

Evidence-Based Initiatives for Organizational Change and Development
Robert G. Hamlin (University of Wolverhampton, UK) Andrea D. Ellinger (The University of Texas at Tyler, USA) and Jenni Jones (University of Wolverhampton, UK)
Business Science Reference • copyright 2019 • 749pp • H/C (ISBN: 9781522561552) • US $495.00 (our price)

Environmental, Health, and Business Opportunities in the New Meat Alternatives Market
Diana Bogueva (Curtin University, Australia) Dora Marinova (Curtin University, Australia) Talia Raphaely (Curtin University, Australia) and Kurt Schmidinger (University of Vienna, Austria)
Business Science Reference • copyright 2019 • 395pp • H/C (ISBN: 9781522573500) • US $225.00 (our price)

Handbook of Research on Business Models in Modern Competitive Scenarios
George Leal Jamil (Informações em Rede e Consultoria Ltda., Brazil) Liliane Carvalho Jamil (Independent Researcher, Brazil) Cláudio Roberto Magalhães Pessoa (FUMEC University, Brazil) and Werner Silveira (Philharmonic Orchestra of Minas Gerais, Brazil)
Business Science Reference • copyright 2019 • 537pp • H/C (ISBN: 9781522572657) • US $295.00 (our price)

IGI Global
DISSEMINATOR OF KNOWLEDGE

701 East Chocolate Avenue, Hershey, PA 17033, USA
Tel: 717-533-8845 x100 • Fax: 717-533-8661
E-Mail: cust@igi-global.com • www.igi-global.com

List of Contributors

Table of Contents

Section 2
De-Internationalization, Offshoring, Backshoring, Nearshoring, Reshoring

Section 3
Internal and External Outcomes of Globalization

Detailed Table of Contents

Restructuring and globalization are very important for every technology sector. It provides key competitive advantages to the companies over their rivals. Telecommunications sector is an important strategic segment of the modern economy. Telecommunications is also an advanced technology sector and its restructuring is essential to optimize its revenues. Now it has been evolved to information and communication technologies (ICT), which is the main driving force of growth worldwide. In fact, ICT has paved the way for modern globalization. Overall, ICT and ICT-enabled sectors are among the main contributors of global economy. This sector has passed through several restructuring and evolves continuously. Its globalization is obvious as it is the main technology which promotes globalization. In this chapter, the authors provide the restructuring of telecommunications sectors since the time of its inception in the early 19th century. They also analyzed the strategic changes that promote the restructuring and globalization of this sector.

A single economic space is created by the conditions of globalization, where corporations become the main economic actors. In this circumstance, the issues of corporate governance, especially the prevention and resolution of corporate conflicts, require the closest attention. In this chapter, the authors will try to answer the question of the possible economic consequences of major corporate conflicts and assess the degree of potential impact on the parameters of company activity: in the first part of the research, key financial indicators, credit ratings capitalization; in the second part of the research, the global economy, investment and economic growth, the dynamics of financial markets, investment climate, capital flows, etc.

Mergers and acquisitions (M&As) are recognized as one of the most popular corporate strategies in recent years. Unlike its popularity, the success rate of mergers and acquisitions is surprisingly low. There are many reasons for failure, but among all, culture integration has emerged as one of the major barriers to an effective merger and acquisition deal. This chapter highlights the fundamentals of this topic with literature review and presents practical and effective guidelines for facilitating cultural integration in merger and acquisition process effectively and efficiently and achieving greater results from the organizational change efforts.

that already have a process of de-internationalization. Five firms cooperate with, presenting six cases. The authors distinguish causes that occur before/after the internationalization process begin and causes related to firm or external to firm. One of the main causes of de-internationalization is the incorrect internationalization process. The Misfit Micro-Location (the wrong choice of place inside a determined country) is a very important cause, which means that, after choosing the country, it is necessary to choose the best place to be located.

The economic reasons that dictated offshoring for countries such as China are vanishing. Customers are increasingly demanding and more informed about the origin and methods of production of the products they buy, and governments are realizing the impact of manufacturing. This new reality is encouraging many companies to relocate their activities and, in some stances, returning manufacturing processes back to their home countries. This rather recent process, known as reshoring poses challenges of all kind with managerial implications in logistics, marketing, strategy, finances, commercial strategy, innovation, and human resources management. Reshoring antecedents are fundamental concepts for the understanding of the sources that may conduct those activities back home. This chapter takes one step in this direction and proposes a comprehensive model of the antecedents of reshoring that can be applied to a specific industry or sector. In particular, the authors examine the important role of economic, marketing, and social/political antecedents.

The main topic of this investigation is the outsourcing of IT services and subsequent analysis of the delivery method based on proximity, examining whether the work would be delivered through a nearshoring model or via an offshoring one. The main goal is therefore to determine the antecedents of the "attitude towards outsourcing," as well as their consequences. The statistical analysis, based on a sample of 88 respondents, shows that the factors that may influence the "attitude towards outsourcing" are strategy, service suppliers, and supplier trust. As a consequence, we have behavioral intention when dealing with a nearshoring vs. offshoring scenario. The study of the details behind the type of the outsourcing options, either nearshoring or offshoring, an individual within an organization is more willing/likely to use, based on behavioral intention, is the main innovative aspect of this research. As per the results of this study, the above was also considered as a valid consequent to the existing models and has shown to be a relevant construct in this context.

The authors address the importance of the operation of manufacturing networks in order to explain why a company brings its previously offshored facilities back. Fundamentally, this chapter stresses the relevance of network operations in the context of relocation, and hence, the linkage of network-manufacturing capabilities to the reshoring phenomenon. First, it focuses on investigating the relevance of strategic objective of international manufacturing to the management/network operations of international manufacturing network (IMN). Second, it explores the role of strategic capabilities of network-manufacturing on the phenomenon of reshoring. The empirical foundation of this research builds on data from multiple in-depth interviews at companies' headquarters in Spain and Sweden. The results showed the relevance of strategic capabilities of network-manufacturing to reshoring. The authors also provide the guidance for decision making in the operation of international manufacturing.

This chapter analyzes whether US outward foreign direct investment contributes to mitigating environmental degradation in host countries or not. This relationship is investigated within the environmental Kuznets curve framework, using dynamic panel data models which include trade openness and environmental regulation as controlling variables. The results lend support to the existence of an environmental Kuznets curve hypothesis. Moreover, the results indicate that capital expenditures from majority-owned foreign affiliates of US multinationals decrease carbon dioxide emissions per capita and provide support for the pollution halo hypothesis. The findings suggest that foreign direct investments carried out by firms with their headquarters based in the United States of America enhance the natural environment. These findings offer some support for host government policies offering generous financial incentives to attract environmentally friendly investments to improve environmental sustainability.

The purpose of this chapter is to analyze the influence of absorptive capabilities on export performance. The author uses a quantitative research approach by conducting a study based on a survey data from 247 Portuguese small and medium-sized enterprises (SMEs) from the textile industry. Findings suggest that absorptive capabilities have a positive and significant influence on export performance. This chapter

the SCM startups assisted in operational area of the SCM where they carried out operational activities and decision making. BMC analysis revealed that startups were asset light and resources held by these startups were the financial funding which the firm secured through venture capitalists and software development teams.

Preface

INTRODUCTION

Actively managing a business portfolio and align it with the business environment is a crucial element of corporate strategy. With the development of the globalization, the increasing role of the financial markets and the growing of international competition, there was an increase in the number of corporate restructuring activities among companies, in general, and of public listed companies, in particular.

Because of this new institutional environment, many American companies engaged in corporate restructuring activities in the 1980s and the 1990s. Existing studies highlight how corporate portfolio management remains an important topic in the strategic agenda of large multinational corporations and that many companies restructure their portfolios in order to adapt and prepare for the upcoming challenges of the future.

One of the objectives of corporate restructuring is shareholder value maximization. However, corporate restructuring is a multifaceted concept comprising organizational, financial and portfolio restructuring.

Organizational restructuring and the reorganization of the company are changes to the organizational structure of firms such as divisional redesign and employment downsizing with the purpose of increasing employees' satisfaction and improve the efficiencies and communication. They require good planning, good preparation in advance to support new organizational goals. Financial restructuring are changes to the capital structure of companies such as leveraged buyouts or leveraged capitalizations with an emphasis on cash flow and on changes in managerial incentives. Finally, portfolio restructuring are changes in the mix of assets including liquidations, divestments seeking to improve the strategic focus, build economies of scale and an efficient management of multiple business units.

With the globalization of the business world, restructuring activities are common place. For example, new business units are added, downsized or offshored. As such, positive or negative impacts of those changes need to be considered. Moreover, as international activities have important consequences in the business world, sectoral changes may occur with important implications for business and other stakeholders alike. As a result, at individual level, companies need to be aware of contextual changes in order to restructure their businesses to deploy best practices and to adapt to new, more challenging business environments.

Restructuring activities may involve different challenges to companies. Some of the main strategies involve:

- Mapping out where the company is and where is heading in the future. This involves deploying a clear strategy where the company is and where it needs to be; a new mission statement and communicating to employees; and a clear perspective of future business portfolio.
- Defining new roles and responsibilities for the business units. This includes the definition of the new changes; the definition of new business acquisitions; the definition of what business units will be closed down; making explicit what businesses are going to be offshored. These new roles need to be based on how differentiated the company needs to be from competitors and how competitive it wants to be. For that, companies need to realign, restructure and reorganize to become more competitive.

This book provides the theoretical structure and some of the latest empirical research in the field of corporate restructuring and globalization being organized into the following sections:

Section 1: Restructuring at a sectorial level and outcomes of restructuring
Section 2: De-internationalization, offshoring, backshoring, nearshoring, reshoring
Section 3: Internal and external outcomes of globalization

These three sections cover a broad set of topics on corporate restructuring and globalization. The first section, "Restructuring at the Level and Outcomes of Restructuring", includes a group of sectoral studies on: the restructuring in the banking industry, the evolution of the restructuring of both the banking and the telecommunications industries. These three chapters embrace a mesoeconomic perspective to restructuring as they deal with, on one hand, how strategic groups in the banking industry managed to deploy their strategies over time and, on the other hand, how restructuring occurred in the financial system and in the telecommunications industry.

This section is complemented by studies about: the consequences of corporate conflicts in the worlds' major economies and involving the major players in world markets; and the measures taken to restructure and turnaround two organizations that went through difficult times in Colombia; and finally a study about cultural integration in Mergers and Acquisitions (M&As) that cover pre- and post-M&A activities that facilitate and support all stakeholders throughout the M&A process.

The second section, "De-Internationalization, Offshoring, Backshoring, Nearshoring, Reshoring", deals with some of the consequences of restructuring as is de-internationalization, or the de-commitment to international operations due to international failure, among others, with an emphasis on small and medium-sized enterprises (SMEs). This section comprises a set of studies dealing with de-internationalization that is a specific understudied aspect of the internationalization process, which addresses restructuring strategies. It is complemented with some studies on offshoring/reshoring and relocation, which is an increasing phenomenon in international business. Although offshoring was initially assumed to increase firms' performance, evidence from the field highlights the difficulties that offshoring create on supply chain management, and organizational restructuring, and how often offshoring activities do not increase firms' performance. These aspects make companies re-think their international strategies and bring back their offshored activities to nearby countries or to the country of origin.

This section is composed of five chapters. The first two chapters deal with the intricacies of de-internationalization of SMEs, their causes and consequences, and how those companies deal with those intricate situations. The following two chapters address offshoring, reshoring and relocation activities and how companies managed to deal with those difficult strategies to compete in international manufacturing networks.

Finally, the third section, "Internal and External Outcomes of globalization", analyzes the outcomes of globalization for economies and firms such as the greenhouse gas spillovers of foreign direct investment (FDI) and the importance of export performance and of intangible resources on SMEs' competitiveness and international performance. The first chapter of this section explores how foreign direct investment impacts greenhouse emissions among US companies. The remaining of the section depicts four chapters dealing with SMEs deploying their activities in international markets, exploring both the resource-based view and the dynamic capabilities of the firms.

In the following paragraphs, the structure of the book is further detailed regarding its sections and chapters.

SECTION 1: RESTRUCTURING AT A SECTORIAL LEVEL AND OUTCOMES OF RESTRUCTURING

Chapter 1, "Strategic Groups in the Portuguese Banking Industry: An Analysis of the 2008-2010 Period", written by Albérico Rosário, Antonio Moreira and Pedro Macedo analyzes the behavior of the retail banking industry in Portugal for the period between 2008 and 2010. The data was collected through the accounting consultation of the reports and accounts of the years 2008, 2009 and 2010, which was a period under heavy economic and financial crisis in Portugal. The results suggest that the retail banking in Portugal has clear differences among players over time as banking institutions reacted with different competitive strategies to the contextual environment that placed a heavy financial burden to all banking institutions in Portugal.

Chapter 2, "The Restructuring of the Financial System in the 21st Century", by Elisabeth Pereira, presents a macro analysis of the process of restructuring of the financial system in the main developed economies such as in Europe and the United States since the 1990s and with an emphasis on the 21st century. From the review of the literature, it can be concluded that the restructuring of the financial system has been influenced by three main factors: the internationalization of the financial markets and its repercussions; the financial innovations; and the regulation of the financial system and its problems.

Chapter 3, "Restructuring and Globalization of Telecommunications Industry", by Sasmita Mohanty, analyzes how the telecommunications industry, one of the main driving forces of growth worldwide, evolved over time. The chapter reviews the technological restructuring, the policy/regulation-oriented restructuring, the economic restructuring and the emergent restructuring in the telecommunications industry and depicts the development of the sector from 1950s onwards. The chapter concludes with the future outlook of this industry.

Chapter 4, "Economic Consequences of Corporate Conflicts", by Mikhail Kuznetsov, Maria Nikishova, Valeria Solovyova, and Konstantin Lukoyanov, examines the features, magnitude of consequences and the conditions to minimize economic damages caused by large corporate conflicts in worlds' major economies such as the United States, Europe and Russia. After analyzing the major conflicts in the last fifteen years, which include examples of large companies such as Volkswagen, Parmalat, or Enron, the authors conclude that corporate conflicts were found to have specific features contingent on the business environment. Corporate conflicts have negative consequences such as market stagnation or economic damage and the main lines of defense against these phenomena include a of strong corporate governance and a reliable judicial system that inspires confidence among all parties involved.

Chapter 5, "Cultural Integration in Mergers and Acquisitions", by Asli Goksoy, highlights the fundamentals of culture integration as a main barrier to successful Merger and Acquisition (M&As) deals. A review of the literature presents the practical and effective guidelines for facilitating cultural integration in M&As processes in order to effectively and efficiently achieve successful organizational changes. For a cultural integration to occur in M&As, it is important not only to recognize the need for a cultural integration in pre-M&A phases, but also, to carry out a culture due diligence process to deploy a cultural integration is the post M&A phase. An internal communication strategy can be carried out to support integration and confidence among employees throughout the restructuration process.

Chapter 6, "Reactivation or Collapse: How Difficult Situations Affect the Organizational Life and Success", by José Mendoza-Guerra, examines two Colombian organizations that suffered a severe drop in performance and were in a difficult situation, identifying the strategies applied to maintain those organizations alive. The chapter highlights the importance of turnarounds strategies for introducing a profound and radical change for correcting situations influencing firms' performance and competitiveness. Crises were found to stem from internal and external sources, but internal sources are easier to solve than the external ones, particularly when the environmental threat comes from increasing competition. While turnaround strategies are often presented in two following stages, contraction and recovery, the analysis underlines the existence of an intermediate moment where both strategies coexist simultaneously.

SECTION 2: DE-INTERNATIONALIZATION, OFFSHORING, BACKSHORING, NEARSHORING, RESHORING

Chapter 7, "De-Internationalization of SMEs: A Case Study", by Antonio Moreira, Pedro Silva, Hugo Gadim and Jorge Mota, presents the results of a case study of a Portuguese SME that de-internationalized from the Moroccan market. A review of the literature is presented on some of the most used internationalization theories and on the causes and main frameworks used to explain the process of de-internationalization. One of the relevant factors found was the SME lack of preparation and knowledge on the challenges of internationalizing using a Greenfield investment. The results of the case study highlight the role of factors such as the lack of knowledge about the target market, the choice of the appropriate mode of entry and existing cultural asymmetries when internationalizing, and of legal issues on the process of de-internationalizing.

Chapter 8, "Causes of De-Internationalization: Evidence of Six Cases", by Raquel Menezes and Helder Pinho, analyzes the cause of de-internationalization based on six case studies. Using grounded theory, two different situations/causes are identified, those that occur before/after the internationalization process begin, and those related to the firm or external to the firm. The chapter concludes that there are two main causes of de-internationalization: one related to and consequence of the incorrect internationalization process; and the other labelled as micro-location misfit related to the wrong choice of place inside the country where the firm internationalized to. The results highlight that firms not only need to choose carefully the mode of entry in international markets, but also to pay close attention to the best place to be located to serve those foreign markets.

Chapter 9, "Proposing an Integrative Model for Reshoring Antecedents", by Joel Vaz, Ana Soares, José Pinho and Susana Costa e Silva, deals with the topic of reshoring, that is, the offshoring of production processes back to the country of origin. After clarifying the overlapping concepts in the field, such as onshoring, backshoring, reshoring, reverse shoring and nearshoring, the main reasons behind reshoring activities are reviewed and an integrative framework proposed that include economic, marketing, and political/social motivations for reshoring activities.

Chapter 10, "The Attitudes Towards Nearshoring vs. Offshoring on the IT Services Industry", by Miguel Pranto and Arnaldo Coelho, analyzes the attitudes of nearshoring versus offshoring activities when outsourcing Information and Technology (IT) services. The chapter determines both the antecedents and consequents of the attitude towards outsourcing. Based on the theory of reasoned action and a questionnaire survey answered by 88 key respondents from companies in the IT industry, the strategy, service suppliers, and supplier trust were found to be the main antecedents of the attitudes towards outsourcing. The consequents include the behavioral intention when dealing with a nearshoring versus offshoring scenario. The conclusions support that outsourcing options are strongly influenced by individuals' behavioral intentions, either in nearshoring or offshoring strategies.

Chapter 11, "The Relationship Between the Relocation and Operation of Global Firms", by Ahmed Sayem, Miguel Ortega-Mier and Andreas Feldmann address the importance of manufacturing operation networks to explain why companies bring back their previously offshored facilities. After reviewing the literature on reshoring from a manufacturing strategy perspective and building on data from in-depth interviews at companies' headquarters in Spain and Sweden, the results emphasize the importance of the strategic capabilities of network-manufacturing reshoring, presenting directions for the decision-making in operating international manufacturing networks.

SECTION 3: INTERNAL AND EXTERNAL OUTCOMES OF GLOBALIZATION

Chapter 12, "Outward US Foreign Direct Investment and Environmental Degradation", by João Bento, Miguel Torres and Paolo Maranzano, examines the impact of FDI on greenhouse gas emissions. On one hand, the pollution haven theory argues that multinationals set up production abroad in the search for cheaper resources at the costs of environmental unfriendly practices. On the other hand, the pollution halo theory supports the notion that FDI spillovers provide host countries with technology that mitigate greenhouse gas emissions. The results of the study support that FDIs contribute to decrease the environmental degradation, highlighting the importance of the United States outwards investment for host economies all over the world.

Chapter 13, "Export Performance: Exploring the Linkage With Absorptive Capabilities", by Orlando Rua, analyzes the link between absorptive capabilities, a two-dimensional construct comprising potential absorptive capabilities and realized absorptive capabilities, and the export performance of the firms. Resorting to survey data from 247 Portuguese SMEs, the findings support that absorptive capabilities have an impact on export performance, showing that the analyzed firms were able to acquire, assimilate and transform new dynamic capabilities, stressing the importance for firms to assess which strategic determinants generate a competitive advantage.

Chapter 14, "Serendipitous Network Internationalization: A Case Study in the ICT Services Sector", by Daniel Polónia and Adriana Miranda, deals with a specific case of internationalization of a service provider company from the Information and Communications Technology (ICT) industry. The chapter explores how a company's internationalization efforts were based on the anticipation of an internal market shock and on the leveraging of serendipitous network connections. The chapter analyzes how the company muddles through to explore overseas markets in low psychic distant markets with very relevant business impact and financial results, highlighting the challenges of SMEs in which market selection scenarios are put down to deploy future perspectives for the company.

Chapter 15, "Linking Intangible Resources and Competitive Advantage", by Orlando Rua, examines the relationship between textile SMEs' intangible resources and two competitive advantages, cost leadership and differentiation. SMEs play an important role in European countries and face distinct challenges than large firms such as lesser tangible resources. Using a quantitative approach and survey data from 247 Portuguese SMEs, the results highlight how intangible resources positively impact both competitive advantages, presenting further evidence for the importance of strategy for small and medium-sized enterprises managers.

Chapter 16, "Supply Chain Startups in India: A Cross Case Comparative Analysis", by Som Bhattacharyya and Apurva Shrey, discusses the importance of supply chain management for firms and the role that supply chain management startups play in the Indian context. Resorting to three models, supply chain driver, supply chain operations reference model and business model canvas, ten Indian startups were analyzed using a cross-case analysis, highlighting that the focus of supply chain management startups are mostly on improving the efficiency and increasing the responsiveness of the supply chain.

As a result of a tremendous effort from all the authors involved in the preparation of the chapters, it is exiting to witness the added value of all the chapters that contribute to the common topic of the book: Corporate Restructuring and Globalization. Moreover, there is a clear complementarity among the chapters of this book.

Corporate Restructuring and Globalization is still an open road as many challenges still lay ahead. We sincerely hope the readers find it very pleased to read Corporate Restructuring and Globalization and that the compilation of chapters hitherto presented are of added value and insightful. Last but not the least, we would like to thank all the authors for their effort in contributing to this book.

Antonio Carrizo Moreira
University of Aveiro, Portugal

Pedro Silva
University of Aveiro, Portugal

Section 1

Restructuring at a Sectorial Level and Outcomes of Restructuring

Chapter 1
Strategic Groups in the Portuguese Banking Industry:
An Analysis of the 2008-2010 Period

Albérico Travassos Rosário
University of Aveiro, Portugal

Antonio Carrizo Moreira
https://orcid.org/0000-0002-6613-8796
University of Aveiro, Portugal

Pedro Macedo
University of Aveiro, Portugal

ABSTRACT

This chapter analyzes the retail banking behavior in Portugal for the period between 2008 and 2010. The data collection took place through the accounting consultation of the reports and accounts of the years under analysis. The selected variables reflect the strategic actions of retail banking during the period under analysis, and it can be argued that retail banking in Portugal has clear differences among players over time. In particular, banking institutions have different competitive strategies, the strategic groups do not have similar resources, and strategies also differ between strategic groups. This reflects the competitive structure of the national retail banking industry.

INTRODUCTION

The organizations of the banking industry have a relevant position in the economy, playing a fundamental and determinant role in economic growth. They are the financial intermediaries between the State, firms, and consumers.

DOI: 10.4018/978-1-5225-8906-8.ch001

In the last 20 years, banking has undergone deep changes that influence strategic business options and significantly shape the future of banking organizations. Within the banking industry it is possible to identify banks that follow similar strategies that can be grouped in several strategic groups (e.g., Amel & Rhoades, 1988; Fiegenbaum & Thomas, 1990; Scannell et al., 2003; Staake et al., 2012; Tsai et al., 2011).

The study of strategic groups (SGs) is based on the foundations of strategic management (Chen & Miller, 2012; Hatten & Hatten 1987; Hervás, Dalmau, & Albors 2006). A strategic group can be defined as a set of companies employing similar strategies within an industry (Porter, 1979), although results and motivations of those companies may differ (Chen & Miller, 2012; Cool & Schendel 1987).

Research on SGs has analyzed several industries, addressing the relationships, rivalry, competitive dynamics and strategic decisions between companies within the strategic group and/or between SGs (e.g., Claver-Cortés et al., 2006; Leask & Parker 2007; Parnell, 2011; Pätäri et al., 2011) as well as the performance and stability differences over time among SGs (e.g., Martins et al., 2010; Más-Ruíz & Sala, 1992; Reger & Huff, 1993). There is also research exploring the similarities between the theory of strategic groups and the resource-based view (e.g., Leask & Parnell, 2005; Martins et al. 2010; Mehra, 1996), and, lastly, research addressing SGs as a strategic tool for the planning and implementation of competitive strategies (e.g., Ebbes et al., 2010).

The studies interpret how strategies influence SGs in a particular industry, evidencing the existence of a certain degree of homogeneity between companies in a same SG and of heterogeneity between SGs (Cool & Dierickx, 1993; Cool & Schendel, 1987; 1988; Zúñiga-Vicente et al., 2004a).

Although there are several studies addressing SGs in the banking industry (Lozano-Vivas & Pastor 2010; Más-Ruíz, 1999; Más-Ruíz et al., 2005; Más-Ruíz & Ruíz-Moreno, 2011; Más-Ruíz et al., 2014; Maudos & Pastor, 2003; Zúñiga-Vicente et al., 2004a; Zúñiga-Vicente et al., 2004b), there is none on the Portuguese banking industry. As such, the main aim of this chapter is to address how SGs are formed in the Portuguese banking industry between the years 2008, 2009 and 2010, which is a period in which the Economic and Financial Assistance Program (FEAP) was implemented in Portugal with serious consequences for the banking industry in Portugal.

The chapter is organized in seven sections. The first section presents the introduction of the chapter. In the second section, strategic groups and the schools of thought behind them are presented. The third section discusses the classification of strategic groups, including strategic groups in the banking industry. The methodological approach, the data and the results are presented in the three following sections. Finally, some concluding remarks are given in the seventh section.

STRATEGIC GROUPS

Strategic Groups and Schools of Thought

An industry can be seen as a combination of clusters, or groups of companies, that follow a similar strategy in accordance with some decision-making variables.

Literature on SGs appeared for the first time during the 1970s, with the identification of significant differences in the characteristics of several companies, although some of those companies followed similar strategies (Hunt, 1972). Several researchers have studied the existence of SGs in various industrial sectors (e.g. Day et al, 1999; Claver et al., 2003; Cool & Schendel, 1987; Finch et al., 2013; Flavián et al., 2002; Mascarenhas & Aaker, 1989; Mayor et al., 2012; McGee & Thomas, 1986; Porter, 1979; 1980;

Tang & Thomas, 1992; Vachani, 1997) determining their formation and influence within the industry (e.g., Claver et al., 2003; Claver-Cortés et al., 2009; Cool & Schendel, 1987; Finch et al., 2013; Kalaf & Bomtempo, 1999; Mayor et al., 2012; Pätäri et al., 2011).

The study of SGs is seen as an analytical instrument for the study of the existing competition in an industry that fosters the implementation of business strategies, being of great importance to the analysis of the competitiveness of companies (Smith et al., 1997).

There are two points of view in the study of SGs: the industrial organization (e.g., Caves & Porter, 1977; Hunt, 1972; Newman, 1978; Oster, 1982; Porter, 1973; 1979) and the strategic management (e.g. Cool, 1985; Hatten, 1974; Patton, 1976). Both strategic thoughts are based on the reference model of the industry analysis.

The point of view of the industrial organization school is focused on a study perspective that takes company size, number of participants of an industry, and degree of vertical integration into account. The main principle of the strategic management school is based on the study of company performance as a way of justifying its existence.

Industrial Organization School

The industrial organization's perspective has taken into account company size (e.g. Más-Ruíz, Ruíz, & Martínez, 2014; Más-Ruiz, Ruiz-Conde, & Calderón-Martínez, 2018; Más-Ruíz & Ruíz-Moreno, 2011; Nicolau-Gonzálbez & Ruiz-Moreno, 2014; Porter, 1973; 1979; Ruíz-Moreno et al., 2010), number of participants in the industry (e.g., Oster, 1982; Porter, 1976), degree of vertical integration (e.g., Mascarenhas 1989; McGee & Thomas, 1986; Newman, 1978) and market positioning (e.g. Hahn & Powers, 2010; Martins et al., 2010; Ramakrishnan, 2010).

The concept of "mobility barriers" between the strategic groups is the basis for the theory of industrial organization. These barriers are an obstacle to companies involved in a specific strategic group (Caves & Porter, 1977; Mascarenhas & Aaker, 1989; Porter, 1980).

SGs are structures separated by mobility barriers and with different strategies. Leask (2004) argues that SGs are stable "structures" separated by mobility barriers, segmenting different corporate groups with different strategies. The performance homogeneity within a strategic group is explained by the "mobility barriers" undertaken by firms from the same strategic group. Such strategic homogeneity within the same group limits the access of other firms to the group, thereby reducing the risk of strategic imitation. Thus, SGs are protected from competition arising from firms outside their group, and act in a way that prevents mobility between SGs. The mobility obstacles depend on the entry cost of a strategic group, i.e. the investment that is necessary in order to overcome the entry barriers of a specific strategic group.

Reger and Huff (1993) question, on one hand, the existence of mobility barriers within the same group, and, on the other hand, whether or not firms within a group are developing a new market niche. They suggest that company strategy is less similar to group strategy the further the positioning of the company is from the core of the group. They concluded that it is possible that mobility barriers and resource heterogeneity exist amongst companies of the same strategic group.

Empirical research regarding SGs from the banking industry has focused on the analysis of performance, analyzing the existence of significant performance differences between SGs over time (e.g. Zúñiga et al., 2004a). Performance differences are the result of: strategic positioning (Cano & Oliva, 2008); asymmetrical rivalry within and between SGs (Más-Ruíz & Ruíz-Moreno, 2011; Más-Ruíz et al., 2014); resource composition (Mehra, 1996); market power, efficiency, and differentiation (Más-Ruíz &

Ruíz-Moreno, 2011); technological innovation and productivity (Epure et al., 2011); and lastly, of the mobility between SGs (Flores-Márquez et al., 2015).

The Strategic Management School

The strategic management school argues that SGs are an analytical tool that groups firms with identical or similar strategies, allowing their comparison. Research focuses on firms from the same industry and their competitive patterns, based on the use of relevant strategic variables as a way of identifying the more relevant SGs of an industry (e.g., Altuntas et al., 2016; Cool, 1985; Cool & Schendel, 1987; Dess & Davis, 1984; Dikmen et al., 2009; Gary & Wood, 2011; Hatten, 1974; Patton, 1976; Oster, 1982; Hatten & Hatten, 1987; Kabanoff & Brown, 2008; Kale & Arditi, 2003; Mascarenhas & Aaker, 1989; Nair & Kotha, 2001; Nicolau-Gonzálbez & Ruiz-Moreno, 2014; Porac et al., 2011; Rhee & Mehra 2006; Schreyögg & Von Reitzenstein, 2008).

A study regarding the American brewing industry revealed the existence of differences that are not due to company size or the number of participants involved in an industry.

For the strategic management school, there are significant differences between SGs. In turn, firms belonging to a strategic group display homogenous and usually stable behaviors over time. Since they follow similar strategies, they compete heavily with each other, which, consequently, makes the study of SGs of great importance to the analysis of the competitive rivalry among companies (Smith et al., 1997).

The main criticism to the SG theory is focused on methodology (Barney & Hoskisson, 1990; Cool & Dierickx, 1993; Ferguson & Ketchen, 1999; Ketchen & Shook, 1996; Leask, 2004; Leask & Parker, 2007), namely regarding its statistical significance and the lack of reliability provided by the results obtained. In turn, Barney and Hoskisson (1990) argue that it has not been proven that a company strategy is determined as a result of the strategic group that it belongs to.

There have been attempts within the banking sector to identify strategic dimensions and to analyze the performance between SGs and within the same strategic group, establishing behavioral links and performance analyses (Tywoniak et al., 2007), as well as the influence of geographical coverage in performance (Márquez & Gutiérrez, 2012).

SGs can be considered a group of organizations or firms from the same industry that follow similar strategies, objectives, characteristics, and market assumptions. In short, the SGs' analysis presents the following characteristics:

- Heavy reliance on the analyst, since they establish the variables that shape SGs;
- Summary of a large volume of information, making it easier to understand the industry and the groups, although losing the individual features of the firm or organization;
- Are largely based on the supply side, with variables that are difficult to obtain.

CLASSIFICATION OF STRATEGIC GROUPS

Empirical research shows that the study of strategic groups is vast and diverse. Several researchers have tried to organize it, contributing with different points of view.

Hatten and Hatten (1987) followed the method of number of used variables, dividing the research into bivariate and multivariate systems. Depending on the theoretical reference, Cool and Schendel (1987) make the distinction between economic research of the industrial organization perspective and of the strategic management view. On the other hand, while Thomas and Venkatraman (1988) used variables on the dual approach rule for the formation of groups, Jegers (1989) established a structure for assessment based on four elements (way of measuring groups; use of data and variables; relationship of groups and industries; and analysis unit – group and/or firm).

Lastly, Reger and Huff (1993) made the distinction between variables arising from theory and variables arising from perceptions of strategists, believing that such perceptions reflect the competitive strategies used by companies.

Studies in the financial area can be divided into two main research areas, taking the financial and the capital investment structures into account.

In this regard, studies that consider the financial structure have the following variables: (i) the use of external financing (Dess & Davis, 1984); (ii) current liquidity (Fiegenbaum & Thomas, 1990); (iii) quick ratio (Sudharshan et al., 1991); (iv) debt-to-equity ratio (Baird et al., 1988); and (v) financial leverage (Fiegenbaum & Thomas, 1990). Studies that consider capital investment structure use, among others: (i) investment diversity (Amel & Rhoades, 1988); (ii) asset profile (Amel & Rhoades, 1988); and, lastly, (iii) new capital investments (Lawless & Tegarden, 1991).

Table 1 empirically classifies strategic groups, taking into account the research criteria and characteristics.

Within the bivariate research, the researcher determines the formation of strategic groups based on predetermined factors, such as company size and pattern of integration. Thus, the formation of strategic groups can be based on criteria determined by researchers, without resorting to statistical methods, with the intention of being used in the production of charts or graphics making the analysis of strategic groups easier. However, the use of a single variable may not reflect the different strategic choices (Amel & Rhoades, 1988).

On the other hand, the multivariate classification uses a set of strategic variables, which are selected based on the knowledge that the researcher has of the industrial sector, using advanced statistical techniques for variable reduction (e.g. factor analysis). This leads to a (possibly) consistent and stable number of groups, allowing for the analysis of the strategies undertaken by firms of the strategic groups.

The cluster analysis is the most frequent technique for the formation of strategic groups, and is usually applied to the original variables or to key strategic dimensions. This method allows us to identify the limits and distances between strategic groups based on the average of the variables, estimating the amount of mobility barriers that exist in strategic groups.

Cool and Schendel (1987) have a different approach for the classification of empirical studies on strategic groups based on two theoretical perspectives: the industrial organization and the strategic management. The main difference of the proposed classification is related to the research target.

The theory of industrial organization uses the concept of strategic groups to prove the heterogeneity between groups and explain competitiveness among them. From a strategic management point of view, the concept of strategic groups does not only seek to demonstrate heterogeneity, but also the existence of similar strategic choices, thus identifying ways to minimize threats and identify competitive opportunities. However, strategic management focuses on the determining factors of the results from firms in an individual manner, limiting research to a specific sector. The main critical area regarding the research is based on the industrial organization theory, noting that results cannot be generalized since they use many variables derived from the concept of business strategy (Cool & Schendel, 1987).

Table 1. Empirical classification of strategic groups

<table>
<tr><th>Criteria</th><th colspan="3">Research Characteristics</th></tr>
<tr><td rowspan="3"></td><td colspan="2">Bivariate classification.</td><td>Based on criteria determined a priori by researchers, not using statistical methods.</td></tr>
<tr><td colspan="2">Multivariate classification.</td><td>Groupings based on direct methodologies (cluster, factor analysis); groupings based on indirect methodologies (combined cluster and factor analysis); multidimensional scaling; logit models; game theory.</td></tr>
<tr><td colspan="3">Industrial organization.
Strategic management.</td></tr>
<tr><td rowspan="8">Inductive approach and deductive approach.</td><td>A priori.</td><td colspan="2">One or few strategic dimensions.</td></tr>
<tr><td rowspan="7">A posteriori.</td><td rowspan="5">With few dimensions.</td><td>To choose a particular industry;</td></tr>
<tr><td>To identify a set of strategic dimensions;</td></tr>
<tr><td>To obtain data related to it;</td></tr>
<tr><td>To use a data reduction technique (e.g., factor analysis);</td></tr>
<tr><td>To analyze the groups regarding the dimensions used.</td></tr>
<tr><td>With many dimensions.</td><td>To confirm the results empirically.</td></tr>
<tr><td>Strategic dimensions.</td><td>With many groups.</td></tr>
<tr><td>Way to measure groups;</td><td colspan="3">Direct and indirect.</td></tr>
<tr><td>Use of data and variables;</td><td colspan="3">Define groups, classify industries and research.</td></tr>
<tr><td>Relation of groups and industries;</td><td colspan="3">One industry, several industries, a posteriori selection of industries.</td></tr>
<tr><td>Unit of analysis;</td><td colspan="3">Differences between groups, industries and companies.</td></tr>
<tr><td rowspan="3">Level of analysis;</td><td colspan="3">Groups, companies and industry.</td></tr>
<tr><td colspan="3">Strategic dimensions proposed by the researcher.</td></tr>
<tr><td colspan="3">Strategic dimensions perceived by managers.</td></tr>
<tr><td rowspan="2">Financial approach.</td><td colspan="2">Financial structure.</td><td>External financing; current liquidity; quick ratio; debt-to-equity ratio; financial leverage.</td></tr>
<tr><td colspan="2">Capital investment structure.</td><td>Diversity of investment; asset profile; new capital investments.</td></tr>
</table>

Source: own elaboration.

Thomas and Venkatraman (1988) propose an approach based on two principles: the specification of the company strategy and the approach for the development of strategic groups.

The approach for strategy specification explains how the researcher establishes the SGs. Thus, the "explanatory power" of the strategic group concept depends on the validity of the scheme that has been implemented in order to specify the firm's strategy. In this context, there are two options to explain strategy, one of which focuses on a few dimensions, being based on functional areas, and the other one using several dimensions to characterize the functional areas of the organization, creating a multidimensional vision of the strategy.

Jegers (1989) proposes the use of five relationship criteria. The first one connects the way that measurements are made in strategic groups, which can be direct, using strategic discriminating variables, and indirect. The second one uses strategic variables, classifying the studied industry based on its strategic homogeneity or heterogeneity. The third one addresses the relation between groups and the industry, separating studies that form strategic groups of an industry and those of several industries, whose approaches are governed by the statistically significant differences between groups, between industries, and between firms.

Reger and Huff (1993) propose a classification of the empirical research on strategic groups based on two points of view: the first, from the executives' perspective, who identify and suggest points of view regarding the dimensions that describe the firm's strategies, and which can be classified as strategic dimensions acknowledged by the managers. The second uses a set of dimensions and variables provided by researchers, and which can be classified as strategic dimensions proposed by the researcher.

Reger and Huff's (1993) line of research is based on the perceptions from executives, managers, or strategists, where they carry out judgments regarding the similarity of strategies of the competition in what concerns their previous history in order to later identify strategic groups. In this regard, the cognitive research of strategic groups is based on the perceptions from firm executives in a specific line of business.

Empirical studies show that the cluster analysis is usually implemented through accounting variables of the balance sheet, as a percentage of total assets. Many empirical studies found significant performance differences between strategic groups (e.g., Altuntas et al., 2016; Cool & Schendel, 1987; Dess & Davis, 1984; Dikmen et al., 2009; Hatten, 1974; Hatten & Hatten, 1987; Huang et al., 2017; Kale & Arditi, 2003; Mascarenhas & Aaker, 1989; Nair & Kotha, 2001; Oster, 1982; Schreyögg & Reitzenstein, 2008).

The establishment of the strategic groups can be carried out through several data sources. Said groups can be classified in accordance with the used criteria, number of used variables, research characteristics, and theoretical framework.

Strategic Groups in the Banking Industry

SGs have been subject to scrutiny in the banking industry. Although Ramsler (1982), Hayes et al. (1983), Passmore (1985), and Azofra and Fuente (1987) carried out the first researches on SGs within the banking industry, Amel and Rhoaes (1988) are the main influencers in that field of research.

Ramsler (1982) studied the 100 largest non-American banks by analyzing product differentiation within the market, size, and geographical scope. In turn, Hayes et al. (1983) look into investment banking by analyzing the connection between the characteristics of the investment bank and the characteristics of individual customers, with variables of customers and banking features. Passmore (1985) and Azofra and Fuente (1987) used financial data from banking in their proposals for the analysis of the sector, whilst Passmore (1985) analyzes a period between 1976 and 1983 using several financial ratios as variables.

Azofra and Fuente (1987) studied 21 banks listed in the stock exchange from 1975 to 1985, resorting to four variables: (i) activity; (ii) expansion; (iii) technological dimension; and (iv) profitability. These first studies focused on the traditional analysis of intra-group homogeneity, and heterogeneity between groups.

The stability of the SGs of the American banking industry was studied for eight years, using fifteen large balance sheet accounts as statistical variables in the group formation analysis. The chosen variables reflect the ownership structure and strategic choices undertaken by directors taking into account the characteristics of consumers, products, and risks. By comparing the averages obtained in each variable from each group, it was concluded that banks had similar targets, regardless (i) of their size; (ii) of the cities where they were located; and (iii) of the different laws in force for each US state. Consumer loans are irrelevant, contrary to the dominant view concerning the selection of the main strategy, claiming that banks are oriented towards the banking consumer. The six identified SGs were considered stable over time, since 70% of banks remained in the same strategic groups during the analyzed periods (Amel & Rhoaes, 1988).

Amel and Rhoaes's (1988) main contribution was the subjective definition of periods of stability, using a cross-section analysis with accounting data of three different years: 1978, 1981 and 1984.

Spanish banking institutions were widely studied (Espitia et al., 1991; Martínez, 1992; Más-Ruíz & Sala, 1992, 1993), although innovation and geographical scope received little attention for the identification of SGs.

The implications associated with product/market and the geographical scopes of Spanish banking institutions from 1983 to 1985 were analyzed by Espitia et al. (1991). In turn, Más-Ruíz and Sala (1992) analyze the expansion of Spanish banking institutions from 1986 to 1989 taking into account the growth in the number of subsidiaries. Martínez (1992) studies the expansion of Spanish banking institutions between 1986 and 1990, also analyzing the cost leadership strategy and the business structure. Más-Ruíz and Sala (1993) also carry out a study on Spanish banking institutions from 1986 to 1989, analyzing the geographical aspects and taking into account their significant presences due to the growth in the number of subsidiaries.

The studies of Reger and Huff (1993) provide an innovative perspective by cognitively analyzing and mapping the individual actions of managers as a result of the external perceptions of reality, thereby creating models and mental representations of markets, competitive environment, competition, and strategic grouping. In that sense, perceptions and beliefs are influenced by available information and the interactions of agents, either as cooperation or competition in the industrial banking sector (Reger & Huff, 1993).

The cognitive school is the foundation for this approach. The principles of psychology look at the analysis of mental processes of business executives or managers based on bounded rationality, arguing that managers develop cognitive maps in decision-making (Bougon, 1983) so as to represent and provide a description of the interpretation in different fields of knowledge, encompassing competitive rivalry.

The cognitive identity of SGs by managers shows consistency regarding performance within the group and a heterogeneous performance between SGs of the American banking industry, during the 1982–1985 period when the 18 largest banks in Chicago were analyzed (Reger & Huff, 1993).

Reger and Huff's (1993) research found that managers of an industry who are part of a specific group perceive the characteristics of companies of the group; however, the mental maps of strategists tend to ignore the conflicting data that is obtained over time regarding environmental changes (Reger & Huff 1993). They reject the explanation that the formed groups are artifactual results of a simple grouping technique, supporting the vision shared amongst strategists.

The main advantage provided by the research of Reger and Huff (1993) was the identification of SGs using an environment simplification cognitive process, through the analysis of, and the interactions with, other competitors. If it is clear that managers of an industry understand SGs, by sharing perceptions on perceived characteristics of the firms, it is necessary to take into consideration that some firms do not follow clear and consistent strategies, changing strategies as events unfold. Consequently, there may be firms without specific strategic positioning inside a group. Additionally, it is not always possible to assign a group to a firm or a firm to a group.

The study of competitive patterns in the US banking industry compares SGs, based on resources and SGs, analyzing rivalry and performance to explain variations of inter-firm performance, determining that the differentiation translates into high heterogeneity.

Companies that follow seemingly different market strategies may have strategic interdependences. Thus, the company can analytically identify its potential rivals, by mapping SGs (Mehra, 1996).

Major regional differences were found in the financial system through the analysis of the strategic positioning of Spanish savings banks using financial data. The empirical research uses an exploratory data analysis to obtain SGs, with a proposal for the combination of an unsupervised neural network, the Self-Organizing Feature Maps (SOFM), with a cluster analysis. This made it possible to find major regional differences in the Spanish financial system and, with a bivariate analysis of the financial ratios, describes the differing aspects of savings banks from different Spanish regions (Serrano-Cinca, 1998).

Research carried out regarding the Spanish banking industry between 1984 and 1991, with a sample composed of twenty-four banks and subdivided into four stable periods, shows that the structure of SGs changes over the years in what concerns number, composition and strategy, thereby granting a dynamic perspective to SGs (Más-Ruíz, 1999).

Based on a concern between financial analysts and policy makers on the high degree of cost dispersion in the banking sector, Tortosa-Ausina (2002) analyzes whether dispersion and specialization factors can influence the dynamic of financial and operating costs of the Spanish banking services. It shows that there is no decrease in the degree of cost dispersion, although the relative position of firms may change.

The most recent studies on SGs redirect their research to the study of internal structure of the groups through the analysis of the complexity of the knowledge structure belonging to a strategic group, composed by the best management teams of the companies and through the assessment of the relationship between complexity of said knowledge structures and firm performance. With a sample of the 76 best banking management teams of three cities in the United States and using a set of fifteen variables, McNamara et al. (2002) found a relevant relationship between the complexity of cognitive SGs and the subsequent performance of the firm, confirming that the strategic structures' development managers know their strategic group and their competitive environment.

The relation between major environmental stressors and the changes that occurred over time in the competitive structure was studied for the Spanish banking system between 1983 and 1997. Performance differences between SGs are stable through time, and there is also strategic stability regarding the group and the firm, although marked by a high degree of strategic instability during periods with major environmental stressors. Since there are geographical constraints in the banking sector competition, SGs are studied in geographically restricted areas, thereby proving the existence of changes in several moments and not only during periods of instability. This confirms the possibility of there being firms that wish to move from one strategic group to another, faced with new environmental conditions (Zúñiga et al., 2004a).

The asymmetrical rivalry between SGs and the degree of response (Más-Ruíz el al., 2005), the rivalry of SGs and its consequence to performance (Más-Ruíz & Ruís-Moreno, 2011) and the asymmetrical rivalry inside and between SGs (Más-Ruíz et al., 2005) were also analyzed in the Spanish banking system. The data information for the formation of SGs of the three studies comes from reports and accounts of the corresponding balance sheets and economic statistical bulletins. The formation of SGs was limited by the size of banking firms, which was determined by the total monetary amount of granted loans.

This new study perspective on inter-firm rivalry assumes that the competitive dynamic is represented in the existing rivalry between firms and, consequently, in the continuous exchange of competitive actions, making it a more appropriate way of explaining the performance and differences between firms.

The rivalry of the industry in a given sector during a deregulated period, the behavior of firms from a strategic group, and their behavior between groups are asymmetrical (Más-Ruíz et al., 2014). Dominant groups expect strong retaliation from firms belonging to that same group, but have a strong strategic desire no minimize responses from firms of smaller groups. In this context, the size of SGs is key within complex industries that are undergoing changes or are part of a deregulated sector. Thus, managers should analyze the competitive environment from the point of view of each competing strategic group (Más-Ruíz et al., 2005). On the other hand, firms of a specific strategic group are able to anticipate rivalry within the core of the group and such competitive behaviors are detected by firms belonging to other SGs (Más-Ruíz & Ruíz-Moreno, 2011).

Strategic decisions are a valid instrument for the analysis of the formation of SGs, with the understanding that these groups can be formed based on the strategic decisions of the companies. Rhee and Mehra (2006) propose a model of two strategic dimensions: one at organizational level and the other at marketing decisions level, using a cluster analysis.

With the aim of analyzing the Colombian banking stability over a period of 10 years (1995/2004), Cano and Oliva (2008) study market stability and its relationship with the average performance of banking firms.

The strategic positioning coming from the industrial economy and strategic management studies, emphasizing external factors that determine strategic behavior of firms and their competitive approach, have some similar characteristics, such as: long-term stability, with high mobility barriers, isolating mechanisms and other common structures of the oligopolistic sector asymmetries, and a fair stability in number and composition of SGs. Cano and Oliva (2008) did not find consistent evidence to prove or deny the relationship between structural differences in performance and the results of firms.

Li (2008) challenges conventional tenets by studying direct competition between foreign and national American banks, exploring the possibility that foreign banks boost the expansion of domestic banks. This research seeks to clarify the competitive interactions between Californian and foreign banks. Results suggest that the presence of foreign banks in a specific segment of the market may represent favorable market opportunities for national banks, thus promoting new entries of national banks. Although Li (2008) shows that foreign banks were not a barrier to the entry of domestic banks, the presence of domestic banks discourages the entry of foreign banks.

The banking industry of the United States has been researched from an evolutionary perspective, and it was concluded that there are significant differences in the performance of firms in all five SGs. The strategic adherence of the groups can be relatively stable through time, co-evolving strategically in the pursuit of different paths over time (DeSarbo et al., 2009).

Although theory predicts that groups differ on performance and their reaction to external shocks, Halaj and Zochowski (2009) researched the Polish banking sector between 1997 and 2005 and showed that the identified groups differ in what concerns profitability and react differently to external shocks, supporting the explanation of earnings in the banking sector. However, no evidence was found regarding the usefulness of SGs in explaining the quality of the bank portfolios, as measured by irregular loans over total loans.

Epure et al. (2011) analyzed changes in productivity and efficiency of Spanish private and savings banks over eight years using two different periods: 1998–2002 and 2002–2006. Results show that productivity improvements of savings banks are partially due to technological innovation, and private banks benefit from efficiency improvements. Therefore, it can be concluded that the economic explanations of the performance of banking groups are the result of primary differences of productivity elements.

The impact of entering the American banking industry through purchase/acquisition was analyzed by Mukherji et al. (2011) between 1995 and 2003. Results argue that incumbents are more inclined to align their strategy of product mixture with that of the competition that entered through purchase/acquisition, as long as: (i) the incumbent is a large firm; (ii) the past performance of the acquirer had been strong; and, lastly (iii) the incumbent's served market is small.

Studying the Venezuelan banking system regarding the performance and geographical coverage during the first semester of 2008, Márquez and Gutiérrez (2012) concluded that: (i) SGs combine behavioral patterns; (ii) the different strategies implemented by banks were not expressed through differentiation; and (iii) the geographical coverage strategy was related to the financial strategy.

A new approach on the theory of SGs uses data envelopment analysis (DEA) to identify groups and performance group leaders. By analyzing over 1,000 branches/subsidiaries of the Canadian banking system, Paradi et al. (2012) refer that management groups are the result of the combination of management preferences, performance goals, and the implementation of similar resources due to market forces. Thus, groups can help firms create opportunities of continuous improvement with the actual development of the best management practices within the groups due to the similar operating characteristics of each strategic group (Paradi et al., 2012).

Empirically we analyzed the actions and competitive responses of Spanish deposit banks and how they compete within and between the SGs, giving rise to the adoption of aggressive strategies. The results provide a deeper understanding of the competitive behavior of firms, since it identifies the different patterns of actions and reactions, depending on the strategic group to which the company belongs (Nicolau-Gonzálbez & Ruiz-Moreno, 2014).

Huang, et al. (2017) explored efficiency differences between strategic groups in the context of transport, the results identified significant differences in efficiency across the four strategic groups (proactive-prudent, conservative-prudent and conservative-chance) prudent ratio showed significant capacity and efficiency, with low leverage compared to other SGs.

Actors can exert pressure on GS members according to organizational practices. Thus, the mode of entry into foreign markets is determined by the previous choices of other companies in the strategic reference group. Más-Ruíz et al. (2018) argue after analyzing 351 foreign direct investments of 30 Spanish banks in 55 countries between the 1986–2008 period they conclude that imitation behavior among members of the SG shows the important role of the group in strategic thinking.

Several empirical studies on the banking system found significant performance differences between SGs (e.g., Cool & Schendel, 1987; Dess & Davis, 1984; Dikmen et al., 2009; Hatten, 1974; Hatten & Hatten, 1987; Huang, et al., 2017; Kale & Arditi, 2003; Mascarenhas & Aaker, 1989; Nair & Kotha, 2001; Oster, 1982; Schreyögg & Von Reitzenstein, 2008). There is a general agreement that professionals are a reliable and valid source for data collection, even within a rapidly changing industry (e.g., Gary & Wood, 2011; Kabanoff & Brown, 2008; McNamara et al., 2002; Porac et al., 2011; Reger & Huff, 1993; Thomas & Carroll, 1994).

The concept of strategic group allows us to group firms from the same industry, enabling the creation of a multidimensional analysis of the competition. This can be used as a way of separating the competition within the retail banking sector, establishing the competing banking firms, and providing the identification of unexplored segments where said banking firms compete or may potentially compete.

The establishment of SGs can be carried out through several data sources and said groups can be classified in accordance with the criteria based on the number of used variables, research characteristics, and, lastly, theoretical framework.

METHODOLOGICAL APPROACH

The empirical study develops a set of steps in the analysis of the retail banking industry, in order to achieve the objectives it proposes. The methodological process of the research is constituted by the following steps: (i) identification of the period; (ii) identification of strategic groups; (iii) characterization of strategic groups; and (iv) analysis of differences between strategic groups.

The first stage of the study involves identifying the analysis period, which was defined as the years 2008, 2009 and 2010, i.e. at the beginning of the critical period the Portuguese economy went through. Periods subjectively determined *a priori* derive from the knowledge and analysis of the industry under study (e.g., Más-Ruíz & Moreno, 2011; Más-Ruíz et al., 2014).

The second step involves a cluster analysis Ward's method (e.g., Martins et al., 2010; Más-Ruíz & Sala, 1992; Pätäri et al., 2011; Reger & Huff, 1993) in order to determine strategic groups from the homogeneity of the corporate conduct. This model uses a hierarchical grouping procedure where similarities are identified to create clusters.

The third stage characterizes the SGs' dimension around which banks try to cluster together, aiming at identifying similar and dissimilar strategies.

The fourth stage involves the analysis of the differences of the main strategic groups, as the strategies of banks between groups may be dissimilar. The change in a group's composition will be the result of a change of the initial strategy, thereby leading to a new strategy similar to that of another group and that may not be followed by the remaining banks in the group.

IDENTIFICATION OF THE SAMPLE, SOURCE OF DATA AND VARIABLES

In this context, based on the aforementioned methodology, this section outlines the study of the Portuguese retail banking sector, with the purpose of analyzing the industry from a longitudinal perspective, as well as the changes occurred during the period under analysis, showing the different strategies of the corporate banking industry. Thus, the Portuguese banking system from 2008 to 2010 was identified using data from statistical bulletins of the Portuguese Banking Association [Associação Portuguesa de Bancos], known hereafter as APB.

Of the 33 financial institutions that integrate APB and that reported their data in 2011, there was a total of 6,306 branches or subsidiaries, with 57,069 employees.

Human resources are divided into 30,680 male employees and 26,389 female employees, 4,574 of which have primary education, 23,066 have secondary education, and 29,429 have higher education. From the total of human resources of all the financial institutions that form APB and reported their data in 2011, 37,206 are connected to the commercial activity and 19,863 to other activities of the financial sector.

Institutions had a total equity amounting to 21,124 Million Euros; total asset amounting to 505,923 Million Euros; a total liability amounting to 484,799.5 Million Euros; and a net result of minus 1,307 Million Euros.

The 33 financial institutions that are part of APB and that reported their data in 2011, are divided into: financial institutions – domestic, with 21 institutions, representing 63% of the total; financial institutions – affiliates with five institutions, representing 15% of the total; and lastly, financial institutions – subsidiaries with seven institutions, representing 21% of the total of institutions that are part of APB.

The information of banking groups was excluded from the total of institutions that compose the group of financial institutions associated with APB, with a license to operate in Portugal, even if the strategic decision of these groups influences the strategic options of the groups' banks, during the analyzed period. Data from electronic and investment banking were also excluded, since their nature is not encompassed in the scope of the study. Institutions that developed their main activity as offshore were equally excluded, and the following institutions were taken out of the analysis due to lack of available data for the financial year of 2008: BPN, EFISA and BPP. BIC was incorporated into BPN and the new entity became Banco BIC Português, S.A. The data from 2011 corresponds to the acquired entity, as published in the 2012 report and accounts. BPP stopped preparing consolidated accounts starting from the financial year ended on December 31st, 2011.

The shareholder structure of retail banking is composed by individual persons, firms, members of governing and institutional bodies, and by the Portuguese State. The Portuguese State has participated in two institutions: Banco Comercial Português, with 3.01% and Caixa Geral de Depósitos, S.A., with 100%.

Table 2 presents the shareholder structure of the financial institutions in retail banking during 2011.

For these reasons, this study focuses on the Portuguese retail banking sector from 2008 to 2010.

The characterization of the retail banking industry is analyzed according to the number of banking entities, number of subsidiaries, number of employees and, lastly, by the amount of the total asset of banking entities for each year (Table 3).

The 20 retail banking institutions that were operating in 2008 counted on a geographical coverage of 5.291 branches/subsidiaries in national territory, with 48,941 employees and a total asset of 434,529.3 Million Euros.

Lastly, we analyze a sample of the Portuguese retail banking system, according to the size of the total assets of each bank operating in Portugal (Table 4).

In accordance with the assets, represented in Millions of Euros from each bank, four types of retail banking entities can be identified, based on the corresponding dimension: (i) very small, with assets lower than 5,000 Million Euros; (ii) small institutions, with assets between 5,000 and 14,999 Million Euros; (iii) medium-sized institutions, with assets between 15,000 and 50,000 Million Euros; and, lastly, (iv) large banking institutions, with banking assets exceeding 50,000 Euros.

Table 2. Shareholder structure of the Portuguese retail banking industry (2011)

Institutions	Private	Businesses	Members of governing and institutional bodies	Institutional	State
Banco BIC Português, S.A. [(1)]	21.00%	60.00%	19.00%		
Banco BPI, S.A.	14.70%	84.40%	0.90%		
Banco Comercial Português	34.31%	22.80%	0.20%	39.86%	3.01%
Banco Espírito Santo, S.A.	16.20%	52.80%	0.20%	30.80%	
Banco Espírito Santo dos Açores, S.A.		32.50%		67.50%	
Banco Finantia, S.A.	3.90%	35.50%	0.80%	59.80%	
BANIF – Banco Internacional do Funchal, S.A.				100.00%	
Caixa Central – Caixa Central de Crédito Agrícola Mútuo, CRL		100.00%			
Caixa Económica Montepio Geral				100.00%	
Finibanco, S.A. [(2)]				100.00%	
Caixa Geral de Depósitos, S.A.					100.00%
Banco Bilbao Vizcaya Argentaria (Portugal), S.A.		100.00%			
Banco Itaú BBA International, S.A.		100.00%			
Banco Popular Portugal, S.A. [(3)]		100.00%			
Banco Santander Consumer Portugal, S.A.		100.00%			
Banco Santander Totta, S.A.	0.10%	99.90%			

Note: (1) Banco BIC was incorporated into BPN and the new entity adopted the corporate name of Banco BIC Português, S.A. The 2011 data are those of the acquired entity, as published in the Annual Report and Accounts of 2012; and (2) Banco Popular Portugal, S.A. ceased to prepare consolidated accounts in December 31, 2011.

Source: own elaboration.

Table 3. Sample characterization

Years	Nº of entities	Nº de branches [(1)]	Nº of workers [(2)]	Total Assets [(3)]
2008	20	5 291	48 941	434 529.3
2009	20	5 389	49 185	461 849.6
2010	18	6 170	54 923	463 911.1

Note: [(1)] National geographic coverage; [(2)] workers in Portugal; [(3)] Million Euros.

Source: own elaboration.

During 2008 and 2009, the number of banking entities of the retail banking system is stable, composed of 20 retail banks, accounting for an increase of the total asset from 434,529.3 in 2008 to 461,849.6 Million of Euros in 2009. Very small banking entities became even smaller due to their assets, which decreased from 19,907.3 in 2008 to 16,963.5 Million of Euros in 2009. The remaining types of banks (small, medium, and large) became larger, whereby large institutions contributed to the total asset growth for the year of 2009 with an asset of 325,823.1 Million Euros.

The number of retail banking entities went from 20 in 2008 to 18 in 2010, with the shift of a large bank to the medium-size bank category, increasing total assets of medium-size banks to 167,079 Million Euros.

The information used to characterize the sample comes from the information provided in balance sheets and individual income statements, which are recorded in the statistical bulletins no. 44, 2008; 45, 2009; 46, 2010; of APB. However, not all accounting data of the balance sheets and individual income statements are consolidated at the time of collecting and processing information.

The selection of variables for establishing the performance ratios is based on the retail banking industry requirement to comply with the FEAP, which is expected to decisively influenced banking behavior regarding its actions *vis-à-vis* the Portuguese economy. Therefore, nine strategic variables and six economic and financial ratios have been considered, as shown in Tables 5 and 6.

Banking performance is largely influenced by the economic profitability of the banking product, with a major impact on banking personnel expenses and banking administrative expenses (Sinkey & Joseph 1992).

RESULTS

The Ward hierarchical technique was used for the identification of strategic groups, in accordance with the proposed methodology. Clusters are formed in order to minimize the internal variation of the strategic group.

Table 7 analyzes the summary of the results regarding the selection of the number of groups for the analyzed period. During the 2008–2010 period, six strategic groups were identified, as presented in Table 7: SG1, is composed of eight banking institutions (BAC; BANIF; BBVA; CCCAM; DEUTSCHE; FINI; MG; BPP); SG2 is composed of two institutions (BIC; BPI); SG3 is composed of four institutions

Table 4. Sample characterization according to size of total assets

Type of retailing bank	Limits of the size of Classes [1]	2008			2009			2010		
		Nº of entities		Assets [1]	Nº of entities		Assets [1]	Nº of entities		Assets [1]
Very small	Lower than 5,000	9	45%	19,907.3	9	45%	16,963.5	7	38%	17,033.0
Small	5,000 – 14,999.9	6	30%	46,863.2	4	20%	39,387.4	6	33%	86,223.1
Medium	15,000 – 50,000	2	10%	87,088.3	3	15%	79,675.6	3	16%	167,079.5
Large	More than 50,000	3	15%	280,670.5	4	20%	325,823.1	2	11%	215,046.8
Total		20		434,529.3	20		461,849.6	18		485,382.3

Note: [1] Million Euros.
Source: own elaboration.

Table 5. Strategic dimension/operationalization of strategic groups

Dimension	Strategic Function	Operationalization	Code
Strategic reach.	Specialization (product/market).	Credit not represented by securities / Total Assets.	V1
		Securitized and non-derecognized credit / Total Assets	V2
		Other credit and values (tittles) / Total Assets	V3
		Overdue credit and interest loan / Total Assets	V4
		Provisions and Impairments / Total Assets	V5
		Call-Demand deposits / Total Liabilities	V6
		Term Deposits / Total Liabilities	V7
	Resources.	Central Bank Resources / Total Liabilities	V8
	Size of the institution.	Total Assets	V9

Source: own elaboration.

Table 6. Result variables

Dimension	Variables	Acronym	Operationalization
Economic and financial dimensions	Economic profitability.	PBMF	Banking product / Financial margin.
		CPMF	Costs with Personnel / Financial margin.
		GGAMF	General administrative expenses / Financial margin.
	Financial profitability.	ROE	Return on Equity (Net results / Shareholder Equity).
		ROI	Return on Investment (Net results / Total Assets).
		GAF	Degree of financial leverage (Operational results / EBIT).

Source: own elaboration.

Table 7. Composition of Strategic Groups during the 2008–2010 period

SG 1	SG 2	SG 3	SG 4	SG 5	SG 6
BAC	BIC	BES	BARCLAYS	BCA	BSC
BANIF	BPI	CGD	BSNP	BPG	
BBVA		BCP	BF		
CCCAM		BST	ITAU		
DEUTSCHE					
FINI					
MG					
BPP					

Source: own elaboration.

(BES; CGD; BCP; BST); SG4 is composed of four institutions (BARCLAYS; BSNP; BF; ITAU); SG5 is composed of two institutions (BCA; BPG); and, lastly, SG6 is composed by one institution (BSC), for a total of 21 banks.

In this point of the empirical research, the different strategies of the aforementioned SGs will be identified. The identification method was chosen based on the proposal of Amel and Rhoades (1988), which is founded on the comparison of average amounts of the strategic variables from each group.

The study focuses only on the analysis of SGs which were observed more than once. In that sense, a detailed analysis of the groups' centroids was carried out, with regard to the average amounts of the national industry, for all strategic groups. The behavior of a SG is analyzed in relation to the strategic variables, using the average of the arithmetic sum of the variables from each strategic group to enhance the defining elements of the strategy implemented by each strategic group. Lastly, we identify the different competitive models in strategic groups over time.

Table 8 presents a summary of the average values of the strategic variables of the national retail banking industry.

Strategic groups can be classified as: "Universal Banking"; "Traditional Banking"; "Specialized Banking"; and "Undefined Banking". Such classification is based on the transposition of an EU directive into the Portuguese legal system by Decree-Law no. 298/92, of December 31st, setting out the purpose or scope of the banking activity in article 4, which, in its broader sense, is called "Universal Banking" (personal banking; corporate banking; institutional banking; investment banking; and specialized financial services), and thus the traditional classification of commercial and savings banks has disappeared. In this context, the strategic features of each SG have been identified, as specified below.

The first group can be characterized as "Universal Banking". It is comprised of small institutions in the first period and very small, small and medium-sized institutions.

The second strategic group may be classified as "Traditional Banking". It is composed of three large institutions and one medium institution. This SG is composed of banking institutions traditionally operating at a national level in all market segments.

Table 8. Behavior of strategic variables over time

Variables	Operationalization	2008	2009	2010	2008–2010
V1	Credit not represented by securities / Total Assets	0.69	0.46	0.46	0.54
V2	Securitized and non-derecognized credit / Total Assets	0.00	0.06	0.07	0.04
V3	Other credit and values (tittles) / Total Assets	0.00	0.02	0.02	0.01
V4	Overdue credit and interest loan / Total Assets	0.00	0.01	0.02	0.01
V5	Provisions and Impairments / Total Assets	0.02	-0.01	-0.02	0.00
V6	Call-Demand deposits / Total Liabilities	0.35	0.15	0.10	0.20
V7	Term Deposits / Total Liabilities	0.00	0.22	0.24	0.15
V8	Central Bank Resources / Total Liabilities	0.02	0.06	0.11	0.06
V9	Total Assets [(1)]	22 569.0	23 092.5	26 965.7	24 209.1

Note: [(1)] Million Euros.

Source: own elaboration.

The third group may be classified as "Specialized Banking". It is comprised of three very small banking institutions and one small institution being difficult to classify according to the strategic variables considered. This group is influenced by the strategic variables' ratio, securitized and non-derecognized credit on total assets and a high central bank resource ratio on total liabilities.

The fourth strategic group is classified as "Undefined Banking", due to being difficult to describe according to strategic variables. BIC is a very small banking institution that started operations in 2009 and incorporated BPN in 2011. Lastly, BPI is a medium-sized institution. In the third period this SG is composed of Novo Banco, which is a large institution.

Table 9 and 10 display the average values of the strategic and economic and financial ratios over time.

The main Portuguese private banking institutions display different behaviors: BPI is part of the strategic group classified as Undefined Banking whilst BCP and BES are part of Traditional Banking.

In the characterization of the composition of the Strategic Groups (Tables 11, 12, 13 and 14) the proposal of Reger and Huff (1993) was used when characterizing the composition of the strategic groups, obtaining SGs according to their structure, distinguishing the following corporate features within the same strategic group: "core" [0;5[; "secondary" [5;10[; "transient" [10;15[; "misfit" [15;20[and, lastly, "idiosyncratic" [20;+∞[, through the average Euclidean square distance seen among individual players. Table 13 provides an analysis of the characterization of the composition of SGs in the period under analysis.

Table 11 allows us to compare the square of the Euclidean distances of the strategic group of Universal Banking, during 2008–2010. Banking institutions of Universal Banking should have developed similar strategies, with the exception of BPP, which presents higher values in most comparisons. Thus, BAC, BANIF, BBVA, CCCAM, DEUTSCHE, FINI and MG banks are classified as "secondary" institutions.

Table 9. Characterization of average values of the strategic variables in strategic groups

Strategic variables	Universal Banking	Traditional Banking	Specialized Banking	Undefined Banking	Average Value
V1 – Credit not represented by securities / Total Assets	0.681	0.553	0.204	0.273	0.285
V2 – Securitized and non-derecognized credit / Total Assets	0.041	0.049	0.000	0.031	0.020
V3 – Other credit and values (tittles) / Total Assets	0.020	0.022	0.002	0.000	0.007
V4 – Overdue credit and interest loan / Total Assets	0.015	0.009	0.000	0.001	0.004
V5 – Provisions and Impairments / Total Assets	-0.007	-0.004	0.000	-0.001	-0.002
V6 – Call-Demand deposits / Total Liabilities	0.215	0.188	0.208	0.078	0.115
V7 – Term Deposits / Total Liabilities	0.252	0.158	0.000	0.092	0.084
V8 – Central Bank Resources / Total Liabilities	0.036	0.053	0.043	0.504	0.106
V9 – Total Assets [(1)]	8 249.2	74 633.9	6.095.5	742.7	14 953.5

Note: [(1)] Million Euros.
Source: own elaboration.

Table 10. Results of strategic groups

Variables	Universal Banking	Traditional Banking	Specialized Banking	Undefined Banking	Average Value
PBMF: Banking product / Financial margin	1.800	1.592	1.951	1.859	0.647
CPMF: Costs with Personnel / Financial margin	0.542	0.490	0.985	0.616	0.204
GGAMF: General administrative expenses / Financial margin	0.366	0.560	0.626	0.679	0.175
ROE: Return on Equity	0.064	-0.887	-0.133	0.049	-0.003
ROI: Return on Investment	0.004	0.000	-0.009	0.001	0.002
GAF: Degree of financial leverage	0.827	0.652	0.946	2.534	1.006

Source: own elaboration.

Table 11. Squared Euclidean distance in the Universal Banking SG

	BAC	BANIF	BBVA	CCCAM	DEUTSCHE	FINI	MG	BPP
BAC	–							
BANIF	9.045	–						
BBVA	4.911	13.236	–					
CCCAM	6.447	7.992	9.825	–				
DEUTSCHE	2.522	12.264	4.262	8.411	–			
FINI	8.341	3.622	9.030	5.665	11.630	–		
MG	4.632	2.565	9.367	4.797	6.157	4.867	–	
BPP	17.185	17.950	7.693	10.802	17.225	8.588	17.343	–

Source: own elaboration.

During the 2008–2010 period, the strategic group of Traditional Banking is composed by BES, CGD and BCP, which were classified as "core". In turn, BST was classified as a "secondary" institution within this strategic group.

The strategic group of Specialized Banking is composed by BARCLAYS, BSNP, BF and ITAU, which can be classified as "secondary".

Lastly, the strategic group of Undefined Banking, which can be difficult to describe, given its "evolution" during the two periods, is composed by two banking institutions: BIC and BPI. These can be classified as "transitional" during the first period.

Table 14 classifies strategic groups, selecting the following variables: number of entities, number of subsidiaries, and number of employees.

In summary, during 2008 to 2010, the national retail banking system was composed by three predominant strategic groups: Universal Banking, Traditional Banking, and Specialized Banking. The identified strategic groups of the Portuguese banking industry reflect the structure of the competitive model of the industry at that time. The Universal Banking strategic group is composed by eight institutions (seven which are characterized as "secondary" and one as "transient"). The Traditional Banking strategic group

Table 12. Squared Euclidean distance in the Traditional Banking SG

	BES	CGD	BCP	BST
BES	–			
CGD	3.880	–		
BCP	2.937	2.565	–	
BST	7.273	7.104	6.356	–

Source: own elaboration.

Table 13. Characterization of the composition of strategic groups in the period under analysis

Classification	Universal Banking	Traditional Banking	Specialized Banking	Undefined Banking
Core	– (1)	BCP; CGD; BES	– (1)	– (1)
Secondary	MG; BAC; FINI; CCCAM; BBVA; DEUTSCHE; BANIF	BST	ITAU; BARCLAYS; BF; BSNP	– (1
Transient	BPP	– (1)	– (1)	BIC; BPI
Misfit	– (1)	– (1)	– (1)	– (1)
Idiosyncratic	– (1)	– (1)	– (1)	– (1)

Note: (1) no data.

Source: own elaboration.

is composed by three institutions which are very close to the "core". The Specialized Banking strategic group is composed by four institutions which are characterized as "secondary".

The challenging conditions faced by the Portuguese economy conditioned the competitive strategies of banks and caused a reorganization of strategic groups of the retail banking. This effect is significant in what concerns the Undefined Banking strategic group, composed by BIC and BPI, with an undefined competitive strategy.

Table 14. Classification of strategic groups

Strategic Groups	Number of entities	Number of Branches (1)	Number of workers (2)	Total Assets (3)
Universal Banking	8 (4)	1 793 (4)	112 025 (4)	65 993.4
Traditional Banking	4	3 159	27 816	330 095.4
Specialized Banking	4	251	2 456	24 382.0
Undefined Banking	2	1 130	7 281	43 816.6

Note: (1) national geographic coverage; (2) Number of workers in Portugal; (3) Million Euros; (4) Finibanco was acquired by Montepio in 2010.

Source: own elaboration.

CONCLUSION

This chapter allowed us to characterize the retail banking industry in Portugal and identify the main SGs and, consequently, its direct or potential competition. It was possible to analyze several entities at once, assessing the effectiveness and efficiency of the banking strategies, as well as the consequences of a specific strategic decision or of any collective movement from the members of a strategic group. This information provides managers with an outlook on competitive actions of members from the several SGs, thereby allowing them to establish any defensive or offensive positioning.

In this context, one can argue that it is possible to obtain a strategic vision of the relative positioning of players in the sector through the SGs analysis, providing them with a systematic assessment process of the strategic ability, taking into account their competitive advantages.

It was possible to conclude that: banking institutions have different competitive strategies; strategic groups do not have similar resources; and strategies also differ between SGs. The selected variables reflect the strategic actions of retail banking during the period under analysis, and it can be argued that retail banking in Portugal has clear differences among players over time.

SGs reflect the competitive structure of the national retail banking industry. The main limitation of this chapter is related to the short time horizon analyzed: only the years 2008, 2009, and 2010, were a period of volatility of the Portuguese economy, in general, and of the banking industry, in particular.

Finally, we have to consider that in future empirical investigations we must evaluate the decomposition of the credit variable not represented by securities, composed of credits to companies, consumption and housing over total assets. It will also be important to assess the effect of inflation and risk on equity accounting valuations and their benefits.

ACKNOWLEDGMENT

This research was supported by the Portuguese national funding agency for science, research and technology (FCT), within the GOVCOPP.

This research was supported by the Portuguese national funding agency for science, research and technology (FCT), within the Center for Research and Development in Mathematics and Applications (CIDMA), project UID/MAT/04106/2019.

REFERENCES

Altuntas, M., Rauch, J., & Wende, S. (2016). Strategic group performance and dynamics under different economic conditions. *The Geneva Papers on Risk and Insurance. Issues and Practice*, *41*(2), 325–347. doi:10.1057/gpp.2015.28

Amel, D. F., & Rhoades, S. A. (1988). Strategic groups in banking. *The Review of Economics and Statistics*, *70*(4), 685–689. doi:10.2307/1935834

Associação Portuguesa de Bancos (APB). (2008). Annual Statistical Bulletins, 44.

Associação Portuguesa de Bancos (APB). (2009). Annual Statistical Bulletins, 45.

Associação Portuguesa de Bancos (APB). (2010). Annual Statistical Bulletins, 46.

Azofra, V., & De La Fuente, J. M. (1987). El Comportamiento estratégico de la banca española durante el período 1975–1985: Una aproximación. *Anales de Estudios Económicos y Empresariales*, *2*, 35–54.

Baird, I. S., Sudharshan, D., & Thomas, H. (1988). Addressing temporal change in strategic group analysis: A three-mode factor analysis approach. *Journal of Management*, *14*(3), 425–439. doi:10.1177/014920638801400306

Barney, J. B., & Hoskisson, R. E. (1990). Strategic groups: Untested assertions and research proposals. *Managerial and Decision Economics*, *11*(3), 187–198. doi:10.1002/mde.4090110306

Bougon, M. (1983). In G. Morgan (Ed.), Uncovering cognitive maps: The selfQ technique,Beyond method: Strategies for social research (pp. 112–144). Academic Press.

Cano, J. E. G., & Oliva, E. J. D. (2008). Grupos estratégicos en la banca colombiana: análisis estático y dinámico. *Innovar: Revista de Ciencias Administrativas y Sociales, 18*,(32),195–226.

Caves, R., & Porter, M. E. (1977). From entry barriers to mobility barriers. *The Quarterly Journal of Economics*, *91*(2), 241–261. doi:10.2307/1885416

Chen, M. J., & Miller, D. (2012). Competitive dynamics: Themes, trends, and a prospective research platform. *The Academy of Management Annals*, *6*(1), 135–210. doi:10.5465/19416520.2012.660762

Claver-Cortés, E., Molina, J. F., & Pereira-Moliner, J. (2006). Strategic groups in the hospitality industry: Intergroup and intragroup performance differences in Alicante, Spain. *Tourism Management*, *27*(6), 1101–1116. doi:10.1016/j.tourman.2005.11.006

Claver-Cortés, E., Molina, J. F., & Tarí, J. J. (2003). Strategic groups and firm performance: The case of Spanish house-building firms. *Construction Management and Economics*, *21*(4), 369–377. doi:10.1080/0144619032000111250

Claver-Cortés, E., Pereira-Moliner, J., & Molina-Azorín, J. (2009). Strategic groups and performance in the Spanish hotel sector. *Service Industries Journal*, *29*(7), 943–961. doi:10.1080/02642060902749567

Cool, K. (1985). *Strategic group formation and strategic group shifts: a longitudinal analysis of the U.S. Pharmaceutical* (Unpublished doctoral dissertation). Purdue University.

Cool, K., & Dierickx, I. (1993). Rivalry, strategic groups and firm profitability. *Strategic Management Journal*, *14*(1), 47–59. doi:10.1002mj.4250140106

Cool, K., & Schendel, D. (1987). Strategic group formation & performance: The case of the U.S. pharmaceutical industry, 1963–1982. *Management Science*, *33*(9), 1102–1124. doi:10.1287/mnsc.33.9.1102

Cool, K., & Schendel, D. (1988). Performance differences among strategic group members. *Strategic Management Journal*, *9*(3), 207–223. doi:10.1002mj.4250090302

Day, G. S., Reibstein, D. J., & Gunther, R. (1999). *A Dinâmica da Estratégia Competitiva*. São Paulo: Editora Campus.

Decree-Law nº 298/92, of 31st of December. Diário da República, Nº 301 — 1.ª series -A — Ministry of Finance.

DeSarbo, W. S., Grewal, R., & Wang, R. (2009). Dynamic strategic groups: Deriving spatial evolutionary paths. *Strategic Management Journal, 30*(13), 1420–1439. doi:10.1002mj.788

Dess, G. G., & Davis, P. S. (1984). Porter's (1980) Generic strategies as determinants of strategic group membership and organizational performance. *Academy of Management Journal, 27*, 467–488.

Dikmen, I., Birgonul, T., & Budayan, C. (2009). Strategic group analysis in the construction industry. *Journal of Construction Engineering and Management, 135*(4), 288–297. doi:10.1061/(ASCE)0733-9364(2009)135:4(288)

Ebbes, P., Grewal, R., & DeSarbo, W. S. (2010). Modeling strategic group dynamics: A hidden Markov approach. *Quantitative Marketing and Economics, 8*(2), 241–274. doi:10.100711129-010-9081-0

Epure, M., Kerstens, K., & Prior, D. (2011). Bank productivity and performance groups: A decomposition approach based upon the Luenberger productivity indicator. *European Journal of Operational Research, 211*(3), 630–641. doi:10.1016/j.ejor.2011.01.041

Espitia, M. A., Polo, Y., & Salas, V. (1991). Grupos estratégicos y resultados en el sector bancario español. *Información Comercial Española, 690*, 189–212.

Ferguson, T. D., & Ketchen, D. Jr. (1999). Organizational configuration and performance: The role of statistical power in extant research. *Strategic Management Journal, 20*(4), 385–395. doi:10.1002/(SICI)1097-0266(199904)20:4<385::AID-SMJ24>3.0.CO;2-X

Fiegenbaum, A., & Thomas, H. (1990). Strategic Groups and Performance: The U.S. Insurance Industry, 1970–84. *Strategic Management Journal, 11*(3), 197–215. doi:10.1002mj.4250110303

Finch, D., McDonald, S., & Staple, J. (2013). Reputational interdependence: An examination of category reputation in higher education. *Journal of Marketing for Higher Education, 23*(1), 34–61. doi:10.1080/08841241.2013.810184

Flavián, C., Haberberg, A., & Polo, Y. (2002). Food retailing strategies in the European Union. A comparative analysis in the UK and Spain. *Journal of Retailing and Consumer Services, 9*(3), 125–138. doi:10.1016/S0969-6989(01)00011-X

Flores-Márquez, S., Rodríguez-Monroy, C., & Flores-Gutiérrez, J. (2015). Identificación y evolución de los grupos estratégicos de la industria bancaria Venezolana. *Interciencia, 40*(3), 165–171.

Gary, M. S., & Wood, R. E. (2011). Mental models, decision rules, and performance heterogeneity. *Strategic Management Journal, 32*(6), 569–594. doi:10.1002mj.899

Hahn, W., & Powers, T. L. (2010). Strategic plan quality, implementation capability, and firm performance. *Academy of Strategic Management Journal, 9*(1), 63–82.

Halaj, G., & Zochowski, D. (2009). Strategic groups and banks' performance. *Financial Theory and Practice, 33*(2), 153–186.

Hatten, K. J. (1974). *Strategic models in the brewing industries* (Unpublished doctoral dissertation). Purdue University.

Hatten, K. J., & Hatten, M. L. (1987). Strategic groups, asymmetrical barriers & contestability. *Strategic Management Journal*, *8*(4), 329–342. doi:10.1002mj.4250080404

Hayes, S. L., Spence, A. M., & Marks, D. V. P. (1983). *Competition in the investment banking industry*. Harvard University Press Cambridge.

Hervás, J. L., Dalmau, J. I., & Albors, J. (2006). 1972–2005: En la cuarta década de la investigación sobre grupos estratégicos ¿Qué hemos aprendido? *Investigaciones Europeas de Dirección y Economía de la Empresa*, *12*(1), 167–205.

Huang, W. H., Chao, S. L., & Chang, C. C. (2017). Assessment of differences in efficiency across strategic groups in the container shipping context: A data envelopment analysis. *International Journal of Shipping and Transport Logistics*, *9*(6), 651–672. doi:10.1504/IJSTL.2017.086934

Hunt, M. (1972). *Competition in the Major Home Appliance Industry, 1960–1970* (Unpublished doctoral dissertation). Harvard University.

Jegers, M. (1989). On the detection of strategic groups and the relation between their occurrence and industry profitability. *Rivista Internazionale di Scienze Economiche e Commerciali*, *36*(6), 497–511.

Kabanoff, B., & Brown, S. (2008). Knowledge structures of prospectors, analyzers, and defenders: Content, structure, stability, and performance. *Strategic Management Journal*, *29*(2), 149–171. doi:10.1002mj.644

Kalaf & Bomtempo, J. V. (1999). Grupos Estratégicos, Competição baseada em Recursos e a Operacionalização da Estratégia. XXIII encontro nacional da ANPAD, Foz do Iguaçu. Anais...Foz do Iguaçu.

Kale, S., & Arditi, D. (2003). Differentiation, conformity, & construction firm performance. *Journal of Management Engineering*, *19*(2), 52–59. doi:10.1061/(ASCE)0742-597X(2003)19:2(52)

Ketchen, D. Jr, & Shook, C. (1996). The application of cluster analysis in strategic management research: An analysis and critique. *Strategic Management Journal*, *17*(6), 441–458. doi:10.1002/(SICI)1097-0266(199606)17:6<441::AID-SMJ819>3.0.CO;2-G

Lawless, M. W., & Tegarden, L. F. (1991). Test of performance similarity among strategic group members in conforming and non-conforming industry structures. *Journal of Management Studies*, *2*, 656–664.

Leask, G. (2004). *Strategic groups & the resource based view: Natural complements enhancing our understanding of the competitive process*. Working paper, Ashton Univ., Birmingham, UK.

Leask, G., & Parker, D. (2007). Strategic groups, competitive groups and performance within the U.K. pharmaceutical industry: Improving our understanding of competitive process. *Strategic Management Journal*, *28*(7), 723–745. doi:10.1002mj.603

Leask, G., & Parnell, J. A. (2005). Integrating strategic groups and the resource based perspective: Understanding the competitive process. *European Management Journal*, *23*(4), 458–470. doi:10.1016/j.emj.2005.06.003

Li, J. (2008). Asymmetric interactions between foreign and domestic banks: Effects on market entry. *Strategic Management Journal*, *29*(8), 873–893. doi:10.1002mj.693

Lozano-Vivas, A., & Pastor, J. T. (2010). Do performance and environmental conditions act as barriers for crossborder banking in Europe? *Omega*, *38*(5), 275–282. doi:10.1016/j.omega.2009.05.002

Márquez, S. L. F., & Gutiérrez, J. O. F. (2012). Strategic groups: Their influence on the performance of the Venezuelan banking industry and its relationship with the geographic coverage. *Dirección y Organización*, *47*, 41–61.

Martínez, R. (1992). *Grupos Estratégicos en el Sector de Cajas de Ahorro Espanolas*. Madrid: Caja de Ahorros de Madrid.

Martins, T. S., Cruz, J. A., Kato, H. T., Silva, W. V., & Silva, E. D. (2010). Análise de grupos estratégicos e desempenho na indústria de bancos comerciais no Brasil. *RCO – Revista de Contabilidade e Organizações – FEA-RP/USP, 4*(9), 100–125.

Más-Ruíz, F. J. (1999). Dynamic analysis of competition in marketing: Strategic groups in Spanish banking. *International Journal of Bank Marketing*, *17*(5), 233–250. doi:10.1108/02652329910292710

Más-Ruíz, F. J., Nicolau-Gonzálbez, J. L., & Ruiz-Moreno, F. (2005). Asymmetric rivalry between strategic groups: Response, speed of response and ex ante vs. ex post competitive interaction in the Spanish bank deposit market. *Strategic Management Journal*, *26*(8), 713–745. doi:10.1002mj.471

Más-Ruíz, F. J., Ruíz, F. M., & Martínez, A. L. (2014). Asymmetric rivalry within and between strategic groups. *Strategic Management Journal*, *35*(3), 419–439. doi:10.1002mj.2102

Más-Ruiz, F. J., Ruiz-Conde, E., & Calderón-Martínez, A. (2018). Strategic group influence on entry mode choices in foreign markets. *International Business Review*, *27*(6), 1259–1269. doi:10.1016/j.ibusrev.2018.05.007

Más-Ruíz, F. J., & Ruíz-Moreno, F. (2011). Rivalry within strategic groups and consequences for performance: The firm-size effects. *Strategic Management Journal*, *32*(12), 1286–1308. doi:10.1002mj.936

Más-Ruíz, F. J., & Sala, J. C. (1992). Identificación de grupos estratégicos en las cajas de ahorros españolas. *Revista Europea de Dirección e Economía de la Empresa*, *1*(3), 9–28.

Más-Ruíz, F. J., & Sala, J. C. (1993). Análisis de la competencia en las cajas de ahorros: Grupos Estratégicos. *ESIC Market*, *79*, 143–167.

Mascarenhas, B. (1989). Strategic group dynamics. *Strategic Management Journal*, *32*(2), 333–352.

Mascarenhas, B., & Aaker, D. (1989). Mobility barriers and strategic groups. *Strategic Management Journal*, *10*(5), 475–485. doi:10.1002mj.4250100506

Maudos, J., & Pastor, J. M. (2003). Cost and profit efficiency in the Spanish banking sector (1985–1996): A nonparametric approach. *Applied Financial Economics*, *13*(1), 1–12. doi:10.1080/09603100110086087

Mayor, M. G., Davo, N. B., & Hera, M. L. (2012). Technological innovation as a determining factor on national competitiveness. *Revista de Economía Mundial*, *31*, 137–166.

McGee, J., & Thomas, H. (1986). Strategic groups: Theory, research and taxonomy. *Strategic Management Journal, 7*(2), 141–160. doi:10.1002mj.4250070204

McNamara, G., Luce, R. A., & Tompson, G. H. (2002). Examining the effect of complexity in strategic group knowledge structures on firm performance. *Strategic Management Journal, 23*(2), 153–170. doi:10.1002mj.211

Mehra, A. (1996). Resource and market based determinants of performance in the U.S. banking industry. *Strategic Management Journal, 17*(4), 307–322. doi:10.1002/(SICI)1097-0266(199604)17:4<307::AID-SMJ820>3.0.CO;2-2

Mukherji, P., Sorescu, A., Prabhu, J. C., & Chandy, R. K. (2011). Behemoths at the gate: How incumbents take on acquisitive entrants (and why some do better than others). *Journal of Marketing, 75*(5), 53–70. doi:10.1509/jmkg.75.5.53

Nair, A., & Kotha, S. (2001). Does group membership matter? Evidence from the Japanese steel industry. *Strategic Management Journal, 22*(3), 221–235. doi:10.1002mj.154

Newman, H. H. (1978). Strategic groups and the structure-performance relationship. *The Review of Economics and Statistics, 60*(3), 417–427. doi:10.2307/1924167

Nicolau-Gonzálbez, J. L., & Ruiz-Moreno, F. (2014). Who performs a stronger response to whom? Detecting individual competitive actions and reactions. *Review of Managerial Science, 8*(3), 385–403. doi:10.100711846-013-0109-1

Oster, S. M. (1982). Intraindustry structure & the ease of strategic change. *The Review of Economics and Statistics, 64*(3), 376–383. doi:10.2307/1925935

Paradi, J. C., Zhu, H., & Edelstein, B. (2012). Identifying managerial groups in a large Canadian bank branch network with a DEA approach. *European Journal of Operational Research, 219*(1), 178–187. doi:10.1016/j.ejor.2011.12.022

Parnell, J. A. (2011). Strategic capabilities, competitive strategy, and performance among retailers in Argentina, Peru and the United States. *Management Decision, 49*(1), 130–155. doi:10.1108/00251741111094482

Passmore, S. W. (1985). *Strategic groups and the profitability of banking*. Research Paper nº 8501. Federal Reserve Bank of New York.

Pätäri, S., Puumalainen, K., Jantunen, A., & Sandstrüm, J. (2011). The interface of the energy and forest sectors—Potential players in the bioenergy business. *International Journal of Production Economics, 131*(1), 322–332. doi:10.1016/j.ijpe.2009.08.015

Patton, G. R. (1976). *A Simultaneous Equation Model of Corporate Strategy: The Case of the U.S. Brewing Industry* (Doctoral Thesis). Purdue University.

Porac, J. F., Thomas, H., & Baden-Fuller, C. (2011). Competitive Groups as Cognitive Communities: The Case of Scottish Knitwear Manufacturers Revisited. *Journal of Management Studies, 48*(3), 646–664. doi:10.1111/j.1467-6486.2010.00988.x

Porter, M. (1973). *Consumer behaviour, retailer power, and manufacturer strategy in consumer goods industry* (Unpublished doctoral dissertation). Universidade de Harvard.

Porter, M. (1976, Winter). Please note location of nearest exit: Exit barriers and planning. *California Management Review*, *19*(2), 21–33. doi:10.2307/41164693

Porter, M. (1979). The Structure within industries and companies' performance. *The Review of Economics and Statistics*, *61*(1), 214–227. doi:10.2307/1924589

Porter, M. (1980). The contributions of industrial organization to strategic management. *Academy of Management Review*, *6*(4), 609–620.

Ramsler, M. (1982). *Strategic groups and foreign market entry in global banking competition* (Unpublished doctoral dissertation). Harvard University, Cambridge, MA.

Reger, R., & Huff, A. S. (1993). Strategic groups: A cognitive perspective. *Strategic Management Journal*, *14*(2), 103–124. doi:10.1002mj.4250140203

Rhee, M., & Mehra, S. (2006). Aligning operations, marketing, and competitive strategies to enhance performance: An empirical test in the retail banking industry. *Omega*, *34*(5), 505–515. doi:10.1016/j.omega.2005.01.017

Ruíz-Moreno, F., Ladrón-de-Guevara, A., & Más-Ruíz, F. J. (2010). Development of a model of price competition in the Spanish loans market. *International Journal of Bank Marketing*, *28*(6), 479–496. doi:10.1108/02652321011077715

Scannell, N. J., Safdari, C., & Newton, J. (2003). An extended application of Factor Analysis in establishing peer groups among banks in Armenia. *Journal of Academy of Business and Economics*, *1*(1).

Schreyögg, J., & Von Reitzenstein, C. (2008). Strategic groups & performance differences among academic medical centers. *Health Care Management Review*, *33*(3), 225–233. doi:10.1097/01.HMR.0000324908.42143.1f PMID:18580302

Serrano-Cinca, C. (1998). From Financial Information to Strategic Groups: A Self–organizing Neural Network Approach. *Journal of Forecasting*, *17*(5-6), 415–428. doi:10.1002/(SICI)1099-131X(1998090)17:5/6<415::AID-FOR705>3.0.CO;2-X

Sinkey, Jr. (1992). *Commercial Bank Financial Management in the Financial Services Industry.* New York: Macmillan Publishing Company.

Smith, K. G., Grimm, C. M., Young, G., & Wally, S. (1997). Strategic groups and rivalrous firm behavior: Towards a reconciliation. *Strategic Management Journal*, *18*(2), 149–157. doi:10.1002/(SICI)1097-0266(199702)18:2<149::AID-SMJ854>3.0.CO;2-O

Staake, T., Thiesse, F., & Fleisch, E. (2012). Business strategies in the counterfeit market. *Journal of Business Research*, *65*(5), 658–665. doi:10.1016/j.jbusres.2011.03.008

Sudharshan, D., Thomas, H., & Fiegenbaum, A. (1991). Assessing mobility barriers in dynamic strategic groups analysis. *Journal of Management Studies*, *28*(5), 429–438. doi:10.1111/j.1467-6486.1991.tb00762.x

Tang, M., & Thomas, H. (1992). The concept of strategic groups: Theoretical construct or analytical convenience. *Managerial and Decision Economics*, *13*(4), 323–329. doi:10.1002/mde.4090130407

Thomas, H., & Carroll, Ch. (1994). Theoretical and empirical links between strategic groups, cognitive communities, and networks of interacting firms. In H. Daems & H. Thomas (Eds.), Strategic groups, strategic moves and performance (pp. 7–29). Oxford, UK: Pergamon.

Thomas, H., & Venkatraman, N. (1988). Research on Strategic Groups: Progress and Prognosis. *Journal of Management Studies*, *25*(6), 537–555. doi:10.1111/j.1467-6486.1988.tb00046.x

Tortosa-Ausina, E. (2002). Financial costs, operating costs, and specialization of Spanish banking firms as distribution dynamics. *Applied Economics*, *34*(17), 2165–2176. doi:10.1080/00036840210138400

Tsai, W., Su, K. H., & Chen, M. J. (2011). Seeing through the eyes of a rival: Competitor acumen based on rival-centric perceptions. *Academy of Management Journal*, *54*(4), 761–778. doi:10.5465/amj.2011.64870138

Tywoniak, S., Galvin, P., & Davies, J. (2007). New Institutional Economics' Contribution to Strategic Groups Analysis. *Managerial and Decision Economics*, *28*(3), 213–228. doi:10.1002/mde.1323

Vachani, S. (1997). Economic Liberalization's Effect on Sources of Competitive Advantage of Different Companies: The Case Groups of India. *International Business Review*, *6*(2), 165–184. doi:10.1016/S0969-5931(96)00044-3

Zúñiga-Vicente, J. Á., Fuente-Sabaté, J. M., & González, I. S. (2004a). Dynamics of the strategic group membership-performance linkage in rapidly changing environments. *Journal of Business Research*, *57*(12), 1378–1390. doi:10.1016/S0148-2963(03)00071-7

Zúñiga-Vicente, J. Á., Fuente-Sabaté, J. M., & Rodríguez-Puerta, J. (2004b). A study of industry evolution in the face of major environmental disturbances: Group and firm strategic behaviour of Spanish banks, 1983–1997. *British Journal of Management*, *15*(3), 219–245. doi:10.1111/j.1467-8551.2004.00416.x

KEY TERMS AND DEFINITIONS

Cluster Analysis: Is a data mining technique that groups together a set of objects or firms in such a way that objects or firms in the same group (called a cluster) are more similar (in some sense) to each other than to those in other groups (clusters).

Competitive Advantage: Is the advantage a firm has over its competitors, which allows the firms to outperform its competitors and thus generate more revenues. The firm with a competitive advantage has an edge over the rivals, which is based on unique resources or capabilities, which allow it to generate more value to the shareholders. The main sources of competitive advantage may be patents, strong distribution network, innovative culture, stronger new product development capabilities, cost-efficient production systems, etc.

Competitive Dynamics: Is the set of actions and reactions in a competitive business environment that rival firms display. The action of an individual firm becomes the key indicator of competitive dynamics as each rival firm enacts this action in order to enhance its competitive advantage *vis–à–vis* its competitors.

Competitive Rivalry: Occurs when two or more firms try and garner favorable market position over its competitors.

Industrial Organization School: Is concerned with the use of economic analysis in studying competition between firms and the evolution of market structure.

Strategic Group: Is a management concept that separates groups of firms within the same industry with similar characteristics, strategies, business models from those with different characteristics, strategies, business models. As a result, strategic groups, within an industry, can be grouped as a dimensional homogeneous construct.

Strategic Management School: Is concerned with the formulation and implementation of the major goals and initiatives taken by an organization's top management, taking into account the resources, competencies and capabilities of the firm and the match of those internal resources to the external environments in which the firm operates.

Chapter 2
The Restructuring of the Financial System in the 21st century

Elisabeth T. Pereira
University of Aveiro, Portugal

ABSTRACT

The financial system on the first decades of the 21st century followed the trend of the last decades of the 20th century with corporate restructuring and international financial markets integration and delocalization being oriented by profits and mergers and acquisitions. The global economy and financial structure changes, in the current century, derived from financial innovations, market deregulation, globalization, technology, market structure changes, regulatory reforms, and (re)formulation of central banks' monetary policy. Currently, the financial system is interconnected, interactive, interdependent, and became over-leveraged. The present chapter focuses on the analysis of the evolution of the financial system and the main determinants of global financial markets restructuring on last decades to explain the relevant changes verified in the financial system in the 21st century. After a literature review, an evaluative and descriptive macro analysis of the financial system is presented to study the process of restructuring of the financial system in the main developed economies.

INTRODUCTION

The first decades of the 21st century reflected the changes occurred in the financial systems in the last decades of the 20th century, with corporate restructuring and international financial markets integration and delocalization; being oriented, essentially, by profits and mergers and acquisitions. These facts had repercussions on the economic and financial crisis verified in the first decade of the 21st century and in the way households and companies demand and supply the financial assets. The global economy and financial structure changes occurred both in the decade of 1990s and in the following first two decades of the current century, resulting from financial innovations, market deregulation, globalization, advances in technology, regulatory reforms of national (governments and national central banks) and international

DOI: 10.4018/978-1-5225-8906-8.ch002

institutions (e.g., the World Bank, the International Monetary Fund (IMF), and the European Central Bank (ECB)), market structures and (re)formulation of central banks' monetary policy.

Currently, global finance is interconnected, interactive and interdependent; and the financial system became over-leveraged. The finance and banking corporate restructuring and business processes have been influenced by the quick growth of financial markets, where companies can rapidly change owners inside the country and across country borders, and also by the emergence of financial markets of increasingly internationally open countries, as for example the countries of former Soviet Union, China, India and other emergent markets, with effects on global finances. The financial market development is positively correlated with the per capita real gross domestic product (GDP) (Beck, Demirgüç-Kunt & Levine, 2010; Mishkin, 2017).

The subject under study, in this chapter, is of great relevance to understanding the changes occurred in the financial system restructuring, which have started in the 1990s in the international financial markets and that is of paramount importance for the proper functioning of the financial, banking and insurance systems. This issue is also at the heart of understanding the functioning of the financial system as a pillar of economic growth and development (Demirgüç-Kunt & Levine, 2010; Bofinger, 2001; Cecchetti, 2006) and as an explanation for the occurrence and contagion of crises that have occurred in recent decades (Lane, 2012). Like was the example's cases of what happened in the United States in the Great Depression of the 1930s, the economic collapse in Thailand and Indonesia with the Asian crisis of 1997 (Lindgren *et al,* 1999), the Russia bond default in 1998, the Korean banks default in 1998 and in United States and European countries with the Subprime crisis after 2007 (Cecchetti, 2006; Abreu *et al.* 2007). So, for the desirable countries' economic growth and development in required a healthy and sustainable financial system (Mishkin, 2017; Pereira, 2019).

To understand the restructuring and competitiveness needs of the financial system over time, it is necessary to provide an overview of the evolution of economies' environment and financial system and the main facts that succeed and that led to the system changes occurred in the last decades, which culminated in the current structure of the financial system. So, the present chapter focus, as main purposes, in an evolutionary causal description and identification of the main determinants of global financial markets' restructuring on the 21st century: international integration and delocalization, capital flows, financial sectors' regulation reforms, global risks interconnections, and ownership changes. A qualitative and descriptive methodology is applied in a macro level perspective. After this, is presented a background of the topics under study and of the financial system until the 1990s, as antecedents with culminating facts leading to the characterization of the financial system on the 21st century, both based on literature, an evaluative and descriptive analysis of the financial system will be presented to study the process of corporate restructuring, integration, regulation, and supervision of the financial system of the main developed economies.

BACKGROUND

The Description of Financial System and Main Concepts

The financial system had its origin on the money functions and on its developments over time, since the primitive society until nowadays. The money had a great development with the appearance of notes and letters of credit on the 15th and 16th centuries, which culminated with the establishment of the first commercial and investment banks and the standardization of the notes' value in the 17th century. But the further development of money and the financial system itself occurred with the Industrial Revolution, in the 19th century, and intensified with the World War I and II, as well as the technological progress and the increasing of international exchanges occurred in the 20th century (Pereira, 2019). These facts have culminated in the imperative development of the banking and financial system to respond to the demand for the intensification of trade and the demand's needs of economies.

Considering the evolution of money, represented in Figure 1, except for the merchandise money all the other types of money require a monetary financial system to support them, which increased his complexity level with the time evolution.

The modes of payment have evolved increasingly rapid over time, as well as the degree of complexity implicit and the geographical coverage of these payments. The great technologic progress applied to the financial system joins in the second half of the 20th century and contributes to the great financial development, and these intensify, in the 21st century, the reaching for a global character that comes to facilitate transactions and diminish the transactions costs, but on the other hand makes the global financial system more complex.

The operationalization of the plastic money, representing the debit and credit cards, only where possible because it is supported by the operation of technology, and in particular by the use of information and communication technologies (ICT). The same occurs with the electronic money, related to the electronic transferences done by the computer or by mobile devices, especially mobile phones (Mishkin, 2017).

The money functions are characterized in three main forms and in one property (Pereira, 2019):

- *Exchange Instrument* or *Payment Method*, which is used for the payment of goods and services, allowing greater efficiency in the process of exchange by reducing transaction costs, leading to specialization and promoting economic efficiency;
- *Unit of Account*, which is used to measure value in the economy eliminating the need to know all relative prices being all the prices expressed in monetary units. The exchange rate, in the international markets, is necessary and very useful to compare international relative prices. And
- *Value Reserve*, which represents the case in which money retains purchasing power over time, allowing to separate the moment of the formation of income from the moment of its application. This function is related to the property of *Liquidity* that is the measure of the facility which an asset is converted into a medium of exchange, and is strictly related to the money market and to the interest rates as the price/cost of opportunity of money holder attributes to the loss or gain of li-

Figure 1. Evolution of money types

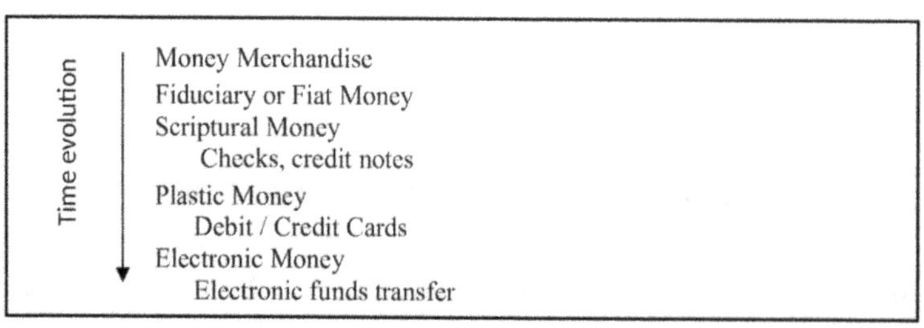

quidity. The money evolution, the technological progress, and financial innovations have strongly influenced the evolution of the three money functions capability over time.

The financial system represents the set of markets and intermediary institutions that coordinate the supply and demand for funds, savings and investment (Pereira, 2019). And it allows:

- The creation of liquidity;
- To minimize transaction costs between savers and investors;
- To minimize the costs of supervising the funds;
- To spread and dilute risks.

The financial system is one of the pillars of the economic development of economic societies, allowing and supporting the possibilities for companies to opt for certain investment projects and ways of securing their financing as well as to consumers to make decisions about the allocation of their available income between savings and consumption (Bofinger, 2001). The financial system mobilizes savers' funds for the productive sector, making it possible to transfer economic resources in time and space, cross borders and between sectors, and facilitating risk management through diversification.

The financial system verifies two distinct types of financial systems that characterize themselves. Some countries, like most of the Eastern European economies and the Asiatic countries (e. g. Germany, Japan, France, Portugal, and most of the European continental countries with the exception for the United Kingdom) base their financial system in the banking system. Other countries, like the Anglo-Saxon economies (e.g. United States and United Kingdom) are more dependents of capital markets (Pereira, 2019).

The banking system is a segment, belonging to the financial system, constituted by several types of banks with special proposes: commercial and business banks, investment banks, specialized banks, cooperative banks, and other financial institutions (special credit agencies, insurance companies, rental associations, investment companies). The central bank represents the national monetary authority, performing also various other functions as being the bank of the banks, the issuer of fiduciary money (notes and coins), international payments regulator and in many countries bank of the State. In the European Union, by the European Central Bank (ECB) statutes the central banks of European member states are not allowed to finance directly the public institutions (Bofinger, 2001; Pereira, 2019).

The financial system is composed of five essential parts (Cecchetti, 2006; Cecchetti & Schoenholtz, 2017):

- **Money:** Money is essential, according to the three money functions, for payments, as a unit of account and as a reserve of value.
- **Financial Instruments:** The financial instruments transfer wealth from the savers to the investors and to transfer the risk to the better equipped to support it. The financial instruments involve legal contracts that grant the right to receive future benefits under certain conditions.
- **Financial Markets:** The financial markets is where take place the purchase and sale of the financial instruments. It can be traded on the money market (market of a short run) and in the capital market (market of a long run). The money market is the market where short-term (less than one year) financial securities are purchased and sold. Examples: treasury bills, savings certificates, commercial paper (issued by companies). The capital market is where long-term financial securities of purchase and sale operations take place. Examples: bonds, equities, mixed securities, loans

- **Financial Institutions:** The financial institutions provide access to the financial markets.
- **Central Banks:** The central banks monitor the financial institutions and through the monetary policy as monetary authority as the target to stabilize the economy. The economic stability improves social well-being and reduces the financial and economic risk in the economy.

The proper functioning of the financial system is essential for the well-functioning of a country's economy or economic zone (Beck & Demirgüç-Kunt, 2009) and for the macroeconomic balance, but for this purpose there must be an active and visible intervention of the monetary authority (Bofinger, 2001). The macroeconomic balance is related to savings and investments required to obtain the economic efficiency on production.

The financial system allows the channeling of savers' funds to investors and includes the direct financing and the indirect financing (Abreu et al, 2007; Bofinger, 2001; Cecchetti, 2006; Mishkin, 2017). In the direct financing, the savers negotiate directly with investors, selling them financial assets. However, this type of financing possesses some kind of inefficiencies at different levels: dimension of savings versus investment needs, maturities, liquidity, difficulties in the risk diversification and the inexistence of multiplier mechanism. The indirect financing compensates the inefficiencies of direct financing, with the financial intermediaries conducting the communication between savers and investors, collecting funds from savers, and transferring these funds to debtors. In this case, the indirect financing allows to reduce the information problems inherits to asymmetric information, both the problems of adverse selection and moral hazard; and the agency problem (principal-agent problem) in the financial market (Abreu et al, 2007).

The financial markets are part of the indirect funding and represent the markets in which an entity with a surplus situation lends funds to an entity that is in a loss. The main functions of financial markets are facilitating the channeling of funds of agents with financing capacity to agents in need of funding and increase the economic efficiency allowing to increase the efficiency in capital allocation (Abreu et al, 2007: Bofinger, 2001; Cecchetti, 2006; Pereira, 2019) . For a summary of the current characterization of the Financial Industry Structure see Table 1.

Nowadays, with the development and the evaluative adaptation of the financial system to the new competitive economic environment (Masciandaro & Quityn, 2013), the financial markets present a set of characteristics: deregulation, relocated, internationalized and globalized, are influenced by psychological factors, are imperfect and dependent of information and have a great influence on economic growth and development (Mishkin, 2017). For proper functioning of financial markets, according to Mishkin (2017) and Bofinger (2001), it should exist low transaction costs, the credibility of the information communicated, and the investors should be properly protected.

The Financial System Until the Decade of the 1990s

The evolution of the financial system, in particular, the banking industry, took place in most of the world economies after the last decades of the 18th century, motivated by the progress from industrial revolutions and the intensification of production and international trade exchanges.

In the United States some important facts that influenced the financial system were the Bank of North America chartered in 1782, the National Bank Act of 1863 that established national banks and the Office of the Comptroller of the Currency in 1863, the Federal Reserve Act of 1913 that created the Federal Reserve system and the Banking Act of 1933 (also known as the Glass-Steagall Act) that created the

Table 1. Summary of financial industry structure

Financial intermediary	Primary Sources of funds (liabilities)	Primary Uses of funds (assets)	Services provided
Bank Companies (Depository and Investment Institutions)	Checkable deposits Savings and time deposits Borrowing from other banks	Cash Loans Securities	Pooling of small savings to provide large loans Diversified deposits accounts Access to payment system Screening and monitoring of borrowers Immediate sales of assets Access to a set of assets allowing diversification Evaluation of firms wishing to issue securities Research and advice for investors
Insurance Companies	Expected claims	Corporate bonds Government bonds Stocks Mortgages	Pooling of risk Screening and monitoring of policy-holders
Securities Companies	Short-term loans	Commercial paper Bonds	Management of asset pools Clearing and settling trades
Mutual-Fund Companies	Shares sold to customers	Commercial paper Bonds Mortgages Stocks Real Estate	Pooling of small savings to provide access to large, and diversified portfolios
Finance Companies	Bonds Bank loans Commercial paper	Mortgages Consumer loans Business loans	Screening and monitoring of borrowers
Pension Fund	Policy benefits to be paid out to future retirees	Stocks Government bonds Corporate bonds Commercial paper	Pooling of employees' and employers' contributions Diversification of long-term investments to ensure future income for retirees
Government Sponsored Companies	Commercial paper Bonds Loan guarantees	Mortgages Farm loans Student loans	Access to financing for borrowers who cannot obtain it elsewhere

(Source: Adapted from Cecchetti, 2006: 345)

Federal Deposit Insurance Corporation and separated the banking and securities industries (Berger et al, 1995; Mishkin, 2017). The Glass-Steagall Act of 1933 was established in result of the Great Depression of the years 1929-1933, after the 9000 bank failures, which annihilated many households' savings and particular deposits at commercial banks, to prevent future depositor losses, provide federal insurance on bank deposits, and, this way, to give credibility to the system (Benston, 1990). The Glass-Steagall Act separated the activities of commercial banks from the securities industries, prohibiting commercial banks from underwriting or dealing in corporate securities and prohibiting investment banks to engage in commercial banking (for more detailed information see Mishkin, 2017, chapter 10). The regulations established by the Glass-Steagall Act were repealed in 1999.

In Europe, due to the different countries that composes it, there were different regulations in the different countries until the creation of the monetary European system, in the decade of 1990s (see Atack & Neal, 2009), which influenced the financial systems of European countries belonging to the European Union and, more specifically, to the Eurozone.

Before the decade of the 1990s, in United States, Europe and in most of the world's advanced economies, the financial system was divided into three distinct segments, resulting from a previous financial structuration after the Great Depression of the 1930s, and that was strictly observed until the decade of 1990s. These three segments were divided into banking, securities and insurance. Each one of the segments, with its specific business proposes, is still now regulated and supervised by proper regulations and national institution's supervisors. Depending on the country, three supervisor models can operate: institutional supervision, supervision by objectives and supervision by a single regulator (Mishkin, 2017; Pereira, 2019).

In the middle of the 1990s took place an integration process of technological, geographical and functional nature of the three segments at the level of institutions, instruments and markets. In the United States, the Congress approved the Reigle-Neal Interstate Banking and Branching Efficiency Act, in 1994, which allow the bank industry to diversify geographically, and made possible the acquisition of branches nationwide (Ceccheti, 2006). In the bank industry, if a bank wants to operate in another state of the country or in another country by acquiring a bank in the desired location when the bank effectuates the purchasing he also acquires the bank's costumers, its employees and the information and knowledge of the business market and legal environment. On November 12, 1999, the Gramm Leach Bliley Act provided a new legal framework for financial companies repealing the Glass Steagall Act's prohibition of mergers between commercial banks and insurance companies or securities companies (Barth, Brumbugh & Wilcox, 2000). According to Barth, Brumbugh and Wilcox (2000), the Glass-Steagall Act was repealed due to three important factors:

1. The increasing weight of empirical evidence findings from academic studies about the little responsibility of securities activities of commercial banks in the traumas of the Great Depression;
2. The extensive experience from other developed countries of banking companies that provide data to support the repeal of Gall-Steagall Act; and
3. The rapid technologic advances that allowed to reduce costs of using data information from one business to other business decreasing the asymmetric information at the same time that reduced the business risk and increased the expected profits.

The mergers and acquisitions, between companies in the financial system, started to take place in the United States and around the world, and led to the globalization of banking and financial industry (Barth, Brumbugh & Wilcox, 2000) and to a national and international change on the way of operating of the several intermediates (Pereira, 2019).

This process was related to the corporate restructuring and international financial markets integration and delocalization, being oriented by increasing of profits and mergers and acquisitions, with effects on the economic and financial crisis verified in the first decade of the 21st century (Barth, Brumbugh & Wilcox, 2000; Mishkin, 2017). According to Cecchetti (2006: 323), the banking industry became more profitable, diminishing the operational costs, increasing the interest rates paid to depositors, and all process of "*the deregulation of the banks was good for the economy* ". However, although some authors point the case of the concentration of different financial activities that reduce insolvency of financial institutions by increasing diversification (Kwan & Laderman, 1999; Barth, Brumbugh & Wilcox, 2000). Other authors concern about the potential risks from expanded banking activities related with the case that the concentration of *"a wide range of activities might increase the risk of insolvency"* (Barth, Brumbugh & Wilcox, 2000: 199).

According to Beck and Demirgüç-Kunt (2009) and Beck, Demirgüç-Kunt and Levine (2010), the integration in global financial markets differ for different income groups, with significate differences between the high-income countries, middle and low income countries. This is based on some indicators like structures, efficiency and stability and trust in domestic banking systems, the activity of capital markets and insurance sectors, and level and relation with financial globalization.

In the last decade of the 1990s, other changes occurred with repercussions on financial markets. At the level of monetary policies of central banks, as consequence of the crises and the high inflation rates of the 1980s, in 1993, Taylor postulated the Taylor Rule (Taylor, 1993) and the central banks of developed countries start using this rule to define their monetary policies and the interest rate. The central bank of New Zealand, followed by the other central banks of developed economies, became politically and economically independent of the government and set inflation targets or bands (mostly between 2% and 5%) as a means of controlling inflation and achieving a desired price stability (Bofinger, 2001; Mishkin, 2017). These facts changed the policies of the central banks and influencing the way is done the inflation management in developed countries.

The Restructuring of the Financial System on the 21st Century

The global economy and financial structure changes occurred in the last decades of the 20th century led to the restructuring of the financial system in the first decades of the current century. This restructuring resulted from the development of the financial markets worldwide, financial innovations and advances in technology, market deregulation, globalization, regulatory reforms, market structures and (re)formulation of central banks' monetary policy. The development and intensification of international trade created needs for the development of the financial system with financial innovations associated to the technologic progress as answer to the increasing competitive environment and leading the process that promoted the changes operated in the financial system (Cecchetti & Schoenholtz, 2017; Masciandaro & Quityn, 2013; Mishkin, 2017).

So, one can say that the restructuring of the financial system, on the 21st century, have been occurred following the observed changes that took place in the last decades of the 20th century, and that are described following and summarize in Figure 2.

Internationalization of Financial Markets and Its Repercussions

At the end of the 20th century, the intensive trade exchanges within most of the countries around the world lead to an explosion in international trade, which had increased the needs to improve the international financial services, initially based on the needs to realize payments between countries and across the national boundaries. And, nowadays, the *"international banking system has adjusted to the needs of an interdependent and globalized world"* (Cecchitti, 2007: 324). Banks of many different nationalities operate in many foreign countries around the world, being the most common approach structure to open foreign branches, and being dependent on factors as the business and legal environment.

From the last decade of the 20th century the banking industry observed a decline in the total number of banks and an increase in the number of banks with branches, a globalization trend and, by the end of the 1990s, in most of the advanced economies, the regulation imposed to segmentation that forbidden the business combinations, between the several financial segments, was repealed (Abreu et al., 2007; Mishkin, 2017). For example, the Citigroup, resulting from a merger, that took place in 1998, between the Citibank, the Traveler's Insurance Company and the investment bank Salomon Smith Barney (Cecchetti, 2006), has currently more than 100 million customers in more than 100 different countries, concentrates its economic activities on deposits and loans as a commercial bank, offer products as a financial institution, and is also an insurance company, a pension fund, a securities broker, and provides mutual funds.

Nowadays, global finance is interconnected, interactive and interdependent; and the financial system became over-leveraged (Bruno & Shin, 2015). The finance and banking corporate restructuring and business integration processes have been influenced by the quick growth of financial markets, where companies can quickly change owners inside the country and across country borders, and also by the emergence of financial markets of increasingly internationally open countries, as for example the countries of former Soviet Union, China, India, and other emergent markets.

The introduction of the new technologies of information and communication, and internet systems in the financial system allow the integration of the financial system in an international way, as well as to get more information about costumers, businesses, countries, and markets (Jayawardhena & Foley, 2000). Is now simpler to get information and to obtain a loan virtually and to a depositor seek the highest return for his savings anywhere in the world if it is more advantageous, or someone who looks for any kind of insurance at the best price quotation in a few minutes or hours by searching on the Internet. In the same way, it is harder for banks and other financial companies to get profits than were some decades ago, once the competition is globally bigger now (Cecchetti, 2006).

The deregulation of financial markets occurred allowed to facilitate the internationalization of financial markets, since deregulation is based on the reduction of institutional control over the functioning of markets, and thus allowed more liberalized markets to increase their efficiency (Abreu et al, 2007). Increased efficiency means that there is increased transparency and the speed with which new information is transmitted to prices (Pereira, 2019).

The new (de)regulation allow the creation of financial holding companies, sometimes also designated for universal banks (Cecchetti, 2006). These large financial companies, according to Cecchetti, (2006), have three main reasons to be created:

- The diversification of business that allows to decrease the risk and increase the profits;
- The dimension of these large firms is enough to take advantage of economies of scale; and
- The economies of scope resulting from the integration of different business in the same company.

For another side, based on the increasing globalization, the growth of international transactions and technological improvements in information and communications technology (ICT), the development of new payment instruments took place. Is, for example, the case of the outsourcing and offshoring of finances and banking, which applications began to take place in the late 1990s (Palugod & Palugod, 2011).

The Financial Innovations

The evolution of the financial system, in the last decades, is strictly related with the evolution of the process of financial innovations, which revolutionized the financial system as one know it today. According to Mishkin (2017: 250), a *"change in the financial environment will stimulate a search by financial institutions for innovations that are likely to be profitable*". Also, the same author states that the changes in the financial system started in the 1960s, when the individuals and institutions have faced drastic changes in the economic environment: high inflation rates, increasing interest rates, increasing unemployment, rapid advances in computer technology, and financial regulations. These circumstances have changed the conditions of market supply and demand, in terms of the conditions prevailing in the financial markets. Which required that financial institutions had to found ai.

Mishkin (2017) suggests a framework for the understanding of why financial institutions develop financial innovations. This author states that financial innovation produce three different basic types of innovations in their search for maximizing their profits:

1. **Responses to Changes in Demand Conditions:** This type of financial innovation is related to the interest rate volatility and to the changes verified in the demand for financial products. The positive relation between interest rates and the demand for financial products and services to reduce the risk which stimulated the search for profitable innovative new financial instruments that allow to obtain a lower interest rate risk. Some examples of this kind of financial innovations are the adjustable rate mortgages and financial derivatives; and the venture capital and start-up funding.
2. **Responses to Changes in Supply Conditions:** This type of financial innovation is related to the improvement in computer, telecommunications and information technology. This technology allowed to decrease the cost of processing financial transactions and create new financial products and services; and for other side made the obtainment of information by the investors more easy and quick. The large and rapid developments in information and communications technology made it possible to develop many innovative financial products and services in the last decades. Some examples of these are the Bank Credit and Debit Cards and their associated services; the Electronic Banking (e-banking) through the automated teller machine (ATM) that allow the customers to get money cash, make deposits, transfer funds and check balances during 24 hours, the home banking that allow trough a telephone or a personal computer establish a connection between the costumer and the bank to carry out transactions, automated banking machine (ABM) which combines in the same location an ATM, an Internet connection to the bank's web site and the telephone link to customer service, a virtual bank that is a new kind of bank institution consisting in a bank with no physical location (also exists virtual insurance firms and virtual security firms); Junk Bonds that allow to have more information about the companies that issue the bonds, becoming easier to investors to obtain financial information about these companies knowing any inherent credit risk that could be associated to this bonds; Commercial Paper Market developments with improvements in information technology; and Securitization. The rapid expansion of the on-line financial services, with the first online stock brokerage platform in the late 1990s, which with the increasing competition brought more user friendly platforms, faster trading, new and complementary services and lower fees.

3. **Avoidance of Existing Regulation:** The financial industry is one of the more regulated industries by government regulations, which leads to financial innovations through the creation of incentives for companies to bypassing regulations that influence their profits negatively, and this way trying to increase their own profitability.

According to Abreu et al (2007), there are two regulation areas that limit the capacity of obtain of bigger profits are the i) the minimum cash reserves, which represent the banks' obligation to keep a percentage of their deposits as reserves. These act as a tax on deposits, since they do not receive interest or are remunerated at rates lower than those of merit. And ii) the restrictions on interest rates. In response to attempts to circumvent the restrictions imposed by cash reserves and interest rate caps, two innovative products have been developed: money market funds and weep accounts that allow banking institutions to escape the formation of reserves.

The financial innovations have created a more competitive environment for the banking and financial industry as answer to the needs of the new economic environment and the new technologic progress, which lead the industry to change dramatically in the 21st century (Mishkin, 2017). The traditional financial intermediation role of banking, based on banks as an intermediary to make loans, that were funded with costumers deposits is no longer at the center of the current financial system. However, this fact is not sufficient to justify the decline in the market share and profitability of banking industry in total lending and as intermediary of assets. As in the other industries, is the profit that moves the companies, and if occurs a decline in profitability the result is the exit from the industry (Abreu *et al,* 2007). This occurred in the decades of 1980s and 1990s, with the observed decline of the traditional banking (Edwards & Mishkin, 1995), which was driven the financial industry to look for new lines of business based on financial innovations, and later, when the law allowed, proceed to mergers and acquisition leading to a concentration of larger financial corporations and financial groups with branches and business around the world and to the banking industry consolidation (see Berger, Demsetz & Strahan, 1999). This situation reflected in the decreasing of the number of commercial banks but in the increase of the dimension of the existing ones – as named by the Federal Reserve of Large, Complex Banking Organizations (LCBOs) (Mishkin, 2017). The existence of the Web and the improvements in the computer and communication technologies, besides strengthening the consolidation, increased the economies of scale and economies of scope. The consolidation took to bigger financial institutions and to the increase of the combination of products and services provided by the financial institutions (Berger, Demsetz. & Strahan, 1999).

The Regulation of the Financial System and Its Problems

The main objectives of the regulation and supervision of the financial system are to control the essential role played by the accumulation of capital and the allocation of financial resources in the process of economic development and the particularities of the financial intermediation activity and the operators involved (Herring & Carmassi, 2008). So, the regulation and supervision intents to prevent and avoid systematic risks, protect consumers and investors, and encourage the stability and efficiency of the financial system in the economy (Bofinger, 2001). For a complete overview of the evolution of financial supervision see Masciandaro and Quityn (2013).

The regulation and supervision of the financial system are based essentially in two types of regulations or supervisions: the prudential regulation and the behavioral regulation (Abreu et al, 2007; Bank of Portugal, 2016). The prudential regulation that is related to solvency concerns and financial soundness of the intervening institutions, it involves government regulation and is crucial to the efficient and well-functioning of the financial system (see Mishkin, 2001). And it is a necessary condition to reduce asymmetric information (Mishkin, 2001; Herring & Carmassi, 2008). The rationale for the prudential supervision is based on the regulations established by all the governments to reduce risk taking to provide for a safety net for the banking system through supervisors monitor banks, otherwise the banks would have an incentive to take excessive risks that could lead to banking – currency and financial – crises (Corsetti, Pesenti & Roubini, 1998; Mishkin, 1999, 2001; Masciandaro & Quityn, 2013).

For another side, the behavioral regulation is associated with the way the business is conducted by financial institutions to its clients (Pereira, 2019). It covers the dissemination of information. This type of regulation is extremely important to prevent crisis situations and if by one way it includes behavioral aspects to prevent crises, for other is policy responses to the recent global financial crisis that lead to changes in systems, procedures and rules in the financial sector (Khan, 2018). According to Khan (2018:5) some examples of the behavioral regulatory approach "*are the Basel III capital and liquidity rules for banks to maintain higher standards; the European Solvency II Directive developing similar capital standards for insurance companies; and IFRS 9 (International Financial Reporting Standards) improving accounting rules by making asset and liability valuation more forward looking, incorporating elements of business models and expected losses*". This author also states that the most notable efforts are the Financial Stability Board's (FSB) work on risk culture (FSB, 2014), the report done by the European Commission (European Commission, 2013) and the World Development Report 2015 (World Bank, 2015). However, ten years after the recent global financial crisis, according to some authors, the policy response on the behavioral regulation seems to not be as effective as it was desirable to be (Khan, 2018; Bainbridge, 2011).

The main reasons for the existence and importance of regulation in an economy is related to prevent and control decision making of the *homo economicus* self-interest focused on companies material incentives explained by the Agency Theory (Jensen & Meckling, 1976), through the existence of legal norms and sanctions (Barth, Brumbugh & Wilcox, 2000; Khan, 2018) and increasing the information available to savers and investors, improving the control of the financial system and ensure the well-functioning and the solidity of the financial system (Mishkin, 2001). For this last issue are relevant the restrictions on market entry, the publication of results, the restrictions on assets and activities, the deposit guarantee, the limits to competition, the limits on interest rates and the solvency ratios.

Under the behavioral regulation, in the United States, President Trump defined in the Executive Order 13772, of February 2017, with "*the core principles for regulating the financial system. These principles include "make regulation efficient, effective, and appropriately tailored"*" (Khan, 2018: 12).

An efficient market is a market in which prices incorporate all available and relevant information for the value of financial assets, and asset prices reflect their fundamental value, then the information available in the market is crucial. The greater the integration in several segments and in several geographic markets, the more difficult it is to have specific information about an asset of a segment in a specific market. Just as dispersion and inter correlation, in addition to hindering the perfect information, also facilitates contagion operations between assets and markets, more easily and faster. So, to prevent from crises, the trend observed, on the last decade, in the United States, in the European Union member states and in the Organization for Economic Co-operation and Development (OECD) countries has been to increase the Regulatory Impact Assessments (OECD, 2012; Khan, 2018). However, this systematic approach has been criticized, once the negative effects of proposed and existing regulations have taken to extra costs higher than the obtained benefits (Hawkesby, 2000; Khan, 2018).

The technological, geographic and functional integration of the three segments of banking, financial and insurance at the level of institutions, instruments and markets and the increasing integration of financial markets has increased the difficulty of maintaining regulation and supervision at a national level (Bank for International Settlements, 1995). The alliances between the various European stock exchanges, mergers and acquisitions between banks, financial companies and insurers around the world advanced economies had a predominant influence in the delocalization and the problems of regulations resulting from these facts. Soto (2012) postulated a causal relationship between money, bank credit and economic cycles, in the functioning of the banking industry relevance for the occurrence of crises.

REGULATIONS AND SUPERVISIONS INFLUENCING THE RESTRUCTURING OF FINANCIAL SYSTEM: CURRENT SITUATION AND RECOMMENDATIONS FOR FUTURE

Soto (2012) presents some suggestions and strategies for a process of banking reform based in a gradual evolution process from a more controlled system, citing the example of the United States and European Union to a least controlled system. However, this approach is not common to all the authors. And the trend observed, in the last years, by the central banks of the most advanced economies are directed to the globalization and decentralization of the financial system, but oriented for a more efficient control sustained by more tight legislation and regulation (Bank for International Settlements, 2017).

There are different regulatory or supervisory models: "single regulator model", "twin or four peaks", "institutional" or by nature of the intermediary (bank, insurance or securities) or by objectives (Cecchetti, 2007; Bofinger, 2001).

The concern with the confidence and soundness of the financial system has created an incentive to regulate the activity of financial intermediaries in general and the banking sector in particular. The existence of problems of asymmetric information, whether of adverse selection, moral hazard or the principal-agent problem, justifies this regulation and supervision that has become tighter in the last decade, and where seven categories of banking regulation are usually identified (Abreu et al, 2007; Mishkin, 2017) Governmental safety net; 2) restrictions on the holding of assets; 3) Own capital requirements; 4) Supervision and audit; 5) Risk management assessment; 6) Protection of consumers and investors; 7) Restrictions to competition.

For the regulation and supervision of the financial system, the *"government officials employ three strategies to ensure that the risks created by the safety net are controlled. Government regulation establishes a set of specific rules for bank managers to follow. Government supervision provides general oversight of financial institutions. And formal examination of banks´ books by specialists provides detailed information on the firm's operation"*(Mishkin, 2007: 370).

Based in Di Giorgio and Di Noia (2008), the current financial regulation and supervision in the United States and in European Union are characterized by different structures. In the United States, the structure of financial regulators and supervisors is complex and is divided into the three segments. For the banking industry there are four federal banking agencies: the Federal Reserve, the Office of the Comptroller of the currency, the Office of Thrifts Supervision and the Federal Deposit Insurance Corporation. For securities segment there are two federal entities: the Securities and Exchange Commission and the Commodity Futures and Trading Commission. For the insurance segment, there is no federal entity, but some state insurance departments are responsible for its regulation and supervision. The Federal Prudential Financial Regulator combines all federal bank charter and consolidates all federal bank regulators in a single prudential regulator. In the European Union, regulation focuses mainly on the banking intermediaries due to the predominant role of this segment in the financial system in continental Europe. The recent actions implemented by the European Commission directives had promoted the *"increasing cross-border financial market integration that first stimulated and then followed the 1992 single market program and adoption of the Euro. However, apart (...) ensure that all financial sectors were adequately regulated and supervised, no European law explicitly deals with the problem of how regulating and supervising financial markets and intermediates. As a consequence, the current picture in the European Union is that a combination of different regulatory approaches*" (Di Giorgio & Di Noia, 2008: 9).

Different European countries have different regulations. The Nordic countries in the North of Europe, the United Kingdom, Austria, Belgium and Germany characterizes to delegate financial regulation and supervision into a unique agency, consistent with the "Single Regulator" supervisor model. In Finland and Luxembourg, a unique agency is responsible for the supervision of banking and securities activities but not for the insurance activities (Di Giorgio & Di Noia, 2008). In the case of Portugal, Spain and Italy there are different specialized institutional supervisors regulating each one of the financial segmented markets. In the Dutch case, the twin-peak model is applied, *"stablishing a single authority for financial market transparency and investor protection, while leaving the supervisory responsibility for microeconomics stability to the central bank"* (Di Giorgio & Di Noia, 2008:9). The other countries in the European Union apply the traditional model.

Mishkin (2017) postulates three basic frameworks for banking and securities industries worldwide: the first framework is the *universal banking* that provides no separation between the banking and securities segments, which exists in Germany, the Netherlands and Switzerland *"in a universal banking system, commercial banks provide a full range of banking, securities, real state, and insurance services, all within a single legal entity"* (Mishkin, 2017: 269). The second framework is the *British-style universal banking system*, exists in the United Kingdom and the other Anglo-Saxon countries more closely to the capital markets orientation like Canada, Australia, and the United States. This framework *"engages in securities underwriting, but it differs from the German-style universal in three ways: Separate legal subsidiaries are more common, bank equity holding of commercial firms are less common, and combinations of banking and insurance firms are less common"* (Mishkin, 2017: 269). The third framework relates to some legal separation of the banking and other financial services industries, and is found in Japan. In this case, the *"major difference between the United States and the Japanese banking systems is that Japanese banks are allowed to hold substantial equity stakes in commercial firms, whereas America banks cannot. In addition, most American banks use a bank holding company structure, but bank holding companies are illegal in Japan"* (Mishkin, 2007: 269).

The existing institutional regulatory differences in the European Union member states can be a barrier to financial integration and to the transmission mechanisms of monetary policy in the case of the common monetary policy of the Eurozone (Ioannidou, 2005; Masciandaro, 2007, 2008; Di Giorgio & Di Noia, 2008; Ceccarelli, Maddaloni & Peydro, 2013), where the principle of minimum harmonization and mutual recognition should be in force inducing the convergence of regulatory behavior and more uniform rules. To overcome this discrepancy and harmonize the regulatory system inducing the convergence in the European Union member states a new definition for financial market regulation and supervision must be implemented based in the adoption of a central regulator and supervisor for the European Union and the United States (see Di Giorgio & Di Noia, 2008). This hypothesis may be sustained in the restructuring observed in the financial system in the last decades with the consolidation of the three financial market segments both in European Union and in the United States. The regulatory and supervisory model by objectives, with all the financial intermediaries and markets being subject of supervision of more than one authority and a central agency supervising the stability of financial system, monetary policy and the prudential regulation – in this case verifying the 4-peak regulatory model by objectives (Di Giorgio & Di Noia, 2008: 22).

The regulatory framework applied at a national or zone level is relevant, but the harmonized regulatory policies to supervise the international dimensions of macro prudential policies and an international level also very important for the well-functioning of international financial systems (Agénor et al, 2017).

FUTURE RESEARCH DIRECTIONS ON THE RESTRUCTURING OF THE FINANCIAL SYSTEM IN THE 21st CENTURY

The restructuring of the financial system is a relevant topic to be a target of future research under the present book's theme, once the financial system is one of the pillar foundations for the well-functioning, economic growth and development of modern economies; and the restructuring of the financial system in strictly related with the developments of technologic progress and innovations and international trade and globalization. This topic is strictly related to funding and the normal development of the productive activities of current economics, being the growth rate of GDP related to the development of the financial system. The restructuring of the financial system as has been verified, in a general way, in all of the world economies resulting from the needs from the new realities of production, international trade, information and globalization leading to a better efficiency to the demand and supply sides, maximizing the needs and utility of costumers and information and profitability for the financial markets business.

So, given the importance of the restructuring of the financial system that has been occurring in constant evolution and adaptation in response to the new needs of the financial market, globalization and technological progress, it is important to study this topic continuously. In addition to the fact that this topic influences the whole productive system and the other sectors of an economy and the world economy, as well as some attributed influence in the occurrence of crises at a national and worldwide levels, given its current characteristics of the liberalization, interconnection, internationalization and consolidation of financial markets. Given these characteristics and the differences across different groups of countries, the regulation and supervision from central banks and international organizations, like the International Monetary Fund (IMF) and the World Bank, are of increased importance for the stability of the financial system and for preventing potential crises (Beck, Demirgüç-Kunt & Levine, 2010).

Special attention must be also paid to this current characteristics and trends on the restructuring of financial systems on the 21st century, which we can add the financial innovations through the technologic progress (e.g. te offshoring and outsourcing of finances and banking in the different income group of countries); the new policies of central banks, IMF and World Bank and the effects of emerging countries, like for example the China on global finances.

Figure 2. Summary of the restructuring of the financial system in the 21st century

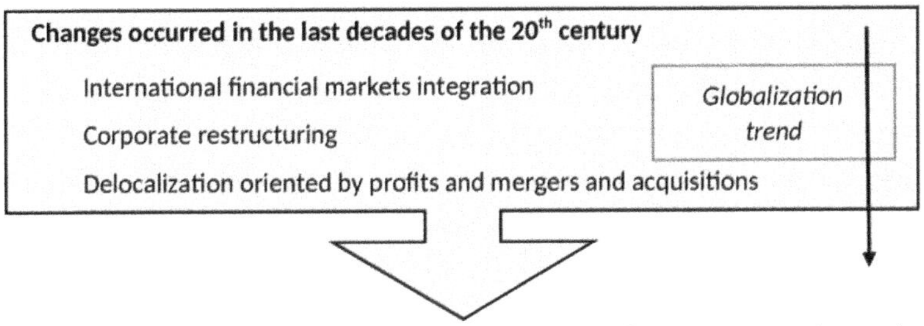

	Consequences and examples
Development of the financial markets	global finance is interconnected, interactive and interdependent
Advances in technologies	introduction of the new technologies of information and communication, and internet systems in the financial system
Market deregulation	facilitated the internationalization of financial markets, increased efficiency and allowed the creation of large financial companies
Increasing globalization	growth of international transactions and technological improvements in ICT, development of new payment instruments. (for example, the case of the outsourcing and offshoring of finances and banking)
Financial innovations	new ways to adapt to the new competitive new economic environment to survive and be able to maximize their own profits, as -responses to changes in demand conditions (examples: the adjustable rate mortgages and financial derivatives; and the venture capital and start-up funding, ...), -responses to changes in supply conditions (examples: credit and debit cards, ATMs, ABMs, virtual banking, junk banks, commercial paper market, securitization,...) -avoidance to existing regulation (examples: money market funds and weep accounts)
Market structures	Changes in the market structures in result of the above trends and the new emergent markets
Regulatory reforms of central banks and international institutions (World Bank, IMF, ...)	regulation and supervision to prevent and avoid systematic risks, protect consumers and investors, and encourage the stability and efficiency of the financial system in the economy (Examples: changing policies of World Bank and FMI, prudential and behavioral regulation and supervisions,...)
(Re)formulation of central bank's monetary policy	Changing policies of central banks in the last 20 years; discretionary monetary policies of EBC to face the recent crisis , Taylor's Rule, ...

CONCLUSION

The restructuration of the financial system has evolved in parallel with the events occurring in the economies and in response to the needs of the demand and supply of the agents involved, which has occurred with the intensification of production and international trade resulting from the industrial revolution, the Great Depression of the periods which followed the great world wars, the great development of markets in the nineties, and the subprime world crisis in the first decade of the twentieth century as important milestones in this evolution.

After the Great Depression, took place a restructuration of the financial system with the implementation of government regulations applied to the separation of the several segments of the financial market as a way to control and better supervise them. In the United States, the Glass-Steagall Act of 1933 separated the activities of commercial banks from the securities industries, prohibiting commercial banks from underwriting or dealing in corporate securities and prohibiting investment banks to engage in commercial banking. These regulations established in the decade of 1930s in many countries were repealed in the decade of 1990s.

Many factors were in the causes of this new restructuring of the financial system in the end of the 20th century, like the intensive trade exchanges within most of the countries around the world that lead to an explosion in international trade which had increased the need for international financial services, the decline in the total number of banks in the banking industry, the technologic progress in the technologies of information and communication and globalization trend.

The new regulation allows the mergers and acquisitions, within the several financial markets, which took to the consolidation and glomeration of financial activities restructuring the corporate finance business allowing the creation of larger international financial holding companies. The finance and banking corporate restructuring and business integration processes have been influenced by the quick growth of financial markets, where companies can quickly change owners inside the country and across country borders, and also by the emergence of financial markets of increasingly internationally tanking to the currently internationalization, sometimes named also globalization, of finance and financial asset with the financial market being interconnected, interactive and interdependent.

The introduction of the new technologies of information and internet systems in the financial system allows the integration of the financial system in an international way, as well as to get more and better information about all the actors and factors acting in the financial markets. Nowadays in more simple and quick get information about a product or a service in any part of the world through the use of the internet, increasing the efficiency of these markets. In the same way, it is harder for banks and other financial companies to get profits, which led to the development of financial innovation in products and financial services to improve the answer to de need and demand of costumers and also to increase the profitability of the business.

The occurred deregulation of financial markets, since this is based on the reduction of institutional control over the functioning of markets have facilitated the liberalization and the internationalization of financial markets, and allowed to increase the economic efficiency. The integration of different business in the same company and the international financial holding companies, that took place in most of the world advance economies, allowed to decrease asymmetric information and take advantage of economies of scale and the economies of scope resulting from.

The restructuring of the financial system has been occurring over the last century, was particularly important in the last three decades. It has verified a constant evolution and adaptation in response to the new needs of the markets, the globalization and the advances in technological progress. Its regulation and supervision are of extreme importance once the finance system is one of the main pillars for the good function and sustainable development of economies. The problems that may occur on its functioning will lead to losses of confidence, and financial and banking crises.

So, the first decades of the 21st century verified the corporate restructuring and international financial markets integration and delocalization being oriented by profits and mergers and acquisitions. The global economy and financial structure changes occurred in this century derived from financial innovations, market deregulation, globalization, technology, regulatory reforms, and market structures and (re) formulation of central banks'. The regulation and supervision became to have a great relevance with the restructuring and the occurrence of the recent global crisis of 2007, as a way to guarantee the solidity and trust in the financial system, in particular, the prudential supervision.

These corporate restructuring facts occurred on the first decades of the 21st century, led to some authors to state that, in a general way, the new paradigm of the new deregulation or financial liberalization of the financial system was good for the economy.

REFERENCES

Abreu, M., Ferreira, C., Barata, L., & Escária, V. (2007). *Economia Monetária e Financeira*. Lisbon: Escolar Editora.

Agénor, P. R., Kharroubi, E., Gambacorta, L., Lombardo, G., & Pereira da Siva, L. A. (2017), *The International Dimensions of Macroprudential Policies, Bank for International Settlements*. BIS Working Papers, Nº. 643, June.

Bainbridge, S. M. (2011). Dodd Frank: Quark Federal Corporate Governance Round II. *Minnesota Law Review*, *95*, 1779–1821.

Bank for International Settlements (1995). 65th Annual Report, 1994–1995.

Bank for International Settlements. (2017). *Understanding Globalisation*. BIS Annual Economic Report, Bank for International Settlements. Accessed in December 05, 2018 on https://www.bis.org/publ/arpdf/ar2017e6.htm

Bank of Portugal. (2016). *White Paper on the Regulation and Supervision of the Financial System*. Bank of Portugal, Governor's Office, Lisbon, Portugal.

Barth, J. R., Brumbugh, R. D., & Wilcox, J. A. (2000, Spring). The Repeal of Glass- Steagall and the Advent of Broad Banking. *The Journal of Economic Perspectives*, *14*(2), 191–204. doi:10.1257/jep.14.2.191

Beck, T., & Demirguc-Kunt, A. (2009). *Financial institutions and markets across countries and over time-data and analysis*. The World Bank. doi:10.1596/1813-9450-4943

Beck, T., Demirgüç-Kunt, A., & Levine, R. (2010). Financial institutions and markets across countries and over time: The updated financial development and structure database. *The World Bank Economic Review*, *24*(1), 77–92. doi:10.1093/wber/lhp016

Benston, G. (1990). *The Separation of Commercial and Investment Banking: The Glass-Steagall Act Revisited and Reconsidered.* Oxford, UK: Oxford University Press. doi:10.1007/978-1-349-11280-7

Berger, A. N., Demsetz, R. S., & Strahan, P. E. (1999, February). The Consolidation of the Financial Services Industry: Causes, Consequences and Implications for the Future. *Journal of Banking & Finance, 23*(2–4), 135–194. doi:10.1016/S0378-4266(98)00125-3

Berger, A. N., Kashyap, A. K., Scalise, J. M., Gertler, M., & Friedman, B. M. (1995). The transformation of the U.S. Banking Industry: What a long strange trip it's been. *Brookings Papers on Economic Activity, 2*(2), 55–201. doi:10.2307/2534612

Bofinger, P. (2001). *Monetary Policy, Goals, Institutions, Strategies, and Instruments* (1st ed.). New York: Oxford University Press.

Bruno, V., & Shin, H. S. (2015). Cross-Border Banking and Global Liquidity. *The Review of Economic Studies, 82*(2), 535–564. doi:10.1093/restud/rdu042

Ceccarelli, M. A., Maddaloni, A., & Peydro, J. L. (2013). Heterogeneous Transmission Mechanism: Monetary Policy and Financial Fragility in the Eurozone. *Economic Policy, 28*(75), 459–512. doi:10.1111/1468-0327.12015

Cecchetti, S. (2006). *Money, Banking and Financial Markets* (2nd ed.). McGraw-Hill.

Cecchetti, S., & Schoenholtz, K. (2017). *Money, Banking and Financial Markets* (5th ed.). McGraw-Hill.

Corsetti, G., Pesenti, P., & Roubini, N. (1999). What Caused the Asian currency and financial crisis? *Japan and the World Economy, 11*(3), 305–373. doi:10.1016/S0922-1425(99)00019-5

Di Giorgio, G., & Di Noia, C. (2008). *Designing a Regulatory and Supervisory Framework for Integrated Financial Markets* (Discussion Paper). Working Paper LUISS Guido Carli.

Didier, T., & Schumkler, S. L. (2014). *Financial Development in Asia: Beyond Aggregate Indicators.* Policy Research Working Paper, Paper 6761, The World Bank.

dos Santos, T. (2001). *O Sistema Financeiro e a Globalização – A Regulação do Sistema Financeiro.* CMVM. Retrieved from www.cmvm.pt

Edwards, F., & Mishkin, F. S. (1995). The Decline of Traditional Banking: Implications for financial stability and regulatory policy. *Federal Reserve Bank of New York Economic Policy Review, 1*(3), 27–45.

European Central Bank (ECB). (2014). *Guide to Banking Supervision.* ECB Banking Supervision.

European Commission. (2013). *Applying Behavioral Sciences to EU Policy-making.* JRC Scientific and Policy Reports, EUR 26033.

European Union. (2013). *European Union Capital Requirements Directive IV, 575/2013.* European Parliament.

Financial Stability Board's (FSB). (2014). Guidance on Supervision Interaction with Financial Institutions on Risk Culture: A Framework for Assessing Risk Culture. Financial Stability Board.

Hawkesby, C. (2000, July). The Institutional Structure of Financial Supervision: A Cost benefit Analysis. *The Journal of International Banking Regulation,* 36-54.

Herring, R. J., & Carmassi, J. (2008). The Structure of Cross Sector Financial Supervision, *Financial Markets. Institutions and Instruments, 17*(1), 51–76. doi:10.1111/j.1468-0416.2007.00132.x

Ioannidou, V. P. (2005). Does Monetary Policy Affect the Central Bank's Role in Bank Supervision? *Journal of Financial Intermediation, 14*(1), 58–85. doi:10.1016/j.jfi.2004.04.002

Jayawardhena, C., & Foley, P. (2000). Changes in the banking sector – the case of Internet banking in the UK. *Internet Research, 10*(1), 19–31. doi:10.1108/10662240010312048

Jensen, M. C., & Meckling, W. H. (1976). Theory of the Firm: Managerial Behavior: Agency Costs and Ownership Structure. *Journal of Financial Economics, 3*(4), 305–360. doi:10.1016/0304-405X(76)90026-X

Khan, A. (2018). *A Behavioral Approach to Financial Supervision, Regulation, and Central Banking.* IMF Working Papers, WP / 18 / 178. International Monetary Fund.

Kwan, S. H., & Laderman, E. S. (1999). On the Portfolio Effects of Financial Convergence – A Review of the Literature, *Economic Review. Federal Reserve Bank of San Francisco., 2,* 18–31.

Lane, P. (2012). The European Sovereign Debt Crisis. *The Journal of Economic Perspectives, 26*(3), 49–68. doi:10.1257/jep.26.3.49

Lewis, M. K., & Mizen, P. D. (2000). *Monetary Economics.* Oxford University Press.

Lindegren, C. J., Balino, J. T., Enoch, C., Gulde, A. M., Quintyn, M., & Teo, L. (1999). *Financial Sector Crisis and Restructuring Lessons from Asia.* IMF Occasional Paper, Nº 188. International Monetary Fund.

Masciandaro, D. (2007). Divide et Impera. Financial Supervision Unification and Central Bank Fragmentation Effect. *European Journal of Political Economy, 23*(2), 285–315. doi:10.1016/j.ejpoleco.2006.02.001

Masciandaro, D. (2008). Unification in Financial Sector Supervision: The Trade Off between Central Bank and Single Authority. *Journal of Financial Regulation and Compliance, 12*(2), 151–169. doi:10.1108/13581980410810768

Masciandaro, D., & Quityn, M. (2013). The Evolution of Financial Supervision: The Continuing Search for the Holy Grail. In *50 Years of Money and Finance: Lessons and Challenges.* SUERF - The European Money and Finance Forum.

Mishkin, F. S. (1999). Lessons from the Asian Crisis. *Journal of International Money and Finance, 18*(4), 709–723. doi:10.1016/S0261-5606(99)00020-0

Mishkin, F. S. (2001). Prudential Supervision: Why Is It Important and What are the Issues? In Prudential Supervision: What Works and What Doesn't. University of Chicago Press.

Mishkin, F. S. (2017). *The Economics of Money, Banking and Financial Markets* (12th ed.). Pearson.

OECD. (2012), Sustainability in Impact Assessment: A Review of Impact Assessment System in Selected OECD Countries and the European Commission. Organisation for Economic Co-operation and Development.

Palugod, N., & Palugod, P. (2011). Global Trends in Offshoring and Outsourcing. *International Journal of Business and Social Science*, *2*(16), 13–19.

Pereira, E. T. (2019). Economia Monetária. *Sílabo Editora. (forthcoming)*

Soto, J. H. (2012). *Money, Bank Credit and Economic Cycles* (3rd ed.). Ludwig Von Mises Institute.

Taylor, J. B. (1993). Discretion versus policy rules in practice. Carnegie-Rochester Conference Series on Public Policy, 39(1), 195-214. doi:10.1016/0167-2231(93)90009-L

World Bank. (2015). *Mind, Society, and Behavioral. World Development Report*. Washington, DC: The World Bank.

ADDITIONAL READING

Atack, J., & Neal, L. (2009). *The Origin and development of Financial Markets and Institutions: From the Seventeenth Century to the Present* (J. Atack & L. Neal, Eds.). New York: Cambridge University Press. doi:10.1017/CBO9780511757419

Bordo, M. D., & Wheelock, D. C. (2007). Stock Market Booms and Monetary Policy in the Twentieth Century. *Federal Reserve Bank of St. Louis Review*, *89*(2), 91–122.

Cecchetti, S., & Schoenholtz, K. (2017). *Money, Banking and Financial Markets* (5th ed.). McGraw-Hill.

Mishkin, F. S. (2017). *The Economics of Money, Banking and Financial Markets* (12th ed.). Pearson.

KEY TERMS AND DEFINITIONS

Asymmetric Information on the Financial Market: Consists in the fact that primary savers and primary borrowers have incomplete information about each other, the level of information being uneven between the contracting parties. If the problem resulting from asymmetric information occurs before the financial transaction we have an adverse selection problem – it occurs when insufficient information about potential borrowers leads to a poor selection of projects for which funding is requested. If the problem resulting from asymmetric information occurs after financial transformation we have a problem of moral hazard – it consists of the risk propensity of the agent contracting a loan to change the initial destination of the funds after the loan is granted. There is also another type of problem associated with asymmetric information, the problem of the principal agent or agency theory.

Behavioral Regulation: It is associated with the way the business is conducted by financial institutions to its clients. It covers the dissemination of information.

Commercial Paper: Is a short-term debt security issued by large banks and corporations.

Commercial Paper Market: Is the market where is transacted the commercial papers.

Conglomeration: Is the process leading to the creation of groups of financial companies operating in the different sectors of the financial system.

Fiduciary Money: The value comes from the trust decreed by the State. Represents the currency in circulation.

Financial System: The financial system represents the set of markets and intermediary institutions that coordinate the supply and demand for funds, savings and investment. The financial system allows 1) the creation of liquidity, 2) minimize transaction costs between savers and investors, 3) minimize the costs of supervising the funds, and 4) spread and dilute risks.

Merchandise Money: Goods that have intrinsic value recognized by the parties involved in the exchange, for example, shells, coffee, cattle, salt, precious metals.

Money: Is an asset generally accepted for payment of goods and services or for payment of debts. Money distinguishes from currency, once money is a general concept that includes currency; and currency represents the fiduciary money of notes and coins.

Money Functions: Exchange instrument or payment method that is used to pay for goods and services, allowing greater efficiency in the process of exchange by reducing transaction costs and eliminates the requirement of double coincidence of needs, leads to specialization and division of labor promoting economic efficiency.

Prudential Regulation: Is related to solvency concerns and financial soundness of the intervening institutions.

Regulation of the Financial System: Consists in the control the essential role played by the accumulation of capital and the allocation of financial resources in the process of economic development and the particularities of the financial intermediation activity and the operators involved. So, the regulation intents to prevent and avoid systematic risks, protect consumers and investors, and encourage the stability and efficiency of the financial system in the economy.

Scriptural or Fiat Money: Instructions to the bank to withdraw funds from the depositor's account and transfer those funds to the person or company whose name is written on the order line. Examples include checks, credit notes.

Securitization: Is the process of transforming illiquid financial assets (e.g., residential mortgages, auto loans, and credit card receivables) into marketable capital market securities. This is one of the most important financial innovations in the past decades.

Unit of Account: Is used to measure value in the economy. It eliminates the need to know all relative prices, and all prices are expressed in monetary units.

Value Reserve: The money retains purchasing power over time, allows to separate the moment of the formation of income from the moment of its use. This function is related to the property of *Liquidity* that is the measure of the facility with which an asset is converted into a medium of exchange. This function results in different money settings (M0, M1, M2, M3, ...). This aggregates depending on the central bank definition.

Chapter 3
Restructuring and Globalization of Telecommunications Industry

Sasmita Mohanty
University of Aveiro, Portugal

ABSTRACT

Restructuring and globalization are very important for every technology sector. It provides key competitive advantages to the companies over their rivals. Telecommunications sector is an important strategic segment of the modern economy. Telecommunications is also an advanced technology sector and its restructuring is essential to optimize its revenues. Now it has been evolved to information and communication technologies (ICT), which is the main driving force of growth worldwide. In fact, ICT has paved the way for modern globalization. Overall, ICT and ICT-enabled sectors are among the main contributors of global economy. This sector has passed through several restructuring and evolves continuously. Its globalization is obvious as it is the main technology which promotes globalization. In this chapter, the authors provide the restructuring of telecommunications sectors since the time of its inception in the early 19th century. They also analyzed the strategic changes that promote the restructuring and globalization of this sector.

INTRODUCTION

Telecommunications industry plays several essential roles in the modern society. Telecommunications has become a basic need in the modern human life. In the business sectors, it has even more important roles. In the modern times, it has been expanded in different forms to be known as the information and communication technologies (ICTs). Due to the essence of ICT, its infrastructure is available in every corner of the world. It has been spread in the form of core, regional, metro and local networks. Most of the access areas are covered through the wireless networks and the core parts are mainly optical fibers. Along with the support of computing, ICTs change the lifestyles and business landscapes which were not possible before their conjugation. The Internet is the clear outcome of the conjugation of these two enabling technologies that has changed the world's communication and business frameworks. That is why, ICT sector is very often regarded as the nervous system of the current world.

DOI: 10.4018/978-1-5225-8906-8.ch003

Telecommunications sector has gone through several stages of evolutions. In the early years, it was started as a point-to-point communication enabling two individuals to communicate. Then came, the broadcasting systems in which the information was transmitted from one source to multiple destinations. Gradually, with the advances of computing, this system evolved in to software enabled multimedia systems. This is how global entertainment and news sectors came into existence. In the last three decades, ICT has disrupted the global businesses several times. First, the arrival of the Internet changed the global business landscapes. The popularity of the mobile communications further enhanced the proliferation of businesses. Mobile communication evolves every decade and it disrupts the global economy in several new ways. The other famous disruptions of the last two decades are: the proliferation of social networks, and arrival of the Internet of things (IoT). It is needless to say that this sector needs regular restructuring with the changing times. New demands propel new inventions in ICT which finally results in restructuring. In ICT, in the recent years, we have witnessed several restructuring at various levels. Some of them are at the foundation level in which the driving technologies themselves have been changed significantly. The others are mainly found at the application and management levels. The changes in the applications are either user or market driven. At the management level, the changes are due to the strategic modifications of the investors to optimize their positions in the market.

Globalization of ICT is a natural choice for the investors. They want larger markets and modern day trade rules facilitate the access to foreign markets. The services landscape in ICT is very much potent in revenue generation. ICT services have evolved in many different ways. The segments which used to generate huge revenue before two decades now have been pushed back by the new services. Globalization brought new enterprises in to the market and at the same time several existing enterprises have disappeared. Irrespective of these changes, ICT sector went up gradually to be the main driver of the global economy. Thus it is clear that restructuring and globalization of ICT sectors are very much significant in the modern world. ICT industry is the main facilitator of the growth and development. The countries which are doing great economically have excellent ICT infrastructure. It is true that the countries which are economically weak are also backward in ICT. Human development index (HDI) and the ICT growth too run in parallel. Countries which are advanced in technology and uses better ICTs have better HDI.

In this chapter, we provide restructuring trends of global telecommunications industry. Restructuring is essential for telecommunications, and we analyze the issues related to it. We show the intensities of globalization in different times and their effects on the market. We present chronological restructuring of telecommunications sector starting from its beginning until the recent years. We present the globalization of telecommunications at different times and its effect of the global trade.

The main objective of this chapter is to provide the overviews of restructuring and globalization in the telecommunications sector since its beginning. Strategic changes in this sector have forced multifaceted restructuring. Globalization is one of the main leading strategies for its expansion. Restructuring and globalization together are very much at the forefront of the telecommunications revolution around the world. We analyzed the past and contemporary literatures to find out the nature of restructuring in different era.

In this chapter, we have eight sections. In Section 2, we review the related literature for this chapter. In Section 3, we provide the methodologies used for this work. In Section 4, we analyze the strategic changes in the telecommunications sector in the last few decades that had motivated the major restructuring in the sector. In Section 5, we show different types of commonly observed restructuring in telecommunications sector. In Section 6, we present the globalization aspects of telecommunications companies. In Section 7, we have discussed the future research directions. We have highlighted the future researches which are important for the growth and restructuring prospects of the ICT sector. Finally, we conclude in Section 8 with the main points.

LITERATURE REVIEW

Telecommunications is a well-researched area. A large number of research activities are being carried on telecommunications management. Its restructuring is very much common since the days of its inception. However, since the beginning of liberalization in the late 1970s and 1980s, restructuring became a key strategic requirement. Based on the strategic changes over the decades, several literatures are available. Since the invention of the telephone, expansion of cross-border telecommunications services continues. Ericsson started its manufacturing of telephone sets and other telecom equipments as early as 1878. Similarly, the cable and wireless started their manufacturing in the 1860s. All these companies globalized their businesses. In the liberalization era, globalization became a key strategic move and become a priority for the leading players of telecommunications operation and equipment vending.

Bruce (1989) studied the restructuring of telecommunications sector in developing countries. Restructuring in developing countries is more important than in the developed countries. In the developing countries, the demand is lower compared to the developed countries and the markets in the developing countries are less exploited. The opportunities for the operators are more in the developing countries as the market is not saturated. However, the prices and other sensitive issues must be planned according to the market dynamics. The costs for infrastructure building and network deployment are costly and the returns may take a long time. Therefore these aspects must be addressed at the planning phase to avoid revenue blackouts. The author has shown the cases of several developing countries where the governmental assistance has been provided and regulatory changes have been passed in favor of restructuring for ICT developments. Bell (1990) analyzed the effects of monopoly in the pre-1980s era and the compared the new scenarios of liberalization and completion. In 1984, AT&T was broken down to 19 smaller companies. British Telecommunications in the UK was privatized in the same year. Similarly, the Japanese telecommunications company NTT was privatized in the 1980s. These are the structural reforms in the telecommunications companies in the 1980s. In some way, these steps removed monopoly from the telecommunications market and introduced competition and liberalization through privatization. The author compared the state of research and development in the two different scenarios. Due to these changes business strategies too were restructured for coping with the new initiatives. Hudson (1991) analyzed the roles of ITU in the development and technical cooperation for the adoption of new technologies in telecommunications. In this work the author focuses the cases of Africa. Traditionally, Africa does not have advanced infrastructure for global communications. There are several reasons behind this such as economical difficulties and lack of political intent. Therefore, international organizations such as ITU have important roles to promote the development in telecommunications in these countries. In fact, ITU is showing increased focus for these developing countries. In many cases it has taken initiative to build networks and motivated for modern restructuring.

Bagley and Hunter (1992), studied different aspects of restructuring in commonly observed industries. According to their findings, restructuring is inevitable in every sector. It is one of the basic needs for the survival of a company. In their study, they analyzed the education system in the US. They suggested that technology plays a key role in the modern restructuring across all the sectors including primary and higher education. Stagliano (1994) presents the roles played by ITU in the regulation, technology adoption and liberalization of the telecommunications industry. ITU as a global organization for the telecommunications standardization and expansion has taken several positive initiatives over the years. It also makes sure that fundamental telecommunications services are available in every country. It played the main role in the telecommunications revolution of 1980s and 1990s. It works as an advisory board for the member countries and explain them about the overall benefits of restructuring. Wellenius and Stern (1994) went through the implementation of reforms in the telecommunications sector for several countries. In their World Bank sponsored documentation they brought forward all the relevant factors of the reforms around the world. According to them the structural reforms for the ICT sectors started in the 1980s. All the developed countries and majority of the developing countries started the structural changes in telecommunications. Both, ICT and information technology (IT) sectors started to grow very fast in those countries. Reforms were implemented as a policy of the government in these countries. These reforms were facilitated by the joint collaboration of the World Bank, the International Telecommunication Union (ITU) and the Commonwealth Telecommunications Organization (CTO). In 1991, these organizations came together and discussed about the roadmap for the reforms in the ICT sector and became very successful. More than forty countries agreed for the reforms and that was a big change in the telecommunications policy changes. In this study, the authors have analyzed the practical aspects of the reforms of Latin America, Asia, Europe and Australia. They included the realities about the investment in ICT sectors, their regulation issues and final implementation in the countries which took part in the initiatives of the World Bank, ITU and CTO.

Levi-Faur (1998), studied the restructuring and globalization of telecommunications in Egypt. In his study he analyzed the case of Etisalat and went through the changes performed over several years. He found that radical changes have been carried on strategically to restructure its businesses across North Africa and the Middle East. He also compared these strategic changes with other sectors. He discovered that no such deeper and broader changes are observed in other technology sectors in the regions where Etisalat provides its services. This study also analyzed the economic impact of the restructuring on the national economy. The impact was clearly positive. The regulations in fact, work as an indirect control over the telecommunications companies. It is also true that the regulations helped in the broader restructuring of the telecommunications businesses. Based on the different regulations of the telecommunications sectors, this work shows that there are normally two types of effects. One is the regulation of the competition and the other is the regulation for the competition. Cogburn (1998) studied the globalization in telecommunications industry of South Africa. This work analyzed the telecommunications industry of South Africa of the 1980s and 1990s. The state of the industry during this time was very much unorganized. South Africa's political restructuring also took place during this time. It was expected that the changed politics would bring new positive aspects to the telecommunications sector. However, the author observed that the politics was playing a hindrance for the changes. In this work, the author proposed several restructuring for the telecom industry. He suggested it is a complex process and needs a changed mindset in the policy making. Graham (1999) studied the modern restructuring of cities around the world. In almost all the countries, cities are pushed for better infrastructure and better quality of life. Telecommunications is one of the prime sectors which play key roles in the modernization of the cities. In fact, ICT has the very basic necessities for several aspects of the city restructuring. Dependence of other sectors on ICT is termed as tele-reliance by the author. Due to the increasing demand on ICT, this sector itself undergoes several restructuring.

Lal, Pitt and Beloucif (2001) studied the European telecommunications market and short listed the major factors responsible for the recent changes. The authors observed that before the 1980s, telecommunications companies used to be very much dormant and their operations used to be limited to only one country. However, the liberalization facilitated globalization and telecommunications became a market-oriented sector. The authors credited the US and the governments of Europe for this liberalization and globalization. European telecommunications markets led strategic changes in the ICT sectors and it was followed by other leading markets. The factors were identified from the European markets and highlighted for this study. These factors were utilized to model the emerging markets.

Chan-Olistad and Jamison (2001) studied the fierce competition in the telecommunications sector that was mainly started after the 1980s. In the developed countries and some select developing countries where several companies operate saw fierce competition among the rivals. This was the first time in the history of telecommunications that such tough completion came to the markets in several countries. The strategic changes were very much focused towards future growth and survival. The authors studied the qualitative aspects of the telecommunications markets considering the new strategic changes observed during the above mentions time period. They studied several strategic factors for these markets and also considered the political economy for the overall restructuring of the ICT sector. One of the most interesting factors they observed was that the companies try all kinds of solutions, including alliances with the rivals. It is remarkable that rivalry through alliances was found to be very much rewarding in the long term. Sakai (2002), studied extensively the global industrial restructuring. The main motivating factor is expansion for long term survival. Revenue increase for innovation is also essential for the company to stay active in the market. Revenues can be increased in several ways. One of them is internationalization. With time, restructuring is inevitable. Without it a company loses its competitive edge over the rivals and over time it moves towards its demise. Bartlett et al. (2002) studied several national telecommunications companies in twenty five different countries. The companies considered in their study were privatized to some extent through public share holdings. They studied the companies' financial and operational status both before and after the privatization process. They observed that post-privatization performances were better than the pre-privatization performances. They further fine tuned the studies to identify the improvement in the performances. They found that regulation and changes in the government policies had significant roles in the performance improvements. Public companies are directly affected by the governmental decisions and normally are slow in restructuring what is decided by the policy makers.

Jin (2005) studied the reforms and restructuring in the ICT sectors in the 1990s and the early twenty-first century. He observed several companies failed despite following the reforms. Then those companies started following different types of restructuring. In the most recent restructuring, the companies took several bold steps which were very much new to the sector. They started to focus on new markets where they did not have presence before failure. This is what the authors called neoliberal globalization. This neoliberal globalization was very much rewarding for several companies. In addition to the strategic changes of the existing companies new startups and spin-offs were the new entrants in the ICT market. Their presence disrupted the ICT market to a large extent. Some of those startups went on to become game changers in the sector. Considering their importance, some of the successful startups were acquired by the big companies of the sector. Similarly several mergers and acquisitions resulted from the fierce competition in the sector. Overall, the restructuring of telecommunications sector became vibrant. It was also found that a few companies could not stand firm in front of the tough competition and failed.

In a few cases the companies were finished forever. According to the author, all these effects are due to the neoliberal globalization across the major markets. Jin (2008) presents the extreme liberalization observed in the telecommunications industry in the early twenty-first century. He started the analysis from the late twentieth century. In the late 1980s, the telecommunications industry saw dramatic changes. New dimensions were established for its rapid expansion. Companies restructured their businesses in many different ways. Globalization was a preferred means of expansion during this period. Internet based services opened new opportunities for both the vendors and operators. Mergers and acquisitions in telecommunications became very common. Some of the mergers and acquisitions were in fact a kind of facilitation of globalization. Foreign direct investment (FDI) in telecommunications increased very fast since the 1990s. It is the effect of globalization on this industry.

Mohanty and Moreira (2014) stressed on the essence of sustainability in global telecommunications. In this study, the authors went through the basics of the current needs of sustainability. They analyzed sector-wise carbon emission at the global scale. They showed that telecommunications is one of the fastest growing sectors in the world. Due to this growth, energy consumption of this sector has grown up very fast. This sector is going to use around 10% of the total power in the next decade. This is huge amount of power, and due to this the carbon footprint from this sector is going to be really huge. In 2014, the telecommunications sector was responsible for almost 2% of the net global carbon emission and has an increasing trend. Green solutions are expected to be followed in the future. In fact, the authors have shown several energy efficient initiatives already in place in current practices in ICT. However, there is a need of deepen the use of green technologies in this sector. Cogburn (2017) studied the modern restructuring of ICT sectors around the world. The authors mention that a new world order has come into existence due to the major changes in the ICT sectors. It has given rise to a new knowledge world. These changes have not happened overnight. Rather continuous restructuring of the ICT sector over the last few decades has contributed to it. The authors have also highlighted the flip sides of these changes and show that several value systems have been degraded due these changes.

He et al. (2017) studied the internationalization of innovation by the global corporations. The authors started with the essence of innovation in the modern businesses. Then they pointed that innovation has become more important due to the globalization of the economy. Chinese firms have been studied in this work. Several Chinese companies have successfully globalized their ventures. They are also using the innovation as one of the driving forces for their growth and restructuring. Like the big global companies, these Chinese companies have also started their innovations bases at overseas destinations. These new initiatives provide positive business perceptions about the Chinese companies and they become popular at overseas destinations. This is one of the most effective ways of making the globalization a success.

Yu (2017) emphasized on the digital transformation for large scale restructuring and globalization. Globalization is a rapid process of fulfilling client demands at very far off places. In order to carry it on successfully digitalization is essential. The author has studied the digital transformation of Chinese economy. He showed that the telecommunications sector in China has changed its digital landscape. That is a really significant achievement for China and that helped the country to progress in its manufacturing and expansion of its economy. Czarnecki and Dietze (2017) analyzed the modern telecommunications industry for the reforms and restructuring points of views. The authors started with the notion that in order to restructure the telecom industry the strategists must understand it clearly. In this article, the authors presented several conceptual and strategic aspects which must be understood properly before applying any kind of restructuring. The value chain in the telecommunications market now has evolved into complex value networks. The restructurings must be done only after understanding the current status and how the new changes will fit into them. Otherwise, the outcomes may not be as expected.

Mohanty and Routray (2017) presented the recent trends of global telecommunications. These trends are mainly motivated by the demand from global population. Consumer electronics plays the main role of driving these demands straight to the customers. The resources such as bandwidth are scarce. There are new bands being introduced for the emerging services. Recent trends show the global bandwidth demand is growing faster than the previous years. Globally, mobile communication is very popular with the total number of subscriptions is about to exceed the global population. However, some parts of the developing world are still not fully connected. In the next decade, it may cover these untouched territories in Africa and elsewhere. Hong (2017) analyzed the post-2008 restructuring in China's online businesses. They started the Internet Plus policy according to which their digital economy got priority over the traditional business platforms. It has developed world class vendor companies such as Huawei and ZTE. It seems that China's plans for a digital restructuring for the future dominance over the online businesses are getting pace. Agur (2018) studied the telecommunications restructuring of independent India. He started his study from 1947 the year in which India achieved its independence and started its own infrastructure. The author has divided the whole period from 1947 until 2018 into three parts: 1947 until 1984, 1984 until 1991 and finally from 1991 until 2018. In the first period from 1947 until 1984 the restructuring was very much slow and dependent on the government policies. In the second period, several initiatives were taken by the government to bring changes in the ICT sector but they were not successful immediately. In the third period, India witnessed the biggest changes in its ICT sector. The liberalization introduced by the government in 1991 brought fruits. The emergence of the private sector in telecommunications was remarkable. These changes were the main driving forces of India's modern telecommunications market which is now very much competitive. Restructuring and globalization over the years have made Indian ICT sector very much matured, forward looking and globally recognized.

Li (2018) presented several positive and revolutionary changes in the global telecommunications sector. Due to the advances in new technologies the Internet of Things (IoT) has arrived. This is termed as the fourth revolution industrialization known as Industry 4.0. In this article, the author has predicted similar changes in the telecommunications sector which is named as Telecommunications 4.0. In this study it has been shown that the analog communication was started more than 100 years back and it was the telecommunications 1.0. With the digital communication the second version came into the industry and the Internet brought the third version. In the current fourth version, with technologies like IoT and 5G many new changes are about to come in the global telecommunications sector. Several new dimensions will be added to the ICT services. There will be several new challenges for the companies in the new landscape. Sapolsky et al. (2018) presented a detailed study of telecommunications revolution in the past, present and also predicted the future trends. It shows the global restructuring of the telecommunications sector over the last several decades. In the past the telecommunications used to be a public service and was controlled by the governments. Regulations were changed due to the competition and this sector too witnessed the LPG transformations. The new technologies in the sector forced several restructuring which were pivotal in the overall changes. Gao (2018) studied the effects of the 2008 world economic recession on the emerging industries including the telecommunications sector. Due to the financial crises in 2008, the global value chain was restructured to cope with the future challenges. As a strategic move global industry relocation was carried out in several sectors. Based on the global supply and demand industry relocations happened to high demand markets. In fact, before the relocations the companies assessed the markets using different measurement tools. It is well known that the global relocation follows the Pareto Principle. Similarly other tools were used for strategic relocation of industries in the post 2008 era.

Lewis (2018) studied the Internet based businesses in China. There are several new opportunities in the online markets in China. Initially, China did not allow the multi-national online giants in China. That is very much according to the Chinese communist principle of maintaining secrecy. However, later they allowed partial openness to the international companies. The controversy with Google China reopened the Chinese policy of hiding information from the public. It was a boon for the domestic Internet-based companies of China. Now several big companies exist in China those do Internet-based businesses. China has even bigger plans for the future. It is clearly visible from the current restructuring in those companies. The recent plans such as Belt and Road Initiatives and Internet Plus clearly show China's ambition to be a superpower in this sector. China engages with ASEAN countries with a special focus in this direction.

METHODOLOGY

In this study, we analyze several telecommunications companies from their beginning till 2018. Several of the old companies have become obsolete now. Some of the companies have been merged with their successful rivals (Mohanty, 2012). We started the analysis from the beginning of the Telegraph era which started in 1831. However, major restructuring in telecommunications was started in the 1980s. Both restructuring and globalization became strategies for long term goals in the 1980s and since then they play key roles in telecommunications planning (Czarnecki & Dietze, 2017). We also analyzed the chronological restructuring and strategic changes in the telecommunications sector. We present all these significant chronological changes in this chapter. We classified the major reasons for restructuring, and found that changing telecommunications technology is the main reason for the restructuring. Technological changes in telecommunications have disrupted the global markets in several ways time and again (Mohanty & Routray, 2017). Especially the mobile communications since the 1990s have changed the global markets and human lives to a large extent (Mohanty & Routray, 2017). We emphasized these disruptions and studied the restructuring of telecommunications companies due to the impact of the mobile technologies. We also studied the future impacts of ICT on the society. For the future research directions we analyzed the technology foresight papers on ICT. Of course we focused the future research directions only for the next decade.

STRATEGIC CHANGES IN TELECOMMUNICATIONS

Telecommunications is one of the largest technology sectors in the world. It has big roles in the day to day lives of people. Revenue wise, it is one of the largest contributing sectors to the global gross domestic product (GDP). It is estimated to be around 5% of the global GDP is from the ICT sector (Mohanty, 2012). This sector is also considered as the backbone of the modern business. All the online commercial activities are dependent on this sector. Due to its importance, its up-gradation is always a priority for government as well as for private companies. Restructuring is always considered a strategic move. However, depending on the contexts it has different goals. For some companies restructuring is required to expand their markets, for some it is essential to survive in the market, for some sustainability is not possible without restructuring. Depending on the contexts, companies restructure their businesses to remain active in the market. In fact modern strategic changes in the telecommunications sector were started in the 1980s, in both Europe and North America. The privatization of British Telecom (BT) and other European telecommunications operators were the beginning of the modern restructuring in a large scale (From & Eliassen, 2007). Similar restructuring was kicked off in the USA through the division of AT&T.

Strategic changes in telecommunications are quite contrasting in the developed countries when compared with the developing countries. Strategically, there are several changes in the telecommunications market of the developed countries. Some of the companies in these developed countries have grown rapidly. Now several of them lead the global communication in the technology and management frontiers. However, some of them have struggled badly to keep their positions intact. Majority of the companies have expanded their coverage areas of services. However, a few of them have done the reverse (Mohanty, 2012). Overall these moves and restructuring are strategy driven to remain competitive in the market. Several big companies have also changed their marketing and cultural aspects of their strategies to compete better. Restructuring in brand building and advertisement too have changed over the last couple of decades in the developed countries. In contrast to the companies in the developed countries, the telecom markets in the developing countries are very much young and unsaturated. The growth rates in several developing countries are in the double digits (Mohanty, 2012). However, large markets in the developing countries are quite versatile with a variety of service providers, operators and customers. The tele-densities of rural and urban areas differ by large margin. That is an attraction for both the domestic and international operators. The growth potentials in the developing countries are still very attractive. However, in developed countries ICT sector is always looking for new innovations to expand the market.

RESTRUCTURING OF TELECOMMUNICATIONS SECTOR

Restructuring of telecommunications is the process or combination of processes to change the technological, management and market related aspects of the telecommunications industry to remain competitive. Restructuring is always a strategic step in the growth and sustainability of a business. Restructuring has several motivating factors. Strategic restructurings are well planned, based on the position of the company in the market. Planned restructuring is done over a period of several years and its main goal is to make the telecom services more attractive and competitive. Intense competition and the intention to provide better services than the competitors may force frequent restructurings (Mohanty, 2012). Some of the restructuring may not be planned. For instance, during the natural disasters, telecom infrastructures are badly affected. The post-disaster restructuring is essential to bring the services back.

Restructuring in telecommunications can be classified in to several types (Ulset, 2007). Here we classify restructuring on the basis of their driving forces. Telecommunications is a technology driven sector. Thus new innovations in ICTs always bring new frontiers and dimensions for this sector. Technology driven restructuring is a continuous process and it happens gradually with every passing year. It is noteworthy that politics and economics also important roles in the restructuring of telecommunications sector. Politics is all about the policy making at the upper level for the approval of the services to the public. Economics is the price decider in the market. If there is only one service provider then the monopoly would keep the prices high, if there is no policy on the price control. On the other hand, competition among multiple service providers normally brings down the price which is very much customer oriented.

Types of Restructuring in Telecommunications

Restructuring is a gradual process. It is an absolute fact that a sector remains competitive as long as the timely restructurings are on course. For telecommunications sector, there are some key motivating factors for restructuring. Normally, the motivating factors are market driven. The three main factors for the restructuring of telecommunication are: technology, telecommunications policy/ regulations, and the economics of the market. However, emergency related events also initiate restructuring. Based on these main factors, we classify telecommunications restructuring in to the following types.

Technological Restructuring

Technology is always the main driving force behind any kind of meaningful restructuring in telecommunications. Technology frames the form and scopes of restructuring. In general, any telecommunications system needs three basic resources: transmitted power, bandwidth and telecom infrastructure. Technology is associated with each of these resources. Transmitted power is needed for every communication and its efficient use is always a benefit for the operators. Therefore in every periodic restructuring, power efficiency is considered for the up-gradation of the telecommunications systems. Bandwidth is a very limited resource. It belongs to the government of the country, and normally, it is auctioned publicly for the allocation to different operators. Presence of many operators makes the spectrum expensive and the services may also become costly. However, it is also noteworthy that large numbers of operators bring healthy competition to the market. Infrastructure is the built environment and the equipment required for the telecommunications operations. Sustainability of the businesses is an essential aspect in the modern world (Mohanty & Moreira, 2014). It is possible only through appropriate restructuring in line with the innovations on resource conservation. Green communications and sustainability issues are really important for the long term success of a telecom company (Routray & Sharmila, 2017). Thus technological restructuring is always a strategic step to remain effective in the telecommunications business.

Policy Oriented Restructuring

In every country, policies are made by the governments. For the telecommunications sector too, the policies are made by the political class. From time to time, governments change the policies on the services, and tariffs of telecommunications sector. Power levels in communications, maximum permissible bandwidth per person, and infrastructural guidelines are prepared by the country's regulators and finally converted

Figure 1. Restructuring in telecommunications

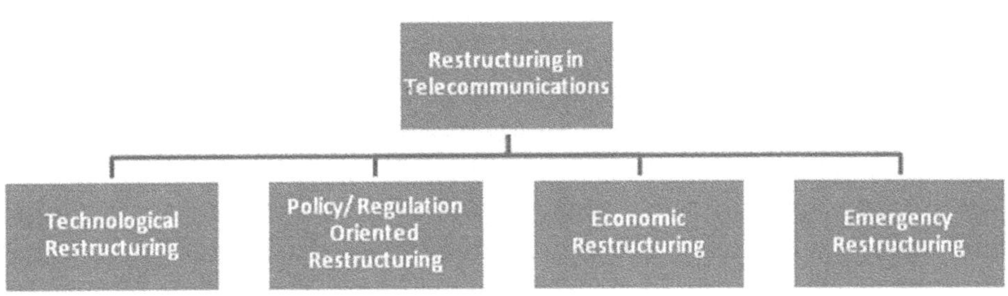

in to regulations for implementation by the governments. The governments auction the resources such as the available bandwidth to the existing operators. Governments also set the policies on the data rates and other performance related aspects. All these proposed changes from the governments are mandatorily implemented by the telecom operators of the country. These are the policy related restructuring. These restructurings are binding and the operators cannot opt out of it.

Economic Restructuring

Economics is the real force behind several restructuring. Economics decides the price through the supply and demand in the market. In case of monopolistic market, the operators can dictate their own terms in the market. This type of monopoly was observed during the pre-liberalization era. However, the presence of multiple operators makes the business very competitive. All the aspects such as tariffs, quality of services, and service maintenances are subject to the competition in the market. All these aspects demand restructuring in telecommunications business to stay relevant in the market. Thus economic restructuring is associated with the market dynamics which is decided by the competition in the market.

Emergency Related Restructuring

Telecom networks are vulnerable to the natural disasters and also suffer from aging related malfunction. An active network cannot be kept out of service for a long time. The malfunctions have to be repaired on time as an emergency. In fact, a normal repairing may not be considered as restructuring. In case of restructuring, the network deployment techniques are altered from the previous ones to improve the robustness of the networks. The main aim is to avoid such damages when a similar disaster strikes. These types of rebuilding services come under the emergency restructuring. Depending on the scale of the disaster, this restructuring can be minor or major. For instance, providing better protection to optical fibers along a coast line for a few kilometers is a minor restructuring. However, rebuilding a network with robust techniques in one or more states after a hurricane or cyclone is a major restructuring. In terms of revenue, a major restructuring is an expensive move. However, emergency restructurings are essential to bring the services back and to resume the day to day operations. A delay in these restructuring may result in revenue loss and customers may switch to the rivals.

Telecommunications Restructuring Until 1950

Telecommunications was started as telegraph in the 1830s. It was based on Morse code and telegraph cables. Initially, telegraph connected only the big cities. Due to the increasing demand, telegraph was extended to the medium and small cities. The restructuring in the 1850s was based on the customer demands. Railways were being built during that time and telegraph companies used the railway tracks to lay the cables along the railway tracks. Even some railway operators started laying their own cables for telegraph and leased them to the telegraph operators. At that time the competition was not very intense as the initial cost for investment in the infrastructure was very high. Later in 1876, telephone was invented by Graham-bell and it needed new kind of cables. The price of voice telecommunications was higher than the telegraph. Co-existence of telephone and telegraph motivated for restructuring around 1900s. That is how, the strategic planning and competition in the telecommunications market in the US gathered pace. Later similar restructuring was followed in Europe and other continents. However, the private companies were very few in number. Most of the telephone and telegraph services were being provided by the public sector companies under the government. In the first decade of the twentieth century, wireless communication was started in the form of Radio. It was very much popular for the long distance broadcasting. Typically, the governments provided the public broadcasting services such as news and public announcements through the radio. It played important roles during the First World War. Commercialization of radio services started during the 1920s, and it became a popular source of entertainment. During the 1920s, television came into the public arena. However, it was very much expensive during the first several years. Silicon-based electronics was started in the late 1940s. It paved ways for economical components for radio and television. This was a big change and television became popular in the 1940s. Both radio and television were very much dependent on the wireless communications. The technological restructuring of the telecommunications sector during the 1920s and 1930s were slow. However, Second World War brought many new inventions in the telecommunications technologies. Transcontinental communications between Europe and North America was mainly through the undersea cables.

Telecommunications Restructuring From 1951 Until 1980

After the Second World War, massive restructuring in all the sectors started in the 1950s. Leaders all around the world focused on political, social and economic stability. Moreover, economic stability was the main priority due to the resources and revenues lost during the war years. Economic development started with the aim of increasing the productivity and to provide employment for the people. Telecommunications sector got a priority due to its importance in the war planning and information management. Infrastructure for telecommunications expanded through the deployment of new networks. Telecommunications companies got bigger and better in the services. However, in most of the countries, telecommunications used to be under the control of the governments (Bell, 1990). Privatization was not very popular and thus the expansion plans and tariff related decisions used to come from the government. Gradually over the years, the telecom companies monopolized due to the absence of competition.

Despite the monopoly of the government-controlled companies, several new initiatives were started during this era. The technological restructuring through research and development used to be funded through the government. Optical communication was developed during the 1960s and 1970s and changed the global telecommunications to a large extent (Routray, 2014). Similarly, digital signal processing and satellite communications too were developed during these years. Satellite communications were the main basis for the international voice and video communication. The price for these services used to be quite high due to the complexities associated with the processes. However, the arrival of optical communications changed that scenario. All the continents were connected with each other through the high capacity optical fibers and the services become economical. Diplomatic differences during the cold war era motivated for better encryption techniques for communications. It became possible though different encryption standards such as data encryption standard (DES).

Telecommunications Restructuring From 1981 Until 1990

In this decade, many surprising changes happened in the telecom sector across the world. Liberalization and privatization started in all the economic sectors. Monopoly of the large companies started diminishing. American Telegraph and Telephone (AT&T) used to be the largest company in the world and it had monopoly over the US telecommunications market. This was found to be against fair competition in the market for the small, medium and private companies. A lawsuit was filed against AT&T and the court in the US ordered for its disintegration. So, the giant AT&T was divided into 19 companies known as baby bells. This is how a huge restructuring came to the sector. New companies found an opportunity to compete. Several new telecom operators and vendors were started after the division of AT&T. Similarly, in Europe privatization in telecommunications was started and several countries followed it (From & Eliassen, 2007). Among them the privatization of BT is the most notable.

Mobile communications were started in 1980s. It induced technological restructuring in several companies. Digital mobile communications started in Europe which was later named as 2G. This was a joint venture of several countries in Europe and the company formed to look after these technologies were named as GSM. This technology became very popular within a few years.

Telecommunications Restructuring From 1991 Until 2000

This decade saw the real growth of ICT in terms of infrastructure and popularity. World Wide Web (WWW) was introduced in 1989. It was the floodgate for telecommunications proliferation. The Internet became popular globally. Online businesses were started over the Internet. ICT started to be a part of part of all important activities of human lives and businesses. The GSM-based mobile communication was started in the 1980s, but its real deployment started in the 1990s. It was the first technology disruption in telecommunications sector. Therefore, the role of the traditional wire line-based telecommunications started losing its importance and in its place people got the mobile services. Mobile services were costly at the beginning. However, due to the large scale competition, the prices came down and it was affordable to the general public. The 2G services helped both individuals and businesses in a whole new fashion. Due to this disruption, land line subscriptions started decreasing and in its place people took new mobile connections.

From the rapid growth of 2G, the operators and vendors were motivated for advancement of the mobile technologies. In fact, their main goal was to provide Internet connectivity through the mobile handsets. Several telecommunications companies came together to form a common mobile research and standardization forum known as Third Generation Partnership Programme (3GPP). They also laid a long term evolution (LTE) goal together. This 3GPP alliance played key roles in the future mobile developments. 2G was not good enough to send anything other than voice. Therefore, the 2G protocols were enhanced through several new packet radio protocols which facilitated the text messaging. The Short Message Service (SMS) was the new dimension of 2G and the new version was called 2.5G (Routray & Sharmila, 2016a). Similar to 2.5G several incremental versions of 2G came to the mobile services. The Internet service provision also started in the 2.9G. Mobile communications induced massive restructuring in telecommunications sector. In fact, it became a disruptive technology and further liberalized the ICT markets.

Telecommunications Restructuring From 2001 Until 2010

The first decade of this century was remarkable for the cellular communications and the restructuring around the mobile communication technologies. The 2G revolution continued into the Twenty-first century and in the developed countries mobile subscriptions approached close to 100%. Technological restructuring continued further and the next generation of mobile communication, i.e., 3G was rolled out.

3G provided enhanced services when compared to the 2G ones. In addition to that it started providing new services such as video and other streaming services. The telecom vendors too found new opportunities in the network building as well as advanced handset design. In both areas the revenues soared significantly which created gigantic mobile operators like Vodafone and Verizon.

Technological restructuring in 2000s was very much relentless. The 3G services were slow in the streaming and other high speed services. This was a bottleneck for the LTE service networks. Contemporary technologies such as WiMAX and 802.11g/n were better than 3G in these aspects. Therefore, the 3GPP started new initiatives for the next advanced version which was named as fourth generation of mobile communications (4G). In 4G, the speed, latency, spectral efficiency and overall throughput were enhanced with respect to 3G. Therefore, it was suitable for streaming and other real time applications. The final version of 4G was finalized in 2009. The rolling out of this advanced version started from the second half of 2009 in the developed countries and a few developing countries. However, the widespread deployment happened only after four to five years.

Telecommunications Restructuring From 2011 Onwards

In the current decade, we see fierce competition among the telecommunications companies in every segment of their businesses. Operators take bold steps to keep the markets with them. Vendors are equally competitive in keeping their revenues intact. Restructuring in the recent days are multi-faceted. The telecommunications value chains between the vendors and operators are observed for each vendor operator pair. For large companies having collaboration with other operators and vendors these value chains turn into value networks.

The current decade is dominated by the widespread technological restructuring across the world. Several new technologies disrupted the markets and changed the traditional framework of telecommunications. In this decade, several value added services were witnessed over the mobile communication platforms. However, the biggest addition was the Internet of things (IoT). It has expanded the domain of the ICT to several new paradigms. Smart cities and smart grids are the outcomes of the IoTs. Through IoTs several new business potentials have been observed over the ICT infrastructure (Ramnath et al., 2017). IoTs are basically sensor driven technologies which can perform computing, communication, storage, actuation of associated components and some domain specific tasks. A connected living environment can be possible through the IoTs. IoT became an integral part of all cellular communication networks. It brought several value added services to the cellular communication businesses (Sharma et al., 2017).

In 2015, the 4G services were substituted by 4.5G which were better than the 4G services. In fact, it was regarded as the hybrid of 4G and 5G services. 4.5G also gave a lot of confidence to the 5G developers in terms of the service performances. Voice communication over the cellular networks found a new technology called Voice over LTE (VoLTE). This new technology provided high quality voice over the LTE networks. The core network capacities increased significantly. Optical fibers were deployed all around the world and it provided superfast connections across the world (Routray, 2014). Internet connectivity increased significantly and it brought dramatic changes in global businesses (Mohanty & Routray, 2017).

Big data became the new buzzword in the ICT in the recent years. With the fusion of computing and communication, several benefits were harnessed. However, the amount of data produced through this was huge. It cannot be processed using the traditional tools (Mohanty & Moreira, 2013). This is called the big data. The importance of big data is that it carries a lot of intelligence which is essential for several applications. Big data are analyzed using special tools known as big data analytics. ICT companies are one of the main generators of big data. The ICT companies are using data analytics to harness the intelligence which can be crucial for their growth and sustainability.

Artificial intelligence (AI) and machine learning are the new dimensions in the ICT platforms. These tools are used to carry out several smart functions. In order to facilitate these new dimensions several restructuring are being proposed for ICT. The Fifth Generation of mobile communication (5G) will have several advanced features which were not available in the previous mobile generations (Routray & Sharmila, 2016b). Some of the 5G new services would use AI. Mobile operating systems are developed to handle these new tasks. Several new versions of these operating systems have been tested for the use in 5G.

GLOBALIZATION OF TELECOMMUNICATIONS MARKET

Expansion of markets is a key motive for restructuring for any large company. It is also an essential strategy to improve the performances of a company. Liberalization and privatization provided a lot of freedom to the telecommunications companies. It also motivated the companies to look for opportunities beyond the national borders. Mainly the companies from the US and Europe started their offshore businesses in their friendly countries (Bruce, 1989). Telecommunications companies too started their international ventures through different means. The telecom equipment vendors easily found partners due to their expertise in making equipments and deploying networks.

Globalization of telecommunications companies can be viewed under two different categories: globalization of vendors and globalization of operators. Telecommunications vendor companies are the telecom equipment and network component builders and they normally deploy the networks. Telecommunications operators are the direct service providers. Therefore they directly deal with the end customers which can be individuals or businesses. They directly collect the revenues from their clients periodically through the post paid services. In case of prepaid services they collect the money in advance. However, the telecom vendors collect their revenue from the operators and it normally come I phases.

Globalization of the telecom vendors' market is as old as the telecommunications industry itself. For instance, telephone was invented in 1876 and Eriksson started manufacturing the telephone sets in 1878 and sold them not only in Sweden but throughout the world. Similarly, just after the invention of Radio, its commercial manufacturing was started by several companies and they sold them globally. Initially, the selling was though some middleman. However, gradually, the manufacturers globalized their manufacturing by opening their bases in several countries. This trend of globalization of telecommunications vendors is still there. However, it has become very much systematic with global marketing and globalization of the markets has created bases in multiple countries. For instance, Eriksson had only a few international bases in the 1970s. Now it has direct business presence in more than fifty countries. Similarly, other vendors such as Nokia networks, Huawei, Cisco, ZTE and Corning are having direct business presence in multiple countries. Without globalization large vendors cannot do good business as the requirements of a single country are not too large for their growth and progress. These days, only small and limited vendoring of some specific components can be done within the geographical limits of a country. Therefore, it is obvious for a vendor company to go for globalization.

Operators have a very much different business perspective. They are not like the vendors who are experts of network deployment. Rather, the operators can just invest for the network building and once it is ready they start the services and collect the tariffs. The competition for the operators is also more direct when compared with those of the vendors. For the operators, the end customer base is very important. Depending on the quality of service and the cost for the services, the operators may lose or retain their customers. These two aspects are also important for an operator when they plan for globalization. Therefore, when an operator enters a new overseas market it must provide something new or something attractive so that they can grab the customers from the existing operators of that new market. Based on the innovative ideas and better technologies, operators go for globalization these days. For instance, the European operators such as Vodafone, Orange and T-mobile have several overseas operations based on their quality of service and advanced technologies. However, it is noteworthy that the competitors of these operators in the overseas countries get better every year (Pedersen et al., 2017). Therefore globalization of the operators is more complex than the globalization of the vendors.

FUTURE RESEARCH DIRECTIONS

Telecommunications is a vibrant technological sector which generates a lot of revenue. Researches on its restructuring and globalization are studied with much interest across the world. Future research directions of telecommunications restructuring too are widely analyzed by the consultants and scholars of the field. In the recent years and near future, there are several important areas in which the telecommunications restructuring researches will be focused. In the following paragraphs we have highlighted these research areas.

Fast and Enhanced Telecommunications Services

Every year new innovations come to the telecommunications sector. Their implementation leads to better services for the end customers. Currently, 5G development is under progress. Through its deployment several performance enhancement will be achieved. Data rates will be increased significantly, latency will be decreased, scalability will be enhanced by several folds, and energy efficiency will be increased (Routray & Sharmila, 2016). Overall, the 5G handsets will provide several new computing and communication facilities which never existed before. A major technological restructuring is going to happen through 5G deployment in the 2020s.

Managed Services for Better Network Management

In the past, the operators used to deploy the network. The revenue for this deployment used to come from their own investment or through the bank loans. It was a burden for the operators. However, this trend has been changed to a large extent. Now, the telecommunications vendors take that role. In several instances, we find that the vendors utilize their expertise to build the networks. Once the network is ready they provide it for use to different operators. The ownership is now largely with the vendors. Operators just rent the networks and pay the fees periodically. The research on the telecommunications value chains and value networks are very much popular these days (Pedersen et al., 2017). In the coming years these concepts would be further developed and would pave the way for more increased roles for the vendors.

Widespread Deployment of Internet of Things

IoT is a game changing technology. In the modern world it has several important roles in our surroundings. In the smart cities all the information will be collected, processed and disseminated by the IoTs. Starting from security to taking care of day to day activities will be executed through the IoTs. In the coming decades, IoT will play key roles in almost all our activities.

Energy Efficiency and Green Technologies

In the recent years, energy efficiency of the telecommunications networks has an increased importance due to the wide spread use of ICT. The net power consumed by the ICT networks and devices is gigantic. Therefore, the current restructuring is very much focused towards energy efficiency. Every operator is now concerned by the high energy bills. Recent advances in the green technologies too have given a boost for its widespread adoption.

Artificial Intelligence and Machine Learning

Artificial intelligence (AI) and machine learning are now very much essential in the telecommunications networks and device management. There are several operations in which human estimation would take a long time and the accuracy may not be that good. In such cases, a machine can be trained to provide optimal results. Several learning theories have been used for machines. Optimal resource allocation and consumption are complex processes in large communication networks. These things can be optimized though AI. Research in this segment of ICT is very much popular and the technological restructuring will be oriented towards these new initiatives.

CONCLUSION

Telecommunications is an essential technology sector which has become an integral part of modern human lives. In the recent years, telecommunications has a role in every aspect of our social activities. It will remain as one of the most widely used technologies. Restructuring of telecommunications is an inevitable requirement. However, in the modern business world of tough competition, restructuring has become a continuous process. Without restructuring, telecommunications companies will lose their competitive edge over their rivals. Even the demise of a company is very much common these days without restructuring. There are four main areas of restructuring in telecommunications. Each of them play essential role in the growth and survival of a company. Globalization is a strategy to expand the market. In addition to the growth, it provides survivability to the companies in the difficult situations. Both restructuring and globalization are important for the telecommunications companies which are large and intend to survive for a long time. The future restructuring will be very much oriented along the managed services. Therefore, the vendors will play important roles in the future restructuring than their traditional roles seen in the past.

REFERENCES

Agur, C. (2018). Re-imagining the Indian state: External forces and the transformation of telecommunications policy, 1947–present. *Global Media and Communication*, *14*(1), 65–83. doi:10.1177/1742766518759794

Bagley, C., & Hunter, B. (1992). Restructuring, constructivism, and technology: Forging a new relationship. *Educational Technology*, *32*(7), 22–27.

Bell, T. E. (1990). From monopoly to competition: Long-term research is vulnerable. *IEEE Spectrum*, *27*(10), 46–50. doi:10.1109/6.58476

Bortolotti, B., D'Souza, J., Fantini, M., & Megginson, W. L. (2002). Privatization and the sources of performance improvement in the global telecommunications industry. *Telecommunications Policy*, *26*(5-6), 243–268. doi:10.1016/S0308-5961(02)00013-7

Bruce, R. R. (1989). Restructuring the telecom sector in developing countries: Some new options for policymakers. *IEEE Technology and Society Magazine*, *8*(4), 16–20. doi:10.1109/44.44528

Chan-Olmsted, S., & Jamison, M. (2001). Rivalry through alliances: Competitive strategy in the global telecommunications market. *European Management Journal*, *19*(3), 317–331. doi:10.1016/S0263-2373(01)00028-7

Cogburn, D. L. (1998). Globalization and state autonomy in the information age: Telecommunications sector restructuring in South Africa. *Journal of International Affairs*, *51*(2), 583–604.

Cogburn, D. L. (2017). From NWICO to Global eCommerce: Telecommunications Restructuring and the GII. In Transnational Advocacy Networks in the Information Society (pp. 53-92). Palgrave Macmillan.

Czarnecki, C., & Dietze, C. (2017). Understanding today's Telecommunications Industry. In *Reference Architecture for the Telecommunications Industry* (pp. 17–54). Cham: Springer. doi:10.1007/978-3-319-46757-3_2

From, J., & Eliassen, K. A. (Eds.). (2007). *The privatisation of European telecommunications*. Ashgate Publishing, Limited.

Gao, X. (2018). *Measuring the Generalized Global Industry Relocation*. Academic Press.

Graham, S. (1999). Global grids of glass: On global cities, telecommunications and planetary urban networks. *Urban Studies (Edinburgh, Scotland)*, *36*(5-6), 929–949. doi:10.1080/0042098993286

He, S., Fallon, G., Khan, Z., Lew, Y. K., Kim, K. H., & Wei, P. (2017). Towards a new wave in internationalization of innovation? The rise of China's innovative MNEs, strategic coupling, and global economic organization. *Canadian Journal of Administrative Sciences*, *34*(4), 343–355. doi:10.1002/cjas.1444

Hong, Y. (2017). Pivot to Internet Plus: Molding China's Digital Economy for Economic Restructuring?
Hudson, H. E. (1991). Telecommunications in Africa the role of the ITU. *Telecommunications Policy*, *15*(4), 343–350.

Jin, D. Y. (2005). The telecom crisis and beyond: Restructuring of the global telecommunications system. *Gazette (Leiden, Netherlands)*, *67*(3), 289–304. doi:10.1177/0016549205052232

Jin, D. Y. (2008). Neoliberal restructuring of the global communication system: Mergers and acquisitions. *Media Culture & Society*, *30*(3), 357–373. doi:10.1177/0163443708088792

Lal, D., Pitt, D. C., & Beloucif, A. (2001). Restructuring in European telecommunications: Modelling the evolving market. *European Business Review*, *13*(3), 152–158. doi:10.1108/09555340110391266

Levi-Faur, D. (1998). The Competition State as a Neomercantilist State: Understanding the restructuring of national and global telecommunications. *Journal of Socio-Economics*, *27*(6), 665–685. doi:10.1016/S1053-5357(99)80002-X

Lewis, D. (2017). China's Global Internet Ambitions: Finding Roots in ASEAN. *Institute of Chinese Studies: Occasional Paper, 14.*

Li, Z. (2018). Telecommunication 4.0: Opportunities and Challenges. In *Telecommunication 4.0* (pp. 107–133). Singapore: Springer. doi:10.1007/978-981-10-6301-5_6

Mohanty, S. (2012). *Strategic changes in the telecommunications sector: Europe vs. India* (Master's thesis). Universidade de Aveiro.

Mohanty, S., & Moreira, A. C. (2014). Sustainability in global telecommunications. *IEEE Potentials*, *33*(5), 29–34. doi:10.1109/MPOT.2013.2292540

Mohanty, S., Moreira, A. C., & Nobre, H. (2013). Marketing Challenges for the Emerging Services of Big Data Technologies and Solutions. *International Conference on Big Data Management and Cloud Computing*.

Mohanty, S., & Routray, S. K. (2017). CE-Driven Trends in Global Communications: Strategic sectors for economic growth and development. *IEEE Consumer Electronics Magazine*, *6*(1), 61–65. doi:10.1109/MCE.2016.2614420

Pedersen, T., Devinney, T. M., Tihanyi, L., & Camuffo, A. (Eds.). (2017). *Breaking up the global value chain: opportunities and consequences*. Emerald Group Publishing. doi:10.1108/S1571-5027201730

Ramnath, S., Javali, A., Narang, B., Mishra, P., & Routray, S. K. (2017). IoT based localization and tracking. In *IoT and Application (ICIOT), 2017 International Conference on* (pp. 1-4). IEEE. 10.1109/ICIOTA.2017.8073629

Routray, S. K. (2014). The changing trends of optical communication. *IEEE Potentials*, *33*(1), 28–33. doi:10.1109/MPOT.2013.2279908

Routray, S. K., & Sharmila, K. P. (2016a). 4.5 G: A milestone along the road to 5G. In *Information Communication and Embedded Systems (ICICES), 2016 International Conference on* (pp. 1-6). IEEE.

Routray, S. K., & Sharmila, K. P. (2016b). Green initiatives in 5G. In *Advances in Electrical, Electronics, Information, Communication and Bio-Informatics (AEEICB), 2016 2nd International Conference on* (pp. 617-621). IEEE.

Routray, S. K., & Sharmila, K. P. (2017). Green initiatives in IoT. In *Advances in Electrical, Electronics, Information, Communication and Bio-Informatics (AEEICB), 2017 Third International Conference on* (pp. 454-457). IEEE. 10.1109/AEEICB.2017.7972353

Sakai, K. (2002). *Global Industrial Restructuring*. OECD Online Library.

Sapolsky, H. M., Crane, R. J., Neuman, W. R., & Noam, E. M. (2018). *The Telecommunications Revolution: Past, Present and Future*. London: Routledge. doi:10.4324/9781351115704

Sharma, L., Javali, A., Nyamangoudar, R., Priya, R., Mishra, P., & Routray, S. K. (2017). An update on location based services: Current state and future prospects. In *Computing Methodologies and Communication (ICCMC), 2017 International Conference on* (pp. 220-224). IEEE.

Stagliano, D. (1994). The ITU's role in the restructuring revolution. *IEEE Communications Magazine*, *32*(11), 48–49. doi:10.1109/35.330226

Ulset, S. (2007). Restructuring diversified telecom operators. *Telecommunications Policy*, *31*(3-4), 209–229. doi:10.1016/j.telpol.2007.01.006

Wellenius, B., & Stern, P. A. (Eds.). (1994). *Implementing reforms in the telecommunications sector: Lessons from experience*. The World Bank. doi:10.1596/0-8213-2606-6

Yu, H. (2017). Networking China: The Digital Transformation of the Chinese Economy. *The China Quarterly, University of Illinois Press*, *231*, 817–819.

ADDITIONAL READING

Ardalan, K. (2017). Driving force of globalization: A multi-paradigmatic look. *Research in International Business and Finance*, *41*, 480–492. doi:10.1016/j.ribaf.2017.05.005

Larson, J. F., & Park, J. (2014). From developmental to network state: Government restructuring and ICT-led innovation in Korea. *Telecommunications Policy*, *38*(4), 344–359. doi:10.1016/j.telpol.2013.10.001

Mohanty, S., & Biswal, S. (2016). Modinomics: The Practical Perspectives (A hype or reality). In *International Conference on Taking India to Greater Heights*, Bangalore, India.

Mohanty, S., Biswal, S., Polonia, D., & Moreira, A. C. (2016). Irrelevant borders: Perspectives of Globalization. In International Conference on Redrawing the boundaries of International relations: going beyond state power, Cuttack, India.

Rodríguez-Ruiz, Ó. (2015). Unions' response to corporate restructuring in Telefónica: Locked into collective bargaining? *Employee Relations*, *37*(1), 83–101. doi:10.1108/ER-03-2014-0029

Williamson, J. G. (1998). Globalization, labor markets and policy backlash in the past. *The Journal of Economic Perspectives*, *12*(4), 51–72. doi:10.1257/jep.12.4.51

Witte, E. (2018). A history of recent German telecommunications policy. In *The Telecommunications Revolution* (pp. 98–101). London, UK: Routledge. doi:10.4324/9781351115704-11

KEY TERMS AND DEFINITIONS

Emerging Segments of Telecommunications Market: These are the new and value-added business segments of telecommunications market. These new segments are strategically important for revenue generation.

Globalization in Telecommunications: It is the process of international expansion of businesses and services of a telecommunication company beyond its original base. It is an important strategic action to remain competitive in the global market.

Managed Service: Managed service is the new paradigm in which the network is built and owned by the vendors, and operators just rent them for their services.

Restructuring: Restructuring is the process or combination of processes to remain effective and competitive in the market.

Restructuring in Telecommunications Industry: It is the market-oriented modernization of telecommunication industry which is essential to remain effective in the market. Without restructuring, the company may lose its markets to its rivals.

Strategic Changes in Telecommunications: It is the combination of all key strategic changes in the telecommunications operators and vendors markets across the world.

Telecommunications Industry: Telecommunication industry comprises of all types of information and communication related companies, businesses and its overall customer base. It is one of the largest modern industrial sectors contributing a significant revenue generation.

Telecommunication Management: This is the overall management of all aspects of telecommunications including revenue, technology, manpower, and infrastructure.

Chapter 4
Economic Consequences of Corporate Conflicts

Mikhail Kuznetsov
Moscow State University, Russia

Maria I. Nikishova
https://orcid.org/0000-0002-8089-1899
Financial University Under the Government of the Russian Federation, Russia

Valeria Solovyova
Center of Corporate Development "Topcompetence", Russia

Konstantin I. Lukoyanov
St. Petersburg State University, Russia

ABSTRACT

A single economic space is created by the conditions of globalization, where corporations become the main economic actors. In this circumstance, the issues of corporate governance, especially the prevention and resolution of corporate conflicts, require the closest attention. In this chapter, the authors will try to answer the question of the possible economic consequences of major corporate conflicts and assess the degree of potential impact on the parameters of company activity: in the first part of the research, key financial indicators, credit ratings capitalization; in the second part of the research, the global economy, investment and economic growth, the dynamics of financial markets, investment climate, capital flows, etc.

INTRODUCTION

Shaping the nature of Russian business, corporate conflicts have had and continue to have a powerful impact on the overall environment of the country - including its investment climate.

In international practice, corporate conflicts are an inevitable part of corporate relations. Depending on the specifics such as the participants, corporate conflicts can lead to both an increase in shareholder value and an increase in the efficiency of companies, as well as have a destructive effect on the economy.

DOI: 10.4018/978-1-5225-8906-8.ch004

The aim of the study is to determine approaches to assessing the impact of corporate conflicts on the investment climate, economic growth and economic development of countries in which large corporate conflicts occurred. This study can be the basis for further study of the economic consequences of corporate conflicts.

The objectives of the study include finding answers to the following questions:

- What are the features of corporate conflicts in the US, Europe, Russia?
- What is the magnitude of possible consequences of large corporate conflicts upon the investment climate, economic growth, and economic development of the country in which the conflict took place?
- What are the conditions for minimizing the potential economic damage caused by large corporate conflicts in the country?

The research method is a desk study of the largest corporate conflicts of the last fifteen years, using, as an example conflicts in the USA, Europe, Russia – included are Volkswagen, Parmalat, Enron, AFK Sistema - Rosneft, NLMK, Norilsk Nickel - Rusal, TNK-BP.

The target audience of the study are teachers, academics, and graduate students, as well as students in the fields of management and corporate governance. The study will also be informative for top management of companies, heads of various organizations and government bodies.

FEATURES OF CORPORATE CONFLICTS IN THE US, EUROPE, RUSSIA

To assess the potential economic consequences of corporate conflicts that go beyond the activities of companies themselves, the authors use the well-known concept of "social costs" (Graaff, 1987), according to which "social costs are the costs that society as a whole incurs from events, actions or political change. They include negative external consequences, but do not take into account the costs that are transfers..." (Deardorff, n.d.). Thus, public costs are private costs plus external consequences.

In this section, the authors try to find an answer to the following questions:

- What are the key features of corporate conflicts in international practice?
- How do corporate conflicts affect the value of the companies involved in the conflict, the investment climate, and the economy?

In international practice, corporate conflicts are a natural part of corporate relations. There are usually two causes of corporate conflicts: differences of opinion and differences in the interests of the parties involved in the conflict.

A large amount of research has been devoted to the study of corporate conflicts. L. A. Bebchuk & M. S. Weisbach (2009), J. Connington (2017), S. Roy (2017), C. Leuz, K. V. Lins, & F. E. Warnock (2009) can be mentioned among international authors dealing with this problem. Among Russian researchers, S. Stepanov & S. Gabdrakhmanov (2011), I. V. Berezinets, Y. B. Ilyina, & D. N. Fakhritdinov (2014), V. Gusakov (2017), O. Kershis & A. Gosh (2017), and others can be identified.

The studies examine the main types of conflicts, their causes and consequences, as well as a comparison of conflicts in Russia, the USA, and Western Europe. The researchers study the causes of conflict with examples of cases, methods of the opposing sides, then draw conclusions and discuss possible scenarios for their settlement.

However, the authors of this study focus on mainly the consequences of corporate conflicts for the companies themselves. In considering corporate conflicts in terms of their impact on the economy, the authors do not limit themselves to confrontation in the "shareholder-management" line, but consider various examples, including major fraud, asset stripping, and company bankruptcy, in order to assess the full range of possible consequences and impact on investment attractiveness.

Corporate Conflicts in the USA

The basis of corporate conflicts in the United States is most often the confrontation between the shareholders and management. As a rule, the reason for opposition between the two is managerial actions that run counter to shareholder interests. At the same time, the board of directors plays an important role in the prevention and settlement of conflicts in the conditions of dispersed ownership.

Research (Bebchuk & Weisbach, 2009, pp. 2-6) also notes the important role of shareholders in corporate governance. For some companies, increasing shareholder rights and intervention in governance, in times of conflict, is part of the necessary reforms to resolve the conflict. For others, the activity of shareholders who potentially have short-term interests is part of the problem, not a solution.

An important role in corporate conflicts in the United States is played by activist shareholders, traditionally being institutional investors, and, more recently, specialized hedge funds. S. Stepanov & S. Gabdrakhmanov (2011, p. 20) believe that the activities of such funds may in some cases have a positive effect on value growth and results of companies.

However, a well-known example of one of the largest bankruptcies in history, Enron, showed that the price of large corporate scandals for society can be very high.

The main accusation (BBC News, 2002) put forward against Enron was gross falsification of statements which misled investors. Giant off-balance debts for more than $ 580 million were discovered only in the fall of 2001, after which rating agencies lowered the company's credit rating to the lowest level, and in one day the company's shares fell by 85% (Hill, 2014).

The wide resonance of the Enron case, both in the United States and around the world, is explained not only by the size of the revealed fraud, but also by the scale of losses for all interested parties. It can be noted that at this particular time - including the time of this scandal - there was a significant decrease in the S&P 500 index. One of the outcomes of the "Enron case" was the adoption by US lawmakers of the Sarbanes-Oxley Act (Bebchuk & Weisbach, 2009, p. 7) which tightened the requirements for financial reporting, the structure and composition of boards of directors, etc.

Corporate Conflicts in Europe

In continental Europe, in conditions of a concentrated ownership structure, the main conflict of interest most often runs along the line between large and small shareholders. Since large owners have the ability to control, appoint and remove the executive management of companies, conflicts with management occur less frequently. A distinctive feature of continental Europe is also the significant role and participation of trade unions within the management of the company, and as a result, within corporate conflicts.

Unlike the United States, conflicts along the lines of controlling owners, e.g. management, are less characteristic of Europe, since in the event of a conflict a majority owner always has the opportunity to dismiss management. Most researchers agree that if a large shareholder aims to maximize the value of a company, it objectively has a positive effect on the well-being of shareholders (Stepanov & Gabdrakhmanov, 2011, pp. 28-29). However, this is not always the case, as evidenced by the examples of Parmalat and Volksvagen.

In 2003-2004, as a result of a scandal, the prices of Parmalat shares and bonds (Enriques & Volpin, 2007) plummeted, and trading of Parmalat shares on the Milan stock market was suspended. At the end of the third quarter of 2003 Parmalat had a cash equivalent of 4.2 billion euros, with debts amounting to about 6 billion euros. The company's outstanding bonds amounted to 7 billion euros (RBC, 2004).

According to experts (Cortes & Rosell, n.d.), the influence of the Parmalat case on the Italian economy was not limited to a decrease in stock quotes and the following negative consequences were noted:

- Italian companies in 2006 experienced great difficulties with access to the Eurobond market. The total amount of bonds issued fell to the level of 1998 (3% of GDP).
- Investors became more cautious when buying unsecured bonds of Italian companies.
- Difficulties in attracting capital to the food industry.
- Reduction in the loan quality portfolios of Italian banks.

Another striking example of the damage that a single corporate scandal can cause to the economy as a whole is "Dieselgate" (Finn, 2015) - a corporate scandal surrounding Volkswagen in 2015, when it turned out that more than 11 million diesel cars around the world were equipped with software which, during tests, emitted dozens of times the amount of harmful gases into the air, in particular, NOx (nitrogen oxides).

As a result of the grand scandal, the company's shares fell significantly, which also affected the Berlin Stock Exchange market index. With "Dieselgate" in the background, Volkswagen sales dropped sharply at the end of 2015 (by 5.2%), and for the whole year global sales fell by 2%, regardless of the fact that over the previous 13 years, the company has shown sales growth.

The scandal with Volkswagen, according to many experts, caused significant damage not only to the company itself, but also to the reputation of corporate Germany (Zlobin, 2017). According to Thomson Reuters (Schwartz, Cremer, Thomasson, & Thomas, 2015), based on research by analyst firm Puls, 49% of Germans believe that Volkswagen's illegal actions undermined the prestige of the "Made in Germany" quality label for a long time, as it was a systematic deception that may have affected the entire industry.

Note that in the considered foreign examples, the basis for conflict resolution is always a thorough preliminary investigation - the consequences of a possible conflict may be too significant.

Features of Corporate Conflicts in Russia

The feature of corporate governance in Russian companies, as well as in Europe, is a high concentration of ownership. Therefore, the main trend of shareholder conflicts, as the history of the last 15 years shows, is the confrontation of large owners in the struggle for control or regarding the adoption of key strategic decisions; there are also frequent conflicts between controlling owners and minority shareholders, some of which are also related to conflicts of major shareholders.

At the same time, in Russia, due to the immaturity of the institutional environment – namely the the law enforcement system, coupled with the underdeveloped practice of pre-trial dispute settlement, the lack of a developed culture of corporate governance (Schwab, 2016, 2017), conflicts are often more acute. The significant role of the state in the economy predetermines a large number of conflicts with the direct or indirect involvement of the state.

An important aspect is the protection of the rights of foreign investors. Foreign investors tend to have less information about the companies in which they invest than domestic investors, and also tend to have fewer political connections or long-term relationships with the company that can potentially replace management (Leuz, Lins, & Warnock, 2009). According to this hypothesis, the quality of management in a firm should be correlated with foreign shareholders in the company. Since good corporate governance makes the firm relatively more attractive to foreigners than to domestic investors, foreigners should have a high proportion of ownership in companies where investors are better protected (Bebchuk & Weisbach, 2009, pp. 20-21).

Conflict of interests between participants in corporate relations, affecting the rights of shareholders, ownership structure, management effectiveness, can lead to reorganization. When a company is reorganized, it is possible to redistribute the company's assets, which in turn can lead to a decrease in the market value of shares. Accordingly, the reorganization of the joint-stock company affects the rights of its shareholders, as it may lead to a depreciation of their securities and a reduction in the scope of the rights granted by such shares. However, reorganization can be not only a radical solution to the conflict, but also the cause of its occurrence. When deciding on reorganization, there may be conflict situations that are related to challenging a decision on reorganization, its outcome, violation of the rights of participants in corporate relations, etc. That is why, according to the Corporate Governance Code (Bank of Russia, 2014), reorganization will be related to a number of significant corporate actions, which should be accompanied by maximum openness and transparency.

Due to the concentrated ownership structure in Russian companies and substantial state participation in the economy, corporate conflicts in Russia can be divided into four basic types (Stepanov & Gabdrakhmanov, 2011, pp. 40-45):

- Between large shareholders (the most typical for Russia in the last 15 years);
- Minority shareholder against majority shareholder;
- Minority shareholder against management / board of directors of a state-owned company;
- Between the main owner and the raider / greenmailer.

Corporate disputes, according to statistics (Savelyev & Bazhenov, 2018), are one of the most unrelated categories of cases. On average, 11–12 thousand corporate disputes per year are considered in arbitration courts, which is 0.6–0.7% of the total number of lawsuits. However, their resolution is a reflection of the development of the Russian institutional environment.

In the cases considered by the authors in this study, the discussion will deal mainly with conflicts between major shareholders. An important question: what is the impact of the largest corporate conflicts on the financial condition and performance of companies participating in conflicts? In order to achieve further research goals, the authors will try to analyze case studies of Russian companies in more detail, in order to show, by the example of Russia, the degree of influence of corporate conflicts on the country's investment climate. Impact assessment is carried out according to the following criteria:

- The company's capitalization compared to market indices,
- Credit ratings
- Key financial figures.

Conflict in TNK-BP

In 2008, a sharp conflict between Russian shareholders of the company and their British partners became public (Papirian, 2010). BP chief executive Robert Dudley reported on the conflict between TNK-BP shareholders on May 26, officially stating that there are disagreements among the shareholders of the joint venture that impeded its normal operation.

Russian shareholders refused to approve the company's financial report for 2007, demanding the dismissal of R. Dudley. According to them, Dudley put the interests of BP above the interests of TNK-BP.

Russian shareholders were also not satisfied with the fact that the leadership of BP did not support their ideas about pursuing a more active expansionist strategy of TNK-BP in the world market (RBC, 2008).

In June 2008 The State Labor Inspectorate filed administrative cases against TNK-BP and R. Dudley personally, relating to the violation of labor laws in terms of salary payment.

Subsequently, in July 2008, 16 vice-presidents and department heads of TNK-BP filed a class action lawsuit for violation of their labor rights. Plaintiffs accused R. Dudley of granting unfounded privileges to foreign employees.

On September 4, 2008, BP and AAP signed a memorandum aimed at resolving the conflict. The parties agreed on the resignation of R. Dudley from the post of CEO, the introduction of three independent directors to the board of TNK-BP, parity on the boards of directors of key subsidiaries, as well as the possibility of conducting a primary placement of 20% share of one of the subsidiaries of TNK-BP. On December 1, 2008 R. Dudley filed a letter of resignation in accordance with the signed memorandum.

In the graph presented in Figure 1, we can note the decline in TNK-BP stock quotes during a conflict situation. At the same time, however, it is necessary to bear in mind the impact on the market during this period of the global financial crisis.

Figure 1. The dynamics of the securities of TNK-BP during the conflict versus market (compiled by the authors)
Source: MFD.ru, 2008 - 2012

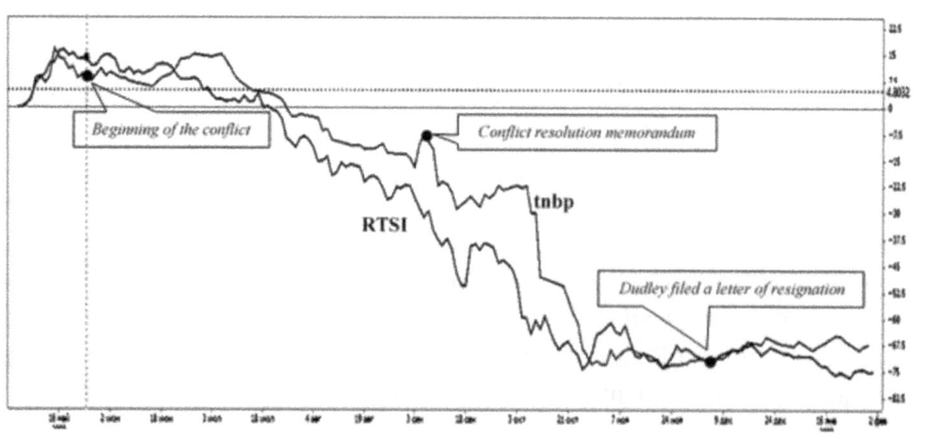

It is also necessary to note the impact of the conflict on the credit rating of the company (Standard & Poor's [S&P], n.d.):

- At the beginning of the conflict, the S&P's TNK-BP rating was at BB+.
- On 08/06/2008 S&P downgraded the company's long-term credit rating and senior unsecured debt rating from "BB+" to "BB".
- On 05/27/09 S&P raised the rating from "BB" to "BB +".
- On 12/07/09 S&P upgraded TNK-BP's long-term and short-term credit rating to BBB-/A-3 from BB +/B, with a stable outlook.

The key financial figures of the Company (taking into account the impact of the global financial crisis) changed slightly at the time of the conflict.

Conflict in MMC Norilsk Nickel

In 2008, one of the most high-profile corporate conflicts in Russia (Berezinets, Ilyina, & Fakhritdinov, 2014) began at Norilsk Nickell, initially between the holding company Interros, owning about 30% of MMC Norilsk Nickel at the start of the conflict, and UC RUSAL, which in April 2008 completed the acquisition of the blocking stake in Norilsk Nickel.

The main reason for the conflict were the different views on the strategy and operational management of the company. From the very beginning of RUSAL's entry into the Norilsk Nickel capital, the stated goal was to merge RUSAL with Norilsk Nickel to create a diversified giant like RioTinto. Later, RUSAL started to criticize the company's strategy developed by the management of Norilsk Nickel, the environmental policy of Nickel and the new CEO of the company.

Another factor that caused the conflict was the varying degree of influence on the operational management of the company with an approximate equality of the shares of the main shareholders: RUSAL representatives could not conduct any of their initiatives on the board of directors of Norilsk Nickel, as the management of Norilsk Nickel was loyal to Interros.

Figure 2. Financial indicators of TNK-BP during the conflict period, millions of dollars (compiled by the authors)
Source: TNK-BP Company Information, 2007 - 2009

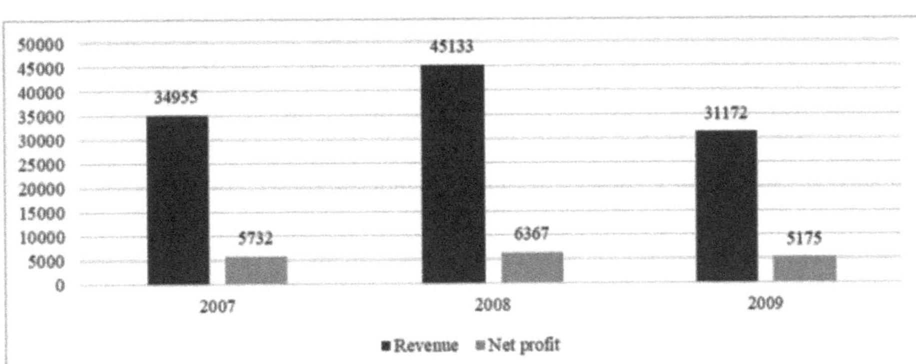

Table 1. Key performance indicators of TNK-BP during the conflict period (compiled by the authors)

Performance indicators	Dynamics at the time of conflict	Dynamics after conflict resolution	Comments
Capitalization of the company compared to the market index	→	↑	The impact of the conflict on the company's capitalization was short-term.
Credit ratings	↓	↑	The credit rating of the company during the conflict was downgraded.
Key financial indicators	→	→	The conflict did not have a significant impact on financial performance (due to the influence of external factors).

Source: TNK-BP Company Information, 2007 - 2012

The conflict ended only in early December 2012, when Millhouse Capital became a shareholder in Norilsk Nickel and took control of 5.87%. RUSAL, Interros and Millhouse Capital signed an agreement aimed at ending the shareholders' conflict over the Norilsk Nickel. According to the agreement, the Board of Directors of Nickel shall consist of 13 people: Interros and RUSAL receive 4 places each, Millhouse Capital 3 places, and independent directors 2 places.

It is worth noting that up to that point, the Russian "blue chip" had never been so close to foreign corporate standards in the level of influence of minority shareholders on the outcome of events. In order to terminate the powers of the current board of directors, it was required that more than 50% of those present at the general meeting of shareholders cast their votes in favor of re-electing the board of directors and only the votes of the minority shareholders were able to help RUSAL regain its lost positions on the board of directors. Moreover, prior to the extraordinary general meeting of shareholders, the opposing parties conducted an extensive "minority tour", trying to convince each of the shareholders in their own right, yet with the final decision being actually left to minority shareholders (Interfax, October 21, 2010).

Figure 3 shows how the price of Norilsk Nickel shares changed during the conflict — the company's securities were traded at a premium to the market.

As can be seen from fig. 4, the company's key financial indicators showed a negative trend during the conflict. Such a significant decline in financial indicators cannot be explained only by fluctuations in the market. Vladimir Putin, who was Prime Minister at the time of the conflict, spoke about the existence of direct economic damage to the company (Ria, 2010). An analysis of the situation shows that the key factors affecting the occurrence of economic damage for the company itself are a reduction in the availability of financing, and as a result, a reduction in investment, which inevitably leads to a decrease in key financial indicators.

Figure 3. Stock quotes for MMC Norilsk Nickel during a conflict versus market (compiled by the authors)
Source: MFD.ru, 2008 - 2012

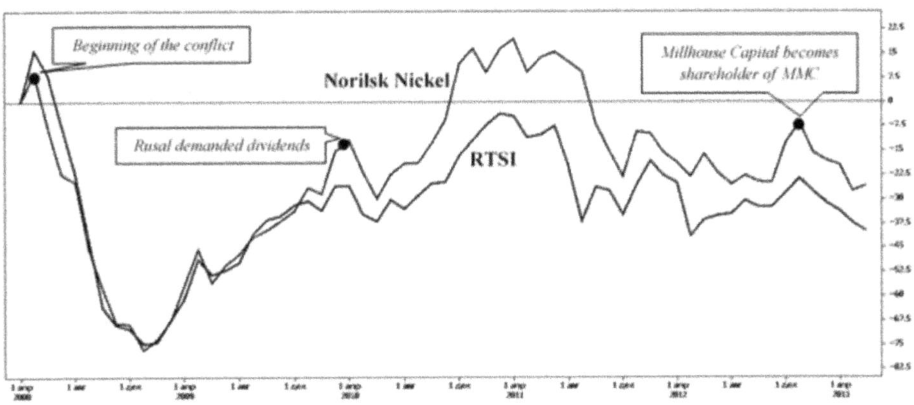

Figure 4. Financial indicators of MMC Norilsk Nickel during the conflict period, millions of dollars (compiled by the authors)
Source: Company data for MMC Norilsk Nickel, 2007 - 2012

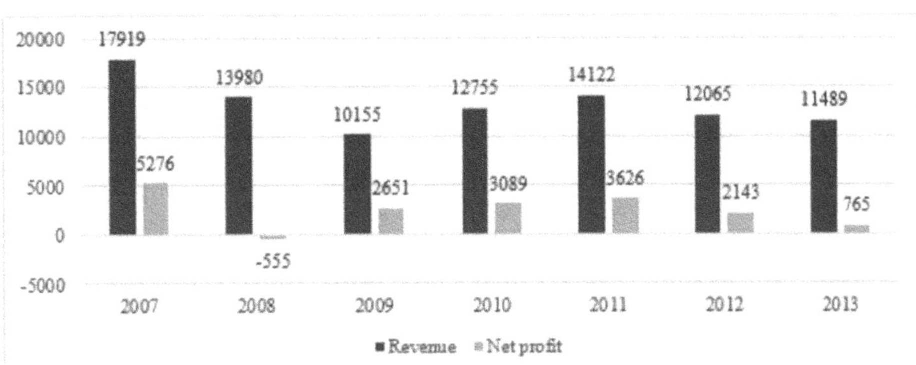

Table 2. Key Performance Indicators of MMC Norilsk Nickel during the conflict period (compiled by the authors)

Performance indicators	Dynamics at the time of conflict	Dynamics after conflict resolution	Comments
Capitalization of the company compared to the market index	↑	↑	The conflict turned out to be beneficial for minorities - each of the parties bought up the company's shares in the struggle for control.
Credit ratings	→	→	The rating during the conflict did not change and remained at the level of BBB-.
Key financial indicators	↓	→	The conflict has affected the financial performance (on the background of the influence of external factors).

Source: Company data for MMC Norilsk Nickel

NLMK vs. Maxi Group

The conflict began in 2007 (Interfax, July 16, 2010), when NLMK acquired from the owner of Maxi-Group N. Maximov a controlling stake in Maxi-Group (50% + 1 share). The amount of the transaction was approximately $600 million and was payable in two tranches. The first tranche of $300 million was paid to the shareholder in January 2008. The second tranche was to be paid after completion of the verification of Maxi-Group and its subsidiaries, and after adjusting the amount of the transaction accordingly.

However, NLMK soon accused former top managers of Maxi-Group of illegally withdrawing funds from the company. According to NLMK, the former management of Maxi-Group misled the customers back in 2007. The fact that NLMK overpaid for the transaction was confirmed by PwC auditors: at the time of sale, Maxi-Group holding's debts significantly exceeded $1.8 billion (Osipov, 2011).

In 2014, the agreement on the purchase of Maxi-Group shares by NLMK was recognized invalid by the court as a transaction made under the influence of fraud by Maximov. An advance payment of a transaction in the amount of 7.3 billion rubles was recovered from Maximov in favor of NLMK (NLMK, n.d.).

As a result, the total expenses of NLMK related to the acquisition of Maxi-Group exceeded 62 billion rubles, and OJSC Maxi-Group was declared bankrupt.

From Figure 5 it can be noted that NLMK shares were trading at a premium to the market. The conflict did not have a significant impact on the quotations of securities.

Despite the fact that the financial performance of NLMK changed due to external factors, the conflict did not have a significant impact, and there was instability of financial performance of Maxi-Group - in 2011 the company was declared bankrupt.

- At the start of the conflict, Standard & Poor's (n.d.) assigned to NLMK a long-term credit rating of "BB+", with the rating outlook "Stable".
- On 24.07.2008 S&P upgraded NLMK's Rating from "BB+" to "BBB-", with a "Stable" outlook.
- On 06.26.2013. S&P downgraded NLMK's Credit Rating from "BBB-" to "BB+", with a "Stable" outlook.

Figure 5. NLMK Stock Quotes during Conflict vs. Market
Source: MFD.ru, 2007 - 2014

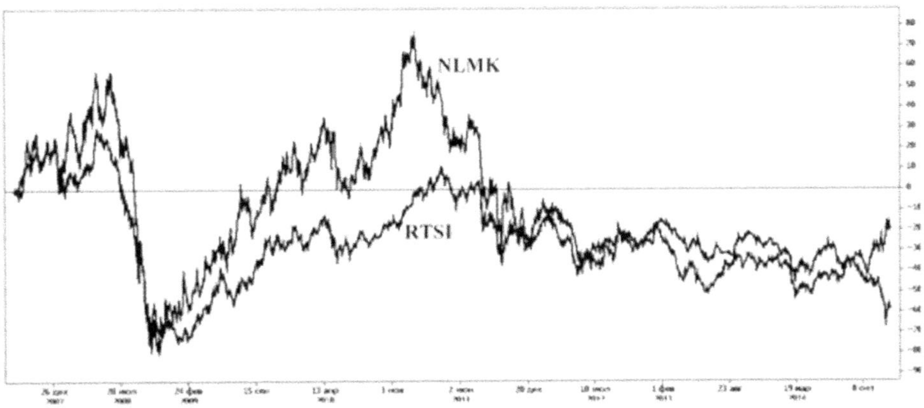

Figure 6. Financial indicators of NLMK during the conflict period, millions of dollars (compiled by the authors)
Source: Company data for NLMK, 2006 - 2015

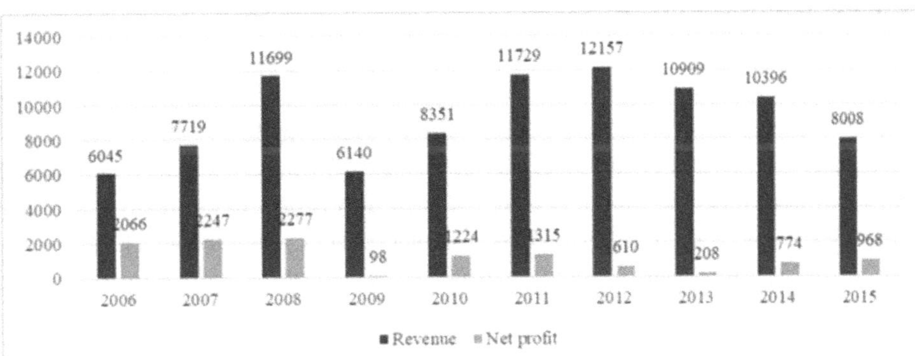

Figure 7. Financial indicators of OJSC Maxi-Group during the conflict period, millions of rubles (compiled by the authors)
Source: Company data for Maxi-Group, 2006 - 2011

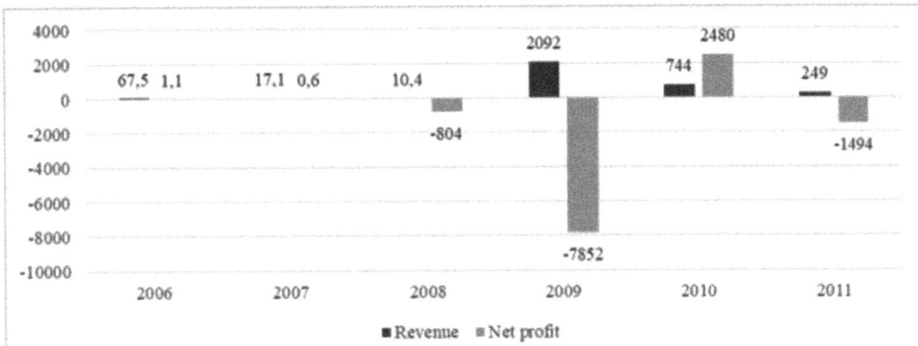

Table 3. Key performance indicators of NLMK and maxi-group during the conflict period (compiled by the authors)

Performance indicators	Dynamics at the time of conflict		Dynamics after conflict resolution		Comments
	NLMK	**Maxi-Group**	**NLMK**	**Maxi-Group**	
Capitalization of the company compared to the market index	→		→		Conflict has little impact on capitalization.
Credit ratings	→		↑		Rating during the conflict changed, due to the influence of external factors.
Key financial indicators	↑	↓	→	↓	The conflict did not have a significant impact on the financial performance of NLMK, and Maxi Group was declared bankrupt.

Source: Company data for NLMK and Maxi-Group, 2006 - 2015

Conflict of AFK Sistema vs. Rosneft

In 2017, the companies NK Rosneft and ANK Bashneft filed a lawsuit against AFK Sistema and its subsidiary Sistema-Invest for the recovery of 106.6 billion rubles, the losses of which allegedly incurred by Bashneft in connection with its reorganization in 2013–2014, when AFK Sistema was its main shareholder. Later, the amount of claims increased to 170.6 billion rubles in connection with the currency reassessment of the claims of the plaintiffs (Vesti Finance, 2017). On August 23, the court decided to recover 136 billion rubles from Sistema. (Fadeeva, Burmistrov, Balashov, Podobedova, & Dzyadko, 2017).

In 2002, the head of the Republic of Bashkortostan issued a decree authorizing the privatization of enterprises of the Bashkir fuel and energy complex (which included Bashneft and its subsidiaries), and in 2003 they were bought by seven private companies. In 2005, AFK Sistema bought minority stakes in the Bashkir fuel and energy complex, and only in March 2009 signed an agreement on the purchase of controlling stakes. The total amount of $2 billion rubles significantly exceeded market quotes of Bashneft and its other enterprises.

After 4 years of operational management in 2013, preparations began for the placement of Bashneft shares on the London Stock Exchange. Prior to placement, AFK Sistema reorganized the oil company. This was due to the loop-back system of share ownership.

In 2014, an investigation was launched into the privatization case of Bashneft against its former owner. The privatization was declared illegal, and all subsequent sales transactions were invalid. In October 2014, the Moscow Arbitration Court decided to withdraw Bashneft shares from AFK Sistema, and in early December the papers became the property of the state.

In May 2016, Russian President V. Putin excluded Bashneft from the list of strategic enterprises. Initially, the company was to be sold at a public auction. Nevertheless, Rosneft bought the company from the state for 329.7 billion rubles.

In May 2017, Rosneft and Bashneft filed two lawsuits. Rosneft considered that Bashneft suffered losses due to reorganization and lost part of its assets. AFK Sistema called the claims unfounded. The company, according to media reports, offered to Rosneft a settlement of the dispute by engaging independent experts, but Rosneft rejected these proposals.

The main hearings on the case took place in July and August 2017. The lawyers of Sistema were dissatisfied with the process: during the process, 3 appeals were made to the judge, which the court did not satisfy. The court refused to satisfy all the other petitions of the defendant, of which, as a matter of fact, there were about 40 total. Rosneft did not complain about the course of the trial. The court finally ruled to recover 136.3 billion rubles from AFK Sistema. News of the lawsuit crashed the stock quotes of AFK Sistema.

Standard & Poor's (n.d.) credit rating of Sistema changed:

- **07/18/2017:** The rating of "BB" level was placed on the CreditWatch Negative list pending a court decision.
- **09/08/2017:** The rating was lowered from "BB" to "BB-" and left on the CreditWatch Negative list due to pressure on liquidity ratios.

Thus, both in international and Russian practice, corporate conflicts are an inevitable part of corporate relations. At the same time, the main participants, conditions of emergence, preferential ways to resolve corporate conflicts differ significantly depending on the model of corporate governance, concentration of property, the role of the state and other stakeholders (for example, trade unions), the quality of corporate governance, and the quality of the institutional environment.

An important difference of the Russian business environment remains the significant role of the state, as well as the preferred means of resolving conflicts.

In Russian conditions of the high value of control over assets and an ownership structure with two or more large shareholders, each of which is not controlling, there is inevitably associated a risk of a conflict between them. Perhaps that is why such companies are few in comparison with companies with sole control. But when wars between large shareholders arise, they, as a rule, gain wide publicity, since the opposing sides have a serious arsenal of recourse.

Figure 8. Stock quotes for AFK Sistema during a conflict versus market (compiled by the authors)
Source: MFD.ru, 2017

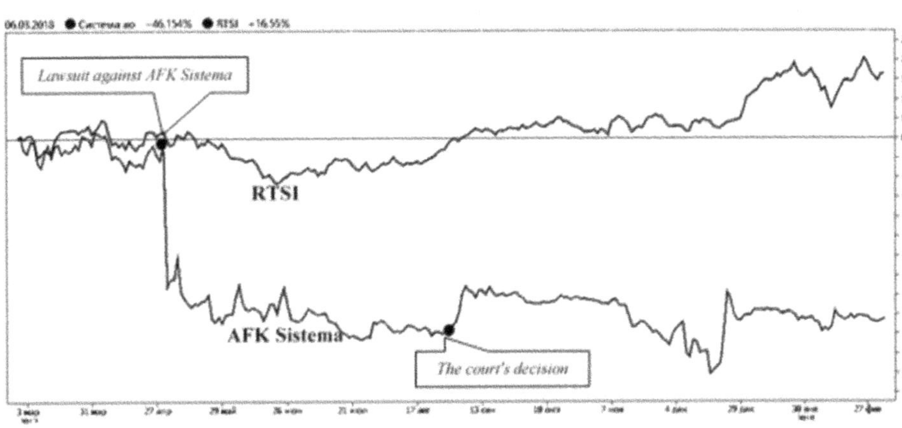

Figure 9. Financial indicators of AFK Sistema during the conflict period, billions of rubles (compiled by the authors)
Source: Company data for AFK Sistema, 2016 - 2017

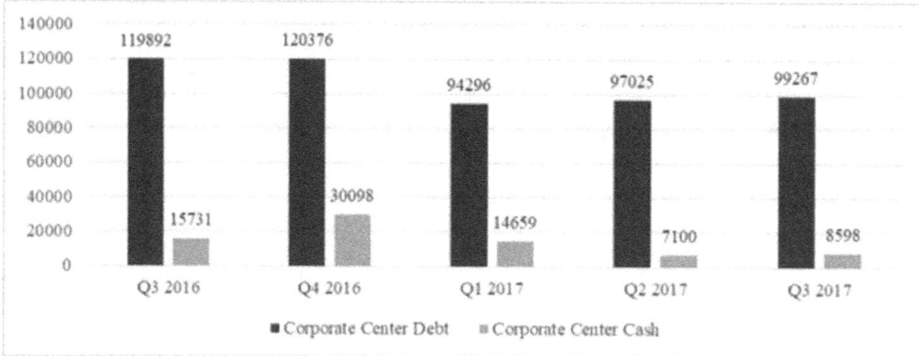

Table 4. Key performance indicators of AFK sistema during the conflict period (compiled by the authors)

Performance indicators	Dynamics at the time of conflict	Dynamics after conflict resolution	Comments
Capitalization of the company compared to the market index	↓	→	The conflict has significantly affected the performance - about 25%.
Credit ratings	↓	→	The rating during the conflict was lowered and placed on the CreditWatch list with a negative outlook.
Key financial indicators	↓	→	The conflict had a significant impact on the investment potential of Sistema (its main activity), reducing liquidity.

Source: Company data for AFK Sistema, 2016 - 2017

Moreover, in each of the analyzed cases, both in Russian and in foreign practices, corporate conflicts affected not only the performance of the companies themselves, but also the economy of the country as a whole. Following the consideration of specific examples, the authors built a matrix for assessing the impact of conflicts on the internal and external environment of the company. The evaluation was made on the basis of the analysis of:

- Financial indicators of companies,
- Stock quotes,
- Credit ratings,
- Market indices at the time of conflict,
- News feeds.

For the formation of the matrix, a 3-point scale for each criterion was used:

- Strong influence - 3 points - a significant negative impact on the stock market, industry indicators, the probability of bankruptcies of companies;
- Moderate impact - 2 points - a drop in market quotes, a decrease in the flow of investment / a negative impact on the company's image, financial indicators;
- Low Impact - 1 point - stability of the stock market / insignificant impact on stock prices, financial indicators.

As can be seen from the above examples and analysis, in practically each of the examples, the impact of corporate conflict on the economy was significant. It can be assumed that in developing economies, in conditions of a weak institutional environment and imperfect law enforcement practice, the costs of corporate conflicts increase due to the low level of trust between participants in corporate relations. What are the mechanisms and the extent of such an impact on the investment climate, stock market capitalization, market valuation of assets, and financial stability?

THE SCALE OF THE POSSIBLE CONSEQUENCES OF CORPORATE CONFLICTS WITH THE EXAMPLE OF THE RUSSIAN ECONOMY

As this study shows, conflicts differ significantly in the degree of their impact on the economy as a whole, depending on the nature and essence of the conflict. Conflicts between shareholders about the business development strategy and dividend policy have a short-term negative impact on some indicators of the company (for example, credit rating, temporary decrease in capitalization and P/E).

However, conflicts related to risks of violation of shareholders' rights, or significant mutual claims of large shareholders, through a long struggle for control over certain assets may have a greater impact on the market.

To assess the impact of corporate conflicts on the economy as a whole, the business and investment climate on the example of Russia, the authors assessed the impact of corporate conflicts, in particular the last conflict of AFK Sistema vs Rosneft, on:

Figure 10. Matrix of influence of corporate conflicts (compiled by the authors)

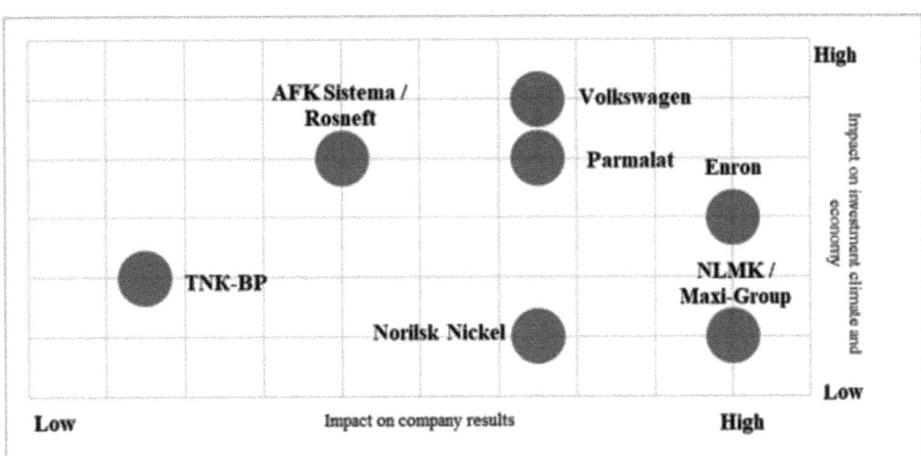

- Market valuation of assets of Russian companies.
- Position in the respective ratings and rankings of the business and investment climate.
- Financial stability

Market Valuation of Russian Company Assets

In assessing the potential impact of corporate conflicts on the economy as a whole, one can pay attention to the impact of conflicts on the market valuation of Russian assets. One of the tools to assess this impact is the MSCI (2017) index, the MSCI Russia Standard Index.

During the last of the reviewed conflict of AFK-System vs Rosneft, the index MSCI Russia showed a significant "draw-down", despite and observed moderate growth of MSCI EM. It should be noted that the dynamics of the Index depends on a number of macroeconomic factors, but it is obvious that the index reflects the general mood of investors. The weight of the AFC-System Index was only 0.46% (MSCI, 2017).

If we analyze the market valuation of Russian companies (Star Capital, 2017) in comparison with both developed and individual emerging markets, it can also be noted that, since 2008, P/E has not risen above 7. In terms of this indicator, Russia is only ahead of China.

At the same time, as a number of studies show (Connington, 2017; Roy, 2017), the low fundamental valuation of Russian assets (in terms of P / E, CAPE Russia is one of the "cheapest" countries in the world) has several reasons. Among the factors contributing to the low score, there are:

- Concentration in several sectors, with a high degree of state participation (the energy sector, the banking sector, etc.), a high dependence of the market on the price of oil,
- International sanctions
- High market volatility.

However, the dividend yield of Russian stocks is one of the highest in the world (Gusakov, 2017) - at a level of 6.0% for 2017.

In exchange traded funds (Roy, 2017) analysts identify the following factors of a negative impact on the valuation of Russian assets (P / E 7.86 - the lowest among all ETF funds):

- International sanctions
- Low oil prices
- Some investors are uncertain about the risks of the possible nationalization of companies with damage to their shareholders.

Comparing the research data (Connington, 2017; Gusakov, 2017) with the dynamics of investments in Russian companies' stocks, it can be assumed that a significant underestimation of Russian stocks (low P/E) actually leads to a lack of potential investments by Russian companies over the past 10 years. At least 30-50% of the current amount of investments by foreign funds - that is, it could amount to $20-30 billion of lost investments in stocks, and taking into account the attraction of debt financing, this could be a loss of $40-60 billion investments needed to ensure high economic growth rates.

Various investor surveys conducted before the events of 2014 and the imposition of sanctions - for example, the JP Morgan report "Investor Opinions of Russian Companies" (2013) - highlighted several key problems affecting the low valuation of Russian assets compared to other developing economies.

As a result of the survey, almost 90% of respondents noted the quality of corporate governance and corruption as key constraints, as well as country risk (83%) and level of transparency (66%). According to survey participants, one of the key problems underlying these risks remains institutional quality.

According to the results of the survey, the average rating based on the "Corporate Governance" factor was 1.8 out of 5, which means that at the time of the study, investors estimated that the situation with corporate governance in Russia was worse than in comparable developing countries. Thus, the quality of corporate governance is still a significant deterrent to attracting foreign investment.

According to a number of studies (Bebchuk & Weisbach, 2009; Khanna & Zyla, 2010), the premium for the quality of corporate governance can range from 5 to 40% of the company's value. This means that the quality of corporate governance in Russia is also a serious factor constraining the growth of the value of Russian companies.

Position in the Ratings and Rankings of the Business and Investment Climate

The dynamics of individual macroeconomic indicators during a period of corporate conflicts can also be an indirect indicator of their impact on the business and investment climate. The authors reviewed indicators such as the Index of Entrepreneurial Confidence (Federal State Statistics Service [FSSS], 2017), the index of competitiveness (World Economic Forum [WEF], 2017), the World Bank's rating of "Doing business" (World Bank, 2017), and the dynamics of the import-export of capital (Bank of Russia, 2017).

The index of entrepreneurial confidence is a qualitative indicator, which, according to the responses of managers about the forecast of output, balance, and demand for it, describes the economic activities of organizations. The indicator is the arithmetic average of the "balances" of answers to questions about the expected output, actual demand and current balances of finished products (the latter with the opposite sign) (FSSS, 2017).

Figure 11. Business confidence index (compiled by the authors)
Source: FSSS, 2017

As can be seen from Figure 11, the index showed a positive trend in the spring of 2017, but in August-October, rolled back to January values. It should be noted that the moment of increase in the indicator from -1 to -3 was at the peak of the last conflict of AFK Sistema and Rosneft.

Since 2013, there has been a positive trend in Russia in the competitiveness index (WEF, 2017) from 4.19 in 2013 to 4.51 in 2017. (from 67 to 43), which is confirmed by the corresponding positions in the World Bank's Doing Business ranking from 111 to 35 in 2017 and the most relevant studies (Ernst and Young, 2015) of the Russian investment climate. In particular, among the positive trends, the authors of the Ernst and Young study (2015, p. 4) note that:

- Frequent changes in legislation raise doubts among foreign investors. 77% of survey participants consider the unstable legal environment as one of the main obstacles to investment in Russia.
- About 90% of survey participants conducting operations in Russia describe the current economic situation as complex, suggesting that the local market will lose some of its attractiveness to investors in the near future.
- The tax system causes a minimum of criticism from foreign investors. There are major improvements in the work of the customs service. However, complex administrative procedures and technical regulations, as well as the inefficient state apparatus and judicial system, create significant difficulties for businesses.
- Many foreign investors noted the reluctance of government officials to maintain communications, slow decision-making, and excessive bureaucratic requirements as constraints. However, the recently introduced mechanisms for the development of improvements in legislation, public administration, the introduction of best practices, at least contribute to the dialogue between government and business.
- While mutual trust is still at a low level, as evidenced by the small number of joint projects, foreign partners note positive changes in management style, which, in their opinion, brings corporate relations to international standards.
- More than 50% of respondents noted that regional administrations are making more efforts to improve the investment climate in comparison with several years earlier, and demonstrate a commitment to creating attractive business conditions for foreign investors.

The last few years have also been marked by significant progress in Russia in the World Bank's "Ease of doing business" rating. In the Doing Business (World Bank, 2017) rating, Russia in 2017 climbed to 35th place in terms of business convenience. For comparison, in 2012, Russia was ranked 120th in the rankings. Improvements to the business environment and product market efficiency, the quantity and quality of education, the innovation environment, and some successes in the fight against corruption, which, however, remains a problematic factor (Schwab, 2016, 2017), contributed to further progress. Also, at a low level, according to the research, is the quality rating of institutions (2017 - 88th, 2018 - 83th place), and the development of the financial market (2017 - 108th, 2018 - 107th place).

Comparing these positions in assessing the quality of institutions, there is a decrease of 5 points from the Ethical behavior of firms. Russia holds the weakest positions in the protection of property rights, the protection of intellectual property, the burden of state regulation. It is noted that the ranking of judicial independence is in a low position, although the effectiveness of conflict resolution is in the 70th place. The authors also emphasize that the country's economy remains very dependent on commodity exports, which also hinders its development.

Table 5. Rating of the quality of institutions, according to the rating of competitiveness in Russia (compiled by the authors)

The Global Competitiveness Report		Rank/ 138 2016 / 2017	Rank/ 137 2017 / 2018
1st pillar: Institutions		*88*	*83*
1.01	Property rights	123	116
1.02	Intellectual property protection	117	93
1.03	Diversion of public funds	92	82
1.04	Public trust in politicians	56	51
1.05	Irregular payments and bribes	83	76
1.06	Judicial independence	95	90
1.07	Favoritism in decisions of government officials	77	66
1.08	Wastefulness of government spending	86	57
1.09	Burden of government regulation	103	79
1.10	Efficiency of legal framework in settling disputes	82	70
1.11	Efficiency of legal framework in challenging regs	91	77
1.12	Transparency of government policymaking	75	70
1.13	Business costs of terrorism	101	94
1.14	Business costs of crime and violence	75	69
1.15	Organized crime	85	86
1.16	Reliability of police services	109	98
1.17	Ethical behavior of firms	65	70
1.18	Strength of auditing and reporting standards	103	100
1.19	Efficacy of corporate boards	73	51
1.20	Protection of minority shareholders' interests	116	111
1.21	Strength of investor protection	63	51

Source: The Global Competitiveness Report, 2016–2018

From the point of view of assessing the impact of corporate conflicts on the investment climate, it is also necessary to pay attention to such an indicator as private sector outflow of capital.

The net outflow of capital by the private sector in January-September 2017, according to the Bank of Russia (2017), formed at the level of US $ 21.0 billion, two times more than in the same period of the previous year. In contrast to the situation of the corresponding period of 2016, net capital outflow was formed due to banking sector operations, which significantly reduced external liabilities. Capital flows related to operations in other sectors were generally balanced.

In a study of the Platform Social Design Center (2017), experts say that the AFK Sistema - Rosneft conflict is not the last corporate conflict in the history of Russian business, and such wars seriously damage Russia's investment climate.

It should be noted that with the improvement of the investment climate, the rise in oil prices, and the strengthening of macroeconomic stability, the export of capital in 2017, however, increased.

Figure 12. The most problematic factors of doing business in Russia (compiled by the authors)
Source: The Global Competitiveness Report, 2016–2018

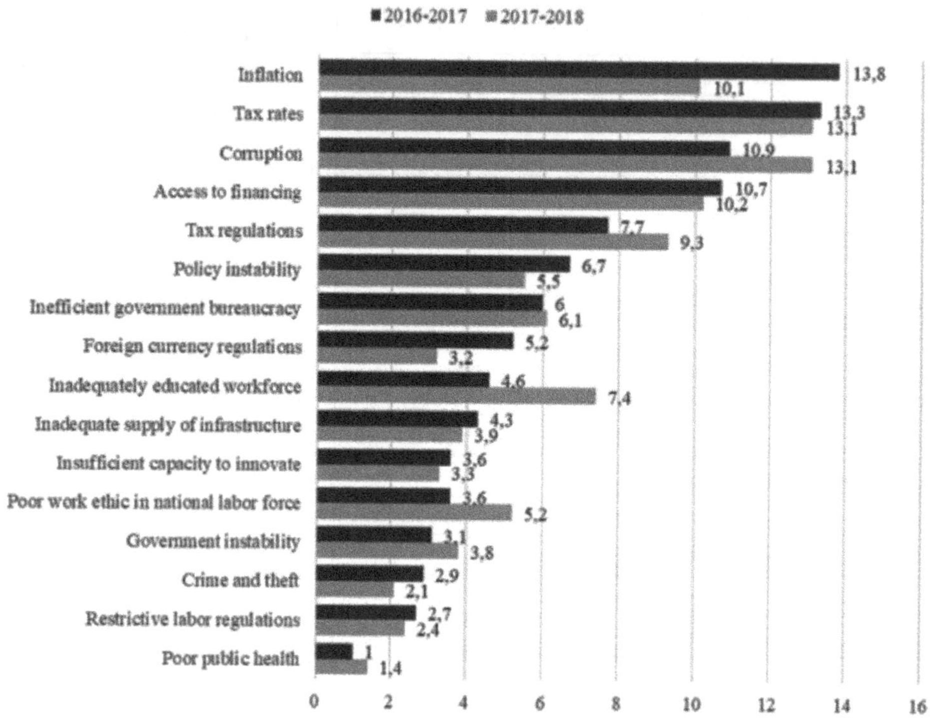

Figure 13. Net import / export of capital by the private sector in 2017, according to the Central Bank (compiled by the authors)
Source: CBR.RU, 2017

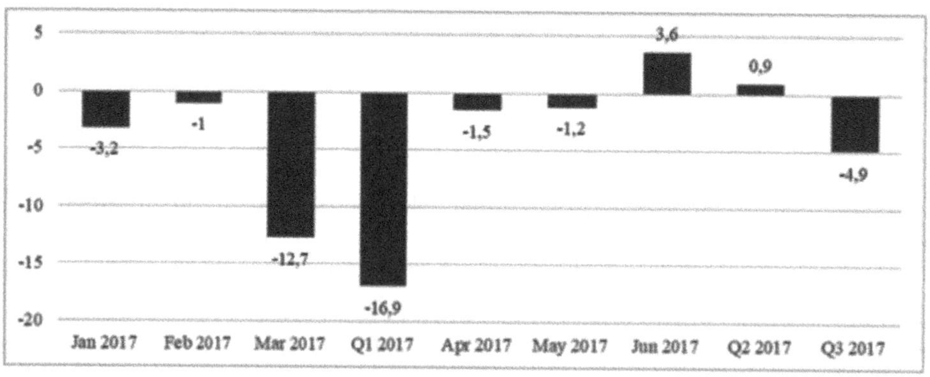

The flow of foreign direct investment is also one of the indicators of the quality of the investment climate. According to the UNSTAD (2018) rating, Russia is in 13th place in terms of the volume of investments among countries with developing economies.

Thus, a comparative analysis of the dynamics of market asset valuations of Russian assets, indicators of the business and investment climate suggests that large corporate conflicts themselves do not lead to a significant decrease in market valuation, but act as indicators of the maturity and quality of the institu-

Table 6. Foreign Direct Investment Flows (compiled by the authors)

FDI flows, by region and economy, 2012–2017 (Billions of dollars)												
	FDI inflows						FDI outflows					
Region/ economy	**2012**	**2013**	**2014**	**2015**	**2016**	**2017**	**2012**	**2013**	**2014**	**2015**	**2016**	**2017**
Russian Federation	30,2	53,4	29,2	11,9	37,2	25,3	28,4	70,7	64,2	27,1	27	36
Developing economies	651,5	648,5	685,3	744	670,2	670,7	362,7	415	458	406,2	406,7	380,8
Developed economies	858,3	693,2	596,7	1141,3	1133,2	712,4	973,7	890,1	731,7	1183,6	1041,5	1009,2

Source: UNCTAD, 2018

tional environment, with traditional problems such as an unstable legal system, a weak judicial system, a weak institution for the protection of property rights, and a low level of protection of shareholders' rights in the first place of the minority shareholders' rights.

Low market valuation of Russian assets has significant economic consequences. A significant "country discount" does not allow Russian companies to receive a level of investment comparable to developed and even with many developing countries. So, if we assume that the Russian IPOs of the last 10 years would have been estimated to be at least 2 times higher than the current (14 P / E), this would mean a significant additional attraction of investments in the Russian economy.

The Impact of Corporate Conflicts on Financial Stability

One of the indicators of the reaction of market participants to corporate conflicts is the Financial Stress Index (FSI). The methodology of the FSI index of the ACRA (2017) rating agency is based on the concepts of systemic risk and financial stability, and implies that the financial system, linking different sectors of the economy, can contribute to the spread of non-payment (regardless of the reasons for their occurrence) under the contracts of agents in some markets to agents for others markets.

Large-scale episodes of this kind (financial crises) can lead to disruption in the functioning of the real sector of the economy (initially due to the occurrence of local liquidity crises), which determines the importance of attention paid to them.

Based on international experience, the Agency ACRA identifies five main external manifestations of financial stress:

1. Uncertainty in the fundamental prices of financial assets or commodities. Correlates with the volatility of prices of financial instruments, forcing agents to react more and faster to any new (even irrelevant) information.
2. Lack of information about the motives and current state of other market participants. It can lead to a misinterpretation of price movements and episodes of a sharp correction of expectations.
3. Asymmetry of information about the quality of assets (the seller knows more) or the quality of the borrower (the borrower is more aware). It appears as a result of the growth of their dispersion and

aggravates the problems of adverse selection and moral hazard, which, in turn, leads to a decrease in trust and credit activity.

4. "Flight into quality" The increase in the probability of loss makes investors prefer less profitable, but at the same time less risky ways of investing, which leads to an often rapid change in their relative prices.
5. "Flight into liquidity" Reducing lending opportunities creates additional incentives to favor the more liquid assets needed to meet the need for covering cash gaps.

As a result of the conflict of AFK Sistema vs. Bashneft "the Financial Stress Index – ACRA", FSI rose significantly on May 3, 2017: by 0.15 percentage points relative to the previous day's level. The sharp decline in AFK Sistema's shares adversely affected financial stability and became the most stressful event for the Russian financial system since mid-March, as well as the first event in several years unrelated to external economic shock. One of the manifestations of financial instability - the uncertainty of the fundamental prices of assets - has significantly increased today, rising by 48 pp relative to its value of yesterday.

Thus, it can be stated that large corporate conflicts can have a short-term "stressful" effect on the market.

SOLUTIONS AND RECOMMENDATIONS

As a result of the study, the authors come to the following solutions:

- Consequences of corporate conflicts can be either positive, or destructive for their participants and the economy as a whole, depending on the nature, course of conflicts, methods and results of their resolution.
- If a corporate conflict ends positively, on a legal plane, there is a high probability that the conflict will have a positive effect on the value of companies and the business environment as a whole.

Figure 14. Index of financial stress by the method of ACRA, 2017 (compiled by the authors)
Source: ACRA, 2017

- In developing economies, in conditions of a weak institutional environment, imperfect law enforcement practices and low level of trust between participants in corporate relations, the costs of corporate conflicts can be high.
- One of the outcomes of corporate conflicts could be the withdrawal of a large foreign investors from the market.
- The reorganization of joint-stock companies is one of the most important decisions that affects their activities and existence, leading to a redistribution of shares in their authorized capitals. This results in corporate conflicts between minorities and minority shareholders. Avoiding a corporate conflict is possible only if a balance is established between the interests of minority and majority shareholders. The balance sheet should be provided with clear legal procedures for decision-making by the management bodies of joint-stock companies, statutory guarantees of the rights of various groups of shareholders, effective, and not formal judicial control.
- In the event of the development of corporate conflicts in a negative scenario in conditions of insufficiently developed institutions in emerging markets, including Russia, macroeconomic consequences can be really significant and can build the following chain of events:
    - Lowering the credit rating of a participating company,
    - Significant decrease in capitalization,
    - Reduced investment,
    - The growth of the index of financial stress, the decrease in the index of entrepreneurial confidence, and as a result - the outflow of portfolio investments,
    - Negative dynamics of stock market indices,
    - Increase in capital outflows,
    - As a general consequence - the long-term market stagnation and a substantial "country discount" for all Russian securities.
- The long-term implications of low asset valuations due to the "country discount" include the fact that companies do not receive a significant amount of investment. In Russia, when compared with other emerging markets, this discount can be estimated at 30-50%; and although a significant part of the discount is a result of geopolitical factors, corporate governance risks and the quality of key institutions also have a significant impact on investor sentiment. For Russia, this could mean a loss of 40-60 billion dollars in potential investments, and therefore, a slowdown in economic growth.

However, is it possible to reduce the potential damage caused by corporate conflicts? It is obvious that it is impossible to "fully insure" against the occurrence of corporate conflicts - their occurrence is inevitable due to the peculiarities of corporate relations, dynamic changes in the external environment, and complication of regulatory requirements. At the same time, both at the company level and at the state level, conditions can be created to minimize the risks of corporate conflicts, and in case of their occurrence, to reduce the negative consequences of such conflicts.

Taking into account the case studies, depending on the level of maturity of the institutional environment, according to the authors, the main efforts should be directed at:

- Increasing the transparency of companies and improving the practice of corporate governance,
- Depending on the development of the institutional environment, the development of effective practice of pre-trial settlement of disputes and the improvement of the judicial system.

The solution of the first task is inherent in the practice and control of compliance by companies with the national Code of Corporate Governance (Bank of Russia, 2014).

In solving the second task, the key role should be played by the state together with the institutions of civil society. A benchmark for creating an appropriate environment can be G20 Approved Guidelines on International Investment Policy (UNCTAD, 2016).

To create an open, transparent and supportive global political environment for investment; to promote coherence in the development of national and international investment policies; and to promote inclusive economic growth and sustainable development, the G20 members offer generally accepted guidelines for the design of investment policies: rules, conditions, investment regulation; legal protection, dispute resolution procedures; compliance with the principles of corporate governance; conditions for cooperation in order to maintain an open and supportive policy environment for investment, etc.

These principles are complementary and should be considered holistically. They can serve as a benchmark for formulating national and international investment policies in accordance with international obligations, taking into account the goals and priorities of national and international development.

FUTURE RESEARCH DIRECTIONS

The authors, studying topics related to factors affecting the investment climate and their consequences, plan to conduct further research on the topic of "The relationship between foreign direct investment and divestment drivers".

CONCLUSION

In this study, the authors attempted to answer the question of how legitimate it is to raise the question of the possible economic consequences of major corporate conflicts, as well as to assess the extent of the possible impact of conflicts on the activities of both the companies and the economy as a whole.

The results of the study showed that corporate conflicts in the United States, Europe and Russia have specific features:

- In the USA, corporate conflicts often occur between shareholders and management, the basis of which is management actions, which go against the interests of shareholders. At the same time, the board of directors plays an important role in the prevention and settlement of conflicts in the conditions of dispersed ownership.
- In Europe, corporate conflicts occur between large and small shareholders and the basis of these disputes are the natural contradictions between the interests of shareholders. In a concentrated ownership structure, trade unions play a significant role in resolving conflicts.
- In Russia, as well as in Europe, there is a high concentration of property. Major conflicts occur between large owners in the struggle for control or in making key strategic decisions. Often, the state is directly or indirectly involved in resolving conflicts.

Possible negative consequences of corporate conflicts can be significant for the economy:

- stock market stagnation;
- low valuation of country assets;
- loss of company reputation, fall of the country's image;
- significant economic damage, bankruptcy of companies, which has a negative impact on the economy as a whole, affecting the interests of many stakeholders.

An analysis of the situation shows that the key factors affecting the occurrence of economic damage for the company itself are a reduction in the availability of financing, and as a result, a reduction in investment, which inevitably leads to a decrease in key financial indicators. The long-term implications of low asset valuations due to the "country discount" include the fact that companies do not receive a significant amount of investment.

Finally, the main "lines of defense" against corporate conflicts, in accordance with international practice, consist of high-quality corporate governance: a strong, professional, independent board of directors, as well as a developed practice of pre-trial settlement of disputes and a reliable judicial system that inspires confidence among all involved parties.

REFERENCES

ACRA. (2017). *ACRA Financial Stress Index* (ACRA FSI RU). Retrieved from https://www.acra-ratings.ru/research/index

Bank of Russia. (2014). Corporate Governance Code. *Bulletin of The Bank of Russia*, *40*(1518), 15.

Bank of Russia. (2017). *External sector statistics.* Retrieved from http://www.cbr.ru/statistics/?PrtId=svs

BBC News. (2002, October 16). *Enron auditor fined $500,000*. Retrieved from http://news.bbc.co.uk/2/hi/business/2334761.stm

Bebchuk, L. A., & Weisbach, M. S. (2009). *The state of Corporate Governance research*. NBER. Working Paper No. 15537.

Berezinets, I. V., Ilyina, Y. B., & Fakhritdinov, D. N. (2014). Corporate conflicts and financial performance of companies. *Bulletin of St. Petersburg University.*, *2*, 100–135.

Connington, J. (2017). Mapped: the world's cheapest stock markets. *Telegraph*. Retrieved from http://www.telegraph.co.uk/investing/shares/worlds-cheapest-markets-2017/

Cortes, A., & Rosell, J. (n.d.). *Parmalat scandal.* Retrieved from https://prezi.com/8xmxofrc2tcw/copy-of-parmalat-scandal/

Deardorff, A. V. (n.d.). "Social cost". *Deardorffs' Glossary of International Economics*. Retrieved from http://www-personal.umich.edu/~alandear/glossary/s.html#SocialCost

Enriques, L., & Volpin, P. (2007). Corporate Governance Reforms in Continental Europe. *The Journal of Economic Perspectives*, *21*(1), 117–140. doi:10.1257/jep.21.1.117

Ernst and Young. (2015). *Investment climate in Russia -Foreign investor perception.* Retrieved from https://www.ey.com/Publication/

Fadeeva, A., Burmistrov, S., Balashov, A., Podobedova, L., & Dzyadko, T. (2017). *The court charged RUR 136 billion from Sistema in favor of Rosneft.* RBC. Retrieved from http://www.rbc.ru/business/23/08/2017/59703cc89a794716007986d7

Federal State Statistics Service. (2017). *Business Confidence Index.* Retrieved from http://www.gks.ru/free_doc/new_site/metod/prom/met_pred-uver.htm

Finn, S. (2015). *WVU Researchers Help Bust Volkswagen for Pollution Violations.* WVPublic. Retrieved from http://wvpublic.org/post/wvu-researchers-help-bust-volkswagen-pollution-violations

Graaff, J. de V. (1987). "Social cost". *The New Palgrave: A Dictionary of Economics*, *4*, 393-395.

Gusakov, V. (2017). Key Trends of the Russian Share Market. *Moscow Exchange.* Retrieved from http://www.oecd.moex.com/s624

Hill, M. (2014). Cautionary Tales From The Enron Of American Churches. *Forbes.* Retrieved from https://www.forbes.com/sites/robasghar/2014/09/16/mars-hill-cautionary-tales-from-the-enron-of-american-churches/#15d4a249583a

Interfax. (2010, July 16). *Corporate Wars: NLMK vs Maksimov.* Retrieved from http://www.interfax.ru/business/145521

Interfax. (2010, October 21). *Finest hour Minority.* Retrieved from https://www.interfax.ru/business/161222

Kershis, O., & Gosh, A. (2017). *Reputation of the country and business: many people - one strategy.* Reputation Capital Group blog. Retrieved from https://reputationcapital.blog/2017/10/reputacija-strany-i-biznesa-mnogo-lic-odna-strategija

Kershis, O., & Gosh, A. (2017). *World leaders in corporate reputation – 2017.* Reputation Capital Group. Retrieved from https://reputationcapital.blog/2017/04/lidery-korporativnoj-reputacii-2017-ana

Khanna, V., & Zyla, R. (2010). *Survey Says.* IFC. Retrieved from https://www.ifc.org/wps/wcm/connect/dbfd8b004afe7d69bcb6bdb94e6f4d75/IFC_EMI_Survey_web.pdf?MOD=AJPERES

Leuz, C., Lins, K. V., & Warnock, F. E. (2009). *Do Foreigners Invest Less in Poorly Governed Firms?* NBER, 2-5.

Morgan, J. P. (2013). *Investor Opinions of Russian Companies.* Depositary Receipts Group. Retrieved from https://www.jpmorgan.com/jpmpdf/1320635528566.pdf

MSCI. (2017). *MSCI Russia index.* Retrieved from http://www.msci.com/

NLMK. (n.d.). *The official position of NLMK.* Retrieved from http://maxi-group.nlmk.ru/

Osipov, I. (2011, February 9). The case of the missing billions. *Forbes.* Retrieved from http://www.forbes.ru/ekonomika-opinion/lyudi/63116-delo-o-propavshih-milliardah

Papirian, G. (2010). BP in Russia: The conflict in TNK-BP and ways to resolve it. *Journal of Economic Policy*, *1*, 184–203.

Platform. (2017). Conflicts in the fuel and energy complex as an indicator of the investment climate. *Key Corporate Conflicts in Russia*, *1*, 25-28.

RBC. (2004, January 20). *"Parmalat case": arrests continue*. Retrieved from http://www.rbc.ru/economics/20/01/2004/5703c0a49a7947dde8e075c8

RBC. (2008, July 16). *TNK-BP will split in two*. Retrieved from http://rbcdaily.ru/industry/562949979036495

Ria. (2010, August 27). *Putin said that Shareholder conflict damages Norilsk Nickel*. Retrieved from https://ria.ru/economy/20100827/269597280.html

Roy, S. (2017). *ETFs With The Lowest Valuations*. ETF. Retrieved from http://www.etf.com/sections/features-and-news/etfs-lowest-valuations?nopaging=1

Savelyev, S., & Bazhenov, A. (2018). Corporate disputes in arbitration courts. Statistics. *Corporate Lawyer*, *10*, 4–5.

Schwab, K. (2016). *The Global Competitiveness Report 2016–2017*. World Economic Forum.

Schwab, K. (2017). *The Global Competitiveness Report 2017–2018*. World Economic Forum.

Schwartz, J., Cremer, A., Thomasson, E., & Thomas, S. (2015, October 4). *Volkswagen to hold extraordinary board meeting on Wednesday: sources*. Thomson Reuters. Retrieved from http://www.reuters.com/article/us-volkswagen-emissions/volkswagen-to-hold-extraordinary-board-meeting-on-wednesday-sources-idUSKCN0RY0P020151004

Standard & Poor's. (n.d.). *S&P Global Ratings*. Retrieved from https://www.standardandpoors.com/

Star Capital. (2017). *Global Stock Market Valuation Ratios*. Retrieved from http://www.starcapital.de/research/stockmarketvaluation

Stepanov, S., & Gabdrakhmanov, S. (2011). *Corporate conflicts in modern Russia and abroad*. National Board of Corporate Governance.

UNCTAD. (2016). Annex III: G20 Guiding Principles for Global Investment Policymaking. *Investment Policy*, 1–2.

UNCTAD. (2018). *World Investment Report – 2018*. Retrieved from https://unctad.org/en/PublicationsLibrary/wir2018_en.pdf

Vesti Finance. (2017, May 5). *The lawsuit of Rosneft crashed shares of Sistema by 25%*. Retrieved from http://www.vestifinance.ru/articles/84936

World Bank. (2017). *Doing Business*. Retrieved from http://www.doingbusiness.org/

World Economic Forum. (2017). *Global Competitiveness Index*. Retrieved from https://www.weforum.org/

Zlobin, A. (2017). The second scandal in two years: Volkswagen, BMW and Daimler were accused of cartel collusion. *Forbes*. Retrieved from http://www.forbes.ru/kompanii/348439-vtoroy-skandal-za-dva-goda-volkswagen-bmw-i-daimler-obvinili-v-kartelnom-sgovore

KEY TERMS AND DEFINITIONS

Board of Directors: A collective management body that provides strategic management of the company.

Corporate Conflict: Open confrontation, in which two or more parties from among the shareholders, managers, members of the board of directors are involved.

Corporate Governance: Structures and processes for the implementation of strategic management and control over the activities of companies.

Corporate Governance Code: Code of voluntary standards and internal regulations that establish and regulate the procedure for corporate relations.

Shareholder: A person who owns shares in a company and therefore gets part of the company's profits and the right to vote on how the company is controlled.

Chapter 5
Cultural Integration in Mergers and Acquisitions

Asli Goksoy
American University in Bulgaria, Bulgaria

ABSTRACT

Mergers and acquisitions (M&As) are recognized as one of the most popular corporate strategies in recent years. Unlike its popularity, the success rate of mergers and acquisitions is surprisingly low. There are many reasons for failure, but among all, culture integration has emerged as one of the major barriers to an effective merger and acquisition deal. This chapter highlights the fundamentals of this topic with literature review and presents practical and effective guidelines for facilitating cultural integration in merger and acquisition process effectively and efficiently and achieving greater results from the organizational change efforts.

INTRODUCTION

The 21st century was driven by new technologies and scientific breakthroughs, innovation and relentless competition. In such a complex business environment, corporate growth represents a key requirement for business success. Despite improved economic conditions in recent years, many corporations are finding it difficult to satisfy their growth expectations and keep their competitive advantage at a desired level. At this point, mergers and acquisitions have become a popular alternative pathway to organic growth promising a multitude of strategic opportunities and an edge that their peers will struggle to replicate. Mergers and acquisitions take place for many strategic business reasons, but the most common reasons for any business combination are economic at their core; improving efficiencies and creating synergy, easy market entry, diversification, cost/risk reduction, to mention just a few.

Mergers and acquisitions tend to be extremely well discussed in literature and planned in terms of financial, strategic and legal aspects in practice. However, research findings show that the risk of failure- fail to achieve the intended goal- is high or in some cases far greater than the chance of success (Christofferson et al., 2004). Merger and acquisition failures can be attributed to a variety of causes. Some are lack of clarity and execution of the integration process, over paying, negotiations errors, but most

DOI: 10.4018/978-1-5225-8906-8.ch005

unsuccessful outcomes are related to soft issues- people side of merger and acquisition, which is often ignored by top-level management. "Incompatible cultures", "incongruent cultural fit" and "misalignment between the two organizations' cultures" are coming in at number one among all. Countless studies demonstrate the link between culture differences and deal failure (e.g., Gomes et al., 2011). Without any doubt, the way the corporate cultures are handled in each phase of merger and acquisition process is crucial to its outcome. More attention and efforts should be spent to evaluate the organizational culture fit properly before going ahead with the transaction in order to increase its rate of success (Appelbaum et al., 2007). The importance of cultural fit for the overall outcome of merger and acquisition integration is at the center of the scientific debate about the impact of corporate culture on the performance of mergers and acquisitions (Santo, 2013).

HR practices, communication, leadership, and management styles, corporate strategies, and many more variables have either direct impact on culture integration in mergers and acquisitions or significantly related to the topic; therefore, culture integration is complex, multifaceted, and incomprehensible, thus change management teams should use well-developed toolkits and strategies for managing the cultural aspects of a deal and be prepared beforehand.

This chapter contributes to change management discipline by providing a framework designed to help executives to manage the integration process successfully throughout the M&A lifecycle and reach the desired outcome in a fast way. This framework presents culture assessment –mainly cultural due diligence- and communication as a crucial component to reducing poor culture-fit as a barrier to M&A success.

This chapter is both important and timely, as it sets the conceptual tone by providing change leaders, practitioners, and scholars a powerful framework for understanding the human side of the change process dynamics, specifically the complexities of cultural integration, and introducing solutions to minimize the relevant risks and obstacles. Finally, a positive consequence of this chapter is the source it can provide for future research.

BACKGROUND

Corporate Culture

Although, the term of "culture" first appeared in the Oxford English Dictionary around 1430, Hawthorne studies in 1930s marked the first systematic attempt to use a concept of culture to understand the work environment. Today, corporate culture has developed tremendously. It has a multidisciplinary foundation in the fields of organizational theory, management, anthropology, and other organizational studies and still attracts significant scholarly attention.

Many researchers have devoted numerous articles to the nature and definitions of culture; however, Schein's view of culture, more than any other view, was widely adopted by researchers in organizational studies. The most common accepted formal definition is-*"A pattern of shared basic assumptions that the group learned as it solved its problems of external adaptation and internal integration that has worked well enough to be considered valid and, therefore, to be taught to new members as the correct way you perceive, think, and feel in relation to those problems"*. Schein's organizational culture model (1980) divides organizational culture into three levels: artifacts (visible), espoused beliefs and values (may appear through surveys) and basic underlying assumptions (unconscious taken for granted beliefs and values). Other definitions are according to Rousseau (2000) corporate culture is a set of commonly experienced stable characteristics of an organization which shows the distinctive features of an organization which differentiates it from others. O'Reilly and Chatman (1996) describe the concept as "a set of norms and values that are widely shared and strongly held throughout the organization". Crémer (1993) defines culture as a stock of shared knowledge and argues that it improves the efficiency of information processing. Lazear (1995) also defines culture as 'shared beliefs, values and technology' and considers a 'genetic' evolutionary model of corporate culture, built on the assumption that culture is contagious, but that management can influence the reproduction rates of the different 'genes.'

In summary, corporate culture in management literature can be described as the blend of the shared values, norms, beliefs, attitudes, standards, symbols, rituals and myths that characterize a company, define how a company functions in its environment and how its employees behave. It is vital and indispensable organizational component that shape corporate's mission, vision, goals, strategies, processes, and structure and affect organizational outcomes such as performance, employee commitment, turnover, and many more.

Mergers and Acquisitions (M&As)

Mergers and acquisitions have been around since 1880s and completed six waves already; each had its own characteristics, shared certain aspects, yet varied in terms of their nature, intensity, and duration and today became a global phenomenon. In return, research in mergers and acquisitions has been ongoing with a high speed thank to substantial interest in academia and practice to the topic and interdisciplinary nature of the concept- a phenomenon not only studied across disciplines such as economics, management, and psychology, but also calls for input from numerous disciplines (Cretin et al., 2015). Today, mergers and acquisitions have become increasingly popular leading growth strategies implemented by thousands of companies in fast changing business landscape. The corporate sector all over the world is restructuring its operations through mergers and acquisitions in order to face challenges posed by the new pattern of globalization (Warter & Warter, 2014), and drivers such as flourishing capital markets, the competitiveness of the environment, industrial innovation, economic expansion, regulatory changes, and the emergence of new technologies.

Planning, executing and integrating a merger and acquisition is a complex process. It requires a significant amount of time, technical expertise and knowledge, leadership experience and assistance from outside resources. It often takes anywhere from six months to several years to complete depending on the size, type and industry. It involves dozens of participants such as consultants, financial advisers, lawyers, government agencies, antitrust specialists, proxy solicitors, escrow agents, banks, insurers and even lobbyists. More importantly, the key players are customers, employees, and competitors who have power to influence the flow of a merger and acquisition.

There are numerous reasons why one company chooses to merge with or acquire another. The literature suggests that the main motives behind making such a deal is to create synergies, gain competitive advantage, diversify, enlarge portfolios and generate new sales, profits and market share. Yet their success is by no means assured. To the contrary, a majority fall short of their expressed attainable goals and growth objectives. Based on a recent analysis of 2,500 high-profile cases by L.E.K. Consulting 60% of the merger and acquisition deals destroy shareholder value (Lewis & McKone, 2016). A global A.T.Kearney study suggests that 58 percent of all mergers, acquisitions, and other forms of corporate restructuring fail to produce results rather than create value (Habeck et al., 2000). In most cases, a failed acquisition can be attributed to several root causes – paying the wrong price, buying for the wrong reason, selecting the wrong partner or buying at the wrong time (Marks, 1997).

Even though there are numerous articles, books and consultant reports published in merger and acquisition management, and most mergers and acquisitions are carefully designed and directed by highly experience executives, mergers and acquisitions still face major challenges to be successful. While some failures can be explained by financial, political and market factors, a substantial number of failures can be explained by neglecting the 'soft factors'- mainly human resource issues, leadership style differences and culture integration- in merger and acquisition process. In other words, while strategic, cost, revenue and legal issues drive most deals, however it is cultural issues that determine the outcome meaning that deal is successful or not. Today, it is clear that how companies handle culture issues in merger and acquisition process is probably the single most decisive factor that can make or break a deal. It is of no surprise that the most often quoted reason for the failure of a merger and acquisition is culture differences (e.g. Papadakis, 2007, Zollo & Meier, 2008). Unsuccessful cultural integration is not just a leading cause of deal failure; it is also an indirect driver for a significant number of other causes, such as delayed integration, retention of key employees, productivity or talent attraction, difficulty in teamwork and coordination (Otterspeer, 2016), and it add costs to the integration process, undermine the ability of firms to achieve synergy and thereby offset the expected financial benefits of the merger or acquisition (Weber, 1996). Therefore, it is essential, if not critical to underestimate the importance of integrating corporate cultures of both sides in a merger and acquisition deal.

Corporate Culture and Mergers and Acquisitions

The impact of corporate culture in merger and acquisition process is twofold. *(1) Corporate culture creates a foundation for change management strategies and has the ability to either support or destroy even the most critical change initiatives.* There is little academic literature on the role that corporate culture plays in the development and success of a firm's merger and acquisition strategy, but one well established research of Bargeron, Lehn, and Smith (2012) summarizes that corporate culture affects the type, if not the volume, of acquisitions made by firms.

Culture functions in a way of self-reinforcing. As a result, while culture can provide a strong foundation for business success in stable environments, it can become a significant impediment to success when executing major change. The self-reinforcing nature of culture will almost always generate resistance toward change, unless the disparity between the existing mindsets and behaviors, and the mindsets and behaviors required realizing the promised benefits of the change is fixed thru appropriate cultural modifications (Conner Partners, 2010).

Corporate culture is critical in employee reaction to change. In an empirical study on the effects of organizational culture on change management, it was discovered that "organizational beliefs, employee attitude and value system, as part of organization culture, has an impact on change management" (Onyango, 2014). He therefore recommended that organizations should ensure that they openly support employee attitudes and pattern of work that promotes change management. There might be specific elements of a culture that an employee likes or dislikes and these influence emotional responses to any type of change. The culture of the organization can also play an important role in both generating emotions during change and influencing their expression or suppression. The affective culture will help or hinder employees' adjustment on an individual level (Smollan & Sayers, 2009).

Types of cultures have also effects on change management. For instance, adaptability culture is flexible in approach to the change process in meeting the demands of the external environment (Muthoni, 2012). Mission culture on the other hand, stresses that the presence of visionary leaders in an organization plays a pivotal role in the change process as they provide direction and stamina to the change process (Hughes, 2005). Additionally, Groysberg and his colleagues recent review of the literature (2018) revealed two primary dimensions for corporate culture in their integrated culture framework: people interactions and response to change. They explained that some corporate cultures emphasize stability—prioritizing consistency, predictability, and maintenance of the status quo—others emphasize flexibility, adaptability, and receptiveness to change. Those that favor stability prefer to maintain status quo rather than accept new ways of doing things resulting in employee resistance to change.

Palthe and Kossek (2003) developed a typology of sub-cultures. Employees' responses to change are often colored by their perceptions of, and engagement in, the sub-culture as well as in the broader organizational culture (Morgan & Ogbonna, 2008). According to Armenakis, Harris and Mossholder (1993), "the cultural memberships may polarize the beliefs, attitudes and intentions of members" through group discourses and undermine readiness for change.

(2) Corporate culture has multi-faceted role in mergers and acquisitions. Corporate culture is a vital intangible asset of a merger and acquisition deal and blending different corporate cultures (cultural integration) is a key part of the overall integration process and a 'must' factor for success.

Countless commentators have targeted culture as an important contributor of merger and acquisition success (e.g. cultural synergy theory and acculturation theory) or failure (e.g., culture clashes theory). Cultural synergy theory is "an approach to managing the impact of cultural diversity, involves a process in which managers form organizational strategies, policies, structures, and practices based on, but not limited to, the cultural patterns of individual organization members and clients" (Adler, 1997, p. 107). Acculturation theory focuses on how different cultures can come together and adapt to each other with positive (or negative) results. By contrast, culture clashes theory states that different cultural background unavoidably causes problems in the integration process (Javidan & House, 2002). Cultural clashes are often blamed for disappointing merger and acquisition outcomes in literature. For instance, Hewitt (2011) shows that 33% of respondents blamed "cultural integration issues" as the reason their deal failed. According to Kroll (2008), 50% of respondents cited "organizational cultural differences" as the most significant post-deal issue they faced. Based on PwC Report of 'Making M&A successful Post-Merger Integration Survey 2017'complexity in execution due to factors like culture and communication issues is 53%. Approximately 65 percent of mergers falter – primarily due to lack of corporate blending, says Alan Smith, CEO of the M&A consulting firm Bay Pacific Group. Finally, KPMG report (2016) states that their survey respondents agree that corporate culture is still a key consideration and 54% say cultural and HR issues are the most consistently challenging integration issues. It is clearly identified and explained in literature that cultural differences matter in merger and acquisition deals and should be handled with special care and timely manner.

Numerous constructs are used to explain the impact of culture on mergers and acquisitions, such as *culture clash, culture gap, cultural fit, cultural conflict, cultural compatibility, cultural collision, cultural discomfort, cultural shock*, and so on due to interdisciplinary nature of the concept (Rotting et al., 2014, p. 136).

Cultural Differences

No corporate culture is the same. With this realty in mind, blending two different companies' habits, traditions, beliefs, values systems, norms, and philosophies under one roof, and stating a fresh unwritten ground rule by saying "from now on, this is the new way we do things around here" is a management challenge. Yet inability to bridge companies' culture differences can undermine even the most scrupulously planned mergers and acquisitions (Miller, 2015). Ability to manage culture is as more important to merger and acquisition success than financial or strategic factors (Cartwright & Cooper, 1996).

Cultural differences of two companies can be an asset (opportunity) or a liability (threat) for management during a merger and acquisition process. It is all about how the nature and extent of those differences is viewed and effectively managed. Cultural differences can be a source of value creation, innovation and learning (Morosini et al., 1998; Vermeulen & Barkema, 2001). Also, if merging cultures are similar or at least complementary, it is less problematic and; therefore, requires less effort to handle situation, simply because the culture similarity between organizations can increase the likelihood of successful merger and acquisition. The greater the sense of coherence between an organization's belief and values and its actions, the stronger the organizations compatibly will be (Cortina, 2015). On the other hand, the cultural difference in merger and acquisition can lead to confusion, hostility, misunderstandings and distrust between the employees of merging organizations, and creates obstacles to raping envisaged integration benefits (e.g. Vaara, 2003). Cultural differences also have been negatively related to the effectiveness of IT systems integration (Weber & Pliskin, 1996), the realization of strategy (Very et al., 1996), and post-merger stock price performance (Chatterjee et al., 1992), positively related to acquired top management turnover, and negatively related to acquired top management commitment (Lubatkin et al., 1999).

Cultural Clash

When corporate cultures are not compatible, organizations typically confront "culture clash". Mirvis and Marks (1992) explain this situation as- *the degree of cultural fit between two companies is a measure of the "shock" that employees will experience by entering a new organizational environment.* Culture clash is what happens when two organizations have different way of operating and beliefs about how to make decisions, supervise, organize, communicate, evaluate, what is really important and valuable, dress code, ways of expressing emotions, office space lay off, leadership styles, and so on. Culture clash can lead to debates, arguments and differing assumptions regarding the internal process of pursuing a business plan (Carleton, 1996).

There are many high-profile deals that allegedly failed due to corporate culture clashes. AOL Time Warner merger turned to be the 'biggest mistake in corporate history' from 'largest merger in American business history' due to cultural differences mismanagement. Insider reports claimed that the cultures were too different and the employees at the two companies seemed to resent one other. Richard Parsons, president of Time Warner says it all: *"I remember saying at a vital board meeting where we approved this, that life was going to be different going forward because they're very different cultures, but I have to tell you, I underestimated how different... It was beyond certainly my abilities to figure out how to blend the old media and the new media culture."* Some other examples include Daimler-Chrysler and Sprint-Nextel, (Bouwman, 2013), U.S.-based advertising giant Omnicom and its French counterpart Publicis (Davies et al., 2014), HP-Compaq, Dollar-Thrifty, Ford-Volvo, and Southern Pacific Rail-Union Pacific Corporation (Appelbaum et al., 2013).

Lack of cultural compatibility between organizations can be a reason for culture clash. Cultural compatibility might seem like a subjective and intangible concept to measure. However, there are scientific managerial tools such as cultural audit, culture survey, and various human resource management techniques to collect and analyze information. Managing culture clashes requires a careful assessment for cultural fit during due diligence in order to take the necessary adjustment on time for the sake of merger and acquisition success, as poor culture-fit has often been cited as one reason why merger and acquisition has not produced the outcomes organizations hoped for (Cartwright & Schoenberg, 2006).

Cultural Fit

The cultural fit is the process of investigating, assessing and defining the cultures of two organizations through a cultural assessment to discover areas of similarity and difference that will influence integration efforts and achievement of strategic objectives (Pellet, 2011). The cultural fit seeks similarities in style such management style preferences, rewarding systems leadership, direction, communication, and organization policies, degree and ways of planning, formalization, reward and sanction modes, time perspective and orientation growth (Bijlsma-Frankema, 2001). The tighter the fit between the organizations is, naturally the higher the chance of a merger and acquisition success (Lubatkin, 1983).

CULTURAL INTEGRATION IN MERGER AND ACQUISITION

The process of integration can be simply defined as "the process of combining two companies into one entity at every level" (Knilans, 2009, p. 39). The primary objective of the integration in a deal is to make more effective use of existing capabilities and resources. Merger and acquisition integration encompasses a wide spectrum of activities ranging from business policies and procedures to information technology, financial reporting (Harrison & Farrell, 2007), decision making and leadership style, ability to change, role definitions, structure, performance evaluation, rewarding systems and many more. Traditionally, when pursuing a deal, focus can be on operational, financial, legal, technical and human aspects; however, cultural integration should be a core focus.

A common general definition of cultural integration is *"cultural integration is a form of cultural exchange in which one group assumes the beliefs, practices and rituals of another group without sacrificing the characteristics of its own culture."* In merger and acquisition talks, consolidating corporate cultures receives relatively little attention, as combining cultures is often a low priority when executives, change agents, and other key actors are busy with the financial and strategic aspects of the deal. First, finding the best partner with a similar or compatible culture is almost never a merger and acquisition criteria when searching a target. Second, during structuring the deal in early stages, there are many factors considered such as antitrust laws, taxes, and forms of financing, but in many cases not corporate culture issues. Finally, after the deal is approved and parties are ready to move forward, the success of the deal still rest on the ability of integrating two cultures which was not considered and discussed previously. At this point, the message is clear: Before the integration process begins every player in the merger and acquisition strategy team should keep in minds that:

1. Corporate culture is considered inherently intangible, but a company's culture will be reflected in tangible, visible, or audible assets such as its dress code, rituals, organizational charts, symbols, business hours, corporate jargon, office setup, employee benefits, interactions, hiring decisions, and many others. In a nutshell, the outcomes of culture can be measurable, and comparable. Once Fukuyama (2017) said '*Workplace culture should have a seat at the table and should be measured, just like sales or ROI. An organization's culture is just as reliable a predictor of success as sales figures; it leads to and magnifies growth.*' With open communication, transparency and trust, data should be collected delicately, and with the proper assessment tools data should turn into quantifiable information.
2. Culture integration process itself is sensitive to time pressure and yet should not be pressured to be completed quickly and process should start as soon as a deal is on the table, not late in the process.
3. Employees once had a cultural fit with their existing organization in some cases may have difficulties in replacing or adjusting their core values, beliefs and collective behaviors with the new ones after the deal is completed, as there is no a one-size-fit. Consequently, this change may end up with resistance and also on the top of this; employee alignment to new company culture may influence worker satisfaction, engagement and retention negatively. This should also be marked and handled as a separate issue with proper human resource strategies.
4. Sometimes, one party in the deal may have more dominate or stronger culture compared to other, and employees in the weaker culture may have a winner/loser perception, thus this situation damages the morale of the employees and cause extreme disruptions. In some other acquisition cases especially, drastic ones such as hostile takeovers, acquired employees are forced to abandon their old distinctive shared principles, norms, values, beliefs, in other words their entire corporate culture and accept a new one take a new organization's identity which results in threatening employees' self-esteem and collective pride. In any case, merger and acquisitions should not be about 'us versus them' or 'I am the boss'. Psychological issues should not be left as a secondary concern, and management team should always have a care-plan, simply because all employees - does not matter from which side they are, are the most important (valuable) asset of any deal.
5. In a typical mergers and acquisitions negotiating involves more than forcing the other party to agree to their own terms; however, negotiation on culture components are not about getting the biggest piece, because corporate culture reveals a sense of employee identity, sense of belonging' therefore, it is all about bringing two sides to an agreement that will make everyone the owner of the new culture.
6. The integration of top management teams (TMTs) should receive extra attention in mergers and acquisitions. They are not only the crucial players in completing the deal process successfully and smoothly, but also proven that negative attitudes of key top managers toward a merger may be a major obstacle to the successful integration of the companies (e.g. Weber & Schweiger, 1992). Additionally, at the beginning of the integration, employees will look at leaders and follow their inspiring messages and guidance. The culture of the combined business can only develop and thrive if top management makes a strong commitment.

In this chapter, cultural integration will be evaluated under two sections; according to Marks and Mirvis (2001); p*re-merger/acquisition phase*: state that pre-merger phase is when the deal is conceived and negotiated by executives and then legally approved by shareholders and regulators and *post-merger/ acquisition* is when the combined entity and its people regroup from initial implementation and new organization settles in. In the literature, stages (phases) of a merger and acquisition process commonly vary between three and seven phases, depending on the method and precision of their division and classification. All of them include the pre-deal decision making phase and the post-deal integration phase, which should be considered together as integrative determinants of merger and acquisition success (Haspelagh & Jemison, 1991).

Cultural Integration in Pre-Merger and Acquisition Phase (Pre-M&A)

A more forceful recognition of cultural aspects in the pre-deal phase is a prerequisite for a successful, but also less painless post-merger integration phase. The main goal of cultural integration in pre-merger and acquisition stage is to make a cultural SWOT analysis- identifying both cultures' strengths and weaknesses, as well as any opportunities and threats that may exist due to cultural issues in a merger and acquisition situation. It will provide us a clear understanding of the risks and challenges the organization is certain to face in the long run in the deal. Cultural assessment of self and potential partner's corporate culture is highly time-consuming, painful, and expensive, and also requires devoted individuals with excellent soft and analytical skills, but extensive amount of research findings have already proven that it is worth to invest the resources in cultural assessment.

Investigating cultural aspects in the pre- merger and acquisition stage is critical for many reasons: 1) It is a 'prerequisite' for the next stages, as it allows a better understanding of the cultural issues related to negotiation, decision-making, due diligence and post-deal integration; 2) Management team can have a better and effective integration/alignment plan to deal with the impact of culture on the other management variables.

Unfortunately, many companies conducting systematic financial analyses in the pre- merger and acquisition stage neglect to examine cultural issues. This shows the lack of importance companies attach to the cultural integration process prior to a merger or acquisition (Warter & Warter, 2017). To emphasize the importance of cultural due diligence, Carleton and Lineberry (2004) and Rosenbloom (2002) consider cultural due diligence should be viewed as a mandatory step to maximize post-merger or acquisition organizational effectiveness and profitability. According to them, cultural due diligence can determine the extent to which change can or cannot occur smoothly within a firm.

Cultural Due Diligence (CDD)

Cultural due diligence is a systemic and research-based methodology to ascertain the degree of cultural alignment or compatibility between companies for significantly increasing the odds of success of mergers, acquisitions, and alliances (Carleton & Lineberry, 2004, p. 54). It intends to offer data enough detailed to determine potential areas of culture clash (Warter & Warter, 2017), and a developed cultural profile including sub-cultures (Gugin, 2013). According to Marks (1999) the main reason for cultural due diligence is to raise awareness of and sensitivity to the cultural issues in a merger.

Reed-Lajoux and Elson (2010) and Gleich and his colleagues (2010) explain that cultural due diligence can be processed in four general steps: integrating cultural criteria into the pre-merger discussions, staffing and preparing the due diligence team with an eye toward cultural issues, adding cultural criteria due diligence data collection, and using formal tools to assess culture fit. Additionally, Carleton and Lineberry (2004) and Schneck (2007) provide a cultural due diligence process model that draws on qualitative and quantitative data by mainly doing an assessment of acquirer and target company cultures, followed by identification of cultural risk/conflict areas, assessment of the difficulty of cultural integration and estimation of the resources required to integrate the two companies.

There are a number of corporate culture diagnostic tools available specifically for merger and acquisition environment; however, measuring culture is a challenging and complicated task due to;

1. Lack of concrete metrics-having an infinite variety of cultural items to measure because of its subjective and perceptual nature of the concept (Weber & Menipaz, 2003),
2. Difficulties in collecting accurate data- e.g. unclearness nature of many elements of culture, as they are taken for granted by employees (Schein, 1985),
3. Bias issues- such as "public" and "private" face of individuals (Goffman 1959),
4. Subjectivity and objectivity of opinions- asking questions about culture is personally and politically sensitive matter, which also brings confidentiality issues to the surface.

Anxiety theory is most relevant at this stage. Information leaks frequently occur, giving rise to various rumors regarding merger possibilities and speculations on various merger scenarios. These rumors can create feelings of uncertainty, threat, and loss of control (Ivancevich et al., 1987). Employees can exhibit a range of negative emotions, including hurt, anger, rejection, and disappointment (Seo & Hill, 2005) making it difficult to collect accurate information. Therefore, it is highly suggested to use multimethod approach to increase the validity and reliability of the findings, and overcome the inherent limitations.

Qualitative and quantitative methodology to understand culture include in-depth interviews, focus groups, customizable employee surveys, workplace observations, annual reports, external ratings, intranet resources, internal newsletters, listening stories, and documentation review (e.g. policy manuals), and company website.

There are more than 70 instruments that are developed by academicians and consultant firms to measure corporate culture. Among all, certain instruments are specific for measuring cultural compatibility. *Organizational Culture Assessment Instrument (OCAI)* developed by Quinn and Cameron based on the Competing Values Framework assesses current and preferred organizational culture and can also be used to guide organizational culture change. The instrument will give the parties in an merger and acquisition scenario a clear picture of the current and desired cultures. *Organizational Culture Inventory (OCI)* developed by Human Synergistics International, provides companies with a visual profile of their current operating cultures based on the behaviors that members believe are needed to "fit in and meet expectations." This tool works especially well if there is already some understanding of the framework from within a leadership development and change context. *Cultural Transformation Tools (CTT)* created by the Barrett Values Centre explains where each organization is at in terms of culture. It maps out all the areas they have in common as well as the areas where they diverge, and addresses the desired merged culture for optimum success (Morrison, 2015).

The cultural dimensions most relevant to an audit might differ for each company; however, eleven different dimensions are discussed by Galphin and Herndon (2000). They are; *strategic direction, key measures and definitions of results, planning and control systems, employee engagement, use and philosophy of information technology, physical environment, historical issues and expectations, organization wide information transfer, information transfer between and among individuals, leaders' and managers' behavior and human capital.* According to Bouchard and Pellet (2002) and Carleton and Lineberry (2004) key cultural domains that include; *leadership and management practices, styles, and relationships, governing principles, formal procedures, informal practices, employee satisfaction, cus-*

tomer satisfaction, key business drivers, organizational characteristics, perceptions and expectations, and how the work gets done in your organization.

Measurements can be industry specific. For example, Scott, and his colleagues (2003) did an extensive research about the quantitative measurement of organizational culture specifically in health care setting. They explained that a range of instruments with differing characteristics are available to researchers interested in organizational culture, all of which have limitations in terms of their scope, ease of use, or scientific properties. They stated that the choice of instrument should be determined by how organizational culture is conceptualized by the research team, the purpose of the investigation, intended use of the results, and availability of resources.

The findings of cultural assessment can be accumulated in a plan with many vital recommendations that can be used in the merger and acquisition road map in the long run, for instance, in decision making such as supporting or reevaluating the decision about which cultural model to implement in the deal. It can serve as a risk analysis; such as signaling the hidden problems related to culture, evaluating the irreconcilable cultural differences and barriers and estimation of resource required in the integration, thus, understanding of other company's culture the sooner they will solve the upcoming problems. Finally, mergers and acquisitions are all about negotiation from beginning to end. Some authors (e.g. Lee et al., 2013) highlighted that the negotiation research has placed great focus on pre-negotiation preparation regarding the other party. During culture assessment, even simple not complex, information gathered about the other party's cultural traits (e.g., personal styles, risk taking, agreement building, and emotionalism, etc.) may provide useful hints and insights about their negotiation styles, preferences and priorities., thus they can be better prepared for the negotiation phase of the deal. As Warter and Warter (2015) said, 'Understanding the nuances of cultural differences will allow a finer understanding of the puzzle of negotiation stage.'

Defining the New Culture

The most important step in the pre-merger phase is the choice of organizational culture (Habeck et al., 2000). The options are: a) to use only one of the partners culture, b) blend the two cultures, and c) create completely a new culture. The choice will depend on the type of the deal, the motive of the deal, the size of the companies, the industries the companies are in, and so forth. Building a shared view of the cultural characteristics to be retained from extensive pre-merger planning to be a well-organized post-merger implementation is the key for success in any given merger and acquisition transaction.

A cultural integration strategy should align with leaders' future-state vision and support the deal's value proposition and targeted business objectives (Deloitte, 2017). Isely (2016) summarized the key facts executives should ask themselves, before developing a culture strategy to support an upcoming merger or acquisition: a) *Deal structure* (e.g., what is being purchased/sold? Share or asset deal?), b) *Business design* (e.g. how will top executives be appointed? Potential impact on workforce?), c) *implementation strategy* (e.g. will businesses be run separately or be integrated?), d) *Culture* (e.g. how far are we from our own aspirational culture? What features about our own culture would we not want to lose? What might a partner bring to our culture that we need more of? What cultural attributes of a potential partner could stop this deal from going ahead?)

Cultural Integration in Post-Merger and Acquisition Phase (Post-M&A)

Pablo (1994) defined post- merger and acquisition integration as the implementation of changes in functional activities, organizational structures and cultures of the two organizations to expedite their consolidation into a functional whole.

Main reasons cultural integration failure in this phase are lack of support from leadership, high level of employee resistance, lack of consensus on desire culture and inconsistent communication. Therefore, integration team should have a game plan.

1. Focus on employee psychology.
    a. *Anxiety and stress are everywhere.* The integration phase can take long time, depending on the amount of changes being made structurally, which continues to drag down employee morale and stability. In other words, living in fear of what is to come is a cause for stress (Ivancevich et al., 1987). During this phase, budgets, space, work assignments, and reporting responsibilities are realigned. Employees are pushed to learn new ways of doing things, meet new performance standards, and adopt new value and belief systems (Marks & Mirvis, 1992). It is expected to face some level of tension, conflict and anxiety in the meantime. Additionally, employees will face *merger syndrome*- consists of feelings of uncertainty and insecurity as a result of the merger or acquisition (Marks & Mirvis, 1985). Anger, frustration, or worry can reduce merger support (Giessner et al., 2006). The integration management team needs to focus on the reasons for anxiety and concerns carefully. Depending on the findings, face to face meetings, mentoring, coaching, training, relationship-building activities, career development sessions, etc. should be offered to employees. Employees, especially in times of stress and challenge, look to management for solutions; therefore, integration management team should demonstrate genuine concern, be honest and transparent, strengthen the trust and open the lines of communication to provide a clear picture of the process. Last, managers should remind themselves that in some cases they themselves could trigger the fear as depending how they present the cultural integration to employees.
    b. *Appreciate the effort.* Cultural integration is a long-term process, also very difficult one. Due to mixed feelings, employees may wonder whether-and how-they will fit into the new corporate culture. To sustain a change effort over the long term, senior leadership must generate short-term wins. At this point, reinforcement of the desired employee behaviors is suggested.
    c. *Be sensitive, but stick to the timetable.* New norms and behaviors are implicit in nature; they develop very slowly and organically. Employees will only accept new values and norms if they feel right (PwC, 2017); therefore, the managers need to be patient and allow employees to take their time to adjust. However, this may end up with delays, and process fall short on completing the integration in a timely manner. As a result, integration team may fell short of finishing post-merger integration on schedule. Once again, proper and sufficient support to employees (e.g., nurturing, communication, making them a part of the process, etc.) needs to be emphasized at this point.
    d. *Be prepared to experience resistance to change.* One of the consequences of having high level of anxiety, stress, fear, uncertainty and insecurity is employee resistance to the combined entity. Moving to unknown area with new managers and new co-workers is stressful and anxiety provoking (Nguyen & Kleiner, 2003). Employee resistance to change will be dependent on

how much of a threat they feel the merger and acquisition poses to their security, which will be directly intertwined with what these employees expect from the newly formed organization (Love, 2000). Reasons for resistance are often based on employee tendencies of attachment towards company values (Ivancevich et al., 1987). Research has shown that the negative and pessimistic reaction of employees towards merger and acquisitions are mostly related to corporate cultures clashing (Spoljarik & Másdottir, 2016). Managers should remember that resistance to change is not a negative phenomenon; but it is normal part of the change process. Change requires leaving the old culture behind, and people need to have the right to mourn before they can adapt new culture and accept changes (Lämsä & Hautala, 2005, p. 189-190).

e. *Remember talent management is a major concern in cultural integration.* During merger and acquisitions, the leaders of both the companies face talent drainage. Unfortunately, this is inevitably. In order to preserve the exceptional employees and maintain their optimum level of task performance, a company must conduct effective one-on-one discussions to capture the hearts and minds of them, make them a part of decision making process, engage to the transaction and implement a way of rewarding such labor.

2. Communication, communication, and followed up by more communication. Communication is a critical tool in helping employees to understand the reasoning behind the merger and acquisition, overcoming resistance, generating commitment, motivating employees, and lowering rumors, wrong interpretations, misunderstandings and information leakage. Tips on communication
   a. Communication in this phase needs to be done *timely* (giving information on time), *continuously* (giving information on a frequent base- at certain time intervals), *strategically* (ensuring the right information gets to employees in ways that make sense to them and also addressing the probable concerns), *candidly* (giving as accurate information as possible), *openly* (encouraging questions and comments) *pertinaciously* (repeating messages over and over again until it is certain they are understood) and *consistently* (using consistent messages that are supportive and compatible to each other).
   b. Measure the impact of the communications and make adjustments as needed to keep the pressure on positive change.
   c. Communication should be two-way: It is not only the team talking, but also integration management team should listen to employees deeply and empathetically, hear them and seek regular feedback from them. Additionally, employees should feel comfortable asking questions and sharing their own feelings and thoughts with integration management team members. Actively listening to employee's ideas and proposals of how best to merge the two companies is important, as it gives some of the power back to the employers (Spoljarik & Másdottir, 2016).
   d. Change agents should be aware of the communication barriers and perception biases.
   e. Audience segmentation is hugely useful. Different departments, different ranks, etc. requires different type of information.
   f. Dysfunctional communication is vicious. For example, giving insufficient or false information can lead to harmful rumors spreading which affects employees' faith in management in a negative way. This can result in employee resistance and can further create social conflicts between employees and management.
   g. Change agents should use different channels;

i. Written communications are useful and necessary, but in emotionally charged situations face to face should be preferred, especially with employees with high stress and anxiety levels.
ii. Symbols and other tangible component of culture can be used to make the new culture feasible, noticeable and realizable in the organization. This can glue the employees of both organizations together by creating synergy and ownership.
iii. Launching an employee website that highlighted the rich history from both companies, featuring a story each month from somewhere in the companies that demonstrated the desired culture already in action can be useful. The culture-in-action stories served to inspire and connect employees (Allan, 2012).

3. *Choose the appropriate leadership.* Transformation leadership is one of the best styles in leading the cultural integration in this phase, because it is consisted of idealized influence, individualized consideration, inspirational motivation, and intellectual stimulation (Kim & Kim, 2014). Nguyen and Kleiner (2003) elaborated the role of transformational leaders for successful integration, which include providing clarity around roles and decision lines, setting directions for the new business, focusing on communication and understanding the emotional, political, and rational issues.

Leaders, in most cases, high level of senior managers or CEOs should be visible and be a role model. Employees interpret the supervisor's actions and use them as their guidelines (Buono & Bowditch, 2003, p. 20). This creates excitement among employees and increases employee trust and confidence for the deal process.

One of the important responsibilities of a leader is the *legitimization* of a merger and acquisition. This is explaining why things need to change and why the change will bring success in the future for the new entity. It should be clear and understood by everyone in both organizations.

4. *Have a perfect blend in integration management team.* The lack of an integration team would slow down the integration process (Laeser, 2014); therefore, it should be carefully designed by top level management and given the resources and authority to take full responsibility of culture integration. It should be consisting of integration managers, middle managers and human resource managers from both parties who have the necessary change management skills and adequate experience. Their priority is to decide on an effective approach for cultural integration, and developing an action plan, to increase employee confidence in the deal in process and create a common vision, and clear set of goals. Responsible managers should possess the key qualities required to facilitate integration, including creativity, transparency, and the ability to meet stakeholders' expectations (Carter & Greer, 2013).

Integration managers influence both value creation and value leakage in merger and acquisition through their actions (Teerikangas et al., 2011). According to Herndon (2017), an integration manager is responsible for coordinating, planning, problem solving, accelerating the process, highlighting the best practices and implementing all requirements to achieve integration. Similarly, HR managers play a critical role by acting as advisors and mentors who help line managers with the integration process (Antila & Kakkonen, 2008). Middle managers are active agents who interpret, mediate, and broker information (Shi et al., 2009) and involve in strategy-making through processes of agenda seeking, proposal selection, information filtering, and implementation (Rouleau & Balogun, 2011). During M&A

deals, employees rely heavily on middle managers for day-to-day direction, details on changes to their department or role, the interpretation of company directives and easing employees through the process (Allan & Clanni, 2012).

5. *Consider the 'clean room (CR)' as a useful option.* Clean teams consist of designated employees from both companies, third-party resources such as lawyers and consultants or mix of both operate under strict protocols to protect confidentiality of their own organizations and prevent information leakage. A clean room can be a highly effective way of gathering information, unlocking synergies, analyzing scenarios, eliminating the uncertainties, minimizing the risks and ensuring that the deal creates value.
6. *Be gentle with cultural flashpoints.* Touching cultural flashpoints is a big risk, however if it is needed to change them, integration team should be clear with reasoning and sensitive to employees' reaction. As Herndon (2017) explained, '"cultural flashpoints are emotionally and historically significant traditions such as pizza lunches, and casual Friday. When you've stepped on them, they blow up."
7. *Pay tremendous attention to shared identity.* Viewed from a social identity perspective, a merger may be defined as 'a formal re-categorization of two social groups as one new group'. Given that this new group incorporates one's former pre-merger group the process can be seen as a continuation of this group. However, the merged group is new. It now also incorporates the merger partner, and thus implies a change in group membership (Van Knippenberg et al. 2002). This interplay between 'new' and 'old' can result in the creation of a shared identity whereby the beliefs, assumptions and values of two previously independent work forces form a jointly determined culture (Larsson & Lubatkin, 2001). However, identity issues become salient as the formal organizational entities cease to exist. In Schweiger et al.'s (1987) study of acquisitions, employees described their feelings of loss of identity and purpose. The pride they had felt in working for their company disappeared, leading to negatives feelings such as strong frustration and confusion as their image of themselves as being successful was shattered. Additionally, when intensive interactions between members of the two organizations increase through work relations, employees may rapidly develop various intergroup biases and experience intergroup conflicts (e.g., Marks & Mirvis, 1992). Those who were more committed to the previous organization may develop strong antagonism and biases toward the other organizational members, who are often perceived as "invading enemies" (Buono & Bowditch, 1989). These inter-organizational conflicts are likely to escalate as people also clash in cultural differences (e.g., Galpin & Herndon, 2000). These points also emphasize one more time why cultural due diligence is vital in pre-merger and acquisition stage. These issues can be deducted with careful analyses.

A shared identity is the ultimate goal of successful *acculturation* -the process of combining cultural systems. Nahavandi and Malekzadeh (1988, p. 81) developed the basis of the approach and defined it as "changes induced in (two cultural) systems as a result of the diffusion of cultural elements in both directions", then Berry (1997) developed the forms as,

- *Integration* occurs when both firms preserve their cultural identities and remain independent and autonomous, except for combining the structural aspect. At the same time, they are willing to be integrated into the other's culture. The flow of cultural elements is balanced because neither tries to dominate the other.

- *Assimilation* is a unilateral process in which one group willingly adopts the identity and culture of the other. This occurs when the members of one organization willingly relinquish their culture and adopt the culture and practices of the other. This often occurs when the members of one organization perceive that their culture and practices are dysfunctional and hindering the organization's performance. Under such a situation, the culture of one organization dominates the other.
- *Separation* involves attempting to preserve one's culture and practices by remaining separate and independent from another group. It is characterized by minimal interaction and contact between both firms.
- *Deculturation* occurs when the members of organizations involved in mergers do not value their own cultures and organizational practices and systems, but do not want to be assimilated into the other's. It results the loss of cultural identity, the refusal to adopt a new one and management as the acquired firm distances and alienates itself due to feelings of confusion, stress and conflict.

As Rajan explained (2010), many factors can influence the corporation choices of acculturation modes. Larsson and Lubatkin (2001) attribute the decision regarding to acculturation modes to four factors; 1) the degree of autonomy or freedom that the acquired firm will be given to make strategic decisions in the company, 2) merger relatedness refers to the similarity in strategy, products, markets and technologies between the two organizations, 3) the relative size of the firm measured by annual sales, employee count or assets of the acquired company. 4) social controls-consists of efforts to improve synergy and socialization in the firm such as transition teams, management involvement and task forces. Nahavandi and Malekzadeh (1988) pointed out in their study that in the mergers, the characteristics of the acquired and the acquiring companies determine which mode of acculturation will be triggered. From the acquired company's point of view, the degree to which members want to preserve their own culture/organizational practices and the degree to which they are willing to adopt the acquirer's culture/ practices will be the key for the choice. On the other hand, in the case of the acquirer, the degree to which the firm values cultural diversity and the degree of relatedness between the two companies will be the determine the mode preference.

8. *Always evaluate the process.* Successful dealmakers are better at tracking the success of cultural integration. It is essential and critical to measure and track process routinely, as it gives an opportunity to overview of the progress throughout the integration process. Sustainability of progress in the cultural integration process requires ongoing action plan execution built upon a clear set of meaningful goals and performance metrics. We should remember, "What gets measured gets done". In addition, keeping these results visible, employees can experience the effectiveness of their collective effort and build confidence in the future culture.

CONCLUSION

Mergers and acquisitions have become one of the leading approaches for organizations to grow globally with other strategic and competitive advantages. However, most often mergers and acquisitions fail to deliver the desired outcome or create value. While strategic issues drive most deals, cultural issues primarily determine the ultimate success or failure in terms of creating anticipated results. The reason is clear. Wrapped in all the excitement of target selection, followed by the anxiety to complete the integration process in order to get the financial benefits of the transaction as quickly as possible, executives in many cases postpone the culture integration for later. However, change management teams should always remember that culture integration is as crucial and vital to deal success as crunching the numbers. It is the key determiner in the management of the human side of the transition process and mitigating many of the risk to reach the goal.

This chapter provides a practical, action-orientated, comprehensive approach which enables change leaders to successfully navigate change challenges. First recommendation is that executives give serious consideration to the cultural integration from the earliest stage of a deal- investing accurate time for cultural assessment through interviews and surveys, observations, and many other reliable tools (The right tools make this process both feasible and effective) and use every available scientific and practical methods to identify what could break the deal. This will give the executives the ability to make culture-related strategic decisions in a healthier way.

Second recommendation is to emphasize the key role of effective strategic communication throughout the M&A process-from due diligence to integration. An internal communication strategy constructed comprehensively can effectively support the cultural integration and confidently convey the value of the deal in terms of employee commitment and business growth.

Final recommendation concerns one of the key aspects of leadership capability; engaging with employees. A further aim for the senior management team is to build the employee identification with the consolidated organization and lay out a strong, positive vision for the future. Executives should focus on creating a shared identity that will bring culture to the forefront of the integration process and can help to prevent fragmentation.

REFERENCES

Adler, N. (1997). International Dimensions of Organizational Behavior (3rd ed.). Cincinnati, OH: South-Western College Publishing.

Allan, S., & Clanni, M. (2012). *Middle managers: Their critical and growing role in M&A transactions, About Towers Watson.* Retrieved January 20, 2018 from https://www.towerswatson.com/

Antila, E. M., & Kakkonen, A. (2008). Factors affecting the role of HR managers in international mergers and acquisitions: A multiple case study. *Personnel Review, 37*(3), 280–299. doi:10.1108/00483480810862279

Appelbaum, S. H., Lefrancois, F., Tonna, R., & Shapiro, B. T. (2007). Mergers 101 (part one): Training managers for communications and leadership challenges. *Industrial and Commercial Training, 39*(3), 128–136. doi:10.1108/00197850710742225

Appelbaum, S. H., Roberts, J., & Shapiro, B. T. (2013). Cultural strategies in M&As: Investigating ten case studies. *Journal of Executive Education, 8*(1), 3. Retrieved from https://digitalcommons.kennesaw.edu/jee/vol8/iss1/3

Armenakis, A. A., Harris, S. G., & Mossholder, K. W. (1993). Creating readiness for organizational change. *Human Relations, 46*(6), 681–703. doi:10.1177/001872679304600601

Bargeron, L., Smith, J., & Lehn, K. (2012). *Corporate culture and M&A activity*. Working paper.

Berry, J. W. (1997). Immigration, acculturation, and adaptation. *Applied Psychology*, *46*, 5–30.

Bijlsma-Frankema, K. (2001). On managing cultural integration and cultural change processes in mergers and acquisitions. *Journal of European Industrial Training, 25*(2/3/4), 192-207.

Bouchard, P. J., & Pellet, L. (2002). *Getting You Shift Together. Making Sense of Organization Culture Change*. CCI Press.

Bouwman, C. S. (2013). The Role of Corporate Culture in Mergers & Acquisitions. In E. Perrault (Ed.), *Mergers and Acquisitions: Practices, Performance and Perspectives*. Hauppauge: NOVA Science Publishers.

Buono, A. F., & Bowditch, J. L. (1989). *The Human Side of Mergers and Acquisitions*. San Francisco: Jossey-Bass.

Buono, A. F., & Bowditch, J. L. (2003). *The Human Side of Mergers and Acquisitions; Managing Collisions Between People, Cultures, and Organizations* (1st ed.). Reprinted by Beard Books, Washington D.C. U.S.A.

Carleton, J. R. (1996). *Cultural Due Diligence*. Vector Group, Inc.

Carleton, J. R., & Lineberry, C. S. (2004). *Achieving Post-Merger Success – A Stakeholder's Guide to Cultural Due Diligence, Assessment, and Integration*. San Francisco: Pfeiffer, an Imprint of John Wiley & Sons.

Carter, S., & Greer, C. (2013). Strategic leadership: Values, styles, and organizational performance. *Journal of Leadership & Organizational Studies, 20*(4), 375–393. doi:10.1177/1548051812471724

Cartwright, S., & Cooper, C. L. (1996). *Managing Mergers, Acquisitions & Strategic Alliances*. Oxford, UK: Butterworth Heinemann, Inc.

Cartwright, S., & Schoenberg, R. (2006). Thirty years of mergers and acquisitions research: Recent advances and future opportunities. *British Journal of Management, 17*(S1), 1–5. doi:10.1111/j.1467-8551.2006.00475.x

Chatterjee, S., Lubatkin, M., Schweiger, D., & Weber, Y. (1992). Cultural differences and shareholder value in related mergers: Linking equity and human capital. *Strategic Management Journal, 13*(5), 319–334. doi:10.1002mj.4250130502

Christofferson, S. A., McNish, R. S., & Sias, D. L. (2004). Where mergers go wrong? *McKinsey Quarterly*. Retrieved May 24, 2018 from https://www.mckinsey.com/business-functions/strategy-and-corporate-finance/our-insights/where-mergers-go-wrong

Conner Partners. (2010). *Corporate culture and its impact on strategic change*. White Papers. Retrieved February 22, 2018 from http://www.connerpartners.com/thought-leadership/white-papers

Cortina, C. (2015). *The role of organizational culture in mergers and acquisitions*. Retrieved January 20, 2018 from https://www.linkedin.com/pulse/role-organizational-culture-mergers-acquisitions-cecilia-cortina/

Crémer, J. (1993). Corporate culture and shared knowledge. *Industrial and Corporate Change*, *3*(3), 351–386. doi:10.1093/icc/2.3.351

Cretin, F., Dieudonné, S., & Bouacha, S. (2015). M&A activity: Where are we in the cycle? *Alternative Investment Analyst Review,* 38-44.

Davies, A., Kim, S., & Abboud, L. (2014). Battle for control destroyed $35-billion Omnicom-Publicis merger. *Reuters*. Retrieved February 3, 2018 from https://www.reuters.com/article/us-omnicom-group-publicis-groupe/battle-for-control-destroyed-35-billion-omnicom-publicis-merger-idUSBREA4713R20140509

Deloitte. (2017). *Safeguarding M&A deal value: Managing culture clash*. Retrieved March 3, 2018 from https://www2.deloitte.com/content/dam/Deloitte/us/Documents/mergers-acqisitions/us-ma-safeguarding-m-and-a-deal-value-managing-culture-clash.pdf

Fukuyama, T. (2017). *Workplace culture should be measured, just like sales or ROI. Uber's issues should have leadership everywhere asking, "How healthy is our culture?"* Retrieved February 3, 2018 from https://www.recode.net/2017/4/18/15327848/workplace-culturemeasurement-metrics-healthy-uber

Galphin, T. J., & Herndon, M. (2000). *The Complete Guide to Mergers and Acquisitions-Process Tools to Support M&A Integration at Every Level*. San Francisco: Jossey-Bass Publishers Inc.

Giessner, S. R., Viki, G. T., Otten, S., Terry, D. J., & Täuber, S. (2006). The challenge of merging: Merger patterns, premerger status, and merger support. *Personality and Social Psychology Bulletin*, *32*(3), 339–352. doi:10.1177/0146167205282151 PMID:16455861

Gleich, R., Kierans, G., & Hasselbach, T. (2010). Value in Due Diligence: Contemporary Strategies for Merger and Acquisition Success. Farnham, UK: Gower.

Goffman, E. (1959). *The Presentation of Self in Everyday Life*. Garden City, NY: Doubleday.

Gomes, E., Weber, Y., Brown, C., & Tarba, S. Y. (2011). *Mergers, Acquisitions, and Strategic Alliances: Understanding the Process*. Melbourne: Macmillan International Higher Education.

Groysberg, B., Lee, J., Price, J., & Cheng, J. Y. (2018, January). *The leader's guide to corporate culture. Harvard Business Review*.

Gugin. (2013). *Cultural due diligence: Identifying your cultural DNA*. Retrieved February 8, 2018 from www.gugin.com

Habeck, M. M., Kroger, F., & Tram, M. R. (2000). *After the Merger: Seven Strategies for Successful Post-Merger Integration*. Harlow: Pearson Education.

Harrison, S., & Farrell, P. (2007). Communication flow in mergers and acquisitions. *The Third Scottish Conference for Postgraduate*, 191-201.

Haspeslagh, P. C., & Jemison, D. B. (1991). *Managing Acquisitions: Creating Value through Corporate Renewal*. New York: The Free Press.

Herndon, M. (2017). *Caution ahead - Cultural flashpoints*. Retrieved February, 25, 2018 from https://www.mapartners.net/insights/caution-ahead-cultural-flashpoints

Hewitt, A. (2011). *Culture integration in M&A- survey findings*. Retrieved April 9, 2018 from www.aon.com/attachments/thoughtleadership/M_A_Survey

Hughes, K. (2005). *IT Fundamentals*. Croydon: Tertiary Press.

Isey, K. (2016). *Culture strategy in M&A: Context is everything*. Retrieved March 22, 2018 from https://www.linkedin.com/pulse/culture-strategy-ma-where-context-everything-karen-isely

Ivancevich, J., Schweiger, D., & Power, F. (1987). Executive action for managing human resources before and after acquisition. *The Academy of Management Executive*, *1*(2), 127–138.

Javidan, M., & House, R. J. (2002). Leadership and cultures around the world: Findings from GLOBE: An introduction to the special issue. *Journal of World Business*, *37*(1), 1–2. doi:10.1016/S1090-9516(01)00068-2

Kim, S., & Kim, J. (2014). Integration strategy, transformational leadership and organizational commitment in Korea's corporate split-offs. *Procedia: Social and Behavioral Sciences*, *109*, 1353–1364. doi:10.1016/j.sbspro.2013.12.637

Knilans, G. (2009). Mergers and acquisitions: Best practices for successful integration. *Employment Relations Today*, *35*(4), 39–46. doi:10.1002/ert.20224

KPMG. (2016). *U.S. executives on M&A: Full speed ahead in 2016*. Retrieved April 27, 2018 from https://assets.kpmg.com/content/dam/kpmg/pdf/.../us-jnet-2016-issue2-article1-EN.pdf

Kroll, M. M. (2008). *M&A beyond borders: Opportunities and risks*. Retrieved April 5, 2018 from https://www.insurancejournal.com/news/international/2008/04/15/89131.htm

Laeser, A. (2014). *Managing Culture Clashes in M&A's*. Hamburg: Anchor Academic Publishing.

Lämsä, A-M., & Hautala, T. (2005). Organisaatiokäyttäymisen perusteet. *Edita*, 189-190.

Larsson, R., & Lubatkin, M. (2001). Achieving acculturation in mergers and acquisitions: An international case study. *Human Relations*, *54*(12), 1573–1607. doi:10.1177/00187267015412002

Lazear, E. P. (1995). Corporate Culture and Diffusion of Values in Trends. In Business Organization: Do Participation and Cooperation Increase Competitiveness. Tubingen.

Lee, S., Adair, W. L., & Seo, S. J. (2013). Cultural perspective taking in cross-cultural negotiation. *Group Decision and Negotiation*, *22*(3), 389–405. doi:10.100710726-011-9272-4

Lewis, A., & McKone, D. (2016). *So many M&A deals fail because companies overlook this simple strategy*. Retrieved May 25, 2018 from https://hbr.org/2016/05/so-many-ma-deals-fail-because-companies-overlook-this-simple-strategy

Love, C. K. (2000). Mergers and Acquisition: The role of HRM Success. *IRC Press-Current Issues Series*, 1-16.

Lubatkin, M. (1983). Mergers and the performance of the acquiring firm. *Academy of Management Review*, *8*(2), 218–225.

Lubatkin, M., Schweiger, D., & Weber, Y. (1999). Top management turnover in related M&A's: An additional test of the theory of relative standing. *Journal of Management*, *25*(1), 55–73.

Marks, M. L. (1997). Consulting in mergers and acquisitions. *Journal of Organizational Change Management*, *10*(3), 261–280.

Marks, M. L. (1999). Adding cultural fit to your diligence checklist. *Mergers & Acquisitions: The Dealermaker's Journal*, *34*(3), 14–24.

Marks, M. L., & Mirvis, P. H. (1985). Merger syndrome: Stress and uncertainty. *Mergers & Acquisitions*, 50-55.

Marks, M. L., & Mirvis, P. H. (1992). Rebuilding after the merger: Dealing with "survival sickness.". *Organizational Dynamics*, *21*(2), 18–32. doi:10.1016/0090-2616(92)90061-Q

Marks, M. L., & Mirvis, P. H. (2001). Making merger and acquisitions work: Strategic and psychological preparation. *The Academy of Management Executive*, *15*(2), 35–47.

Miller, F. (2015). Addressing culture differences in M&A. *The Wall Street Journal*. Retrieved January 12, 2018 from http://deloitte.wsj.com/cio/2015/06/18/addressing-culture-differences-in-ma/

Mirvis, P. H., & Marks, M. L. (1992). *Managing the Merger. Making It Work*. Prentice Hall.

Morgan, P. I., & Ogbonna, E. (2008). Sub-cultural dynamics in transformation: A multi-perspective study of healthcare professionals. *Human Relations*, *6*(1), 39–65. doi:10.1177/0018726707085945

Morosini, P., Shane, S., & Singh, H. (1998). National cultural distance and cross border acquisition performance. *Journal of International Business Studies*, *29*(1), 137–158. doi:10.1057/palgrave.jibs.8490029

Morrison, S. (2015). *Culture assessments for mergers and acquisitions*. Retrieved January 12, 2018 from https://talentmanagement360.com/culture-assessments-for-mergers-and-acquisitions/

Muthoni, E. (2012). *Effects of Organization Culture on Strategy Implementation in Commercial Banks in Kenya* (Dissertation). University of Nairobi.

Nahavandi, A., & Malekzadeh, A. (1988). Acculturation in mergers and acquisitions. *Academy of Management Review*, *13*(1), 79–90. doi:10.5465/amr.1988.4306790

Nguyen, H., & Kleiner, B. (2003). The effective management of mergers. *Leadership and Organization Development Journal*, *24*(8), 447–445. doi:10.1108/01437730310505876

O'Reilly, C. A., & Chatman, J. A. (1996). Culture as social control: Corporations, cults, and commitment. In B. M. Staw & L. L. Cummings (Eds.), Research in organizational behavior: An annual series of analytical essays and critical reviews (pp. 157-200). Elsevier Science/JAI Press.

Onyango, W. P. (2014). Effects of organization culture on change management: A case of the vocational training centre for the blind and deaf sikri. *European Journal of Business and Management*, *6*(34), 204–214.

Otterspeer, W. (2016). *The impact of cultural differences on the performance of mergers and acquisitions* (Dissertation). Radboud University Nijmegen.

Pablo, A. L. (1994). Determinants of acquisition integration level - a decision- making perspective. *Academy of Management Journal, 37*(4), 803–836.

Palthe, J., & Kossek, E. L. (2003). Subcultures and employment modes: Translating HR strategy into practice. *Journal of Organizational Change Management, 16*(3), 287–308. doi:10.1108/09534810310475532

Papadakis, V. (2007). Growth through mergers and acquisitions: How it won't be a loser's game. *Business Strategy Series, 8*(1), 43–50. doi:10.1108/17515630710686879

Pellet, L. (2011). *M&A 2011 style.* The cultural fit factor. Retrieved March 11, 2018 from http://chiefexecutive.net/ma-2011-style-the-cultural-fit-factor/

PwC Report. (2017). *Making M&A successful post-merger integration survey.* Retrieved March 12, 2018 from https://www.pwc.com/us/en/services/deals/library/ma-integration-survey.html

Rajan, H. C. (2010). *Double-layered acculturation in cross-border mergers &acquisitions: Examining the role of national culture.* The 11th International Conference on HRD Research and Practice Across Europe.

Reed-Lajoux, A., & Elson, C. (2010). *The Art of M&A: Due Diligence: Navigating Critical Steps and Uncovering Crucial Data.* Maidenhead, UK: McGraw-Hill.

Rosenbloom, A. H. (2002). Due Diligence for Global Deal Making: The Definitive Guide to Cross-Border Mergers and Acquisitions, Joint Ventures, Financings, and Strategic Alliances. Princeton: Bloomberg Press.

Rotting, D., Reus, T., & Tarba, S. Y. (2014). The Impact of Culture on Mergers and Acquisitions: A Third of a Century of Research. In C. L. Cooper & S. Finkelstein (Eds.), *Advances in Mergers and Acquisitions (Advances in Mergers and Acquisitions. Emerald Group Publishing Limited.*

Rouleau, L., & Balogun, J. (2011). Middle managers, strategic sensemaking, and discursive competence. *Journal of Management Studies, 48*(5), 953–983. doi:10.1111/j.1467-6486.2010.00941.x

Rousseau, D. M. (2000). Assessing Organizational Culture: The case for Multiple Methods. In B. Schneider (Ed.), *Organizational climate and culture.* San Francisco: Jossey-Bass.

Santo, R. D. (2013). *The impact of human factors on M&A performance, and the importance of careful culture and knowledge integration* (Dissertation). Alaidos University of Applied Sciences Switzerland.

Schein, E. H. (1980). *Organizational Psychology.* Prentice-Hall.

Schein, E. H. (1985). *Organizational Culture and Leadership.* San Francisco, CA: Jossey-Boss.

Schneck, O. (2007). *Cultural due diligence. Warum Unternehmensübernahmen scheitern.* Kredit & Ratingpraxis.

Schweiger, D. M., Ivancevich, J. M., & Power, F. R. (1987). Executive actions for managing human resources before and after acquisition. *The Academy of Management Executive, 1*, 127–138.

Scott, T., Mannion, R., Davies, H., & Marshall, M. (2003). The quantitative measurement of organizational culture in health care: A review of the available instruments. *Health Services Research, 38*(3), 923–945. doi:10.1111/1475-6773.00154 PMID:12822919

Seo, M. G., & Sharon, H. N. (2005). Understanding the human side of merger and acquisition: An integrative framework. *The Journal of Applied Behavioral Science*, *41*(4), 422–443. doi:10.1177/0021886305281902

Shi, W., Markoczy, L., & Dess, G. G. (2009). The role of middle management in the strategy process: Group affiliation, structural holes, and tertius iungens. *Journal of Management*, *35*(6), 1453–1480. doi:10.1177/0149206309346338

Smollan, R. K., & Sayers, J. S. (2009). Organizational culture, organizational change and emotions: A qualitative study. *Journal of Change Management*, *9*(4), 435–457. doi:10.1080/14697010903360632

Spoljarik, M., & Másdottir, H. K. (2016). *Merger Failure within the Integration Process & the Contributing Extent of Human Resources* (Dissertation). School of Economics & Management, Lund University.

Teerikangas, S., Very, P., & Pisano, V. (2011). Integration manager's value-capturing roles and acquisition performance. *Human Resource Management*, *50*(5), 651–683. doi:10.1002/hrm.20453

Vaara, E. (2003). Post-acquisition integration as sense-making: Glimpses of ambiguity, confusion, hypocrisy, and politicization. *Journal of Management Studies*, *40*(4), 859–894. doi:10.1111/1467-6486.00363

Van Knippenberg, D., Van Knippenberg, B., Monden, L., & Lima, F. (2002). Organizational identification after a merger: A social identity perspective. *British Journal of Social Psychology*, *41*(2), 233–252. doi:10.1348/014466602760060228 PMID:12133226

Vermeulen, F., & Barkema, H. (2001). Learning through acquisitions. *Academy of Management Journal*, *44*, 457–176.

Very, P., Lubatkin, M., & Calori, R. A. (1996). Cross-national assessment of acculturative stress in recent European mergers. *International Studies of Management & Organization*, *26*(1), 59–86. doi:10.1080/00208825.1996.11656674

Warter, I., & Warter, L. (2014). *Latest trends in mergers and acquisitions research. the new pattern of globalization.* Buletinul Instititilui Politehnic Din Iasi, Publicat de, Universitatea Tecnica, Gheorgehe Asachi din Iasi, Tomul LX (LXIV), Fasc.2 Sectia Constructii De Maasini.

Warter, I., & Warter, L. (2015). Intercultural negotiation in mergers and acquisitions. the integration of the cultural dimension into the negotiation domain. BULETINUL INSTITUTULUI POLITEHNIC DIN IASI Publicat de Universitatea Tehnică „Gheorghe Asachi" din Iasi, Tomul LXI (LXV). *Fasc.*, *1*, 2015.

Warter, I., & Warter, L. (2017). Cultural due diligence in M&A: Importance of soft risks factors. *Annals of Spiru Haret University. Economic Series*, *2*, 38–61.

Weber, Y. (1996). Corporate cultural fit and performance in mergers and acquisitions. *Human Relations*, *40*(9), 1181–1202. doi:10.1177/001872679604900903

Weber, Y., & Menipaz, E. (2003). Measuring cultural fit in mergers and acquisitions. *International Journal Business Performance Management*, *5*(1), 54–72. doi:10.1504/IJBPM.2003.002100

Weber, Y., & Pliskin, N. (1996). The effects of information systems integration and organizational culture on a firm's effectiveness. *Information & Management*, *30*(2), 81–90. doi:10.1016/0378-7206(95)00046-1

Weber, Y., & Schweiger, D. M. (1992). Top management culture conflict in mergers and acquisitions: A lesson from anthropology. *International Journal of Conflict Management*, *3*(4), 1–17. doi:10.1108/eb022716

Zollo, M., & Meier, D. (2008). What is M&A performance? *The Academy of Management Perspectives*, *22*(3), 55–77. doi:10.5465/amp.2008.34587995

KEY TERMS AND DEFINITIONS

Corporate Culture: The beliefs and behaviors that determine how a company's employees and management interact and handle outside business transactions.

Cultural Clash: A conflict arising from the interaction of people with different cultural values and beliefs.

Cultural Differences: Various beliefs, behaviors, practices, and expressions considered unique to members of an organization.

Cultural Due Diligence (CDD): A diagnostic process conducted to ascertain the degree of cultural alignment or compatibility between companies that are party to a merger or acquisition.

Cultural Fit: Alignment of two organizations' cultures mainly beliefs, values, and goals.

Cultural Integration: Blending of two or more different cultures.

Merger and Acquisition: A general term that refers to the consolidation of companies or assets through various types of financial transactions.

Pre-Merger and Acquisition Phase (Pre-M&A): Phase of a M&A process when the deal is conceived and negotiated by executives and then legally approved by shareholders and regulators.

Post-Merger and Acquisition Phase (Post-M&A): Phase of a M&A process when the combined entity and its people regroup from initial implementation and new organization settles in.

Chapter 6
Reactivation or Collapse:
How Difficult Situations Affect the Organizational Life and Success

José María Mendoza Guerra
Universidad Simón Bolívar – Barranquilla, Colombia

ABSTRACT

This chapter is structured for contrasting how differentially firms applying strategies of contraction/reactivation reach converse results and how management models may impact the organizational life and success in these circumstances. It analyzes two organizations in difficult situation in Colombia (Aluminios Reynolds Santo Domingo and Hospital Niño Jesus in Barranquilla city), and it identifies strategies to be applied for maintaining alive these organizations, evaluates management styles accompanying the formulated strategies, and reveals the organizational denouement. In this work two styles for confronting turnaround are identified: classic, applied in a ruptured and aggressive way with strong reduction of direct cost; and inclusive, integrating members of the firm around the problem solution and socially building a strategy as a solution. For the empirical analysis, the case method is used accompanied by qualitative techniques as interviews, documental material, and observation.

INTRODUCTION

This chapter compares how different firms that apply retrenchment or recovery strategies reach distinct results, and how, under these circumstances, management models used may impact organizational life and success. It analyzes two Colombian organizations that are facing difficulties: Aluminios Reynolds Santo Domingo, founded in 1955, and Hospital Niño Jesus, founded in 1952 in Barranquilla city. This chapter identifies applicable strategies that can keep these organizations alive, evaluates management styles accompanying these formulated strategies, and reveals each organization's denouement.

Businesses often encounter difficult situations. In fact, the number of businesses that have declined worldwide exceeds those that have grown (Pearce & Robbins, 1993). Because of intense global competition, turnaround as a retrenchment or recovery strategy is relatively contemporary (Behnt, 1983; Pearce & Robbins, 1993).

DOI: 10.4018/978-1-5225-8906-8.ch006

In the academic literature regarding turnarounds, the dominant strategy to turn businesses around is a drastic reduction in costs or a sale of assets, as well as possible layoffs. In this chapter, we confirm that other managerial options exist to confront difficult business situations.

THEORETICAL BACKGROUND

Four important factors impact the success of a business: the environment, path dependence, human interrelationships, and management.

- The environment is affected by variables and actors that impact companies' results.
- Path dependence influences the consistency of organizational behavior, which itself may generate resistance to changes (Leonard-Barton, 1992).
- Human relationships promote positive conflicts (reasonable pluralism, according to Rawls, 2001), based on human differences, and stimulate common action.
- Management defines future behavior and sustains an equilibrium with the environment.

Together, all these factors help organizations achieve their goals. These effects are integrated in Equation 1.

$$R = F(E, P, I, D)$$

where:

E: environmental state or scenario
P: path dependence
I: interrelationships
D: direction

With these facts, organizations may either grow, survive, or fail. Quickly increasing situations are typical in management (Penrose, 1959) and could occur in favorable external conditions. Ansoff (1988) proposed four strategic categories: penetration, product development, market development, and diversification. Survival takes place in highly competitive environments (red ocean, Kim & Mauborgne, 2005), where the probability of failure is high. This chapter considers this topic.

An organization responds systematically to the outside world by means of development, leanness, and turnarounds. Development implements a growth strategy and requires an amplified structure, a proactive leadership, and the monitoring of results. Leanness (Socconini, 2013) eliminates waste, keeps costs low to maximize a company's competitive position, maintains the functioning of business in a complicated environment, and creates value for clients. It comprises the entire organization, controls costs, and increases productivity. The goal of a turnaround is to confront a difficult situation, recover a business health, and establish different ways for keep it afloat.

A turnaround, which confronts an organization's difficult situation, generally is accompanied by the following characteristics:

- It is integral in scope.
- It has a negative impact that challenges organizations.
- It is urgent, requiring rapid solutions.
- It has a duration and it takes time.
- It uses scarce resources that need to be reallocated.

This complicated circumstance may be generated by two contingencies: 1) a change in the environment or 2) mistakes by an organization's management (internal error)

Several organizational characteristics are presented in this type of situation.

- Losses or insolvencies
- Anxiety
- A critical organizational climate
- Problems with internal governance
- Lack of hope (Kanter, 2003)
- Incredibility of stakeholders
- Employee turnover

To better understand a "turnaround," several definitions are provided in Table 1.

These different proposals allow an analysis of a turnaround's essential elements. A turnaround negatively affects performance (competitiveness, sales, and profitability), significantly changes an organization, requires resilience and other efforts for recovery (reaching breakeven and more) (Grotberg, 2001, 2003; Tengblad, 2018; Xiao & Cao, 2017), and needs corporate adaptations.

Types of Difficult Situations

While turnarounds are characterized by total, critical, and radical changes (Schmitt, 1994), difficult circumstances can be graded. These gradations, and their respective application strategies, are presented in Table 2.

Hofer (1980) notably postulated that the more severe a retrenchment, the more costs and assets are reduced.

Table 1. Definitions of turnaround

Schmitt (1994)	Implies to introduce profound and radicals changes for correcting situations affecting the firm performance, its competitiveness and its capacity for generating profit or usually for transforming enterprises in deficit into profitable enterprises.
Khandwalla (1998)	To reach at least a breakeven from a loss situation.
Suzuki (1985)	Series of rescue efforts aimed at arresting the declining trend of business activities of a firm.
Barker & Buheim (1997)	Increased organizational adaptation to its industry or micro niche leading to a recovery in performance and an increase in resources within the firm.
Slatter & Lovett (1999)	Refers to those firms or operating units whose financial performance indicates that firm will fall in the foreseeable future unless short-term corrective actions are taken.

Table 2. Turnaround severity and strategies (Hofer, 1980; Pandit, 2000)

Severity	Strategy
Low	Austerity (including a lean company) and productivity
Medium	Cost reductions and product eliminations
Critical	Disinvestment and elimination of the business

When severity is low, two effective actions are eliminating waste and augmenting efficiency (O'Neill, 1986). When it is medium, the key is to eliminate indirect costs and, if possible, to diminish direct costs and to sell products or assets. In a critical situation, when these actions are insufficient, drastic actions are needed, such as cutting business lines and reducing direct costs, including downsizing and reengineering processes and systems.

Causes of a Business Crisis

Turnarounds are motivated by crises, events that threaten and destroy an organization's routines (Giddens, 1984). Crises disrupt an organization's life-cycle, including disasters that have a highly negative impact (Allen & Toder, 2004).

Crises can originate internally or externally. Hanschilst (2000) identified possible internal causes, such as a manager's personality, the value creation process, the nature of an institution, and governance. Chanchai, Abebe, and Lipay (2013) also included financial issues, decision-making, and operational and human dysfunction. Other authors believe that internal factors determine crises (i.e., Bibeualt, 1999), and that crises decrease stock values (Flanagan & O'Shaughnessy, 2005). Bourdieu (2000), regarding French real estate industries, identified succession problems, path dependence, strategic mistakes, and conflicts (among directives or referents to decentralization) as internal factors, and the general economic situation as external factors. Separately, Skoenberg, Collier, and Bowman (2013) connected crises with the strategies of rival firms.

Turnaround Phases

As a dynamic phenomenon, turnarounds have durations and different stages of development (Bebault, 1982). Miller (1986) established three steps in a turnaround: a strategy crisis, a liquidity crisis, and bankruptcy. Most researchers of turnaround theory focus on two key events: retrenchment and recovery.

Retrenchment is a negative position where an organization strongly reduces costs for savings, eliminates poor products, divests assets, and withdraws from marginal markets to improve productivity. Hambrick and Schecter (1983) call this *operational strategy*. As a result of these activities, more efficient use of resources (Pearce & Robbins, 1993) increases earnings. At the end of this course of action, having achieved a better financial position, firms raise their competitiveness and profitability by working on quality, services, and agility. The difficulty of this strategy requires managing human resources to avoid a negative impact on an organization's psychology. Companies need to motivate people and provide emotional support and cooperation. In a crisis stage, conflicts can increase, generating problems of power that negatively affect the possibility of reactivation. To control conflict and its destructive capacity, managers must integrate employees, create a confident climate to improve expectations, motivate, be optimistic, and emphasize positive aspects needed for moving forward.

When these actions are successful, a second phase (recovery) can be undertaken, where it is possible to use the surplus to invest in resurgent activities that elevate a company's value, such as better quality and innovation. (On a small scale, these activities can be initiated in the first (contraction) phase). Hambrick and Schecter (1983) call this *entrepreneurial strategy,* which requires exploration as a preface for growth (Håkonsson, Eskildsen, Argote, Mønster, Burton, & Obel, 2015; Murrow, Johson, & Busenitz, 2004).

A turnaround strategy presumes a problem of adaptability (Reeves & Deimler, 2011; Volberda, 1997; Watiez, 2000), or more precisely, an ability to readapt to challenges, because a situational change may necessitate a new strategic position. When the change is provoked by a slowdown in the environment, its impact on an adaptation is stronger. The re-adaptation may require a new strategy, an adjustment to the organizational structure, or a modification to external stakeholder relationships (the ecosystem). This directly implies organizational resilience, the capacity to resist a difficult environmental situation as a means to adapt and to recover from the effects of a crisis or turbulence (Schneider, 2006). Here as in the cases studied in this book, resilience means an ability performed well in a threatened organization. Organizational resilience is referred to as the follows:

- The psychological health of people, a mechanism for resistance.
- Learning from one's mistakes (Schneider, 2006), because an error always causes a negative effect.
- Having perspectives or hopefulness about the future, because the possibility of surmounting a poor circumstance energizes an organization.
- Perseverance. Moving ahead in a difficult situation is basic to maintain the effort in permanent pressing that, similarly, is based on a behavior oriented by patience.
- Solidarity. Surmounting a crisis requires organizational energy. Thus, cooperative behavior is critical for exceptional performance.

The re-adaptation implied in recuperation must be accompanied by innovation, creativity, and energy, because new circumstances require new ideas and hard work for their implementation. In either an internal or an external environmental shift, emergent states need to be reconfigured to meet the prior environment.

Time is also important in a difficult situation. An effective turnaround strategy depends upon an anticipated action that presupposes a dynamic monitoring capability (Teece, Pisano, & Shuen, 1997; Teece, 2011), implying early detection and analysis of a situation. This also requires prospecting the evolution and making opportune decisions (responsiveness). Timely intervention depends on the situation. In a low state of crisis, a rapid and anticipated intervention can speedily attack difficulties, but a high critical situation requires additional time. In general, success depends upon rapid action.

Thus, timing is obviously important. Chanchai, Abebe, and Lipay (2013) studied opportune actions during initial retrenchment phases, including constraining product portfolios or eliminating markets. Without opportune activities, a situation may be complicated and would require more difficult actions, such as downsizing and reengineering.

The main problem in a turnaround is the dynamic transition from retrenchment to recovery. And as such is a social energy trouble. Unambiguously, organizational success in a complicated crisis demands energy that compromises employees (motivation and resilience), processes (more productivity), structure (organic), and management (more integrative).

The Consequences of Distressed Enterprises

It is logical to hope a turnaround provides noxious consequences into the organization and its stakeholders (Freeman, 1984; Freeman & McVea, 2001). Outcomes include:

- **Financial Injury**: The first impact is damage to financial results: profits, liquidity and solvency, and a roll reduction.
- **Reputation**: External stakeholders react to a firm's information, which can affect their good will. Clients can have doubts about the quality, continuity, or opportunity of a firm's services, provision of goods, and post-sale service. Shareholders may see no future dividends, suppliers may not be paid on time, and a company may lose prestige. Downsizing generally has a negative impact on a company's reputation (Flanagan & O'Shaughnessy, 2005; Love & Kraatz, 2009; Zyglidopoulos, 2005). Zhulz and Johann (2018) discovered that this negative effect is of 0.15 in average. However, shareholders recognize that a legitimate downsizing can be the only way to save a firm (Ferrari, 2018).
- **Organizational Climate**: Climate is affected by disturbances to the state of a firm: fear of losing one's job, the impact of payment difficulties (Harrigan, 2012), loss of loyalty and commitment (Cameron, 1994), the stress of work, resource demands and value creation (Boyd, Tuckey, & Winefield, 2014). This may increase employee turnover and absenteeism, which could potentially harm an organization. Lopez, Chambel, and Diaz-Valdez (2018) noted that survivors of a downsized firm reported high levels of irritability, guilt, distress, and fear, and lower levels of enthusiasm, pride, interest, and attention. A corporate restructuring changes the balance between employees and employers, which also may affect stakeholders (Ferrari, 2018) and remaining employees.
- **Emotional Intelligence:** (Goleman, 1998, 2000). Crises impact a firm's emotional life. Specifically, employees can be affected by the possibility of losing employment during a retrenchment in an organization without a solid future. In such a circumstance, resilience is necessary. A downsizing strategy may alter the reconfiguration of a company's human network, creating the possibility of changing the control of information (Sussking, Moore, & Katmar, 2018).
- **Innovation**: Cascio (2010) noted four ways that a downsizing affects innovation. It increases the risk aversion of remaining employees, reduces resources for innovation, restricts the number and morale of innovators, and raises the work charge of the survivors.

It is obvious that an austerity strategy is required. Fortunately, these problems can be attacked in different ways:

- Consider how crises affect the confidence of outside stakeholders (Chanchai, Abebe, & Li, 2013) by means of the dynamic capability of monitoring or sensing and the behavior of the key external actors (Teece, 2011).
- Adopt a practical view for designing solutions and putting them into action.
- Practice perseverance, a quality needed for surmounting a difficult situation, and require a sustained effort where many barriers need to be overcome. Perseverance is based on patience and hopefulness, aspects that condition an effective performance.
- Control the emotional life of an organization. This is basic because of the need to undermine the stress, anxiety, and anguish provoked by an organizational slowdown.

Because turnaround problems can involve many distinct difficulties in an organization, an effective turnaround requires an amplified framework, principally a sound, simple financial strategy.

Management Styles in a Turnaround

Two management styles exist in turnarounds: classic and inclusive.

A Classic Turnaround

A classic turnaround strategy is ruptured and aggressive. Generally, it uses the following actions:

- Downsizing, with a strong reduction of direct costs, including personal expenses.
- Outsourcing, which lowers operational expenses while maintaining or augmenting the value of products and services.
- Sale of product lines to generate income and reduce costs.
- Sale of assets for cash.
- Refinancing debt to improve repayment terms in a reactivation.

These financial strategies focus on costs, disinvestments, and financings.

All turnarounds, though, has a human risk for the organizational climate, especially autocratic leadership, technocratic decision-making, *tête-a-tête* control, top-down communications, and penalties. Without participation, people feel powerless and helpless (Cascio & Wynn, 2004).

An Inclusive Turnaround

An inclusive turnaround is based on different actions founded in social constructivism (Berger & Luckmann, 1966) and applied to organizations. In this construct, the people who build the corporate revival place a high value on human talent:

- Create a wide committee of clients, unions, executives, and the surrounding community, incorporating individual personalities and inter-organizational networks (Capaldo, 2007).
- Use a communications system for constructing and diffusing the strategy.
- Provide factual information, sensitize people about the situation, and avoid defensive behavior (Senge, 1990). This requires endomarketing.
- Build positive future expectations that strengthen hopefulness in a revitalization and promote optimism.
- Integrate members of the firm around the problem's solution by looking ahead to the objective of recovering the company. This task keeps tacit an alignment work (Norton & Kaplan, 2008).
- Build a solution using general assemblies and committees, in which everyone participates.
- Incentivize people to achieve results.
- Monitor the situation and make corrections if necessary.

In short, an inclusive style attacks crises by accumulating enough energy to produce a drastic change that an emergency requires (from retrenchment to recovery). This is impossible without the cooperation of human resources management. Similarly, inclusive management strategies create an amplified organizational base, which allows everyone to participate in the recovery (Schonberger, 1986) and stimulates a cooperative spirit (Arendt, 1998). In addition, an inclusive approach may facilitate innovation that transforms the company to reach reactivation. Innovation is a core ingredient for reengineering (Hammer & Champy, 1993) and reinventing a firm (Hamel & Prahalad, 1994; Naisbitt, & Abundene, 1985). This method maintains the organizational climate, minimizes negative consequences for employee relations, and overall reduces the pain that crises may cause.

METHODOLOGY

To understand corporate crises, two organizations were selected: an industrial enterprise (Aluminios Reynolds Santo Domingo), and a social organization (Hospital Niño Jesus), which suffered a drop in performance. The former saw increased competition when Colombia opened its economy (an external, environmental event), while the hospital had management problems (an internal issue) that impacted its surplus.

Our methodological approach was based on diverse, reliable, and valid research techniques, including interviews, observations, and document analysis. For each method, different instruments were used to collect data and information, such as interview guides, day books, observation notes, and document protocols. Quality guaranty to labor was based in saturation in the questioning cases, and triangulation, using different information inputs, including employees, general and second-line managers, and ex-employees. Likewise, boards of directors' acts and financial statements (the Financial Corporation of North, COFINORTE for Aluminios Reynolds Santo Domingo and the finance department of Hospital Niño Jesus) were consulted. Six internal executives were interviewed (four still working and two retired) at Aluminios Reynolds Santo Domingo. At Hospital Niño Jesus, documents were consulted, and the average length of each interview was one hour and 30 minutes. In addition, the physical infrastructure, operational process, and employee behavior were observed.

RESULTS

Crisis Appearance

The management crisis at Hospital Niño Jesus took place between 2003 and 2008 because of ineffective management. In 2004–2005, the Minister of Social Protection liquidated ESE Hospital Niño Jesus in the Department of Atlántico because of its budget deficit, which exceeded 2.5 trillion pesos, without the possibility of finding alternative financing and achieving an operational balance. This problem had an internal origin, which impacted the hospital's climate. Its recovery-director, David Pelaez, noted that "the workers operated without commitment, absolutely dissatisfied, without academic growth, or labor update, together with the fact that they were owed the payment of the economic obligations, therefore they faced difficulties to attend at home the basic family needs: food, public services, leases or housing mortgage financing, education of children.... ."

Aluminios Reynold Santo Domingo began restructuring in 1990 because of the threat presented by its main rival in Colombia (Alumina) and the presence of international competitors. Thus, its crisis had external causes.

Strategy

The strategies applied by each organization, while different, followed the two types of turnaround noted above and in the turnaround literature. Aluminios Reynolds Santo Domingo intended to overcome its crisis using a classic strategy and management model, while the hospital applied a more participatory model.

Aluminios Reynolds' strategy is shown in Figure 1. The company used distinct strategies for specific effects. It expanded its plant and marketing efforts, caught up with international technology and management, and adopted international standards for evaluating performance (a development strategy) (Ansoff, 1988). An informant said: "the company did benchmarking against other plants of the world and reached high levels of performance" based on a technological advance. In deceleration moment, the firm lost dynamics, focusing on efficiency and reducing creation of value, applying a management system concentrated on a hierarchical and authoritarian leadership; an interviewer said: "The company had a decade without investing in technology and was losing the international reference; it was affected by the withdrawal of the Reynolds Company, reducing competitive advantage in technology."

The situation became more complicated with the government's opening of the Colombian economy. This external factor (declination) increased the presence of an internal competitor (Alumina, founded in 1960), which, in addition to several external competitors, intensified competition and complicated the firm's outlook. In response, Alumina strengthened its technological development (focusing on extrusion technology) and improved its marketing strategy. This reaction was caused by a more open economy that altered market dynamics. In addition, internal factors, such as the rupture with an international partner, destroyed organizational resistance.

Figure 1. Evolution of Aluminios Reynolds' strategy

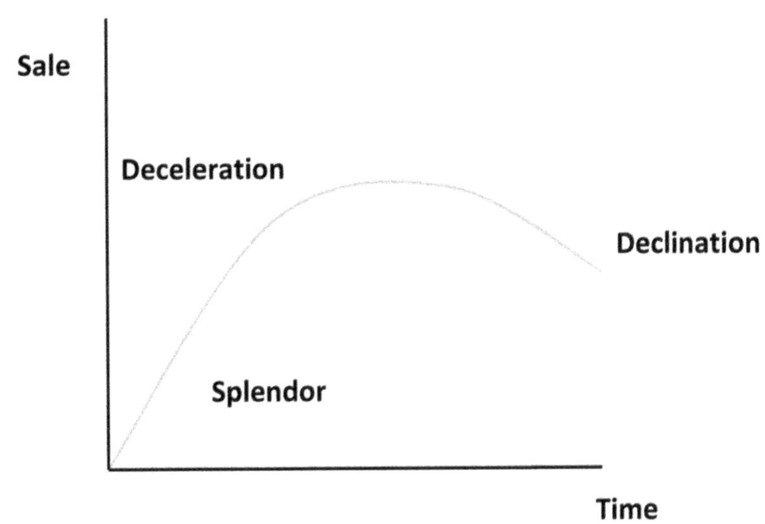

In 1996, Reynolds Santo Domingo attempted improving its management based on quality (after Colombia initiated this program in the 1980s). The company obtained several quality register approvals, such as UL GN59, NTC 1798, and ICONTEC, by applying preventive maintenance, modernizing technology with new equipment, and beginning a strategy of internationalization toward Andean Pact nations and Central America. It also initiated a revised marketing policy that included a TIC application (ERP BAAN IV, web pages, and ecommerce). At the same time the company cut staff. An informant said: "over the period 1990 to 1991, the roll dropped from 900 to 600 workers." Aluminios utilized a classic style to confront a difficult situation, incorporating Reynolds' modern and international management model. In spite of these efforts, Aluminios continued to decline and was unable to become resilient, at least in part because of an unfavorable economic environment (Hamel & Valikangas, 2003).

In contrast, the hospital adopted a behavior, shown in Figure 2, incorporating the following facts and events at the starting:

- Salaries unpaid
- High debt with suppliers
- Operational difficulties
- Undermotivated employees

Using a more humanistic turnaround approach, the following actions were applied:

- Employees were sensitized about the situation.
- Employees understood the problem and conceded one hour of labor to the hospital.
- The technology was modernized.
- Social networks were built as a strategy.
- Client services were improved.
- Better use was made of human capital.
- Medical specialists conformed to a cooperative method of outsourcing.

Figure 2. Evolution of hospital Niño Jesus strategy

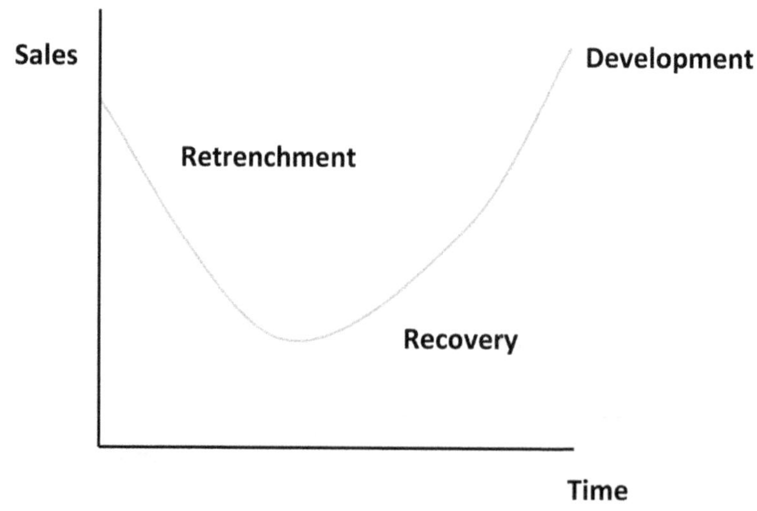

As a reactivation mechanism, marketing actions were applied, such as changing the corporate image and a visit program for communities and institutions. Furthermore, a client service system was initiated based on close client-hospital relationships (Patch & Mylander, 2010). This allowed the hospital to recover, an event that became a successful model in the Colombian health care system. Niño Jesus adopted an anthropological paradigm (Ribes, 2001), emphasizing human talent and participation. One employee said: "Everybody gave their contribution and a decision was democratically made when more than one alternative were presented as a best road." Another informant commented: "The doctor (Director) was friendly with the workers and considered the hospital was a family where everybody must go hospital ahead" and added: "We supported the Director, we continued working and things were improving." Clearly this style is inclusive. The alignment and integration efforts, based on an open and participative management, created a positive organizational climate that avoided the conflicts that generally accompany corporate crises. This rapidly led to a reactivation phase. As a service enterprise, employee interactions are important to create value for patients, and a management style based on employees' responses had a major impact in the recovery.

Unsurprisingly, the hospital's' financial results improved. Over a five-year period, income rose from $3,280,000,000 to $10,000,000,000, an annual increase of 26.6%. An operational surplus of about $3,800,000,000 allowed the hospital to pay its debts and salaries.

DIFFERENCES

Both these two organizations experienced crises that were addressed with a strategy of savings, which had financial, organizational, and emotional impacts.

However, each company's different approach led to the disparate results. Ultimately, the hospital became the best performer in its market. In contrast, an aggressive competitor to Aluminios notably increased international competition, (Porter, 1980) or be in a red ocean (Kim & Mauborgne, 2005), which depressed ROI. The hospital's issues were managerial, and as a local business, it benefited from growing demand.

A participative model of management facilitated integration and the hospital's recovery. A participative leadership style elevates the motivation needed for a difficult situation. By contrast, its absence (the classic turnaround style), adopted by Aluminios, did not generate the necessary high levels of organizational energy to move the business forward.

Table 3. Differences between the two enterprises

Topic	Aluminios	Hospital
Enterprise	Industrial	Service
Competition	High competition	A few rivals
Management model	Classic	Inclusive
Motivation	Low	High
International	International connection	Local market

Aluminios, which began as an international firm, lost its competitive edge when Columbia opened its economy. Aluminios then returned to the international market by expanding into Andean Pact countries and Central America, its natural neighbors.

Because of the distinct strategies adopted by each company, their results differed significantly. Aluminios did not survive and was sold to its main competitor (Alumina). Hospital Niño Jesus, meanwhile, remains in full operation, despite the critical situation of the health care system of Colombia.

CONCLUSION

This research confirms that a crisis may have either an internal or an external origin. The former case (Hospital Niño Jesus) was easier to solve than the latter one (Aluminios Reynold Santo Domingo) because an environmental threat can meaningfully change the competitive environment.

The difference between an industrial and a service company can influence whether to apply a classic or a participative turnaround model. A service organization such as a hospital creates value by serving the needs of its clients (patients). Consequently, a participative management system is more aligned to this type of institution.

Organizational success is a core topic in turnarounds, which this chapter addresses. Surviving in a crisis is a complex problem involving several internal and external factors. The key actions are as follows:

- To understand the situation, scan the environment (a dynamic capability, according to Teece, 2011) and perform an organizational analysis.
- Formulate an adequate strategy, combining retrenchment and recovery.
- Manage time and implement opportunities.
- Generate organizational energy (easier with an inclusive turnaround style).

The two cases presented highlight several causes for organizational failure.

- A drastic situation is very difficult to surmount (true for both organizations).
- Previous internal problems may complicate the situation (i.e., for Aluminios, conflicts among partners).
- Timing scarcity for opportunely moving as in Aluminios Reynold Santo Domingo laggards the reactivation and even do it impossible.
- Poor human resources management hinders recoveries.

A successful recovery requires organizations to muster an extraordinary emotional, physical, rational, and creative effort. Both cases show the large amount of work a turnaround requires.

In a turnaround, management needs to understand the complexity of the situation and formulate an adaptable turnaround strategy that is carried out in practice. A competitive strategy for confronting a clever rival and alliances with international partners require special solutions.

The positive potential of an international market, as an alternative to a competitive national market, requires a high learning curve. Nevertheless, when Colombia opened its economy in the 1990s, an opportunity was presented for Aluminios Reynold Santo Domingo. A turnaround demands organizational energy. This was provided in the case of Hospital Niño Jesus but did not occur in the case of Aluminios because of its choice of turnaround strategy.

DISCUSSION

The classic approach has dominated the turnaround literature. Pearce & Robbins (1993) showed that a more involved turnaround style may provide better results for service businesses. Nevertheless, the inclusive style for managing a crisis has scarcely been studied by lecturers, despite its importance as a tool for saving an organization in a more humane manner. Overall, turnarounds need to be more explored more fully in the strategic literature.

We prefer an inclusive turnaround style to a classic one. Its effectiveness is motivated by the high organizational cooperation that it generates, and by the minimal changes to an organization's culture and employee relations (Santana, Valle, & Galan, 2018).

Generally, a turnaround strategy takes place in two stages: retrenchment and recovery, in linear succession. This study notes that an intermediate moment exists (just before reactivation) when both strategies coexist, in which some resources required to improve performance are generated in the first stage. Both organizations use these two strategies in a similar manner. Some recovery actions do not need much money and can be anticipated in the first step. Later, when a surplus exists, the recovery comes to fruition.

In strategic management, a company's dynamic capabilities have been recognized as tools for responding to the environment. Teece (2011) maintained that a key dynamic capability is taking advantage of environmental opportunities. However, it also is important to have the resources to react to a crisis. We suggest that this capability is *resilience*, the ability to overcome difficult circumstances (adversity). This capability must go accompanied of respective routines for practice ends (Federwoski, 2007).

Researchers generally have a pessimistic attitude about turnarounds. Crises are negative, and recovery implies turmoil, but a difficult situation can be overcome with organizational energy and aligning people toward success. However, this result presumes an inclusive style that raises motivation by promoting participation.

The strategic literature largely does not recognize the role of leadership, even though it is central in an inclusive-style turnaround. This is clear in the hospital case, where intervention by the Director stimulated a reactivation.

The general literature regarding turnarounds concentrates on retrenchment and finance. However, other positive aspects, such as motivation and hope, help surmount a crisis. Likewise, imagination and reasoning seek alternative solutions (improvements and innovations) and strengthen productivity and efficiency by using resources wasted in earlier periods, prior to the crisis.

Finally, both cases studied in this chapter indicate the importance of internal situations prior to a crisis (Bibeualt, 1999). The negative impact of poor management and an inept strategy may complicate a firm's survival.

REFERENCES

Ansoff, H. I. (1988). *New Corporate Strategy*. New York: Wiley.

Arendt, H. (1998). *The Human Condition*. Chicago: University of Chicago. doi:10.7208/chicago/9780226924571.001.0001

Barker, V., & Duheim, I. (1997). Strategic Change in the Turnaround Process. Theory and Empirical Evidence. *Strategic Management Journal*, *18*(1), 13–38. doi:10.1002/(SICI)1097-0266(199701)18:1<13::AID-SMJ843>3.0.CO;2-X

Behnt, R. (1983). The fundamentals of Cutback Management. In R. Zeckhauser & D. Leebaert (Eds.), *What role for government: lessons from policy research*. Duke University Press.

Berger, P., & Luckmann, T. (1966). *The Social Construction of Reality: A Treatise of Sociology of Knowledge*. New York: Doubleday.

Bibault, D. (1982). *Corporate Turnaround: How Managers Turn Losers into Winners*. New York: McGraw-Hill.

Bibeualt, D. (1999). *Corporate Turnaround*. Washington, DC: Beard.

Bourdieu, P. (2000). *Les Estructures Sociales de L'economie*. Paris: De Seuil.

Boyd, C., Tuckey, M., & Winefield, A. (2014). Perceived effects organizational downsizing and staff cuts on the stress experience: The role of resources. *Stress and Health*, *30*(1), 53–64. doi:10.1002mi.2495 PMID:23868509

Cameron, K. (1994). Strategic for successful organizational downsizing. *Human Resource Management*, *33*(2), 189–201. doi:10.1002/hrm.3930330204

Capaldo, A. (2007). Network structure innovation: The leveraging of dual network as a distinctive relational capability. *The Journal of Strategic Management*, *28*(6), 585–608. doi:10.1002mj.621

Cascio, W. (2010). *Employment Downsizing and its Alternatives: Strategies for Long-term Success*. Alexandria, VA: Society for Human Resources Management.

Cascio, W., & Wynn, P. (2004). Managing a downsizing process. *Human Resource Management*, *43*(4), 425–436. doi:10.1002/hrm.20034

Chadwick, C., Hunter, L., & Walson, S. (2014). Effects of downsizing practices on the performance of hospitals. *Journal of Strategic Management*, *25*(5), 405–427. doi:10.1002mj.383

Chanchai, T., Abebe, M., & Li, Z. (2013) A Temporal Approach to Successful Turnaround in Declining Firms. *Academy of Management Annual Meeting Proceedings*, *2013*(1).

Federwoski, R. (2007). Routines in a turnaround - What are they good for. *International conference on corporate routines: Empirical Research and Conceptual Foundations*.

Ferrari, M. (2018). The structure and dynamics of the CEO's "small world" of Stakeholders: An application to the industrial downsizing. *Technological Forecasting and Social Change*, *140*, 147–159. doi:10.1016/j.techfore.2018.04.006

Flanagan, J., & O'Shaughnessy, K. (2005). The effect of layoffs on firm reputation. *Journal of Management*, *31*(3), 445–463. doi:10.1177/0149206304272186

Freeman, R. (1984). *Strategic Management: A Stakeholder Approach*. Boston: Pitman.

Freeman, R., & McVea. (2001). *Strategic management; a stalkholder approach*. Pitman.

Giddens, A. (1984). *The Constitution of Society, Outline of the Theory of Structuration*. Cambridge, UK: Polity.

Goleman, D. (1998). *Working with Emotional Intelligence*. New York: Bantam.

Goleman, D. (2000). Leadership that gets results. *Harvard Business Review*, *78*(2), 78–89.

Grotberg, E. (2003). *Resilience for Today*. Westport, CT: Praeger.

Håkonsson, D., Eskildsen, E., Argote, L., Mønster, D., Burton, R., & Obel, B. (2015). Exploration versus exploitation: Emotions and performance as antecedents and consequences of team decisions. *Strategic Management Journal*, *37*, 935–1001.

Hambrick, D., & Schecter, S. (1983). Turnaround Strategy for mature industrial-product Business Units. *Academy of Management Journal*, *26*(2), 231–248.

Hamel, G., & Prahalad, C. K. (1994). *Competing for the Future*. Boston: Harvard Business School Press.

Hamel, G., & Valikangas, L. (2003, September). The Quest for resilience. *Harvard Business Review*, 52–63. PMID:12964393

Hammer, M., & Champy, J. (1993). Reengineering the Corporation. New York: Academic Press.

Harrigan, K. (2012). *A Turnaround Strategy Framework. Columbia Casework*. New York: Columbia University.

Hofer, C. (1980). Turnaround strategies. Analytical concepts. *The Journal of Business Strategy*, *1*(1), 19–31. doi:10.1108/eb038886

Kanter, R. (2004). *Confidence*. Random House.

Khandwalla, N. (1998). *Effective Turnaround of Sick Enterprises (Indian Experience): Text and Cases*. London: Commonwealth secretariat.

Kim, W., & Mauborgne, R. (2005). *Blue Ocean Strategy*. Boston: Harvard Business Press.

Leonard-Barton, D. (1992). Core capabilities or core rigidities: A paradox in managing new product development. *Strategic Management Journal*, *13*(S1), 111–125. doi:10.1002mj.4250131009

Lopez, S., Chambel, M., & Diaz-Valdez, A. (2018). Job insecurity, procedural justice and downsizing survivors affects. *International Journal of Human Resource Management*. doi:10.1080/09585192.2018.1482939

Love, E., & Kraatz, M. (2009). Character, conformity or the bottom line? How and why downsizing affected corporate reputation. *Academy of Management Journal*, *52*(2), 314–335. doi:10.5465/amj.2009.37308247

Miller, D. (1986, November). Common syndromes of business fail. *Business Horizons*, 43–53.

Murrow, J., Johson, R., & Busenitz, L. (2004). The effects of cost and assets retrenchment on Firm Performance: The Overlooked Role of Firm's Competitive Environment. *Journal of Management*, *30*(2), 198–208.

Naisbitt, J., & Abundene, P. (1985). *Reinventing the corporation*. Megatrends.

Norton, R., & Kaplan, D. (2008). *Execution Premium*. Barcelona: Deusto.

O'Neill, H. (1986). An analysis of %Turnaround in Commercial Bank. *Journal of Management Studies*, *23*(2), 165–188. doi:10.1111/j.1467-6486.1986.tb00418.x

Pandit, N. (2000). Some recommendation to improved research in corporate turnaround. *M@n@gement*, *3*(2), 31-56.

Patch, A., & Mylander, M. (2010). *Gesundeheit! Bringing good health to you, the medical system, and society through physician, service, complementary therapies, humor and joy*. Rochester, VT: Healing Arts Press.

Pearce, J. II, & Robbins, K. (1993). Toward an Improved Theory and Research of Business Turnaround. *Journal of Management*, *19*(3), 613–636. doi:10.1177/014920639301900306

Penrose, E. (1959). *The theory of the growth of the firm*. Oxford, UK: Oxford University Press.

Porter, M. (1980). *Competitive Strategy*. New York: The Free Press.

Rasheed, H. (2002) Grow or Retrenchment Strategy Choice for Declining Entrepreneurial Firms: The Effect of Performance and Resources. *Journal of Business and Enterpreunership*.

Rawls, J. (2001). *Justice as Fairness*. Boston: Harvard.

Reeves, M., & Deimler, M. (2011). *Adaptability: The New Competitive Advantage*. Boston: Harvard Business Press.

Ribes, A. (2001). *Modelo antropológico para humanizar las organizaciones. Papeles de ética, Economía y Dirección, n 6*. Universidad de Valencia.

Santana, M., Valle, R., & Galan, J. (2018). Sources of decline, Turnaround Strategy, and HR Strategies and Practices: The Case of Iberia Airlines. *Economic and Industrial Democracy*. doi:10.1177/0143831X18772356

Schmitt, G. (1994). *Turnaround*. Buenos Aires: Atlántida.

Schneider, B. (2006). Resiliencia: Cómo Construir Empresas en Contextos de Inestabilidad. Bogotá: Norma.

Schonberger, R. (1986). *World Class Manufacturing*. New York: The Free Press.

Senge, P. (1990). *The Fifth Discipline: The Art and Practice of the Organizational Learning*. New York: Doubleday.

Skoenberg, R., Collier, N., & Bowman, C. (2013). Strategy for business turnaround and recovery: A review and synthesis. *European Business Review*, *25*(3), 243–262. doi:10.1108/09555341311314799

Slatter, S., & Lovett, L. (1999). *Corporate Turnaround*. London: Pinguin.

Socconini, L. (2013). Lean Company. Bogotá: Norma.

Sussking, A., Moore, O., & Katmar, K. (2018). *Organization Downsizing: How Communication Networks Connect with the Employee Performance*. Retrieved from https://scholarship.sha.cornell.edu/chrpubs/255

Suzuki, N. (1985). *The Cross National Comparison of Turnaround Strategies The USA and Japan*. Academic Management Proceeding.

Teece, D. (2011). Dynamic capabilities. Oxford, UK: Oxford.

Teece, D., Pisano, G., & Shuen, A. (1997). Dynamic capabilities and strategic management. *Strategic Management Journal*, *18*(7), 509–533. doi:10.1002/(SICI)1097-0266(199708)18:7<509::AID-SMJ882>3.0.CO;2-Z

Tenbglad, S. (2018). Organizational resilience: Theoretical Framework. In S. Tenbglad & M. Oudhuis (Eds.), *The Resilience Framework: Work, Organization and Employment*. Singapore: Springer.

Volberda, H. (1997). Building a Flexible Organization for Fast-moving Markets. *Long Range Planning*, *2*(30), 169–183. doi:10.1016/S0024-6301(96)00110-0

Watiez, J. (2000). Flexibilité et adaptation de l'organisation á l'environnement: La flexibilité en tanque réponse a l'asymétrie intra et intra entreprise. *Finance Contrôle Stratégie*, *5*(1), 217-254.

Xiao, L., & Cao, H. (2017). Organizational Resilience: The theoretical model and Research Implication. *IYM Conference 04021*. 10.1051/itmconf/20171204021

Zhulz, A., & Johann, S. (2018). Downsizing and the Fragility of Corporate Reputation: An Analysis of Impact on contextual factors. *Scandinavian Journal of Management*, *34*(1), 40–50. doi:10.1016/j.scaman.2017.11.004

Zyglidopoulos, S. (2005). The impact of downsizing on corporate reputation. *British Journal of Management*, *16*(3), 253–259. doi:10.1111/j.1467-8551.2005.00460.x

Section 2

De-Internationalization, Offshoring, Backshoring, Nearshoring, Reshoring

Chapter 7
De-Internationalization of SMEs:
A Case Study

Antonio Carrizo Moreira
https://orcid.org/0000-0002-6613-8796
University of Aveiro, Portugal & University of Beira Interior, Portugal

Pedro Silva
University of Aveiro, Portugal

Jorge Mota
University of Aveiro, Portugal

Hugo Oliveira Gadim
University of Aveiro, Portugal

ABSTRACT

Existing literature has devoted high attention to the topic of internationalization. A common assumption is that companies progressively commit to international operations; however, with the increase of competition in international markets, there may be a backwards perspective towards international operations. In this chapter, the topic of de-internationalization is examined, and a case study of a Portuguese SME that de-internationalized conducted. The featured case highlights the drivers and the main challenges of internationalization, as well as the factors and the difficulties in a de-internationalization process. The chapter findings highlight the need to expand the existing research on the topics of de-internationalization and re-internationalization.

DOI: 10.4018/978-1-5225-8906-8.ch007

INTRODUCTION

The internationalization and expansion to foreign markets is a key topic in the field of international business (Griffith, Cavusgil, & Xu, 2008). With the development of the globalization process, the internationalization of business activities has acquired a greater relevance. As a result, the topic of internationalization has gathered increasing attention from the scientific community since the 1960s (Benito, 2005; Ribau, Moreira, & Raposo, 2015). A common assumption is that the international development of companies follows an incremental outward path (Sousa & Tan, 2015).

Actions such as divestments, market exits, downsizing of operations and de-commitment to international operations contradict this notion (Benito & Welch, 1997). The possibility of a negative evolution of international operations has remained far less explored in the literature than that of expanding operations (Freeman, Deligonul, & Cavusgil, 2013). While there have been several theories put forward to explain the process of internationalization (Ribau, Moreira, & Raposo, 2015), the same has not happened regarding the negative development of international operations (Kotabe & Ketkar, 2009). Moreover, there have been few attempts in the literature to explain the de-internationalization process of companies (Benito, 2005; Silva & Moreira, 2019). Existing research has also examined specific forms of de-internationalization, particularly, export withdrawal (Pauwels & Matthyssens, 1999) but the understanding of the strategic antecedents of other forms of de-internationalization, particularly the ones involving the reversal of international operations with higher levels of commitment, have been less explored.

Among the reasons that may help explain the lack of research in de-internationalization is the fact that while internationalization is associated with growth, a de-internationalization implies a contraction process and may be negatively related with failure (Benito & Welch, 1997; Karakaya, 2000). In addition, expansion outward activities such as mergers and acquisitions are received with enthusiasm, contrariwise to contraction activities such as divestments (Silva & Moreira, 2019).

Small and medium-sized enterprises (SMEs) are increasingly internationalizing, which can be explained by the opening of new markets that were previously closed (Hessels & Parker, 2013; Onkelinx & Sleuwaegen, 2008; Ribau, Moreira, & Raposo, 2018a) and the existence of support programs to foster SMEs growth by country governments and the European Union (OECD, 2009). The spread of both the globalization process and the availability of new information and communication technologies have made internationalization easier for companies with fewer resources, allowing them to provide support for distant markets and the ability to easily communicate with potential customers, suppliers and international partners (Keupp & Gassmann, 2009). As a result, a higher number of companies are internationalizing driven by an increase in domestic competition, a limited internal market and a search for new market opportunities, growth, or simply to follow an international expansion path (Keupp & Gassmann, 2009; Kuivalainen, Sundqvist, Saarenketo, & McNaughton, 2012). However, internationalization may not guarantee the survival of the company because the risks and costs involved in the process can be substantial (Onkelinx & Sleuwaegen, 2008; Ribau, Moreira, & Raposo, 2018a).

This chapter focuses on the topic of de-internationalization, particularly of SMEs. The focus of the research on SMEs stems from the fact that when compared to large companies or multinational corporations (MNCs), SMEs traditionally have fewer resources, less research and development activities, face higher uncertainties and barriers to innovation (Zeng, Xie, & Tam, 2010), and are less connected to international knowledge networks (OECD, 2017). Because SMEs do not have abundant resources, they face higher difficulties managing and planning their internationalization process (European Commission, 2003) due to managers lack of technical capabilities and limited time availability. In 2015, SMEs[1] represented 99%

of all enterprises in the European Union (Eurostat, 2018); thus, SMEs are well-suited and of interest to conduct research in the field of de-internationalization. The literature on SMEs de-internationalization is also limited, as most of the existing research focuses on MNCs (Turcan, 2003; Turcan 2013).

Considering the abovementioned gaps, the objective of this chapter is to address the process of de-internationalization of a SME in Portugal, particularly:

- How the company managed its de-internationalization process;
- What happened after its de-internationalization;
- How the company made up for the loss of an external market;
- How the company faced re-internationalization after a market exit.

To achieve these research objectives, an exploratory case study of an SME that de-internationalized from Morocco was conducted, exploring the main reasons as to why the company de-internationalized. The results of this chapter seek to contribute to the discussion of an under-researched topic such as de-internationalization, and to provide companies with knowledge on what can go wrong on an internationalization process. It will also contribute to identify the underlying causes of a de-internationalization decision and to bring clarity into the internationalization/de-internationalization relationship.

The chapter is structured as follows. After this introduction, the following section presents the literature on internationalization and de-internationalization. Then, the methodology used is described and the case study presented, after which follows the analysis and discussion of the main findings. The chapter ends with the conclusions, its limitations and the future research proposals.

THEORETICAL BACKGROUND

In this section, the literature on internationalization is reviewed such as the main theories for firms' internationalization, the reasons to engage in international activities and the choice among the various modes of entry. Then, the literature on de-internationalization is reviewed approaching topics such as the modes of exit like export withdrawal, market exit, reverse internationalization or re-internationalization.

Internationalization

Internationalization is "*the process of increasing involvement in international operations*" (Welch & Luostarinen, 1988; p. 36). Internationalization allows companies to have access to markets other than the domestic one, and to take advantage of their capabilities to create value for the company and to address market needs based on their competences and capabilities. Internationalization happens whenever there is a flow or an exchange of raw materials, finished and semi-finished goods, services, money, people or even ideas between two different countries (Etemad, 2004).

A company's decision-making to expand abroad is one of the most important strategic moves to a company's growth. However, the international business environment is more complex and difficult than the domestic market and the probability of failure in an external market is higher due to increasing competition and the lack of market knowledge, among others. The increasing number of companies that internationalize their activities has been evolving over time by the spread of the globalization process in which companies are embedded today. Furthermore, the internationalization is an important factor for the survival of SMEs (Lee, Kelley, Lee, & Lee, 2012; Ribau, Moreira, & Raposo, 2018b).

Theories of Internationalization

Several theories have been put forward to explain the process of internationalization of firms but among the most consensual ones are the Uppsala model, Dunning's eclectic paradigm or the network theory (Ribau et al., 2015).

The *Uppsala model* is an internationalization stage model based on the assumption that firms follow a sequential pattern of entry into foreign markets and an increasing commitment to each market. The increase of commitment is an important factor in the Uppsala model (Johanson & Wiedersheim-Paul, 1975; Johanson & Vahlne, 1977) as firms intensify their commitment to a certain foreign market as their experience on that market grows. Accordingly, firms first gain experience in the domestic market and then gradually move to culturally and geographically more distant markets. Likewise, firms begin international operations using a low level of commitment to international activities such as exports and then gradually move to higher modes of commitment to international activities such as Greenfield investment.

Dunning's eclectic paradigm discusses the importance of Ownership, Location and Internalization (OLI) variables in foreign direct investment (FDI) decisions (Dunning, 1988). Accordingly, firms only engage in FDI when the following three advantages are simultaneously met:

1. Ownership advantage: the firm should own an asset (e.g., a patent, a copyright, the reputation of the brand, etc.) that has enough value to offset the costs of engaging in international production;
2. Locational advantage: there must be an advantage to the firm to operate in a certain location such as favorable transportation costs, tariffs or labor costs;
3. Internationalization advantage: it should be more profitable to the firm to maintain international activities within its boundaries (e.g., to protect its ownership advantage, an asset or know how) than to engage in modes of internationalization such as alliances or licensing.

When one of these OLI conditions is not met, it may be more profitable for firms to engage in other modes of internationalization other than FDI. For example: (1) without the ownership advantage, it may be difficult for the firm to produce enough value to maintain its activity at all; (2) without a location advantage, it may be more profitable to manufacture in the home market and to export to foreign markets rather than to manufacture abroad; and (3) without an internalization advantage, the firm could license its production process to a partner that would instead manufacture that good.

The *network theory* assumes that firms should not be understood as standalone actors in an industrial system as these are composed by: actors (e.g., individuals, firms and groups), activities and resources (e.g., tangible and intangible resources). According to the network theory, the actor (firm) is dependent on the resources controlled by other actors, establishing with them long-term relationships that go beyond the mere transaction. The relationships held by the firm in its domestic network can be used as a connection to other networks located in other countries (Johanson & Mattsson, 1988). Entering a new market constitutes an opportunity for the firm to develop new relationships, thus, internationalization is understood as the evolution of the firm's network. The network theory is among the most well-accepted to explain the internationalization process of SMEs (Ahokangas, 1998).

Reasons for Internationalization

There are various endogenous and exogenous reasons for the internationalization of companies. The literature presents several factors for the internationalization of companies (Keupp & Gassmann, 2009; Kontinen & Ojala, 2010; Kuivalainen et al., 2012; Ribau et al., 2018b).

Dunning (1993) argues that the main reasons for the internationalization includes: the search for new markets, resources, efficiency and strategic resources.

- The *search for markets* focuses on the demand side to find new markets that the company can explore, allowing the company to gain access to new target markers. The saturation of the domestic market may trigger companies to search other options to sell its products and increase its income by selling in international markets.
- The *search for resources* involves searching for a resource, tangible or intangible, such as know-how, that is not available in the company's country of origin. Nowadays, companies often seek for cheap hand labor to decrease production costs and maximize profits. Companies may also search for highly skilled human resources or countries which have cutting-edge technology.
- The *search for efficiency* seeks to rationalize the investment structure established by the company to increase its competitiveness through the management of multiple production facilities, and to optimize the value chain and maximize the efficiency of the company's resources (Dunning, 1993).
- The *search for strategic resources* involve the search for intangible resources which may include the company's core technologies and competencies (Dunning, 1993). These intangible strategic resources can be patents, knowledge and other skills of employees that are necessary for the development of a competitive advantage.

Dunning (2000) notes that that the search for new markets and resources is among the most important reasons for firms to internationalize. However, the internationalization occurs more because of opportunities encountered by the company, than by threats from competitors. Companies internationalizing for the first time favor the search for new markets and resources, whereas companies that have already internationalized often seek to continue to expand their activity and favor the efficiency and the strategic resources to gain a competitive advantage (Dunning, 2000)

Modes of Entry in International Markets

The mode of entry into the foreign markets is one of the most important critical strategic decisions firms must take when entering foreign markets (Young et al., 1989). The choice of the mode of entry in the foreign market is a complex and difficult decision to undertake. The choice of the mode of entry can make the business thrive or alternatively, lead to its termination. Although Rothaermel et al. (2006) consider three main ways to enter foreign markets – exports, licenses and/or direct investment – they can be expanded into the following ones (Aliouche & Schlentrich, 2011; Pla-Barber & León-Darder, 2004; Rodríguez, 2002): exports, licensing, franchising, strategic alliances, joint ventures or wholly owned subsidiaries.

- *Exports* can be classified as direct and indirect (Simões, 1997). Indirect export occurs when a company is not responsible for the sale of the product that manufactures and instead, uses an intermediary to carry out the business, i.e., the sale is made to a third party who in turn makes the international sale. The advantage of this type of internationalization is that the company only has to deal with the intermediary. On the other hand, the company's commitment is very low and there is a lack of control over the commercialization of the product in the foreign market (Simões, 1997). Direct export occurs when the company makes the decision to internationalize, selling its products directly in the foreign market. An advantage of direct over indirect exports is a greater control over the products sold. However, in direct sales, the company must be aware of the legal procedures and there is a higher commitment from company in terms of human and financial resources (Simões, 1997). Export is considered the first step for entering international markets, thus, serving as a platform for future expansions of the company. Export is the initial step and can be complemented with other modes of entry (Kogut & Chang, 1996). It is considered as the most used entry mode by SMEs because of the lack of resources these companies have, and the low level of risk and commitment required.
- *Licensing* is an agreement between two parties where one party assigns the right over an intangible property (e.g. a patent) to another party for a specified period. The party that wants to use the intangible property pays a monetary sum to benefit from the agreement (Hill, 2007). Traditionally, the license is granted for a particular region or country, nonetheless, each agreement has different characteristics, depending on the agreement between the parties.
- *Franchising* is a contractual agreement between two parties in which the franchisor authorizes the franchisee to use its image, among other things. The franchisor provides the image, know-how and other tangible and intangible goods to the franchisee, and the franchisee in turn, yields a percentage of its sales or profits to the franchisor. This agreement allows the franchisee to use the franchisor's name and image to create a business, however, the franchisee is also obliged to accept some rules of how to run its business, the type of products provided and the locations of the assets.
- *Strategic alliances* are a set of voluntary agreements between companies, characterized by reciprocity or by combining efforts and skills between the various actors. Yoshino & Rangan (1995) argue that no company is isolated in the business world and that it is important to establish relationships with other companies.
- *Joint-ventures* are a relationship between two parties that agree to participate jointly in a project, with the risk being shared between the two, although it is possible that there may be differences according to the contract. A joint-venture can be beneficial because the two companies can complement their skills, allowing each company to focus on what it does best.
- *Wholly owned subsidiaries* include two types of strategies, Greenfield investment and acquisitions. Greenfield investments are more complex and potentially costlier, but in turn allow a full control of the activities and have a higher potential to generate above average returns. Acquisitions allow a fast mode of entering a foreign market and expand the international activities, representing a lower risk than Greenfield investments because the outcomes can be estimated more accurately. Acquisitions are attractive when there are already well-established companies in operation but have some disadvantages such as problems in integrating two companies' cultures and control systems.

The mode of entry depends on degree of commitment to international operations as some modes require a higher commitment to international operations than others (e.g., wholly owned subsidiary requires a higher commitment than exports) (Aliouche & Schlentrich, 2011; Pla-Barber & León-Darder, 2004).

De-Internationalization

De-internationalization should be considered as a viable strategic option by managers (Turcan, 2011). The topic of de-internationalization can be associated to different terminologies such as closure, shut-down, dissolution, insolvency, mortality, exit, divestment or bankruptcy (Turcan, 2013). De-internationalization may have a negative connotation since the term is usually associated with the failure of a company's internationalization process.

Welch and Luostarinen (1988; p. 37) mention about internationalization that "*once a company has embarked on the process, there is no inevitability about its continuance*", i.e., internationalization is not a non-reversal activity nor the solution to all companies' issues. Turcan (2011) organized de-internationalization into total and partial. Total de-internationalization includes the termination of commercial exchanges and the focus on the market of origin. Partial de-internationalization includes the reduction of international operations, market optimization and a change of the mode of entry chosen by the company.

Mellahi (2003) defines de-internationalization as a voluntary decrease in international operations. According to Reiljan (2004), this definition does not include the involuntary process, which is based on the external unpredictability such as the beginning of a war, or a coup d'état. Reiljan (2004) argues that de-internationalization can be voluntary, where the company proactively takes the initiative to de-internationalize, or involuntary, where the company reacts to market changes. De-internationalization can also report to a complete withdrawal from the market and the full discontinuation of the exports, or partial, such as withdrawing only some products from a market with the purpose of decreasing the commitment of the company to the external market without meaning its complete abandonment from the foreign market.

Benito and Welch (1997; p. 17) argue that the "*probability of complete withdrawal from international operations declines as the commitment to these operations increases*", i.e., a total de-internationalization is more likely to happen in the first stages of the internationalization process because the level of commitment to international operations is lower, however, a partial de-internationalization has a higher likelihood of occurring both in the initial and final stages of internationalization as shown in figure 1.

Pauwels and Matthyssens (1999) argue that de-internationalization can happen because of endogenous or exogenous factors. Endogenous factors involve the lack of commitment to the market or a poor implementation of the business strategy. Exogenous factors refer to situations outside the control of the company, where the company's strategy is no longer adjusted to the market because of changes in the environment. The authors conclude that a company's withdrawal from international activities should not necessarily be considered a failure as it can be the outcome of a change in the business strategy. Pauwels & Matthyssens (1999; p. 32) claim "*that a successful strategic withdrawal may lead to a better strategic foundation of the entire international market portfolio.*" In other words, when a company withdraws from a market it may obtain relevant information that may be helpful in future internationalization processes.

Boddewyn (1979) identified several reasons that lead to the divestment of foreign operations: financial considerations, poor pre-investment analysis, adverse environmental conditions, lack of fit and resources, structural and organizational factors, external initiating pressures and foreignness and national differences. Based on Boddewyn's work, Reiljan (2004) organized the de-internationalization factors

Figure 1. Probability of total and partial de-internationalization
Source: Benito & Welch (1997)

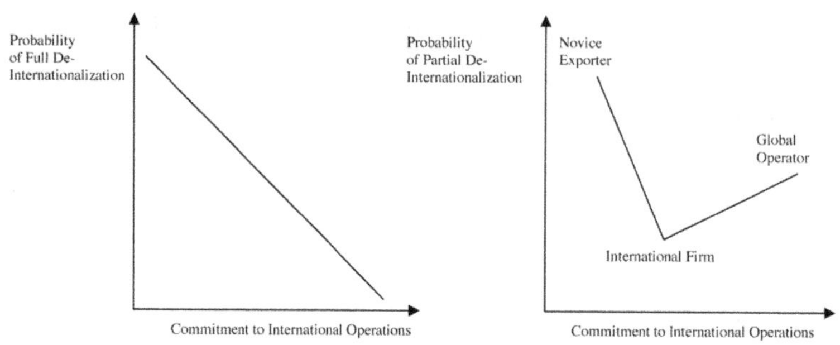

into three main categories: lack of international experience; change in strategy; and poor performance or increase in costs. Table 1 provides an overview of the three main categories.

- **Lack of international experience.** Decision errors on the pre-internationalization activity are usually made by companies that lack international experience because they "*often do not realize the necessity of a careful target market selection process and tend to underestimate the importance of a thorough analysis of the target market*" (Reiljan, 2004; p. 61). This is because companies overestimate the importance of a selection process and an in-depth analysis of the target market. Poor decisions can be made if data collection is misdirected or if there is insufficient data to make an adequate decision. De-internationalization can also be avoided if the company conducts more market research and is more careful planning before venturing into internationalization. The choice of the entry mode into a target market can also be a reason for de-internationalization (Reiljan, 2004). SMEs often invest few resources in foreign markets because they want to ensure that they have the possibility of leaving the market at the lowest possible cost to the company (Bonaccorsi, 1992) and as a result, tend to avoid investments abroad that could have been successful (Reiljan, 2004).
- **Change in the strategy.** Changes in market conditions or strategic changes are identified as external factors of de-internationalization (Welch & Wiedersheim-Paul, 1980). Accordingly, the development of foreign markets need to be monitored regularly to make informed strategic decisions as much as possible (Reiljan, 2004). Elango (1998) states that positive changes may be possible such as a rapid growth of the domestic market. Withdrawals from markets can be caused after a company obtains a more in-depth knowledge about that particular market. Based on companies' acquired knowledge through internationalization processes, companies may recognize that the entry mode used could not have been the most suited to that particular market. Thus, the company can withdraw temporarily or permanently from that market (Reiljan, 2004). Other factor presented by Boddewyn (1983) is 'following the leader', i.e., to follow stakeholders such as clients or suppliers that have abandoned certain market for various reasons.
- **Poor performance or increase in costs.** Reiljan (2004) identified a third group of factors including financial considerations such as weak performance which has been recognized as an important reason for exiting a market (Pauwels & Matthyssens, 1999; Torneden & Boddewyn, 1974).

Table 1. Groups of reasons for de-internationalization

Category	Reasons for divestment of foreign operations
Lack of international experience	Insufficient pre-internationalization analysis
	No previous outward or inward internationalization
	Too rapid and/or early expansion to the foreign market
	Inadequate interpretation of market signals
	Decrease in the value of previous experience and knowledge due to the rapid changes in target market
	Choice of inappropriate target market and/or operational mode
	Misfit or product and/or insufficient adaptation to the market
	Insufficient attention to foreign markets (focusing on sporadic export)
Change in the strategy	Focusing on core markets and/or core activities
	Change of target markets due to increase in demand at home and/or insufficient growth in the target market
	New managers and/or owners with different strategic perspectives
	Constraints of manufacturing capacity, scarcity of resources and qualified personnel
	Maturing of the product in the target market
	Change of operational mode
	(De-)internationalization of related industries
	External shock (including government intervention)
Poor performance or increase in costs	Increase in production costs
	Increase in transportation costs and/or tariffs
	Increase in competition (from the home country, host country or third country)
	Poor performance

Source: Reiljan (2004)

Figure 2 presents the variables that might influence the decision to de-internationalize.

Reiljan's (2004) de-internationalization decision framework proposes several factors that contribute to a company's de-internationalization. The impact of these reasons varies according to the stage or degree of internationalization of a company.

The *reasons for internationalization* are related with the mode of entering a market, i.e., the entry mode chosen can affect the decision to de-internationalize a company. As the commitment to international operations increases, there is the possibility of a change in the mode of internationalization as the company invests more in own branches. This can change the mode of entry to a next level, e.g., from exports to a Greenfield investment. The *knowledge from external sources* includes the knowledge gathered by other actors in the market. The knowledge from external sources can concern to contacts that the company has collected through its internationalization process into a certain market. The *costs related to the de-internationalization* can represent a burden to the company's exit from the market. Companies may choose to remain in a market because of the high sunk costs of withdrawing from that market as occasionally, the costs of exit can be higher than those of entering a market. Because of the investment made and the commitment to the international operations, companies are often reluctant to divest because of the sunk costs they have already incurred. On the other hand, with the increase in the international experience, the company may be able to decrease the costs of a complete or partial exit from the market. The impact of the costs of the de-internationalization on the decision-making depends on the level of commitment and the experience of the company on foreign operations.

The remaining factors may have an impact on the timing of the de-internationalization. The *lack of foreign experience* is more important in the early stages of an internationalization process because the market research may not correspond to the real market conditions. However, during the internationalization processes, companies are simultaneously collecting data from the market. The *increase in costs and poor performance* is more likely to occur after a long period of time and the possibility that they will lead to de-internationalization is unlikely in the beginning of the international activities. In the case of MNCs with large-scale international activities, the impact of the costs on de-internationalization is moderate, as these companies use transfer prices or their bargaining power (among others) to offset the effects of higher costs – thus, the impact of the costs and performance is more significant after the middle of the internationalization process. The *change in the strategy* is more likely to happen in the final stages of internationalization as MNCs may want to restructure their international activities and focus on their core activity. These factors may influence de-internationalization because whenever companies internationalize, they may learn they were not as competitive as they wanted to be or that they do not have enough capacity to respond quickly to environmental changes. There are several ways to de-internationalize: export withdrawal, market exit, inverse internationalization, or a re-internationalization.

Export Withdrawal

Export withdrawal can be defined as the abandonment or the discontinuation of a product or market (Matthyssens & Pauwels, 2000). This type of de-internationalization can be compared with a withdrawal from the market or a complete exit from the internationalization of the company (Porter, 1976). Export withdrawal can report to the discontinuation of a product from a market or the exit of the company from that market. Pauwels & Matthyssens (1999) note that export withdrawal is more likely in SMEs

Figure 2. Framework for de-internationalization decisions
Source: Reiljan (2004)

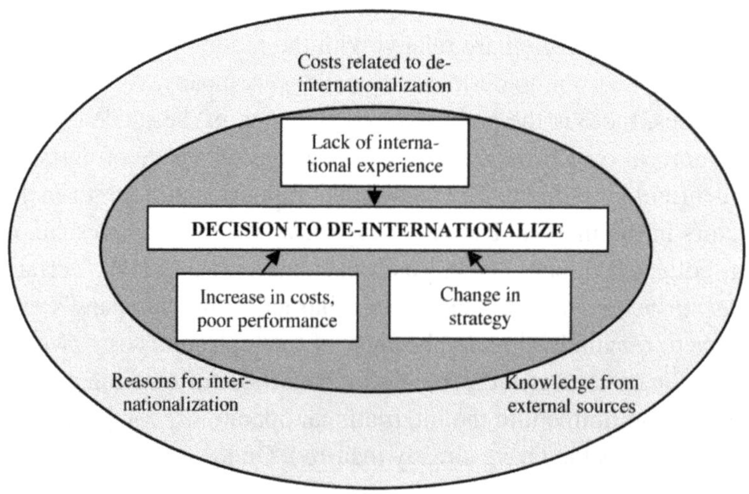

because these companies typically use exports as the main internationalization mode since they have scarce resources and exports are among the entry modes that require the fewer resources and levels of commitment from companies.

Pauwels and Matthyssens (1999) argue that exports withdrawal should not be necessarily seen as a failure because a re-evaluation of the portfolio may be necessary so that the resources can be used more effectively in other markets. Welch and Wiedersheim-Paul (1980) claim that exports are often seen as an experiment by companies. In the case of SMEs, exports can be understood as a stage in the internationalization process. According to Bonaccorsi (1992), only a few exporting companies hold a stable export activity as industrial SMEs exhibit a high export and market mobility. This phenomenon can be explained by the fact that SMEs accept orders from foreign companies for economic reasons, thus, after the first export and inherent sale, exports might be technically withdrawn since the results or the mode of entry were not as strategic as the company wanted to be.

Crick (2004) found differences in the companies that discontinued exports such as the duration of the de-internationalization, i.e., one group considered the discontinuation of short-term exports while the other group considered the discontinuation of the long-term exports. Crick (2004) classified the first group as disappointed companies and the second group as disinterested companies. Figure 3 presents Crick's typology of companies that discontinued exporting activities.

Market Exit

For Benito and Welch (1997) when companies exit international markets, they normally do it inverting the internationalization process with the aim of reducing the commitment and activities in a particular market. Exiting from a market means that the product is no longer available in the target market. According to Karakaya (2000), different actions can be taken such as the discontinuation of a product or product line, the closing of subsidiaries, or the sale of all the assets in a certain country. These actions

Figure 3. Companies participating in Crick's study
Source: Crick (2004)

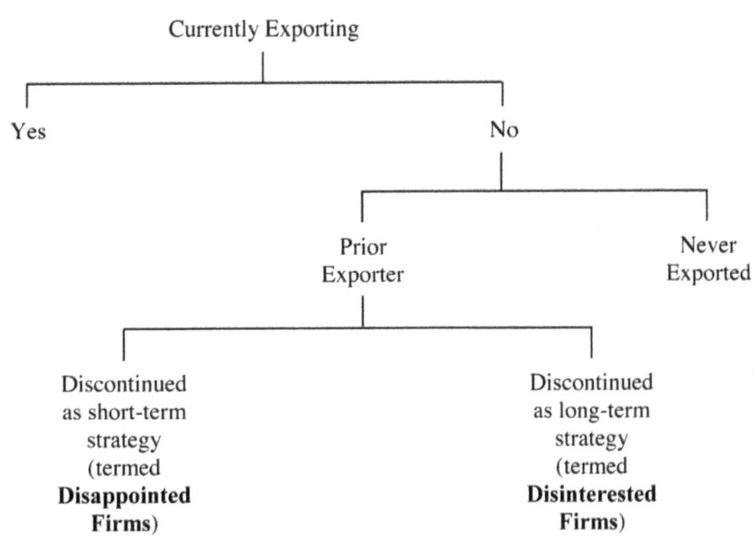

may be indicative that those products no longer generate profits for the company, that the products are going to be replaced by new models, or because of the bankruptcy of the company (Karakaya, 2000).

A market exit can be voluntary or involuntary. Voluntary exits aim to free resources which can later be invested in more attractive markets (Karakaya, 2000; Matthyssens & Pauwels, 2000). Hadjikhani (2015) argues that in extreme cases, the involuntary exit from the market may be due to a war that has started in the country where the company was internationalizing.

Reverse Internationalization

The literature on internationalization has generated models including various aspects of companies, industries and geography such as the Uppsala model, the network-based model and the born global perspective. These concepts are based on a positive/forward movement of internationalization (Gnizy & Shoham, 2014). Oppositely, reverse internationalization is described as negative/backward movement of internationalization (Gnizy & Shoham, 2014).

Gnizy and Shoham (2014) use the term reverse internationalization (RI) to describe a negative/backward change in foreign markets leading companies to decrease their involvement and exposure to international operations. According to (Gnizy & Shoham, 2014; p. 263) a "*RI is common in a world of globalization and rapid changes in which firms opt or are forced to abandon or reduce their level of involvement in foreign markets.*" The authors argue that RI is a multidimensional construct based on four dimensions: the number of foreign active markets; the width/length of the product lines; the stage of internationalization; and the pace of internationalization.

The first dimension is the *number of active foreign markets.* Some authors consider exiting from a market as a reverse internationalization (e.g., Pauwels & Matthyssens, 2004). Gnizy and Shoham (2014) interviewed international executives of international companies that mentioned that although they were in some markets, they were exiting from others in what they understood as a reverse action to that of internationalization. The second dimension is the *width/length of the product lines.* For Gnizy and Shoham (2014), withdrawing a product at different stages of its life cycle reflects a downsizing of the international portfolio of products. Benito (2005) notes that divestment can be seen from the point of view of the product life cycle. Gnizy and Shoham's (2014) study's interviewees understood a reduction in the length and width of the product line in one or more markets as a reverse internationalization. The third dimension is the *stage of the internationalization.* RI is also considered when switching to a lower degree of commitment to the internationalization mode and to a lower degree of committed resources to the internationalization of the company (Gnizy & Shoham, 2014). Benito and Welch (1997) note that the company's commitment affects the decision to have a reverse internationalization. Pauwels and Matthyssens (2004) argue that a cease in the commitment generally leads to an exit from the market. Gnizy and Shoham (2014) see a backward movement in the process of internationalization as a RI. The fourth dimension is the *pace of internationalization.* Zorzini, Stevenson, and Hendry (2011) argue that internal and external conditions influence the pace at which companies commit their resources to foreign markets. Gnizy and Shoham (2014) argue that negative changes or a stagnation in the pace of internationalization may be indicative of a market withdrawal or RI barriers.

Re-Internationalization

Luostarinen (1979) was one of the first to define re-internationalization as a withdrawal from inward and outward international operations before a subsequent international re-entry. Welch and Welch (2009; p. 568) conceptualize re-internationalization "*as a process involving a period of international business activity, then exit from international operations, followed by a time-out period of some duration, then a process of international re-entry, concluding with successfully renewed international operations.*"

Vissak (2006) notes that de-internationalization can be followed by a new internationalization processes, in other words, a re-internationalization. Vissak (2006; p. 4) states that re-internationalization can be full or partial, "*a firm might return to all the markets from which it retreated, but it can also only decide to re-enter only one or some of them. Similarly, it may decide to use the same operation modes it used before or only some of them or even use a different mode: for instance, it may have exported to a certain country before, but now it may decide to establish a production subsidiary.*" Vissak (2006) argues that a company should only re-internationalize if its business environment becomes favorable, if the company develops unique resources and capabilities, if its new managers are more oriented to internationalization, and if the company was able to create new and retain previously valuable network relationships.

Welch and Welch (2009) developed a framework on the process of re-internationalization based on the influences of Johanson & Vahlne (1977, 1990) that internationalization is guided by the relationship between market knowledge and the commitment of resources in the foreign market. According to Welch and Welch (2009), the re-internationalization is a process that initially implies an international experience, then leaving the market for a period of time where the company has no involvement in international operations, and eventually re-internationalize based on renewed international operations. Figure 4 exhibits Welch and Welch (2009) re-internationalization process, which is explained below:

- **Initial international experience.** McGrath (1999) argues that a failure may also bring benefits, allowing the company a greater facility to recognize what failed than to explain a successful outcome, i.e., it is easier to identify and modify an error in the process than to change something that worked for a certain market, but may eventually not work in a different market. When a company de-internationalizes, it gains an intangible knowledge that can use later. The acquired knowledge depends on each company, but may include knowledge about external relations, management skills and attitudes towards internationalization factors which may be considered the company's international heritage. The acquired knowledge comes from the initial internationalization of the company and its positioning in the international market. The international heritage includes the length of internationalization, the number of markets and the degree of committed resources to international operations. According to Roth (1995), companies that have a short internationalized lifetime can obtain some knowledge that can be helpful when re-internationalizing, but the level of knowledge obtained is less than that of companies with a higher level of commitment regarding the duration of the internationalization, the number of markets served, and the degree of resources committed.

- **Exit process.** Besides the international heritage, the exit process of a company may also influence the decision to re-internationalize. The decision to withdraw from the international market may occur after a decrease in international sales, but also because of an external cause to the company that forces it out of the market. The exit from an international market inevitably involve the dissolution of existing relations that the company had in that market. For SMEs, the exit process can be simpler since decision-making is often undertaken by the company's owner and its implementation is relatively quick (Rao & Naidu, 1993). In some cases, the exit can be traumatic because of the investment made by the company which may lead to its later closure. Likewise, the consequences of that failure can make companies not to consider the possibility of re-internationalization for some time.
- **International time-out stage.** Crick (2004) classified de-internationalized companies into two groups: those that discontinued their export activity based on a short-term strategy (disappointed), and those that discontinued their export activity based on a long-term strategy (disinterested), as referred before. Re-internationalization seems to be more appealing to companies that have a strong commitment to international operations. In this case, these companies were not too traumatized by the exit process and may have retained (or even extended) their international heritage, networks, employees and other resources developed during their internationalization. For companies that do not intend to re-internationalize because of their (poor) international experience, they may have to undergo major internal and external changes before considering a re-internationalization. These changes may include orders from foreign companies, a recessive domestic market and in some cases, a change of leadership that may bring to a new attitude towards internationalization. The period without international operations (i.e., away from the international markets) can be beneficial to some companies that have de-internationalized since it allows them to hire new employees, to conduct internal restructures and to reshape its network.
- **Re-entry process.** Regardless of exiting from international operations, some companies may have the desire to re-enter the international market driven by several reasons that make them look to internationalization under a new perspective. The re-entry process can be driven by internal and external triggers and the renewed interest in international opportunities may be the outcome of strategic changes. The knowledge acquired by the company in the initial process will help the company in the process of re-entry as the management team is more aware of the causes that made the initial internationalization more difficult. There can be a difference regarding the initial internationalization of the company as it now has prior knowledge on how the internationalization process works – allowing the re-entry process to be faster. During a re-entry process of a re-internationalization, the expansion process is faster because the company makes use of its larger base of knowledge (than the one it had previously).

According to figure 4, during the initial process of internationalization, the company obtains knowledge about the market – which the literature designates as international heritage. When a company de-internationalizes, the knowledge obtained thus far is changed as it may undergo a 'more or less' turbulent de-internationalization. After the company leaves the market, it goes through a period of retraction where it focuses in its domestic/original market. Dependent on the nature of the previous internationalization activities of the company and on the resources recovered, the company may have collected information about some markets it had contact with – which can be used latter. The recovered assets may later

Figure 4. Re-internationalization process
Source: Welch & Welch (2009)

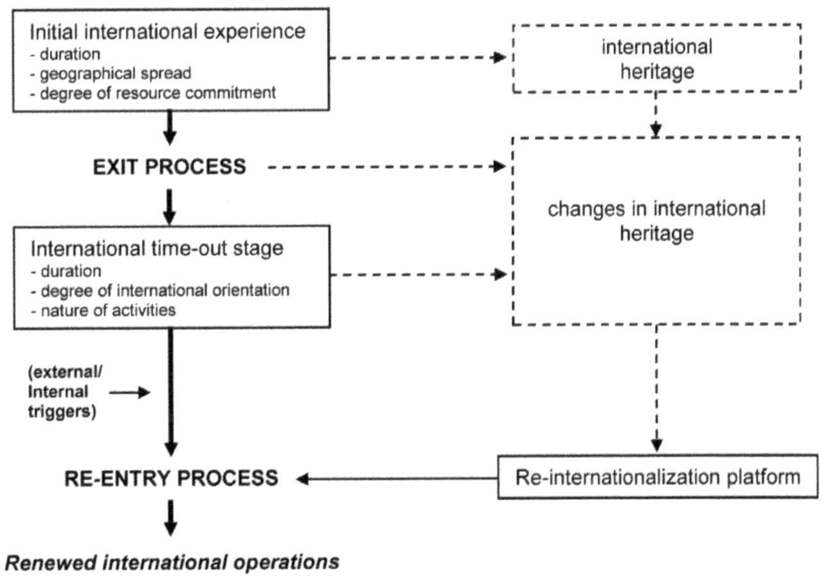

constitute an added value for the company and contribute to build a greater confidence for a stronger process of re-entry.

After the review of the literature on internationalization and de-internationalization, the following section presents the methodology used to conduct the research.

METHODOLOGY

The empirical section of this chapter focuses on a Portuguese SME that de-internationalized from Morocco. Because the objective of this study is to explore and describe a specific case related to a de-internationalization of a SME, a qualitative approach was used. The qualitative approach is more descriptive and interpretative and was considered more suited for this case since this method allowed an in-depth understanding of the phenomena, i.e., the de-internationalization process. A single case was used on the analysis. The choice of a case study was based on the possibility that the research could gain a deeper understanding of the organizational and managerial process. The use of the case study is also adequate when answering questions such as 'how' and 'why' (Yin, 1994) as is the case of this research. A theoretical sample technique was chosen because the researchers were already aware of a SME that de-internationalized its activities abroad and after contacting its responsible, he showed openness to participate in the research. In addition, the featured firm met the following criteria:

- It was an SME;
- It held international operations;
- It has de-internationalized;
- It was in Portugal and thus, accessible to the researchers.

The primary data used in the analysis was semi-structured interviews to the company's owner. The analysis of the company's brochures and reports allowed the researchers to triangulate the data and to deepen the analysis.

THE CASE STUDY

The objective of this chapter is to contribute to increase the knowledge about the topic of the de-internationalization of SMEs. Because de-internationalization is a highly sensitive and confidential topic often seen with dislike by managers, the anonymity of the company was preserved, therefore and henceforth we will call the featured company TANGO.

TANGO was founded in 1989 by two partners. However, the history of the company began years before when one of the partners created a single member company. Later, it joined a partnership creating a new company in 1982. In these early stages, the company focused on marketing and technical assistance of sewing machines. In 1986, the two partners acquired another company (alongside with its portfolio of customers) expanding its operations beyond sewing machines to machinery and components for the footwear industry. In 1989, because of the company's need to operate in multiple industries, the previous company was shut-down and a new one was created with a different designation but maintaining its existing structure. TANGO began its activity with the production of computer numerical control (CNC) machines and the commercialization of CNC equipment, particularly for the footwear industry.

TANGO's portfolio of activities includes marketing services, the commercialization of CNC machines and the development of complete industrial solutions, i.e., from the creation of the layouts to the installation of the production lines. Table 2 presents an overview of TANGO's key information.

According to its owner, among the objectives of TANGO are:

- Anticipating and satisfying its customer needs through an innovation-based policy;
- Maintaining a high-quality product standard;
- Developing and building long-lasting partnership relationships;
- Adapting to the demands of globalization.

TANGO's internationalization process began in 2004 when the company chose to internationalize to Morocco. The main reason to internationalize to the Moroccan market was the evolution and flow of the footwear industry from Northern European countries (England, Netherlands, Italy, Spain and Portugal) to southern European countries and particularly to North African countries (Morocco, Algeria

Table 2. TANGO's general information

Year of foundation	1989
Core industry	Footwear
Core business	Commercialization and development of CNC machines for the textile and footwear industries
Size (employees)	97
Main product	CNC machines
Market position	Leader on the domestic market of CNC machines

and Tunisia) because of the availability of cheaper hand labor factors. TANGO saw in the Moroccan market an opportunity to make business because Chinese companies were also entering this market at the time. Nonetheless, and to differentiate from its competitors, TANGO sought to introduce higher quality products than those offered by competition in those markets. Besides the search for new markets to sell its products, other of the reasons for TANGO's internationalization to Morocco was its proximity to the Portuguese market. Finally, the Moroccan market was also considered attractive for TANGO because the Portuguese domestic market was becoming saturated.

In the early stage of its internationalization process, TANGO established a strategic alliance with a Moroccan entrepreneur who knew the local market and held activities in the manufacturing of footwear components. The entry mode chosen was the establishment of a subsidiary to supply CNCs to the Moroccan market. TANGO was responsible for the know-how and the production of the CNC machines whereas its Moroccan partner was responsible for the bureaucratic, legal and market issues. Later, a third Portuguese partner joined this strategic alliance. We will BETA call this strategic alliance between these three parties. BETA focused on a higher product quality and avoided competing with Chinese companies which were competing with low prices achieved due to economies of scale.

BETA went through difficulties in its internationalization process initially because of cultural asymmetries between Portugal and Morocco. BETA experienced difficulties in the management of human resources, namely regarding the recruitment or personnel and the levels of absenteeism. Regardless the support provided by its Moroccan partner, TANGO/BETA's manager soon realized: "*that they entered a new world without having made a thorough study on the difficulties they would encounter*" (TANGO's manager).

BETA's difficulties increased when its Moroccan partner went into bankruptcy. This situation bought about administrative issues to BETA since its 'daily life' activities required the signature and agreements between the three parties involved in the strategic alliance. The existing cultural differences between the three parties were further aggravated by this issue. Later that year and shortly after the Moroccan partner entering into bankruptcy, the Portuguese partner also went into bankruptcy and TANGO was left alone with a subsidiary that was not able to manage administratively.

BETA 'ceased' operations in 2013 with heavy losses for TANGO. Even though BETA does not hold any commercial or administrative activity, the company is still active in the Moroccan market because it was not able to present a requirement signed by the former three partners to formalize its closure. Despite all these setbacks, TANGO remained committed to international operations and in 2013 successfully created a wholly owned company to export components for the Moroccan market and footwear industry. Figure 5 presents the timeline of TANGO's main events.

ANALYSIS AND DISCUSSION

One of the reasons for TANGO's internationalization was the search for new markets because of the saturation of its domestic market. Among the various modes of internationalization, TANGO chose to enter the Moroccan market through a strategic alliance and a Greenfield investment.

The internationalization process of TANGO does not fully fit the Uppsala theory of internationalization. Accordingly, TANGO internationalized to a geographically close country but a culturally distant one but more importantly, TANGO's internationalization process began with a high degree of commitment to international operations as is the establishment of a subsidiary abroad (without any previous

Figure 5. TANGO's timeline and main events

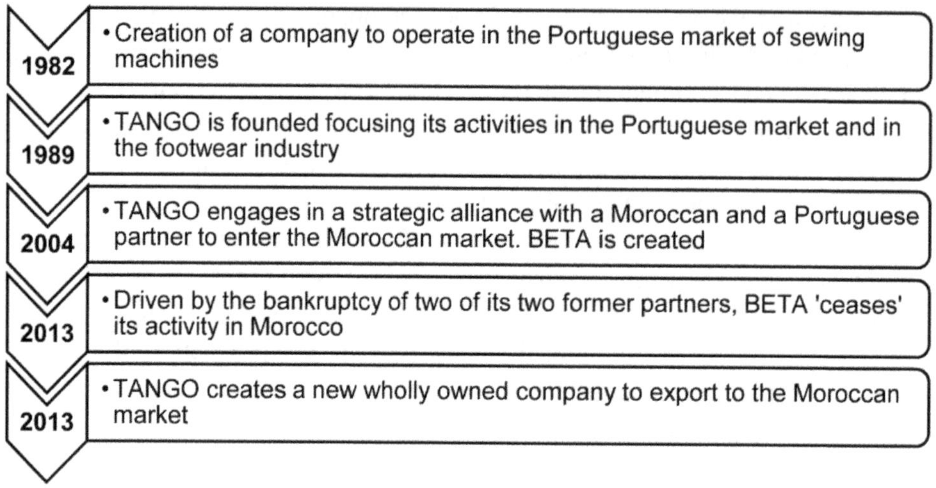

international experience). However, based on the network theory, TANGO could have made use of its network and existing relationships to engage in a strategic alliance with its foreign partner.

The lack of experience of TANGO in international market and the company's entry mode conditioned its international path. According to Turcan (2011), one can assume that TANGO partially de-internationalized because it changed its internationalization mode from a Greenfield investment to exports, i.e., TANGO decreased its level of commitment to the Moroccan market but did not fully abandoned it.

While Benito and Welch (1997) argue that a partial de-internationalization is more likely in the beginning and latter stages of an internationalization process, TANGO's internationalization process did not follow the traditional pattern of a gradual increase of commitment to international operations. Instead, in the case of TANGO, both its lack of experience and entry mode were important reasons for its de-internationalization. This case highlights the complexity of de-internationalization and the need to examine partial and full de-internationalization as the outcome of the interplay between entry mode and international experience, rather than based on the international experience exclusively.

It can be assumed that the de-internationalization process of TANGO was caused by the lack of international experience of the company, as it failed to carefully assess the target market and underestimated the need of an in-depth analysis of that market but also, because of the entry mode chosen, which was not the most suited one as seen.

Welch & Welch (2009; p. 568) note that re-internationalization "*considers companies that have withdrawn from international operations but maintain domestic business activity before re-engaging in international market activity*". The featured case differs from the existing theory on re-internationalization. TANGO's re-internationalization process does not include the 'exit process' nor the 're-entry process' stages as proposed by Welch & Welch (2009) since TANGO has not effectively left the Moroccan market from a legal standpoint. TANGO's activities in the Moroccan market were based on a strategic alliance between three parties and a subsidiary called BETA. BETA's activities began to decline because of exogenous factors to TANGO such as the bankruptcy of two of its strategic alliance partners. Nonetheless, during the turbulent period undergone by BETA, TANGO remained committed to the Moroccan market to the point that it created a new wholly owned company to export to this market. The results however support Welch and Welch (2009) claim that a re-internationalization is a process that implies a previous international experience and that the knowledge gathered through a failed international experience is an important factor that determines the chances of success of a re-internationalization. Accordingly, during the re-internationalization, TANGO's managerial team was aware of the causes that went wrong in the initial internationalization and changed its *modus operandi*.

Crick (2004) presented two categories of companies that have withdrawn export activities: disappointed and disinterested. The first seek to re-internationalize in the short term whereas the later in the long term. In the case of TANGO, the company remained legally international for the whole period, however, its international activity decreased as the company sought for a new strategy to re-internationalize. TANGO initially engaged in a strategic alliance and a Greenfield investment but because of issues with its partners and acquired market knowledge, decreased the level of commitment of its international operations and changed from FDI to exports.

The case of TANGO highlights the importance of selecting the adequate mode of entry, the need to properly know the target market before internationalizing and the need for assistance and support when engaging in foreign operation. It also underlines the legal difficulties in de-internationalization as due to disagreements between its former strategic alliance partners, TANGO was not able to legally close its foreign subsidiary. While Crick (2004) conceptualizes export withdrawing companies as disappointed or disinterested companies, in the featured case, TANGO entered the market through a strategic alliance and a Greenfield investment, remaining committed to internationalization for the whole period and re-internationalized using a lower level of commitment to foreign operations.

One can argue, according to Reiljan (2004), that TANGO did not go through the pre-internalization process and internationalized as soon as an opportunity emerged. This internationalization was based on the market knowledge of the Moroccan partner, which led to the involvement of a third partner. This insufficient pre-internationalization analysis was complemented by a large cultural difference between Portugal and Morocco.

According to the information gathered on the interviews, there were no problems in terms of costs or scarcity of resources, so that operations in Morocco, despite the cultural differences, were running smoothly. The market target/segment was not a problem either. However, the mode of entry was a heavy burden to TANGO as, according to was referred in the interviews, the cost of entry became real burden as soon as the other two partners were bankrupt, as TANGO realized there were two options at the table: to withdraw and leave the Moroccan market behind or to stay and try to internalize marketing and operational knowledge and keep in touch with the Moroccan market. Closing down BETA's activities would mean a total withdrawal and closure of all operations in Morocco. Moreover, it would mean losing future sales to Morocco and refocusing all activities in the Portuguese market that was shrinking. It could also mean a negative/traumatic experience that could jeopardize internationalization processes. Staying in Morocco would mean difficult times ahead but not all the investment would be wasted as BETA could still save the Moroccan market and would not need to invest in expanding relational marketing activities and to invest again in tearing entry barriers.

Although TANGO cannot be considered a disappointed firm or a disinterested firm, as it never withdrew from the Moroccan market, TANGO'S owner argued in the interview that with the experience he went through, it would have been much more adequate to have used exports as entry mode than Greenfield investment that lead to the partnership. However, he also claimed that had TANGO used exports to the Moroccan market to maintain internationalization costs low, TANGO'S experience would not be as broad and rich as it was culturally and business wise.

It is important to mention that one of the main challenges in the internalization process is the high expectation of most managers. Although one can claim that TANGO'S owner was certainly driven when embracing internalization through an alliance process, being overly dependent on their partners is a huge risk, which was the case of TANGO. Moreover, as soon as the Moroccan partner went bankrupt, TANGO realized that its entry in the Moroccan market was a gamble as TANGO needed to assure all activities in which it lacked most of the core competences. A more rational decision, and a less risky one, would have been to have opted for a safer entry mode as export is, which is what the Uppsala model prescribes and is usually expected by SMEs.

CONCLUSION

This chapter addresses the topic of the de-internationalization process of a Portuguese SME. In the theoretical background, internationalization was found to be driven by the search of market, resources, efficiency and strategic resources. The entry mode was also found to have an impact on the process of de-internationalization.

This chapter highlights the reasons for an SME's internationalization such as the search for new markets for its products, the proximity to the target market and the saturation of its domestic market. The case also highlights the main challenges of internationalization, particularly for SMEs, such as the difficulties leading with cultural asymmetries, the importance of choosing the adequate mode of entry and the need to know the target market.

In the case of TANGO, while the strategic alliance was initially beneficial as one of the partners had knowledge of the target market and contributed to solve bureaucratic issues, its bankruptcy and existing cultural issues increased the difficulties of running a subsidiary abroad. It should be emphasized how TANGO's manager realized too late that the company was not prepared to internationalize with that degree of commitment such as a Greenfield investment. The findings also highlight existing challenges when de-internationalizing such as legal issues, which did not allowed TANGO to formerly shut down its foreign subsidiary.

The findings of this chapter underline the challenges of internationalizing to developing and culturally distant countries and the need to increase the knowledge on the drivers of de-internationalization, particularly on SMEs as they often have few resources than large companies.

LIMITATIONS AND FUTURE RESEARCH DIRECTIONS

One of the limitations of this research stems from its qualitative nature. The findings are based on a single case study, nonetheless, this approach also allowed the discussion of the intricacies of a real case of a de-internationalization. Future studies could focus on the various challenges of de-internationalizing from developed and developing countries, as well as the decision-making of the re-entry process such as: which markets de-internationalized companies choose to re-enter afterwards and whether they choose a higher or lower level of commitment to international operations compared to their previous internationalization experience.

REFERENCES

Ahokangas, P. (1998). *Internationalisation and resources: an analysis of processes in Nordic SMEs.* Academic Press.

Aliouche, E. H., & Schlentrich, U. (2011). A model of optimal international market expansion: The case of US hotel chains expansion into China. In M. Tuunanen, J. Windsperger, G. Cliquet, & G. Hendrikse (Eds.), *New Developments in the Theory of Networks. Franchising, Alliances and Cooperatives* (pp. 135–154). Heidelberg, Germany: Physica. doi:10.1007/978-3-7908-2615-9_9

Bauer, M. W., & Gaskell, G. (2000). *Qualitative researching with text, image and sound: a practical handbook.* London: Sage publications. doi:10.4135/9781849209731

Benito, G. R. G. (2005). Divestment and international business strategy. *Journal of Economic Geography, 5*(2), 235–251. doi:10.1093/jnlecg/lbh041

Benito, G. R. G., & Welch, L. (1997). De-internationalization. *Management International Review, 37*, 7–25.

Boddewyn, J. J. (1979). Foreign divestment: Magnitude and factors. *Journal of International Business Studies, 10*(1), 21–27. doi:10.1057/palgrave.jibs.8490786

Boddewyn, J. J. (1983). Foreign direct divestment theory: Is it the reverse of FDI theory? *Weltwirtschaftliches Archiv, 119*(2), 345–355. doi:10.1007/BF02706431

Bonaccorsi, A. (1992). On the relationship between firm size and export intensity. *Journal of International Business Studies, 23*(4), 605–635. doi:10.1057/palgrave.jibs.8490280

Cassell, C., & Symon, G. (2004). *Essential guide to qualitative methods in organizational research.* London: Sage Publications Inc. doi:10.4135/9781446280119

Crick, D. (2004). U.K. SMEs' decision to discontinue exporting: An exploratory investigation into practices within the clothing industry. *Journal of Business Venturing, 19*(4), 561–587. doi:10.1016/S0883-9026(03)00032-6

Denscombe, M. (2010). *The Good Research Guide: For Small-Scale Social Research Projects: For small-scale social research projects.* Leicester, UK: McGraw-Hill.

Dunning, J. H. (1988). The eclectic paradigm of international production: A restatement and some possible extensions. *Journal of International Business Studies, 19*(1), 1–31. doi:10.1057/palgrave.jibs.8490372

Dunning, J. H. (1993). *The Globalization of Business.* London: Routledge.

Dunning, J. H. (2000). The eclectic paradigm as an envelope for economic and business theories of MNE activity. *International Business Review, 9*(2), 163–190. doi:10.1016/S0969-5931(99)00035-9

Elango, B. (1998). An empirical examination of the influence of industry and firm drivers on the rate of internationalization by firms. *Journal of International Management, 4*(3), 201–221. doi:10.1016/S1075-4253(98)00011-8

Etemad, H. (2004). Internationalisation of small and medium-sized enterprises: A grounded theoretical framework and an overview. *Canadian Journal of Administrative Sciences*, *21*(1), 1–21. doi:10.1111/j.1936-4490.2004.tb00319.x

EUR-Lex. (2003). *Definition of micro, small and medium-sized enterprises*. Retrieved from https://eur-lex.europa.eu/eli/reco/2003/361/oj

European Commission. (2003). *Observatory of European SMEs 2003*. Luxembourg: Author.

Eurostat. (2018). *Statistics on small and medium-sized enterprises*. Retrieved November 27, 2018, from https://ec.europa.eu/eurostat/statistics-explained/index.php/Statistics_on_small_and_medium-sized_enterprises

Fisher, C. M. (2010). *Researching and writing a dissertation: an essential guide for business students*. Harlow, UK: Pearson Education.

Freeman, S., Deligonul, S., & Cavusgil, T. (2013). Strategic re-structuring by born-globals using outward and inward-oriented activity. *International Marketing Review*, *30*(2), 156–182. doi:10.1108/02651331311314574

Gnizy, I., & Shoham, A. (2014). Explicating the Reverse Internationalization Processes of Firms. *Journal of Global Marketing*, *27*(4), 262–283. doi:10.1080/08911762.2014.917755

Griffith, D. A., Cavusgil, S. T., & Xu, S. (2008). Emerging themes in international business research. *Journal of International Business Studies*, *39*(7), 1220–1235. doi:10.1057/palgrave.jibs.8400412

Hadjikhani, A. (2015). A Note on the Criticisms Against the Internationalization Process Model. In *Knowledge, Networks and Power* (pp. 64–87). London: Palgrave Macmillan. doi:10.1057/9781137508829_3

Hessels, J., & Parker, S. C. (2013). Constraints, internationalisation and growth: A cross-country analysis of European SMEs. *Journal of World Business*, *48*(1), 137–148. doi:10.1016/j.jwb.2012.06.014

Hill, C. W. L. (2007). *International Business: Competing in the global marketplace* (6th ed.). New York, NY: McGraw-Hill/Irwin.

Johanson, J., & Mattsson, L. (1988). Internationalization in industrial systems — a network approach. In P. J. Buckley & P. N. Ghauri (Eds.), *The internationalization of the firm: a reader* (pp. 303–321). London: Academic Press.

Johanson, J., & Vahlne, J.-E. (1977). The Internationalization Process of the Firm—A model of knowledge development and increasing foreign market commitments. *Journal of International Business Studies*, *8*(1), 23–32. doi:10.1057/palgrave.jibs.8490676

Johanson, J., & Vahlne, J.-E. (1990). The mechanism of internationalisation. *International Marketing Review*, *7*(4). doi:10.1108/02651339010137414

Johanson, J., & Wiedersheim-Paul, F. (1975). The internationalization of the firm—Four swedish cases. *Journal of Management Studies*, *12*(3), 305–323. doi:10.1111/j.1467-6486.1975.tb00514.x

Karakaya, F. (2000). Market exit and barriers to exit: Theory and practice. *Psychology and Marketing*, *17*(8), 651–668. doi:10.1002/1520-6793(200008)17:8<651::AID-MAR1>3.0.CO;2-K

Keupp, M., & Gassmann, O. (2009). The past and the future of international entrepreneurship: A review and suggestions for developing the field. *Journal of Management*, *35*(3), 600–633. doi:10.1177/0149206308330558

Kogut, B., & Chang, S. J. (1996). Platform investments and volatile exchange rates: Direct investment in the US by Japanese electronic companies. *The Review of Economics and Statistics*, *78*(2), 221–231. doi:10.2307/2109924

Kontinen, T., & Ojala, A. (2010). The internationalisation of family businesses: A review of extant research. *Journal of Family Business Strategy*, *1*(2), 97–107. doi:10.1016/j.jfbs.2010.04.001

Kotabe, M., & Ketkar, S. (2009). Exit Strategies. In M. Kotabe & K. Helsen (Eds.), *The Sage Handbook of International Marketing*. London: Sage Publications.

Kuivalainen, O., Sundqvist, S., Saarenketo, S., & McNaughton, R. (2012). Internationalisation patterns of small and medium-sized enterprises. *International Marketing Review*, *29*(5), 448–465. doi:10.1108/02651331211260331

Lee, H., Kelley, D., Lee, J., & Lee, S. (2012). SME Survival: The impact of internationalization, technology resources and alliances. *Journal of Small Business Management*, *50*(1), 1–19. doi:10.1111/j.1540-627X.2011.00341.x

Luostarinen, R. (1979). *Internationalization of the firm: an empirical study of the internationalization of firms with small and open domestic markets with special emphasis on lateral rigidity as a behavioral characteristic in strategic decision-making* (Vol. 30). Academic Press.

Matthyssens, P., & Pauwels, P. (2000). Uncovering international market-exit processes: A comparative case study. *Psychology and Marketing*, *17*(8), 697–719. doi:10.1002/1520-6793(200008)17:8<697::AID-MAR3>3.0.CO;2-T

McGrath, R. G. (1999). Falling forward: Real options reasoning and entrepreneurial failure. *Academy of Management Review*, *24*(1), 13–30. doi:10.5465/amr.1999.1580438

Mellahi, K. (2003). The de-internationalization process: A case study of Marks and Spencer. In C. Wheeler, F. McDonald, & I. Greaves (Eds) Internationalization (pp. 150–162). The Academy of International Business. doi:10.1057/9780230514638_10

Merriam, S. B. (1998). *Qualitative research and case study applications in education. Revised and expanded from: Case study research in education*. San Francisco, CA: Jossey-Bass Publishers.

OECD. (2009). *Top Barriers and Drivers to SME Internationalisation*. Retrieved from http://strathprints.strath.ac.uk/15845/

OECD. (2017). *Meeting of the OECD Council at Ministerial Level*. Retrieved from https://www.oecd.org/mcm/documents/C-MIN-2017-8-EN.pdf

Onkelinx, J., & Sleuwaegen, L. (2008). *Internationalisation of SMEs*. Leuven, Belgium: Flanders DC Studies.

Pauwels, P., & Matthyssens, P. (1999). A strategy process perspective on export withdrawal. *Journal of International Marketing*, *7*(3), 10–37. doi:10.1177/1069031X9900700304

Pauwels, P., & Matthyssens, P. (2004). Strategic flexibility in export expansion: Growing through withdrawal. *International Marketing Review*, *21*(4/5), 496–510. doi:10.1108/02651330410547162

Pla-Barber, J., & León-Darder, F. (2004). La internacionalización de la industria hotelera española. Formas de entrada y factores determinantes. *Papeles de Economía Española*, *102*(102), 193–206.

Porter, M. E. (1976). Please Note Location of Nearest Exit: Exit Barriers and Planning. *California Management Review*, *19*(Winter), 21–33. doi:10.2307/41164693

Rao, T. R., & Naidu, G. M. (1993). Are the stages of internationalization empirically supportable? *Journal of Global Marketing*, *6*(1–2), 147–170. doi:10.1300/J042v06n01_08

Reiljan, E. (2004). *Reasons for de-internationalization: an analysis of Estonian manufacturing companies*. Universitas Tartuensis.

Ribau, C., Moreira, A. C., & Raposo, M. (2015). Internationalisation of the firm theories: A schematic synthesis. *International Journal of Business and Globalisation*, *15*(4), 528–554. doi:10.1504/IJBG.2015.072535

Ribau, C. P., Moreira, A. C., & Raposo, M. (2018a). Categorising the internationalisation of SMEs with social network analysis. *International Journal of Entrepreneurship and Small Business*, *35*(1), 57–80. doi:10.1504/IJESB.2018.094264

Ribau, C. P., Moreira, A. C., & Raposo, M. (2018b). SME internationalization research: Mapping the state of the art. *Canadian Journal of Administrative Sciences*, *35*(2), 280–303. doi:10.1002/cjas.1419

Rodríguez, A. (2002). Determining factors in entry choice for international expansion. The case of the Spanish hotel industry. *Tourism Management*, *23*(6), 597–607. doi:10.1016/S0261-5177(02)00024-9

Roth, K. (1995). Managing international interdependence: CEO characteristics in a resource-based framework. *Academy of Management Journal*, *38*(1), 200–231.

Rothaermel, F. T., Kotha, S., & Steensma, H. K. (2006). International market entry by U.S. internet firms: An empirical analysis of country risk, national culture, and market size. *Journal of Management*, *32*(1), 56–82. doi:10.1177/0149206305277793

Schutt, R. K. (2014). *Investigating the social world: The process and practice of research*. London: Sage Publications.

Silva, P., & Moreira, A. (2019). The evolution of corporate divestment: Towards a new research paradigm? In C. Dogru (Ed.), *Handbook of Research on Contemporary Approaches in Management and Organizational Strategy* (pp. 292–316). Hershey, PA: IGI Global.

Simões, V. C. (1997). *Estratégias de internacionalização das empresas portuguesas (ICEP–Inves)*. Lisboa: ICEP.

Sousa, C., & Tan, Q. (2015). Exit from a Foreign Market: Do poor performance, strategic fit, cultural distance, and international experience matter? *Journal of International Marketing, 23*(4), 84–104. doi:10.1509/jim.15.0003

Torneden, R. L., & Boddewyn, J. J. (1974). Foreign divestment: Too many mistakes. *The Columbia Journal of World Business.*

Turcan, R. (2003). De-internationalization and the small firm. In *Internationalization* (pp. 208–222). London: Palgrave Macmillan. doi:10.1057/9780230514638_13

Turcan, R. (2011). De-internationalization: A conceptualization. AIB-UK & Ireland Chapter Conference "International Business: New Challenges, New Forms, New Practices."

Turcan, R. (2013). The Philosophy of Turning Points: A Case of De-Internationalization. In T. M. Devinney, T. Pedersen, & L. Tihanyi (Eds.), Philosophy of Science and Meta-Knowledge in International Business and Management (pp. 219–235). Emerald Group Publishing Limited. doi:10.1108/S1571-5027(2013)0000026014

Vissak, T. (2006). *Re-internationalization: A conceptual framework and some evidence from Estonia.* Retrieved from https://www.impgroup.org/uploads/papers/5805.pdf

Welch, C., & Welch, L. (2009). Re-internationalisation: Exploration and conceptualisation. *International Business Review, 18*(6), 567–577. doi:10.1016/j.ibusrev.2009.07.003

Welch, L., & Luostarinen, R. (1988). Internationalization: Evolution of a concept. *Journal of General Management, 14*(2), 34–55. doi:10.1177/030630708801400203

Welch, L., & Wiedersheim-Paul, F. (1980). Initial exports–a marketing failure? *Journal of Management Studies, 17*(3), 333–344. doi:10.1111/j.1467-6486.1980.tb00407.x

Yin, R. (1994). *Case study research: Design and methods* (2nd ed.). Newbury Park, CA: Sage.

Yoshino, M., & Rangan, S. (1995). *Strategic Alliances: An Entrepreneurial Approach to Globalization.* Boston, MA: Harvard Business School Press.

Young, S., Hamill, J., Wheeler, C., & Davis, J. R. (1989). *International market entry and development: Strategies and management.* Englewood Cliffs, NJ: Prentice-Hall.

Zeng, S. X., Xie, X. M., & Tam, C. M. (2010). Relationship between cooperation networks and innovation performance of SMEs. *Technovation, 30*(3), 181–194. doi:10.1016/j.technovation.2009.08.003

Zorzini, M., Stevenson, M., & Hendry, L. (2011). *A contingency-based approach to internationalization: a multi-case study analysis in Argentina.* LUMS Working Papers.

ADDITIONAL READING

Bernini, M., Du, J., & Love, J. H. (2016). Explaining intermittent exporting: Exit and conditional re-entry in export markets. *Journal of International Business Studies, 47*(9), 1058–1076. doi:10.105741267-016-0015-2

Dominguez, N., & Mayrhofer, U. (2017). Internationalization stages of traditional SMEs: Increasing, decreasing and re-increasing commitment to foreign markets. *International Business Review, 26*(6), 1051–1063. doi:10.1016/j.ibusrev.2017.03.010

Fletcher, R. (2001). A holistic approach to internationalisation. *International Business Review, 10*(1), 25–49. doi:10.1016/S0969-5931(00)00039-1

Onkelinx, J., Manolova, T. S., & Edelman, L. F. (2016). The Consequences of de-internationalization: empirical evidence from Belgium. In *In Global Entrepreneurship: Past, Present & Future* (pp. 45–66). Emerald Group Publishing Limited. doi:10.1108/S1571-502720160000029006

Trąpczyński, P. (2016). De-internationalisation: A review of empirical studies and implications for international business research. *Baltic Journal of Management, 11*(4), 350–379. doi:10.1108/BJM-08-2015-0153

Turner, C., & Gardiner, P. D. (2007). De-internationalisation and global strategy: The case of British Telecommunications (BT). *Journal of Business and Industrial Marketing, 22*(7), 489–497. doi:10.1108/08858620710828863

KEY TERMS AND DEFINITIONS

Commitment: The effort and time invested in order to continue in a certain relationship.

De-Commitment: A decrease or a movement backwards regarding the existing level of commitment.

Divestment: The partial or complete disposal of a company's resources such as a whole company, a segment of business, a division, a subsidiary, a unit, or a tangible asset like machines, or intangible such as marketing activities.

International Business: All the activities such as the trade of goods, services, technology, capital, skills, and knowledge between two countries.

Internationalization: A strategy where a company performs business activities outside its country of origin.

Market Entry Mode: Strategy chosen to enter a foreign market involving a higher or a lower risk and commitment of a company's resources.

Market Exit: The strategic decision to abandon a certain country or market because of financial losses, a decrease in the profitability or a change in the business strategy.

Strategic Alliance: An agreement between at least two parties which usually have complementary resources or skills and share a common goal while remaining independent companies.

ENDNOTE

1 The category of SME is made up of enterprises which employ fewer than 250 persons and which have an annual turnover not exceeding EUR 50 million, and/or an annual balance sheet total not exceeding EUR 43 million (EUR-Lex, 2003).

Chapter 8
Causes of De-Internationalization:
Evidence of Six Cases

Raquel Meneses
University of Porto, Portugal

Helder Pinho
University of Porto, Portugal

ABSTRACT

Until a few years ago, internationalization was seen as a self-feeding process, resulting from decisions based on accumulated knowledge. De-internationalization is not an option. However, the reality shows us that enterprises have done international divestment. To this date, the research on de-internationalization remains somehow scarce and needs additional research. The authors want to understand the causes of de-internationalization. They use the grounded theory methodology, studying six Portuguese cases that already have a process of de-internationalization. Five firms cooperate with, presenting six cases. The authors distinguish causes that occur before/after the internationalization process begin and causes related to firm or external to firm. One of the main causes of de-internationalization is the incorrect internationalization process. The Misfit Micro-Location (the wrong choice of place inside a determined country) is a very important cause, which means that, after choosing the country, it is necessary to choose the best place to be located.

INTRODUCTION

Existing literature recognises that internationalisation leads to more internationalisation, due to the accumulation of experience, increased connections and networks and stronger commitment to foreign firms. Therefore, the internationalisation of firms is presented as a self-feeding process, in order to begin the process, the only solution is internationalisation, as a means of growth.

DOI: 10.4018/978-1-5225-8906-8.ch008

In practice, we see many cases of Portuguese firms with international divestment, for example, Sonae and Jerónimo Martins in Brazil and Parfois in Spain, amongst other cases. Portugal is not an exception, according to Padmanabhan (1993) divestiture has increased dramatically since the early eighties (Padmanabhan, 1993). This evidence questions the existing literature, as these firms leave foreign markets and do not display progressive growth as expected. However, "despite compelling empirical evidence of de-internationalisation, academic research lags behind" (Turcan, 2017, p. 1), even knowing that almost half of foreign direct investment is divested (Wan, Chen, & Yiu, 2015). Overwhelming evidence of this gap between literature and reality has led to the development of this study.

LITERATURE REVIEW

Research on the internationalisation of companies intensified with the rapid growth of international trade and foreign direct investment in the 1960s. Since this time, a large number of researchers have analysed factors which have had an impact on the internationalisation process, the influence of internationalisation on the company and the home economy, threats and opportunities of internationalisation, and several other problems related to the international activities of the company. Until a few years ago, all approaches viewed internationalisation as a self-feeding process. The Stage Model was the dominating approach towards explaining internationalisation. This model is based on organising learning processes (Johanson & Vahlne, 1977). Firms tend to begin international investment in countries with a short psychic distance to the home country. This similarity with the home country reduces the risk of the internationalisation process, because the company has experience of operating in a similar reality. With the accumulation of experience in these markets, firms tend to invest in the farthest countries, making small steps for a safe internationalisation process.

The evolution of international trade brings with it other theories such as the Network Approach, the International Entrepreneurship Perspective and the Born Global Firms. The Network Approach supports the principle that business networks play a fundamental role in the internationalisation process. Business networks are defined as an interconnected set of trade relationships with other actors in business, suppliers and customers, affecting new internationalisation processes (Johanson & Mattson, 1988; Johanson & Vahlne, 2003). These business networks influence how initial market entry is selected, its mode and any development on an international level.

Firms are not faceless, and it is important to emphasise the role of the entrepreneur, since opportunities are recognised as a result of entrepreneurial alertness and ability to adapt to surprises. The International Entrepreneurship Approach places more importance on the role of entrepreneurs than on other variables such as the firm's size and age. Additionally, Schweizer, Vahlne and Johanson (2010) reinforce the role of entrepreneurs adding a more holistic view to Johanson and Vahlne's model (2009), the studies on entrepreneurship and opportunity identification and development (Ardichvili, Cardozo, & Soray, 2003), studies on effectuation by Sarasvathy (2001) and the literature on dynamic capabilities (Sapienza, Autio, George, & Zahra, 2006).

Another theory explaining the internationalisation process is the Born Global Firms, also designed as International New Ventures. This perspective was supported by Rennie (1993) and developed by Oviatt and McDougall (1994), Chetty and Campbelt-Hunt (2004). The Born Global Firms are companies that internationalised within two years from inception and whose home market represents less than 25%. In this case, the growth of internationalisation is rapid, although it is gradual in the Uppsala Model.

For this precocious internationalisation, it is necessary for someone to have international experience. In this model the founder has extensive experience in relevant markets, usually acquired in other companies. The internationalisation process takes place more rapidly because of the advanced internationalisation knowledge obtained in multiple markets in which the company internationalises.

None of these models has the option of leaving these markets or de-internationalisation, so success in all of the markets that the firms enter is assumed.

The idea that a continuous internationalisation process is not inevitable was first introduced by Welch and Luostarien (1988). De-internationalisation is "any voluntary or forced action that reduces a company's engagement in or exposure to current cross border activities" (Benito & Welch, 1997, p. 9), and it does not consider relocation to its home country or in/out-sourcing. De-internationalisation is not about reshoring or backshoring. Turcan (2013, p. 221) notes that this is an understudied phenomenon, since de-internationalisation "appears to be one of those areas that, while important, is either not convenient, or is perhaps undesirable, to research", maybe because it is human nature not to broach failures. However, it is important to note that de-internationalisation is not synonymous with failure (Vissak & Francioni, 2013; Trąpczyński, 2016; da Silva & Moreira, 2019), and concept de-internationalisation as the reverse of internationalization is a misconception (Trąpczyński, 2016) since it could be strategic-driven, pursuing non-previous existing opportunities (da Silva & Moreira, 2019). To Wan et al (2015, p. 207), "international divestment is, and should be, treated as a vital part of the internationalisation process", creating new important knowledge to a potential re-entry (Surdu, Mellahi, Glaister, & Nardella, 2018; Surdu, Mellahi, & Glaister, 2018; Gong, Zhang, & Xia, 2017).

Mellahi (2003) and Benito (1997) distinguish between deliberate (voluntary) or forced divestment (involuntary, e.g nationalizations, expatriations, confiscations ...). Nevertheless, the process of de-internationalisation is always a very painful process. As Onkelinx, Manolova and Edelman (2016) note, exports can be more easily reversed, while other ways of entry often imply sunk costs, resulting in the reverse process being harder.

Welch and Welch (2009) present the phenomenon of re-internationalisation. Re-internationalisation can be defined as withdrawal from inward and outward international operations by a company before subsequent international re-entry. Basically, the 'act' of re-internationalisation is conceptualised as a process involving a period of international business activity, then exit from international operations, followed by a time-out period of some duration, then the process of international re-entry, concluding with successfully renewed international operations. The definition of re-internationalisation that Welch and Welch (2009) propose is confined to the organisational rather than individual level of analysis. In other words, it considers companies that have withdrawn from international operations but maintain domestic business activity before re-engaging in international market activity. Nevertheless, they recognise the importance of individual entrepreneurs as part of the general re-internationalisation scene. They may sell a company after ceasing international operations, or cease operations altogether, but subsequently re-start international business activity as part of the new enterprise. As such, they provide some information and knowledge for the process of re-internationalisation; they bring with them a wealth of experience. The principal way to carry out re-internationalisation is when a company is sold and the former managers create a new company in which presumably some of the effects of their former international involvement will be retained within the company, despite any loss of international experience associated with the change of ownership. Of course, the new owners may be responsible for a change in the way in which international involvement is approached, constituting the trigger for re-entry. This approach has four stages: the initial international experience, the process output, time without international experience and the new international influences that will lead the process of re-entry into international markets. It is important to know how the previous exit process occurred and the reasons for this exit.

DE-INTERNATIONALISATION

The term de-internationalisation has been forgotten for many years, while the internationalisation process has gained significant attention. Mellahi (2003) defined de-internationalisation as a voluntary process of decreasing participation in international operations due to organisational decline at home or abroad, as a way to increase profits under non-crisis conditions. From another perspective, Chetty (1999) stated that de-internationalisation in one dimension can incept internationalisation in other areas. This idea was also supported by Dass (2000), as firms have a limited amount of resources and multiple projects competing for resources and one type of diversification may be substituted by another. For example, a firm can reduce the number of markets in order to increase the number of products.

De-internationalisation can be full or partial (Benito & Welch, 1997). Full de-internationalisation is more likely to take place in the first stages of the internationalisation process because the level of commitment is reduced and tends to increase. While partial de-internationalisation tends to occur in the first or late stages of internationalisation.

There are several different reasons as to why firms decide to de-internationalise, in line with Reiljan (2004), the main reasons are classified into four groups (Table 1) as follows: (1) Lack of international experience caused by limited number of entrepreneurs with international experience; the entrepreneur does not completely understand the differences between countries and an analysis of the market is not sufficient. Usually this kind of reason appears at the beginning of the internationalisation process; (2) Change in strategy caused by a change of the foreign owner's plans or modification of strategy in the gradual development of the international market. A change in strategy usually occurs in the last stages of the internationalisation process; (3) Poor performance and/or increased costs originating from an increase in competition or production costs. This set of reasons tends to appear at the middle stage of internationalisation; (4) Other reasons, include external shocks. It is important to point out that different reasons can have simultaneous effects and are interrelated. Another important aspect is that the role of the entrepreneur is decisive in the two first reasons, because their level of knowledge and their decisions affect the process of de-internationalisation. Thus, we can deduce that de-internationalisation activities can lead to increased entrepreneurial actions to identify new opportunities in other market segments in order to promote the creation of wealth in the future.

Reiljan (2004) presents three different factors that influence the importance of the different sets of the de-internationalisation reasons: Knowledge from external sources, this factor tends to decrease the effect of the lack of previous international experience. The influence of this factor tends to diminish because the firm gradually improves its own knowledge; the second factor is the reason for the internationalisation of the firm, several reasons for internationalisation exist and their importance depends on the development of the internationalisation process; the last factor is the cost related to de-internationalisation, this cost is higher as more time goes by in the internationalisation process due to the level of commitment between the firms. On the other hand, as their international experience increases firms are able to minimise costs more effectively. Consequently, the influence of this factor is ambiguous and the effect depends on the level of commitment and experience of the firm.

Table 1. Reasons leading to de-internationalisation (Reiljan, 2004, 147)

LACK OF INTERNATIONAL EXPERIENCES	Insufficient pre-internationalization analysis
	Too rapid and/or early expansion to the foreign market
	Lack of knowledge
	Inadequate interpretation of market signals
	Choice of inappropriate target
	Choice of inappropriate operational mode
	Misfit of product and/or insufficient adaptation to the market
	Decrease in the value of previous experiences and knowledge due to the rapid changes in target market
	No previous inward internationalization
	Insufficient attention to foreign market (focusing on sporadic export)
CHANGE IN STRATEGY	Focusing on core markets
	Focusing on core activities
	Change of (foreign) owner's strategy
	New managers with different strategic perspectives
	Increase in demand at home
	Scarcity of resources and qualified personnel
	Constraints of manufacturing capacity
	Inadequate growth in target market
	Maturing of the product in the target market
	Change of operational mode
POOR PERFORMANCE AND INCREASE IN COSTS	Increase in production costs
	Increase in transport costs and tariffs
	Increase in competition (from the home country, host country, or third country)
	Poor performance
OTHER REASONS	(De)internationalization of related industries
	External shocks (including government interventions)
	Existence of foreign owner

Divestment is (Duhaime & Grant, 1984) the decision to reduce significantly the assets (company, business unit or division) held by the company, and foreign divestment "occurs when a company: ceases to possess net competitive advantage; no longer finds it profitable to internalise its advantages; and it is no longer profitable to utilise its internalised net competitive advantage abroad," (Panibratov & Brown, 2018a, 359). Such operations are executed with the utmost secrecy and confidentiality (Hamilton & Chow, 1993), thus hindering the study of these cases. The decrease of assets can be made through alienation (Mitchell, 1994; Chang & Singh, 1999) or by restructuring (Bergh & Lawless, 1998). The divestment would thus be associated with the dismantling of a relationship of ownership (Vale, 2001). Other authors associated divestment to the closure of production plants (Clark & Wrigley, 1997). However, the cessation of manufacturing activities is possible while maintaining the establishment and maintenance of the property (close the industrial activity and maintain the property as a logistics centre). This generally corresponds to the transformation of subsidiaries to mere commercial subsidiaries (Simões, 1987; 1992). On the other hand, there may be a change of ownership without significant change in the current activity of a firm.

Additionally, consider two types of divestment, divestment in the first case (in general terms) can be seen from the perspective of the evolution of the subsidiary. In this case, the closure of the subsidiary is part of the same process that may lead to its establishment as a centre of excellence (Holm & Pedersen, 2000). There are a number of common elements that lead to divestment, the strengthening (or not) of the autonomy of the subsidiary (Simões, Biscaya, & Nevado, 2001) and the establishment of centres of excellence (Simões & Nevado, 2000).

This in turn leads to the second aspect to consider concerning divestment: the analysis of divestment should be based on the interaction between endogenous and contextual factors. The endogenous factors consist of two parts: one associated with the multinational group (strategy, logic of action, innovation, rationalisation of activities, distinctive competencies), the other belonging to the subsidiary and its inclusion in the group. The contextual factors are also divided into two groups: sectoral aspects (structure of competitive forces, technological trajectories) and local aspects, connected with the attraction capacity of the investment territory.

Benito distinguishes between deliberate and forced divestment. The first corresponds to strategic situations that lead to voluntary liquidation or sale of all or part of operations abroad. Forced divestment corresponds to a change of ownership through the reduced shareholding position of the investor (expropriation, nationalisation and confiscation). The same author, Benito, subdivides the divestment process into four possible forms, according to the way they are carried out and the final results at a structural and organisational level. The concept of divestment disturbs business movements changing existing relationships, which can range from small and gradual adjustments, to the complete and permanent disruption of activities.

International divestment processes are beginning to be more common and the need to develop an explanation for such events is more and more evident. Corporate divestment is tied closely to the restructuring of a firm, as it is a tool which can be used to reconfigure and adapt to any new competitive challenges. In this sense, (Freitas, 1998) argues that investment and divestment are two sides of the same coin, driven by the dynamics of competition and the nature of the life cycle of products.

Viewing divestment as the closure of production units, Watts and Stafford (1986) and later Watts (1991) present the theory that a distinction is made between closure by suppression (i.e., the company leaves the business, moving away from the line of products concerned or opts to outsource) and selective closure (when production is transferred to or retained in other production units). Mata and Portugal (1997 and 2000) distinguish between "exit", which corresponds to the sale of the company or sale of the shares in the Portuguese company and "closure" in which the subsidiary is liquidated. Mariotti and Piscitello (1997) consider two types of divestiture - failure and restructuring. The first reflects the failure of the subsidiary, while the second is linked to broader strategies in terms of the restructuring of the company's business portfolio. Hennart et al. (1998), analysing the longevity of joint ventures of Japanese companies in the United States, examine the case of liquidation (i.e., the process of closing the subsidiary).

Given the evidence presented, it is possible to put forward a generic typification and ample forms of international divestment. This typification forms part of the intersection of two dimensions (property and business of the subsidiary). The size of the property determines the prospect of "traditional" divestment – as supported by Duhaime and Grant's (1984) definition, or the maintenance of a branch within the group. The extent of the activity determines the continuation of the normal activity of the company, or alternatively, its closure and possible downgrading. Quadrant one is the only one that does not portray a divestment situation, as the property and the business remain intact. Quadrant two considers the sale of the property by the company, whilst maintaining the activity of the firm. The strategic restructuring of local, regional or global firm assets is the cause of this divestment. Usually this restructuring takes place due to difficulties within the group or the poor performance of the subsidiary. However, in certain situations the company's strategic restructuring leads to the partial or total sale of the "crown jewel" to fund a new activity. In the case of certain mergers, the duplication of activities occurs, thus leading to the sale of one of the activities. In the third quadrant, companies reduce or terminate activity in this country, but retain ownership of it. This quadrant includes three situations: recession in situ, technological downgrading and dilution of relevance. The recession in situ, term taken from Vale (2001), reflects a down-sizing of the company's structure, by reducing the number of employees and decreasing productive activity. Technological downgrading occurs when a company decides to produce low-end products, which are not intensive in skilled labour and technology. Technological downgrading also occurs in situations where subsidiaries compete. This is due to the lack of competitiveness of one subsidiary, making it impossible to go ahead with the production of the new product, leaving it with obsolete technology. The dilution of relevance results in a change in the philosophy of the company that changes the distribution network of its products, as well as the location of the production units. These changes lead to the production units becoming mere business units, leading to reduced employment in these firms. In the last quadrant, there is a reduction in property and business activity. This quadrant integrates all types of divestment considered by Watts and Stafford (1986) and Watts (1991), abandoning a business, outsourcing, abandoning the range of products, selective closure and keeping other plants in operation and finally, cessation of production in the country. In the last case, the affiliate is sold as it is unable to meet demand and fails to meet the objectives of the firm. Besides the poor performance of the subsidiary, other reasons may lead to closure: the relative size of establishments (Watts & Stafford, 1986) or markets, as well as the income provided by alternative uses of space (Clark & Wrigley, 1997).

METHODOLOGY

The methodology of qualitative research grounded theory, first proposed by Glaser and Strauss (1967), was adopted throughout this work. The logic behind this approach is to place emphasis on the theory as a process and not to test the hypotheses already given. In this work, we used an abductive approach,

Table 2. Relation between reducing/maintaining the activity and property

Activity/Property	Maintaining	Reducing
Maintaining	• "Business as usual" (no divestment)	• Forced divestment • Sale of subsidiary • Sale of joint venture position • Partial sale of participation
Reducing	• Recession in situ • Technological downgrading • Dilution of relevance (abandonment of industrial activity; Focus in activities of low value)	• Sale of subsidiary • Sale of position with reduction or downgrading activity

described by Denzin (1978, p. 110) as an approach that "combines the deductive and inductive models in development of propositions and theory building". The methodological process was based on the Pandit's (1996) five phases. A literature review was the starting point to selected a theoretical sample. Then, a rigorous protocol was developed to go to the field. Information about the cases was collected, one by one, and ordered chronologically, to get a holistic vision and a better understanding of all phenomenon. This study applied mix codification, combining codes from theory (table 3 was the starting point) with emergent codes. The process ended when marginal improvements are very small, reaching theoretical saturation.

Thus, the final result of this research is a consequence of the interaction between successive relevant theoretical frames and empirical evidence.

As Strauss and Corbin (1990) suggested, studies using the grounded theory methodology should build a "relevant" sample related to the phenomenon under study, which will then be defined by the analysis which follows. So, at this study a theoretical sampling is used.

The requirements are as follows, to:

- Be based in Portugal;
- Have international experience;
- Have at least one case of international divestment.

Firm A is a brand created in 1994, offering consistently good value for money in a wide and dynamic range of fashion accessories (necklaces, rings, earrings, bracelets, scarves, handbags, wallets, sunglasses, travel bags, shoes, among others), within an attractive and vibrant space that enhances the buying experience. The process of brand internationalisation began in Spain, as this country is psychic and geographically the closest market to Portugal. In the very first year (2005), this brand opened eight shops. However, a few years later, they closed four or five shops. Although the beginning was not as auspicious as expected, the Spanish market is now one of the most important markets. This interview took place with the CEO (Mr. SM).

Firm B and C are part of a large Portuguese group, which has a wide range of businesses; firm B specialises in retail and firm C is a specialist in shopping centre management. Concerning both firms, Mr. AP was interviewed.

It was during Mr. AP's leadership that Firm B first began its internationalisation process, in the 1990s. The first markets were Brazil and Greece. Firm B believed that the Brazilian market was very similar to the Portuguese one and they applied the same business model there. However, this turned out not to be true, and in 2005 firm B was sold to the Wall Mart Group.

Firm C was founded in 1989, and it began its internationalisation process in 1999 in Spain, Greece, and Brazil. In 2008, Firm C reached 50 shopping centres with the opening of the first two shopping centres in Italy. However, the success of internationalisation temporarily took a step backwards with the closure of the M40 Shopping Centre in Madrid. Once again, they replicated domestic experience in an international market and had problems.

Firm D, founded in 1996, produces cork stoppers. Its founders have extensive knowledge of the cork industry gained through working in the world's leading cork company for many years. Firm D internationalised from the very beginning and is one example of a firm that is Born Global. The firm has invested in a number of markets such as Chile, Argentina, Bulgaria, Hungary, Spain, Italy and France. All of these countries boast good quality wines, with large scale production (reasons to be chosen). Due to financial problems, the firm had to sell their subsidiary in Argentina1. The person interviewed in this firm was the CFO (Mr. AS).

Firm E was founded in 1984, with a production capacity of 500 pairs of shoes per day, with a total of 50 employees. From the beginning, this production was mostly exported and the principal target was the European Union. Firm E is the other Born Global case; the firm was created with the intention of operating in international markets. The person interviewed in this company was the owner, Mr. FF. In Spain, the initial strategy was to open a warehouse in Madrid, but that strategy was not successful because the ideal place to sell shoes in Spain is Alicante, where the main shoe businesses and distributors are located. There was also a case of international divestment in Pakistan by Firm E, where they stepped down as partners in a firm that makes shoes. Firm E however still maintains relationships with this firm; buying leather for its production in Portugal.

Types of De-Internationalisation of the Firms Studied

All the firms studied followed a process of de-internationalisation. However, the way in which they de-internationalised was very different (Figure 1).

Firm C built a shopping centre in Madrid, the M40. However, this commercial centre was only successful for the first 3 months, while it was a novelty. After this period of time, people's affluence began to decrease, because they preferred other commercial centres. Over evaluation of the location was the reason for the closure of the M40, according to AP. Therefore, we consider the mode of de-internationalisation of the M40 to be failure, due to the ceasing of trade.

Figure 1. Modes of de-internationalisation of the firms studied (adapted from Turcan, 2011)

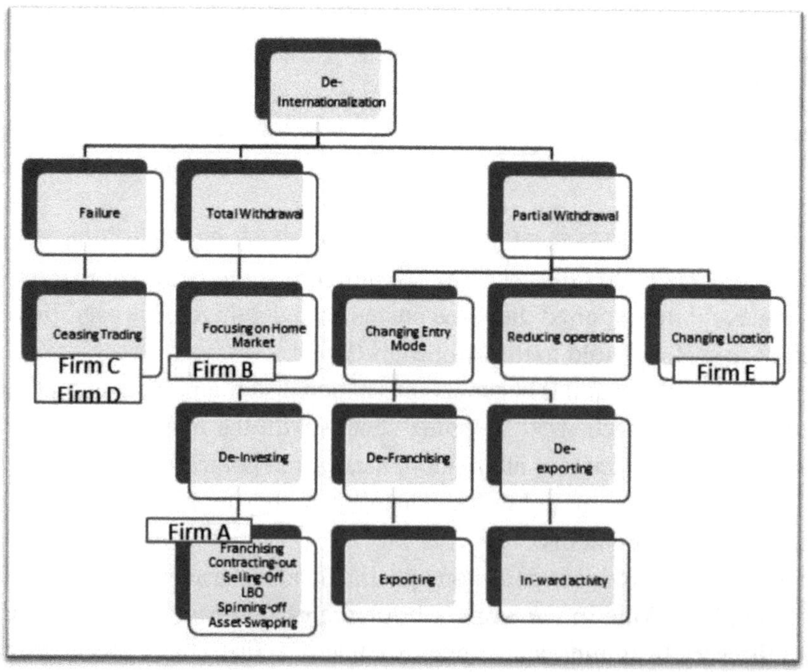

Source: Adapted from Turcan (2011)[1]

Firm D had a successful subsidiary in Argentina, with an Argentinean partner, but capital needs led the firm to sell its shares to their major competitor. This took place because of the crisis in Portugal and the reduction of credit supply by banks to firms. This reduction caused firm has to sell some assets to maintain their activities in other countries. In spite of the firm's success in Argentina, we consider that it was failure that led to ceasing business in that country. It is a failure because the internationalisation process grew faster than its possibilities to internationalise.

Firm B left the Brazilian market in 2005, selling its position to the Wall Mart group. The entry process was achieved through the acquisition of small firms in local cities.

The owners of these small firms could not open firms for some years, however following this period, they opened new shops and began to compete. This competition would normally not be a problem, if they competed under the same circumstances. However, in a market such as Brazil where a parallel economy exists, this kind of economy was only possible for small firms with a restricted number of employees.

Firm A de-internationalised in Spain. According to MS, the reasons for this were the pretended "similarities" to the Portuguese market, the store concept and the location of stores. He thought that Spanish market was similar to the Portuguese market, so he could copy the business model and it would be successful. After this first entry into the market, they corrected the errors and today the Spanish market is a very important one. In the beginning, they opened their own shops, but now most shops are franchised. This allows them to be in more markets with more shops, but they are limited to the decision of the franchisees to open more shops. We consider de-internationalisation to be a partial withdrawal, as a consequence of changing the entry mode to franchising.

Firm E also followed a de-internationalisation process in Spain. The firm began to internationalise in Madrid through a warehouse, which was open for three years. However, sales did not correspond to expectations; after they were informed that Alicante was a more suitable place to sell shoes in Spain, the firm changed its location to Alicante. Today Spain is a successful market.

To conclude, from the five firms that de-internationalised, the authors identified four different modes of de-internationalisation.

Only one de-internationalisation mode led two companies to failure and consequently to cease trading. In some cases, the withdrawal was temporary and they are now operating in prosperous markets.

CODIFICATION

The reasons studied by Reiljan (2004) and presented in Table 1 were the starting point for codification. However, new variables were identified. With the exclusion of some variables, such as ones that were new but that had little relevance, the external validation was improved, establishing a criterion by which the results of the study could be generalised, as Pandit (1996) suggested.

Each of the cases was studied in detail, and the interviews took place without any kind of interference from the interviewer. The respondent approached the various themes freely, with more focus placed on the process of internationalisation and the "why" and "how" of it all. By analysing this issue, the goal is to identify variables that had acted as facilitators of this process.

Other sources were articles in journals, sites and theses, in order to obtain more information about the de-internationalisation of these firms.

CATEGORIES FROM LITERATURE

As shown in Table 1, after studying the existing literature, four sets of reasons which influence the de-internationalisation decision were used. Interviews found empirical evidence for all of these four sets. Table 3 presents the first set, Lack of International Experience.

The most cited cause is 'insufficient pre-internationalisation analysis' with thirteen references, such as "In hindsight, analysing the business, the principal reason for the withdrawal of Firm B was the competitive characteristics of the Brazilian market that are very specific", as said by AP.

'Inadequate interpretation of market signals' is referred to ten times, one such example which clearly demonstrates this is AP's comment, the Group "grows through the acquisition of small units, however this growth was made through acquisitions which then failed. This was because the deal was carried out on the basis of business value, a value that no longer existed at the time they were acquired". This occurred due to insufficient interpretation of the Brazilian Market.

Two causes have nine references, 'insufficient attention to foreign market and choice of inappropriate mode'. One example that justified the second mode was explained by SM, from Firm A, "We began a few years ago with our own stores and what happened at the beginning was like banging our head against a brick wall, because we thought that Spain and Portugal were the same. The shopping centres were opening in Spain; so, we decided we should go and open some stores because it seemed to be an easy option".

There are two causes which are not referred to, 'a decrease in the value of previous experience and knowledge due to the rapid changes in the market and misfit of product and/or insufficient adaptation to the market'. These causes of de-internationalisation are viable, however in the firms we examined these causes were not given as reasons for the de-internationalisation process.

The second category is the Change in Strategy (Table 4).

The causes with the most references are 'scarcity of resources and qualified personal' and 'change of operational mode'. These two reasons are closely related because the scarcity of resources can lead to a change of operational mode. MS said, "The greatest difficulty we have when opening stores abroad is human resources," and "Franchising is a model that has advantages for us, because the franchisee

Table 3. Lack of international experience

Name	Source	Reference
Lack of international experience		
Insufficient pre-internationalisation analysis	3	13
Too rapid and early expansion in the foreign market	4	6
Lack of knowledge	2	6
Inadequate interpretation of market signals	3	10
Choice of inappropriate target market	3	4
Choice of inappropriate operational mode	4	9
Misfit of product and or insufficient adaptation to the market	0	0
Decrease in the value previous experiences and knowledge due to the rapid changes in target market	0	0
No previous inward internationalisation	2	4
Insufficient attention to foreign market (focusing on sporadic export)	3	9

Table 4. Change in strategy

Name	Source	Reference
Change in Strategy		
Focusing on core markets	1	1
Focusing on core activities	2	5
Change of (foreign) owner's strategy	1	1
New managers with different strategic perspectives	1	2
Increase in demand at home	0	0
Scarcity of resources and qualified personnel	3	7
Constraints of manufacturing capacity	3	4
Inadequate growth in target markets	2	3
Maturing the product in the target market	0	0
Change of operational mode	2	7

[Local Franchiser] is in the local market and knows the market. The operation is, in principle, more effective than what we could achieve and we do not have the resources to go to 40 countries." The other node given more relevance was, 'Focusing on core activities', as described by AP, "In 2003 or 2004, the Group had a strategy that needed resources from Firm B, for example, with the aim of increasing its stake in Portucel." Furthermore FF, owner of Firm E, points out that "We made a deal, to come away and leave the factory in Pakistan and still continue to buy leather from them. It was a positive experience, because firstly we solved the problem of a lack of good quality leather, available at a good price. Secondly, it demonstrated that one aspect that was suitable in relation to the supply of skins, was not suitable in the field of finished products."

The third category is Poor Performance and Increase of Costs (Table 5).

In this node, 'poor performance' has four references. One example of these references was made by AP, "I was responsible for market entry. We insisted on it and invested in it, and I am sorry it happened. Particularly, as I think all the resources that Firm C used in this market would have been more effectively used in other markets".

Finally, the fourth category is Other Reasons (Table 6).

Table 5. Poor performance and increase of costs

Name	Source	Reference
Poor performance and increase of costs		
Increase in production costs	1	1
Increase in transport costs and tariffs	1	1
Increase in competition (from the home country, host country, or third country)	1	1
Poor performance	3	4

Table 6. Other reasons

Name	Source	Reference
Other reasons		
(De)internationalisation of related industries	0	0
External shocks (including government interventions)	1	1
Existence of foreign owner	0	0

One reference was made to the node 'Other Reasons' by AP in relation to the failure of Firm C, "There are some other frustrations that are related to the situation and the market itself, I am talking about Romania. Romania was a target of the crisis like other countries. The 2008 crisis also affected Romania, but we always have to think about what is being considered." In this situation, the cause of failure was the international crisis (External Shocks), that led to a decrease of sales in shopping centres.

New Emerging Categories

This research identified the causes of the de-internationalisation process presented in the literature but some new categories also emerged (Table 7).

In addition to the causes of de-internationalisation proposed by Reiljan (2004), some others that led to the de-internationalisation of the firms studied emerged. The new emerging cause the most often referred to was, 'High Expectations', with 24 references (referred to by all firms). AS, from Firm D, points out that "Our difficulty in terms of internationalisation is not in terms of product, because technically this company came to stimulate smaller companies facing the market because it came the turn to the markets and we invested significantly in technology, branding, quality and research, we knew that the question of taste was a situation that had to be solved, so we invested in a unit that cost 12 M€ in the south. Maybe today ...".

Regarding Firm C, AP states that, "There was a fundamental overestimation of the location. La Fortuna is a relatively poor neighbourhood with little commercial interest. It has limited purchasing power, but our assessment was the following: it is not relevant to be in la Fortuna, because the market that matters is in the City of Madrid. This is guaranteed, because of the M40, where thousands of cars pass every day. The mall has a high level of visibility, with direct access from the M40 to the shopping area, a positive and straight-forward advantage. We would be established there, but it will be as if we were in

Table 7. New emerging causes of de-internationalisation

Name	Source	Reference
Emerged nodes		
Unfair competition	3	7
High expectations	4	24
Currency devaluation	1	1
Pressure due to external factors / environment	3	12
Lack of capital	3	9

the centre or even better, because there are no traffic jams and the shopping centre is easily accessible for cars. However, this turned out not to be true".

FF also referred to a similar situation where the advantages of the location were overestimated, "We had an experience in Spain, which went on for 4-5 years, where we had to pull out, because we were no longer interested. However, today we are in Spain and our business is successful. The location was poor. After three years, we realised that the ideal place for selling shoes in Spain is Alicante".

SM also indicated that poor store concept and location were the reasons for failing when entering the Spanish market as demonstrated below, "After entering the Spanish market, 4-5 shops then had to be closed. At the time, it was more than half of our stores. I believe, we initially opened eight stores, but I am not sure as it was a long time ago. It took place a number of years ago. Now our investment in the Spanish market is successful, we have franchisees and company stores as well. The store concept and location has greatly improved."

It is important to emphasise that in most cases 'High Expectations' are a result of misfit of the Micro-Location. With regard to the cases which took place in Spain, it is evident that Firm A, Firm B and Firm E, made a mistake when they chose the first locations to begin the internationalisation process. In all cases, the subsequent alteration of location brought with it increased profit and better results.

The second node with more references is the 'Environment of Decisions,' referred twelve times. This node refers to decisions that are taken due to the pressure of external factors such as other markets, financial pressure and administrative pressure. AS, from Firm D, explains that, "About one year ago [the World Cork Leader Group] took over our partnership in Argentina. We had an excellent company, with an excellent image and performance, but had some difficulty adapting the product due to this crisis. Furthermore, we believe that it was not fair to penalise the company, which boasted an excellent performance. We sold our shares to this Group, and then went on to solve other issues. The pressure that the financial system places on businesses, leaves no margin for error. We left Argentina, not due to the market, but because of the financial crisis".

AP also said, "Therefore, the image that surrounded the issue is an image reflecting the pressure to "diversify." This happens in all companies; the decisions are always surrounded by external factors. This fact made the Group decide that it was more beneficial to put the capital used in Brazil, in other places, with much regret of my part".

'Lack of capital' was referred to by three interviewees as reasons for de-internationalisation.

One such case was mentioned by AS, "the problem arose with the crisis, because banks went to firms and informed them about drastic steps that would have to be taken such as current accounts closing and lines of credit being reduced to half the amount and later closed. The company was not prepared for this shock; when implementing an internationalisation project, such aspects are not always considered. Yes, we thought, we had a business plan, but as a result of completing deep research, I decided I wanted to open a company in Chile, knowing that I needed capital. However, I soon learnt that long-term investments require long-term capital. In Portugal, I still question what financial products are available for SMEs that want to establish a company in Chile or Argentina and need 6-7 years to make a return on these investments? I wonder what financial products are available? I approached the bank, they liked the project, but for an investment, you need to have collateral. Therefore, we had to arrange a mortgage. The business was in Chile, but I cannot use an asset based in Chile as collateral. I wanted to make my investment considering all of these issues, but eventually I decided not to make the investment".

Another cause of de-internationalisation identified through these interviews was, 'Unfair Competition' mainly in South American markets. AS said, "Argentina also suffers from the issue of tax evasion because the tax burden is very high." And AP points out, "The name given in Brazil as a key feature that led to the departure of Firm B is tax evasion." This happens because small units can escape taxes, because they are in a restricted, familiar environment and can avoid paying taxes. When a large group buys small shops and builds a big group, they cannot avoid paying taxes, and for that reason they cannot compete with them, despite having economies of scale in the distribution and supply processes. Additionally, FF comments that some customers in Spain want to buy goods without an invoice, but we did not allow this, "We opened a store in Madrid, with a team of salesmen, but customers only wanted to buy items without having an invoice issued. We were there for three years without success".

The cause of de-internationalisation with the least number of references is 'Currency Devaluation.' It was only referred to once by AS, "While today volatility is more controlled, currency remains very volatile. The currency issue is fundamental in the process of internationalisation. It is clearly felt in the Latin American markets that were based on the U.S. dollar". Although AP did not refer to this problem directly in his interview, we found a reference made to it in Carvalho (2009, p. 49) that said, "strong political and economic instability and the high interest rates, resulted in a sharp depreciation of the Brazilian currency, contributing to a decrease in value of Firm B's Consolidated Model. This resulted in a loss of 1.271 million, a decrease of 23% since 2001." Thus, Firm B experienced the problem of Currency Devaluation in its Brazilian businesses too.

Following the presentation of all of these new causes of de-internationalisation, an additional category called Misfit or Poor Adjustment of Entry Mode was created. This new category includes 'High Expectations' with a focus on the cause of 'Misfit of Micro-Location', 'Environment of Decision's and 'Lack of Capital'.

'Unfair Competition' and 'Currency Devaluation' stay outside this category because they do not depend on the entry mode but on changes in the market. Misfit or Poor Adjustment of Entry Mode Category incorporate situations such as overestimation of the advantages of the location, overestimation of the market, capital needs due to numerous markets, environments of decisions because a promising opportunity can lead to withdrawal from one of the markets, changes in the financial market that lead to changes in the financial conditions available to firms.

CONCLUSION

It is interesting to note that all reasons for de-internationalisation referred to by Reiljan (2004) were found in these cases. However, with this study five new causes of de-internationalisation emerged. These are 'High Expectations' with a focus on 'Misfit Micro-Location, Environment of decisions, Lack of Capital due to the Economic Crisis, Currency Devaluation and Unfair Competition'. These causes are diversified; however, three of them go into a new category, called Misfit or Poor Adjustment of Entry Mode. These findings make it possible to complete the causes of de-internationalisation.

As Turcan (2003, p. 211) demonstrated, "Thus, the process of cross-border activity of the firm can be defined as cause – effect relationship between internationalisation and de-internationalisation, whereby a firm cannot de-internationalise (effect) without having internationalised (cause)". All these causes are related to the internationalisation process. Thus, one of the main causes of de-internationalisation is the incorrect internationalisation process.

The new variables explain most cases of de-internationalisation. The cause 'Unfair Competition' is an external factor, because the company cannot control the payment of taxes from firms to the government. Burt, Coe and Davies (2019), studying the European retails exiting from Asia, talk about the resistance of local players. In the same vein, Coe, Lee, and Woo (2017) analised Tesco decision to sell its very successful subsidiary Homeplus, and noted the same local resistance with the re-regulation of South Korean market. Firm should check, before internationalising to any market, the market conditions, the taxes, the GDP growth, the local animosity and future perspectives. Pretended similarities are a wrong starting point, and sometimes transferring the experience obtained in the domestic market to the international one is very difficult. The companies should also analyse the location inside the country, the traditions of the population, how they carry out businesses (tax evasion tradition). These measures can help a firm to avoid unpleasant surprises, like the situation of Firm B in Brazil.

Another new cause is 'High Expectations,' which is more internal than external.

When a firm begins to internationalise, the team responsible thinks that the internationalisation process will be a success, so they design large projects. Unfortunately, not all projects are successful and larger projects have a higher risk of loss. This puts in evidence the role of appropriate managing and the importance of communication and public relations, as Mellahi (2003) noted when studying the case of Marks and Spencer.

One high expectation comes from the government, who invites firms to internationalise, as it appears to be the only solution to overcome a crisis. However, internationalising is not as simple as that. It is necessary to have a product and/or service that can be exported, funds, a good team, a good concept, knowledge, an alert entrepreneur able to deal with surprises and availability to satisfy customers.

In this study, the most common cause was the Misfit Micro-Location, that means the wrong choice of place inside a determined country. So, after choosing the country, it is necessary to choose the best place to be located to internationalise. In International Business, the term International Market Selection is often referred to and it is very important, however we suggest companies should place more relevance on the selection of the place inside the country or city, it is crucial for the success of the firm's internationalisation.

The cause 'Currency Devaluation' is external to the firm; however, the firm can minimise this risks. For example, Firm D began to carry out all billing in Euros, reducing the risk of two currency devaluations ARS/USD and USD/EUR.

The cause 'Environment of decision' is internal to the firm. This cause means decisions that the administration makes in determined situations. These decisions are not consensual and easy to make. Funds available to the firm are not unlimited, so the decision to enter a market can lead to withdrawal from another market. In this kind of decision, the last months in the market are of interest and the profits from the years before are forgotten. The last new cause 'Lack of Capital' includes situations of capital needs to invest in multiple markets, but especially situations where the financial crisis has led to a reduction of financial conditions available to firms. Alexander and Quinn (2002) have already noted the negative effect of domestic crisis in the Arcadia and Marks and Spencer internationalization process. However, in this study, the problem is the reduction of credit lines, discount lines and current accounts makes the sustainability of firms and their foreign markets difficult. AS suggests that the government should make agreements with banks to accept real warranties from foreign countries and also provide special conditions to projects which are economically viable. He [AS] also suggests agreements should be in place between countries to make the process of internationalisation easier.

The combination of three of these five new causes, 'Unfair Competition, High Expectations and Environment of Decisions' creates a new cause of de-internationalisation called Misfit or Poor Adjustment of Entry Mode.

Table 8 presents a new matrix that includes all causes of de-internationalisation used by Reiljan (2004) and the new causes which emerged from this study.

This matrix separates causes according to if they are before or after internationalisation. Columns were drawn up showing whether the start of the of de-internationalisation process was caused by internal factors within the firm or external factors.

The result of this separation is presented in Table 8, which demonstrates that most of the causes are internal to firms and occur before the start of the internationalisation process. This happens because firms do not have a well-defined entry plan. It is interesting to note that in our study, the firms did not carry out market studies of the market that they were planning to enter. The second group with more causes of de-internationalisation is external to the firm and occurred after the internalisation process started. The third group with a higher number of causes of de-internationalisation is internal to the firm and occurred after the internationalisation process started. 'Lack of Capital' is integrated into this group because this can come from multiple projects when firms do not have enough funds or there is a change in conditions with banks which leads to difficulties in companies. In the last situation, it is considered as external to the firm.

However, it was expected mores causes in this group. None of the firms studied admitted to errors in the management of the internationalisation process. The authors believe that the omission of these errors affects the studies carried out on this subject.

Table 8. The start of the de-internationalisation causes.

TIMING	
BEFORE	**AFTER**
• Insufficient pre-internationalisation analysis • Too rapid and 7 or early expansion to the foreign market • Lack of knowledge; • Inadequate interpretation of market signals • Choice of inappropriate target market • Choice of inadequate operational mode • Misfit of product and / or sufficient adaptation to the market • No previous inward internationalisation • Insufficient attention to foreign market • Constraints of manufacturing capacity • High expectations	• New managers with different strategic perspectives • Inadequate growth in target market • Poor performance • Change of operational mode • Focusing on core markets • Focusing on core activities • Existence of foreign owner • Lack of capital
• Maturing of the product in the target market • Unfair competition • Scarcity of resources and qualified personnel	• Decrease in the value of previous experience and knowledge due to the rapid changes in target market • Increase in production costs • Increase in transport costs and tariffs • Increase in competition • Environment of decisions • (De)internationalisation of related industries • External shocks (including government interventions) • Increase in demand at home • Currency devaluation

The group with fewer categories is external to the firm and it occurs before starting the process of internationalisation. This group includes 'Unfair Competition' and 'Scarcity of resources and qualified personnel' because usually these conditions are already present in the market but firm didn't considered them.

Table 8 shows the most common causes of de-internationalisation until now, helping firms that are beginning internationalisation now to avoid these errors.

One limitation of this study relates to the sample size. Although the size is justified by the theoretical saturation reached, it would be interesting to test the new variables identified from a larger universe of companies. Another limitation is that the study was only developed in Portugal, a country with a small open economy and facing an economic crisis that worsened the financial situation of firms. In some cases, it led to the closure of these firms.

This study falls under a topic which firms find difficult to approach because it searches and raises questions about the causes of de-internationalisation. People generally do not like to share bad experiences and try to justify them by referring to external factors. This is a further limitation of this study, because interviewees could be biased. As Panibratov and Brown (2018b, p. 920) note, "of all the various types of activity, divestment is the most likely to be under-recorded with firms", as people believe it has a negative impact on the firm's reputation.

The present study tried to identify the causes that led to de-internationalisation, based on a qualitative methodology, the Grounded Theory Methodology. It is recommended carrying out this study with a larger number of sample companies, therefore a quantitative confirmatory study.

Future researchers should also examine the Micro-location of firms in foreign countries as a cause of successful internationalisation. Until now, the choice of market was studied and not the location inside a specific country. One more suggestion goes to the study of Re-internationalisation phenomenon further, because in some of our cases this phenomenon occurred. Welch and Welch (2009) carried out a study about the phenomenon of Re-internationalisation, however new research based on Misfit Micro-Location would also be enlightening. Procher and Engel (2018) noted that investments in some subsidiaries create pressures to divest in others, so study the competitive arena (namely the intersubsidiary competition) must be studied in future works.

This is a qualitative work, the main purpose of which is not to confirm any theory or hypothesis but rather to expand the theory. In this regard, the greatest contribution of this study is the presentation of five more causes that lead to de-internationalisation and the development of a new table (Table 8 - The start of de-internationalisation causes). Thus, this study has contributed towards a better understanding and more in-depth knowledge of the de-internationalisation problem, helping to reduce the rate of companies failing when pursuing the internationalisation process.

REFERENCES

Alexander, N., & Quinn, B. (2002). International retail divestment. *International Journal of Retail & Distribution Management*, *30*(2), 112–125. doi:10.1108/09590550210418137

Ardichvili, A., Cardozo, R., & Souray, R. (2003). A theory of entrepreneurial opportunity identification and development. *Journal of Business Venturing*, *18*(1), 105–123. doi:10.1016/S0883-9026(01)00068-4

Benito, G. (1997). Divestment of foreign production operations. *Applied Economics*, *29*(10), 1365–1377. doi:10.1080/00036849700000027

Benito, G. (2005). Divestment and international business strategy. *Journal of Economic Geography*, *5*(2), 235–251. doi:10.1093/jnlecg/lbh041

Benito, G., & Welch, L. (1997). De-internationalization. *Management International Review*, *37*(2), 7–25.

Bergh, D. D., & Lawless, M. W. (1998). Portfolio Restructuring and Limits to Hierarchical Governance: The Effects of Environmental Uncertainty and Diversification Strategy. *Organization Science*, *9*(1), 87–102. doi:10.1287/orsc.9.1.87

Burt, S., Coe, N. M., & Davies, K. (2019). A tactical retreat? Conceptualising the dynamics of European grocery retail divestment from East Asia. *International Business Review*, *28*(1), 177–189. doi:10.1016/j.ibusrev.2018.05.010

Chang, S. J., & Singh, H. (1999). The impact of modes of entry and resource fit on modes of exit by multibusiness firms. *Strategic Management Journal*, *20*(11), 1019–1035. doi:10.1002/(SICI)1097-0266(199911)20:11<1019::AID-SMJ66>3.0.CO;2-9

Chetty, S., & Campbelt-Hunt, C. (2004). A Strategic Approach to Internationalization: A Traditional Versus a "Born-Global" Approach. *Journal of International Marketing*, *12*(1), 57–81. doi:10.1509/jimk.12.1.57.25651

Chetty, S. K. (1999). Dimensions of Internationalisation of Manufacturing Firms in the Apparel Industry. *European Journal of Marketing*, *33*(1/2), 121–142. doi:10.1108/03090569910249201

Clark, G. L., & Wrigley, N. (1997). Exit, the firm and sunk costs: Reconceptualizing the corporate geography of divestment and plant closure. *Progress in Human Geography*, *21*(3), 338–358. doi:10.1191/030913297674898950

Coe, N. M., Lee, Y. S., & Wood, S. (2017). Conceptualising contemporary retail divestment: Tesco's departure from South Korea. *Environment & Planning A*, *49*(12), 2739–2761. doi:10.1177/0308518X17733265

da Silva, P. M. F., & Moreira, A. C. (2019). The Evolution of Corporate Divestment: Towards a New Research Paradigm? In *Handbook of Research on Contemporary Approaches in Management and Organizational Strategy* (pp. 292–316). IGI Global. doi:10.4018/978-1-5225-6301-3.ch015

Dass, P. (2000). Relationship of Firm Size, Initial Diversification, and Internationalization with Strategic Change. *Journal of Business Research*, *48*(2), 135–146. doi:10.1016/S0148-2963(98)00097-6

Denzin, N. (1978). The logic of naturalistic inquiry. New York: Sociological Book.

Duhaime, I., & Grant, J. (1984). Factors Influencing Divestment Decision-making: Evidence from a Field Study. *Strategic Management Journal*, *5*(4), 301–318. doi:10.1002mj.4250050402

Engwall, L., & Wallenstal, M. (1988). Tit for tat in small steps: The internationalization of Swedish banks. *Scandinavian Journal of Management*, *4*(3/4), 147–155. doi:10.1016/0956-5221(88)90006-1

Freitas, J. A. (1998). *Determinantes do desinvestimento em Portugal*. GEPE - Ministério da Economia.

Glaser, B., & Strauss, A. (1967). *The discovery of Grounded Theory*. London. *Weidenfeld and Nicholson*, *24*(25), 288–304.

Hamilton, R., & Chow, Y. (1993). Why Managers Divest: Evidence from New Zealand's largest companies. *Strategic Management Journal*, *14*(6), 479–484. doi:10.1002mj.4250140606

Hennart, J.-F., Kim, D.-J., & Zwng, M. (1998). The Impact of Joint Venture status on the Longevity of Japanese Stakes in US Manufacturing Affiliates. *Organization Science*, *9*(3), 382–395. doi:10.1287/orsc.9.3.382

Holm, U., & Pedersen, T. (2000). *In The Emergence and Impact of MNC Centres of Excellence – A Subsidiary Perspective*. London: Macmillan.

Johanson, J., & Mattsson, L. G. (1988). *Internatianalisation in Industrial Systems-A Network Approach. Strategies in Global Competition.* Croom Helm.

Johanson, J., & Vahlne, J.-E. (1977). The internationalization process of the firm: A model of knowledge development and increasing foreign market commitments. *Journal of International Business Studies*, *8*(1), 23–32. doi:10.1057/palgrave.jibs.8490676

Johanson, J., & Vahlne, J.-E. (2003). Business relationship learning and commitment in the internationalization process. *Journal of International Entrepreneurship*, *1*(1), 83–101. doi:10.1023/A:1023219207042

Johanson, J., & Vahlne, J.-E. (2009). The Uppsala internationalization process model revisited—From liability of foreignness to liability of "Outsidership". *Journal of International Business Studies*, *40*(9), 1411–1431. doi:10.1057/jibs.2009.24

Mariotti, S., & Piscitello, L. (1997). Divestment as fa ilure or part of a restructuring strategy: evidence from the italian MNEs. *Proceedings of the 23rd Conference of EIBA*.

Mata, J., & Portugal, P. (1997). The Exit Mode of Foreign Entrants: The Impact of Entry and Post-Entry Strategies. Paper delivered at the 6º Encontro de Economia Industrial, Lisbon, Portugal.

Mata, J., & Portugal, P. (2000). Closure and Divestiture by Foreign entrants: The impact of entry and post-entry strategies. *Strategic Management Journal*, *21*(5), 549–562. doi:10.1002/(SICI)1097-0266(200005)21:5<549::AID-SMJ94>3.0.CO;2-F

Mellahi, K. (2003). The de-internationalization process: a case study of Marks and Spencer. In *Internationalization* (pp. 150–162). London: Palgrave Macmillan. doi:10.1057/9780230514638_10

Mitchell, W. (1994). The dynamics of evolving markets: The effects of business sales and age on dissolutions and divestitures. *Administrative Science Quarterly*, *39*(4), 575–602. doi:10.2307/2393772

Onkelinx, J., Manolova, T. S., & Edelman, L. F. (2016). The Consequences of De-Internationalization: Empirical Evidence from Belgium. In Global Entrepreneurship: Past, Present & Future (pp. 45-66). Emerald Group Publishing Limited. doi:10.1108/S1571-502720160000029006

Oviatt, B. M., & McDougall, P. P. (1994). Toward a theory of international new ventures. *Journal of International Business Studies*, *25*(1), 45–64. doi:10.1057/palgrave.jibs.8490193

Padmanabhan, P. (1993). The impact of European divestment announcements on shareholder wealth: Evidence from the UK. *Journal of Multinational Financial Management*, *2*(3/4), 185–208.

Pandit, N. R. (1996). The creation of theory: A recent application of the grounded theory method. *Qualitative Report*, *2*(4), 1–15.

Panibratov, A., & Brown, T. (2018a). Mitigating divestment stigma: A legitimation perspective. *Kybernetes*, *47*(5), 920–936. doi:10.1108/K-12-2017-0470

Panibratov, A., & Brown, T. (2018b). Foreign divestments from Russia: An exploration of the mediating factors. *Strategic Change*, *27*(4), 359–367. doi:10.1002/jsc.2208

Procher, V. D., & Engel, D. (2018). The investment-divestment relationship: Resource shifts and inter-subsidiary competition within MNEs. *International Business Review*, *27*(3), 528–542. doi:10.1016/j.ibusrev.2017.10.004

Reiljan, E. (2004). *De-Internationalization motives: A Theoretical Framework*. Retrieved from http://www. mattimar. ee/publikatsioonid/ettevottemajandus/2004/11_Reiljan.pdf

Rennie, M. W. (1993). Born Global. *The McKinsey Quarterly*, *4*, 45–53.

Rennie, M. W. (1993). Born Global. *The McKinsey Quarterly*, (4): 45–53.

Sapienza, H. J., Autio, E., George, G., & Zahra, S. A. (2006). A capabilities perspective on the effects internationalization on firm survival and growth. *Academy of Management Review*, *31*(4), 914–933. doi:10.5465/amr.2006.22527465

Sarasvathy, S. D. (2001). Causation and effectuation: Toward a theoretical shift from economic inevitability to entrepreneurial contingency. *Academy of Management Review*, *26*(2), 243–288. doi:10.5465/amr.2001.4378020

Schweizer, R., Vahlne, J.-E., & Johanson, J. (2010). Internationalization as an entrepreneurial process. *Journal of International Entrepreneurship*, *8*(4), 343–370. doi:10.100710843-010-0064-8

Simões, V., & Nevado, P. (2000). MNE centres of excellence and acquisitions: long evolutionary paths or capturing opportunities. *MESIAS Project.*

Simões, V. C. (1987). Capital extranjero y empleo: Comparación del comportamiento de las mayores empresas industriales. *Información Comercial Española*, *643*, 121–132.

Simões, V. C. (1992). European Integration and the pattern of FDI inflow in Portugal. In Multinational Investment in Modern Europe (pp. 256-297). Academic Press.

Simões, V. C., Biscaya, R., & Nevado, P. (2001). Subsidiary Decision-Making Autonomy: Competences, Integration and Local Responsiveness. In Network Knowledge in International Business. Academic Press.

Strauss, A., & Corbin, J. (1990). *Basics of qualitative research: Grounded theory procedures and techniques*. Sage Publications.

Surdu, I., Mellahi, K., & Glaister, K. W. (2018). Once bitten, not necessarily shy? Determinants of foreign market re-entry commitment strategies. *Journal of International Business Studies*, 1–30.

Surdu, I., Mellahi, K., Glaister, K. W., & Nardella, G. (2018). Why wait? Organizational learning, institutional quality and the speed of foreign market re-entry after initial entry and exit. *Journal of World Business*, *53*(6), 911–929. doi:10.1016/j.jwb.2018.07.008

Trąpczyński, P. (2016). De-internationalisation: A review of empirical studies and implications for international business research. *Baltic Journal of Management*, *11*(4), 350–379. doi:10.1108/BJM-08-2015-0153

Turcan, R. V. (2013). The philosophy of turning points: A case of de-internationalization. In *Philosophy of science and meta-knowledge in international business and management* (pp. 219–235). Emerald Group Publishing Limited. doi:10.1108/S1571-5027(2013)0000026014

Turcan, R. V. (2017). *De-internationalization: Evolution of the Concept*. Paper presented at McGill International Entrepreneurship Conference: Speed, Diversity, Complexity in International Entrepreneurship, Galway, Ireland.

Vale, M. (2001). *Desinvestimento: Caracterização e Literatura de Referência*. DivesT project.

Vissak, T., & Francioni, B. (2013). Serial nonlinear internationalization in practice: A case study. *International Business Review*, *22*(6), 951–962. doi:10.1016/j.ibusrev.2013.01.010

Wan, W. P., Chen, H. S., & Yiu, D. W. (2015). Organizational image, identity, and international divestment: A theoretical examination. *Global Strategy Journal*, *5*(3), 205–222. doi:10.1002/gsj.1101

Watts, H. (1991). Plant Closures in Urban Areas: Towards a Local Policy Response. *Urban Studies (Edinburgh, Scotland)*, *28*(5), 803–817. doi:10.1080/00420989120080941

Watts, H., & Stafford, H. (1986). Plant Closure and the multiplan firm: Some conceptual issues. *Progress in Human Geography*, *10*(2), 206–227. doi:10.1177/030913258601000203

Welch, C. L., & Welch, L. S. (2009). *Re-internationalisation: Exploration and conceptualisation*. Academic Press.

Welch, L. S., & Luostarinen, R. (1988). Internationalization: Evolution of a concept. *Journal of General Management*, *14*(2), 34–55. doi:10.1177/030630708801400203

ADDITIONAL READING

Burt, S., Dawson, J., & Sparks, L. (2003). Failure in international retailing: Research propositions. *International Review of Retail, Distribution and Consumer Research*, *13*(4), 355–373. doi:10.1080/0959396032000129471

Mlody, M. (2016). Backshoring in Light of the Concepts of Divestment and De-internationalization: Similarities and Differences. *Entrepreneurial Business and Economics Review*, *4*(3), 167–180. doi:10.15678/EBER.2016.040312

Palmer, M. (2005). Retail multinational learning: A case study of Tesco. *International Journal of Retail & Distribution Management*, *33*(1), 23–48. doi:10.1108/09590550510577110

Perlmutter, H. V. (2017). The tortuous evolution of the multinational corporation. In *International Business* (pp. 117–126). Routledge. doi:10.4324/9781315199689-7

Song, S. (2014). Subsidiary divestment: The role of multinational flexibility. *Management International Review*, *54*(1), 47–70. doi:10.100711575-013-0198-8

Song, S., & Lee, J. Y. (2017). Relationship with headquarters and divestments of foreign subsidiaries: The hysteresis perspective. *Management International Review*, *57*(4), 545–570. doi:10.100711575-017-0317-z

Sousa, C. M., & Tan, Q. (2015). Exit from a foreign market: Do poor performance, strategic fit, cultural distance, and international experience matter? *Journal of International Marketing*, *23*(4), 84–104. doi:10.1509/jim.15.0003

Vida, I., & Obadia, C. (2008). The dark side of internationalisation: Dysfunctional behaviours in foreign subsidiaries. *Transformations in Business & Economics*, *7*(2), 130–143.

KEY TERMS AND DEFINITIONS

De-Internationalization: Total or partial, voluntary or involuntary exit of a company from an extern/foreign market.

Inter-Subsidiary Competition: Competition among multiple subsidiaries of the same mother-company regarding strategic options, investment choices for example.

International Market Selection: Process of choosing the right market for a company to internationalize.

Misfit of Micro-Location: Wrong choice of determining a place to be located after choosing a country, due to the fact that it is not only necessary to choose the best country but also the best place inside it.

Recession in Situ: Decrease of the size of a company's structure, by reducing the number of employees and decreasing productive activity.

Technological Downgrading: The decision from a company of producing low-end products that are not intensive in skilled labor or technology.

Unfair Competition: Situation in what local companies have privileged conditions comparing to international companies, considering both legal or less legal ways in that market.

ENDNOTE

[1] Firm D has already ceased its activity.

Chapter 9
Proposing an Integrative Model for Reshoring Antecedents

Joel Pedroso Vaz
Universidade Lusíada Norte, Portugal

Ana Maria Soares
https://orcid.org/0000-0001-5714-2876
University of Minho, Portugal

José Carlos M. R. Pinho
University of Minho, Portugal

Susana Costa e Silva
https://orcid.org/0000-0001-7979-3944
Católica Porto Business School, Portugal & Wrocław University of Economics, Poland

ABSTRACT

The economic reasons that dictated offshoring for countries such as China are vanishing. Customers are increasingly demanding and more informed about the origin and methods of production of the products they buy, and governments are realizing the impact of manufacturing. This new reality is encouraging many companies to relocate their activities and, in some stances, returning manufacturing processes back to their home countries. This rather recent process, known as reshoring poses challenges of all kind with managerial implications in logistics, marketing, strategy, finances, commercial strategy, innovation, and human resources management. Reshoring antecedents are fundamental concepts for the understanding of the sources that may conduct those activities back home. This chapter takes one step in this direction and proposes a comprehensive model of the antecedents of reshoring that can be applied to a specific industry or sector. In particular, the authors examine the important role of economic, marketing, and social/political antecedents.

DOI: 10.4018/978-1-5225-8906-8.ch009

INTRODUCTION

In the past years, understanding the strategic direction of manufacturing has become the focus of a large scale debate (Ellram, 2013). Taking advantage of the goods manufacturing wave, Obama's administration developed a series of interesting initiatives with the goal to attract American companies to manufacture again their products/brands on the home soil (Gray, Skowronski, Esenduran, & Rungtusanatham, 2013; Regalado, 2013; Plumer, 2013). The same pattern is seen in Europe in which several countries have assumed the capital interest of attracting European companies to manufacture back home by providing the necessary financial and infrastructural support (Foresight, 2013; Veugelers, 2013).

Currently, the reshoring phenomenon received plenty attention from the popular press especially in the U.S. (United States of America) (Ellram, Tate, & Petersen, 2013). However, despite the growing practice of reshoring, only recently has the concept captured the attention of the academic community (Ellram et al., 2013; Fratocchi, Mauro, Barbieri, Nassimbeni, & Zanoni, 2014), especially after the phenomenon brought to the attention of the academic community by Kinkel, Lay, & Maloca (2007). The diversity of interest in this topic has spawned a profusion of overlapping concepts, such as onshoring, backshoring, in shoring, reverse shoring, and nearshoring that limits our understanding of this phenomena (Fratocchi et al., 2013). Nevertheless, there is a generalized consensus among researchers that reshoring describes a manufacturing location decision based on moving, entirely or partially, the previously offshoring production processes back to their home original country (Ellram, 2013; Gray et al., 2013). Foerstl, Kirchoff, & Bals (2016) define the phenomenon as the relocation of value creation tasks from offshore to geographically closer locations and although this broad definition is correct, it simultaneously includes two closer though different dimensions: reshoring and nearshoring. In a simple way it is possible to define reshoring as the return from a previous offshoring decision (Fratocchi et al., 2013), bringing manufacturing activities or services from broader countries back to the original country (Initiative, 2015). Reshoring is basically the opposite, i.e., production movement of an offshoring decision (Arlbjørn, Mikkelsen, Schlichter, & Thoms, 2013; Ellram, 2013; Gray et al., 2013)

Despite the fact that reshoring is more advanced in the U.S. where several companies are already admitting to reshore their manufacturing operations (Gray et al., 2013; Sirkin, Zinser, & Hohner, 2011), some manufacturing sectors in Europe are also reshoring (Foresight, 2013; Fratocchi & Silva, 2018; Fratocchi et al., 2014; Fratocchi et al., 2015; Kinkel & Montalvo, 2014), a trend which is expected to keep growing with the development of technological capacities, efficiency, productivity, robotics and nanotechnology (Veugelers, 2013) and the increasing direct or indirect consumers' pressure, for faster, higher quality and safe products while creating jobs for the local society in a sustainable way (Naitove, 2013; Plumer, 2013; Tseng, 2011). Also, there seems to exist some political pressures to move production processes in that direction (Regalado, 2013).

Notwithstanding its growing importance in Europe, however, in our view there is a dearth of research about this topic, including the evaluation in different sectors most affected and the evolution of this phenomenon over time. Previous studies have established a connection between a number of scopes that may impact on reshoring (Foresight, 2013; Sirkin et al., 2011).

This study aims to deepen knowledge in this area and to identify Reshoring motivations. To the best of our knowledge, research about the reshoring phenomenon is scarce and fragmented. This paper aims at reviewing the literature about reshoring and proposes an integrative Model of the variety of antecedents of reshoring. Specifically, this study aims at analyzing the following research questions: 1) How and which economic factors exercise a major influence in reshoring; 2) How and which marketing factors exercise a major influence in reshoring; 3) How and which political/social factors exercise a major influence in reshoring.

Economic factors, marketing related and political/social factors are identified as relevant antecedents for reshoring decisions. However, current studies do not clarify from the company perspective, the specific factors behind each dimension and how each factor exercises its influence on the reshoring decision. In fact, literature is not consensual about the major determinants of reshoring. While several studies maintain that reshoring is associated with the economic dimension as a major antecedent (see Ellram et al., 2013; Foresight, 2013; Fratocchi et al., 2013; Fratocchi et al., 2014; Fratocchi & Silva, 2018; Gray et al., 2013; Sirkin et al., 2011; Veugelers, 2013), others argue that companies often justify reshoring decisions with the need to be closer to their customers (Foroohar, 2013; Naitove, 2013; Plumer, 2013; Regalado, 2013; Tseng, 2011; Wadhwa, 2012). Still others emphasize the importance of political and social factors (Ellram et al., 2013; Foresight, 2013; Siza, 2014; Veugelers, 2013). We accept that reshoring is fundamentally a location decision rather than a concern with the company's management on whom is in fact manufacturing the production (Ellram, 2013).

This paper is divided into three major sections. The first section presents the reshoring phenomenon and identifies different motivations as potential reshoring antecedents. In the second part of this paper we propose a number of research propositions and a Conceptual Framework for the understanding of reshoring antecedents. The third and last part of this work addresses several theoretical and practical contributions.

RESHORING: IN SEARCH OF A DEFINITION

Companies seek the best and most efficient way to produce their goods, either internally (domestically) or externally (by offshoring). As means of transportation, communication and technology evolved, companies started to outsource and offshore their production especially to low cost countries in what was the first big scale step towards global manufacturing internationalization and global supply chains (Hutzel & Lippert, 2014; Liao, 2012). Irrespective of their importance for world economy (Kinkel & Maloca, 2009), outsourcing and offshoring are also important competences for a company, especially because they provide a better focus on the core of business (Bettis et al., 1992 cit in Arlbjørn & Mikkelsen, 2014; Dachs, Ebersberger, Kinkel, & Waser, 2006). Offshoring may be an important strategic advantage for companies regardless of their dimension and location (Kinkel & Maloca, 2009). Additionally, consumers also perceive numerous benefits of companies' offshoring, particularly and most importantly, the lower price of the products they are consequently able to buy (Hutzel & Lippert, 2014). In fact, this approach democratized the consumption of goods that were, before, an exclusive of some segments of the market.

In recent years we have been witnessing a deep change with regard to the offshoring phenomenon. Furthermore, there is an intense worldwide discussion about how, why, and where companies decide to locate their manufacturing activities (Ellram, 2013). By 2005, the term reshoring started to be used by popular press and raised public attention in the U.S. for a new reality, which started to be associated with a possible solution for resolving a number of problems faced by industrialized nations, in particular the unemployment and other problems resulting from the global crisis. Hence, national governments, policy makers and academics became increasingly interested in the reshoring phenomenon and what it can mean for several economies (Kinkel, 2014) to overcoming a recessionary period.

Prior to this, it is inevitable to define what reshoring is. Indeed, its definition is not consensual among authors due to the profusion of other interrelated concepts (Arvidsson, Magnusson, & Nilsson, 2014; Arlbjørn & Mikkelsen, 2014). For example, nearshoring and backshoring are similar terms often used to refer the same phenomenon (Cottrill, 2014). But there are others that address the same phenomenon, such as Intelli-Sourcing (Fine, 2013), on-shoring, in-shoring, reverse shoring (Fratocchi et al., 2013). Therefore, using so many different terms (many times with similar concepts) and by using the concept definition that is often not given or clearly explained, writers generate greater confusion about the theme (Arlbjørn & Mikkelsen, 2014). And this imprecision, as stated by Gray et al. (2013) is not exclusive to reshoring, the term offshoring is by itself imprecise: does it refer only to companies that have their own facilities in other countries and manufacture there? Or does it also include foreign outsourcing for those companies, which do not own foreign manufacturing plants but count on foreign companies that produce their products at a lower cost? (Gray et al., 2013) Several authors define offshoring as a move of part of the company to a foreign country (Contractor, Kumar, Kundu, & Pedersen, 2010; Arlbjørn & Mikkelsen, 2014). This assertion is supported by other authors who do not clearly distinguish external outsourcing from offshoring. For the purpose of this work, it is irrelevant if the company is producing directly in a foreign country (classic offshoring) or if the company has outsourced the production with a foreign supplier. The best way to clearly define reshoring is to take out of the equation the bond between internal or external production (outsourcing) and to establish that offshoring refers to both external outsourcing and own company production plants installed in foreign countries. We argue that reshoring is fundamentally a location decision rather than a concern with whom is manufacturing the production (Ellram, 2013). This way, we tend to follow a dual approach to the phenomenon. On one hand, considering it a location advantage option on the basis of the Eclectic Paradigm of Dunning (1998); and, on another hand, assuming that it is part of the strategic intent of the firm, following several strategic management theories. Under these, it is upon firm's internal decision, as well, the choice to relocate activities (Fratocchi et al., 2016; Fratocchi & Silva, 2018.

As a result of these postulations, it is possible to define reshoring as the return of a previously offshoring production (Fratocchi et al., 2013). In other words, reshoring refers to bringing manufacturing and services activities back to home country from overseas (Initiative, 2015). Thus, reshoring refers to as moving the production in the opposite direction of offshoring and outsourcing (Arlbjørn & Mikkelsen, 2014). Reshoring is also pointed as a change of policy of manufacturing location decision from a previous decision, moving the manufacturing processes to firm's home country (Cottrill, 2014). Kinkel & Maloca (2009) developed a complete and elucidative definition of this key concept: "*Accordingly, backshoring* (i.e. reshoring) *will be defined as a re-concentration of parts from own foreign locations as well as from foreign suppliers to the domestic production site of the company*". Reshoring refers to moving the manufacturing back to the home country after it has been offshored (Ellram, 2013; Gray et al., 2013). Reshoring is a manufacturing location decision regarding the production and the market the company intends to serve (e.g. GE reshored from China to U.S. to meet U.S. demand) (Gray et al., 2013) aiming at establishing a physical proximity with the company's market (Sirkin et al., 2011).

Reshoring phenomenon is actually a relevant topic for either academics and practitioners (Tate, 2014) and a trend topic among the popular press, having originated many consulting studies (Ellram et al., 2013). In spite of still being a taboo or a non-admitted matter for some companies, considering that it can be seen as an expensive international long term project failure (Fratocchi et al., 2014; Kinkel, 2014; Kinkel & Maloca, 2009), some companies flag the decision of reshoring as a patriotic option (Lewis, 2013). And, even if there are other reasons upon which the decision is made, most of the times there are several intricate reasons that base the ultimate decision to relocate activities. As reporting negative decisions is not very common (Silva & Silva, 2012) and may be interpreted as a failure, it is difficult to confirm when reshoring decisions are taken with the intent to correct an earlier managerial decision (Kinkel & Maloca, 2009; Gray et al., 2013). In some of these circumstances, several other reasons may be invoked, namely contingency factors, as the global financial crisis.

Additionally, after the global financial crisis, there was a global awareness that this global event, which can be framed between 2008-2012, had created the ideal conditions for companies to reflect about their global manufacturing strategy and how to move forward (Ellram et al., 2013; Ellram, 2013; Lahidji & Tucker, 2014; Tate, 2014). Reshoring became in such a context a relevant issue because it was generally admitted that most offshoring decisions were taken under faith, intuition or low valid basis (Kinkel & Maloca, 2009) that were not at place any longer. This is because, not just conditions back home of these multinational firms deteriorated, but also because some of those cost conditions were not so appealing. To these cost-based conditions, others were added and reshoring became at some companies' agenda on the basis of an intricate number of criteria that are worth to disentangle.

Fine (2013) maintains that in the future global companies will not put so much emphasis in low cost production but rather in their reputation, ethical behavior and sustainable production (Ellram, 2013). Yet, it is advised that each company must reflect seriously on their position, goals, products, and market before opting for a reshoring decision. For some companies, being closer to their customers becomes highly important; for others, having a competitive price is the core of their business. Thus, there may be very different motivations for reshoring decisions, and these cannot be equally and lightly evaluated (Tate, 2014). At the same time, at the macro-level, the future is equally challenging for each country. Consistent with current predictions, over the next 10 years there will be nearly two billion more consumers than today (mainly from China, India and Brazil). There will be an increasing demand for new product and services, thereby significant challenges will be posed to numerous countries and their organizations (Lahidji & Tucker, 2014).

According to Fratocchi et al., (2014) and Kinkel (2014), there is a lack of knowledge about the topics surrounding reshoring, the most salient being connected with motivations for reshoring, effects of reshoring for the companies, markets, and countries involved, and reshoring evolution over time. In fact, just a small fraction of the puzzle is known about the magnitude, impact, barriers, and motivation factors of reshoring (Lahidji & Tucker, 2014; Arlbjørn & Mikkelsen, 2014).

Despite few empirical studies have already been successfully applied under different markets, methodologies, sectors and conditions (see Table 1), it is still difficult to clearly distinguish among the real factors that may provoke a reshoring decision.

This paper focuses its attention on three major antecedents of reshoring: economic, marketing, and, political and social.

ECONOMIC ANTECEDENTS

China offered during many years a vast number of economic advantages for American and European manufacturing companies, including low-cost labor, subsidies, flexible employment laws, artificial low currency, significant government incentives, rapid growth of internal market, and cheap land to build companies' plants (Sirkin et al., 2011). These incentives seduced many western companies to move their manufacturing operations to China. By 2011 China represented approximately 21% of the global exports

Table 1. Reshoring empiracal investigation

Author(s)	Area(s)	Methodology(ies)
Arlbjørn, Mikkelsen, Schlichter, & Thoms (2013); Arlbjørn & Mikkelsen (2014)	Reshoring in Denmark	Qualitative and Quantitative
Arvidsson et al. (2014)	Reshoring in Sweden	Qualitative
Bossche et al. (2014)	Reshoring in U.S.	Quantitative
Canham & Hamilton (2013)	Offshoring, Reshoring and homeland manufacturing in New Zealand	Quantitative
Dachs et al. (2006)	Offshoring and Reshoring in Europe	Quantitative
Distler et al. (2014)	Offshoring and Reshoring in Apparel and Clothing	Quantitative
Ellram et al. (2013)	Offshoring and Reshoring in U.S.	Quantitative
Fratocchi, Equizi, et al. (2013); Fratocchi et al. (2014)	Reshoring	Qualitative and Quantitative
Kinkel (2012); Kinkel (2014)	Reshoring in Germany	Quantitative
Kinkel & Maloca (2009)	Reshoring in Germany	Qualitative and Quantitative
Lahidji & Tucker (2014)	Reshoring and Employment in the U.S.	Qualitative
Frank Prevos (2013)	Reshoring in Netherlands and Belgium	Qualitative and Quantitative
Sirkin et al. (2011)	Reshoring in U.S.	Quantitative
Tate et al. (2014)	Manufacturing location decision processes	Quantitative
Veugelers (2013)	Manufacturing in Europe	Quantitative

(Lewis, 2013) and millions of jobs were transferred from America and Europe to China (Wadhwa, 2012). Britain had in 1966 about nine million manufacturing jobs and, by 2011, there were less than three million jobs (Foresight, 2013) and similar results were observed in U.S. manufacturing with three million jobs lost since the 1950's (Regalado, 2013).

In the past years, the benefits of offshoring to China became less clear. The experiences exchanged among companies which had offshored, and the evidence of scientific studies and new tools to compare the real costs of manufacturing abroad or at home, led companies to question their decision to offshore to China.

From 1999 to 2006, Chinese wages raised around 150% departing from an average wage per hour of \$0.50 in 2000 and in 2015 was nearly \$4.50 and it is notorious that U.S.' salaries did not raise at the same percentage over the last years (Sirkin et al., 2011). Salaries in China were expected to erode gradually in the next 5 to 10 years (Kinkel & Montalvo, 2014). In fact, the low salaries were and are still being considered an important reason to offshore (Kakabadse & Kakabadse, 2000). Simultaneously, it has been identified in China and India that semi qualified or qualified human resources are insufficient, and, as it happens in all markets, when the availability of a good or resource is scarce, it tends to become more expensive (Tate, 2014). Another globally economic aspect, regards the middle class emancipation in emergent countries: some manufacturing functions are becoming less desired which is bringing many difficulties to hire low cost workers (Tate, 2014).

The manufacturing costs difference between U.S. and China is falling and the same is happening along other emergent markets (Tate, 2014). Although salaries are an important reason and motivation for offshoring decisions, the experience and accumulated knowledge through many years, weakened offshoring option and reshoring decision started to make sense and to become a concrete option in the manufacturing location decision process (Gray et al., 2013; Sirkin et al., 2011).

However, economic costs are relevant, other studies justify how and why companies' practical experience weakened the option of manufacturing through offshoring (Gray et al., 2013; Sirkin et al., 2011) and studies have been demonstrating that impacts on cost saving, service efficiency, and/or productivity improvement are mostly short-termed (Amiti & Wei, 2009). In practice, many managers came to the conclusion that the advantages of offshoring were offset by a number of problems: midnight phone calls, delivery delays, IP leakage, communication issues and misunderstandings, constant travels, inventory expenses, quality control problems, supply disruptions, political conflicts, and intellectual protection violation (Fratocchi et al., 2013; Gray et al., 2013; Plumer, 2013; Regalado, 2013; Sirkin et al., 2011). Supplier risks are amplified when dealing with international markets. For instances, a quality problem with a certain product in a domestic and controlled market can be hard to overcome for a company but the same problem on a global market scale can be fatal for the company (Roth & Diamantopoulos, 2008).

If you're a U.S. company and the advantage is only $7 per hour, suddenly it may be worth staying at home. If I stay there, I have lower inventory costs, lower transportation costs. I'm closer to my market, I can have a higher-quality production and I can keep my technology. Dan North cit in Plumer, 2013

In fact, based on the transaction cost theory (Williamson, 1985), it may be very difficult to account precisely for all the costs involved with the manufacturing process, especially when there are considerable physical and mental distances (Kinkel, 2014; Kinkel & Maloca, 2009). Furthermore, as the World's population keeps growing, a huge short term boom in manufacturing processes is expected because the demand shall increase due to the new consumers of emerging economies (Veugelers, 2013). To face this growth, new technologies are expected to make the difference in lowering manufacturing costs in a short future: 3D printers, robotics, nanotechnology, smart communication systems and Big Data (Veugelers, 2013). 3D printers are inclusively pointed out as the revolutionary weapon for home manufacturing which enable the creation of several small companies and new jobs (Foresight, 2013; Plumer, 2013; Wadhwa, 2012).

The idea that more developed countries must be essentially service economies is being questioned. It is indeed important for a country to be able to manufacture efficiently products and services simultaneously (Tate, 2014). Manufacturing shall be one of the key points for industrialized countries to face their regrowth after a global financial crisis that affected recently the global economy (Foresight, 2013). However, despite the positive forecast made by Manufacturing Europe's Future (Veugelers, 2013) the distance between the U.S. and the majority of European countries is significant and may keep growing. The U.S. shall soon become one the most powerful manufacturing countries in the World and, to achieve that, an integral and comprehensive strategy was planned and executed. The main difference between the U.S. and European countries was the huge investment on efficiency, productivity and the recently declared government incentives (Deloitte, 2012; Sirkin et al., 2011).

A number of economic related antecedents and motivations can be identified as contributing to company's decision to reshore. Table 2 summarizes the previously reviewed contributions.

Given the discussion above, we propose the following propositions for the Economic dimensions:

Table 2. Summary of economic antecedents

Concepts	Authors
Hand Labor Cost	(Arvidsson et al., 2014); (Bossche et al., 2014); (Dachs et al., 2006); (Distler et al., 2014); (Ellram, 2013); (Fratocchi et al., 2013); (Kinkel, 2014); (Kinkel & Maloca, 2009); (Kinkel & Montalvo, 2014); (Plumer, 2013); (Regalado, 2013); (Sirkin et al., 2011); (Schumpeter, 2013).
Flexible Employment	(Dachs et al., 2006); (Foresight, 2013); (Fratocchi et al., 2013); (Kinkel, 2014); (Plumer, 2013); (Sirkin et al., 2011); (Veugelers, 2013).
Shipping Costs	(Arvidsson et al., 2014); (Bossche et al., 2014); (Dachs et al., 2006); (Ellram et al., 2013); (Foroohar, 2013); (Kinkel, 2014); (Naitove, 2013); (Plumer, 2013); (Regalado, 2013); (Sirkin et al., 2011); (Tseng, 2011).
Currency	(Ellram et al., 2013); (Fratocchi & Silva, 2018); (Hutzel & Lippert, 2014); (Sirkin et al., 2011).
Midnight Phone Calls	(Gray et al., 2013)
Delivery Delays	(Gray et al., 2013)
IP Leakage	(Gray et al., 2013)
Communication Issues and Misunderstandings	(Gray et al., 2013); (Dachs et al., 2006); (Fratocchi & Silva, 2018); (Sirkin et al., 2011).
Constant Travels	(Gray et al., 2013); (Sirkin et al., 2011).
Inventory Expenses	(Bossche et al., 2014); (Sirkin et al., 2011).
Quality Control Problems	(Arlbjørn & Mikkelsen, 2014); (Dachs et al., 2006); (Fratocchi et al., 2013); (Fratocchi et al., 2014); (Kinkel & Maloca, 2009); (Kinkel & Montalvo, 2014); (Lahidji & Tucker, 2014); (Naitove, 2013); (Regalado, 2013); (Sirkin et al., 2011).
Supply Disruptions	(Ellram et al., 2013); (Sirkin et al., 2011); (Tseng, 2011).
Intellectual Property Abuses	(Ellram et al., 2013); (Sirkin et al., 2011).
Productivity & Efficiency	(Arlbjørn & Mikkelsen, 2014); (Bossche et al., 2014); (Deloitte, 2012); (Distler et al., 2014); (Ellram et al., 2013); (Foroohar, 2013); (Fratocchi et al., 2013); (Fratocchi & Silva, 2018); (Lewis, 2013); (Plumer, 2013); (Sirkin et al., 2011); (Tseng, 2011).
Technology	(Arlbjørn & Mikkelsen, 2014); (Distler et al., 2014); (Foroohar, 2013); (Plumer, 2013); (Regalado, 2013); (Schumpeter, 2013); (Sirkin et al., 2011); (Wadhwa, 2012); (Veugelers, 2013).

P1: Labor costs have a relevant influence on the decision of reshoring.
P2: Supply costs have a relevant influence on the decision of reshoring.
P3: Productivity has a relevant influence on the decision of reshoring.

Besides economic reasons, there are also marketing and consumer related antecedents for reshoring. In the next section, we will discuss how and why consumer and marketing related factors may influence companies to re-shore and how companies perceive and act upon those influences.

MARKETING ANTECEDENTS

Many companies are reshoring in order to get closer to their customers or being able to produce higher quality products to better satisfy more demanding customers (Fratocchi et al., 2014; Fratocchi & Silva,

2018; Naitove, 2013). Companies such as Caterpillar, GE, Lenovo, Apple, Walmart, Boeing, GM, Google, among others, are moving manufacturing processes, entirely or partially, back to the U.S. in order to become closer to their customers (Foroohar, 2013; Plumer, 2013; Regalado, 2013; Tseng, 2011; Wadhwa, 2012) and also in Europe this phenomenon has been receiving attention (Martínez-Mora & Merino, 2014; (Di Mauro, Fratocchi, Orzes, & Sartor, 2018).

An important argument relates to the consumer perspective about the origin of products. The Country of Origin Effect (COE) had been introduced by Schooler in 1965 (Dinnie, 2003) and has been studied for almost 50 years. The concept of COE refers to the consumers' perception of the Brand Name and Country of Origin Image (COI). In fact, consumers' perception of product quality is strongly influenced by two important factors: source country and seller's brand name (Han & Qualls, 1985). It is possible to verify this consumer phenomenon in almost all products – from automobiles (e.g. recently Opel developed a whole new communication strategy based on the idea of communicating their German born brand), televisions, and other supplies. At the same level, COI is also important to correctly define the consumer equation of product origin. Part of the products' performances are interpreted by consumers depending on the COI perception, and this means that there is a previous expectation about product satisfaction and perception of quality depending on the COI (Josiassen, Lukas, & Whitwell, 2008).

COI was first described as a halo effect that consumers unconsciously use to evaluate the products which they are less familiar with (Bilkey & Nes, 1982 cit in Josiassen et al., 2008). The halo effect has been studied for many years and frame-worked as a psychological field definition that finds common traces with marketing and consumer behavior. In short, it explains how a special bond and effective connection between product/brand/COE based on a previous experience is formed (Beckwith, Kassarjian, & Lehmann, 1978). Yet, there is still a difference between a belief and a real attitude which means that, regardless of the created bond it does not always gets translated into real attitudes (Erickson, Johansson, & Chao, 1984).

Thus, COI directly influences the way the product is previously and posteriorly evaluated by the customer and how this influence may also play a role in companies' decisions to reshore.

There is a consensus that a customer evaluates a product by the brand name and the source country image (Han & Qualls, 1985). Consumers may not know a particular brand but if they notice that the product is, for example, *Made in Germany*, they will evaluate it favorably (Josiassen et al., 2008) and this suggests that despite the importance of brand name, in the product evaluation process, the source country has a greater effect on the purchasing process (Han & Qualls, 1985). This perception allowed Han & Qualls (1985)to conclude that companies should evaluate better their consumer' perceptions before advancing to joint ventures in other countries. Due to the Halo Effect, consumers unconsciously categorize countries by their image (COI) and demonstrate divergent perceptions regarding quality, behavior, and intention to purchase (Josiassen et al., 2008). Those important evaluation factors should be considered by companies in the internationalization process since the customer is more likely to buy a product manufactured in a country with a positive image (Dinnie, 2003).

Despite COE misinterpretation, unawareness and disorientation pointed out by Samiee et al. (2005), other studies indicate that "*Made in*" awareness is becoming relevant. A 2012 survey developed by Perception Research Services International (PRS) concluded that 83% of the American consumers noticed the "*Made in USA*" on the product packaging. At the same time, it was observed that most of those shoppers – 76% - stated that they were more attracted and willing to buy the product after noticing the label "*Made in USA*" (Research, 2012). In the PRS study, consumers revealed that their main motivation to buy American products was to "help the economy" and at the same time associated the products with higher quality and safety. In parallel, the study also verified the perception of products labeled as "*Made in China*". Results showed that 57% were less likely to purchase "*Made in China*" products and the main concerns regarded Safety and Quality. It was also confirmed that "*Made in China*" products were often associated with cheaper prices (Research, 2012).

Whether it is for quality assurance, to boost the economy, or out of patriotism, buying American-made products is becoming quite fashionable among U.S. Shoppers. Asher cit in Research, 2012

Another current and relevant concern that affects consumption is the growing awareness of production on the environmental. Companies and countries are becoming more concerned about their production footprints. The act of protecting the environment affects customers' opinion about a company/brand. Furthermore, offshoring means travelling and shipping. For those reasons, reshoring is a good alternative from both perspectives (companies and customers) since it enables the reduction of environmental footprints and responds to one of the customers growing concerns: sustainability. Customers are more demanding for information about the materials used to produce the goods they consume (Gray et al., 2013). After all, reinforcing what has been mentioned previously with WWF (2012) clarify environmental warnings, it is possible to obtain an equation that it is a win-win option for all the involved parties. And yet, one important question that may position this trend along or deviate from it, with Green Consumer is: *How much more are customers really willing to pay for American products?* (Bossche et al., 2014).

Another important point in the reshoring equation is the constant growth of product customization. Companies are increasingly creating products that are partially or totally personalized by customers. Customers enjoy customization and the possibility to input their own character into a product. This enhances the importance of proximity: rarely is a customer willing to wait for 2 or 3 months (production and shipping time from China for example) to receive a customized product. This means that companies and production centers need to be near final markets in order to respond quickly to those demands (Foresight, 2013).

Finally, another interesting and strongly driving force of reshoring are "buy national" campaigns. Such campaigns intend to promote the purchase of nationally produced products convincing customers of their quality and the role of local manufacturing for the benefit of national economy (AEP, 2014).

Thus, the marketing-related factors have also addressed in the literature for their role in companies' decision to bring manufacturing processes back to their original countries. Table 3 sums up marketing reasons to reshore which are becoming more important since watchful companies respond to customers' needs.

Considering the aforementioned discussion, we propose the following propositions for the Marketing dimension:

P4: Customer proximity has a relevant influence on the decision of reshoring.
P5: Country of origin has a relevant influence on the decision of reshoring.
P6: Quality perception has a relevant influence on the decision of reshoring.
P7: Sustainability has a relevant influence on the decision of reshoring

Political and Social factors may also play a determinant role in the reshoring decision as examined in the next chapter.

Table 3. Summary of Marketing antecedents

Concepts	Authors
Customer Physical Proximity	(Arlbjørn & Mikkelsen, 2014); (Arvidsson et al., 2014); (Bossche et al., 2014); (Dachs et al., 2006); (Foresight, 2013); (Kinkel, 2014); (Kinkel & Maloca, 2009); (Lahidji & Tucker, 2014); (Plumer, 2013); (Sirkin et al., 2011).
Country of Origin Effect	(Almeida, Alves, & Miguel, 2011); (Dinnie, 2003); (Elango & Sethi, 2007); (Han & Qualls, 1985); (Josiassen et al., 2008).
Seller's Brand Name	(Almeida et al., 2011); (Han & Qualls, 1985); (Josiassen et al., 2008); (Samiee et al., 2005).
Country of Origin Image	(Almeida et al., 2011); (Bossche et al., 2014); (Han & Qualls, 1985); (Josiassen et al., 2008); (Roth & Diamantopoulos, 2008).
Customer Quality Perception	(Fratocchi et al., 2013); (Han & Qualls, 1985); (Josiassen et al., 2008); (Roth & Diamantopoulos, 2008).
Halo Effect	(Beckwith et al., 1978); (Dinnie, 2003); (Erickson et al., 1984); (Han & Qualls, 1985); (Josiassen et al., 2008).
Buying Attitudes	(Josiassen et al., 2008); (Research, 2012); (Roth & Diamantopoulos, 2008).
Made in Awareness	(AEP, 2014); (Almeida et al., 2011); (Lewis, 2013); (Research, 2012).
Safety & Quality	(Almeida et al., 2011); (Bossche et al., 2014); (Dachs et al., 2006); (Fratocchi et al., 2014); (Josiassen et al., 2008); (Plumer, 2013); (Research, 2012).
Environmental Awareness and Footprints	(Distler et al., 2014); (Ellram, 2013); (Ellram et al., 2013); (Gray et al., 2013); (Schumpeter, 2013).
Sustainability	(Ellram, 2013); (Foresight, 2013); (Schumpeter, 2013).
Product Customization and Fast Customer Response	(Bossche et al., 2014); (Deloitte, 2012); (Distler et al., 2014); (Ellram et al., 2013); (Foresight, 2013); (Fratocchi et al., 2014); (Kinkel, 2014); (Kinkel & Montalvo, 2014); (Naitove, 2013); (Schumpeter, 2013); (Sirkin et al., 2011).
National Campaigns promoting National Products	(AEP, 2014); (Lewis, 2013).

POLITICAL AND SOCIAL ANTECEDENTS

Subsidies and funds provided by countries to the economy (or sectors) are embracing with contradictory visions capable of boosting companies or destroy them (Mitra & Webster, 2008). Yet, there are countries like U.S. that were able to reorganize its manufacturing sector through correct strategies and governmental incentives (Ellram et al., 2013; Foresight, 2013), where new centralized policies promoted internal manufacturing by decreasing taxation and energy costs for companies who manufacture in U.S. (Bailey & De Propris, 2014), and the same was applicable also for companies that offshored and intended to reshore their manufacturing processes (Bals, Daum, & Tate, 2015).

Is a country interested in internal manufacturing and in captivating companies to produce internally? Yes, and due to several reasons. As companies were transferring their local manufacturing processes to offshoring (directly or by outsourcing), many work stations were lost and many companies started to generate significant part of the production value in a foreign country (Hutzel & Lippert, 2014). This meant that the industrialized countries were charging less companies taxes (for created and richness value), and at the same time deal with increasing costs derived from more unemployment or precarious employment (Hutzel & Lippert, 2014).

A common issue that affects European small and medium enterprises (SMEs) regards the difficulty to access financial resources (e.g. bank financing) required to invest and create new structures. This problem is more significant when taking into account the lack of strategies and policies emanated by European institutions (Foresight, 2013). Creating a standardized European policy for attracting European companies to return their production to Europe reducing trade barriers may led these companies to reshore, to grow, to create new jobs and to innovate. For example, as the U.S. successfully did with energy costs, providing electricity 40% to 70% cheaper than Europe and Japan (Foroohar, 2013; Bossche et al., 2014). This would result in higher company efficiency enabling companies to review their internationalization strategy and to assure that a quality product and process is delivered to the final customer (Veugelers, 2013).

Although many international companies may have already reshored, the employment impact in each country is not expected to be significant since the new manufacturing is creating fewer but more skilled jobs (Veugelers, 2013). In the 1980s, about 25% of the employment in the U.S. was directly related to manufacturing but those figures are not likely to repeat ever (Wadhwa, 2012). Improvements in work efficiency allied with technology transformed a sector that represents the same economic impact even if with many fewer workers (Tseng, 2011). A Liao (2012) study also noted that workers and company relationships improved when the company opted to reshore, creating higher happiness levels and productivity (Liao, 2012).

Albeit some optimistic visions predicting the creation of more than 3 million jobs in the U.S. caused directly by reshoring companies (Sirkin et al., 2011), and the fact that the number of manufacturing jobs is realistically increasing in the U.S. and in England (Foroohar, 2013; Schumpeter, 2013) a contradictory effect caused by sector self-regulation is expected (Gray et al., 2013) and as the technology evolves, more companies will be created but employing fewer workers (Schumpeter, 2013). A study on German companies realized that the impact of reshoring on national employment is irrelevant since, from 2004 to 2005 12.000 new jobs were created by reshoring but, in the same period, 86.000 were lost by offshoring (Kinkel, 2014).

Another risk that companies face when offshoring regards different political environments (Foresight, 2013). The political environment is important for a company but it is even more important when the company is dealing directly (as importer or exporter) with multiple countries (Roe, 2003). The supply interruption risk, despite not being one of the major concerns for American and European companies (Ellram et al., 2013) can be very prejudicial for a company image (Sirkin et al., 2011). Plus, political conflicts can appear when less expected and cause immediate and severe consequences for the involved companies, as with the recent example of European Union and American sanctions to Russia (Siza, 2014).

The majority of the authors point to Government Incentives and Unemployment as the stronger political and social antecedents (Table 4). Still, as previously mentioned, Political Conflicts may become a huge obstacle for offshoring and consequently a potential antecedent for a reshoring decision.

Given the aforementioned discussion, we propose the following propositions for the Political and Social antecedents:

P8: Government incentives have a relevant influence on the decision of reshoring.
P9: Political conflicts have a relevant influence on the decision of reshoring.
P10: Unemployment has a relevant influence on the decision of reshoring.

Table 4. Summary of political and social antecedents

Concepts	Authors
Government Incentives	(Deloitte, 2012); (Elango & Sethi, 2007); (Ellram et al., 2013); (Foresight, 2013); (Fratocchi et al., 2014); (Hutzel & Lippert, 2014); (Plumer, 2013); (Regalado, 2013); (Schumpeter, 2013); (Sirkin et al., 2011); (Wadhwa, 2012); (Veugelers, 2013).
Political Conflicts	(Foresight, 2013)
Unemployment	(Dachs et al., 2006); (Foresight, 2013); (Foroohar, 2013); (Gray et al., 2013); (Hutzel & Lippert, 2014); (Kinkel, 2014); (Plumer, 2013); (Regalado, 2013); (Schumpeter, 2013); (Wadhwa, 2012); (Veugelers, 2013).

PROPOSED MODEL

As referred along this paper, although many authors from different countries have studied the reshoring phenomenon under different activity sectors and external environments, most of the reshoring theory is not yet fully developed and that gap takes more profound significance when regards to terms like: reshoring concept, reshoring amplitude, reshoring investigation model, conceptual framework and most important, due to its direct impact for academic and professional, the antecedents of reshoring and their individual impact in a reshoring decision.

Taking as base all the dimensions and sub dimensions presented during this paper, we developed the following comprehensive model (Figure 1) which intends to represent the antecedents of reshoring.

In every scientific study, knowing barriers and limits may work as an interesting indicator of the path that investigators can take. That indicative path shall allow the investigator to focus her / his study in other more relevant topics, constructing more advanced theories and variables testing. This model and this study intend precisely to design a common model that can be used by investigators, independently of their origin or sector in evaluation, to measure and evaluate reshoring activities. Only by using common measures will be possible to understand deeply the reshoring phenomenon and to compare / upgrade results prevenient from different and multiple locations and industries.

CONCLUSION

This article proposes an integrative model of the variety of antecedents of reshoring, which is currently considered by many authors a growing trend although the analysis of its antecedents require a thorough understanding. Traditionally, the offshoring academic debate documents how firms are able to disaggregate their value chains into discrete, value-adding activities, each of which may be located in different geographic locations to benefit from specific local endowments (Buckley, Doh, & Benischke, 2017). While this debate of offshoring is relevant, we believe that this research stream has reached a point that requires a different angle and new arguments to pursue. Therefore, the proposed model captures the variety of factors identified in the literature about the re-shoring, which represents a new angle of offshoring, under three main groups of antecedents: economic, marketing and political/social motivations. This model offers a starting point for further studies in this topic, specifically empirical quantitative studies, carried out in different industries aiming to contribute to the understanding of the drivers of reshoring.

In Europe the study of this topic is still in an early stage, although in the US it is already a well-known phenomenon. Over the last five to seven years, only 50 major companies reshored in the U.S. and major

Figure 1. Conceptual framework

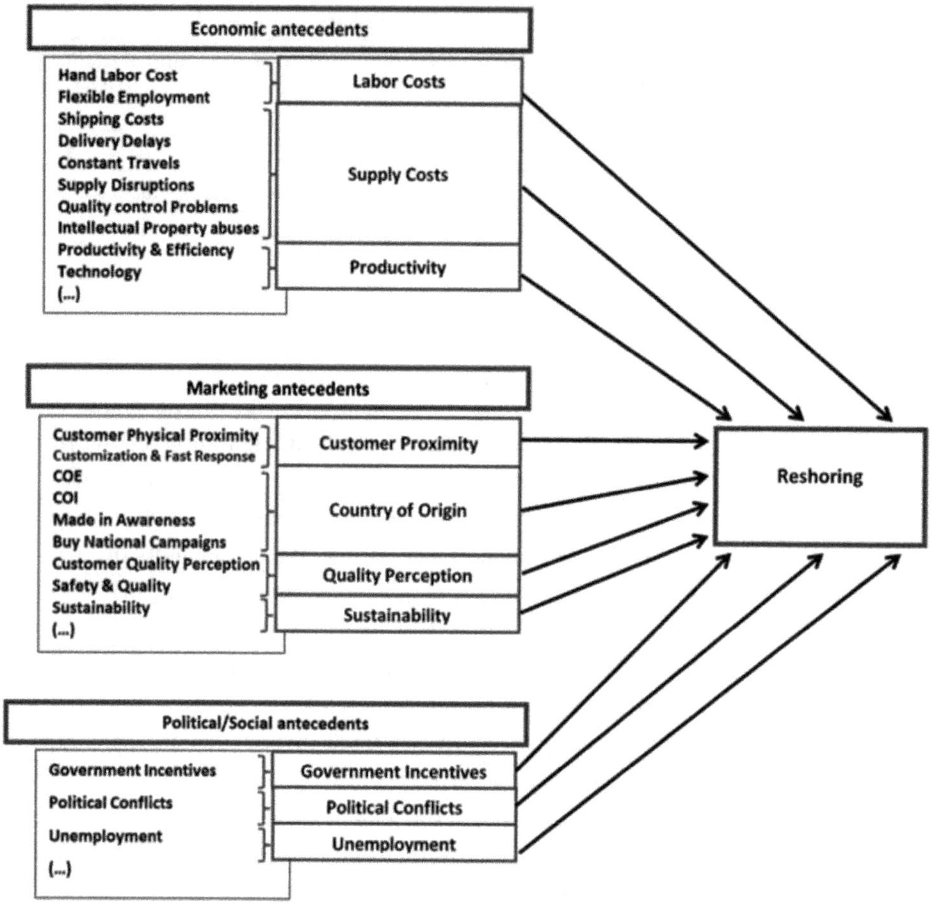

companies like Google and Apple, that have announced their coming back, started indeed domestic production centers but the core of the manufacturing still is being produced as offshore (Cottrill, 2014). This phenomenon assumes a crucial importance in International Business and International Marketing. However, at this stage there is still few data available to characterize this reality and sometimes the existing data is not correctly classified and easily accessible which hinders research Lahidji & Tucker, 2014). For instance, in the UK, in 2012 one in six manufacturers have reshored entirely or part of their production (Groom, 2013 cit in Arvidsson et al., 2014).

In Sweden, despite the fact that the term reshoring is not well known by many company managers, they claim that they would like to produce more in Sweden under the proper conditions (Arvidsson et al., 2014). In Denmark from a sample of 873 companies, 23,7% claim to have already offshored and from those, 21,5% have already reshored (i.e. according to the author's definition of insourced, offshored, and backshored) (Arlbjørn & Mikkelsen, 2014). In Germany, during the period of four to five years, four out of six companies that were offshoring decided to reshore (Kinkel & Maloca, 2009). Also in Germany, from 400 to 700 companies reshore per year, yet taking the years 2010 to 2012, this corresponds to only 2% of German Manufacturing (Kinkel, 2014). According to Dachs et al. (2006), in 2003 the UK was the European country with higher reshoring quota, 20%, followed by Austria 16%, France 15% and Switzerland 12% (Dachs et al., 2006).

These authors concluded that local supply is strategically more sustainable, economically advantageous, and creates a positive impact on the country of origin employment rates. Currently, it is easier to follow global manufacturing trends, and managerial habits, to manufacture in mass serving global markets. However, success in not guaranteed.

We believe that this study contributes to the advance of this specific field. Identifying and understanding the different antecedents for companies decision to relocate their manufacturing operations is an important topic that was not properly addressed in the literature. Therefore, developing and proposing an integrative model that contributes to better understanding this phenomenon is a worth research field to investigate in the area of international business. More research on this topic is needed and more cases need to be deeply analyzed. The use of qualitative research is fundamental for the systematization of findings. The case studies should cover companies from different locations, different business sectors and that allow to study in depth the phenomenon specifically whether initial outsourcing was conducted through firm's operations abroad or through subcontracting, whether all activities are performed in outsourcing or just some, and also whether decisions are made to relocate to the home market or to another one, different from the initial outsourcing location.

REFERENCES

AEP. (2014). *Compro o que é nosso.* Retrieved February 7, 2015, from http://www.compronosso.pt/index.php?option=com_content&task=view&id=2&Itemid=2

Almeida, C. Q., Alves, H. M. B., & Miguel, R. A. L. (2011). *A Imagem das Marcas Portuguesas de Vestuário Image of the Portuguese Fashion Brands. Vida Económica.* Lisboa: Vida Económica.

Amiti, M., & Wei, S. J. (2009). Service offshoring and productivity: Evidence from the US. *World Economy, 32*(2), 203–220. doi:10.1111/j.1467-9701.2008.01149.x

Arlbjørn, J. S., & Mikkelsen, O. S. (2014). Backshoring manufacturing: Notes on an important but under-researched theme. *Journal of Purchasing and Supply Management, 20*(1), 60–62. doi:10.1016/j.pursup.2014.02.003

Arlbjørn, J. S., Mikkelsen, O. S., Schlichter, J., & Thoms, L. (2013). *Danske producenters udflytning og hjemtagning af produktion.* Kolding.

Arvidsson, I., Magnusson, A., & Nilsson, K. (2014). *Reshoring, a trend in Sweden?* Umea School of Business and Economics.

Bailey, D., & De Propris, L. (2014). Manufacturing reshoring and its limits: The UK automotive case. *Cambridge Journal of Regions, Economy and Society, 7*(3), 379–395. doi:10.1093/cjres/rsu019

Bals, L., Daum, A., & Tate, W. (2015). From Offshoring to Rightshoring: Focus on the Backshoring Phenomenon. *AIB Insights, 15*(4), 3–8.

Beckwith, N. E., Kassarjian, H. H., & Lehmann, D. R. (1978). Halo Effects in Marketing Research: Review and Prognosis. *Advances in Consumer Research. Association for Consumer Research (U. S.), 5*, 465–467.

Bossche, P. Van den, Gupta, P., Gutierrez, H., & Gupta, A. (2014, January). Solving the Reshoring Dilemma. *Supply Chain Management Review*, 26–33.

Buckley, P. J., Doh, J. P., & Benischke, M. H. (2017). Towards a renaissance in international business research? Big questions, grand challenges, and the future of IB scholarship. *Journal of International Business Studies, 48*(9), 1045–1064. doi:10.105741267-017-0102-z

Canham, S., & Hamilton, R. T. (2013). SME internationalisation: Offshoring, "backshoring", or staying at home in New Zealand. *Strategic Outsourcing, 6*(3), 277–291. doi:10.1108/SO-06-2013-0011

Contractor, F. J., Kumar, V., Kundu, S. K., & Pedersen, T. (2010). Reconceptualizing the firm in a world of outsourcing and offshoring: The organizational and geographical relocation of high-value company functions. *Journal of Management Studies, 47*(December), 1417–1433. doi:10.1111/j.1467-6486.2010.00945.x

Cottrill, K. (2014). *Reshoring: New Day, False Dawn, or Something Else?* Retrieved January 24, 2015, from https://ctl.mit.edu/news/reshoring-new-day-false-dawn-or-something-else

Dachs, B., Ebersberger, B., Kinkel, S., & Waser, B. R. (2006). *Offshoring of production – a European perspective. European Manufacturing Survey*. Retrieved from http://www.isi.fraunhofer.de/isi-en/i/projekte/fems.php

Deloitte. (2012). *The reshoring of America - How can we take advantage of it?* Samson Bélair/Deloitte & Touche.

Di Mauro, C., Fratocchi, L., Orzes, G., & Sartor, M. (2018). Offshoring and backshoring: A multiple case study analysis. *Journal of Purchasing and Supply Management, 24*(2), 108–134. doi:10.1016/j.pursup.2017.07.003

Dinnie, K. (2003). Country-of-Origin 1965-2004: A Literature Review. *Journal of Customer Behaviour, 3*(2), 165–213. doi:10.1362/1475392041829537

Distler, J., Fernández-Seara, J., Gottstein, H., Haemmerle, V., Rasch, S., & Rohrhofer, S. (2014). *Apparel at a Crossroads - The End of Low-Cost-Country Sourcing*. Academic Press.

Dunning, J. H. (1998). Location Enterprise : The Multinational Neglected Factor? *Journal of International Business Studies*, 45–66. doi:10.1057/palgrave.jibs.8490024

Elango, B., & Sethi, S. P. (2007). An Exploration of the Relationship between Country of Origin (COE) and the Internationalization-Performance Paradigm. *Management International Review, 47*(3), 369–392. doi:10.100711575-007-0021-5

Ellram, L. M. (2013). Offshoring, Reshoring and the Manufacturing Location Decision. *The Journal of Supply Chain Management, 49*(2), 1–3.

Ellram, L. M., Tate, W. L., & Petersen, K. J. (2013). Offshoring and Reshoring: An update on the manufacturing local decision. *The Journal of Supply Chain Management*, *49*(2), 14–22. doi:10.1111/jscm.12019

Erickson, G. M., Johansson, J. K., & Chao, P. (1984). Image Variables in Multi-Attribute Product Evaluations: Country-of-Origin Effects. *The Journal of Consumer Research*, *11*(2), 694–699. doi:10.1086/209005

Fine, C. (2013). Intelli-Sourcing to Replace Offshoring as Supply Chain Transparency Increases. *The Journal of Supply Chain Management*, *49*(2), 6–7. doi:10.1111/jscm.12018

Foerstl, K., Kirchoff, J. F., & Bals, L. (2016). Reshoring and insourcing: Drivers and future research directions. *International Journal of Physical Distribution & Logistics Management*, *46*(5), 492–515. doi:10.1108/IJPDLM-02-2015-0045

Foresight. (2013). *The Future of Manufacturing: A new Era of opportunity and challenge for the UK*. London: Author.

Foroohar, R. (2013). *How "Made in the USA" is Making a Comeback*. Retrieved from http://business.time.com/2013/04/11/how-made-in-the-usa-is-making-a-comeback/

Frank Prevos. (2013). *Backshoring of Dutch Manufacturing Firms*. Amsterdam Business School, University of Amsterdam.

Fratocchi, L., Ancarani, A., Barbieri, P., Di Mauro, C., Nassimbeni, G., Sartor, M., … Zanoni, A. (2015). Manufacturing Back-Reshoring as a Nonlinear Internationalization Process. In Progress in International Business Research (pp. 365–403). Emerald Group Publishing Limited. doi:10.1108/S1745-886220150000010011

Fratocchi, L., Ancarani, A., Barbieri, P., Di Mauro, C., Nassimbeni, G., & Sartor, M. (2016). Motivations of manufacturing reshoring: an interpretative framework. *International Journal of Physical Distribution & Logistics Management, 46*(2), 153–176.

Fratocchi, L., Di Mauro, C., Barbieri, P., Nassimbeni, G., & Zanoni, A. (2014). When Manufacturing Moves Back: Concepts and Questions. *Journal of Purchasing and Supply Management*, *20*(1), 54–59. doi:10.1016/j.pursup.2014.01.004

Fratocchi, L., Equizi, S., Nassimbeni, G., Sartor, M., Ancarani, A., Di Mauro, C., … Vignoli, M. (2013). Manufacturing Back-shoring: Theoretical Conceptualization and Empirical Evidence. In *15th Conference of the International Academy of Management and Business* (pp. 1–10). Retrieved from http://beachvolleyball.guidedbees.com/~ruben/EDSI/papers/dimauro_manufacturing.pdf

Fratocchi, L., & Silva, S. C. L. da C. e. (2018). Manufacturing Back-Shoring and Direct Brand Creation in the Footwear Industry. In P. Thorvald & K. Case (Eds.), Avances in Manufacturing Technology XXXII (pp. 461–466). doi:10.3233/978-1-61499-902-7-461

Gray, J. V., Skowronski, K., Esenduran, G., & Rungtusanatham, M. J. (2013). The Reshoring Phenomnon: What supply chain academics ought to know and should do. *The Journal of Supply Chain Management*, *49*(2), 27–33. doi:10.1111/jscm.12012

Han, c. M., & Qualls, W. J. (1985). Country-Of-Origin Effects and Their Impact Upon Consumers' Perception of Quality. *Historical Perspective in Consumer Research: Natitional and International Perspectives*, 162–167.

Hutzel, T., & Lippert, D. (2014). *Bringing Jobs Back to the USA. CRC Press.* doi:10.1201/b17056

Initiative, R. (2015). *Reshoring Initiative - Bringing Manufacturing Back Home.* Retrieved January 31, 2015, from http://www.reshorenow.org/what-is-reshoring/

Josiassen, A., Lukas, B., & Whitwell, G. J. (2008). Country-of-origin contingencies: Competing perspectives on product familiarity and product involvement. *International Marketing Review*, *25*(4), 423–440. doi:10.1108/02651330810887477

Kakabadse, N., & Kakabadse, A. (2000). Critical Review--Outsourcing: A Paradigm Shift. *Journal of Management Development*, *19*(8), 668–728. doi:10.1108/02621710010377508

Kinkel, S. (2012). Trends in production relocation and backshoring activities: Changing patterns in the course of the global economic crisis. *International Journal of Operations & Production Management*, *32*(6), 696–720. doi:10.1108/01443571211230934

Kinkel, S. (2014). Future and impact of backshoring-Some conclusions from 15 years of research on German practices. *Journal of Purchasing and Supply Management*, *20*(1), 63–65. doi:10.1016/j.pursup.2014.01.005

Kinkel, S., Lay, G., & Maloca, S. (2007). Development, motives and employment effects of manufacturing offshoring of German SMEs. *International Journal of Entrepreneurship and Small Business*, *4*(3), 256. doi:10.1504/IJESB.2007.013251

Kinkel, S., & Maloca, S. (2009). Drivers and antecedents of manufacturing offshoring and backshoring-A German perspective. *Journal of Purchasing and Supply Management*, *15*(3), 154–165. doi:10.1016/j.pursup.2009.05.007

Kinkel, S., & Montalvo, C. (2014). Setting the scene: Global value chains, re-shoring activities, global innovation networks, and their impact on global innovation platforms. In *6CP Conference* (pp. 1–28). Hertogenbosch.

Lahidji, B., & Tucker, W. (2014). The Case for Re-shoring Manufacturing Jobs. XXVI Convegno annuale di Sinergie, Manifattura: quale futuro? doi:10.7433/SRECP.2014.29

Lewis, M. (2013). *Made in the USA, Again: 3 Firms Bringing Jobs Home.* Retrieved from http://www.dailyfinance.com/2013/08/30/made-in-the-usa-again-companies-reshoring-jobs/

Liao, W. C. (2012). Inshoring: The geographic fragmentation of production and inequality. *Journal of Urban Economics*, *72*(1), 1–16. doi:10.1016/j.jue.2012.01.001

Martínez-Mora, C., & Merino, F. (2014). Offshoring in the Spanish footwear industry: A return journey? *Journal of Purchasing and Supply Management*, *20*(4), 225–237. doi:10.1016/j.pursup.2014.07.001

Mitra, S., & Webster, S. (2008). Competition in remanufacturing and the effects of government subsidies. *International Journal of Production Economics, 111*(2), 287–298. doi:10.1016/j.ijpe.2007.02.042

Naitove, M. H. (2013). *"Reshoring" is not a myth.* Retrieved from http://www.ptonline.com/articles/reshoring-is-not-a-myth

Plumer, B. (2013). *Is U.S. manufacturing making a comeback - or is it just a hype?* Retrieved from http://www.washingtonpost.com/blogs/wonkblog/wp/2013/05/01/is-u-s-manufacturing-set-for-a-comeback-or-is-it-all-hype/

Regalado, A. (2013). *Made in America, Again.* Retrieved from http://www.technologyreview.com/news/509326/made-in-america-again/

Research, P. (2012). *2012 Survey Results: Made in the USA Matters to Shoppers.* Academic Press.

Roe, M. J. (2003). *Political Determinants of Corporate Governance: Political Context, Corporate Impact* (No. 451). Economics and Business Discussion Paper Series.

Roth, K. P., & Diamantopoulos, A. (2008). *Advancing the Country Image Construct* (No. 12288). Academic Press.

Samiee, S., Shimp, T. A., & Sharma, S. (2005). Brand origin recognition accuracy: Its antecedents and consumers' cognitive limitations. *Journal of International Business Studies, 36*(4), 379–397. doi:10.1057/palgrave.jibs.8400145

Schumpeter. (2013). *Manufacturing - The factory of the future.* Retrieved from http://www.economist.com/blogs/schumpeter/2013/10/manufacturing

Silva, S. C., & Silva, M. F. (2012). Failure is a stepping stone for success. *International Review on Public and Nonprofit Marketing, 9*(2), 153–179. doi:10.100712208-012-0084-2

Sirkin, H. L., Zinser, M., & Hohner, D. (2011). *Made in America.* Again - Why Manufacturing Will Return to the U.S.

Siza, R. (2014). *Novas sanções europeias contra a Rússia entram em vigor esta sexta-feira.* Retrieved from http://www.publico.pt/mundo/noticia/novas-sancoes-europeias-contra-a-russia-entram-em-vigor-esta-sextafeira-1669404

Tate, W. L. (2014). Offshoring and reshoring: U.S. insights and research challenges. *Journal of Purchasing and Supply Management, 20*(1), 66–68. doi:10.1016/j.pursup.2014.01.007

Tate, W. L., Ellram, L. M., Schoenherr, T., & Petersen, K. J. (2014). Global competitive conditions driving the manufacturing location decision. *Business Horizons, 57*(3), 381–390. doi:10.1016/j.bushor.2013.12.010

Tseng, N.-H. (2011). *Made (again) in the USA: The return of American manufacturing.* Retrieved from http://finance.fortune.cnn.com/2011/06/29/return-of-american-manufacturing/

Veugelers, R. (2013). *Manufacturing Europe's future* (Vol. 21). Bruegel Blueprint Series.

Wadhwa, V. (2012). *The End of Chinese Manufacturing and Rebirth of U.S. Industry*. Retrieved from http://www.forbes.com/sites/singularity/2012/07/23/the-end-of-chinese-manufacturing-and-rebirth-of-u-s-industry/

Williamson, O. E. (1985). *The Economic Institutions of Capitalism*. New York: Free Press; doi:10.2307/2392889

WWF. (2012). *Living Planet Report 2012*. WWF.

KEY TERMS AND DEFINITIONS

Backshoring: A synonym of reshoring; to repatriate production to the home country.

Country of Origin Effect: Psychological effect that describes consumers' perception towards a brand or product based on its origin.

Country of Origin Image: Initially labelled as Halo Effect, it is a psychological and unconscious evaluation of a product and a country based on a previous experience.

Manufacturing: The process of making/producing goods using manual labor or machinery, normally on a large scale.

Nearshoring: Similar to reshoring to some extent, however, while reshoring strictly refers to returning the production to the original country, nearshoring implies that manufacturing processes are returned to countries near the original production country.

Offshoring: Regards to the practice of moving partially or totally production processes, employees, activities or certain manufacturing functions to other foreign countries, normally low cost, as a way to lower costs. For this study purposes, there were no need to differentiate the two common types of offshoring: offshoring by outsourcing or offshoring by internal production.

Onshoring: A synonym of reshoring; to repatriate production to the home country.

Outsourcing: Refers to the process of purchasing or subcontracting goods, services or manufacturing processes from an external source, commonly known as supplier.

Reshoring: It is the process of returning previously offshored manufacturing processes to the original country.

Chapter 10
The Attitudes Towards Nearshoring vs. Offshoring on the IT Services Industry

Samuel Pranto
Universidade de Coimbra, Portugal

Arnaldo Coelho
Universidade de Coimbra, Portugal

ABSTRACT

The main topic of this investigation is the outsourcing of IT services and subsequent analysis of the delivery method based on proximity, examining whether the work would be delivered through a nearshoring model or via an offshoring one. The main goal is therefore to determine the antecedents of the "attitude towards outsourcing," as well as their consequences. The statistical analysis, based on a sample of 88 respondents, shows that the factors that may influence the "attitude towards outsourcing" are strategy, service suppliers, and supplier trust. As a consequence, we have behavioral intention when dealing with a nearshoring vs. offshoring scenario. The study of the details behind the type of the outsourcing options, either nearshoring or offshoring, an individual within an organization is more willing/likely to use, based on behavioral intention, is the main innovative aspect of this research. As per the results of this study, the above was also considered as a valid consequent to the existing models and has shown to be a relevant construct in this context.

INTRODUCTION

The growing interest in the outsourcing of IT services arises from the fact that we are currently dealing with an increasingly demanding market, where products and/or associated services undergo a faster and reduced life-cycle, due to constant innovation. In order to achieve the necessary flexibility to innovate with the required quality and speed, companies use subcontracting of specialized services from specialist supplier companies (Bernstorff, 2003).

DOI: 10.4018/978-1-5225-8906-8.ch010

IT services outsourcing is a global-scale business with exciting growth prospects and is already driving very large sums of money. According to Gartner, in 2013, a worldwide spending of approximately $288 billion was expected, driven by an expected growth of 5.1%. This trend remained constant, according to the Computer Economics' IT Outsourcing Statistics 2016/2017, which states that the budget available for IT outsourcing rose, in 2016, 10.6%.

Research in areas such as distributed work, global strategy and economic geography, show that, despite the present phenomenon of globalization that we currently experience, service and/or product delivery location still represents a major factor in decision-making. (Kiesler & Cummings, 2002) argue that proximity is critical to the development of group interactions and for building social connections; technology alone is insufficient to recreate the same facilities in a remote environment (Willcocks, Lacity, & Sauer, 2017).

Proximity outsourcing, which has been used extensively over the past two decades for software development, is presently being addressed for more elaborate and complex purposes. (Guedes, 2015) states that the benefits that can be derived from the use of outsourcing services, namely nearshoring, in Digital Transformation projects are very positive, and when compared with a traditional delivery model, it is shown that they offer substantial financial advantages, and an increase in ROI, without significant loss of quality or added risk. Thus, the adoption of this delivery model significantly reduces the cost of implementing the projects, while at the same time guarantees the same quality standards to the client, with a lower total final cost (Hahn, Bunyaratavej, & Doh, 2011).

Also, (Porter, 1998) argues that although the ease of obtaining capital, resources, and information at a global level is appealing, there is evidence that there is a competitive advantage in proximity, especially in areas such as knowledge and relationships (McIvor, 2010).

Given that the decision to outsource IT services entails high strategic and economic risks, as (Schneider & Sunyaev, 2016) state, a study is needed to support IT market decision-makers, such as project managers, delivery executives, service providers, and other professionals that may somehow be related to the theme. When they are provided with useful and up-to-date information that facilitates their understanding of the market, they can make better decisions, and influence their institutions positively (Tate, 2014).

The main goal of this research is to understand the relationship between the customer and the IT service provider, and their preferences regarding the delivery method. It will study consumer attitude towards outsourcing services taking into account the following factors: strategy, environment, project indicators, cost, service providers, suppliers trust, opportunistic behaviors. Subsequently, it offers a deeper analysis on the preference for nearshoring vs. offshoring.

OUTSOURCING, IT SERVICES OUTSOURCING, OFFSHORING AND NEARSHORING

Outsourcing

With the increase of competitiveness, companies are focused in having the best collaborators in order to deliver products/services of excellence. Obtaining employees who can leverage corporate competitiveness, in turn, creates a variety of outsourcing opportunities, which has grown exponentially, becoming one of the biggest businesses of the future.

Outsourcing had been for many years an underutilized resource, until the early 1990s, when strategic vision finally changed, so much that companies began to delegate even core functions such as production, logistics, product design and other innovation-related activities. Since then, subcontracting has been viewed as one of the most advanced ways for companies to follow. In this context, outsourcing has gained a strong position as organizations, concerned with minimizing costs, increasing productivity and competitiveness, have begun to restructure internal processes (Pedriali, 2004). Thus, outsourcing as a method of subcontracting has assumed a preponderant role in IT and has contributed to the new context that is currently characterizing the labor market.

Following this trend, it was necessary to establish a transparent partnership between client and service provider (Pedriali, 2004). In this way, partnerships were created between companies in the different sectors of activity, to implement new tools in outsourcing.

Outsourcing has become crucial in this new situation, by developing the conditions that emerged from this new world economic order. Outsourcing is an original English term, a neologism that in business environment is characterized as a management technique through which a third party, mostly a company, is interposed in the typical relationship of work (employee versus employer). It is intended, therefore, not the interposition in the traditional employment relationship, of a worker as a third party, but of a company that will assume the service or activity (Cherchiglia, 2004). According to Cherchiglia, outsourcing can be defined as the process by which the company, intending to achieve higher quality, productivity and cost reduction, transfers to a different company a certain service or production of a specific product. Certain activity is no longer performed by employees of company "A" to be executed by company "B", called "outsourced" (Cherchiglia, 2004). That is, through a process of transferring functions/activities from the "origin company" to the "destination company" (subcontracted). These functions may include phases of the "origin-company" process itself, or only underlying activities/services, such as cleaning and maintenance services, food preparation and distribution for company employees, security services, material handling, shipping and marketing of final products, among others (Cherchiglia, 2004). Outsourcing means passing on responsibility to third parties for the execution of an activity or set of activities (Araújo, 2011). Araújo also emphasizes that subcontracting cannot have as consequence or purpose the exemption of social and legal charges. For him, subcontracting is not a way to reduce the benefits granted to an organization's employees, nor to mass resignation or reduction of wages.

These changes in the production process, which have evolved from restructuring and industrial transition processes, have been shown to be a preponderant factor in competitiveness. Achieving greater competitiveness, translated into greater performance in terms of quality and productivity, has been the main objective of companies that use outsourcing services. As a result, this reorganization implies a simplification of the organizational structure, through the elimination of hierarchical levels, sectors, as well as administrative and operational areas, in the search for greater efficiency in decision-making.

Outsourcing also ensures good results for businesses as it allows a review of the company's organizational structure. Companies often have very intricate organizational structures and are immersed in routines/processes and resources that could be put to a better use in other activities or dismissed to other companies. Therefore, outsourcing becomes an incentive for the organization to highlight what is fundamental to its existence (Araújo, 2014). In other words, specialized companies may take over non-essential tasks for the business itself, and to transfer onto these some of the activities and services is a strategic option.

Therefore, outsourcing and cooperation between companies are inseparable. The main goal is to optimize production, quality, profit and competitiveness, through a process of horizontalization, thus simplifying the organizational structure, so that companies can focus their efforts on the best methodology for obtaining the end-activity product. In addition, it allows for a reduction of the final price of the product or service, by reducing labor and preventive costs. Another outcome is that there will also be a greater specialization of service providers (Cherchiglia, 2004).

Today, outsourcing is widely regarded as a strategic tool when it is used to add value, as well as to transform a business. Subcontracting adds a new link to the supply chain and this is usually equivalent to an extra guarantee ("The Reality of IT Outsourcing in 2018 - ITChronicles," 2018)

IT Services Outsourcing

IT companies turn to outsourcing for a several of reasons. Entities overseeing the industry attribute this to two main reasons. The first is due to a change in business strategy, where most companies have abandoned the diversification of their service/product portfolio and have focused on core competencies. Administrations today focus on competencies that stand out from the competition by looking at them as competitive advantages, outsourcing virtually all other activities that do not bring added value. The second reason is that it is difficult to quantify the value that corporate IT departments bring to the structure. This is, however, considered as an essential cost, but to be minimized through outsourcing (Dibbern, Goles, Hirschheim, & Jayatilaka, 2004).

These two factors, focusing on a new business strategy and perceived high IT costs, have led many administrations to accept several million-dollar outsourcing contracts for IT services. So, the question that remains for these administrations is where they are going to procure these services and not how to outsource.

Offshoring

Commonly mistaken, the terms outsourcing, and offshoring refer to different things. This distinction can be made based on two criteria: location of the place of execution of the task (in the country of origin or foreign), and responsibility for the execution of the task (in-house or external). Whenever a task is performed by an external entity, rather than within the structure itself, we can say that this is an outsourcing case. Since this external entity may be in the country of origin or located abroad, in the latter we are facing an international outsourcing activity.

However, whenever a task or service that took place at the company's country is moved abroad, it is automatically characterized as offshoring. Therefore, offshoring may include tasks or services performed by parent company subsidiaries or by independent suppliers through contracts signed between them (Bottini, Ernst, & Luelbker, 2007). In more detail, there are two main offshoring types that can be distinguished between the captive model and the "outsourced" model. The first one is characterized by the usage of a service center that is owned or managed by the main company, the second one by contracting a third-party company or labor, that can provide the services needed (Lewin & Peeters, 2006). Another definition of the captive model and the "outsourced" model was presented by (Nieto & Rodríguez, 2011), where she/he states that the first one is performed by affiliate firms abroad, and the second one through arm's length relationships with independent foreign suppliers.

Table 1. Table that distinguishes outsourcing types according to localization and accountability

		Location
		National
Accountability	In-house	Local Production
	External	Outsourcing

Source: adapted from Bottini et al. (2007)

Historically-wise, it may be relevant to say that it was Kodak, in the late 1980s, who first made the offshoring of IT services abroad through IBM (Yadav & Gupta, 2008).

Nearshoring

There is currently a great interest in offshoring in the software development sector, as it has been like that for some years now. One can say that this practice has already achieved some maturity, as to have even become a segmented activity by now already. A wide range of terms characterizing the different delivery models have since emerged based on "shoring" and "sourcing" such as "farmshoring", "two-shoring", "best-shoring", etc. (Carmel & Abbott, 2007).

One of the most prominent terms among those described above is nearshoring. The term nearshore first appeared in the IT world at the hands of PRT, a software development company founded on the island of Barbados in 1995. PTR founder was a shrewd marketeer who, in order to differentiate his company from those based in India, decided to use the term "near", as opposed to "far", to emphasize the advantages associated with the proximity of the United States.

Erber & Sayed-Ahmed, (2005) states that literature often refers the concept of nearshoring as service outsourcing applied to locations of greater proximity to the country of origin from which IT services can be decentralized. As an example, if the country of origin of IT services is the US, Mexico and Canada would be nearshore locations. In Europe, if the company's country of origin is Germany, we would have Ireland and Portugal as nearshore locations. In addition, the remaining services that were not decentralized are considered onshore services.

A more concise definition of nearshoring was presented by (Fratocchi, Di Mauro, Barbieri, Nassimbeni, & Zanoni, 2014), that is: "*Nearshoring denotes repatriating value creation tasks from the foreign host country to a location closer to, but not within, the borders of the home country*". Along with this definition a more illustrative example is presented below to help to understand the differences between offshoring and nearshoring.

Table 2. Table that illustrates the differences between nearshoring and offshoring

Location	Definition	Example
A foreign country placed in the firm's region	Nearshoring	A French company locates its (in-/out-sourced) production activity in Romania
A foreign country far away from the firm's home region	Offshoring	An Italian company locates its (in-/sourced) production activity in India

Source: adapted from Fratocchi et al. (2014)

CONCEPTUAL DEVELOPMENT AND RESEARCH HYPOTHESIS

Strategy

According to the strategy definition put forth by Chandler, strategy is determinant for the attainment of the company's long-term goals, for the adoption of action plans, and the allocation of resources necessary for the pursuit of these same objectives (Chandler, 1962; Quinn & Mccann, 1980).

Quinn (1999), point to the existence of two strategic approaches that, when properly combined, allow for companies to promote their skills and resources beyond the levels obtained through other strategies. They are: concentration of the company's core resources on its core competencies, and outsourcing activities where there is no strategic need or special capacity. Thus, the company can direct its resources to the processes and methods that bring competitive advantages and subcontract other activities so that it can make the most of it without the need of further investment.

Given the need to obtain specific and sophisticated information technologies, companies have opted to outsource services to external operators that have the necessary know-how and human resources (Bandeira, 2009; Dibbern et al., 2004). Several variables were considered in the reviewed literature regarding Strategy and Outsourcing in decision-making. This study focused on access to human resources, considering that outsourcing of resources makes it easier to access certain resources (Mozzini, 2011).

H1: There is a relationship between Strategy and Attitude Towards Outsourcing.

Environment

Factors such as power relations, economic and business interests and policies play a key role in an organization's decision-making (Pfeffer, 1981, 1982). From an organizational perspective, there is a hierarchy with structured levels of decision-making power. This power is essential to make intentions into a reality. Power and politics are crucial in decision-making in the IT sector (Markus, 1983), especially when it comes to outsourcing decisions (M. Lacity & Hirschheim, 1993).

The intrinsic risks associated with cross-border relocation of part, or all, of one, or a set, of IT services may stem from geopolitical stability and/or instability. Areas that are in latent conflict or at risk of war with bordering countries, uncontrolled sovereign debt, and unstable in the foreign exchange market are some of the factors that must be considered (Aron, Clemons, & Reddi, 2005; Willcocks et al., 2017).

DiMaggio & Powell (2000) define institutional isomorphism as "the major factors that a business organization must take into consideration are other organizations". In addition to companies having to compete in the market for resources and clients, organizations also must compete for political power and institutional legitimacy to obtain the much-desired socio-economic returns (Dibbern, 2003). Among others, this theory says that companies in general will tend to mimic (isomorphism) other companies in the same sector that are successful and have superior results (Mozzini, 2011).

H2: There is a relationship between the environment and the attitude towards outsourcing.

IT Project Indicators

ERP implementations, and/or major changes in the existing or non-existing software infrastructures within companies are complex projects involving substantial amounts of resources. These projects are usually subject to tight chronological scheduling and often unforeseen activities need to be conducted. As such, it is not uncommon for these projects to be fully successful, hence it is imperative to measure their success (Akkermans & Van Helden, 2002; Mary C. Lacity, Khan, Yan, & Willcocks, 2010).

In order to consider the decision to outsource (Bandeira, 2009; McFarlan & Nolan, 1995; Mozzini, 2011), the following seven factors must be taken into account: Complexity; Specificity; Difficulty of imitation/substitution; Value generation; Performance; Flexibility; and Operational Risk.

In order for a decision to be made it is necessary to design, at the start of a project, a detailed analysis taking into account the above-mentioned indicators, thus ensuring that the decision to subcontract was correct. This analysis also allows for the assessment of the actual needs of the type of subcontracting to be done, and requirements and knowledge procured to achieve success in the project at hand.

After the choice for subcontracting and the type of subcontracting to be done, it is advisable to carry out another analysis focusing on performance monitoring, in order to verify if any of the indicators are not being fulfilled, or if any of the indicators that initially had no impact on the subcontracting decision, can now have a negative impact and need to be resorted to subcontracting (Cooke-Davies, 2002).

H3: There is a relationship between the IT Project Indicators and the Attitude Towards Outsourcing.

Cost

According to Coase and Wiliamson, market use entails costs, and economic efficiency can be achieved through a comparative analysis of production costs and transaction costs. The success of a business depends on the efficiency of transaction management (Coase, 2012; Oliver E. Williamson, 1975, 1981).

Overall cost reduction was for a long time the main advantage in the decision to outsource, since by doing this, the company could use the remaining unspent money resources in other business operations. However, it is not only cost and profit that should be taken into consideration, but also the strategic aspects of the process. These undoubtedly influence outsourcing, but, in turn, should be controlled by costs (Dibbern, 2003). Outsourcing is a strategy to reduce costs, accelerate delivery, and gain access to skilled labor (Haq, Raza, Zia, & Khan, 2011).

H4: There is a relationship between Cost and Attitude Towards Outsourcing.

Service Suppliers

According to Kohn & McGinnis (1997), the ability of an external logistics operator to meet the needs of an organization has a greater influence on the outsourcing decision than any other fact. This is of significant importance, taking into account the need for companies to add value to their business (Mary C. Lacity et al., 2010). Companies that hire external services, when deciding to outsource, wish to have access to state-of-the-art products, services and technology, and qualified human resources (Guedes, 2015). In addition of having a solid reputation and experience in the field, suppliers must offer specific services, ensure the necessary geographic coverage, and have the essential resources.

Therefore, to ensure the highest levels of quality and productivity, the drafting of contracts and the development of relationships must also encourage a state of partnership and increase the flexibility of agreements. Nevertheless, some difficulties may arise at times between the management of the models of the provided services and the development of this relationship (Prado, 2009). Supplier-customer relationship is determinant when it comes the need to be registered in a contract (Goles & Chin, 2005). This contract, in addition to clarifying the roles played by each party, is also limited by the uncertainty of an unknown future, or by extrajudicial mechanisms, and based on the confidence and understanding of each one, but which acts as a guarantee that future behavior will remain constant and as agreed upon.

H5: There is a relationship between Service Providers and Attitude Towards Outsourcing.

Supplier Trust

The confidence in projects executed by in-house resources, compared with those carried out by outsourcing, is generally higher (Currie & Willcocks, 1998). Regarding the possibility of opportunistic behavior, the need for safeguards against work done by the company's own workers is lower than towards external workers (Dibbern et al., 2004).

In this sense, both supplier and client must obtain a minimum of mutual trust in order to overcome the lack of knowledge and encourage the exchange of information and experience between them, leading to a "learn to cooperate" interaction. For this to happen, it is necessary a management of relations, through the introduction of monitoring and coordination mechanisms, establishing transparency in the agreement, opening space for trust and demanding exchange of information among agents. Therefore, it is useful to pinpoint and analyze the links that may exist between mechanisms of formalization, trust, and mutual understanding.

Well-drafted contracts drastically reduce further discussions around the scope of projects, and the dimension of risks both parties are taking, and as such they increase cooperation and trust levels between them (Willcocks et al., 2017). There is a social design that indicates that good governance of projects increases the likelihood of a greater sense of trust and cooperation, which may come to fill or resolve disputes arising out of omitted or poorly-drafted contracts (Goo, Kishore, Rao, & Nam, 2009).

H6: There is a relationship between Supplier Trust and Attitude Towards Outsourcing.

Opportunistic Behaviours

Williamson (1985) defines opportunistic behavior as the "pursuit of self-interest with willfulness," which is sometimes "flagrant, such as lies, theft and deception", and in many circumstances understood through "more subtle of deception". The author also argues that opportunism may arise *ex ante* or *ex post* to contracts. The former, *ex ante*, can manifest itself through the opposite selection, in which agents are unable to identify the risks or, even when knowing them, deprive themselves of divulging their true situation. The latter, *ex post* opportunism, is related to the lack of activities, or to the agent's inability to minimize risks, which raises concerns about how to guide compliance problems during relationships.

Opportunism is based on the concept of uncertainty linked to the behavior of individual agents, since human behavior also influences the performance of economic activities and is reflected in the analysis of transaction cost savings. If there were no opportunism, the transactions would automatically adapt, by means of simple preconceived rules, when unexpected episodes occur. However, to speak of the absence of opportunism is almost hypothetical, since in the real economic world its use is almost permanent, although not all conflicts of interest necessarily derive from opportunist attitudes. For this, it is enough that the agents express their divergent attitudes in legal behavior grounded and agreed upon by both parties.

In commercial relations it can be assumed that both parties act opportunistically, taking one side advantage(s) at the expense of the other(s) (Goo et al., 2009). The probability of opportunistic behavior is lower in a company, due to the existence of a hierarchy, than when it operates with agents in the market. The central argument regarding opportunistic behavior, as whether it exists or not, based on the existence of governance conditions that may be internal, hybrid or even external (Dibbern et al., 2004).

The opportunistic or unilateral renegotiation of changes in contracts can happen when the customer is confronted with limited supplier choices (Lacity & Willcocks, 2001). In this scenario, the customer is obliged to pay the proposed price, whichever is due to reduced or non-existent trading capacity. This is considered a strategic risk and occurs when the provider thinks he can offer his services in the way that suits him/her best. Notwithstanding, it may also be considered opportunistic behavior when the customer, as described above, has little bargaining capacity regarding the work and/or services provided by a supplier (Aron et al., 2005).

H7: There is a relationship between Opportunistic Behavior and Attitude Towards Outsourcing.

Behavioural Intention to Use Nearshoring vs. Offshoring

According to TRA (Theory of Reasoned Action), an individual's behavior is determined by the intention to engage in this behavior and in turn the intention is determined by the individual's attitudes and their subjective norms in relation to a certain behavior. The subjective norms are linked to the perception an individual has of what the most important people in his social circle think as to whether he or she should perform a certain behavior.

Fishbein & Ajzen (1975) defined the attitude as an acquired predisposition that responds favorably or unfavorably to a given object. The behavior of an individual can be predicted taking into account the attitudes that he has to similar behavior. The relevant attitudes for this analysis are those specific to the object of study and are not sufficient to consider the generality of the individual's attitudes (Ajzen, 1988; Fishbein & Ajzen, 1975).

In 1989, Davis presented the TAM (Technology Acceptance Model) theory, that is an extension of TAR (Theory of Reasoned Action) proposed by Fishbein and Ajzen in 1975. TAM is one of the most influential theories in information systems and explains how users are receptive to new technologies. This model is based on two factors, PU (Perceived Usefulness) and PEU (Perceived ease of use). PU defines the level at which the individual believes that when using a particular system, it would help him/her improve the performance of a task. Likewise, the PEU defines individual perception that the use of a particular system is easier and reduces the effort associated with the performance of a task (Davis, 1989). Contrary to TRA, TAM is a more specific model, developed to explore and predict the acceptance and behavior of an individual using information systems (Petrick, 2004).

Therefore, the attitude towards using Outsourcing is assumed to positively influence the intention to increase the level of Outsourcing. Based on TRA, we define the attitude towards Outsourcing as the overall evaluative appraisal, made by an employee who is empowered to decide whether to use outsourcing, either nearshore or offshore. In the end, the more positive the attitude towards Outsourcing is, the greater the intention to increase the level of Outsourcing for that current project will be present (Gewald, Wüllenweber, & Weitzel, 2006).

Based on these theories and going further on how behavioral intention can influence an individual to choose between nearshore and offshore, Thelen (2011) explains that an individual's sense of choice is inherent in the behavior associated with referencing a type of service from one individual to another, that is, the decision to procure a particular service is associated with individual perception by reference to another individual's reference. Taking in consideration that an individual's intention in performing a behavior, which ultimately determines whether or not he/she will perform it, is influenced by social pressures, or subjective norms, that arise from the individual's perception of how he is judged by others when he has this specific behavior (Vallerand, Deshaies, Cuerrier, Pelletier, & Mongeau, 1992), we think that for professionals that can, and are willing to outsource IT services, can have their behavior influenced by the above between choosing a nearshoring or offshoring model for their projects.

H8: There is a relationship between the Attitude Towards Outsourcing and the Behavioral Intention of using Nearshoring Vs. Offshoring.

CONCEPTUAL MODEL

Based on the model proposed to be tested in this research, we have identified as antecedents of Attitude Towards Outsourcing the following: Strategy, IT Project Indicators, Cost, Service Suppliers, Supplier Trust, and Opportunistic Behaviors. As possible consequents of Attitude Towards Outsourcing we can identify Behavioral Intention to use Nearshoring vs. Offshoring. The conceptual model is represented in Figure 1 with the previously listed hypothesis:

METHODOLOGY

Sample and Data Collection

This study is based on the assessment of the answers to a questionnaire presented to European employees of IT companies with decision-making power to influence the choice of the type of outsourcing they are willing to work with.

The respondents of the study were contacted through corporate social networks and through LinkedIn. The criteria used to build the sample were: individuals who worked in an IT company, holding a professional position of Project Manager, Delivery Executive, Manager, Consultant, or Solution Architect. Sales professionals were left out, since they could handle delivery of services in an indirect way, or not as directly as the professionals listed above. Within these criteria we have contacted more than 400 professionals and asked them to answer the questionnaire. 103 professionals have replied but only 88 questionnaires were validated, since 15 professionals declared to belong to the category "Others", meaning that they might not be in a position to directly influence the outsourcing decision.

Figure 1. Conceptual model

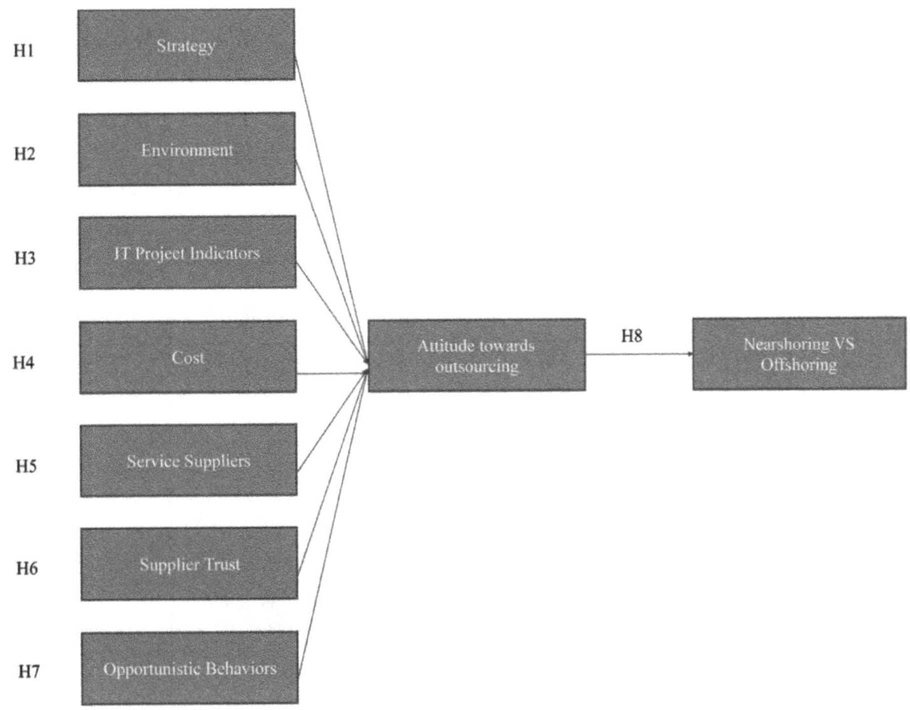

Measures

In accordance with the goals set for this study, we decided for a quantitative approach to analyze the data collected by the questionnaire. For the variables from 1 to 7 we presented multiple choice questions, operationalized through 7-point Likert scales, ranging from 1 ("totally disagree") to 7 ("totally agree"). For variable "Attitude towards outsourcing" was used a semantic differential scale. Finally, for variable 8, to assess proximity and/or distance, we allowed the respondent to choose only between nearshoring and offshoring, following on Putrevu & Lord's (1994) research to assess Purchase Intention, but also with a 7-point scale. In the table below are the scales that were used and their respective references:

Validity

Table 3 shows the results of the EFA and Cronbach alphas. Results show that variables present good psychometric characteristics. Variables are unidimensional, and alphas are above 0.7.

Fornell & Larcker (1981) criterion has been commonly used to assess the degree of shared variance between the latent variables of the model. According to this criterion, the convergent validity of the measurement model can be assessed by the Average Variance Extracted (AVE) and Composite Reliability (CR).

In table below the determination of these values for the constructs can be found, and according to them some comments can be made. All values for CR are above 0.7 which can be considered acceptable, regarding AVE all values are above 0.5, specially the values for CON and NVO that are above 0.7 which means that can be considered very good.

Table 3. Scales used for the questionnaire and respective source authors

Scale	Questions	Source Author(s)
Strategy	• Is the decision to outsource IT services influenced by the organization's strategy and is the process a core competency or not? • Is the decision to outsource IT services influenced by the strategy of accessing specific resources? • Is the decision to outsource services influenced by the strategic risk involved in the respective project?	(Bandeira, 2009) (Mozzini, 2011)
Environment	• Is the decision to use outsourcing of IT services influenced by the internal political environment (employees and administration)? • Is the decision to outsource IT services influenced by the successful environment of companies that opted for the same strategy (isomorphism)? • Is the decision of outsourcing IT related to the uncertainty of the external geopolitical environment?	(Bandeira, 2009) (Mozzini, 2011)
IT Project Indicators	Do the following project characteristics relate to the decision of outsourcing IT services? • Complexity of the project • Know-how of the resources (IT or human resources) • Capacity to generate value from the respective project • Performance of the project activities • Difficulty in implementing the project • Flexibility of the organization in relation to leverage the existing human resources capacity (e.g. knowledgeable resources/multipliers) • Operational risk of the project	(Bandeira, 2009) (Mozzini, 2011)
Cost	• Is the decision to outsource IT services influenced by the cost of the project(s)? • Is the decision to outsource IT services influenced by the management of the overall budget? • The decision behind choosing outsourcing of IT services, depends on the costs associated to it?	(Bandeira, 2009) (Mozzini, 2011)
Service Suppliers	• Is the decision to outsource services influenced by the availability of service providers capable of performing the activities that will be outsourced? • Is the decision to outsource services influenced by the availability of service providers that provide the necessary resources? • Is the decision to outsource services influenced by the availability of service providers operating in markets where the contracting company already operates? • Is the decision for outsourcing services influenced by the availability of similar suppliers operating with similar technologies to that of the contracting company? • Is the decision to outsource services influenced by the reputation of service providers available in the market?	(Bandeira, 2009) (Mozzini, 2011)
Supplier Trust	• The (external) IT service providers make beneficial decisions to us under any circumstances? • The (external) IT service providers is/are sincere at all times? • The (external) IT service providers make has always provided us a completely truthful picture of the relevant IT services?	(Goo, 2009)
Opportunistic Behaviors	Both parties, in a relationship between external service provider and contractor... • ...share the risks that can occur in the process of business? • ...have collective responsibility of benefits and risks • ...effectively carry out services that the other is dependent on?	(Goo, 2009)
Attitude towards outsourcing	Overall having outsourced IT services is: • Bad/Good • Negative/Positive • Harmful/Beneficial • Foolish/Wise • Illogical/Logical • Worthless/Valuable	(Dibbern, 2003)
Nearshoring VS Offshoring	• It is very likely that I will use an IT outsourcing service of the type: Nearshoring/ Offshoring • My next experience when outsourcing IT services will be of the type: Nearshoring/Offshoring • Most likely the next time you will need to outsource IT services, these will be of the type: Nearshoring/Offshoring	(Putrevu & Lord, 1994)

Table 4. Scales, variables and corresponding statistical analysis

Scale	Variables	No of questions	KMO	Bartlett's Test	% explained variation	Cronbach alpha
Strategy	Est1, Est2, Est3	3	0,667	0,000	65,130	0,731
Environment	Amb1, Amb2, Amb3	3	0,642	0,000	69,235	0,773
IT Project Indicators	Ind1, Ind2, Ind3, Ind4, Ind5, Ind6, Ind7	7	0,782	0,000	64,777	0,782
Cost	Cst1, Cst2, Cst3	3	0,634	0,000	57,891	0,734
Service Suppliers	For1, For2, For3, For4, For5	5	0,835	0,000	60,388	0,833
Supplier Trust	Con1, Con2, Con3	3	0,709	0,000	79,973	0,875
Opportunistic Behaviors	Cmp1, Cmp2, Cmp3	3	0,635	0,000	66,453	0,742
Attitude towards outsourcing	Att1, Att2, Att3, Att4, Att5, Att6	6	0,738	0,000	56,439	0,844
Nearshoring VS Offshoring	NvO1, NvO2, NvO3	3	0,768	0,000	91,249	0,952

Table 5. Table with the variance extracted (AVE) and composite reliability (CR) values

	S.D.	EST	AMB	IND	CST	FOR	CON	CMP	ATT	NVO	AVE	CR
EST	1,341	0,731									0,651	0,848
AMB	1,561	0,443	0,773								0,692	0,87
IND	1,049	0,686	0,507	0,782							0,567	0,901
CST	1,155	0,484	0,246	0,589	0,634						0,579	0,804
FOR	1,320	0,425	0,650	0,519	0,525	0,833					0,604	0,884
CON	1,767	0,315	0,517	0,273	0,190	0,362	0,875				0,799	0,923
CMP	1,463	0,553	0,467	0,431	0,316	0,328	0,674	0,742			0,664	0,855
ATT	1,135	0,515	0,569	0,519	0,476	0,634	0,574	0,502	0,844		0,565	0,885
NVO	1,991	0,444	0,583	0,335	0,296	0,517	0,747	0,626	0,548	0,952	0,912	0,969

RESULTS

Hypotheses testing was carried out using multiple linear regression, based on stepwise approach. The model of the antecedents of Attitudes Towards Outsourcing produced the following results:

Results show that variables "Environment", "IT Project Indicators", "Cost" and "Opportunistic Behaviors" will be excluded. According to the data obtained the variables that explain "Attitude towards outsourcing" are: "Strategy", "Service Suppliers" and "Supplier Trust". The model presents an R^2 of 0.581.

The model of the relationship between Attitudes Towards Outsourcing and Nearshoring VS Offshoring produced the following results:

Results show that there is a relationship between attitudes towards outsourcing and nearshoring VS offshoring (r=0,548; p==.000) and the model explains 0.301 of the variance of the dependent variable.

Figure 2. Attitude towards outsourcing

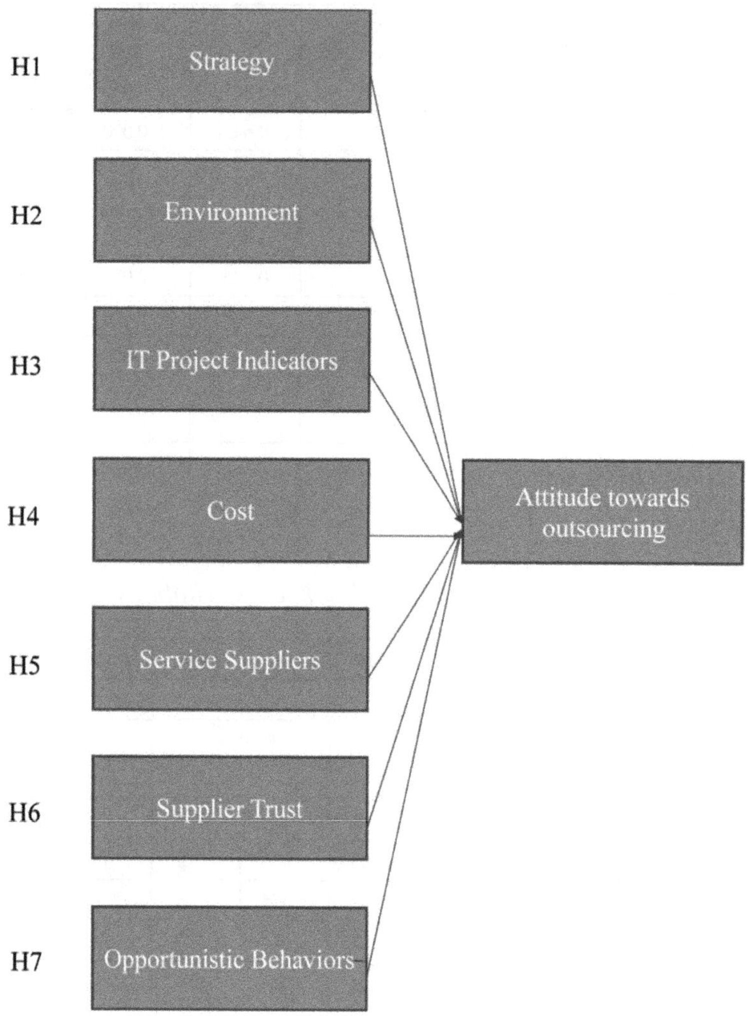

Table 6. Results of the hypothesis test of the sub model "attitude towards outsourcing"

R^2	R^2 *adjusted*	F	*Variable*	B	Beta *standardized*	T	Sig.	Durbin Watson
0,581	0,566	38,842	(*constant*)	1,294		3,336	0,001	1,945
			Strategy	0,195	0,230	2,896	0,005	
			Service Suppliers	0,351	0,408	5,046	0,00	
			Supplier Trust	0,227	0,354	4,586	0,00	

Figure 3. Sub model "nearshoring Vs offshoring"

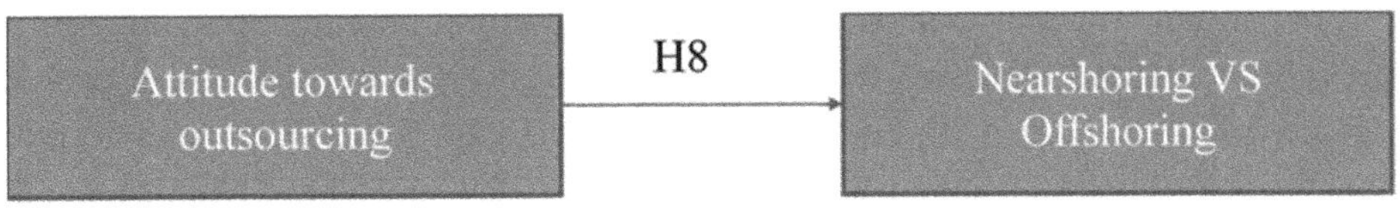

Table 7. Results of the hypothesis test of the sub model "nearshoring Vs offshoring"

R^2	R^2 *adjusted*	F	*Variable*	B	Beta *standardized*	T	Sig.	Durbin Watson
0,301	0,293	36,968	(constant)	-0,956		-1,145	0,256	1,466
			Attitude towards outsourcing	0,962	0,548	6,080	0,000	

DISCUSSION AND CONCLUSION

Throughout the analysis of the results obtained from this survey study, it can be concluded that the constructs "Strategy", "Service Suppliers", and "Supplier Trust" are antecedents of "Attitude Towards Outsourcing". Regarding the variables Strategy and Service Suppliers both Bandeira (2009) and Mozzini (2011), and Goo et al. (2009) for Supplier Trust, have found similar positive results in their studies. Comparing the obtained results with these authors' own results, has helped in validating the findings of the current study. The corroboration of these hypotheses allows us to conclude that a positive attitude towards IT Services Outsourcing results from a sum of some pinpointed factors, namely those linked to a Strategic approach, a positive view towards IT Service Suppliers and, finally, a positive attitude of Trust placed in the IT Service Suppliers.

The results regarding "Environment", "IT Project Indicators", "Cost" and "Opportunistic Behaviors", according to the study sample, do not influence "Attitude Towards Outsourcing". When compared to the results obtained in Bandeira (2009) and Mozzini (2011) for Environment, IT Project Indicators, and Cost, and with Goo et al. (2009) for Opportunistic Behaviors, we can conclude that, for these four variables, the aforementioned authors obtained positive results, contrary to what might be expected. On these four variables and their influence in IT Service Outsourcing there is considerable literature. As for the latter, Opportunistic Behavior, in fact, not that many authors consider it as an influence in the Attitude Towards Outsourcing. Despite all the bibliographical references analyzed and studied, it was not possible to prove, with the present study, the direct influence of these factors in "Attitude Towards Outsourcing". Perhaps, and from this sample, companies are more focused on their core businesses and consequently on the relationships with suppliers and the success of their strategies maybe is more important for them.

From a managerial point of view, from this study, it can be concluded that it could be more important for companies to find the right partner and the right producer for their work, partners that are aligned with their core strategies and also considered trustful from a supplier perspective, to ultimately concentrate on what is critical for business and what they are really good and unique.

The main innovative aspect of this study is directly linked to hypothesis H8, which tests the relationship between Attitude Towards Outsourcing and the Behavioral Intention of using Nearshoring Vs. Offshoring. A positive Attitude Towards Outsourcing is directly related with a higher probability of an offshoring choice, which is in line with Dibbern's research published in 2003. Another innovate aspect of this study is the use of an innovative framework, composed by several marketing related constructs and based on the TRA (Theory of Reasoned Action).

CONTRIBUTIONS AND SUGGESTIONS FOR FURTHER STUDIES

Contributions

This paper offers three main contributions to the field: 1. It introduces and measures Attitudes Towards Outsourcing; 2. It uses the variable Attitudes Towards Outsourcing to mediate the relationship between the main determinants and choosing between nearshoring and offshoring; 3. It uses a unique way of operationalizing outsourcing regarding a nearshoring/offshoring choice. The main innovative aspect of this study is the use of a model that includes Attitude Towards to address the different hypotheses around outsourcing, as well as Behavioral Intention to address which modality is most likely to gather greater preference.

As an additional contribution, and for researchers, this study brings together topics related to outsourcing, namely nearshoring and offshoring, through an extensive review of the literature available.

Finally, and for IT professionals, this study is expected to offer a positive contribution, particularly near those in decision-making positions in a given company. It is desirable, that with this study, they are able to see their task, of deciding whether or not to outsource IT services, more effectively. Likewise, it can also help to clarify the best location from where the services should be delivered, either nearshore or offshore.

LIMITATIONS AND SUGGESTIONS FOR FURTHER RESEARCH

In spite of the results obtained and commented above, at the end of this study some limitations were found, and some suggestions are also given when considering future works on the topic of Outsourcing Services in IT.

The first major limitation found was that we chose to use a convenience-based sample. Even though it proved more convenient and more feasible in terms of time and logistics, this method has some limitations when compared to a random sample. Likewise, even though the initial number of questionnaires sent to the target respondents was considerably high, the response rate fell short of what was expected.

In addition to this, it can be observed that the data was collected cross-sectionally, and measurement of variables occurred within a specific time-frame, thus preventing the analysis of changes that could occur in different time points. The data collected was based on the perceptions, opinions and subjective evaluations of the interviewed professionals.

Focusing on the statistical analysis, another limitation is related with using linear regressions, since we were not allowed to test the model from an end-to-end perspective, and only by splitting it in two sub models, and analyzing those. It is suggested that, in a future study, we use a structural equation modeling in order to analyze the model as a whole.

Another suggestion is that the study can be replicated with another sample, this time more comprehensive, since, as we have mentioned before, the sample used here was a very homogeneous one, which can be in itself considered a limitation. The fact that the present sample is not very heterogeneous, especially in the diversity of companies, has not allow us to draw more valuable conclusions from the respondents' business data and their answers.

The second suggestion, still related to business data, is to carry out a study focusing on a particular professional category. In this survey, several professional categories were addressed, and it is known that they individually entail different objectives, and where some may focus more on cost, such as project managers, others may focus on other factors, such as indicators of IT projects, abundantly discussed here.

The third suggestion will be to redo the study using other, additional, variables that may be relevant to the topic, such as "Management Commitment", "Past Experience", "Effort Expectancy", thus analyzing in-office management effort.

The fourth and final suggestion would be to carry out the survey study in other geographic areas of the planet. This particular study focused on European professionals, especially Central Europe's, and in assessing their views on outsourcing of IT services, but it would be equally valid to undergo the same research in the USA, for example, or in Australia.

REFERENCES

Ajzen, I. (1988). *Attitudes, personality, and behavior*. Milton Keynes, UK: Open University Press.

Akkermans, H., & Van Helden, K. (2002). Vicious and virtuous cycles in ERP implementation: A case study of interrelations between critical success factors. *European Journal of Information Systems*, *11*(1), 35–46. doi:10.1057/palgrave.ejis.3000418

Araújo, L. (2011). Organização, Sistemas e Métodos e As Tecnologias de Gestão Organizacional - Vol. 1. Atlas.

Araújo, L. (2014). Gestão de Pessoas - Estratégias e Integração Organizacional. Atlas.

Aron, R., Clemons, E. K., & Reddi, S. (2005). Just Right Outsourcing: Understanding and Managing Risk Introduction : objectives of this paper. *International Conference on System Sciences*, 1–10. 10.1109/HICSS.2005.368

Bandeira, R. (2009). *Fatores de Decisão de Terceirização Logística: Análise baseada na percepção dos executivos*. Universidade Federal Do Rio Grande do Sul. Retrieved from http://hdl.handle.net/10183/17636

Bernstorff, V. (2003). Influenciar a escolha dos profissionais de outra empresa para realizar tarefas para a sua organização garante o sucesso da terceirização da tecnologia da Informação? *EnANPAD*.

Bottini, N., Ernst, C., & Luelbker, M. (2007). *Offshoring and the labour market : What are the issues.* Economic and Labour Market Paper.

Carmel, E., & Abbott, P. (2007). Distance Matters. *Communications of the ACM, 50*(10), 139–178.

Chandler, A. D. (1962). Strategy and Structure. *Business History Review*. doi:10.15347/wjm/2014.010

Cherchiglia, M. (2004). *Terceirização do trabalho nos serviços de saúde: alguns aspectos conceituais, legais e pragmáticos.* CADRHU.

Coase, R. (2012). The nature of the firm. In The Economic Nature of the Firm: A Reader (3rd ed.). Academic Press. doi:10.1007/978-3-642-27922-5_22

Cooke-Davies, T. (2002). The "real" success factors on projects. *International Journal of Project Management, 20*(3), 185–190. doi:10.1016/S0263-7863(01)00067-9

Currie, W. L., & Willcocks, L. P. (1998). Analysing four types of IT sourcing decisions in the context of scale, client/supplier interdependency and risk mitigation. *Information Systems Journal, 8*(2), 119–143. doi:10.1046/j.1365-2575.1998.00030.x

Davis, F. D. (1989). Perceived Usefulness, Perceived Ease of Use, and User Acceptance of Information Technology. *Management Information Systems Quarterly, 13*(3), 319–340. doi:10.2307/249008

Dibbern, J. (2003). *The Sourcing Of Application Software Services: Empirical Evidence Of Cultural, Industry And Functional Differences (Information Age Economy).* Physica-Verlag.

Dibbern, J., Goles, T., Hirschheim, R., & Jayatilaka, B. (2004). Information systems outsourcing: A survey and analysis of the literature. *The Data Base for Advances in Information Systems, 35*(4), 6–102. doi:10.1145/1035233.1035236

DiMaggio, P. J., & Powell, W. W. (2000). The iron cage revisited institutional isomorphism and collective rationality in organizational fields. *Advances in Strategic Management, 17*, 143–166. doi:10.1016/S0742-3322(00)17011-1

Erber, G., & Sayed-Ahmed, A. (2005). Offshore outsourcing. A global shift in the present IT Industry. *Inter Economics, 40*(2), 100–112. doi:10.100710272-005-0141-8

Fishbein, M., & Ajzen, I. (1975). *Belief, Attitude, intention and behaviour. Belief, Attitude, Intention, and Behavior: An Introduction to Theory and Research.* doi:10.1016/j.ecolecon.2004.07.008

Fornell, C., & Larcker, D. F. (1981). Evaluating Structural Equation Models with Unobservable Variables and Measurement Error. *JMR, Journal of Marketing Research, 18*(1), 39–50. doi:10.1177/002224378101800104

Fratocchi, L., Di Mauro, C., Barbieri, P., Nassimbeni, G., & Zanoni, A. (2014). When manufacturing moves back: Concepts and questions. *Journal of Purchasing and Supply Management, 20*(1), 54–59. doi:10.1016/j.pursup.2014.01.004

Gewald, H., Wüllenweber, K., & Weitzel, T. (2006). The influence of perceived risks on banking managers' intention to outsource business processes-a study of the German banking and finance industry. *Journal of Electronic Commerce Research, 7*(2), 78–97.

Goles, T., & Chin, W. W. (2005). Information Systems Outsourcing Relationship Factors: Detailed Conceptualization and Initial Evidence. *The Data Base for Advances in Information Systems*, *36*(4), 47–67. doi:10.1145/1104004.1104009

Goo, K. Rao, & Nam. (2009). The Role of Service Level Agreements in Relational Management of Information Technology Outsourcing: An Empirical Study. *Management Information Systems Quarterly*. doi:10.2307/20650281

Guedes, J. F. (2015). Maximizing return on investment without increasing project risks - Near-shoring as a key practice on a business transformation programme: Case study on a training project for a global consumer goods company. *2015 10th Iberian Conference on Information Systems and Technologies, CISTI 2015*. 10.1109/CISTI.2015.7170387

Hahn, E. D., Bunyaratavej, K., & Doh, J. P. (2011). Impacts of Risk and Service Type on Nearshore and Offshore Investment Location Decisions. *Management International Review*, *51*(3), 357–380. doi:10.100711575-011-0078-z

Haq, S., Raza, M., Zia, A., & Khan, M. N. A. (2011). Issues in Global Software Development: A Critical Review. *Journal of Software Engineering and Applications*, *04*(10), 590–595. doi:10.4236/jsea.2011.410069

Kiesler, S., & Cummings, J. N. (2002). What do we know about proximity and distance in work groups? A legacy of research. In *Distributed work* (Vol. 1, pp. 57–80). Boston, MA: MIT Press; doi:10.1161/HYPERTENSIONAHA.107.103572

Kohn, J. W., & McGinnis, M. A. (1997). Logistics strategy: A longitudinal study. *Journal of Business Logistics*.

Lacity, M., & Hirschheim, R. A. (1993). *Information Systems Outsourcing: Myths, Metaphors and Realities*. Wiley Series in Information Systems.

Lacity, M. C., Khan, S., Yan, A., & Willcocks, L. P. (2010). A review of the IT outsourcing empirical literature and future research directions. *Journal of Information Technology*, *25*(4), 395–433. doi:10.1057/jit.2010.21

Lacity, M. C., & Willcocks, L. (2001). Global Information Technology Outsourcing: In Search of Business Advantage. New York: John Wiley & Sons, Inc.

Lewin, A. Y., & Peeters, C. (2006). Offshoring Work: Business Hype or the Onset of Fundamental Transformation? *Long Range Planning*, *39*(3), 221–239. doi:10.1016/j.lrp.2006.07.009

Markus, M. L. (1983). Power, politics, and MIS implementation. *Communications of the ACM*, *26*(6), 430–444. doi:10.1145/358141.358148

McFarlan, F. W., & Nolan, R. L. (1995). How to manage an IT outsourcing alliance? *Sloan Management Review*. doi:10.1016/0024-6301(95)91610-5

McIvor, R. (2010). Global Services Outsourcing. In *Global Services Outsourcing* (pp. 1–6). Cambridge, UK: Cambridge University Press; doi:10.1017/CBO9780511844911.001

Mozzini, S. (2011). *Fatores de decisão de terceirização em tecnologia da informação*. Universidade Federal do Rio Grande do Sul.

Nieto, M. J., & Rodríguez, A. (2011). Offshoring of RD: Looking abroad to improve innovation performance. *Journal of International Business Studies*, *42*(3), 345–361. doi:10.1057/jibs.2010.59

Pedriali, M. (2004). Business Process Outsourcing: uma importante ferramenta estratégica da terceirização. Anais do Congresso Brasileiro de Custos-ABC.

Petrick, J. F. (2004). The roles of quality, value and satisfaction in predicting cruise passengers' behavioral intentions. *Journal of Travel Research*, *42*(4), 397–407. doi:10.1177/0047287504263037

Pfeffer, J. (1981). *Power in organizations*. Pitman Pub. Retrieved from https://books.google.pt/books?id=pSe3AAAAIAAJ

Pfeffer, J. (1982). *Organizations and organization theory*. Pitman. Retrieved from https://books.google.pt/books?id=xy1VAAAAMAAJ

Porter, M. E. (1998). Clusters and the new economics of competition. *Harvard Business Review*. doi:10.1042/BJ20111451 PMID:10187248

Prado, E. P. V. (2009). Terceirização de Serviço de TIC: Uma avaliação sob o ponto de vista do fornecedor. *Revista Eletrônica de Administração*, *15*(3), 653–678.

Putrevu, S., & Lord, K. R. (1994). Comparative and Noncomparative Advertising : Attitudinal Effects under Cognitive and Affective Involvement Conditions. *Journal of Advertising*, *23*(2), 77–90. doi:10.1080/00913367.1994.10673443

Quinn, J. B. (1999). Strategic Outsourcing : Leveraging Knowledge Capabilities. *MIT Sloan Management Review*. doi:10.1074/jbc.M608048200

Quinn, J. B., & Mccann, J. E. (1980). Strategies for Change : Logical Incrementalism. *Academy of Management Review*. doi:10.2307/257320

Schneider, S., & Sunyaev, A. (2016). Determinant Factors of Cloud-Sourcing Decisions: Reflecting on the IT Outsourcing Literature in the Era of Cloud Computing. *Journal of Information Technology*, *31*(1), 1–31. doi:10.1057/jit.2014.25

Tate, W. L. (2014). Offshoring and reshoring: U.S. insights and research challenges. *Journal of Purchasing and Supply Management*, *20*(1), 66–68. doi:10.1016/j.pursup.2014.01.007

The Reality of IT Outsourcing in 2018 - ITChronicles. (2018). Retrieved January 5, 2019, from https://www.itchronicles.com/practices/the-reality-of-it-outsourcing-in-2018/

Thelen, S. T., Yoo, B., & Magnini, V. P. (2011). An examination of consumer sentiment toward offshored services. *Journal of the Academy of Marketing Science*, *39*(2), 270–289. doi:10.100711747-010-0192-7

Vallerand, R. J., Deshaies, P., Cuerrier, J. P., Pelletier, L. G., & Mongeau, C. (1992). Ajzen and Fishbein's Theory of Reasoned Action as Applied to Moral Behavior: A Confirmatory Analysis. *Journal of Personality and Social Psychology*, *62*(1), 98–109. doi:10.1037/0022-3514.62.1.98

Willcocks, L. P., Lacity, M. C., & Sauer, C. (2017). *Outsourcing and offshoring business services*. Springer. doi:10.1007/978-3-319-52651-5

Williamson, O. E. (1975). *Markets and hierarchies: analysis and antitrust implications: a study in the economics of internal organization*. The Free Press. doi:10.2139srn.1496220

Williamson, O. E. (1981). The Economics of Organization: The Transaction Cost Approach. *American Journal of Sociology*, *87*(3), 548–577. doi:10.1086/227496

Williamson, O. E. (1985). *The Economic Institutions of Capitalism: Firms, Markets, Relational Contracting*. Free Press. Retrieved from https://books.google.pt/books?id=lj-6AAAAIAAJ

Yadav, V., & Gupta, R. K. (2008). A paradigmatic and methodological review of research in outsourcing. *Journal of Information Technology Research*, *1*(4), 41–61. doi:10.4018/jitr.2008100104

KEY TERMS AND DEFINITIONS

Attitude Towards Outsourcing: The overall evaluative appraisal, made by an employee who is empowered to decide whether to use outsourcing, either nearshore or offshore type.

Behavioral Intention: Individual intention to use a delivery method that directly affects the overall delivery type.

IT Outsourcing: Management technique through which a third party, mostly a company, is interposed in the typical relationship of work.

IT Services: The use of technical, business applications and know how that allows organizations to create, manage and optimize their business processes and information.

Nearshoring: Service outsourcing applied to locations of greater proximity to the country of origin from which IT services can be decentralized to.

Offshoring: Whenever a task or service that took place at the company's country is moved abroad.

Outsourcing: Whenever a task is performed by an external entity, rather than within the organization structure itself.

Theory of Reasoned Action: Individual behavior is driven by behavioral intentions where behavioral intentions are a function of an individual's attitude toward the behavior and subjective norms surrounding the performance of the behavior.

Chapter 11
Relationship Between the Relocation and Operation of Global Firms

Ahmed Sayem
https://orcid.org/0000-0002-5446-8966
Shahjalal University of Science and Technology (SUST), Bangladesh

Miguel Ortega-Mier
Universidad Politécnica de Madrid (UPM), Spain

Andreas Feldmann
Royal Institute of Technology (KTH), Sweden

ABSTRACT

The authors address the importance of the operation of manufacturing networks in order to explain why a company brings its previously offshored facilities back. Fundamentally, this chapter stresses the relevance of network operations in the context of relocation, and hence, the linkage of network-manufacturing capabilities to the reshoring phenomenon. First, it focuses on investigating the relevance of strategic objective of international manufacturing to the management/network operations of international manufacturing network (IMN). Second, it explores the role of strategic capabilities of network-manufacturing on the phenomenon of reshoring. The empirical foundation of this research builds on data from multiple in-depth interviews at companies' headquarters in Spain and Sweden. The results showed the relevance of strategic capabilities of network-manufacturing to reshoring. The authors also provide the guidance for decision making in the operation of international manufacturing.

DOI: 10.4018/978-1-5225-8906-8.ch011

INTRODUCTION

Since the mid of twentieth century, manufacturing offshoring has renowned as a strategy for achieving competitive advantage. In recent decades, manufacturing in offshore facilities faced increasing pressures from changes in the cost structure, customer patterns, supplier's policy, host regulations, etc. (Tate, 2014). Thus forcing companies to handle complex issues when considering their presence in international manufacturing (Strom & Levy, 2013). Research on the importance of operation of global firms can help to gain insights into how to manage activities in dispersed facilities and how the network-related advantages are achieved through the operation of international manufacturing network. A manufacturing network is defined as a group of globally dispersed facilities of one multinational corporation that delineates a certain style of organisational structure for the whole network and holds responsibility and control over those facilities (Cheng et al., 2015; Colotla et al., 2003). Management of activities in international manufacturing network plays an important role in the performance and profitability of global companies (Ferdows, 1997). Research has validated the contribution of network coordination to attain competitive advantages of international manufacturing. It has also suggested that strategic objectives, such as competitive priorities of manufacturing in globally disperse facilities, are highly important for setting and implementing global manufacturing strategy. Meanwhile, the impact of such strategic objective/s on management of global operation is still unexplored, especially for determining the mechanisms of coordination.

Aside from the management of global firms, over the last ten years, the phenomenon of relocation of dispersed facilities has attracted attention from both the researchers and practitioners. Popular press have highlighted that several firms are facing challenges in operating their dispersed facilities (e.g. Wilkinson et al., 2015). Research on relocation or reshoring generally focuses on perspectives external to the firms in order to explain why a company brings its previously offshored facilities back. Specifically, research has mainly focused on its reasons which are mostly linked to economic factors; for instance, increased cost structure, lack of skilled human resources, product quality etc. (Foerstl et al., 2016; Fratocchi et al., 2016). However, in this context elements relating to the operation of dispersed facilities (for instance, capabilities of network manufacturing) have been less investigated and this work addresses that gap. Accordingly, this chapter stresses the relevance of global operation to the phenomenon of manufacturing relocation.

The remaining part of the chapter proceeds as follows. Next section illustrates relevant literature on manufacturing strategy and theoretical perspectives of reshoring is reviewed in order to show what research has been done. The third section is concerned with the methodology used for this study. In addition, this section introduces the conceptual framework. At the end of this section, a brief overview of studies cases are illustrated. Next section present the cross-case analysis in tabulated form, and discussion on network-manufacturing capabilities is carried out. Then we analyze the impact of strategic objectives (first research question) and relevance of operational issues to reshoring (second research question). Finally, we conclude this chapter by discussing our results and implications.

RELATED LITERATURE

Manufacturing Strategy and Its Deployment in Networks

There are several reasons for firms to choose international manufacturing. Researchers have addressed the issues of going abroad in the company's strategy for manufacturing. Most prior studies in the development of international manufacturing configuration, management's role -particularly in manufacturing- has been neglected (Dunning, 1988). Moreover, prior studies have approached international investment decisions from finance and economics perspective rather than internally generated priorities linked to manufacturing. Early literature on manufacturing networks came from factory management literature and tended to perceive the network as a number of individual factories (Shi & Gregory, 1998). Dubois et al. (1993) attempted to merge two complementary streams of research from the international business and manufacturing strategy literature through the development and application of a framework. They establish a link between international sourcing decisions and manufacturing strategy decisions. Miltenburg (2005) creates a framework for international manufacturing, which is very similar to the framework for formulating a manufacturing strategy (Miltenburg, 2009). Miltenburg (2009) attempted to incorporate several aspects of international manufacturing into one framework.

The research matter of this chapter combines the topics of international business and manufacturing strategy literature. Manufacturing strategy (MS) has been interpreted by various researchers. Skinner (1964; 1969) is the pioneer in defining the concept of MS, who refers this to exploiting certain properties of the manufacturing function as a competitive weapon thus helps to derive a competitive advantage from manufacturing. Hayes and Wheelwright (1984) defined MS as a consistent pattern of decision making in the manufacturing function which is linked to the business strategy. Eventually, the business strategy defines how the functional areas required to cooperate in order to achieve desired competitive advantages (Miltenburg, 2005). Hill (1986) views manufacturing strategy as a coordinated approach, which strives to achieve consistency between functional capabilities and policies for success in the marketplace.

On the one hand there is content related area address issues like manufacturing capabilities, strategic choices, competitive priorities, best practices and performance measurement; and on the other hand, there is process related area refers to the way the strategic manufacturing decisions are made (Dangayach & Deshmukh, 2001). According to Boyer and Lewis (2002), there is general agreement among researchers about the competitive priorities (cost, quality, delivery, and flexibility) being the content of manufacturing strategy. Competitive priorities guide the structural and infrastructural decisions for manufacturing, and those lead to the development of manufacturing capabilities. That is, manufacturers ability to compete on the dimensions of competitive priorities relative to competitors in its target markets. Process aspects of manufacturing strategy include design, development and implementation of MS. An investigation made by Marucheck et al. (1990), concluded that the formulation of manufacturing strategies mostly follows general conceptual models. In addition, the implementation process is less structured and more behaviorally oriented process than strategy formulation. Mills et al. (1995) have given a detailed framework for strategy process, which has been tested (Platts et al., 1998). The frameworks for strategy process usually propose a particular approach for implementing the developed MS; however, do not discuss in detail about how and where decisions on manufacturing strategy are made. Moreover, they merely consider explicitly or talked about how the process is affected when there are multiple facilities involved in a manufacturing process. Hence, more research is needed on the implementation part of the MS, especially considering how the decisions be made in the multi-facility manufacturing.

Theoretical Perspectives of Reshoring

International trade theories, international business theories, and strategic management theories have been adopted to explain the production location decisions, and the same could also be possible to explain the reshoring phenomenon (Fratocchi et al., 2016).

International trade theories focus on the relevance of production cost differences and the factor endowments between countries. In addition, these theories points on the specialization of production and cross-border transactions. According to Martínez-Mora and Merino (2014), reshoring decisions reflect the changes in the availability and cost of factors between countries when they change the factor endowments as well as competitive advantages; hence, restore the attractiveness of production in the home country. Mcivor (2013) studied the transaction cost and capability perspective on (re)location decision and concluded that efficiency of governance structure and the search for competitive advantage are issues when making a location decision. Williamson (2008) points to the high coordination and incentive costs that firms may face in the offshore location as compared to the home country. Moreover, some scholars (e.g. Kinkel & Maloca, 2009; Mcivor, 2013) highlighted that geographical and cultural distance could raise the risk of opportunistic behavior by the offshore facility. All these results in an unsustainable cost to foster the decision to reshore manufacturing facilities from dispersed locations. Sayem, Feldmann, & Ortega-mier (2019) showed that competitive advantage of network-manufacturing operation be gained through access to resources as well as capabilities to deploy those resources, and how such capabilities forces the companies in taking the decision to reshore. Hence, resource-based view (RBV) and the transaction cost theory as well be advocated to explain reshoring.

Internalization theory of Buckley and Casson (1976), and the eclectic paradigm of Dunning (1980) were developed with the aim to explain the international expansion decisions of firms. Internalization theory looks direct control over firm-specific, knowledge-based scarce resources, and capabilities in the most effective way for a firm to internationalize its activities. This theory applies the concept of transaction-cost and resource-based view theories to explain the efficiency aspects of MNC (Rugman, 2010). While the eclectic paradigm aims to explain the choice regarding international production by asking three questions: why -clarified by ownership advantage, how -internalization of know-how and value-adding activities, and where -the locational issues. Ownership advantage refers to the intangible assets of a company, for example, the management model and innovative capacity. Locational advantage relates to the benefits in the input of production regarding price, quality and productivity, as well as the lower cost of transportation and communication. Internalization-incentive advantage indicates the advantage gained from controlling specific activities by the company as its core competence, rather than transferring or outsourcing these activities to others. 'The final decision on which a firm should locate its production will depend on the character of its advantages and the extent to which one location helps to internalize intermediate product markets better than another" (Meijboom & Vos, 1997, p.794). These theories have also been applied to the international reconfiguration of firms (Fratocchi et al., 2016). For instance, a recent study by Ellram (2013) reports that reshoring can originate from changes in location-specific advantages, more precisely changes in the characteristics of the home and host locations. Dachs and Kinkel (2013) explain the reshoring from the perspective: deterioration over time of ownership and internalization advantages on which the initial offshoring decisions were made. Hence, these can be described according to Dunning's eclectic paradigm. Martínez-Mora and Merino (2014) highlights the governance choice -the cost of managing ownership in a distant location- as an element for relocation decision of international companies. In addition, Buckley and Casson (2011) observe that (re)location of facilities and the ownership influence each other.

In contrast to the views presented in the above two paragraphs indicate reshoring decision is reflected as their rational reaction to changing conditions (Gray et al., 2013), there are literature show the reshoring decision as a correction of prior misjudgments (e.g. Kinkel & Maloca, 2009) or as a more strategic and deliberate response to exogenous or endogenous changes (Fratocchi et al., 2015; Martínez-Mora and Merino, 2014). In addition, Kinkel and Maloca (2009) emphasize that SMEs can suffer from lack of know-how, and competent personnel for cross-border management during the planning and implementation of internationalization initiatives. In a similar vein, Gray et al. (2013) also highlighted that the decision-making process of production location choice is affected by inappropriate selection criteria; for example, little consideration of total cost analysis. Firms under this category tend to base their internationalization decision on simple, static criteria that do not adequately account for the impact of the dynamics and the uncertainties of offshoring. Once they gain experience from operating abroad, updated assessment of the critical factors pushes them to revise their prior decisions. On the other hand, Mugurusi and de Boer (2014) demonstrated that reshoring is a key strategic choice, "more than just a geographical shift of operations. It is also a reconfiguration of systems." (p.291). In their review, Fratocchi et al. (2016) mentioned three (out of sixteen) motivations or drivers of reshoring are an example of strategic choice linked to the home country: subsidies for reshoring, higher flexibility in the home country, and high unemployment rate in the home country.

RESEARCH DESIGN AND METHODOLOGY

The aim of this research is to test the relevance of manufacturing-network operation to the contemporary phenomenon of relocation. Insights gained from extant research, this research starts with a frame of thought for mapping coordination practices within manufacturing network and for investigating the linkage of network operations with relocation (see. Figure 1). With reference to the (Sayem, Feldmann, & Ortega-Mier, 2018), we formulate first research question.

- **Research Question One:** How does the strategic objective of international manufacturing affect the management of IMN? This question emphasis on the consideration of competitive priorities and the focus of offshored facilities in the coordination of activities of international manufacturing. As discussed by Santos (2000) and Ward et al. (1998) we consider four basic elements of competitive priorities: cost, quality, flexibility, and delivery lead-time.

Figure 1. Conceptual framework developed as part of this chapter

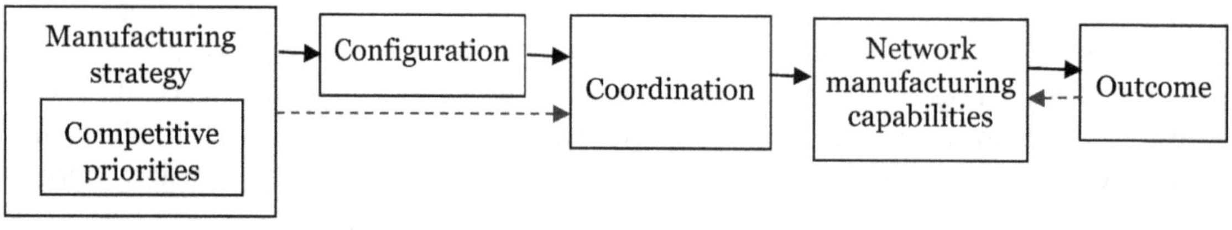

The second part of the analysis is to investigate the relevance of operational issues to the relocation choice. Therefore, research question 2 is formulated as,

- **Research Question Two**: How do the capabilities linked to network operation infer the reshoring phenomenon? This question stressed on a better understanding of relocation phenomenon in order to understand how the problems arose in operations of dispersed facilities, and whether the capabilities derived from the operations can link to the relocation decisions.

The case study as a research methodology is useful for studies that require in-depth descriptions and focus on how or why a social phenomenon works (Voss, Tsikriktsis, & Frohlich, 2002; Yin, 2009). Since manufacturing networks are such complex systems, there may be several alternative explanations for observed outcomes. In this context, the use of case studies can prove favorable (Stuart, McCutcheon, Handfield, McLachlin, & Samson, 2002). Although case studies can be used for exploratory as well as confirmatory research, it is especially suited for exploratory studies. One of its strengths is the ability to adjust the data collection during the research process (Stuart et al., 2002).

Posed questions were investigated using a case-based methodology that combines multiple in-depth interviews conducted in some European-based companies (headquartered in Spain and Sweden) that has experience on offshored manufacturing as well as on relocation of facilities from dispersed locations, e.g. China, Thailand, and India. A multiple-case design was chosen to enhance external validity. Data were collected via interviews with semi-structured questionnaires, and study of company reports. Qualitative data were analyzed following a theory building process proposed by Miles and Huberman (1994), to refine the emerging research concept.

Case Selection

This study is based on in-depth case studies in multiple companies, in which cases are selected based on suitability for illuminating and revealing the phenomenon of interest, thereby extending relationships and logic among attributes (Eisenhardt & Graebner, 2007). Case selection was performed in two actions. First, we searched for companies from different industry sectors and different business orientations. Those companies had already offshored a range of their manufacturing activities and operating dispersed facilities in their network. In fact, accessibility is very important (Patton, 1990), hence the final selection was based on accessibility i.e. we had the best data access regarding coordination of multiple facilities in their networks. In selecting the cases, access to the companies and their particular characteristics were factors taken into consideration. Four companies from different industries were selected for an in-depth analysis while ensuring that views were captured from multiple business areas. According to Barratt, Choi, and Li (2011), the number of cases is considered acceptable for a multiple case-study research; meanwhile, a small sample was chosen because of the expected difficulty in obtaining comprehensive information from a large number of cases. The unit of analysis in this study is the targeted product/product line at the manufacturing plant and its corresponding network.

Data Collection and Analysis

The data were collected in two steps from different sources. First, documents from secondary sources, such as company reports and presentation materials for stakeholders, were collected and analyzed to obtain knowledge about the companies as well as their manufacturing networks. Second, the information was collected by direct interviews to obtain the views of activity-management in their manufacturing networks. Multiple interviews were conducted with business development manager, international operations manager, production manager and factory managers in order to achieve triangulation of perceptions. Network operation and capabilities were explored using semi-structured interviews with four executives per network, hence a total of 16 interviews were conducted. All interviews were recorded and fully transcribed. In order to improve rigour, a set of semi-structured questionnaires was prepared in advance and sent to each interviewee before the interview session to make sure they were properly prepared. There were two researchers present at each interview to reduce bias and generate a more reliable dataset (Eisenhardt, 1989; Yin, 2009). This provided a fine-grained picture of the case companies' instances of how the manufacturing in intra-firm dispersed facilities was coordinated, and the information about the elements of competitive priorities. We created a database for individual case consisting of archival records and interview transcripts. Based on the written description of studied cases, the key characteristics of the companies are presented in Table 1. Company names are undisclosed to comply with their request.

Data analysis was carried out simultaneously with the data collection, which provided the flexibility to make relevant adjustments throughout the process (Eisenhardt, 1989). Extensive pattern matching was used to categorize the data. Each case was analyzed and described in a dedicated report. Data analysis and coding were conducted manually by two members of the research to ensure inter-coder reliability (Duriau, Reger, & Pfarrer, 2007). To increase the reliability of the findings, an explanation of each case was tested twice by looking into the field notes to see how well supported they were. The interview scripts were coded and supported by documentary evidence to develop themes and categories using the within-case analysis approach. In the coding process, categories were selected based on the indicators linked to operational performance, mechanisms of coordination and the attributes linked to network manufacturing capabilities (see Table 2). Thematic analysis is defined as the process of encoding qualitative information in order to determine themes that are used to describe, and organize possible observations or interrupt aspects of a phenomenon (Boyatzis, 1998). Each case was described in terms of two main categories (operation in network manufacturing and network manufacturing capabilities). The cross-case analysis identified commonalities and differences among the studied cases. Moreover, cross-case analysis between different cases was conducted to improve the external validity of the studies, as this analysis allows searching for common evidence.

CROSS-CASE ANALYSIS

Table 3 summarizes the main issues of the operation of disperse facilities in network manufacturing raised from the within-case analysis. Moreover, observations are presented in remarks column. Matching empirical findings on the operations of network manufacturing with the capability dimensions generated the following reflections.

- **Accessibility:** The studied companies aimed at benefiting mostly from access to lower-cost of production inputs, and a proximity to the market-focused offshoring of Company-A and Company-D. As reported by the interviewees, Companies -B and -C do not have difficulties regarding the expected levels of accessibilities into targeted lower-cost of production inputs. However, difficulties in acquiring target resources in the case of Company-A is reflected as an increased production

Table 1. Summary of cases

Cases	Sector/ product	Revenue (mln €)	Company size *	Home and Offshore location	Primary motive of offshoring	Manufacturing network [with reference to Shi and Gregory's (1998) classification]
Company A	Toy	50	Medium	Spain, China, Mexico	Cost of production, Market seeking	Global-integrated for cost seeking. Multi-domestic for market seeking.
Company B	Sports, Games	38	Small-medium	Sweden, China, Lithuania	Lower cost of production	Global-integrated manufacturing configuration
Company C	High tech	285	Medium	Sweden, France	Product specialization	Somewhere in-between multi-domestic and globally integrated configuration.
Company D	High tech	10	Large	Sweden, Malaysia	Proximity to market	Multi-domestic manufacturing configuration

* According to the definition of European Commission, small < 50 and medium < 250 employees.

Table 2. Coding categories

Operational performance indicators (Santos, 2000; Ward et al., 1998)	Mechanisms of coordination (Martinez & Jarillo, 1989)	Dimensions of network manufacturing capabilities (Colotla et al., 2003; Shi & Gregory, 1998; et al., 2018)
Cost efficiency Quality Delivery speed Volume, design and product mix flexibility	Formal mechanisms: structure, centralization vs. decentralization, and formalization. Informal mechanisms: continuous relationships between facilities.	Network dispersion Extent of competences Knowledge exchange Degree of duplication

cost. This increase was mainly due to higher (than expected) wages in the host location, whereas other production inputs were at the expected level. Once an offshore decision has been made it is necessary to improve the capabilities in strategic resource access, such as, apart from the access to a lower cost-of-production they need to maintain high performing employees.

- **Thriftiness:** Thriftiness is defined as the ability to achieve economies of scope and avoid duplication of work in a manufacturing network. All the cases display a significant duplication of activities, extra control mechanisms and very little network learning and economies of scope. For example, in the case of Company-A and Company-D, limited integration between home and host facilities acts as a barrier to achieve the advantage from the centralized management of R&D and purchasing. Whereas, Company-C highlighted a relationship between engineering know-how's transfer and additional work performed in multiple facilities. Moreover, Companies -A and -C failed to establish the sharing as well as to develop the production competencies in their dispersed facilities, which they tried to mitigate through direct travel. Interviewees of Company-B opine that they required extra effort on control mechanisms; which was to protect the unexpected changes in raw materials and errors in the products. The above insights reaffirm the association between developments of thriftiness ability, with an emphasis on the economics of scope, and the success of manufacturing in dispersed facilities.

Table 3. Selected issues and remarks per cases

Cases	**Selected issues of intra-firm network operation**	**Remarks**
Company A	Limitations in sharing production-related competencies. Excessive communication than that planned. Home facility-based control of multiple activities. Longer lead time.	Weak integration between facilities. Lack of interdependencies. Low network integration.
Company B	Direct and indirect control in purchasing activities. Similar types of mistakes in host operation. Excessive communication for information sharing. Limitations in knowledge about the host suppliers. No alternative ways to teach employees.	Decreased network integration. Insufficient transfer of managerial skills. Inadequate knowledge transfer between managers of home and host facilities. Limited learning opportunities.
Company C	Extra travel from home to host facilities, for process management. Both planned and unplanned coordination. Repetitive similar types of mistakes. Cultural differences and different mindsets. Communication misunderstandings. Unable to adjust the long-haul lead time.	Inadequate process mobility. Incomplete/inefficient transfer of engineering know-how. Insufficient transfer of managerial skills. Decreased flexibility in communication. Barriers to transfer and learning. Networking inefficiency.
Company D	Home facility based R&D decides about the product architecture and development. Home facility centric system integration. Few planning meetings among top managers acts a formal coordination. Centralized coordination of purchasing and material management.	Difficulties in quality assurance. Excessive administrative tasks to ensure formal mechanisms. Limited scope for transfer of managerial skills.

- **Learning:** Learning, in the perspective of manufacturing in intra-firm dispersed facilities, is stimulated when one facility is affected by the knowledge of the others (Sayem et al., 2019). Company-A showed that a lack of interdependency restricts its learning abilities within the network. To explain the limited learning ability of Company-B, it appears that knowledge transfer between the home-based manager and the dedicated manager in the host facility was poor, which are apparent from the extra travel and not having detailed knowledge of the host suppliers. Company-C and Company-D reveals a flawed learning ability, which is reflected as the inefficient transfer of engineering know-how's from home to host facilities. Furthermore, each facility specialized in a selected range of products. Since no similar product was produced in two facilities, there was no possibility to bring production employees from another facility to provide more in-depth knowledge of the processes.
- **Mobility:** Mobility is the ability to transfer products, processes or managerial skills between facilities. In Company-C inadequate levels of process mobility are reflected by the increased number of problem-oriented complexities. In the cases of Company-A, -B and -D, though there were managerial movements to ensure quality, the mobility of managerial skill was limited. Which were due to repetition of similar types of mistakes in their host facility production. Meanwhile, Company-B was searching to increase the degree of product duplication hence to obtain the benefits of network-manufacturing mobility.

RESULTS

Strategic Objectives Affect the Management of IMN

In the management of international manufacturing networks, the competitive priorities and the focus of offshored facilities were explained as central in setting strategic objectives of network operation. Moreover, both of these affect the mechanisms applied in the coordination of intra-firm manufacturing network. Out of four elements of competitive priorities, two (namely 'quality' and 'flexibility') proved to have most critical. In order to ensure these two priorities, the management of IMN needs to employ -in varying levels- both the formal and informal mechanisms of coordination. For instance, it was shown that the formal mechanisms (as a means of product architecture and product instructions) of coordination were linked to ensure the 'quality' of product. In addition, the informal mechanisms (e.g. virtual exchange of process knowledge, and informal meetings) were promised to enhance the common understanding of product strategy, and to fulfil the specific need for 'conformance quality'.

Flexibility in product design and variety are the most common types that the companies would like to share with their host facilities. In such, informal mechanisms (e.g. virtual exchange among system-sensitive members) were the most important to share the profound understanding of development knowledge and production competencies. Moreover, it was shown that formal mechanisms, (e.g. predefined work procedure and planned meeting among the members of a global team) are critical for effective coordination of network-manufacturing. On the other hand, coordination of dispersed facilities intended for delivery-dependability and speed, are mostly managed with informal mechanisms (e.g. problem-oriented coordination). Meanwhile, coordination mechanisms those intended to ensure a reduced cost are mostly through formal mechanisms.

When we come to the consideration of mechanisms for coordination with the intent to strategic focus of dispersed facilities, formal mechanisms stand as a building block in the coordination of both market-focused and low-cost focused offshore facilities. On the other hand, informal mechanisms are not prevalent in the same ways as the formal. It is noted that informal mechanisms has varying level of preference depending upon the focus-type as well as the elements of competitive priorities. Furthermore, taking together competitive priorities (quality, flexibility, lead-time, and cost) and mechanisms of network coordination, the findings suggest that low-cost focused network-manufacturing has expressed more intensity towards the use of both formal and informal mechanisms of coordination, than as required for market-focused type. Indeed, it appears that though the formal mechanisms are equally vital for both focus types, coordination of low-cost focused offshored facilities showed more preference towards the informal mechanisms than that of market-focused.

Operational Issues and Reshoring

The second research question deals with an increasingly important phenomenon of global manufacturing: 'reshoring'. It has highlighted that the network operation of manufacturing firms are influenced by the management of activities in dispersed facilities due to a lack of competitiveness in international production. In other words, operational issues vis-à-vis the network-management has notable influence on the phenomenon of reshoring. Out of four capability dimensions, two dimensions (vis. thriftiness and learning capabilities) as determined by the 'extent of competencies', 'network-integration' and 'knowledge exchange', were found to be most relevant in considering their manufacturing facilities back from dispersed location. Exactly, these capabilities showed a predominant influence in ensuring the quality of products manufactured in network facilities. The dimensions of network-manufacturing capabilities, which are linked to the management of dispersed facilities, influences the companies to rethink about existing network dispersion.

DISCUSSION

The results provide empirical support for the proposed linkage between strategic objectives of international manufacturing and the management of disperse facilities of a company (RQ 1). Following the literature, manufacturing strategy acts as a competitive weapon that helps to derive a competitive advantage. In other words, individual company's strategic vision and the core of competitive advantage are mirrored in the decision of its manufacturing strategy. In which, core of competitive advantage be operationalised along the factors: cost, quality, delivery, and flexibility. For instance, a defined combination of these factors (e.g. product with high quality, extended flexibility, and fast delivery) acts as guiding vehicle for a company's manufacturing strategy. Considering dependency nature of competitive priorities and network goals (cf. Colotla et al., 2003), network coordination needs to cover the translated goals from different priorities of a company. The result provide clear support for that relevance of network coordination, specifically in the selection of mechanisms for coordination, to a set of priorities linked to network goals. This means that translated or derived network goals are predecessors of coordination in international manufacturing. Moreover, when comparing the coordination for the market-focused from that of low-cost focused disperse facilities, the link to formal mechanisms is dominant one; hence network manufacturing coordination are built upon formal mechanisms as the essential step. Then, the choice regarding varying level of informal mechanisms are built upon both focus of offshoring dimension and target dimension/s of competitive priorities. Therefore, there are prevailing relationship of strategic objectives with network management via competitive priorities.

The results show that having network manufacturing capabilities, specifically thriftiness and learning capabilities has a direct positive influence on the decision of reshoring. The reason behind this might be that quality assurance as the essential priority implies that frequent exchange of knowledge and extent of competencies need to be build and ensure continuously, which is likely easier if the facilities are located in nearby location of home facility. The findings also showed that dimensions of network manufacturing capabilities has influence on better performance in quality, flexibility and cost. Moreover, network integration via coordination of disperse facilities play a central role in the success of global operation. Thus, the second research question express its relevance to infer the contemporary phenomenon of reshoring, from the operations perspective of network manufacturing.

CONCLUSION

This chapter intended to explore the craft of manufacturing-network management, and the role of operation of dispersed facilities to infer the phenomenon of relocation. Firstly, we addressed the interaction between operations of multiple facilities vis-à-vis coordination of global firms and strategic objective/s of international manufacturing. It has explained that competitive priorities and the focus of offshored facilities affects the mechanisms applied in the coordination of facilities of a global firm. Moreover, we have identified that 'quality' and 'flexibility' are two most critical elements of competitive priorities in determining mechanisms for coordination. As a note, management of global firms need to employ both the formal and informal mechanisms (in varying levels) of coordination, in order to ensure the highlighted priorities.

Following on, it has investigated the phenomenon of relocation through looking at the interaction of resources and activities in multiple facilities of a global firm. Especially, it has identified that network operation of manufacturing firms are influenced by the management of activities in dispersed facilities due to a lack of competitiveness in international production.

This chapter contributes in several insights to the research areas of network manufacturing strategy, and to practitioners in international manufacturing operations. The results are aimed at providing insights on activity management in international manufacturing, and how they are relevant to the phenomenon of relocation. In this first implication of this research is the manifestation of the competitive priorities and focus of offshore facilities as essential elements to consider when studying the mechanisms to coordinate network manufacturing operations. Next, we concluded by highlighting the relevance of strategic capabilities of network-manufacturing to reshoring.

LIMITATIONS AND FUTURE RESEARCH

The result of our study should be viewed in the light of following limitations. Firstly, the selected cases for this study are limited to the context of industries. Research should consider firms from several industries to introduce the possibility of industry-specific findings. Moreover, studies that include a larger sample of companies might be useful to assess the extent to which the relationship derived from this study can be generalized. Secondly, we adopted a multiple case study design and performed qualitative analysis. Despite several actions were taken to enhance the validity and reliability of the outcome (for instance, multiple source of evidence, interviews and analysis conducted by more than one researcher, detailed case study protocol, interview report checked by the interviewees), it would be interesting to develop a testable hypothesis that could be investigated using data from a large-scale survey. Additionally, this would allow examining the differences across different types of offshore manufacturing. Finally, as a proposal for future research, we suggest longitudinal case studies on companies that have offshoring and consequent reshoring experience in order to understand the decision scenario and its consequences on reshoring decisions.

REFERENCES

Arlbjørn, J. S., & Mikkelsen, O. S. (2014). Backshoring manufacturing: Notes on an important but under-researched theme. *Journal of Purchasing and Supply Management*, *20*(1), 60–62. doi:10.1016/j.pursup.2014.02.003

Barratt, M., Choi, T. Y., & Li, M. (2011). Qualitative case studies in operations management: Trends, research outcomes, and future research implications. *Journal of Operations Management*, *29*(4), 329–342. doi:10.1016/j.jom.2010.06.002

Belderbos, R., & Zou, J. (2006). Foreign investment, divestment and relocation by Japanies electronics firms in East Asia. *Asian Economic Journal, 20*(1), 1–27. doi:10.1111/j.1467-8381.2006.00222.x

Boyatzis, R. E. (1998). *Transforming qualitative information: Thematic analysis and code development*. Sage Publications, Inc.

Boyer, K. K., & Lewis, M. W. (2002). Competitive Priorities: Investigating the need for trade-offs in operations strategy. *Production and Operations Management, 11*(1), 9–20. doi:10.1111/j.1937-5956.2002.tb00181.x

Buckley, P. J., & Casson, M. (2011). Marketing and the multinational: Extending internalisation theory. *Journal of the Academy of Marketing Science, 39*(4), 492–508. doi:10.100711747-010-0243-0

Buckley, P. J., & Casson, M. C. (1976). *The Future of the Multinational Enterprise*. London: The Macmillan press. doi:10.1007/978-1-349-02899-3

Cheng, Y., Farooq, S., & Johansen, J. (2015). International manufacturing network: Past, present, and future. *International Journal of Operations & Production Management, 35*(3), 392–429. doi:10.1108/IJOPM-03-2013-0146

Colotla, I., Shi, Y., & Gregory, M. J. (2003). Operation and performance of international manufacturing networks. *International Journal of Operations & Production Management, 23*(10), 1184–1206. doi:10.1108/01443570310496625

Dachs, B., & Kinkel, S. (2013). Backshoring of production activities in European manufacturing – Evidence from a large-scale survey. In *20th International Annual EurOMA Conference* (pp. 7–12). Dublin, Ireland: Academic Press.

Dangayach, G., & Deshmukh, S. (2001). Manufacturing strategy: Literature review and some issues. *International Journal (Toronto, Ont.), 21*(7), 884–932.

Dubois, F. L., Toyne, B., & Oliff, M. D. (1993). International Manufacturing Strategies of U.S. Multinationals: A conceptual framework based on a four-industry study. *Journal of International Business Studies*, 307–333.

Dunning, J. H. (1980). Towards an eclectic theory of international production: Some empirical tests. *Journal of International Business Studies, 11*(1), 9–31. doi:10.1057/palgrave.jibs.8490593

Dunning, J. H. (1988). The eclectic paradigm of international production: A restatement and some possible extensions. *Journal of International Business Studies, 19*(1), 1–31. doi:10.1057/palgrave.jibs.8490372

Duriau, V. J., Reger, R. K., & Pfarrer, M. D. (2007). A Content Analysis of the Content Analysis Literature in Organization Studies: Research Themes, Data Sources, and Methodological Refinements. *Organizational Research Methods, 10*(1), 5–34. doi:10.1177/1094428106289252

Eisenhardt, K. M. (1989). Building Theories from Case Study Research. *Academy of Management Review, 14*(4), 532–550. doi:10.5465/amr.1989.4308385

Eisenhardt, K. M., & Graebner, M. E. (2007). Theory Building From Cases: Opportunities and Challenges. *Academy of Management Journal, 50*(1), 25–32. doi:10.5465/amj.2007.24160888

Ellram, L. M. (2013). Offshoring, reshoring and the manufacturing location decisions. *The Journal of Supply Chain Management, 49*(2), 3–5. doi:10.1111/jscm.12023

Ellram, L. M., Tate, W. L., & Petersen, K. J. (2013). Offshoring and reshoring: An update on the manufacturing location decision. *The Journal of Supply Chain Management, 49*(2), 14–22. doi:10.1111/jscm.12019

Ferdows, K. (1989). Mapping international factory networks. In K. Ferdows (Ed.), *Mapping International Manufacturing*. New York: North Holland.

Ferdows, K. (1997). Made in the World: The Global Spread of Production. *Production and Operations Management, 6*(2), 102–109. doi:10.1111/j.1937-5956.1997.tb00418.x

Foerstl, K., Kirchoff, J. F., & Bals, L. (2016). Reshoring and insourcing: Drivers and future research directions. *International Journal of Physical Distribution & Logistics Management, 46*(5), 492–515. doi:10.1108/IJPDLM-02-2015-0045

Fratocchi, L., Ancarani, A., Barbieri, P., Di Mauro, C., Nassimbeni, G., Sartor, M., … Zanoni, A. (2015). Manufacturing Back-Reshoring as a Nonlinear Internationalization Process. Academic Press.

Fratocchi, L., Ancarani, A., Barbieri, P., Di Mauro, C., Nassimbeni, G., Sartor, M., ... Zanoni, A. (2016). Motivations of manufacturing reshoring: An interpretative framework. *International Journal of Physical Distribution & Logistics Management, 46*(2), 98–127. doi:10.1108/IJPDLM-06-2014-0131

Fratocchi, L., Di Mauro, C., Barbieri, P., Nassimbeni, G., & Zanoni, A. (2014). When manufacturing moves back: Concepts and questions. *Journal of Purchasing and Supply Management, 20*(1), 54–59. doi:10.1016/j.pursup.2014.01.004

Gray, J. V., Skowronski, K., Esenduran, G., & Rungtusanatham, M. J. (2013). The reshoring phenomenon: What supply chain academics ought to know and should do. *The Journal of Supply Chain Management, 49*(2), 27–33. doi:10.1111/jscm.12012

Hayes, R. H., & Wheelwright, S. C. (1984). *Restoring our competitive edge: Competing through manufacturing*. New York: Wiley.

Hill, T. J. (1994). Teaching Manufacturing Strategy. *International Journal of Operations & Production Management, 6*(3), 10–20. doi:10.1108/eb054762

Kinkel, S. (2012). Trends in production relocation and backshoring activities: Changing patterns in the course of the global economic crisis. *International Journal of Operations & Production Management, 32*(6), 696–720. doi:10.1108/01443571211230934

Kinkel, S., & Maloca, S. (2009). Drivers and antecedents of manufacturing offshoring and backshoring—A German perspective. *Journal of Purchasing and Supply Management, 15*(3), 154–165. doi:10.1016/j.pursup.2009.05.007

Martinez, J. I., & Jarillo, J. C. (1989, Fall). The evolution of research on coordination mechanisms in multinational corporations. *Journal of International Business Studies, 20*(3), 489–514. doi:10.1057/palgrave.jibs.8490370

Martínez-Mora, C., & Merino, F. (2014). Offshoring in the Spanish footwear industry: A return journey? *Journal of Purchasing and Supply Management*, *20*(4), 225–237. doi:10.1016/j.pursup.2014.07.001

Marucheck, A., Pannesi, R., & Anderson, C. (1990). An Exploratory Study of the Manufacturing Strategy Process in Practice. *Journal of Operations Management*, *9*(1), 101–123. doi:10.1016/0272-6963(90)90148-7

Mcivor, R. (2013). Understanding the manufacturing location decision: The case for the transaction cost and capability perspectives. *The Journal of Supply Chain Management*, *49*(2), 23–26. doi:10.1111/jscm.12010

Mefford, R. N. (2010). Offshoring, lean production and a sustainable global supply chain. *European Journal of International Management*, *4*(3), 303–315. doi:10.1504/EJIM.2010.033006

Meijboom, B., & Vos, B. (1997). International manufacturing and location decisions: Balancing configuration and co-ordination aspects. *International Journal of Operations & Production Management*, *17*(8), 790–805. doi:10.1108/01443579710175565

Miles, M. B., & Huberman, A. M. (1994). *Qualitative Data Analysis: an expanded sourcebook* (2nd ed.). Academic Press.

Mills, J., Platts, K., & Gregory, M. (1995). A framework for the design of manufacturing strategy processes: A contingency approach. *International Journal of Operations & Production Management*, *15*(4), 17–49. doi:10.1108/01443579510083596

Miltenburg, J. (2005). *Manufacturing Strategy: How to formulate and implement a winning plan* (2nd ed.). New York: Productivity Press. doi:10.4324/9781482278392

Miltenburg, J. (2009). Setting manufacturing strategy for a company's international manufacturing network. *International Journal of Production Research*, *47*, 6179–6203.

Mugurusi, G., & de Boer, L. (2014). Conceptualising the production offshoring organisation using the viable systems model (VSM). *Strategic Outsourcing*, *7*(3), 275–298. doi:10.1108/SO-10-2014-0026

Norton, R., & Rees, J. (1979). The product cycle and the spatial decentralization of American manufacturing. *Regional Studies*, *13*(2), 141–151. doi:10.1080/09595237900185121

Patton, M. Q. (1990). *Qualitative evaluation and research methods* (2nd ed.). Thousand Oaks, CA: Sage Publications, Inc.

Pennings, E., & Sleuwaegen, L. (2000, May). International relocation: Firm and industry determinants. *Economics Letters*, *67*(2), 179–186. doi:10.1016/S0165-1765(99)00269-4

Platts, K. W., Mills, J. F., Bourne, M. C., Neely, A. D., Richards, A. H., & Gregory, M. (1998). Testing manufacturing strategy formulation processes. *International Journal of Production Economics*, *56–57*, 517–523. doi:10.1016/S0925-5273(97)00134-5

Porter, M. E. (1986). Changing patterns of international competition. *California Management Review, XXVIII*(2), 9–40. doi:10.2307/41165182

Porter, M. E. (1994). The Role of Location in Competition. *International Journal of the Economics of Business, 1*(1), 35–40. doi:10.1080/758540496

Rugman, A. M. (2010). Reconciling internalization theory and the eclectic paradigm. *Multinational Business Review, 18*(2), 1–12. doi:10.1108/1525383X201000007

Santos, F. C. (2000). Integration of human resource management and competitive priorities of manufacturing strategy. *International Journal of Operations & Production Management, 20*(5), 610–628. doi:10.1108/01443570010318986

Sayem, A., Feldmann, A., & Ortega-Mier, M. (2018). Coordination in International Manufacturing: The Role of Competitive Priorities and the Focus of Globally Dispersed Facilities. *Sustainability, 10*(5), 1314. doi:10.3390u10051314

Sayem, A., Feldmann, A., & Ortega-mier, M. (2019). Investigating the influence of network-manufacturing capabilities to the phenomenon of reshoring: An insight from three case studies. *BRQ Business Research Quarterly, 22*(1), 68–82. doi:10.1016/j.brq.2018.07.001

Shi, Y., & Gregory, M. (1998). International manufacturing networks— To develop global competitive capabilities. *Journal of Operations Management, 16*(2-3), 195–214. doi:10.1016/S0272-6963(97)00038-7

Skinner, C. (1964). Management of International Production. *Harvard Business Review, 42*(5), 125–136.

Skinner, C. (1969). Manufacturing: Missing link in Corporate Strategy. *Harvard Business Review, 3*, 163–145.

Strom, M., & Levy, M. (2013). Going beyond reshoring to right-shoring. PwC.

Stuart, I., McCutcheon, D., Handfield, R., McLachlin, R., & Samson, D. (2002). Effective case research in operations management: A process perspective. *Journal of Operations Management, 20*(5), 419–433. doi:10.1016/S0272-6963(02)00022-0

Tate, W. L. (2014). Offshoring and reshoring: U.S. insights and research challenges. *Journal of Purchasing and Supply Management, 20*(1), 66–68. doi:10.1016/j.pursup.2014.01.007

Tate, W. L., Ellram, L. M., Schoenherr, T., & Petersen, K. J. (2014). Global competitive conditions driving the manufacturing location decision. *Business Horizons, 57*(3), 381–390. doi:10.1016/j.bushor.2013.12.010

Voss, C., Tsikriktsis, N., & Frohlich, M. (2002). Case research in operations management. *International Journal of Operations & Production Management, 22*(2), 195–219. doi:10.1108/01443570210414329

Ward, P. T., McCreery, J. K., Ritzman, L. P., & Sharma, D. (1998). Competitive Priorities in Operations Management. *Decision Sciences, 29*(4), 1035–1046. doi:10.1111/j.1540-5915.1998.tb00886.x

Wilkinson, S., Gregory, M., & Arnold, P. (2015). Reshoring manufacturing- Time To Seize the Opportunity. EY Building a Better Working World, 1–24.

Williamson, O. E. (2008). Outsourcing: Transaction cost economics and supply chain management. *The Journal of Supply Chain Management*, *44*(2), 5–16. doi:10.1111/j.1745-493X.2008.00051.x

Yin, R. K. (1994). *Case Study Research: Design and Methods* (2nd ed.). Thousand Oaks, CA: Sage Publications.

Yin, R. K. (2009). *Case study research: design and methods* (4th ed.). Sage Publications.

Section 3

Internal and External Outcomes of Globalization

Chapter 12
Outward US Foreign Direct Investment and Environmental Degradation

João Bento
https://orcid.org/0000-0002-1145-9664
University of Aveiro, Portugal

Miguel Torres
University of Leeds, UK

Paolo Maranzano
https://orcid.org/0000-0002-9228-2759
University of Milano-Bicocca, Italy

ABSTRACT

This chapter analyzes whether US outward foreign direct investment contributes to mitigating environmental degradation in host countries or not. This relationship is investigated within the environmental Kuznets curve framework, using dynamic panel data models which include trade openness and environmental regulation as controlling variables. The results lend support to the existence of an environmental Kuznets curve hypothesis. Moreover, the results indicate that capital expenditures from majority-owned foreign affiliates of US multinationals decrease carbon dioxide emissions per capita and provide support for the pollution halo hypothesis. The findings suggest that foreign direct investments carried out by firms with their headquarters based in the United States of America enhance the natural environment. These findings offer some support for host government policies offering generous financial incentives to attract environmentally friendly investments to improve environmental sustainability.

DOI: 10.4018/978-1-5225-8906-8.ch012

INTRODUCTION

There is worldwide concern that climate change presents serious risks with the potential to impact human activities (Stern & Stern, 2015). Many countries are collectively taking action to reduce global pollutant emissions and implement an adequate set of incentives to support green technology investments.

Foreign direct investment (hereafter FDI) by firms with their headquarters based in the United States of America accounts for a large share of global FDI (United Nations Conference on Trade and Development, 2018). The United States is the largest trading and investment partner for almost all other countries in the global economy, providing important sources of FDI to host economies. The economic rationale behind FDI is that multinational enterprises (hereafter MNEs) are capable to transfer technology that reduces environmental degradation in recipient countries. The study asks the question of whether foreign investment activities from the United States of America affect the environmental conditions in recipient countries and if it has the potential to enhance local environmental sustainability.

This study aims at understanding how MNEs may impact the natural environment of host countries seeking to attract FDI. Public opinion seems to be that any country may come under pressure to lower its environmental standards as governments seek to attract or retain economic activities and investors inside their national borders, propelling a "race to the bottom" on key regulations in areas such as environmental protection. Many environmentalists are concerned about the environmental consequences of corporate business activities around the world, where pollution-intensive industries seek countries with weak environmental standards, turning these locations into "pollution havens" (Eskeland & Harrison, 2003). On the contrary, the argument of the "pollution halo" refers to the possibility that MNEs and their FDI activities constitute an important vehicle for the transfer of green technology and economic development, reducing the impact upon the natural environment (Porter & Linde, 1995).

If investment abroad raises income, it allows countries to attain greater output leading to an increase in emissions while at the same time triggering countervailing tendencies by facilitating the introduction of "greener technologies" and influencing individual preferences for an unpolluted environment (Kozul-Wright & Fortunato, 2012). A number of scholars have attempted to answer the question of how MNEs are or will be impacted by the main requirements and regulations related to environmental issues (Pinkse & Kolk, 2012). However, few researchers have provided empirical evidence on how MNEs can contribute to environmental sustainability.

The purpose of this study is to explore the empirical relationship between FDI and the natural environment. This is done by testing the validity of the environmental Kuznets curve (hereafter EKC) on a panel dataset comprising 97 countries from 2004-2013. The EKC posits an inverted-U function between environmental degradation and income per capita. The Generalized Method of Moments panel estimator is used to obtain consistent and efficient estimates. This estimation method exploits the time-series variation in the data and controls for unobserved country-specific effects and endogeneity of the explanatory variables. In so doing, the research findings contribute to the debate on globalization and the natural environment. Critics of globalization assert that FDI is bad for the natural environment because it encourages the location of polluting industries in countries with poor environmental regulations. This question is also interesting because there is less research into the possibility of positive externalities from FDI and their impact on the natural environment. If, however, FDI is good for the natural environment, this weakens arguments for restricting foreign investment.

LITERATURE REVIEW

The theory behind the EKC concept has its roots in the hypothesized relationship between per capita income and income inequality. The EKC curve represents the relationship between environmental degradation and per capita income. It is represented as an inverted U-shaped curve similar to the original curve proposed by Simon Kuznets concerning the relationship between income inequality and economic growth (Kaika & Zervas, 2013). The EKC posits that in the early stages of economic development, environmental pressure increases as output increases up to a certain threshold of wealth is reached – the turning point, after which the relative impact of pollution declines. Environmental improvement is likely to occur because, as economic growth proceeds, people value cleaner water, improved air quality, and a generally better natural environment, relating it to utility and consumer choice. Environmental decay, or degradation, is expected to occur due to greater use of natural resources and the operation of less efficient and relatively polluting technologies, while environmental effects of growth are disregarded.

Interest in EKC started in the early 1990s with the study of the potential impacts of the North American Free Trade Agreement (Grossman & Krueger, 1995). The EKC has been estimated for a variety of pollutants (Dinda, 2004). Most empirical studies estimate the EKC using time series-cross sectional data or panel data and confirm the existence of the EKC for carbon dioxide emissions (Selden & Song, 1994) although there are different outcomes in the literature (Galeotti, Lanza, & Pauli, 2006).

Studies on the EKC have been criticized on their theoretical basis, empirical validity and even the interpretation of some of the research results. The theoretical foundation of the EKC has been challenged and the cause of the downturn of the EKC has been questioned in terms of how it could be directly related to an environmental improvement and a decrease of emissions, or whether it is a consequence of changes in trade patterns. Moreover, the validation of the EKC is not without its econometric problems and several aspects have been criticized, such as the statistical properties of the variables and estimation methods (Stern, 2004).

The EKC literature also focuses on the impact of international trade on shaping the relationship between economic growth and the natural environment. In particular, the pollution haven hypothesis has been tested, which posits that emission reductions observed in developed nations are partly the result of shifting “dirty” production to developing nations with lax environmental standards (Kearsley & Riddel, 2010). To mitigate environmental degradation, governments usually put stricter environmental regulations and pollution control in place, which may encourage domestic production of pollution-intensive goods to delocalize to other countries, commonly low-income countries with relatively lax environmental standards. The displacement of industries occurs because of differences in the stringency of environmental regulation and it relates to the shift of manufacturing industries from developed to developing countries due to increasing costs for industries to meet environmental requirements. Generally such costs are lower in developing countries and therefore these countries have the potential to develop comparative advantages in the production of pollution-intensive goods (Cole, 2004). Countries on different levels of development differ in the stringency of environmental standards due to the fact that industrialized countries have more specialized and developed institutions that work to enforce environmental legislation (Mani & Wheeler, 1998).

In light of the EKC theory, it has been suggested that the shape of the curve does not entirely depend on the increase in income, but might also be explained by international trade and investment. Developed countries have usually a comparative advantage in the production of capital-abundant goods. Given that trade liberalization results in increasing specialization of industrial goods for which a country possesses a comparative advantage, the impact of trade openness on the natural environment is not the same in every country. If a country specializes in cleaner production, trade liberalization will result in increased production in environmental friendly sectors and less production in other sectors. This in turn will lead to less environmental degradation. The opposite goes for a country that specializes in dirty production.

Advances in technology also contribute to environmental improvements, causing emissions to decline over time. Emissions decline due to technological and structural changes; the abatement in emissions can be attributed to shifts in new techniques for production and this explains why countries will follow the EKC pattern. FDI has become a key factor in facilitating technology transfer and hence economic growth, as foreign firms can transfer both technology and knowledge to host country firms by this means. The relationship between FDI and the natural environment will also depend on the extent to which externalities from foreign firms exist (Newman, Rand, Talbot, & Tarp, 2015). The economic reasoning behind this argument is embedded in the pollution halo hypothesis. It suggests that FDI is accompanied by cleaner technology and improved environmental-management practices that augment the environmental quality of host countries. Moreover, environmental regulation stringency can encourage efficiency innovation and guide production procedures towards being more environment-friendly (Porter & Linde, 1995). The rise in environmental regulation stringency still has a modest deterrent effect on FDI capital inflow in China. Empirical evidence reveals that the internationalization of green R&D by multinational firms increases with the host country's stringency of environmental regulation, market size and research and development intensity, and lower wages for scientists and engineers in the host country (Noailly & Ryfisch, 2015). The pollution halo hypothesis is also confirmed using Chinese city-level data and FDI reveals important spatial technological spillover effects which improve overall air quality (Jiang, Zhou, Bai, & Zhou, 2018).

By contrast, the pollution haven hypothesis posits that FDI prompts relocation to host countries, usually with less developed economies and weaker environmental regulations, to reduce the costs of complying with applicable environmental regulations. It is worth mentioning one empirical study that has provided evidence to support this argument by analyzing the industrial sulfur dioxide emissions in China's 29 provinces (He, 2006). Significant influence of FDI on the EKC relationships is also found in a study on Chinese provinces (He & Yao, 2017). The pollution haven hypothesis is certified to be true for FDI among Belt & Road Initiative member countries (Liu & Kim, 2018).

Moreover, both the pollution halo and pollution haven hypotheses are validated for low income countries where foreign companies employ less polluting technology while lax environmental regulations might attract FDI (Kim & Adilov, 2012). FDI has also a significant negative effect on carbon intensity in different host countries while controlling for different income levels (Shao, 2017).

Recent studies have investigated the existence of causal relationships between environmental quality, FDI and economic growth (Abdouli & Hammami, 2017; Omri & Kahouli, 2014) but do not yield consistent results (Yildirim, 2014). The literature on the relationship between FDI and pollutant emissions has also centered its attention on explaining regional differences and found support for the pollution halo hypothesis (Zhang & Zhou, 2016). Furthermore, the impact of FDI on environmental pollution has been investigated with a large sample of highly heterogeneous countries including France, Germany, Sweden and the United Kingdom (Zugravu-Soilita, 2015). The study concluded that FDI is associated with a reduction in pollution in countries with low capital endowments and high environmental regulation and that FDI increases pollution in countries with high capital endowments and low environmental regulation.

According to the literature presented above, this study tests the EKC hypothesis as follows:

H1: Environmental degradation increases with per capita income, and after economies have reached a certain level of development, emissions decline.

According to the "gains from trade hypothesis", trade allows countries to attain more of what they want, which includes environmental goods in addition to market-measured output (Frankel & Rose, 2005). The effect of trade liberalization on the environment points towards freer trade being good for the environment (Copeland & Scott Taylor, 2013). Overall, the empirical results in this area are mixed, and trade leads to a reallocation of pollution from the poor country to the rich country, rather than in the opposite direction (Antweiler, Copeland, & Taylor, 2001). The sign of the environmental effect of trade openness is not clear-cut (Atici, 2009; Cole, 2006). On this basis, the following research hypothesis is proposed:

H2: Free trade can lead to increases in the volume of trade and output, such that emissions will be worse in more open economies.

Many less developed countries present poor environmental outcomes, weak environmental standards if any, a growing specialization towards pollution-intensive goods and high pollution levels. FDI is instrumental in the diffusion of environmentally superior innovations and performances, because MNEs incorporate environment-efficient technologies in their investments. Adaptation of cleaner technologies encouraged by investment in environmental R&D will benefit the environment (Neumayer, 2001). According to the Porter hypothesis presented above, the introduction of stricter regulation and well-enforced regulation would benefit both the natural environment and the firm. Well-crafted environmental regulations create external pressure on firms which force them to come up with new design and development of products and services that contribute positively to their international competitiveness. Environmental regulation would push firms to overcome market failures and to pursue otherwise neglected investment opportunities (Rubashkina, Galeotti, & Verdolini, 2015). Therefore, the following hypothesis is proposed in this study:

H3: Environmental regulation makes any support for fossil fuels economically less viable; hence use of renewable energy benefits the natural environmental in host countries.

FDI is instrumental in the diffusion of environmentally superior innovations and performance since multinationals often incorporate environment-efficient technologies in their foreign operations. Theoretical and empirical literature exploring the effects of FDI on host economies has emphasized the importance of technology transfer and spillovers deriving from the foreign operations of MNEs (Narula & Driffield, 2012). Firms co-evolve with their environment (Dunning, 2009) and organization theory has long explored the extent to which firms are selected in or out based on their viability in a particular competitive environment, and the extent to which firms engage in adaptive responses in order to maintain or enhance their viability (Cantwell, Dunning, & Lundan, 2015). Therefore, the following hypothesis is stated:

H4: FDI by multinational enterprises will generate benefits for the natural environment in host countries through the transfer of clean technologies and production practices to their foreign affiliates.

METHODOLOGY

Econometric Model and Data

This section describes the econometric model to assess the relationship between FDI and the natural environment. The EKC regression model can be written in the following form:

$$\ln\left(\frac{E}{P}\right)_{it} = \beta_0 + \beta_1 \ln\left(\frac{Y}{P}\right)_{it} + \beta_2 \ln\left(\frac{Y}{P}\right)_{it}^2 + \beta_3 \ln\left(\frac{X+M}{Y}\right)_{it} + \beta_4 \ln\left(REG\right)_{it} + \beta_5 \ln\left(FDI\right)_{it} + \varepsilon_{it}$$

E is emissions, *P* is population, *Y* represents income, *X* are exports, *M* are imports, *REG* is environmental regulation and *FDI* stands for outward FDI. The first term on the right hand side is the intercept parameter, which varies across countries *i* and time *t*. The residual ε it is the random error term, representing other causes of environmental degradation and *ln* indicates natural logarithms.

Table 1 summarizes all variables and sources of statistical data. The dependent variable is the measure of environmental degradation. Equation (1) is estimated with carbon dioxide emissions from total fuel consumption. These are emissions from the burning of fossil fuels and cement manufacturing measured in metric tons per capita. The dependent variable is computed by dividing carbon dioxide emissions by total population of country *i* in time *t*. Carbon dioxide is known as a greenhouse gas — a gas that absorbs and emits thermal radiation, creating the "greenhouse effect".

Income per capita, measured by per capita gross domestic product valued at constant 2011 US dollars, based on purchasing power parity, figures among the independent variables. The effects of trade openness and energy use that embody pollution are incorporated in the regression model to capture several environmental impacts (Suri & Chapman, 1998). Trade openness is computed as the sum of nominal exports and imports of goods and services measured as a share of gross domestic product. The specification of the econometric model further controls for environmental regulations to reduce emissions by including the share of final energy consumption derived from renewable energy sources. All data is retrieved from the databank of World Bank World Development Indicators.

The coefficient of interest here is β_5, the partial effect of FDI on environmental degradation. FDI is measured in current US dollars and constitutes capital expenditures from majority-owned subsidiaries of US MNEs (outward FDI). A capital-expenditure-based proxy is used to capture the foreign activity of MNEs instead of FDI flows (Desai, Foley, & Hines, 2006). National accounts do not normally record capital expenditures by foreign-owned firms. Instead, national balance of payments statistics are typically employed as a proxy for foreign investment activity. This study uses data on capital expenditures because they represent changes in the fixed assets of foreign affiliates whereas FDI flows, by contrast, only record the provision of financial flows from foreign investors to host country firms in which they hold a majority equity share.

The statistics on activities of multinational enterprises used here provide a picture of the overall activities of US affiliates of foreign parents and contain a wide variety of indicators of their financial structure and operations. Data published by the US Department of Commerce on the operations of MNEs with their headquarters based in the United States of America is a comprehensive source for foreign capital expenditures abroad. This data is collected through mandatory surveys on US MNEs by the US Bureau of Economic Analysis (hereafter, BEA). The BEA collects data at the firm level through its surveys on FDI and then uses it to produce aggregated tabular data on MNEs operations for release to the general public. The BEA data contains information on US firms alone. BEA collects FDI data on a consistent basis on foreign affiliates located around the world through its annual and benchmark surveys to make sure the data on the activities of US MNEs is reliable and valuable.

The main reason for using macroeconomic and microeconomic data in the same regression is because BEA data has notable features that distinguish it from other data sources. BEA data on FDI are drawn from all foreign affiliates and the BEA filings profile all of the firm's activity abroad every year. Moreover, reporting in BEA data follows usually accepted US accounting principles and the financial information collected is filed through US entities used to those practices. In addition to providing various financing and operational data for MNEs, the BEA data constitutes a unique source of information on FDI around the world. Finally, the BEA data are available for download at the country level, but access to the firm-level data is restricted to researchers working directly under the auspices of the BEA.

The EKC postulates an inverted U-shaped relationship between income per capita and per capita emissions. To determine the shape of the EKC, it is important to inspect the signs and magnitudes of the regression coefficients β_1 and β_2. The EKC relation exists under the condition that $\beta_1 > 0$ and $\beta_2 < 0$. If $\beta_2 < 0$, there is an inverted U-shaped relationship and the EKC is concave. If $\beta_2 > 0$, this implies a convex U-shaped relationship and the EKC is not validated. According to the EKC theory, emissions increase up to a certain level as income goes up (in the initial stages of industrialization) and start to decrease beyond a threshold as countries become richer. In order to validate the EKC hypothesis, the coefficients are required to be statistically significant and β_1 should be larger than the absolute value of β_2.

The impact of environmental regulation and trade openness are captured by the coefficients β_3 and β_4, respectively. These variables enter the EKC equation to control for the omitted variable bias and to check for the robustness of the results.

Estimation Technique

Dynamic panel data methods are employed to exploit the time-series along with the cross-country dimension of the data. The panel dataset is strongly balanced and consists of yearly observations for 97 countries from 2004-2013. The list of countries is presented in Appendix 1. Following Antweiler, Copeland & Taylor (2001) and Grossman & Krueger (1991), a panel data methodology is adopted. This approach offers advantages over conventional methods, such as ordinary least squares regressions, because it controls for country-specific effects and for the potential endogeneity of explanatory variables. This approach improves the estimated coefficients and their standard errors in the regression model.

The endogeneity problem that plagues EKC regressions is addressed in this study. If explanatory variables are endogenous then causality may run in both directions so that the regressors may be correlated with the error term. The Generalized Method of Moments is used to estimate a dynamic panel data model capable of correcting for bias caused by endogenous explanatory variables. The original estimator entitled Difference Generalized Method of Moments (Diff-GMM) deals with this inherent endogeneity by transforming the data to remove time-invariant country characteristics (fixed effects) but at the cost of introducing a correlation between the error term and the explanatory variables. One disadvantage of the first difference transformation is that it magnifies gaps in unbalanced panels and lagged levels are often rather weak instruments for first-differenced variables. This motivates an alternative approach that modifies the estimator to include lagged levels as well as lagged differences. The expanded estimator, commonly termed System Generalized Method of Moments (Sys-GMM), combines the regression in a system to overcome these drawbacks (Baltagi, 1995).

The consistency of the Generalized Method of Moments estimator depends on the validity of the instruments. To address this issue, two specification tests are used in both estimation approaches. The first is the Sargan test of over-identifying restrictions to ascertain the overall validity of the instruments. The second test examines the hypothesis that the error terms in the regression models are not first-order and second-order serially correlated. This approach has one potential limitation, which is the likely importance of country-level unobserved heterogeneity. Heterogeneity is restricted to the intercept but is not allowed in the slope coefficients. This method works under the assumption that all explanatory variables are valid instruments, provided there is no second order autocorrelation in the first-differenced idiosyncratic error terms.

RESULTS

Table 2 provides summary descriptive statistics for all variables included in the study. Table 3 shows the pairwise correlation matrix. The output of the bivariate Pearson correlation coefficient and corresponding significance tests suggest that per capita carbon dioxide emissions are positively correlated with per capita income, and, positively correlated with FDI. Overall, positive correlation is reported among the indicators of environmental degradation and trade openness, while a negative correlation exists among per capita carbon dioxide emissions and environmental regulation.

Table 4 presents the regression results of the dynamic panel models. The Hansen-Sargan tests do not suggest rejection of the instrumental validity at conventional levels. The tests for no autocorrelation indicate absence of second-order serial correlation in the first-differenced errors and valid instruments. The estimation results are robust to alternative model specifications and the signs and magnitudes of the coefficients are generally maintained. The relationship between FDI and environmental degradation is confirmed when allowing the dependent variable to vary with trade openness and environmental regulation.

The regression results validate *H1* and provide evidence for the EKC hypothesis. In addition, the statistical significance of the lagged dependent variable displays a positive sign at the 1% level. This means that higher carbon dioxide emissions do occur continuously from the past to the future. Carbon emissions rise first with higher per capita income, but at a decreasing rate, until a threshold is reached after which emissions decline. Per capita income is positive and the quadratic term of per capita income is negative. Both coefficients associated with income are statistically significant at conventional levels. These results suggest an inverted U-shaped pattern, where previously rising carbon dioxide emissions start to decline as per capita income continues to grow. This result is in line with prior literature (Galeotti, Manera, & Lanza, 2009).

Table 4 shows that *H2* is validated. In accordance with earlier evidence, more free trade leads to more pollution (Antweiler et al., 2001). This result supports the pollution haven hypothesis and the argument can be made that trade openness causes a relocation of polluting activities to countries with weaker environmental standards (Copeland & Scott Taylor, 2013).

The research hypothesis *H3* is supported by the data. The estimated coefficients for the variable that captures environmental regulation have the expected signs and are statistically significant. It is likely that countries will choose to reduce the level of emissions as they become wealthier (Carson, 2010). Such findings also indicate that individuals and governments become less willing to accept higher carbon dioxide emissions at higher income levels, particularly because they want a clean environment and healthy living.

Additionally, hypothesis *H4* is fully supported. The variable capturing FDI always has a negative and statistically significant impact on the level of emissions. This outcome provides evidence to support the pollution halo hypothesis and demonstrates that foreign investments contribute to the upgrading of energy efficiency and clean technologies. This result is in line with prior literature that found support for the pollution halo hypothesis (Jiang et al., 2018; Liu & Kim, 2018; Zugravu-Soilita, 2015).

DISCUSSION OF RESULTS

Several implications can be drawn from these results. The findings highlight the importance of FDI from the US in host economies around the world. They are in support of the argument that there is an emerging ambivalence in overseas capital investment as FDI appears to be sensitive to rising abatement costs, yet the investment recipients are countries with comparably stringent environmental standards or "greener countries" (Vogel & Kagan, 2004). Moreover, the results support the view that multinationals become a vehicle for deploying cleaner technologies and promote more resource-efficient business activities to the FDI recipient countries. Furthermore, the findings support those found in the study for the OECD countries and China (Noailly & Ryfisch, 2015).

The international investment of MNEs driving the economic globalization process, particularly in FDI and production abroad, plays a key role in issues ranging from economic growth to environmental concerns for countries around the world. This poses the question of whether US MNEs and their foreign affiliates can help to mitigate environmental degradation. The research findings contribute to the debate on the corporate social responsibility of MNEs whereby companies integrate social and environmental concerns into their business operations (Ghauri & Yamin, 2009). Much of FDI is directed into resource extraction, infrastructure and manufacturing operations, and therefore it is important to address its implications on environmental degradation. Governments have very often undermined the willingness to raise environmental standards and it has been left to consumer, shareholder, and community pressure to improve corporate behavior and ensure corporate social responsibility in the interest of enterprises. Unless environmental concerns are already a core component of a firm's economic competitiveness or identity, there is little support that enterprises and foreign production operate to higher environmental standards than their domestic counterparts when these pressures are absent. In face of intense international competition, governments play a key role in fostering "green" FDI which can involve transferring cleaner technologies and management processes to enterprises already operating in the host market, which in turn can translate into environmental and economic benefits.

The results presented here suggest that MNEs help to reduce environmental degradation, possibly through the transfer of environmentally friendly and energy-saving technology into host economies. MNEs can be regarded as key players in helping authorities promote environmental sustainability and achieve internationally agreed environmental goals. The study also contributes to ongoing trade and investment negotiations such as the initiative in the Transatlantic Trade and Investment Partnership. Trade and investment issues such as the investor-state dispute settlements, regulatory cooperation mechanisms, and a separate chapter on energy remain highly controversial on both sides. This highlights the strategic importance of environmental provisions on any trade and investment partnership. Hence, negotiators of economic agreements should introduce specific environmental clauses into international investor protection and liberalization treaties. For instance, international trade negotiations should pay more attention to business-government interactions, and particularly to MNEs and host government relations, to find ways to cut emissions and to protect the natural environment. There remains a need for closer monitoring of environmental challenges within trade, investment negotiations from an environmental protection perspective, and their implications for environmental sustainability.

CONCLUSION

The EKC hypothesis is validated when investigating the link between FDI and environment degradation. The answer to the research question of whether US majority-owned foreign affiliates contribute to mitigating environmental degradation in host countries or not is investigated, controlling for trade openness and environmental regulation. As a result, this study supports the pollution halo hypothesis and suggests that FDI is accompanied by green technologies which improve the natural environment. For this reason, governments should encourage clean technology transfer to domestic companies through FDI in order to fuel economic activity and tackle environmental pressures.

This study is not without limitations. The influence of the structure of MNEs and FDI on environmental degradation when compared to other types of FDI that do not take the form of MNEs needs to be taken into account. In fact, the estimated models do not distinguish between equity and non-equity modes of entry into foreign markets. The relationship between FDI and the natural environment might potentially be greater through non-equity entry modes, contractual agreements, and outsourcing. In this particular case, there is no direct presence in the host country and hence no environmental liability. Moreover, the findings are obtained at the aggregate level while FDI as a cause of pollution might be more related to certain types of industries. Future studies could target this issue.

REFERENCES

Abdouli, M., & Hammami, S. (2017). Investigating the causality links between environmental quality, foreign direct investment and economic growth in MENA countries. *International Business Review*, *26*(2), 264–278. doi:10.1016/j.ibusrev.2016.07.004

Antweiler, W., Copeland, B. R., & Taylor, M. S. (2001). Is free trade good for the environment? *The American Economic Review*, *91*(4), 877–908. doi:10.1257/aer.91.4.877

Atici, C. (2009). Carbon emissions in Central and Eastern Europe: Environmental Kuznets curve and implications for sustainable development. *Sustainable Development*, *17*(3), 155–160. doi:10.1002d.372

Baltagi, B. H. (1995). *Econometric analysis of panel data*. John Wiley & Sons.

Cantwell, J., Dunning, J. H., & Lundan, S. M. (2015). An evolutionary approach to understanding international business activity: The co-evolution of MNEs and the institutional environment. In J. Cantwell (Ed.), *The eclectic paradigm* (pp. 192–223). London: Palgrave Macmillan UK. doi:10.1007/978-1-137-54471-1_8

Carson, R. T. (2010). The environmental Kuznets curve: Seeking empirical regularity and theoretical structure. *Review of Environmental Economics and Policy*, *4*(1), 3–23. doi:10.1093/reep/rep021

Cole, M. A. (2004). Trade, the pollution haven hypothesis and the environmental Kuznets curve: Examining the linkages. *Ecological Economics: The Journal of the International Society for Ecological Economics*, *48*(1), 71–81. doi:10.1016/j.ecolecon.2003.09.007

Cole, M. A. (2006). Does trade liberalization increase national energy use? *Economics Letters*, *92*(1), 108–112. doi:10.1016/j.econlet.2006.01.018

Copeland, B. R., & Scott Taylor, M. (2013). *Trade and the environment: Theory and evidence*. Princeton University Press.

Desai, M. A., Foley, C. F., & Hines, J. R. Jr. (2006). Capital controls, liberalizations, and foreign direct investment. *Review of Financial Studies*, *19*(4), 1433–1464. doi:10.1093/rfs/hhj041

Dinda, S. (2004). Environmental Kuznets curve hypothesis: A survey. *Ecological Economics: The Journal of the International Society for Ecological Economics*, *49*(4), 431–455. doi:10.1016/j.ecolecon.2004.02.011

Dunning, J. H. (2009). Explaining changing patterns of international production. In defense of the eclectic theory. *Oxford Bulletin of Economics and Statistics*, *41*(4), 269–295. doi:10.1111/j.1468-0084.1979.mp41004003.x

Eskeland, G. S., & Harrison, A. E. (2003). Moving to greener pastures? Multinationals and the pollution haven hypothesis. *Journal of Development Economics*, *70*(1), 1–23. doi:10.1016/S0304-3878(02)00084-6

Frankel, J. A., & Rose, A. K. (2005). Is trade good or bad for the environment? Sorting out the causality. *The Review of Economics and Statistics*, *87*(1), 85–91. doi:10.1162/0034653053327577

Galeotti, M., Lanza, A., & Pauli, F. (2006). Reassessing the environmental Kuznets curve for CO2 emissions: A robustness exercise. *Ecological Economics: The Journal of the International Society for Ecological Economics*, *57*(1), 152–163. doi:10.1016/j.ecolecon.2005.03.031

Galeotti, M., Manera, M., & Lanza, A. (2009). On the robustness of robustness checks of the environmental Kuznets curve hypothesis. *Environmental and Resource Economics*, *42*(4), 551–574. doi:10.100710640-008-9224-x

Ghauri, P. N., & Yamin, M. (2009). Revisiting the impact of multinational enterprises on economic development. *Journal of World Business*, *44*(2), 105–107. doi:10.1016/j.jwb.2008.05.010

Grossman, G. M., & Krueger, A. B. (1995). Economic growth and the environment. *The Quarterly Journal of Economics*, *110*(2), 353–377. doi:10.2307/2118443

He, J. (2006). Pollution haven hypothesis and environmental impacts of foreign direct investment: The case of industrial emission of sulfur dioxide (SO2) in Chinese provinces. *Ecological Economics: The Journal of the International Society for Ecological Economics*, *60*(1), 228–245. doi:10.1016/j.ecolecon.2005.12.008

He, X., & Yao, X. (2017). Foreign direct investments and the environmental Kuznets curve: New evidence from Chinese provinces. *Emerging Markets Finance & Trade*, *53*(1), 12–25. doi:10.1080/1540496X.2016.1138813

Jiang, L., Zhou, H.-F., Bai, L., & Zhou, P. (2018). Does foreign direct investment drive environmental degradation in China? An empirical study based on air quality index from a spatial perspective. *Journal of Cleaner Production*, *176*, 864–872. doi:10.1016/j.jclepro.2017.12.048

Kaika, D., & Zervas, E. (2013). The environmental Kuznets curve (EKC) theory — Part A: Concept, causes and the CO2 emissions case. *Energy Policy*, *62*, 1392–1402. doi:10.1016/j.enpol.2013.07.131

Kearsley, A., & Riddel, M. (2010). A further inquiry into the pollution haven hypothesis and the environmental Kuznets curve. *Ecological Economics: The Journal of the International Society for Ecological Economics*, *69*(4), 905–919. doi:10.1016/j.ecolecon.2009.11.014

Kim, M. H., & Adilov, N. (2012). The lesser of two evils: An empirical investigation of foreign direct investment-pollution trade-off. *Applied Economics*, *44*(20), 2597–2606. doi:10.1080/00036846.2011.566187

Kozul-Wright, R., & Fortunato, P. (2012). International trade and carbon emissions. *European Journal of Development Research*, *24*(4), 509–529. doi:10.1057/ejdr.2012.15

Liu, H., & Kim, H. (2018). Ecological footprint, foreign direct investment, and gross domestic production: Evidence of Belt & Road initiative countries. *Sustainability: Science Practice and Policy*, *10*(10), 3527. doi:10.3390u10103527

Mani, M., & Wheeler, D. (1998). In search of pollution havens? Dirty industry in the world economy, 1960 to 1995. *Journal of Environment & Development*, *7*(3), 215–247. doi:10.1177/107049659800700302

Narula, R., & Driffield, N. (2012). Does FDI cause development? The ambiguity of the evidence and why it matters. *European Journal of Development Research*, *24*(1), 1–7. doi:10.1057/ejdr.2011.51

Neumayer, E. (2001). Trade liberalisation, economic growth and the environment. *Journal of Environmental Policy and Planning*, *3*(3), 245–254. doi:10.1002/jepp.73

Newman, C., Rand, J., Talbot, T., & Tarp, F. (2015). Technology transfers, foreign investment and productivity spillovers. *European Economic Review*, *76*, 168–187. doi:10.1016/j.euroecorev.2015.02.005

Noailly, J., & Ryfisch, D. (2015). Multinational firms and the internationalization of green R&D: A review of the evidence and policy implications. *Energy Policy*, *83*, 218–228. doi:10.1016/j.enpol.2015.03.002

Omri, A., & Kahouli, B. (2014). Causal relationships between energy consumption, foreign direct investment and economic growth: Fresh evidence from dynamic simultaneous-equations models. *Energy Policy*, *67*, 913–922. doi:10.1016/j.enpol.2013.11.067

Pinkse, J., & Kolk, A. (2012). Multinational enterprises and climate change: Exploring institutional failures and embeddedness. *Journal of International Business Studies*, *43*(3), 332–341. doi:10.1057/jibs.2011.56

Porter, M. E., & Linde, C. van der. (1995). Toward a new conception of the environment-competitiveness relationship. *The Journal of Economic Perspectives: A Journal of the American Economic Association, 9*(4), 97-118.

Rubashkina, Y., Galeotti, M., & Verdolini, E. (2015). Environmental regulation and competitiveness: Empirical evidence on the Porter hypothesis from European manufacturing sectors. *Energy Policy, 83*, 288–300. doi:10.1016/j.enpol.2015.02.014

Selden, T. M., & Song, D. (1994). Environmental quality and development: Is there a Kuznets curve for air pollution emissions? *Journal of Environmental Economics and Management, 27*(2), 147–162. doi:10.1006/jeem.1994.1031

Shao, Y. (2017). Does FDI affect carbon intensity? New evidence from dynamic panel analysis. *International Journal of Climate Change Strategies and Management, 34*, 27–43.

Stern, D. I. (2004). The rise and fall of the environmental Kuznets curve. *World Development, 32*(8), 1419–1439. doi:10.1016/j.worlddev.2004.03.004

Stern, N., & Stern, N. H. (2015). *Why are we waiting? The logic, urgency, and promise of tackling climate change*. MIT Press.

Suri, V., & Chapman, D. (1998). Economic growth, trade and energy: Implications for the environmental Kuznets curve. *Ecological Economics: The Journal of the International Society for Ecological Economics, 25*(2), 195–208. doi:10.1016/S0921-8009(97)00180-8

United Nations Conference on Trade and Development. (2018). *World Investment Report 2018*. Author.

Vogel, D., & Kagan, R. A. (2004). *Dynamics of regulatory change: How globalization affects national regulatory policies*. University of California Press.

Yildirim, E. (2014). Energy use, CO2 emission and foreign direct investment: Is there any inconsistence between causal relations? *Frontiers of Energy and Power Engineering in China, 8*(3), 269–278.

Zhang, C., & Zhou, X. (2016). Does foreign direct investment lead to lower CO2 emissions? Evidence from a regional analysis in China. *Renewable & Sustainable Energy Reviews, 58*, 943–951. doi:10.1016/j.rser.2015.12.226

Zugravu-Soilita, N. (2015). How does foreign direct investment affect pollution? Toward a better understanding of the direct and conditional effects. *Environmental and Resource Economics, 66*(2), 293–338. doi:10.100710640-015-9950-9

KEY TERMS AND DEFINITIONS

Environmental Kuznets Curve: Hypothesized relationship between environmental quality or environmental degradation and economic development.

Foreign Affiliate: Details the economic operations of foreign direct investment-based enterprises.

Multinational Enterprise: An enterprise producing goods or delivering services in more than one country.

Panel Data: Longitudinal data or cross-sectional time series data.

Pollution Halo: Hypothesis that posits that multinational enterprises supply advanced technology to countries and accordingly cause lower carbon emissions.

Pollution Haven: Hypothesis that posits that polluting industries will relocate to jurisdictions with less stringent environmental regulations.

Sustainability: Process of meeting the needs of the present without compromising the ability of future generations to meet their needs.

United States of America: A federal constitutional republic made of 50 states and a federal district.

APPENDIX

The countries included in the sample are Algeria, Angola, Argentina, Australia, Austria, Azerbaijan, Bahamas, Bahrain, Belgium, Bermuda, Bolivia, Brazil, Bulgaria, Cambodia, Cameroon, Canada, Chile, China, Colombia, Costa Rica, Côte d'Ivoire, Croatia, Cyprus, Czech Republic, Denmark, Dominican Republic, Ecuador, Egypt, El Salvador, Equatorial Guinea, Estonia, Fiji, Finland, France, Gabon, Germany, Ghana, Greece, Guatemala, Honduras, Hong Kong, Hungary, India, Indonesia, Iraq, Ireland, Israel, Italy, Jamaica, Japan, Jordan, Kenya, Korea Republic, Latvia Lebanon, Liberia, Libya, Lithuania, Luxembourg, Macao, Malaysia, Malta, Mexico, Morocco, Netherlands, New Zealand, Nicaragua, Nigeria, Norway, Pakistan, Panama, Paraguay, Peru, Philippines, Poland, Portugal, Qatar, Romania, Russian Federation, Saudi Arabia, Serbia, Singapore, Slovak Republic, Slovenia, South Africa, Spain, Sweden, Switzerland, Thailand, Trinidad and Tobago, Turkey, Ukraine, United Arab Emirates, United Kingdom, Uruguay Venezuela, Vietnam.

Table 1. Variables and sources of statistical data

Variable	Proxy	Unit	Description	Data Source
Environmental degradation	Carbon dioxide emissions from total fuel consumption	metric tons per capita	Emissions from burning of fossil fuels and the manufacture of cement, and produced during consumption of solid, liquid, and gas fuels and gas flaring	World Bank World Development Indicators and Carbon Dioxide Information Analysis Center, Environmental Sciences Division, Oak Ridge National Laboratory, Tennessee, United States
Income	Per capita gross domestic product	constant 2011 US dollars per capita	Aggregate output at purchaser's prices computed as the sum of gross value added by all resident producers plus any product taxes and minus any subsidies not included	World Bank World Development Indicators
International trade	Trade openness	percent of total gross domestic product	The sum of exports and imports of goods and services measured as a share of gross domestic product	World Bank World Development Indicators
Environmental regulation	Renewable energy consumption	percent of total final energy consumption	Share of renewable energy in total final energy consumption	World Bank World Development Indicators
Multinational enterprises	Foreign investment activity	current US dollars	Capital expenditures by majority-owned foreign affiliates of US multinational enterprises	United States Department of Commerce and Bureau of Economic Analysis

Table 2. Summary statistics

	Mean	Standard Deviation	Minimum Value	Maximum Value	Coefficient of Variation
$ln(E/P)_{it}$	1.38	1.11	-2.00	4.16	0.80
$ln(Y/P)_{it}$	9.72	0.96	6.36	11.82	0.09
$ln[(Y/P)_{it}]^2$	95.53	18.29	40.52	139.92	0.19
$ln[(X+M)/Y]_{it}$	4.45	0.52	3.09	6.12	0.11
$ln(REG)_{it}$	2.43	1.61	-5.07	4.51	0.66
$ln(FDI)_{it}$	5.83	2.24	0.00	10.42	0.40

Note: the coefficient of variation is the standard deviation-to-mean ratio.

Table 3. Correlation matrix

	$ln(E/P)_{it}$	$ln(Y/P)_{it}$	$ln[(Y/P)_{it}]^2$	$ln[(X+M)/Y]_{it}$	$ln(REG)_{it}$	$ln(FDI)_{it}$
$ln(E/P)_{it}$	1					
$ln(Y/P)_{it}$	0.88*	1				
$ln[(Y/P)_{it}]^2$	0.87*	0.99*	1			
$ln[(X+M)/Y]_{it}$	0.18*	0.21*	0.23*	1		
$ln(REG)_{it}$	-0.62*	-0.53*	-0.51*	-0.29*	1	
$ln(FDI)_{it}$	0.35*	0.38*	0.37*	-0.23*	-0.17*	1

Note: * indicates significance at the 0.05 level.

Table 4. Results of GMM regressions

	Dependent Variable: $ln(E/P)_{it}$					
	Estimation Method					
	Sys-GMM			Diff-GMM		
Explanatory Variable						
Lagged $ln(E/P)_{it}$	0.70 (0.00)	0.71 (0.00)	0.71 (0.00)	0.29 (0.00)	0.31 (0.00)	0.24 (0.00)
$ln(Y/P)_{it}$	0.91 (0.00)	0.96 (0.00)	1.01 (0.00)	1.31 (0.00)	1.56 (0.00)	0.98 (0.00)
$ln[(Y/P)_{it}]^2$	-0.03 (0.00)	-0.04 (0.00)	-0.04 (0.00)	-0.05 (0.00)	-0.06 (0.00)	-0.03 (0.00)
$ln[(X+M)/Y]_{it}$		0.06 (0.00)	0.05 (0.00)		0.06 (0.00)	0.08 (0.00)
$ln(REG)_{it}$			-0.04 (0.00)			-0.21 (0.00)
$ln(FDI)_{it}$	-0.01 (0.00)	-0.01 (0.00)	-0.02 (0.00)	-0.01 (0.00)	-0.02 (0.00)	-0.01 (0.00)
Intercept	-5.21 (0.00)	-5.56 (0.00)	-5.54 (0.00)	-7.07 (0.00)	-8.44 (0.00)	-5.29 (0.00)
Observations	772	768	760	647	644	639
No. countries	97	97	95	94	94	92
Sargan test [1]	$X^2(131)$ = 94.34 (0.99)	$X^2(131)$ = 94.33 (0.99)	$X^2(131)$ = 90.58 (0.99)	$X^2(107)$ = 90.52 (0.87)	$X^2(107)$ = 91.34 (0.86)	$X^2(107)$ = 86.65 (0.92)
AR(1) test [2]	-3.48 (0.00)	-3.49 (0.00)	-3.44 (0.00)	-3.20 (0.00)	-3.27 (0.00)	-3.04 (0.00)
AR(2) test [3]	0.04 (0.97)	0.24 (0.81)	0.28 (0.78)	-0.52 (0.60)	-0.29 (0.77)	-0.42 (0.67)

Note: Values in parenthesis are estimated p-values.
[1]Sargan test of over identifying restrictions and valid specification.
[2] [3]First and second order serial correlation tests. All models are statistically significant at the 0.01 level.

Chapter 13
Export Performance:
Exploring the Linkage With Absorptive Capabilities

Orlando Lima Rua
Polytechnic of Porto, Portugal

ABSTRACT

The purpose of this chapter is to analyze the influence of absorptive capabilities on export performance. The author uses a quantitative research approach by conducting a study based on a survey data from 247 Portuguese small and medium-sized enterprises (SMEs) from the textile industry. Findings suggest that absorptive capabilities have a positive and significant influence on export performance. This chapter presents further evidences of the strategies that SMEs managers should pursue and policy makers should promote. This study deepens our understanding and provides novel insights into strategic management literature, since it combines multiple factors and has obtained the importance of each construct in SMEs business growth.

INTRODUCTION

The Resource-Based View (RBV) emphasizes that the ownership of strategic resources enables companies to gain competitive advantage (Monteiro, Soares & Rua, 2017). Recent studies have shifted the focus on tangible resources to intangible resources, which are deemed more important from a strategic viewpoint and more relevant for business performance and success (Bakar and Ahmad, 2010; Morgan *et al.*, 2006). Barney (1995, p. 66) developed the VRIO model (Valuable, Rare, Imitable, Organisation) and suggested that, in order to create sustained competitive advantage and discover unique resources and capabilities, "managers must look inside their firm for valuable, rare and costly-to-imitate resources, and then exploit these resources through their organization". This theory is based on the assumption that the source of competitive advantage is obtained from firms' resources based on two assumptions: 1) strategic resources are heterogeneously distributed across firms; and 2) these differences are stable overtime (Barney, 1991).

DOI: 10.4018/978-1-5225-8906-8.ch013

Several strategic management scholars argue that RBV has basically "in-ward" orientation. Although this theory recognizes that "the value of the firm's resources and capabilities is determined by the market context within which the firm is operating" (Barney, 2001, p. 645), it does not address the processes of converting resources and capabilities into customer value (Möller, 2006).

Resource-based scholars argue that resources form the basis of firm strategies (Barney, 1991) and intangible resources are more likely than tangible resources to produce a competitive advantage, since they are often rare and socially complex, thereby making them difficult to imitate (Hitt, Bierman, Shimizu, & Kochhar, 2001). Thus, intangible assets are considered strategic variables (Amit & Schoemaker, 1993) and can consequently create sustainable value. Firms with valuable, scarce, and nonsubstitutable resources can gain at least temporary advantages by using those resources to develop and implement product-market strategies (Hsu & Ziedonis, 2013).

Another body of literature in the field of strategic management has focused on dynamic capabilities (Barreto, 2010). The firms' success depends not only on its' resources and capabilities, but also the ability to adapt itself to the industry contingencies and markets in which operates. Firms may possess resources but must display dynamic capabilities otherwise shareholder value will be destroyed (Bowman & Ambrosini, 2003). It is in this context that emerges the Dynamic Capabilities View (DCV) (Amit & Schoemaker, 1993; Teece et al., 1997) to support the adjustment to environmental change. DCV is not divergent but rather an important stream of RBV to gain competitive advantage in increasingly demanding environments (Ambrosini & Bowman, 2009; Barreto, 2010; Eisenhardt & Martin, 2000; Wang & Ahmed, 2007). Monteiro, Soares and Rua (2017) defend that in versatile markets, firms' capabilities should be dynamic and managers must display the ability to ensure consistency between business environment and strategy in order to continuously renew skills.

Firms may possess resources but must display dynamic capabilities otherwise shareholder value will be destroyed (Bowman & Ambrosini, 2003). It is in this context that emerges the DCV (Amit & Schoemaker, 1993; Teece, Pisano & Shuen, 1997) to support the adjustment to environmental change. The literature suggests that resources and capabilities are related to each other (Dhanaraj & Beamish, 2003; Morgan, Kaleka & Katsikeas, 2004). Integration, reconfiguration and learning resources only become significant when resources are abundant (Wu & Wang, 2007), thus improving firms' dynamic capabilities. Monteiro, Soares and Rua (2017) defend that in versatile markets, firms' capabilities should be dynamic and managers must display the ability to ensure consistency between business environment and strategy in order to continuously renew skills.

Our study is responsive to the call of Sousa, Martínez-López and Coelho (2008) which suggests that, in the context of international markets, firms' survival and expansion, and consequent economic growth of many countries, is strongly dependent on a better understanding of the determinants that influence export performance. In fact, the factors that set off SME growth (including exporting) are still in need of research (Stouraitis et al., 2017). So, the purpose of this paper is to broad the boundaries of strategic management literature and test the following research question: —— *Does absorptive capabilities positively influence small business export performance?*

THEORETICAL FRAMEWORK

Absorptive Capabilities

Cohen and Levinthal (1990) presented a definition of Absorptive Capability (ACAP) most widely cited by academic research, as the firm's ability to identify, assimilate and exploit new knowledge. Thus, this ability access and use new external knowledge, regarded as an intangible asset, is critical to success and depends mainly on prior knowledge level, since it is this knowledge that will facilitate the identification and processing of new one. This prior knowledge not only includes the basic capabilities, such as shared language, but also recent technological and scientific data or learning skills. By analysing this definition is found that absorptive capability of knowledge only three dimensions: the ability to acquire external knowledge; the ability to assimilate it inside; and the ability to apply it.

Zahra and George (2002) divided ACAP in Potential Absorptive Capability (PACAP) and Realized Absorptive Capability (RACAP). PACAP reflects the firms' ability to acquire and assimilate knowledge that is vital for their activities. Knowledge identification, acquisition and assimilation is related to routines and processes that permit to analyse, process, interpret and understand external information. RACAP includes knowledge transformation and exploitation, where transformation is the ability to develop routines that facilitate the integration of newly acquired knowledge in existing one. Knowledge exploitation are routines which enhance existing skills or create new ones by incorporating acquired and transformed knowledge internally.

In order to cope and enhance each ACAP dimension, Jansen, Van Den Bosch and Volberda (2005) argue that firms need to develop organizational mechanisms which enable them to synthesize and apply newly acquired knowledge. Thus, there are coordination mechanisms that increase the exchange of knowledge between sectors and hierarchies, like multitasking teams, participation in decision-making and job rotation. These mechanisms bring together different sources of expertise and increase lateral interaction between functional areas. System mechanisms are behaviour programs that reduce established deviations, such as routines and formalization. Socialization mechanisms create a broad and tacit understanding of appropriate rules of action, contributing to a common code of communication.

Export Performance

Literature on export performance is extensive but arguably it has not yet achieved the consensus required to prescribe exporting strategies to small firm (Casey & Hamilton, 2014). Exporting is an early phase in the internationalisation model established by Johanson and Vahlne (1977, 2009), grounded on the assumption that new exporters can gradually engage with foreign markets, depending their exploitation strategy on knowledge and other resources. This export research, however, was not pertinent for small exporters (Casey & Hamilton, 2014), since its unit of analysis was large firms.

In a fairly recent literature review, Sousa *et al.* (2008) conclude that, along with internal capabilities and competencies, the main determinants of export performance are firm size and international experience. Actually, internationalization processes have mainly been studied with reference to multinational corporations and less for SMEs, because smallness is usually considered a problem, as these firms often have a disadvantage in resource access (Musso & Francioni, 2014). This, however, does not support small firm managers in search of a growth strategy through exporting.

Conversely, the number of small firms operating in international markets has increased and represents the majority of firms in most countries, and therefore, they play an important role in the economic growth of their countries. As a consequence, the internationalization process of SMEs has become a topic of academic and governmental attention (Musso & Francioni, 2014).

Hence, the development of exports is of great importance, both at macro and micro levels. Exporting contributes to economic and social development of nations, helps the industry progress, increases productivity and creates jobs. At firms level, through market diversification, exports provide an opportunity for them to become less dependent on the domestic market, gaining new customers, exploiting economies of scale and achieving lower production costs while producing more efficiently (Okpara, 2009).

Exports is a more attractive way to enter international markets, especially for SMEs, in comparison with other alternatives, such as joint ventures, which involve spending a large number of resources (Dhanaraj & Beamish, 2003; Fuchs & Köstner, 2016; Piercy, Kaleka & Katsikeas, 1998), does not create high risk and commitment and allows greater flexibility in adjusting the volume of goods to different export markets (Lu & Beamish, 2002).

On one hand, export activity fulfils certain business goals, which may be economic (such as increasing profits and sales) and/or strategic (such as diversification of markets, gaining market share and increasing brand reputation) (Cavusgil & Zou, 1994). On the other hand, export motivation may result from proactive or reactive actions. For example, proactive actions are advantage of profit, introduction of a single product, technological advantage, exclusive information, commitment of management, tax benefits and economies of scale. Reactive motivations are identifying competitive pressures, excess production capacity, sales decrease or saturation in the domestic market and proximity of customers and landing ports (Stouraitis et al., 2017; Wood & Robertson, 1997).

Hypothesis Derivation

Teece *et al.* (1997, p. 516) defined dynamic capabilities as the "firm's ability to integrate, build, and reconfigure internal and external competences to address rapidly changing environments". Dynamic capabilities thus reflect firms' ability to achieve new and innovative export forms. ACAP is a dynamic capability found in organizational processes that enables firms to reconfigure their core resources, react to environmental dynamics and build competitive advantage (Zahra & George, 2002). The heterogeneity of resources and capabilities leads to performance imbalances and affects firms' ability to design and implement competitive strategies (Barney, 1991; Peteraf, 1993). Thus, this theory suggests that heterogeneous resources and capabilities have a direct effect on firms' performance (Makadok, 2001; Teece et al., 1997). Thus, we tested the following hypothesis:

H1: Absorptive capabilities influences positively with export performance.

METHODOLOGY

Sample and Data Collection

The population of this empirical study has been drawn from Portuguese textile industry firms. Electronic questionnaires were used as primary data sources and were carried out over the period of February 16 to April 30, 2016, and were applied to firm's top managers. The identification of companies was done through the Portugal's Textile Association (Associação Têxtil de Portugal) database (ATP, 2014). So, in this study we use a non-probabilistic and convenient sampling.

A total of 247 complete and validated questionnaires accounting for 25% per cent of the population were obtained. This response rate is considered quite satisfactory, given that the average of top management survey response rates are in the range of 15%-20% (Menon & Bharadwaj, 1999).

Statistical Analysis

We used PLS-SEM path modelling to test our hypothesis, specifically the software SmartPLS 3.0 (Hair et al., 2013; Sarstedt et al., 2014). We believe that the PLS-SEM path modelling is best suited to estimate our research model since: 1) this study focuses on prediction and explanation of constructs variance (in our case 2); 2) our research model has a complex structure; 3) the relationship between absorptive capabilities and export performance; 4) this study uses first and second-order reflective constructs; and 5) the sample (n=247).

Measures

This study uses well-validated scales from previous studies to operationalize the key constructs and adapted them to the particular context of our empirical setting.

Independent variable - According to Zahra and George (2002), ACAP construct is divided in Potencial Absorptive capabilities (PACAP) e Realized Absorptive capabilities (RACAP). To measure this construct we use Jansen et al.'s (2005) scale.

Dependent variable – This construct was measured using Okpara's (2009) measurement instrument.

All constructs were assessed on a five-point Likert scale.

RESULTS

Non-Response Bias and Common Method Bias

In this study we performed a univariate test of significance (*t*-test), to examine existing differences between respondents who answered our questionnaire quickly and those who did not. The results ($p<0.05$) showed the absence of significant differences between the two groups of respondents. Hence, we can assure that our sample is free from non-response bias. The methods used to reduce the risk of common method-bias were several. In the survey design itself, already validated in previous investigations, short and concise items were used to reduce misunderstandings. A pre-test was conducted to a group of several university experts and business specialists. Similarly, following the recommendation of Podsakoff el al. (2003), a distribution of items of dependent and non-consecutive independent variables was used. Finally, before assessing the relationships between dependent and independent variables, Harman's single-factor test was performed. Unrotated factor analysis using the eigenvalue-greater-than-one criterion revealed six factors, the first explaining 17.0 percent of the variance. This suggests that common method bias is not a serious threat to the validity of our study.

Next, in order to analyse and interpret the PLS-SEM results, we will: 1) assess the measurement model; and 2) evaluate and test the structural model.

Evaluation of Measurement Model

Results from Table 1 show that the measurement model meets all general requirements. First, all reflective items have a load higher than 0.707, which means that the reliability of individual indicators ($loading^2$) are higher than 0.5. Second, all composite reability values and Cronbach's alpha values are higher than 0.70, suggesting acceptable model reliability. Third, the average variance extracted (AVE) values of all constructs are higher than 0.50, indicating an adequate convergent validity and implying that our set of indicators represent the same underlying construct (Hair et al., 2013).

Finally, regarding discriminant validity, this paper presents two necessary approaches: 1) the first approach suggests that the AVE should share more variance with its assigned indicators than with any other construct - Fornell-Larcker criterion (Fornell & Larcker, 1981); and 2) the second approach suggests that no item should have a higher factor load with another construct than with the one which is assign to measure. The results shown in Table 2 confirm the existence of discriminant validity in our study.

Evaluation of Structural Model

Once the measurement model is defined and validated in all its components, we will proceed and create the second order model, following previous research (e.g., Zahra & Garvis, 2000), where the latent variables of the measurement model behave as constructs' measurement variables. Specifically, Absorptive capabilities (acquisition, assimilation, transformation and exploitation) and Export performance.

In the following tables 3 and 4, we present the results of reliability, convergent validity and discriminant validity corresponding to the second order model. All data confirm the strength of our model.

Since the fundamental objective of our PLS-SEM technique is the prediction of Export Performance, the quality of our theoretical model will be determined by measuring the strength of each path (β), that is the relationship between Absorptive Capability (AC) in the predictability of the endogenous construct Export Performance (EP).

Results from Table 5 indicate that firms with dynamic capabilities achieve superior export performance, thus AC, that is the acquisition, assimilation, transformation and exploitation influence significantly and positively export performance (EP), supporting H1 (β=0.479; p<0.001).

DISCUSSION AND CONCLUSION

The main goal of this study was to analyse the influence of absorptive capabilities on export performance. The central context of this research is on SMEs, which constitute the vast majority of firms in Portugal, as in most word economies. Thus, we conducted an empirical research based on a sample of 247 firms, which were applied a questionnaire in order to exploit data to test hypothesis, using proceedings and statistical techniques. It is important to note that firms evaluated intangible resources, absorptive capabilities, innovation and export performance relative to their major competitors in the export market(s), so the results should be interpreted based on these two aspects.

Table 1. Measurement model

First-order constructs	Items	Factor loading	Item loading	Cronbach's Alpha	Composite reliability	AVE
ABSORPTIVE CAPABILITIES						
	ACAQ1	0.729	0.531			
	ACAQ2	0.694	0.482			
Acquisition*	ACAQ3	0.830	0.689	0.782	0.850	0.532
	ACAQ4	0.687	0.472			
	ACAQ6	0.698	0.487			
	ACAS1	0.819	0.671			
Assimilation	ACAS2	0.932	0.869	0.847	0.907	0.766
	ACAS3	0.871	0.759			
	ACTR2	0.827	0.684			
	ACTR3	0.873	0.762			
Transformation*	ACTR4	0.795	0.632	0.874	0.908	0.665
	ACTR5	0.854	0.729			
	ACTR6	0.721	0.520			
	ACEX1	0.791	0.626			
	ACEX2	0.765	0.585			
	ACEX3	0.866	0.750	0.897	0.922	0.663
Exploitation	ACEX4	0.836	0.699			
	ACEX5	0.703	0.494			
	ACEX6	0.909	0.826			
Export Performance						
	DEXP1	0.873	0.762			
	DEXP2	0.889	0.790			
Export Performance	DEXP3	0.837	0.701	0.927	0.945	0.775
	DEXP4	0.915	0.837			
	DEXP5	0.887	0.787			

* The variables ACAQ5 and ACTR1 corresponding to Acquisition and Transformation were excluded from the measurement model due to low values. Accordingly, values lower than 0.7 generate a low correlation and threaten the reliability of the scale.

Source: Own.

This study demonstrated that the firms' absorptive capabilities has a positive and significant influence on their performance. The results of this study does confirm that dynamic capabilities, specifically absorptive capabilities, enable firms to achieve superior long-term performance (Teece, 2007) (H1 supported). Thus, the analysed firms are able to acquire, assimilate, transform and dynamic capabilities.

This ones can take a variety of forms and be involved in different functions, but the most important common characteristics are that they are higher level capabilities which provide opportunities for knowledge gathering and sharing, constant updating the operational processes, interaction with the environment, and decision-making evaluations (Easterby-Smith, Lyles, & Peteraf, 2009). However, the existence of

Table 2. Latent constructs correlation (Fornell-Larcker Criterion)

Constructs/ Dimensions	1.	2.	3.	4.	5.
1. Acquisition	**0.730**				
2. Assimilation	0.307	**0.875**			
3. Exploitation	0.357	0.656	**0.815**		
4. Export performance	0.390	0.466	0.584	**0.880**	
5. Transformation	0.412	0.620	0.848	0.640	**0.816**

Source: Own.

Table 3. Convergence validity and reliability indexes of the second-order model

Constructs	Cronbach's Alpha	Composite Reliability	AVE
Absorptive capabilities	0.849	0.900	0.694
Export performance	0.927	1.000	0.775

Source: Own.

Table 4. Discriminant validity index of the second-order model

Constructs	Absorptive capabilities	Export performance
Absorptive capabilities	0.662	
Export performance	0.650	0.880

Source: Own.

Table 5. Significant testing results of the structural model path coefficients

	Original Sample (O)	Sample Mean (M)	Standard Deviation (STDEV)	T Statistics (|O/STDEV|)	P Values	2.5%	97.5%
H1. AC -> EP	0.479	0.487	0.039	12.306	0.001*	0.413	0.567

*p<0.001

Source: Own.

common features does imply that any particular dynamic capability is exactly alike across firms, rather they could be developed from different starting points and take unique paths (Eisenhardt & Martin, 2000).

Theoretically, this study contributes to the literature of absorptive capabilities that leverage firm performance (e.g., Cabral et al., 2015; Damanpour et al., 1989). We also highlight the contribution of this study to the theory of strategic management. It is known that strategy includes deliberate and emergent initiatives adopted by management, comprising resource and capabilities used to improve business performance (Nag, Hambrick & Chen, 2007). In order to remain competitive, firms must assess which strategic determinants give them an advantage over their competitors. The findings are a contribution to clarify the influence of intangible resources and absorptive capabilities in small firms export performance.

Additionally, our findings provide guidance to business practitioners, since they indicate that absorptive capabilities are predictors of export performance. Firms are a bundle of resources and capabilities (Peteraf, 1993), it is essential to understand and identify which resources are relevant to gain competitive advantage and superior performance. Business owners must be able to systematically analyse the changes that arise in their target market(s) and to incorporate this knowledge into their processes, to identify the present and future needs and market trends, anticipate changes in demand and seek new business opportunities.

By building on the literature of strategic management, this study aims to support the strategic development of business management policies designed to increase firms' performance in foreign markets and add value to the current context of change.

The fact that the research does not consider the effect of control variables such as age, location and target market of the respondents can be seen as a limitation. Also, the fact that the sampling is non probabilistic and convenience is a limitation. Therefore we advise prudence in the generalization of results.

Further studies with a longitudinal perspective would be of added value to investigate why these differences persist. In other words, to find how and why some small exporters become highly successful while others, in the same industry, struggle to raise their export strengths.

REFERENCES

Ambrosini, V., & Bowman, C. (2009). What are dynamic capabilities and are they a useful construct in strategic management? *International Journal of Management Reviews*, *11*(1), 29–49. doi:10.1111/j.1468-2370.2008.00251.x

Amit, R., & Schoemaker, P. (1993). Strategic assets and organizational rent. *Strategic Management Journal*, *14*(1), 33–46. doi:10.1002mj.4250140105

ATP. (2014). *Plano Estratégico Têxtil 2020 – Projetar o Desenvolvimento da Fileira Têxtil e Vestuário até 2020*. V. N. de Famalicão: ATP.

Bakar, L. J. A., & Ahmad, H. (2010). Assessing the relationship between firm resources and product innovation performance: A resource-based view. *Business Process Management*, *16*(3), 420–435. doi:10.1108/14637151011049430

Barney, J. (1991). Firm Resources and Sustained Competitive Advantage. *Journal of Management*, *17*(1), 99–120. doi:10.1177/014920639101700108

Barney, J. (1995). Looking inside for competitive advantage. *The Academy of Management Perspectives*, *9*(4), 49–61. doi:10.5465/ame.1995.9512032192

Barney, J. (2001). Resource-based theories of competitive advantage: A ten-year retrospective on the resource-based view. *Journal of Management*, *27*(6), 643–650. doi:10.1177/014920630102700602

Barreto, I. (2010). Dynamic Capabilities: A Review of Past Research and an Agenda for the Future. *Journal of Management*, *36*(1), 256–280. doi:10.1177/0149206309350776

Bowman, C., & Ambrosini, V. (2003). How the Resource based and the Dynamic Capability Views of the Firm Inform Corporate level Strategy. *British Journal of Management*, *14*(4), 289–303. doi:10.1111/j.1467-8551.2003.00380.x

Cabral, J. E. O., Coelho, A. F. M., Coelho, F. J. F., & Costa, M. (2015). Capabilities, innovation, and overall performance in brazilian export firms. *RAM. Revista de Administração Mackenzie*, *16*(3), 76–108. doi:10.1590/1678-69712015/administracao.v16n3p76-108

Casey, S. R., & Hamilton, R. T. (2014). Export performance of small firms from small countries: The case of New Zealand. *Journal of International Entrepreneurship*, *12*(3), 254–269. doi:10.100710843-014-0126-4

Cavusgil, T., & Zou, S. (1994). Marketing strategy-performance relationship: An investigation of the empirical link in export market ventures. *Journal of Marketing*, *58*(1), 1–21. doi:10.1177/002224299405800101

Cohen, W., & Levinthal, D. (1990). Absorptive Capacity: A New Perspective on Learning and Innovation. *Administrative Science Quarterly*, *35*(1), 128. doi:10.2307/2393553

Damanpour, F., Szabat, K. A., & Evan, W. M. (1989). The relationship between types of innovation and organizational performance. *Journal of Management Studies*, *26*(6), 587–601. doi:10.1111/j.1467-6486.1989.tb00746.x

Dhanaraj, C., & Beamish, P. W. (2003). A Resource-Based Approach to the Study of Export Performance. *Journal of Small Business Management*, *41*(3), 242–261. doi:10.1111/1540-627X.00080

Easterby-Smith, M., Lyles, M. A., & Peteraf, M. A. (2009). Dynamic Capabilities: Current Debates and Future Directions. *British Journal of Management*, *20*(1), S1–S8. doi:10.1111/j.1467-8551.2008.00609.x

Eisenhardt, K. M., & Martin, J. A. (2000). Dynamic capabilities: What are they? *Strategic Management Journal*, *21*(10–11), 1105–1121. doi:10.1002/1097-0266(200010/11)21:10/11<1105::AID-SMJ133>3.0.CO;2-E

Fornell, C., & Larcker, D. F. (1981). Evaluating structural equation models with unobservable variables and measurement error. *JMR, Journal of Marketing Research*, *18*(1), 39–50. doi:10.1177/002224378101800104

Fuchs, M., & Köstner, M. (2016). Antecedents and consequences of firm's export marketing strategy: An empirical study of Austrian SMEs (a contingency perspective). *Management Research Review*, *39*(3), 329–355. doi:10.1108/MRR-07-2014-0158

Hair, J., Hult, G. T. M., Ringle, C. M., & Sarstedt, M. (2013). *A primer on Partial least Squares Structural Equation Modeling (PLS-SEM)*. SAGE Publications, Inc.

Hitt, M., Bierman, L., Shimizu, K., & Kochhar, R. (2001). Direct and moderating effects of human capital on strategy and performance in professional service firms: A resource-based perspective. *Academy of Management Journal*, *44*(1), 13–28.

Hsu, D. H., & Ziedonis, R. H. (2013). Resources as Dual Sources of Advantage: Implications for Valuing Entrepreneurial-Firm Patents. *Strategic Management Journal*, *34*(7), 761–781. doi:10.1002mj.2037

Jansen, J. J. P., Van Den Bosch, F. J., & Volberda, H. W. (2005). Managing Potential and Realized Absorptive Capacity: How Do Organizational Antecedents Matter? *Academy of Management Journal*, *48*(6), 999–1015. doi:10.5465/amj.2005.19573106

Johanson, J., & Vahlne, J.-E. (1977). The internationalization process of the firm-a model of knowledge development and increasing foreign market commitments. *Journal of International Business Studies*, *8*(1), 23–32. doi:10.1057/palgrave.jibs.8490676

Johanson, J., & Vahlne, J.-E. (2009). The Uppsala internationalization process model revisited: From liability of foreignness to liability of outsidership. *Journal of International Business Studies*, *40*(9), 1411–1431. doi:10.1057/jibs.2009.24

Lu, J. W., & Beamish, P. W. (2002). The Internationalization and Growth of SMEs. *ASAC*, *2002*, 86–96.

Makadok, R. (2001). Toward a synthesis of the resource-based and dynamic-capability views of rent creation. *Strategic Management Journal*, *22*(5), 387–401. doi:10.1002mj.158

Menon, A., Bharadwaj, S., Adidam, P. T., & Edison, S. W. (1999). Antecedents and consequences of marketing strategy making: A model and a test. *Journal of Marketing*, *63*(April), 18–40. doi:10.1177/002224299906300202

Möller, K. (2006). Role of competences in creating customer value: A value-creation logic approach. *Industrial Marketing Management*, *35*(8), 913–924. doi:10.1016/j.indmarman.2006.04.005

Monteiro, A., Soares, A. M., & Rua, O. L. (2017). Entrepreneurial orientation and export performance: The mediating effect of organisational resources and dynamic capabilities. *Journal of International Business and Entrepreneurship Development*, *10*(1), 3–19. doi:10.1504/JIBED.2017.082749

Morgan, N., Kaleka, A., & Katsikeas, C. S. (2004). Antecedents of Export Venture Performance : A Theoretical Model. *Journal of Marketing*, *68*(1), 90–108. doi:10.1509/jmkg.68.1.90.24028

Musso, F., & Francioni, B. (2014). International strategy for SMEs: Criteria for foreign markets and entry modes selection. *Journal of Small Business and Enterprise Development*, *21*(2), 301–312. doi:10.1108/JSBED-10-2013-0149

Nag, R., Hambrick, D., & Chen, M. (2007). What is strategic management, really? Inductive derivation of a consensus definition of the field. *Strategic Management Journal, 955*, 935–955.

Okpara, J. (2009). Entrepreneurial orientation and export performance: Evidence from an emerging economy. *Int. Rev. Bus. Res. Papers*, *5*(6), 195–211.

Peteraf, M. (1993). The cornerstones of competitive advantage: A resource-based view. *Strategic Management Journal*, *14*(3), 179–191. doi:10.1002mj.4250140303

Piercy, N., Kaleka, A., & Katsikeas, C. (1998). Sources of competitive advantage in high performing exporting companies. *Journal of World Business*, *33*(4), 378–393. doi:10.1016/S1090-9516(99)80081-9

Podsakoff, P. M., MacKenzie, S. B., Lee, J. Y., & Podsakoff, N. P. (2003). Common method biases in behavioral research: A critical review of the literature and recommended remedies. *The Journal of Applied Psychology*, *88*(5), 879–903. doi:10.1037/0021-9010.88.5.879 PMID:14516251

Sarstedt, M., Ringle, C. M., Smith, D., Reams, R., & Hair, J. F. Jr. (2014). Partial least squares structural equation modeling (PLS-SEM): A useful tool for family business researchers. *Journal of Family Business Strategy*, *5*(1), 105–115. doi:10.1016/j.jfbs.2014.01.002

Sousa, C. M. P., Martínez-López, F. J., & Coelho, F. (2008). The determinants of export performance: A review of the research in the literature between 1998 and 2005. *International Journal of Management Reviews*, *10*(4), 343–374. doi:10.1111/j.1468-2370.2008.00232.x

Stouraitis, V., Harris, M., Harun, M., & Kyritsis, M. (2017). Motivators of SME initial export choice and the European Union regional effect in manufacturing. *International Journal of Entrepreneurial Behaviour & Research*, *23*(1), 35–55. doi:10.1108/IJEBR-05-2015-0120

Teece, D. J. (2007). Explicating dynamic capabilities : The nature and microfoundations of (sustainable) enterprise performance. *Strategic Management Journal*, *1350*(13), 1319–1350. doi:10.1002mj.640

Teece, D. J., Pisano, G., & Shuen, A. (1997). Dynamic capabilities and strategic management. *Strategic Management Journal*, *18*(7), 509–533. doi:10.1002/(SICI)1097-0266(199708)18:7<509::AID-SMJ882>3.0.CO;2-Z

Wang, C., & Ahmed, P. K. (2007). Dynamic capabilities: A review and research agenda. *International Journal of Management Reviews*, *9*(1), 31–51. doi:10.1111/j.1468-2370.2007.00201.x

Wood, V. R., & Robertson, K. R. (1997). Strategic orientation and export success: An empirical study. *International Marketing Review*, *4*(6), 424–444. doi:10.1108/02651339710192975

Wu, L.-Y., & Wang, C.-J. (2007). Transforming resources to improve performance of technology-based firms: A Taiwanese empirical study. *Journal of Engineering and Technology Management*, *24*(3), 251–261. doi:10.1016/j.jengtecman.2007.05.002

Zahra, S., & Garvis, D. (2000). International corporate entrepreneurship and firm performance: The moderating effect of international environmental hostility. *Journal of Business Venturing*, *15*(5-6), 469–492. doi:10.1016/S0883-9026(99)00036-1

Zahra, S., & George, G. (2002). Absorptive capacity: A review, reconceptualization, and extension. *Academy of Management Review*, *27*(2), 185–203. doi:10.5465/amr.2002.6587995

ADDITIONAL READING

Ambrosini, V., & Bowman, C. (2009). What are dynamic capabilities and are they a useful construct in strategic management? *International Journal of Management Reviews*, *11*(1), 29–49. doi:10.1111/j.1468-2370.2008.00251.x

Aulakh, P. S., Kotabe, M., & Teegen, H. (2000). Export strategies and performance of firms from emerging economies: Evidence from Brazil, Chile, and Mexico. *Academy of Management Journal*, *43*(3), 342–361.

Barney, J. (1991). Firm Resources and Sustained Competitive Advantage. *Journal of Management*, *17*(1), 99–120. doi:10.1177/014920639101700108

Barney, J. (2001). Resource-based theories of competitive advantage: A ten-year retrospective on the resource-based view. *Journal of Management*, *27*(6), 643–650. doi:10.1177/014920630102700602

Barreto, I. (2010). Dynamic Capabilities: A Review of Past Research and an Agenda for the Future. *Journal of Management*, *36*(1), 256–280. doi:10.1177/0149206309350776

Hofer, K. M., Niehoff, L. M., & Wuehrer, G. A. (2015). The effects of dynamic capabilities on value-based pricing and export performance. *Advances in International Marketing*, *25*, 109–127. doi:10.1108/S1474-797920140000025005

Monteiro, A. P., Soares, A. M., & Rua, O. L. (2017). Linking intangible resources and export performance: The role of entrepreneurial orientation and dynamic capabilities. *Baltic Journal of Management*, *12*(3), 329–347. doi:10.1108/BJM-05-2016-0097

Sousa, C. M. P., Martínez-López, F. J., & Coelho, F. (2008). The determinants of export performance: A review of the research in the literature between 1998 and 2005. *International Journal of Management Reviews*, *10*(4), 343–374. doi:10.1111/j.1468-2370.2008.00232.x

KEY TERMS AND DEFINITIONS

Absorptive Capabilities: Firm's ability to identify, assimilate, and exploit new knowledge.

Dynamic Capabilities View: Firms' capabilities should be dynamic, and managers must display the ability to ensure consistency between business environment and strategy in order to continuously renew skills.

Export Performance: Profitability indicators such as growth in sales, profit, activities and operations, and performance in general concerning the export activity.

Potential Absorptive Capability: Reflects the firms' ability to acquire and assimilate knowledge that is vital for their activities.

Realized Absorptive Capability: Includes knowledge transformation and exploitation, where transformation is the ability to develop routines that facilitate the integration of newly acquired knowledge in existing one.

Resource-Based View: Theory based on the assumption that the source of competitive advantage is obtained from firms' resources.

SME: Small and medium-sized enterprises.

Chapter 14
Serendipitous Network Internationalization:
A Case Study in the ICT Services Sector

Daniel Ferreira Polonia
https://orcid.org/0000-0001-8194-4713
University of Aveiro, Portugal

Adriana Marques Miranda
University of Aveiro, Portugal

ABSTRACT

This chapter addresses the internationalization case of an ICT (information and communication technology) company in the services sector. After an initial review of the theoretical framework on the internationalization of SMEs, where it is found that the subject is still under-researched, and an analysis of the criteria these companies follow to select markets to be addressed, the case of a company whose internationalization efforts were based on the anticipation of an internal market shock and on the leveraging of serendipitous network connections, with very relevant business impact and financial results, is analyzed. The case study ends with a "what-if" approach, where the taken approach is confronted with a more structured "textbook-like" theoretical scenario of market selection, with significant differences arising from the comparisons made.

INTRODUCTION

In a context of economic instability, there is an increasing need for companies to broaden their horizons and expand their business. Over the last decades, there has been an ever-decreasing number of barriers to trade, as well as very significant progress in information and communication technologies.

The combination of these two factors has caused an increasing number of service companies to change their strategies, pursuing internationalization initiatives in order to diversify markets. However, one of the recurrent problems they face is the choice of target markets and the criteria underlying that decision, as well as the alliances they must forge so that they can achieve a sustainable internationalization process.

DOI: 10.4018/978-1-5225-8906-8.ch014

In this chapter we will revisit the theoretical framework concerning internationalization of service companies and the criteria they follow to select the markets where they start the process. After analyzing the possible strategies to implement this process, a case study of the initial efforts of internationalization of a Portuguese ICT (Information and Communication Technology) SME (Small and Medium Enterprise) is presented and a comparison is made between the choices made and the indications that a theoretical matrix pointed to.

With this background structure, and starting from this introductory section, the following sections are structured as follows:

Firstly, a review of the state of the art is carried out, starting with an analysis of the main theories on the internationalization process and of an analysis of how chance and serendipity play a role in these processes. Afterwards, it is studied the case of internationalization in services and the approaches that can be taken in the selection of the destination markets, namely through the use of a bi-dimensional matrix encompassing risk and opportunities in the destination markets.

Subsequently, a brief presentation of the ICT sector in Portugal is made, followed by a case study of the GAMMA company, starting with the characterization of the context where the company operated at the beginning of the internationalization process, the *modus operandi* it followed in its internationalization process and the business and financial results achieved.

Using a "what-if" methodology, this approach is then compared with a theoretical approach based on a risk-opportunity matrix that allows the identification of the markets that best fit the nature and the objectives of the organization, based on the concepts previously discussed.

The final section analyzes how literature anticipated (or not) the moves described in the case study and enables a reflection on how intuitive, serendipitous moves in the internationalization process lead to successful results.

Literature Review

The strategic option to internationalize is often made by firms in order to leverage a certain competitive advantage that the firm owns and that, according to its strategy, believes it can be replicated elsewhere (Stanisauskaite & Kock, 2016). Other motives may include the need to follow competitor or customers, pursuing specific opportunities abroad, or the need to retain greater control of the value chain where the company is inserted (Bradley, 2005; Hutchinson, Alexander, Quinn, & Doherty, 2007). More recently, Cuervo-Cazurra (2015) has argued that there are four reasons for overseas expansion: the first is to sell more - that is, the company exploits the existing resources to obtain better conditions in the destination market; the second is to buy better-sell better, in which the company exploits existing resources to avoid the lack of conditions of the country of origin; the third is to upgrade, exploring new resources to obtain better conditions in the host country; finally the fourth is to escape, in which the company explores new resources to avoid the lack of conditions of the country of origin. Whatever is the underlying motive, the option for an internationalization strategy involves expanding and creating an integrated network of contacts and partners located at home and in the destination markets where the firm seeks to expand (Dominguez, 2016; Luostarinen, 1979; Welch & Luostarinen, 1988).

In an integrative analysis of internationalization theories, Ribau et al (2015) identified the main schools of thought on the subject. The analysis starts with the pioneering research on the nature and causes of nations' wealth by Adam Smith (1776), and indicates that, parallel to Smith's work are two other traditional theories that explain the flow of goods between countries in terms of comparative advantage. These theories are David Ricardo's theory of comparative advantage, which argues that comparative advantage can arise because of productivity differences and Hecksher and Ohlin's (1933) theory that the comparative advantage stems from the combination of differences in industry in terms of intensity and abundance.

Following a chronological analysis, World War II marked the beginning of a new era in the development of international trade theories, which may be called the modern era. For the first time, the company became the unit of analysis in the 50's with the post-war multinational company growth. From the end of this decade, economic thinking gave rise to new approaches, the first being the product life cycle theory (Vernon, 1966) and other theories that emanated from it.

These theories are divided into two broad groups: economic and behavioral.

On one hand, economic approaches are focused on the analysis of foreign direct trade and foreign investment of multinationals and their involvement in international markets. From this principle, it was derived the internalization theory (P. Buckley & Casson, 1976; Chetty & Blankenburg Holm, 2000) and the transaction costs theory (Willianson, 1975), with the former focusing on the links between the development and production of the offer and the latter focusing on the links between production facilities and on the assumption that markets are competitive, upon which there are many suppliers, agents and distributors. The transaction costs theory predicts that companies integrate when the specificity of assets is high, in order to maintain control over the specific advantages they offer to the market and, according to Hennart (1991), transaction cost theory postulates that the choice between full and partial ownership will depend on the costs and benefits of joint ventures over the full ownership of wholly owned subsidiaries. The approach to transaction costs is useful in explaining vertical integration decisions, i.e. how firms assess whether or not to establish a production subsidiary in an external market (Erramilli & Rao, 1993; Whitelock, 2002).

The Eclectic Paradigm, developed by Dunning (1988), synthesizes elements of both theories (Cantwell, Dunning, & Lundan, 2010) and offers a holistic structure through which it is possible to identify and evaluate the importance of the factors that influence both the initial act of foreign production by the companies as the growth of such production. The theory was conceived to convey the idea that a full explanation of transnational corporate activities needs to draw on several strands of economic theory and that foreign direct investment is just one of a number of possible channels of participation each of which is determined by a number of common factors.

This theory, also known as OLI (Ownership - Location - Internalization) theory, is an attempt to analyze the companies motivations for internationalization based on the ownership advantages, unique to a particular company that enables it to take advantage of international investment opportunities; in the location advantages that are country-specific and are especially attractive to foreign investors (and when they do not exist they lead to simple export of the goods); and where internalization advantages are the benefits that come from producing the product or service using internal resources (and when they do not exist, lead to the licensing of the production).

On the other hand, behavioral approaches, founded on the behavioral theory of the firm (Cyert & March, 1963), explained the motivations for internationalization based on the behavior and experiences of the firm and of its decision-makers.

The Uppsala model, developed by Johanson and Vahlne (1977), is based on an evolutionary, sequential and linear model with growing international involvement, explaining the characteristics of the internationalization process of a company based on empirical observations from studies in international business at Uppsala University, which shown that Swedish companies generally develop their international operations in small steps, rather than making large investments of foreign production at isolated points in time. Typically, companies start by exporting to a country through an agent, then they establish a sales subsidiary and eventually, in some cases, they start production in the host country. For the aforementioned authors, the key characteristic of the Uppsala model is that companies develop their activities abroad over time and incrementally, relying on the development of their knowledge and this development is explained by the concept of "psychic distance" (Ribau et al., 2015), in which companies first expand to psychically closer markets and expand into more distant markets as their development increases. The model describes the internationalization stages of companies taking into account the company's accumulation of knowledge in foreign markets and the availability of resources to enter them and it has been extensively supported (Gankema, Snuif, & Zwart, 2000; Welch & Luostarinen, 1988) and criticized. Andersen (1993) pointed to the fact that the model, although it describes the process of international expansion, does not explain the motive upon which firms embark on each stage of the model nor the way that globalization is affecting it.

These criticisms led to the emergence of a complementary theory, based on a relational-based perspective among market players (Håkansson & Snehota, 2006) where the business activities consist of a cumulative process in which relationships are continually established, maintained, developed, and broken in order to provide a satisfactory and short-term economic return, thus creating positions that ensure survival and long-term development of the company. Through the activities in the network, the company develops relationships that guarantee its access to important resources (such as technical resources, planning, knowledge, social, economic and legal resources) and the sale of its products and services (Johanson & Mattsson, 2015). Markets are thus portrayed as systems of relations among, for example, clients, suppliers, competitors, family and friends. According to the network perspective, the nature of the relations between the parties will influence decisions, and the network will involve the exchange of resources among its different members (N. Coviello & Munro, 1997). Chetty and Holm (2000) conclude that the characteristics of the company, and of the decision maker, influence how the company will respond to the initiatives of its network relationships. In small and medium enterprises, the manager plays an important role in identifying the stimuli for internationalization. Furthermore, Ruzzier et al. (2006), argue that the complementarities in the network participants are built initially at a domestic level and then are expanded and developed in other countries.

In spite of its popularity, none of these two theories explained the adoption of innovative and risky behaviors at cross border level (McDougall & Oviatt, 2000). The explanation of the motives underlying the actions of open-minded managers and entrepreneurs was systematized as the born global and the born-again global firms, where rapid internationalization movements are performed in order to detect and capture unique opportunities at international level.

The born global firm emerged from the shortening of the investment decision process, empowered by Information and Communication Technologies, that allows large and small companies to be present in international markets (N. Coviello, 2015), thus challenging the classical behavior theories. These firms are characterized as young, entrepreneurial companies with a strong culture of innovation and a strong tendency to internationalize, eventually achieving a sustainable performance in foreign markets (Knight & Cavusgil, 2004), counter balancing the shortage of financial or human resources with the existence of intangible skills based on knowledge of foreign markets, since the very beginning of their international evolution.

In order to typify the companies that began their existence only addressing the internal market not showing any signs of interest in external markets and that, as a result of an unexpected, external shock, have a sudden need to rapidly address other markets using the competitive advantages they have amassed while serving the domestic market and that can be replicated in other countries (Schueffel, Baldegger, & Amann, 2014). The unexpected, external shock can be of multiple natures, mostly arising from changes in management or from sudden crisis in the demand in the internal market leading to proactive and flexible modes of entry, sometimes omitting stages in the internationalization process.

These sudden changes make that the strategy formation is not as systematic in these cases as it is assumed previously, namely in the staged approach where management teams anticipate and react to internal and external factors with a premeditated strategy. In the case where it is necessary a contingency approach, it is grounded on personal networks which act as communication infrastructures where common interests are shared (Hallen, 1992). These networks are used in order to support the beginning of the firm internationalization, in particular to select and expand into foreign markets as they facilitate the acquisition of experimental knowledge about these markets (Lindqvist, 1997).

In an analysis of how firms started their internationalization process, Crick and Spence (2005) observed that some of them commenced their overseas sales for serendipitous, unplanned reasons, noting that, although the case of firms starting exporting after the receipt of an unsolicited order had been studied, the influence of other issues that might be termed “chance” or “serendipitous” events has been somehow overlooked.

In any case, even if a serendipitous encounter was the main catalyst for internationalization, the firm still has the need to have the offer ready for overseas development and ensure that the human and financial resources are in place to enable the opportunity to be pursued.

Internationalization in the Services Sector

Much of the literature on international business has assumed the perspective of manufacturing companies. In the last two decades and following the emergence of the professional services companies (N. E. Coviello & Martin, 1999), literature has started to pay attention to the internationalization of service firms, which evidently raised the necessity to define what is a service (P. J. Buckley, Pass, & Prescott, 1992).

Although products and services have a common characteristic (they can be transacted between two entities), there are several characteristics of services that differentiate them from manufactured goods (Javalgi & Martin, 2007).

The main differences rely on the fact that services are intangible in the sense that they cannot be touched, seen, or physically transported; they are also are inseparable from their users, i.e. in international service companies, this feature increases the need to establish and maintain a local presence in each market (Lovelock & Wirtz, 2007); furthermore services are perishable and cannot be stored like manufactured goods; and services are heterogeneous in the sense that the production of services can vary widely from place to place, from service provider to service provider, and from moment to moment (Frazer Winsted & Patterson, 1998).

This is a challenge for all companies that want to enter new markets, especially international ones, due to linguistic and cultural barriers. Since service industries involve a much higher level of social interaction, both in production and consumption, compared to manufacturing, therefore it is not surprising that the cultural issues are frequently addressed in the discussions on the internationalization of services (Asakawa, Ito, Rose, & Westney, 2013).

The globalization process, together with other factors such as information and communication technologies, have led service companies to have the opportunity to create and expand their international presence in broader geographic horizons than the ones that were previously within reach (Contractor, Kundu, & Hsu, 2003; Rodríguez & Nieto, 2012).

However, in spite of the considerable amount of research, there are still areas in the internationalization of SMEs (Small and Medium Enterprises) that need more focus and attention (Ribau, Moreira, & Raposo, 2018) such as the ones related to the way that service SMEs ignite and maintain the internationalization process, with new research being necessary to clarify how international expansion affects SMEs performance and how successful internationalization strengthens SME internal resources.

Market Selection Criteria

As described by Papadopoulos and Martín (2011), international business is carried out in an increasingly globalized environment characterized by fewer barriers, increased competition and greater opportunities for expansion. Yet despite the general trend towards globalization, the specific environments in which a company operates are the result of the various strategic decisions that shape the entire internationalization process.

Entering new markets, particularly in foreign markets, involves a major commitment of strategic, technical, management and financial resources. Due to resource constraints, the firm has to make a strategic decision about which market to enter and allocate resources accordingly (He & Wei, 2011).

Thus, companies seeking to expand overseas are faced with the complex task of screening and evaluating foreign markets. Markets differ in terms of market attractiveness, due to variations in the economic and commercial environment, growth rates, political stability, consumption capacity, receptivity to foreign products, and other factors (Knight & Cavusgil, 2004).

For Bradley (2005) in the selection phase, there can be three possible approaches: The opportunistic selection, where market opportunities arise in a casual and unplanned manner and must be carefully implemented; the systematic selection, in which the company becomes aware of opportunities by evaluating and comparing the various available market alternatives; and finally, the combination of the first two approaches, in which there is an evolution from an opportunistic selection to a systematic selection.

The selection of the best markets from a large number of different markets with different levels of capacity and potential is a complicated and time-consuming task, requiring multiple decision criteria and many approaches (Farzipoor Saen, 2011). Sakarya et al. (2007) argue that the traditional market selection analysis is based on purely macroeconomic and political factors and does not take into account the dynamism of an emerging market and the future potential resulting from rapid changes, as well as the national attributes that affect specific sectors and the market responsiveness. For the same author, in order to develop a fair analysis for emerging markets, a number of criteria must be taken into account, such as market potential, cultural dimensions to measure distance the competitive analysis of the sector, as well as general indicators of risk.

One of the most used criteria to describe national cultures are the four dimensions, developed by Hofstede (1983) and that can occur in almost every possible combination and are largely independent of each other. The considered dimensions were "individualism versus collectivism" where the fundamental question involves the relationship between individuals in which at one end are societies in which individuals are supposed to care about their own interests and immediate family (individualism); and at the other end are societies in which the bonds between individuals are very tight, and people should take care of the interest of their group and not have different opinions and beliefs (collectivism); "large or small distance from power" where the fundamental question is related to the fact that people are unequal in physical and intellectual capacities. In societies far removed from power, societies let inequalities grow over time, in terms of power and wealth, while other societies (with little distance from power) try to minimize these inequalities and strive to equalize the power; "strong or weak aversion to uncertainty" where the fundamental question is related to how society manages the uncertainties about the future, since, in some societies, people take risks fairly easily and are tolerant of behaviors and opinions different from their own, and these societies are characterized by low aversion to uncertainty and in other societies it is present a higher level of anxiety in relation to the unpredictability of the future, which manifests itself in greater nervousness, emotionality and aggressiveness, being such societies characterized by high aversion to uncertainty; finally the fourth dimension is related to "masculinity versus femininity" is related to the division of roles between the sexes in society. In societies characterized by greater masculinity values are based on the importance of exhibitionism, achievement, achieving something invisible, where the public hero is the successful and the entrepreneur. In societies characterized by greater femininity, relationships with people are placed before money, caring for quality of life, preserving the environment and helping others.

According to Daniels et al. (2014) companies should collect and analyze data using external sources such as government agencies and reports from specialized agencies and associations, that must be complemented by internal analysis. In order to compare countries, graphs with important country variables

Figure 1. Matrix of opportunity and risk
Source: Adapted from Daniels et al. (2014)

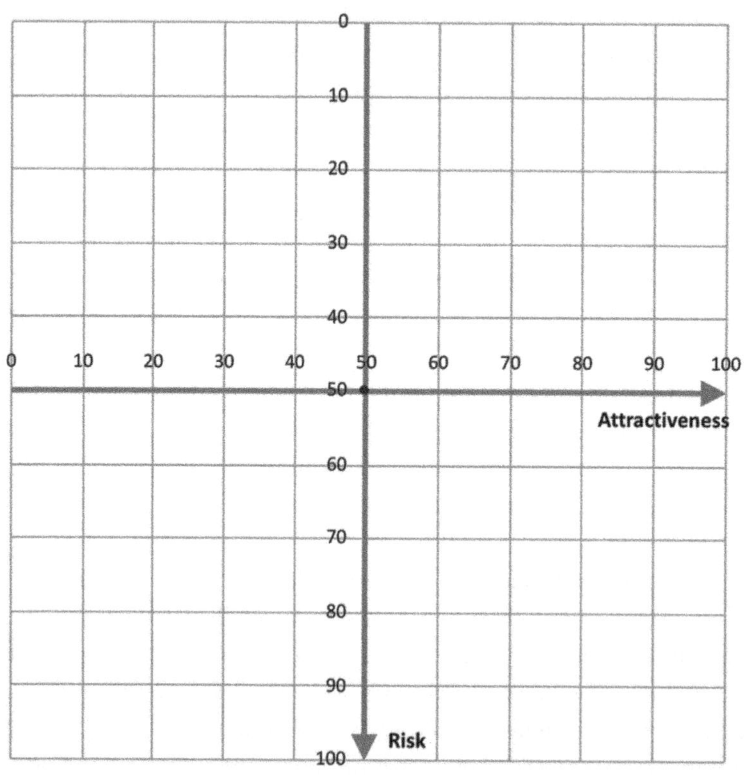

or matrices with punctuated indicators can be used, where the countries are then evaluated according to these indicators.

By using bi-dimensional matrices, managers can identify certain indicators, assign weights, and then evaluate each country based on weighted indicators. One of the most frequently used matrices is the bi dimensional matrix that shows the relationship between risk and opportunity in markets.

The ICT Sector in Portugal

In a prospective study of the ICT sector, carried out by InovaRia (2011), it is argued that in a highly competitive business environment, it is essential that companies take on the capacity to develop state-of-the-art technological products and services with significant added value. As with all other offers, the success of technology offering is measured by their market acceptance. In this sense, it is crucial that companies in the ICT sector define their strategic orientations in the light of the opportunities that are prospected in the national and international markets. From an economic and business perspective, the definition of short- and medium-term strategies, which guarantee the sustained development of the ICT sector and the economic aggregate associated with it, is one of the decisive factors for the competitiveness of companies in the sector.

Another prospective study carried out by the Portuguese FCT (Fundação para a Ciência e Tecnologia) Foundation for Science and Technology (2014) revealed some important data on the ICT sector. In this study it is revealed that the ICT sector represents, in Portugal, 6% of Gross Value Added and 3.7% of turnover and 1.6% of the employed people, serving mainly the national market, but also the Spanish, Dutch, German and Chinese markets. Furthermore, it is indicated that the global ICT sector has shown significant growth in overall and aggregate terms in recent years in terms of added value and employment, with the United States, the European Union, Japan, China, India and Brazil positioning as the main global markets in the ICT sector, with significant growth in the BRIC (Brazil, Russia, India and China) and Middle East markets.

The InovaRia study, went farther and, after questioning the decision makers in these companies, concluded that most of them had an internationalization strategy, with a budget and resources allocated to this effort. However, most of them found that it was necessary to have social, legal and fiscal information regarding the destination markets, showing great concern for the effects of corruption propensity in the destination markets. As barriers to the internationalization process, the decision makers mentioned the need to adapt the services portfolio to the specificities of the destination markets and the lack of experience in internationalization processes, thus lacking the adequate staff and the contacts needed for a first approach. Due to this fact, most of the interviewees mentioned that they prefer to start their internationalization process in Portuguese speaking countries in Africa (Angola, Mozambique, Cape Verde) and in America (Brazil). Also, most of the questioned decision makers regretted the fact that there is little cooperation between companies in the sector, pointing to the need to create larger companies that can operate at a global scale, in order to penetrate in advanced markets and establish a presence in growing markets.

Both studies, have concluded that the Portuguese companies in the sector have the need to develop concerted actions in order to create synergies when accessing international markets, thus operating at a larger scale and reducing the costs associated with the internationalization process. This process must be aligned with the ability to broaden the service portfolio, that must be wrapped in a brand, specifically created for the destination market, repositioning the offers and differentiating from the competition.

The GAMMA Company Case Study

GAMMA is a company incorporated in the year 2000 in order to coordinate the activity of several ICT companies operating at a regional scale since the beginning of the 1990s. This provided the organization with a critical dimension that brought together highly qualified human resources in developing and implementing advanced solutions in ICT, particularly what concerns system integration.

Through the provision of turn-key solutions, GAMMA strongly focuses on innovation, with a dynamic corporate culture based on technological specialization and permanent training of its workers in order to provide high quality services to its customers and develop specific proprietary know-how in that areas it operates. This philosophy is extensible to the suppliers, that are considered partners of the organization and with whom the company aligns its policies and objectives.

With a business proposition focused guaranteeing a high return on the investment made in the solutions it presents, the focus on customer needs and its business processes is kept through a set of methodologies and tools that guarantee the continuous improvement and efficiency of its activity, namely through the implementation of a certified Quality Management System (ISO 9001) and of an Information Security Management System (ISO/IEC 27001).

Based on the time series from 2006 thru 2017, it is possible to analyze the behavior of the company in terms of gross revenues and the number of employees for the last twelve years.

Figure 2. GAMMA company basic data (turnover and employees) (2006-2017)
Source: SABI database (Bureau Van Dijk, n.d.)

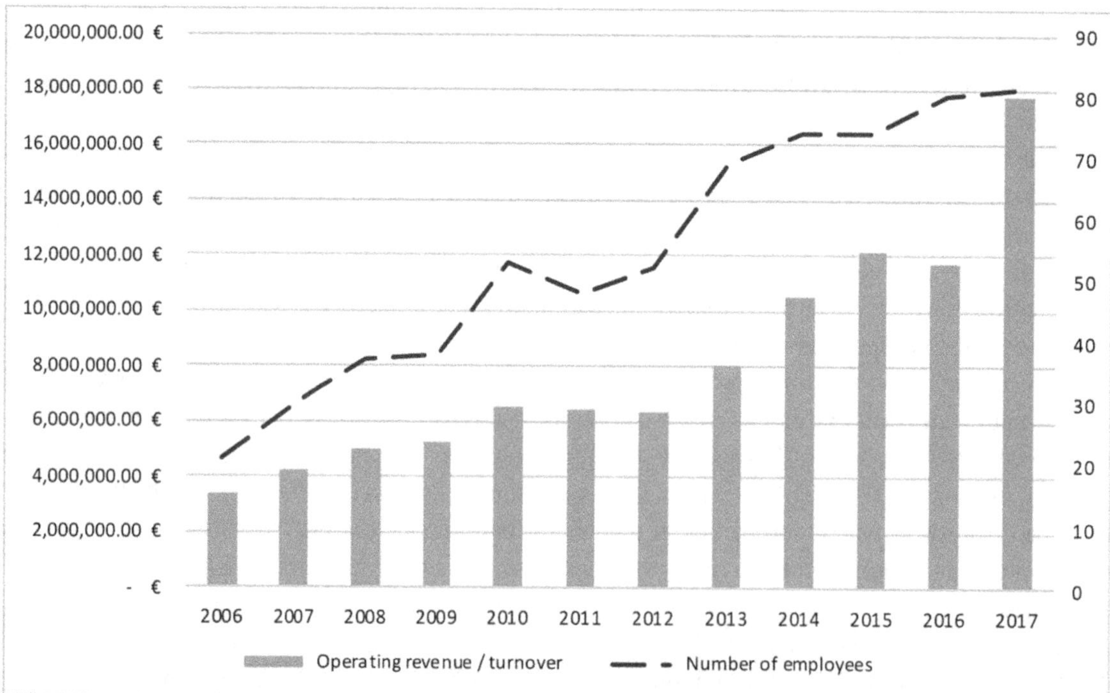

GAMMA Internationalization Process Overview

The internationalization process of the GAMMA company started discreetly in the year 2007 through exports to EU and non-EU (African) markets. These efforts continued through export until the year 2010, mostly as demands from clients that were at the time starting their internationalization process. The company saw these opportunities as a laboratory where it could test some concepts and acquire know how and contacts in the destination markets.

In the year 2010, foreseeing a decrease in the internal market activity, the company started to address the internationalization process more systematically, leveraging the contacts it made in the previous years. In the next year, and as a result of the country bankruptcy, that led to an IMF rescue and the implementation of strong austerity measures, the internal market suffered a contraction, leading to an 8% decrease in revenues from the internal market from 2010 thru 2012. This fact led the company to increase the already relevant internationalization efforts, especially in Spain, Gambia and Algeria where, although the company was not physically present, it had contacts from previous exports of telecommunications material and the remote provision of services that served as the entry points to these markets. In April 2010, the company also addressed the Portuguese speaking countries in Africa, by joining another Portuguese ICT company. This joint venture was extended in May 2011 to other 5 ICT companies, with the resulting ZETTA company aiming to address the Angolan, Mozambican and Cape-Verdean markets. In Cape Verde it was created the ZETTA CV company, in Mozambique it was created the ZETTA MZ company and in Angola, due to issues surrounding company ownership legislation, it was used an existing company, that we will call IOTA, created in April 2008. This arrangement, through a joint venture created with other companies already present in these markets, allowed GAMMA to tighten its commercial bonds and start a systematic internationalization process, with similar value propositions to those presented in the domestic market, standing out of the competition by focusing on customer and employee satisfaction, as well as service effectiveness, that lead to long-term relationships between the involved parties.

For undisclosed reasons, the joint venture came to an end in 2015. Although the joint venture ceased to exist, GAMMA has kept the ability to provide services in the previously addressed markets, being interesting to analyze the case of Angola, where in April 2014 was created the MU company, a partnership between a local citizen and the IOTA company that, in April 2015, sold its shares and left the partnership.

As of today, the MU company is presented as the most relevant example of internationalization by the GAMMA company, with its headquarters in Luanda hosting 8 permanent workers. Other than this, the company is also present in the markets of Algeria, Botswana, Cape Verde, Gambia, Mozambique, Namibia, Senegal, Spain and Zambia.

In Table 1, it is presented a detailed timeline of the events surrounding the internationalization of the GAMMA company.

Analyzing the publicly available data of the GAMMA company in the SABI database (Bureau Van Dijk, n.d.), it can be analyzed how the internationalization process affected the P&L (Profit and Loss) statement of the company.

Starting in 2007 with a very residual activity, the systematic efforts of internationalization held from 2010 onwards had an almost immediate effect in the P&L statement of the company. From 2007 thru 2010, the weight of exports in the total turnover averaged yearly 1,78% and in 2011, as a result of the described efforts it rose to 4,33%, continuing to grow rapidly until 2014, where it stabilized around a value of 10%, that it has kept until 2017.

Table 1. Relevant dates in the GAMMA company internationalization process

Date	Event
October 2000	GAMMA company incorporated in Portugal
September 2007	ZETTA company incorporated in Portugal
April 2008	IOTA company incorporated in Angola
May 2010	GAMMA company member joins board of ZETTA company
May 2011	5 other members of ICT companies joint the board of ZETTA company
April 2014	MU company incorporated in Angola as a partnership between a local citizen and the IOTA company
April 2015	IOTA company leaves the MU company partnership
October 2015	Board of the ZETTA company reconfigured and company renamed
Late 2018	MU company headquartered in Luanda hosting 8 permanent workers

Source: Portuguese and Angolan Official Company Registrars

Figure 3. Exports (as a percentage of the annual turnover of the GAMMA company) (2006-2017)
Source: SABI database (Bureau Van Dijk, n.d.)

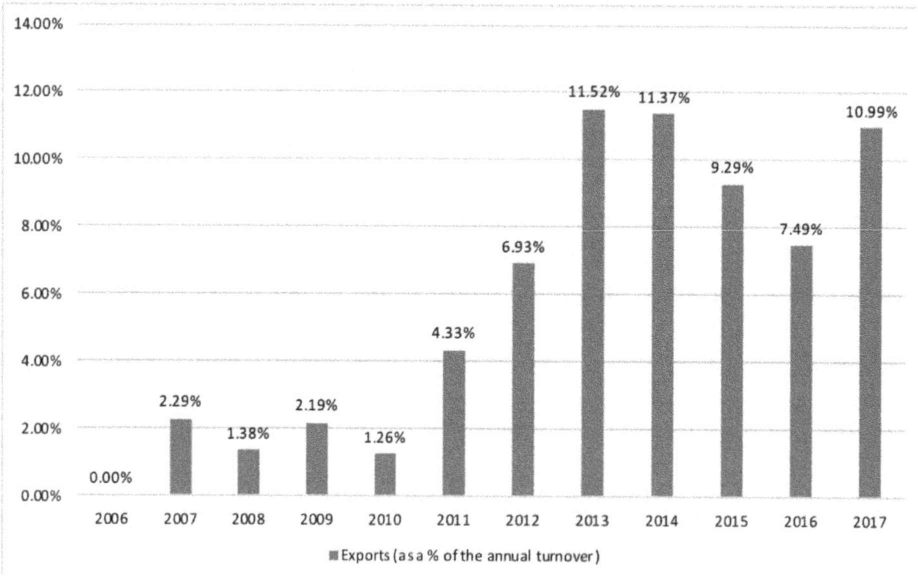

A Methodology for Market Attractiveness Analysis

As seen previously, the internationalization process of the GAMMA company was based on casuistic methods, mostly following demands from customers and in joint ventures with other companies already installed in the destination markets. However, it is reasonable to analyze if the results on the choices of destination markets would have been different if the company chose a more structured and analytical, textbook-like approach to the internationalization process.

To answer that question, it is proposed a methodology to obtain and systematize market information, using a market selection matrix that takes into account the destination markets´ opportunities and the

Figure 4. Export ratio from EU and Non-EU markets
Source: SABI database (Bureau Van Dijk, n.d.)

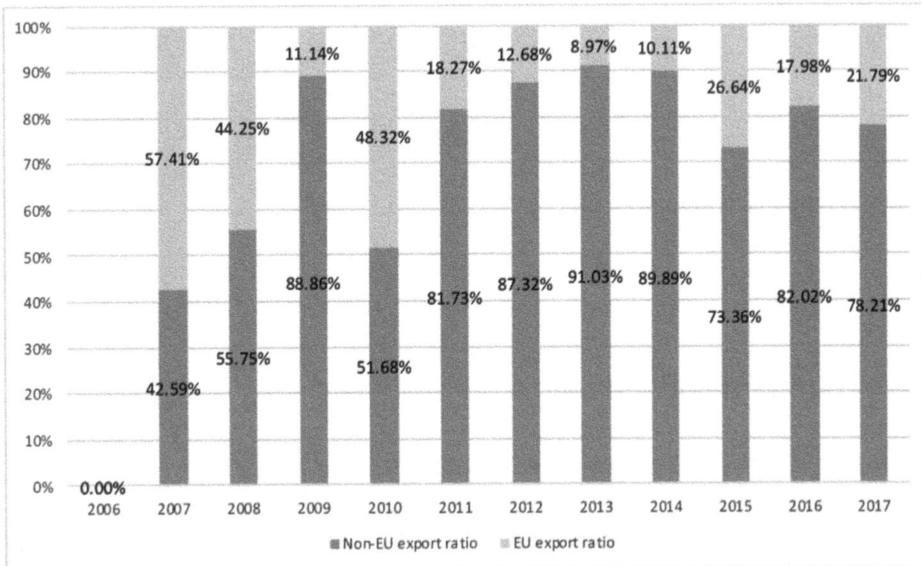

risks, based on Daniels et al., (2014), gathering the critical information for the organization. This matrix was created based on the literature review made in the second section of this chapter, complemented by the choice of the attractiveness and risk variables relevant to the GAMMA company and thus ascertaining the potential of the destination markets.

This matrix is one of the tools available to the decision maker for a systematic and thoughtful selection of markets, allowing the decision maker and the company to carry out a logical procedure that, in the end, allows the choice of the most interesting and relevant market(s) for the internationalization process.

For the filling of the matrix it is necessary to carry out a logical sequence of data collection and processing. For this, steps were defined, taking into account the models with the various stages of the process of evaluation of foreign markets presented by the authors mentioned in the literature review, namely in the sub-section "Market selection criteria".

Firstly, the various countries to be analyzed must be identified. According to Daniels et al. (2014) this number should vary between 5 and 8 countries, and this identification should be made on the basis of a screening of potential markets, i.e.: markets that have, in their characteristics, the potential for the organization's offer to be well received.

Then, an analysis and selection of attractiveness and market risk indicators must be carried out, always taking into account the sector in which the company operates. As described in the literature review, several indicators such as demographic, economic, political, industry-specific and cultural ones must be taken into consideration.

Lastly, a critical analysis must be carried out for each market, in relation to the chosen indicators, in order to choose only one or those that offer the best conditions for company success.

Although this tool is very useful for the systematic selection of markets, it has some limitations. As a first clear limitation is the (un)availability of data collection for some countries in a uniform way, which sometimes makes it difficult to choose the indicators as well as the countries themselves, causing discrepancies in the process. Other limitations are related to the difficulty of adapting the indicators to the factors of attractiveness and/or risk, that is, some indicators may function ambivalently, both as attractiveness and risk factors.

The construction of the matrix is done using Microsoft Excel, in order to be able to apply a set of formulas that simplified the whole process of data collection and processing.

In the construction of the matrix, the following four steps were performed:

1. Selection of countries and indicators;
2. Gross Data collection;
3. Data homogenization;
4. Weighting of homogenized data.

Selection of Countries and Indicators

As argued in the literature review, in the process of evaluating markets, it is necessary to screen potential markets and then select those that may be most interesting to the company under study.

As for the selection of the potential markets, the GAMMA company had executed several projects in Angola, Mozambique and Cape Verde and other specific projects in Spain, France, Belgium, England, Algeria, Gambia and Guinea-Bissau. In addition, the company had also had experiences in remote support for other countries such as Brazil, Germany, the Netherlands and Poland. By analyzing geographically, the markets where the GAMMA company wanted to carry out its activity, one can conclude that in Europe, Spain, and in Africa, Algeria, Angola, Cape Verde, Gambia and Mozambique were the main targets with Portugal being used as a reference.

Regarding the indicators used to prepare the matrix, the factors described in the literature review were taken into account, among them attractiveness (those that make a market appealing to internationalization) and risk factors (those that could affect entry into another country).

In the factors of attractiveness, a demographic indicator was chosen - the population, an economic one - the GDP (Gross Domestic Product) growth rate and three indicators with ICT sector-specific information, among them the availability of technology, the absorption of technology at the enterprise level and the FDI (Foreign Direct Investment) and technology transfer level.

These attractiveness indicators were chosen since "Population" provides a clear perception of the market size of each country, with larger values commanding a larger attractiveness; the "GDP growth rate" is a relevant indicator since it helps to have a perception about the economic growth of the country, as well as to show if the country is a producer of goods and services. In what regards the "Availability of the latest technologies" - it is essential to understand the degree of use of new technologies in the country being studied. This indicator is based on The Global Competitiveness Report (Schwab & Sala-i-Martin, 2015) of the World Economic Forum where the answer to the question: "In your country, to what extent are the latest technologies available?" can range from 1 (not available at all) up to 7 (widely available). In the same report is measured the "Absorption of technology at the company level" that allows to verify the degree of use of new technologies at the company level considering that the answer to the question: "In your country, to what extent do companies adopt the new technologies?" can range from 1 (never) up to 7 (adopt extensively). Finally, in what regards "FDI and technology transfer" is the indicator that allows to evaluate the degree of foreign investment in the technology sector and is obtained from the Global Competitiveness Report where the answer to the question: "To what extent does FDI bring new technologies to your country?" can range from 1 (nothing) up to 7 (to a large extent, the FDI is a fundamental source of new technologies in my country).

In the risk factor, it was selected a political factor - political stability and absence of violence / terrorism, two economic factors - the perception of corruption and the rate of inflation and finally cultural proximity indicator.

These risk factors were chosen based on the following criteria: "Political stability and absence of violence / Terrorism" is an important factor because it reflects the perception of the probability that government is unstable and / or may be overthrown by non-constitutional or violent means, including politically motivated violence and terrorism. According to World Bank's analysis (Kaufmann, Kraay, & Mastruzzi, 2013) the figures for this indicator range from -2,5 (countries with low political stability and a higher propensity for violence and terrorism) up to 2.5 (for countries with a high political stability and less propensity for violence and terrorism). As for the "Perception of Corruption", means that having commercial relations with that can country can range from "reliable clients, banks and justice application" or if one should "take extra care in all negotiations with that country". The figures were based on a report from International Transparency (2014). The "Inflation rate" is considered because since the inflation rate consists of the generalized rise of prices, then a high value in this indicator can mean an accelerated loss of purchasing power by the country economic agents and indicate some economic instability and/or social unrest.

Finally, it was chosen an indicator of cultural proximity, based on the work of Geert Hofstede, and whose data for these dimensions came from The Hofstede Center (Hofstede, n.d.).

Matrix Creation

In order to be able to manage and make flexible the use of the matrix, it was incorporated a weighting functionality that allows, according to the circumstances, to differentiate the relevance of each of the indicators. It was not possible to find studies that differ scientifically the relative weight of each of the factors, and taking into account that the attribution of these weights will result from empirical experiences of the users of the tool and considering, in addition, that this tool is in a first phase of use, it was decided to assign equal importance to all items, and, as a result of the experience and knowledge accumulated by users, this value can be adjusted in future iterations.

After collecting the gross data from the above-mentioned sources, the data was homogenized so the it could be compared and weighted, with equal weighting factors for all the five attractiveness dimensions and for all the four risk dimensions.

According to the methodology previously proposed the following graphical representation of the positioning of the selected countries according to the risk-attractiveness binomial was reached. (Raw and homogenized data can be found in Table 2 in Appendix 1.)

Data Analysis

From the data obtained, and given the fact that this was an exercise where it was intended to analyze the internationalization process using a rational approach, a few comments are necessary:

As for Portugal, although it was presented in the analysis, it serves merely as reference country.

Spain represents the country with the highest total attractiveness value, which is derived from the high values it presents in the population (it is even the most populous country under analysis) and generous

Figure 5. Matrix of opportunity and risk
Source: Adapted from Daniels et al. (2014)

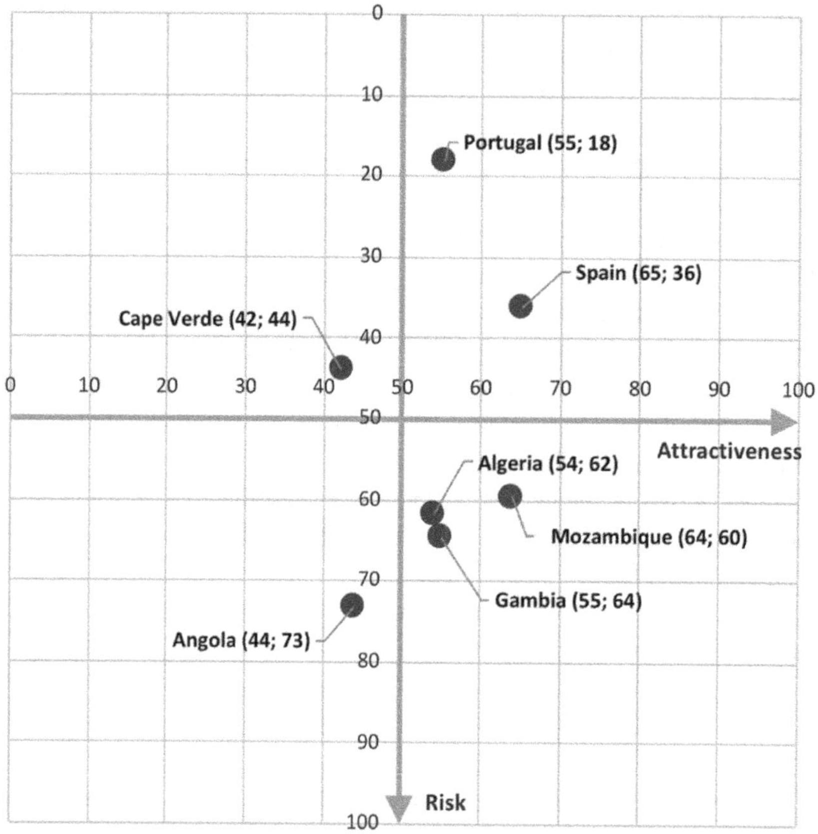

values in the indicators with specific characteristics of the information technology sector. In addition, it is the country with the lowest risk value, which allows us to conclude that Spain, considering only this analysis matrix, was positioned as the most interesting country for the internationalization of the GAMMA company.

Algeria stands out as the second most populous country under analysis and because it has one of the lowest values in indicators with specific characteristics of the information technology sector. In terms of risk, the fact that it has the most unfavorable ratings of all countries with regard to the indicator of political stability deserves special mention.

Angola stands out in almost all the indicators as the least attractive and most risky of the countries. It is also the country with the most unfavorable values in what concerns the ICT sector and, at the same time, it presents very unfavorable values regarding political stability, the perception of corruption and the rate of inflation, which makes the country that presents the greatest risk.

Cape Verde, in terms of attractiveness stands out as having the smallest population in the countries under analysis, presenting intermediate values for the other indicators, which, based only on this analysis, positions it as the least attractive country. On the other hand-side, it has a very favorable rating in political stability and in the perception of corruption. However, it is the second most culturally distant country in Portugal (which is still a point of reflection on how the matrix is elaborated and the different weights attributed to the factors).

Gambia presents intermediate values in general, but it is positive for being the second country with the highest value for the GDP growth rate. However, it is also the second country with the most unfavorable values both in the perception of corruption and in the rate of inflation, which makes it the second most risky country.

Finally, Mozambique has the highest GDP growth rate in all the countries under analysis and presents intermediate values in the remaining indicators, making it the second most attractive country. However, it stands out because of its proximity to culture, which is even more culturally distant from Portugal (which, as in the case of Cape Verde, is still a reason for reflection).

From the foregoing, it can be concluded, based only on the information contained in this matrix, that the most interesting country for the internationalization of the company in question would be Spain, for presenting itself as the most attractive and least risky country. On the other hand, the country that presents itself as less interesting would be Angola, with low values of attractiveness and with a high risk.

Once again, and as a point of reflection in future iterations, the study showed that the least interesting country for the internationalization of the company under analysis is where the presence of the company is being strengthened through the creation of a company in Luanda.

Algeria, Gambia, and Mozambique represent relatively interesting markets for the internationalization of the company, given their intermediate values for attractiveness and risk indicators. With regard to Cape Verde, it has become a low-risk country, although it represents a country with a low attractiveness.

In short, this analysis allowed us to understand how each country positions itself in terms of risk and attractiveness, allowing a summary analysis to the company of these factors. Of course, this analysis does not take into account other factors such as the business links of the company being studied in the markets and, frequently, in the case of SMEs, turns out to be one of the main factors that induces the choice of a given market.

Final Remarks

After analyzing the data collected and based on the theoretical framework discussed earlier it is possible to say that the GAMMA company structured its internationalization process based on the need to circumvent the anticipated shrinkage of the domestic market, that suffered from economic instability precisely when the company was starting its internationalization process in a more systematic way. Anticipating this shrinkage, the GAMMA company management decided to expand the size of the addressable market, entering new and larger markets that could fulfil the limitations presented by the domestic market.

Another reason was the need to stay close to customers, following their internationalization path and providing services in external markets, taking into consideration that installing a company where the ICT sector is still underdeveloped may represent an opportunity for the company to succeed, given the small number of competitors.

As for the internationalization models, and taking into account all the theories addressed, in fact those in which the GAMMA company seems to integrate are, according to Johanson and Vahlne (2009) the network model, as it integrated into a group of companies whose activities and relationships with customers, suppliers and competitors are continuously developed; and the Uppsala model, since the company has developed its international operations over time in small steps, having started exporting to several countries and afterwards installing itself through the creation of a new company in Angola, which is a market where it had already accumulated knowledge.

Regarding the forms of internationalization, and according to the literature review and the information obtained, it is possible to identify that the first form of access to external markets has been the export of goods and services, with several projects in various European and African countries; followed by the creation of a joint venture with national partners, which integrated six independent companies, forming the ZETTA company and under which these partners shared information, resources and knowledge; and finally the creation of a new subsidiary in Luanda, which allowed it to set up a new operation in this country.

Among the several obstacles to entry into the target countries of internationalization of the company under study were the legislative barriers, such as the complexity of tax systems, tight market control, investment applications, visa problems, and the lack of specialized professionals; furthermore, linguistic and sociocultural barriers, especially felt in Algeria, which, because it is an Arab country, has a culture and religion that differ greatly from Portuguese habits; and technological barriers, in the most concrete cases in Algeria and Angola, which are technologically less developed countries and where IT and telecommunications infrastructures are not up to western standards.

This process revealed that the expert recommendations, notably both InovaRia (2014; 2011) studies and the FCT (2014) study, were taken into consideration, through the development of concerted actions in order to create synergies in the access to international markets, operating at a larger scale and diluting the costs associated with the process, and also broadening the service portfolio and creating a specific brand for the destination markets.

FUTURE RESEARCH DIRECTIONS

The present case can bring relevant new information to a field that, as mentioned previously by Ribau et al (2018), is in need of research in order to clarify how international expansion affects SMEs performance and how successful internationalization strengthens SME internal resources.

In this case it is clear that the internationalization process was enhanced due to the correct forecast made in 2010 that the internal market would suffer a significant convulsion during the following years, which led to the promotion of proactive internationalization policies.

From the actions taken, the most important conclusion that can be derived is that it is relevant to understand the informal connections between the agents in the market, even when they appear to be competitors, since these connections can leverage bonds and enable actions in distinct markets where rivalry is set aside, and synergies are created among apparent competitors.

As such, it is now relevant to discover if this was a one-off serendipitous movement or if it was replicated by other service companies in the same markets, creating temporary alliances that enabled the market entrance and that were, once the objective was achieved, disbanded.

Also, it can be of interest to find if the proposed tool can be refined, both by introducing calibration effects into the weight of each variable and by introducing new variables that allow a clearer perception of the paths that can be taken by the decision makers in the abovementioned situations.

CONCLUSION

Nowadays, internationalization is seen as a fundamental process for organizational expansion, a source of innovation and knowledge, and the possible creation of competitive advantage in an increasingly globalized world. It is necessary to take into account that to operate domestically is very different from operating at an international level, because entering foreign markets requires overcoming several obstacles, which can condition success and compromise the company.

International expansion enables companies to increase their number of customers, their sales volume and gain access to new resources. In this way, it is fundamental to determine the attractiveness of a market, that is, to consider and evaluate several indicators that allow to know if this market is attractive or not.

In the study carried out, it can be concluded that, among all the countries under analysis, the most attractive markets are Spain, first followed by Mozambique, and those with the highest risk are primarily Angola and then Gambia. Thus, the results analyzed through the indicators used in the matrix, showed that the country with the highest risk is precisely the one that was chosen to be the first country in which the GAMMA company created a new company - Angola. Even so, the fact that this country is the one with the most unfavorable values, especially in the ICT indicators, may represent an opportunity for Portuguese companies in the area to take advantage of this market, which is still very little developed in this sector.

In addition, emerging markets continue to be attractive as a growth driver and continue to attract the ICT industry as they continue to be sources of growth and scale. At the same time, the high level of population and GDP growth in these markets is leading to the emergence of new consumers in the middle and upper middle classes, leading to an increase in the demand for increasingly advanced services.

This research received no specific grant from any funding agency in the public, commercial, or not-for-profit sectors.

REFERENCES

Andersen, O. (1993). On the Internationalization Process of Firms: A Critical Analysis. *Journal of International Business Studies*, *24*(2), 209–231. doi:10.1057/palgrave.jibs.8490230

Asakawa, K., Ito, K., Rose, E. L., & Westney, D. E. (2013). Internationalization in Japan's service industries. *Asia Pacific Journal of Management*, *30*(4), 1155–1168. doi:10.100710490-012-9325-5

Bradley, F. (2005). *International marketing strategy*. Pearson Education.

Buckley, P., & Casson, M. (1976). *The future of the multinational corporation*. London: Macmillan.

Buckley, P. J., Pass, C. L., & Prescott, K. (1992). The internationalization of service firms: A comparison with the manufacturing sector. *Scandinavian International Business Review*, *1*(1), 39–56. doi:10.1016/0962-9262(92)90035-5

Bureau Van Dijk. (n.d.). *Sabi - Spain and Portugal financial company information and business intelligence - BvD*. Retrieved March 4, 2018, from https://www.bvdinfo.com/en-us/our-products/company-information/national-products/sabi

Cantwell, J., Dunning, J. H., & Lundan, S. M. (2010). An evolutionary approach to understanding international business activity: The co-evolution of MNEs and the institutional environment. *Journal of International Business Studies*, *41*(4), 567–586. doi:10.1057/jibs.2009.95

Chetty, S., & Blankenburg Holm, D. (2000). Internationalisation of small to medium-sized manufacturing firms: A network approach. *International Business Review*, *9*(1), 77–93. doi:10.1016/S0969-5931(99)00030-X

Contractor, F. J., Kundu, S. K., & Hsu, C.-C. (2003). A three-stage theory of international expansion: The link between multinationality and performance in the service sector. *Journal of International Business Studies*, *34*(1), 5–18. doi:10.1057/palgrave.jibs.8400003

Coviello, N. (2015). Re-thinking research on born globals. *Journal of International Business Studies*, *46*(1), 17–26. doi:10.1057/jibs.2014.59

Coviello, N., & Munro, H. (1997). Network relationships and the internationalisation process of small software firms. *International Business Review*, *6*(4), 361–386. doi:10.1016/S0969-5931(97)00010-3

Coviello, N. E., & Martin, K. A.-M. (1999). Internationalization of Service SMEs: An Integrated Perspective from the Engineering Consulting Sector. *Journal of International Marketing*.

Crick, D., & Spence, M. (2005). The internationalisation of 'high performing' UK high-tech SMEs: A study of planned and unplanned strategies. *International Business Review*, *14*(2), 167–185. doi:10.1016/j.ibusrev.2004.04.007

Cuervo-Cazurra, A., Narula, R., & Un, C. A. (2015). Internationalization motives: Sell more, buy better, upgrade and escape. *Multinational Business Review*, *23*(1), 25–35. doi:10.1108/MBR-02-2015-0009

Cyert, R. M., & March, J. G. (1963). *A behavioral theory of the firm*. Retrieved from https://books.google.pt/books/about/A_Behavioral_Theory_of_the_Firm.html?id=9PydngEACAAJ&source=kp_cover&redir_esc=y

Daniels, J. D., Radebaugh, L. H., & Sullivan, D. P. (2014). *International business: Environments and operations*. Addison-Wesley.

Dominguez, N. (2016). Risk-seeking behaviours in SMEs' internationalization. In The Changing Global Economy and Its Impact on International Entrepreneurship. Academic Press.

Dunning, J. H. (1988). The Eclectic Paradigm of International Production: A Restatement and Some Possible Extensions. *Journal of International Business Studies*, *19*(1), 1–31. doi:10.1057/palgrave.jibs.8490372

Erramilli, M. K., & Rao, C. P. (1993). Service Firms' International Entry-Mode Choice: A Modified Transaction-Cost Analysis Approach. *Journal of Marketing*, *57*(3), 19.

Farzipoor Saen, R. (2011). International market selection using advanced data envelopment analysis. *IMA Journal of Management Mathematics*, *22*(4), 371–386. doi:10.1093/imaman/dpr011

FCT. (2014). *Estratégia Nacional de Investigação e inovação para uma especialização inteligente 2014-2020 – Diagnóstico de Apoio às Jornadas de Reflexão Estratégica*. Retrieved from https://www.fct.pt/esp_inteligente/docs/TIC_ENEI_Lisboa.pdf

Frazer Winsted, K., & Patterson, P. G. (1998). Internationalization of services: The service exporting decision. *Journal of Services Marketing*, *12*(4), 294–311. doi:10.1108/08876049810226964

Gankema, H. G. J., Snuif, H. R., & Zwart, P. S. (2000). The internationalization process of small and medium-sized enterprises: An evaluation of stage theory. *Journal of Small Business Management*, *38*(4), 15.

Håkansson, H., & Snehota, I. (2006). No business is an island" 17 years later. *Scandinavian Journal of Management*, *22*(3), 271–274. doi:10.1016/j.scaman.2006.08.001

Hallen, L. (1992). *Infrastructural networks in international business*. Företagsekonomiska Institutionen vid Uppsala Universitet.

He, X., & Wei, Y. (2011). Linking market orientation to international market selection and international performance. *International Business Review*, *20*(5), 535–546. doi:10.1016/j.ibusrev.2010.10.003

Hecksher, E., & Ohlin, B. (1933). *Interregional and international trade*. Cambridge, MA: Harvard UniversityPress.

Hennart, J.-F. (1991). The Transaction Costs Theory of Joint Ventures: An Empirical Study of Japanese Subsidiaries in the United States. *Management Science*, *37*(4), 483–497. doi:10.1287/mnsc.37.4.483

Hofstede, G. (1983). The Cultural Relativity of Organizational Practices and Theories. *Journal of International Business Studies*, *14*(2), 75–89. doi:10.1057/palgrave.jibs.8490867

Hofstede, G. (n.d.). *Compare countries - Hofstede Insights*. Retrieved December 29, 2018, from https://www.hofstede-insights.com/product/compare-countries/

Hutchinson, K., Alexander, N., Quinn, B., & Doherty, A. M. (2007). Internationalization Motives and Facilitating Factors: Qualitative Evidence from Smaller Specialist Retailers. *Journal of International Marketing*, *15*(3), 96–122. doi:10.1509/jimk.15.3.96

InovaRia. A. (2011). *Análise do Comportamento das Empresas Portuguesas de Tecnologias de Informação e Eletrónica face à Internacionalização*. Retrieved from http://anetie.pt/wp-content/uploads/2017/09/Estudo_Internacionalização_ANETIE.pdf

InovaRia; Sociedade Portuguesa de Inovação. (2014). *Estudo Prospetivo do setor TICE*. Retrieved from http://www.pofc.qren.pt/ResourcesUser/2013/Publicacoes/Setor_TICE_EstudoPropectivo.pdf

International Transparency. (2014). *Corruption Perceptions Index 2014-results*. Author.

Javalgi, R. G., & Martin, C. L. (2007). Internationalization of services: Identifying the building-blocks for future research. *Journal of Services Marketing*, *21*(6), 391–397. doi:10.1108/08876040710818886

Johanson, J., & Mattsson, L.-G. (2015). Internationalisation in Industrial Systems — A Network Approach. In *Knowledge, Networks and Power* (pp. 111–132). London: Palgrave Macmillan UK. doi:10.1057/9781137508829_5

Johanson, J., & Vahlne, J.-E. (1977). The Internationalization Process of the Firm—A Model of Knowledge Development and Increasing Foreign Market Commitments. *Journal of International Business Studies*, *8*(1), 23–32. doi:10.1057/palgrave.jibs.8490676

Johanson, J., & Vahlne, J.-E. (2009). The Uppsala internationalization process model revisited: From liability of foreignness to liability of outsidership. *Journal of International Business Studies*, *40*(9), 1411–1431. doi:10.1057/jibs.2009.24

Kaufmann, D., Kraay, A., & Mastruzzi, M. (2013). *The Worldwide Governance Indicators (WGI) project*. World Bank.

Knight, G. A., & Cavusgil, S. T. (2004). Innovation, organizational capabilities, and the born-global firm. *Journal of International Business Studies*, *35*(2), 124–141. doi:10.1057/palgrave.jibs.8400071

Kumar, V., Stam, A., & Joachimsthaler, E. A. (1994). An Interactive Multicriteria Approach to Identifying Potential Foreign Markets. *Journal of International Marketing*.

Lindqvist, M. (1997). Infant multinationals: internationalisation of small technology-based firms. In *Technology, innovation and enterprise* (pp. 303–324). Springer. doi:10.1007/978-1-349-25770-6_10

Lovelock, C., & Wirtz, J. (2007). *Services Marketing: People, Technology, Strategy. Upper Sadle River*. Pearson Prentice Hall.

Luostarinen, R. (1979). *Internationalization of the firm: an empirical study of the internationalization of firms with small and open domestic markets with special emphasis on lateral rigidity as a behavioral characteristic in strategic decision-making* (Vol. 30). Helsinki School of Economics.

McDougall, P. P., & Oviatt, B. M. (2000). International entrepreneurship: The intersection of two research paths. *Academy of Management Journal*, *43*(5), 902–906.

Papadopoulos, N., & Martín Martín, O. (2011). International market selection and segmentation: Perspectives and challenges. *International Marketing Review*, *28*(2), 132–149. doi:10.1108/02651331111122632

Ribau, C. P., Moreira, A. C., & Raposo, M. (2015). Internationalisation of the firm theories: A schematic synthesis. *International Journal of Business and Globalisation*, *15*(4), 528–554. doi:10.1504/IJBG.2015.072535

Ribau, C. P., Moreira, A. C., & Raposo, M. (2018). SME internationalization research: mapping the state of the art. *Canadian Journal of Administrative Sciences/Revue Canadienne Des Sciences de l'Administration*, *35*(2), 280–303.

Rodríguez, A., & Nieto, M. J. (2012). The internationalization of knowledge-intensive business services: The effect of collaboration and the mediating role of innovation. *Service Industries Journal*, *32*(7), 1057–1075. doi:10.1080/02642069.2012.662493

Ruzzier, M., Hisrich, R. D., & Antoncic, B. (2006). SME internationalization research: Past, present, and future. *Journal of Small Business and Enterprise Development*, *13*(4), 476–497. doi:10.1108/14626000610705705

Sakarya, S., Eckman, M., & Hyllegard, K. H. (2007). Market selection for international expansion. *International Marketing Review*, *24*(2), 208–238. doi:10.1108/02651330710741820

Schueffel, P., Baldegger, R., & Amann, W. (2014). Behavioral patterns in born-again global firms: Towards a conceptual framework of the internationalization activities of mature SMEs. *Multinational Business Review*, *22*(4), 418–441. doi:10.1108/MBR-06-2014-0029

Schwab, K., & Sala-i-Martin, X. (2015). *World Economic Forum's Global Competitiveness Report, 2014-2015*. Academic Press.

Smith, A. (1776). *An inquiry into the wealth of nations*. London: Strahan and Cadell.

Stanisauskaite, V., & Kock, S. (2016). The dynamic development of international entrepreneurial networks. In The Changing Global Economy and Its Impact on International Entrepreneurship. Academic Press. doi:10.4337/9781783479849.00012

Vernon, R. (1966). Product Life-Cycle Theory. *The Quarterly Journal of Economics*.

Welch, L. S., & Luostarinen, R. (1988). Internationalization: Evolution of a concept. *Journal of General Management*, *14*(2), 34–55. doi:10.1177/030630708801400203

Whitelock, J. (2002). Theories of internationalisation and their impact on market entry. *International Marketing Review*, *19*(4), 342–347. doi:10.1108/02651330210435654

Willianson, O. E. (1975). Markets and hierarchies: analysis and antitrust implications. New York: Academic Press.

ADDITIONAL READING

Coviello, N. (2015). Re-thinking research on born globals. *Journal of International Business Studies*, *46*(1), 17–26. doi:10.1057/jibs.2014.59

Cuervo-Cazurra, A., Narula, R., & Un, C. A. (2015). Internationalization motives: Sell more, buy better, upgrade and escape. *Multinational Business Review*, *23*(1), 25–35. doi:10.1108/MBR-02-2015-0009

Dominguez, N. (2016). Risk-seeking behaviours in SMEs' internationalization. In A. Zucchella (Ed.), *Etemad H. Denicolai S. Hagen B* (pp. 66–95). The Changing Global Economy and Its Impact on International Entrepreneurship.

Johanson, J., & Mattsson, L.-G. (2015). Internationalisation in Industrial Systems — A Network Approach. In *Knowledge, Networks and Power* (pp. 111–132). London: Palgrave Macmillan UK. doi:10.1057/9781137508829_5

Ribau, C. P., Moreira, A. C., & Raposo, M. (2015). Internationalisation of the firm theories: A schematic synthesis. *International Journal of Business and Globalisation*, *15*(4), 528–554. doi:10.1504/IJBG.2015.072535

Ribau, C. P., Moreira, A. C., & Raposo, M. (2018). SME internationalization research: mapping the state of the art. *Canadian Journal of Administrative Sciences/Revue Canadienne Des Sciences de l'Administration, 35*(2), 280–303.

Stanisauskaite, V., & Kock, S. (2016). The dynamic development of international entrepreneurial networks. In A. Zucchella (Ed.), *Etemad H. Denicolai S. Hagen B* (pp. 119–135). The Changing Global Economy and Its Impact on International Entrepreneurship. doi:10.4337/9781783479849.00012

KEY TERMS AND DEFINITIONS

Born Again Global: Companies that are initially focused on the domestic market and that, as a result of an external shock, change their strategy and focus in international markets.

Cultural Dimensions Theory: Developed in the 1970s by Geert Hofstede, is a framework that describes the effects of a society´s culture on the values of its members, and how these values relate to behavior, using a structure derived from factor analysis.

Eclectic Paradigm: Is a theory grounded on a three-tiered framework (a comparative advantage, an ownership advantage and an internalization advantage) that analyses, for a given company, if it is beneficial to pursue foreign direct investment. Is based on the assumption that institutions will avoid transactions in the open market when internal transactions carry lower costs.

ICT Services: Information and communication technologies that provide access to information through telecommunications systems.

Joint Ventures: A business arrangement in which two or more parties agree to pool their resources to accomplish a specific task. It is not like a partnership agreement because this has a definite end to it as it focuses on a single project or undertaking.

Market Screening: A process used to evaluate markets according to its compatibility with overall competencies and business objectives of the company.

Network Theory: Analyses the industrial systems through three variables: actors (individuals, firms or groups); activities and resources (physical or intangible). Describes the industrial markets of SMEs as firms' networks and the basic assumption of this theory rests on the assertion that the actors (firms) are dependent on resources controlled by other parties.

Psychic Distance: Perceived difference between countries (home and abroad) that is independent of space and time factors and takes mostly into consideration cultural aspects of business.

Serendipity: Recognizing "chance" opportunities and being ready to take advantage of them, encompassing a temporal, relational, and analytical element.

Uppsala Model: Explains the process of internationalization of companies based on how organizations learn and the impact of learning on the companies' international expansion. This theory defends that the companies' internationalization process is carried out in stages, from non-regular exports to the establishment of companies abroad.

APPENDIX

Table 2. Cultural proximity

Cultural proximity	Portugal	Spain	Algeria*	Gambia**	Cape Verde	Angola	Mozambique
Distance from power	63	57	80	77	75	83	85
Individualism/Collectivism	27	51	38	20	20	18	15
Masculinity/Femininity	31	42	53	46	15	20	38
Uncertainty avoidance	99	86	68	54	40	60	44
Rating	**0**	**54**	**81**	**81**	**94**	**79**	**96**

* Arab country
** Western Africa Country

Table 3. Raw data

Raw	Indicators/Countries	Portugal	Spain	Algeria	Gambia	Cape Verde	Angola	Mozambique
Attractiveness factors	Population	10 813 834	47 737 941	38 813 722	1 925 527	538 535	19 088 106	24 692 144
	GDP growth rate	1,0%	1,3%	4,0%	7,4%	1,0%	3,9%	8,3%
	Technology availability	6,30	5,60	3,40	4,80	4,70	3,20	4,30
	Technology absorption	5,60	4,90	3,40	4,50	4,60	2,90	4,20
	FDI and technology transfer	5,20	4,70	3,90	4,50	4,70	3,90	4,60
Risk factors	Political stability	0,75	-0,01	-1,34	0,01	0,78	-0,38	0,35
	Perception of Corruption	63	60	36	29	57	19	31
	Inflation rate	0,0%	0,0%	2,5%	5,6%	0,4%	7,5%	3,0%
	Cultural proximity	0	54	81	81	94	79	96

Table 4. Homogenized data

Weighted	Indicators/Countries	Portugal	Spain	Algeria	Gambia	Cape Verde	Angola	Mozambique
Attractiveness factors	Population	21,63	95,48	77,63	3,85	1,08	38,18	49,38
	GDP growth rate	10,00	13,00	40,00	74,00	10,00	39,00	83,00
	Technology availability	90,00	80,00	48,57	68,57	67,14	45,71	61,43
	Technology absorption	80,00	70,00	48,57	64,29	65,71	41,43	60,00
	FDI and technology transfer	74,29	67,14	55,71	64,29	67,14	55,71	65,71
Risk factors	Political stability	35,00	50,20	76,80	49,80	34,40	57,60	43,00
	Perception of Corruption	37,00	40,00	64,00	71,00	43,00	81,00	69,00
	Inflation rate	0,00	0,00	25,00	56,00	4,00	75,00	30,00
	Cultural proximity	0	54	81	81	94	79	96

Table 5. Weighted data for attractiveness factors

	Indicators/Countries	Weight	Portugal	Spain	Algeria	Gambia	Cape Verde	Angola	Mozambique
Attractiveness factors	Population	20%	4,33	19,10	15,53	0,77	0,22	7,64	9,88
	GDP growth rate	20%	2,00	2,60	8,00	14,80	2,00	7,80	16,60
	Technology availability	20%	18,00	16,00	9,71	13,71	13,43	9,14	12,29
	Technology absorption	20%	16,00	14,00	9,71	12,86	13,14	8,29	12,00
	FDI and technology transfer	20%	14,86	13,43	11,14	12,86	13,43	11,14	13,14
	Total	100%	55,18	65,12	54,10	55,00	42,22	44,01	63,91

Table 6. Weighted data for risk factors

	Indicators/Countries	Weight	Portugal	Spain	Algeria	Gambia	Cape Verde	Angola	Mozambique
Risk factors	Political stability	25%	8,75	12,55	19,20	12,45	8,60	14,40	10,75
	Perception of Corruption	25%	9,25	10,00	16,00	17,75	10,75	20,25	17,25
	Inflation rate	25%	0,00	0,00	6,25	14,00	1,00	18,75	7,50
	Cultural proximity	25%	0,00	13,50	20,25	20,25	23,50	19,75	24,00
	Total	100%	18,00	36,05	61,70	64,45	43,85	73,15	59,50

Table 7. Final rating

Indicators/Countries	Portugal	Spain	Algeria	Gambia	Cape Verde	Angola	Mozambique
Attractiveness	55,18	65,12	54,10	55,00	42,22	44,01	63,91
Risk	18,00	36,05	61,70	64,45	43,85	73,15	59,50

Chapter 15
Linking Intangible Resources and Competitive Advantage

Orlando Lima Rua
Polytechnic of Porto, Portugal

ABSTRACT

The purpose of this chapter is to analyze the linkage between intangible resources and competitive advantage. The author uses a quantitative approach based on a survey data from 247 Portuguese small and medium-sized enterprises (SMEs) from the textile industry. Findings suggest that intangible resources have a positive and significant influence on competitive advantage, either by cost leadership or differentiation. This chapter presents further evidences of the strategies that SMEs managers should pursue and policy makers should promote. This study deepens our understanding and provides novel insights into strategic management literature, since it combines multiple factors and has obtained the importance of each construct in SMEs business growth.

INTRODUCTION

Penrose (1959) mentions that the Resourced-Based View (RBV) argues that the competitive advantage of any organization is based on the set of resources and the role they play in its strategy. It can then be said that competitive advantage is based not only on the final product or service placed on the market, but mostly on a clear identification of available resources (Wernerfelt, 1984), and on how they are optimized (Penrose, 1959).

The Industrial Revolution created a market where the success and value of a firm were established by its ability to obtain, use and sell physical resources (Tsai, Lu & Yen, 2012). However, the Information Society has brought with it a new reality in which physical goods give way to intangible values, such as knowledge, culture and technology (Fakhrutdinova et al., 2014), and in which the main source of value creation market is based on immaterial pillars (Tsai et al., 2012).

According to the Economic Theory, intangible resources are based on the relation between society and property, which in itself has neither a material form nor a recognizable value, but which has the capacity to generate profit and competitive advantage (Fakhrutdinova et al., 2014).

DOI: 10.4018/978-1-5225-8906-8.ch015

Exploring intangible resources among SMEs has inherent scholarly value, since these firms tend to be constrained in their tangible assets; possessing intangible resources take on particular strategic significance and can form the basis for competitive advantage (Anderson & Eshima, 2013).

Resource-based scholars argue that resources form the basis of firm strategies (Barney, 1991) and intangible resources are more likely than tangible resources to produce a competitive advantage, since they are often rare and socially complex, thereby making them difficult to imitate (Hitt, Bierman, Shimizu & Kochhar, 2001). Thus, intangible assets are considered strategic variables (Amit & Schoemaker, 1993) and can consequently create sustainable value. Firms with valuable, scarce, and nonsubstitutable resources can gain at least temporary advantages by using those resources to develop and implement product-market strategies (Hsu & Ziedonis, 2013).

So, the purpose of this paper is to broad the boundaries of and strategic management literature and test the following research question: —— *Does intangible resources positively influence small business competitive strategies, either by cost leadership or differentiation?*

THEORETICAL FRAMEWORK

Intangible Resources

Wernerfelt (1984) argues for the existence of two typologies of organizational resources: tangible - all that is touchable, and intangibles - which by contrast are immaterial goods related to the history and culture of the organization itself. Fakhrutdinova et al. (2014), generalizing, argue that intangible resources are "all intangible products with the potential to respond to needs and generate profits" (p. 83), such as brand, patents or knowledge (Dyer & Singh, 1998).

There is a consensus in the literature that the source of competitive advantage is much more associated with intangible resources, since these are scarcer and socially complex, making their imitation difficult (Barney, 1991; Hitt et al., 2001). Consequently, intangible resources are considered strategic resources (Amit & Schoemaker, 1993).

Intangibles have three interesting features that distinguish them from tangible resources (Molloy et al., 2011). First, intangibles do not deplete or deteriorate with use, conferring benefits for an undefined period of time, contrasting with tangible resources, which have expected depreciation (Cohen, 2005). Second, multiple managers can simultaneously use intangibles. For example, the brand is available for use to all managers. Finally, intangibles are immaterial, which makes them difficult to exchange and cannot be separated from their owner. Indeed, to get hold of a brand, firms must often acquire the entire organization (Marr & Roos, 2005).

Empirical research identified six types of resources that are particularly important sources of competitive advantage, especially in international ventures: reputational resources; access to financial resources; human resources; cultural resources; relational resources; and informational (knowledge) resources (Morgan, Vorhies & Schlegelmilch, 2006).

Intangible resources are based upon knowledge or information, such as organisational culture, product reputation, firm's brand, their abilities are unlimited (Pearson, Pitfield & Ryley, 2015), having a much broader range of use in international markets (Fernández-Olmos & Díez-Vial, 2015).

These resources are created through core competencies such as "organizational structure, employee knowledge, centripetal strength of the employer, capacity for innovation and development, consumer dimension, brand recognition and market share", resulting in "the dynamic capacity of the organization" (Tsai et al., 2012, p. 67). Kayo (2002) argue that intangible resources can be classified into the following categories: 1) human resources: knowledge, talent, skills, experience, top management, key employees and training; 2) innovation resources: research and development, patents, secret formulas, and technological knowledge; and 3) relational resources: brand value, trademarks, copyrights, customer relationships, suppliers, licensing agreements and franchising.

Competitive Advantage

Ansoff (1965) appears as the first author to try to define competitive advantage, referring to it as the individual and superior characteristics of an organization compared to the rest in the same market. However, it is Porter who is referred to as a reference author, who defined competitive advantage as "the fundamental basis for superior long-term performance" (Porter, 1985, p. 11). Based strictly on the perception of superior value by customers, which can be achieved through superior characteristics with prices equivalent to the rest of the market or lower prices of equivalent benefits (Porter, 1985).

Although the concept of competitive advantage is deeply rooted in the business sector (South, 1981; Baaij, Bosch & Volberda, 2004; Barney, 1997; Grant, 1998) as a differentiating factor in business performance (Zott & Amit 2008; Ceccagnoli, 2009), there is still no clear definition of its determinants (Sigalas & Pekka-Economou, 2013; Ma, 2000; Arend, 2003; Rumelt, 2003; O'Shannassy, 2008), making it often difficult to understand and manage (Markides, 2000) and used in disparate contexts (O'Shannassy, 2008; Sigalas, 2015). Sigalas et al. (2013) characterize this reality as the conceptual phenomenon of competitive advantage.

Newbert (2008) advocates using Barney's definition of competitive advantage, "a degree to which business exploits opportunities, neutralizes threats, and reduces costs". For Sigalas et al. (2013, p. 324) it refers to the "superior ability of industry to exploit opportunities, counteract competitive threats, and reduce costs". Barney (1991, p. 102) defines competitive advantage as "the implementation of a strategy that adds value, which is not being simultaneously implemented by a current or potential competitor, that its benefits can not be duplicated" and that allows you to replicate the profits countless times. Peteraf and Barney (2003) argue that competitive advantage happens whenever "the company manages to create more economic value than the competitive equilibrium" (p. 314). In the same perspective, but in a less demanding current, Sigalas et al. (2013) concludes that this happens when the organization manages to "create more economic value than its less efficient competitor" (p. 324).

The increased intensity of business competition has forced firms to adopt a non-traditional management techniques and tools. Maintaining competitive advantage is a dynamic and infinite activity (Hung, Yang & Lien, 2010).

How firms achieve and sustain competitive advantage? This is the fundamental question in the field of strategic management (Teece et al., 1997). Porter (1985) considers simply a matter of creating value for customers and doing it better than competition.

Porter's model to classify firm strategies remains the most commonly supported and acknowledged framework in strategic management literature (Allen et al., 2006). Porter proposed four competitive strategies: broad cost leadership, broad differentiation, cost focus and differentiation focus. While cost leadership or differentiation is defined as dominant competitive strategies, focus is not a standalone strategy and "is not sufficient for above-average performance' (Porter, 1985, p. 15). Consequently, there is a tendency in the literature to recognise two main sources of competitive advantage: a) cost leadership – reaching lower costs than competitors and b) differentiation – creating more value for customers than the average firm (Lechner & Gudmundsson, 2014). Furthermore, and according to Porter, the two logics of differentiation and cost leadership are incompatible.

Hence, we can reduce the study of competitive strategy to differentiation and cost leadership, especially if the competitive strategy is related to other strategic elements of firm's behaviour. Differentiation means to fulfil customers' needs in a unique way, based on speed, customer service and flexibility, which is consistent with innovative approaches and characteristics of entrepreneurial firms. Cost leadership requires substantial financial resources (to invest in tangible assets), is based on process innovation, learning curve benefits, economies of scale and standardization, and seems to be less appropriate for small firms, given the resource constraints (Lechner & Gudmundsson, 2014).

Sustainable competitive advantage represents firm's competitive maintenance on the long run, whose performance is above average, resisting the dynamic evolution of competition, consumers and industry (e.g., Amit & Schoemaker, 1993; Peteraf, 1993; Porter, 1985).

Hypotheses Derivation

RBV argues that competitive advantages are obtained from firms' resources based on two assumptions: 1) strategic resources are heterogeneously distributed across firms; and 2) these differences are stable overtime (Barney, 1991). Barney (1995, p. 66) suggested that, in order to create sustained competitive advantage and discover unique resources and capabilities, "managers must look inside their firm for valuable, rare and costly-to-imitate resources, and then exploit these resources through their organization". Peteraf (1993) considers resources to be the cornerstone of competitive advantage.

H1: Intangible resources are positively associated with cost leadership.
H2: Intangible resources are positively associated with differentiation.

METHOD

Sample and Data Collection

The population of this empirical study has been drawn from Portuguese textile industry firms. Questionnaires were used as primary data sources and were carried out over the period of February 16 to April 30, 2016. The identification of companies was done through the Portugal's Textile Association (Associação Têxtil de Portugal – ATP) database. So, in this study we use a non-probabilistic and convenient sampling.

A total of 247 complete and validated questionnaires accounting for 25% per cent of the population were obtained. This response rate is considered quite satisfactory, given that the average of top management survey response rates are in the range of 15%-20% (Menon & Bharadwaj, 1999).

Statistical Analysis

We used PLS-SEM path modelling to test our hypothesis, specifically the software SmartPLS 3.0 (Hair el al., 2013; Sarstedt el al., 2014). We believe that the PLS-SEM path modelling is best suited to estimate our research model since: 1) this study focuses on prediction and explanation of constructs variance (in our case 2): 1) intangible resources and competitive advantage; 2) our research model has a complex structure; 3) the relationship between intangible resources and competitive advantage; 4) this study uses first and second-order reflective constructs; and 5) the sample (n=247).

Measures

This study uses well-validated scales from previous studies to operationalize the key constructs and adapted them to the particular context of our empirical setting.

Independent variables – Following Morgan et al. (2006), in the intangible resources construct we included six dimensions: reputational resources; access to financial resources; human resources; cultural resources; relational resources; and informational resources.

Dependent variable – Competitive strategy was measured through two dimensions, differentiation and cost leadership, using Morgan et al. (2004)'s scale.

For intangible resources and competitive advantage, the decision-makers were asked to assess the relative position of their firm vis-à-vis their competitors. All constructs were assessed on a five-point Likert scale.

RESULTS

Non-Response Bias and Common Method Bias

In this study we performed a univariate test of significance (*t*-test), to examine existing differences between respondents who answered our questionnaire quickly and those who did not. The results ($p<0.05$) showed the absence of significant differences between the two groups of respondents. Hence, we can assure that our sample is free from non-response bias. The methods used to reduce the risk of common method-bias were several. In the survey design itself, already validated in previous investigations, short and concise items were used to reduce misunderstandings. A pre-test was conducted to a group of several university experts and business specialists. Similarly, following the recommendation of Podsakoff et al. (2003), a distribution of items of dependent and non-consecutive independent variables was used. Finally, before assessing the relationships between dependent and independent variables, Harman's single-factor test was performed. Unrotated factor analysis using the eigenvalue-greater-than-one criterion revealed six factors, the first explaining 17.0 percent of the variance. This suggests that common method bias is not a serious threat to the validity of our study.

Next, in order to analyze and interpret the PLS-SEM results, we will: 1) assess the measurement model; and 2) evaluate and test the structural model.

Evaluation of Measurement Model

Results from Table 1 show that the measurement model meets all general requirements. First, all reflective items have a load higher than 0.707, which means that the reliability of individual indicators (loading^2) are higher than 0.5. Second, all composite reability values and Cronbach's alpha values are higher than 0.70, suggesting acceptable model reliability. Third, the average variance extracted (AVE) values of all constructs are higher than 0.50, indicating an adequate convergent validity and implying that our set of indicators represent the same underlying construct (Hair et al., 2013).

Finally, regarding discriminant validity, this paper presents two necessary approaches: 1) the first approach suggests that the AVE should share more variance with its assigned indicators than with any other construct - Fornell-Larcker criterion (Fornell & Larcker, 1981); and 2) the second approach suggests that no item should have a higher factor load with another construct than with the one which is assign to measure. The results shown in Table 2 confirm the existence of discriminant validity in our study.

Evaluation of Structural Model

Once the measurement model is defined and validated in all its components, we will proceed and create the second order model, following previous research (e.g., Zahra & Garvis, 2000), where the latent variables of the measurement model behave as constructs' measurement variables. Specifically, Intangible Resources (reputational, financial, human, cultural, relational and informational resources), Competitive Advantage-Cost and Competitive Advantage-Differentiation (product and service).

In the following tables 3 and 4, we present the results of reliability, convergent validity and discriminant validity corresponding to the second order model. All data confirm the strength of our model.

Results from Table 5, regarding the effect of intangible resources on firms' competitive strategies, remarkably our findings confirm that the possession of intangible resources influences the development of both cost leadership and differentiation (product or service). That is, the possession of reputational, financial, human, cultural, and relational and information resources support competitive strategies design by firms. According to statistical data, these intangible resources are more significant on differentiation (β=0.723; p-value<0.001), confirming H2. Similarly, H1 is also supported by the model (β=0.525; p-value<0.001).

DISCUSSION AND CONCLUSION

The main purpose of this study was to analyze the influence of intangible resources on competitive advantage. The central context of this research is on SMEs, which constitute the vast majority of firms in Portugal, as in most word economies. Thus, we conducted an empirical research based on a sample of 247 firms, which were applied a questionnaire in order to exploit data to test hypothesis, using proceedings and statistical techniques.

Newbert (2007) argues that, because of their rareness, intangible resources are critical to gain competitive advantage and its ownership is an important factor in the SMEs ability to implement strategies that lead to superior performance. On this point, we conclude that globally intangible resources have a positive and significant impact on competitive advantage, either cost leadership or differentiation (H1 and H2 supported). This is due to the fact that these resources are valuable, rare and inimitable, and

Table 1. Measurement model

First-order constructs	Items	Factor loading	Item loading	Cronbach's Alpha	Composite reliability	AVE
INTANGIBLE RESOURCES						
	REP1	0.928	0.861			
Reputational resources	REP2	0.915	0.837	0.905	0.934	0.779
	REP3	0.847	0.717			
	REP4	0.835	0.697			
	FIN1	0.940	0.884			
Financial-resources	FIN2	0.962	0.925	0.964	0.974	0.902
	FIN3	0.942	0.887			
	FIN4	0.956	0.914			
	HUM1	0.875	0.766			
Human-resources	HUM2	0.889	0.790	0.932	0.952	0.832
	HUM3	0.943	0.889			
	HUM4	0.939	0.882			
	CULT1	0.922	0.850			
Cultural-resources	CULT2	0.914	0.835	0.891	0.932	0.821
	CULT3	0.880	0.774			
	REL1	0.963	0.927			
Relational-resources	REL2	0.916	0.839	0.951	0.965	0.872
	REL3	0.934	0.872			
	REL4	0.922	0.850			
	INF1	0.875	0.766			
Informational-resources	INF2	0.822	0.676	0.881	0.917	0.734
	INF3	0.864	0.746			
	INF4	0.866	0.750			
	VCC1	0.884	0.781			
COMPETITIVE ADVANTAGE						
	VCC2	0.816	0.666	0.900	0.931	0.771
Cost	VCC3	0.952	0.906			
	VCC4	0.855	0.731			
	VCP1	0.875	0.766	0.924	0.946	0.814
Product	VCP2	0.903	0.815			
	VCP3	0.929	0.863			
	VCP4	0.902	0.814			
	VCS1	0.863	0.745			
Service	VCS2	0.923	0.852	0.886	0.921	0.746
	VCS3	0.865	0.748			
	VCS4	0.799	0.638			

Source: Own.

Table 2. Latent constructs correlation (Fornell-Larcker Criterion)

Dimensions	1.	2.	3.	4.	5.	6.	7.	8.	9.
1. Cost	.878								
2. Cultural resources	.260	.906							
3. Financial resources	.670	.511	.950						
4. Human resources	.373	.810	.636	.912					
5. Informational resources	.480	.557	.496	.666	.857				
6. Product	.303	.711	.485	.731	.524	.902			
7. Relational resources	.447	.698	.622	.715	.606	.649	.934		
8. Reputational resources	.404	.639	.589	.660	.459	.789	.656	.882	
9. Service	.319	.502	.465	.589	.540	.814	.599	.555	.864

Source: Own.

Table 3. Convergence validity and reliability indexes of the second-order model

Constructs/Dimensions	Cronbach's Alpha	Composite Reliability	AVE
1. Intangible resources	.963	.929	.687
2. Competitive advantage-differentiation	.940	.951	.907
3. Competitive advantage-cost	.901	.927	.761

Source: Own.

Table 4. Discriminant validity index of the second-order model

Constructs/Dimensions	1.	2.	3.
1. Intangible resources	.829		
2. Competitive advantage-differentiation	.726	.952	
3. Competitive advantage-cost	.535	.326	.873

Source: Own.

Table 5. Significant testing results of the structural model path coefficients

Hypotheses	Original Sample (O)	T Statistics (|O/STDEV|)	P Values	2.5%	97.5%	Results
H1. IR -> CAC	0.525	10.917	0.001*	0.428	0.614	Supported
H2. IR -> CAD	0.723	17.448	0.001*	0.634	0.797	Supported

*p<0.001

Source: Own.

are dully organized to be converted into competitive advantage (Barney, 1995), which is why they are considered the cornerstone of competitive advantage (Peteraf, 1993), and are taken into consideration in the development and implementation of product-market strategies (Hsu & Ziedonis, 2013). Thus, this study demonstrated that the firms' intangible resources has a positive and significant influence on their competitive advantage.

As reported by the ATP (2014), globalization pressures, such as textile trade liberalization, have considerably affected the industry. The textile sector is being subjected to strong pressures in a fast-changing business environment due to market volatility and strong competition world-wide. The key success factors of the industry are related primarily with cost (labour, energy, transport), but also with geographical location (flexibility, responsiveness, proximity service), knowledge (know-how, experience, technical expertise, research and development, networking) and recognition (tradition, brands, quality). Therefore, we acknowledge that the sector is developing strong differentiation factors. Firms in these mature markets must look for ways to stay competitive and develop strategies that enables them to differentiate themselves from other firms.

We highlight the contribution of this study to the theory of strategic management. It is known that strategy includes deliberate and emergent initiatives adopted by management, comprising resource and capabilities used to improve business performance (Nag, Hambrick & Chen, 2007). In order to remain competitive, firms must assess which strategic determinants give them an advantage over their competitors. The findings are a contribution to clarify the influence of intangible resources in small firms export performance.

Additionally, our findings provide guidance to business practitioners, since they indicate that intangible resources is predictor of competitive strategies and performance. The research has also shown the positive influences of generic strategies on firm performance. So, for small firm managers, competitive strategy does matters and the development of one type of competitive advantage, alongside with firm's resources, is a major performance driver.

The study is not without its limitations. The fact that the research does not consider the effect of control variables such as age, location and target market of the respondents can be seen as a limitation. Finally, the fact that the sampling is non probabilistic and convenience is a limitation. Therefore we advise prudence in the generalization of results.

Firstly, this study has been based on a mature sector, as is the textile sector in Portugal. The results obtained should be understood in this context. For this reason, new research could be done in more modern industries to test again the proposed relations. Second, given the irregular nature of business growth, a snapshot survey may not be able to capture strategy and performance variations over long periods of time. As such, further studies with a longitudinal perspective would be of added value to investigate why these differences persist. In other words, to find how and why some small exporters become highly successful while others, in the same industry, struggle to raise their export strengths.

REFERENCES

Allen, R. S., Helms, M. M., Takeda, M. B., White, C. S., & White, C. (2006). A Comparison of Competitive Strategies in Japan and the United States. *S.A.M. Advanced Management Journal*, *71*(1), 24–34.

Amit, R., & Schoemaker, P. (1993). Strategic assets and organizational rent. *Strategic Management Journal*, *14*(1), 33–46. doi:10.1002mj.4250140105

Anderson, B. S., & Eshima, Y. (2013). The influence of firm age and intangible resources on the relationship between entrepreneurial orientation and firm growth among Japanese SMEs. *Journal of Business Venturing*, *28*(3), 413–429. doi:10.1016/j.jbusvent.2011.10.001

Ansoff, I. (1965). *Corporate Strategy*. New York: McGraw Hill.

Arend, R. (2003). Revisiting the logical and research considerations of competitive advantage. *Strategic Management Journal*, *24*(3), 279–284. doi:10.1002mj.285

ATP. (2014). Plano Estratégico Têxtil 2020 – Projetar o Desenvolvimento da Fileira Têxtil e Vestuário até 2020. V. N. de Famalicão: ATP.

Baaij, M., Bosch, F., & Volberda, H. (n.d.). The international relocation of corporate centres - Are corporate centres sticky? European Management Journal, 22(2), 141–149.

Barney, J. (1991). Firm Resources and Sustained Competitive Advantage. *Journal of Management*, *17*(1), 99–120. doi:10.1177/014920639101700108

Barney, J. (1995). Looking inside for competitive advantage. *The Academy of Management Perspectives*, *9*(4), 49–61. doi:10.5465/ame.1995.9512032192

Ceccagnoli, M. (2009). Appropriability, preemption, and firm performance. *Strategic Management Journal*, *30*(1), 81–98. doi:10.1002mj.723

Cohen, J. A. (2005). *Intangible Assets: Valuation and Economic Benefit*. Hoboken, NJ: Wiley.

Dyer, J. H., & Singh, H. (1998). The Impacts of Customer Interaction and Social Capital on New Service Development Performance. *Academy of Management Review*, *23*(4), 660–679. doi:10.5465/amr.1998.1255632

Fakhrutdinova, E., Kolesnikova, J., & Yurieva, O. K. (2014). Current trends of realization of the intellectual capital and problems of intellectual migration. *Procedia Economics and Finance*, *14*(1), 326–332.

Fernández-Olmos, M., & Díez-Vial, I. (2015). Intangible resources, export channel and performance: Is there any fit? *Journal of Business Economics and Management*, *16*(5), 1013–1033. doi:10.3846/16111699.2012.726928

Fornell, C., & Larcker, D. F. (1981). Evaluating structural equation models with unobservable variables and measurement error. *JMR, Journal of Marketing Research*, *18*(1), 39–50. doi:10.1177/002224378101800104

Grant, R. M. (1998). *Contemporary strategy analysis: concepts, techniques, applications*. Malden, MA: Blackwell.

Hair, J., Hult, G. T. M., Ringle, C. M., & Sarstedt, M. (2013). *A primer on Partial least Squares Structural Equation Modeling (PLS-SEM)*. SAGE Publications, Inc.

Hitt, M., Bierman, L., Shimizu, K., & Kochhar, R. (2001). Direct and moderating effects of human capital on strategy and performance in professional service firms: A resource-based perspective. *Academy of Management Journal*, *44*(1), 13–28.

Hsu, D. H., & Ziedonis, R. H. (2013). Resources as Dual Sources of Advantage: Implications for Valuing Entrepreneurial-Firm Patents. *Strategic Management Journal*, *34*(7), 761–781. doi:10.1002mj.2037

Hung, R., Yang, B., Lien, B., McLean, G. N., & Kuo, Y.-M. (2010). Dynamic capability: Impact of process alignment and organizational learning culture on performance. *Journal of World Business*, *45*(3), 285–294. doi:10.1016/j.jwb.2009.09.003

Kayo, E. K. (2002). *A estrutura de capital e o risco das empresas tangível e intangível-intensivas: uma contribuição ao estudo da valoração de empresas*. Tese (Doutorado em Administração). FEA/USP.

Lechner, C., & Gudmundsson, S. V. (2014). Entrepreneurial orientation, firm strategy and small firm performance. *International Small Business Journal*, *32*(1), 36–60. doi:10.1177/0266242612455034

Ma, H. (2000). Competitive advantage and firm performance. *Journal of Global Competitiveness*, *10*(2), 15–32. doi:10.1108/eb046396

Markides, C. (2000). Cross talk: Strategy and management: Constantinos Markides discusses strategic innovation, an interview by Peter Mang. *European Management Journal*, *18*(4), 357–366.

Marr, B., & Roos, G. (2005). A strategy perspective on intellectual capital. In *Perspectives on intelectual capital* (pp. 28–52). New York: Routledge. doi:10.1016/B978-0-7506-7799-8.50007-3

Menon, A., Bharadwaj, S., Adidam, P. T., & Edison, S. W. (1999). Antecedents and consequences of marketing strategy making: A model and a test. *Journal of Marketing*, *63*(April), 18–40. doi:10.1177/002224299906300202

Molloy, J. C., Chadwick, C., Ployhart, R. E., & Golden, S. J. (2011). Making Intangibles "Tangible" in Tests of Resource-Based Theory: A Multidisciplinary Construct Validation Approach. *Journal of Management*, *37*(5), 1496–1518. doi:10.1177/0149206310394185

Morgan, N., Kaleka, A., & Katsikeas, C. S. (2004). Antecedents of Export Venture Performance : A Theoretical Model. *Journal of Marketing*, *68*(1), 90–108. doi:10.1509/jmkg.68.1.90.24028

Morgan, N., Vorhies, D. W., & Schlegelmilch, B. B. (2006). Resource–performance relationships in industrial export ventures: The role of resource inimitability and substitutability. *Industrial Marketing Management*, *35*(5), 621–633. doi:10.1016/j.indmarman.2005.05.018

Nag, R., Hambrick, D., & Chen, M. (2007). What is strategic management, really? Inductive derivation of a consensus definition of the field. *Strategic Management Journal*, *955*, 935–955.

Newbert, S. (2007). Empirical research on the resource-based view of the firm: An assessment and suggestions for future research. *Strategic Management Journal*, *146*(2), 121–146. doi:10.1002mj.573

Newbert, S. (2008). Value, rareness, competitive advantage and performance: A conceptual level empirical investigation of the resource-based view of the firm. *Strategic Management Journal*, *29*(1), 745–768. doi:10.1002mj.686

O'Shannassy, T. (2008). Sustainable competitive advantage or temporary competitive advantage: Improving understanding of an important strategy construct. *Journal of Strategy and Management*, *1*(2), 168–180. doi:10.1108/17554250810926357

Pearson, J., Pitfield, D., & Ryley, T. (2015). Intangible resources of competitive advantage: Analysis of 49 Asian airlines across three business models. *Journal of Air Transport Management*, *47*, 179–189. doi:10.1016/j.jairtraman.2015.06.002

Penrose, E. T. (1959). *The Theory of the Growth of the Firm*. New York: John Wiley.

Peteraf, M. (1993). The cornerstones of competitive advantage: A resource-based view. *Strategic Management Journal*, *14*(3), 179–191. doi:10.1002mj.4250140303

Peteraf, M., & Barney, J. (2003). Unravelling the resource-based tangle. *Managerial and Decision Economics*, *24*(1), 309–323. doi:10.1002/mde.1126

Podsakoff, P. M., MacKenzie, S. B., Lee, J. Y., & Podsakoff, N. P. (2003). Common method biases in behavioral research: A critical review of the literature and recommended remedies. *The Journal of Applied Psychology*, *88*(5), 879–903. doi:10.1037/0021-9010.88.5.879 PMID:14516251

Porter, M. (1985). *The Competitive Advantage: Creating and Sustaining Superior Performance*. Free Press.

Rumelt, R. (2003). *What in the world is competitive advantage*. Working Paper No. 2003-105. University of Califórnia. Los Angeles: The Anderson School.

Sarstedt, M., Ringle, C. M., Smith, D., Reams, R., & Hair, J. F. Jr. (2014). Partial least squares structural equation modeling (PLS-SEM): A useful tool for family business researchers. *Journal of Family Business Strategy*, *5*(1), 105–115. doi:10.1016/j.jfbs.2014.01.002

Sigalas, C. (2015). Competitive advantage: The known unknown concept. *Management Decision*, *53*(9), 2004–2016. doi:10.1108/MD-05-2015-0185

Sigalas, C., & Pekka Economou, V. (2013). Revisiting the concept of competitive advantage: Problems and fallacies arising from its conceptualization. *Journal of Strategy and Management*, *6*(1), 61–80. doi:10.1108/17554251311296567

South, S. (1981). Competitive advantage: The cornerstone of strategic thinking. *The Journal of Business Strategy*, *1*(4), 15–25. doi:10.1108/eb038908

Teece, D. J., Pisano, G., & Shuen, A. (1997). Dynamic capabilities and strategic management. *Strategic Management Journal*, *18*(7), 509–533. doi:10.1002/(SICI)1097-0266(199708)18:7<509::AID-SMJ882>3.0.CO;2-Z

Wernerfelt, B. (1984). A resource-based view of the firm. *Strategic Management Journal*, *5*(2), 171–180. doi:10.1002mj.4250050207

Zahra, S., & Garvis, D. (2000). International corporate entrepreneurship and firm performance: The moderating effect of international environmental hostility. *Journal of Business Venturing*, *15*(5-6), 469–492. doi:10.1016/S0883-9026(99)00036-1

ADDITIONAL READING

Aulakh, P. S., Kotabe, M., & Teegen, H. (2000). Export strategies and performance of firms from emerging economies: Evidence from Brazil, Chile, and Mexico. *Academy of Management Journal, 43*(3), 342–361.

Barney, J. (1991). Firm Resources and Sustained Competitive Advantage. *Journal of Management, 17*(1), 99–120. doi:10.1177/014920639101700108

Monteiro, A., Soares, A. M., & Rua, O. L. (2017). Entrepreneurial orientation and export performance: The mediating effect of organisational resources and dynamic capabilities. *Journal of International Business and Entrepreneurship Development, 10*(1), 3–19. doi:10.1504/JIBED.2017.082749

Monteiro, A. P., Soares, A. M., & Rua, O. L. (2017). Linking intangible resources and export performance: The role of entrepreneurial orientation and dynamic capabilities. *Baltic Journal of Management, 12*(3), 329–347. doi:10.1108/BJM-05-2016-0097

Penrose, E. T. (1959). *The Theory of the Growth of the Firm*. New York: John Wiley.

Peteraf, M. (1993). The cornerstones of competitive advantage: A resource-based view. *Strategic Management Journal, 14*(3), 179–191. doi:10.1002mj.4250140303

Peteraf, M., & Barney, J. (2003). Unravelling the resource-based tangle. *Managerial and Decision Economics, 24*(1), 309–323. doi:10.1002/mde.1126

Rua, O. L., & França, A. (2017). Assessing the relationship between Entrepreneurial Orientation, Reputational Resources and Absorptive Capability: A resource-based approach. *Periodica Polytechnica Social and Management Sciences, 26*(1), 30–37. doi:10.3311/PPso.10206

Rua, O. L., & França, A. (2018). The Linkage Between Intangible Resources and Export Performance: The mediating effect of Innovation. *International Journal of Innovation, 5*(3). doi:10.5585/iji

KEY TERMS AND DEFINITIONS

Competitive Advantage: Based on the strategies of broad cost leadership, broad differentiation, cost focus, and differentiation focus.

Intangible Resources: Considered strategic resources, including six dimensions: reputational resources, access to financial resources, human resources, cultural resources, relational resources, and informational resources.

Resource-Based View: Theory based on the assumption that the source of competitive advantage is obtained from firms' resources.

SME: Small and medium-sized enterprises.

Chapter 16
Supply Chain Startups in India: A Cross Case Comparative Analysis

Som Sekhar Bhattacharyya
National Institute of Industrial Engineering, India

Apurva Shrey
National Institute of Industrial Engineering, India

ABSTRACT

Supply chain management (SCM) has become a critical business function. SCM has become such a specialized function that dedicated firms on SCM has emerged. Startups in SCM domain target to reduce the inefficiencies through technological interventions and innovative business models. This chapter focuses on 10 Indian supply chain startups. These startups were analyzed based on supply chain drivers, supply chain operation reference model (SCOR), and using business model canvas (BMC). The case data was collected through secondary sources and analyzed through the cross-case analysis. It was found that the SCM startups were focusing more on transportation driver. SCOR model analysis demonstrated that the SCM startups assisted in operational area of the SCM where they carried out operational activities and decision making. BMC analysis revealed that startups were asset light and resources held by these startups were the financial funding which the firm secured through venture capitalists and software development teams.

INTRODUCTION

Startup has become a buzz word globally. The dictionary meaning of the word "Startup" indicated a flourishing business enterprise (Merriam Webster,2017). According to Government of India (GOI), an entity was defined as a startup when it has been established for not more than seven years since the date of incorporation. Additionally, the turnover shouldn't have increased beyond INR 25 crores in these 7 years. Last but not the least criteria were that it should be working with innovation, development, deployment and commercialization of new processes or new products driven by intellectual property and technology (Department of Industrial Policy and Promotion, Ministry of Commerce and Industry, 2017). Startup has also been defined as a company which is in initial stages of foundations and is often backed

DOI: 10.4018/978-1-5225-8906-8.ch016

by funding from the founders as they fund the venture to gain market share of products or services for which they believed that there exists a demand. (Macaulay, 2017). The short-term financing generally came from the founders and the long-term financing came from the Venture Capitalists (VC). VCs are lured by venture potentiality of the company (Investopedia,2018). Another way of looking at a startup was as an entrepreneurial venture which has been fast emerging and aimed to meet the demand through innovative business model. (Rao, 2017) Startups have the capability and the business model to scale up the business footprints.

Startups in India

It has been reported that the decade of 2010s in India has been best suited for the growth of startups as India has been judged as the fastest growing economy by Central Statistics Organization (CSO) and International Monetary fund (IMF) (Indian Brand Equity Foundation, 2018). The current Indian growth rate in Gross Domestic Product (GDP) has been around 7% (Economic survey, 2016-17). India has been the third largest startup base in the world. It 2016 India had around 4,750 technology startups and about 1,400 new start-ups being founded in 2016 (Momentous rise of Indian Startup Ecosystem, NASSCOM, 2015). It has been reported that the GOI schemes were supporting the environment for the growth of the startups (Agarwal, 2017). Recently, the GOI had initiated a campaign of “Startup India” which aimed at building a strong ecosystem for nurturing entrepreneurial growth in India (Economic Survey, Ministry of Finance, Government of India, 2016-17). One can also note that for India, Moody’s rating for ease of doing business had improved (Press Information Bureau, Government of India, Ministry of Finance, 2017) and the improvement was the result of government initiatives which had made entry and exit from business easy for the companies (Workloft, 2017). Startups have been driven by innovation and this emphasized the need for protection on intellectual property rights. GOI for the first time adopted a comprehensive National Intellectual Property Rights (NIPR) policy to lay future roadmap for intellectual property (Economic Survey, Ministry of Finance, Government of India, 2016-17). Thus, the importance of startups in India has become significant in present day scenario.

Significance of Supply Chain Startups

Supply Chain Management (SCM) has been defined as the material and informational interchanges in logistical process, stretching from acquisition of raw materials to delivery of finished products to end users (vendors, service providers, and customers) as links in the supply chain (Council of SCM, CSCMP Glossary,2013). Another widely accepted definition was that SCM is the design and coordination of a network through which organizations and individuals get, use, deliver, and dispose of material goods; acquire and distribute services; and make their offerings available to markets, customers, and clients (LeMay et al.,2017). Thus, one can comprehend that coordination in supply chain was necessary for a responsive as well as an efficient strategy. (Singh, 2011)

The term supply chain restructuring has been used in terms of streamlining operations, elimination of redundancies for cost savings and becoming responsive to customer demands. The supply chain restructuring has its core in manpower, technological interventions and flow of information. Thus, these are the areas in which startups helps firms in achieving cost effective and efficient supply chain.

Over the years, firm managers have been focusing more on improving the efficiency and responsiveness of supply chain using technological interventions and innovative business models (Berttram & Schrauf, 2016) The definition of last mile has been changed over the years through advancement in technology, internet and robotics (Huppe, 2017). In the present-day context, consumers have become the new last mile for companies. (Joerss, 2016) Thus, business strategies and business models have been carved around this hypothesis. Some of the most prominent business models on startups are discussed by (Tomaro, 2015). These are Warby Parker model, Marketplace model and On-demand model.

1. Warby Parker Model is the business model in which startup eliminates the need of middle men and gives the startup an advantage of controlled pricing.
2. Marketplace Model is the model where startup brings the supply and demand to a single platform. The advantages of this model are that it has zero overhead and minimal inventory.
3. On-demand Model is the model that allows startups to leverage new technologies and it utilizes existing infrastructure. The penetration of smartphones in Indian market has been an advantage for the on-demand model.

Promising startup verticals in India in this decade are based on Internet of Things (IoT), Healthtech, Hyperlocal aggregation and e-commerce according to National Association of Software and Services Companies report (NASSCOM-Zinnov,2015). Startups in supply chain addresses the area of business gap ("What role are Startups playing in the Digital Transformation of Supply Chain Management?", 2017). Technologies such as Artificial Intelligence (AI), Big Data (BD), Machine Learning (ML), IoT, 3D printing and wearables have led to a surge into transitioning and including the daily activities of firms to be encompassed and completed within the domain of SCM (Kodiak Community 2017). Thus, some of the SCM startups were leveraging data analytics for increased visibility in the SCM domain (Holloway, 2015). Thus, SCM as a business domain had witness increase in both scale and scope.

Therefore, a study on supply chain startups in India carries a lot of significance and it can provide insights to firm managers to improve upon the extant lacunae. Startups explored the idea gaps extant in the business landscape and then attempted to scale it. (Vanga, 2017) After reaching a certain volume and funding, startups expand to exploit the developed firm resources and capabilities (Adams, Alexander, & Oberg, 2014). As growth rate of India's GDP has been healthy, there will be more number of jobs required in near future. (Woetzel, 2017) India was one of the most job creators in the year 2016, in the Asia and Pacific region (World Employment and Social Outlook Report,2017) however this achievement was outweighed by the growing population of India.

So, there is a need for more job creators and startups created jobs (Dvorkin, 2017). As more and more millennials are coming in working population age group, India is going to retain the top spot with 18.6% of global workforce (Giudice & Lu, 2017).

Thus, need for creation of jobs has been an obvious reality in India. SCM domain has remained very inefficient in terms of technological interventions and operations in Indian context so far (Moneylife Digital Team, 2010). Thus, a study on these startups will provide managers the idea about which part of supply chain have been focused more by the startups and which have been blinded. The insight from this study could help SCM managers with options to focus their resources towards strengthening the lacking areas.

LITERATURE REVIEW

The authors for literature review gave a string search of "Supply Chain"/"Supply Chain Management"/"SCM" and "Startups" in the databases of Emerald insight, ProQuest, Elsevier Science Direct, Taylor Francis and EBSCO Journal databases. Some of these journals searched were specifically, "The International Journal of Logistic management", "Journal of SCM", "International Journal of Physical Distribution & Logistics Management". Journals available on these databases were searched. The articles on SCM from online sources such as Wiley online library, MIT Sloan and ResearchGate were also reviewed. SCM has been defined in somewhat correlated manner in different texts. Table 1, is a summarization of the various definitions of SCM.

Table 1. Literature and methodology review on SCM

S. No.	Authors	Methodology	Findings
1.	LeMay, Helms, Kimball and McMahon, (2017)	Reviewed the current definitions of SCM in practical and analytical usage from journals and textbooks.	Proposed definitions and discussed the areas for future research.
2.	Ellram and Cooper (2014)	Followed a structured, systematic literature review methodology.	Examined five perspectives on SCM, regarding the way that SCM was viewed as a discipline and as a functional process, philosophy, and governance structure.
3.	Larsen (1999)	Discussed three aspects of the SCM using available literature.	Introduced three different perspectives on SCM namely the transaction cost approach, the network perspective and the resource-based view.
4.	Lummus, Krumwiede and Vokurka (2001)	Examined the historical definition of logistics and SCM terms and current practitioner view of the term.	Proposed the hierarchy for relationship between logistics and SCM.
5.	Carter, Rogers, and Choi (2015)	Conceptually developed six foundational premises on SCM using available literature.	Developed a theory on SCM and its potential future research agendas and managerial implications.
6.	Chen and Paulraj (2004)	Critically analyzed main areas of SCM using available literature and performance metrics present in extant literature.	Developed a research framework for improved understanding of SCM.
7.	Svensson (2007)	Analyzed literature available on both SCM and sustainable SCM and compared them to draw the conclusions.	Formulated a comprehensive model of sustainable SCM which represented SCM as a loop chain.
8.	Pounder, Bowell and Worrell (2014)	Analyzed secondary data from online databases, digital libraries, books, journals and conference papers.	Provided a strategic, historical perspective of the principles of SCM and the external factors influencing SCM.
9.	Mentzer et. al. (2000)	Defined different aspects of marketing, relationship marketing and SCM based on the literature available.	An integrated framework of the relationships between marketing concept, market orientation, relationship marketing, and SCM was proposed.
10.	Harland (1996)	Three level of analysis was done namely network level analysis, dyad level analysis and chain level analysis. A mismatch tool was designed to address the gaps between purchasing organization and the supplier.	Provided an integrated framework for locating SCM research. It also provided clarification and coordination of disparate research work existing in area of SCM.

The literature available on SCM provided a detailed perspective of the terms, its definitions, its relationship with other terminologies. The authors also discuss about the literature of SCM specific to the Indian perspective as local factors comes into play and those factors influence the working of the supply chain function of a company. This has been tabulated in table 2.

In table 2, the focus has been narrowed down to the literature available on supply chain domain which were specific to the Indian context.

Continuing with literature review research papers highlighting the Supply Chain Drivers (SCD), Supply Chain Operations Reference (SCOR) model and Business Models Canvas (BMC) were also thus reviewed. The SCOR model stood for supply chain operations reference model. The model illustrated the interlinkages between the different areas of supply chain such as Plan, Source, Make, Deliver and Return. These areas of supply chain were valid for every member of supply chain i.e. suppliers, manufacturers and distributors. A Business model has been defined as a logical basis in which the businesses create value and deliver them. The model has various components or headers linked to each other.

Customer segment indicated that for which type of the customers the organization is creating the value.

Value proposition indicated the value which the startups would be offering to their customers.

Channels depicted the different types of methods used by startups to communicate with the customers. Customer relationships indicated how the startups connected with its customers to aid.

Revenue streams indicated exactly how the startups are generating revenues from the customers.

Key resources provided details about the important assets which are needed to run the business and generate profit.

Table 2. Literature and methodology review on SCM in Indian context

S. No.	Authors	Methodology	Findings
1.	Sahay and Mohan (2003)	Survey questionnaire was designed to capture the facts, figures and responses about SCM practices.	SCM strategies in Indian companies should align themselves with the business strategy. Technological intervention could play a major role in this area of SCM integration
2.	Srivastava (2006)	Observation and informal interviews of middle and top management were conducted	Logistics and SCM practices were influenced by factors such as the type of industry, firm size, its position in the supply chain, supply chain length and the type of supply chain.
3.	Sahay, Gupta and Mohan (2006)	Questionnaire was used to collect data and statistical analysis was performed on it	Indian organization should align its SCM strategy, their activities with business goals and strategy.
4.	Sahay and Mohan (2006)	Data was collected through survey questionnaire and was used to establish impact of usage of 3PL services on business performance through statistical analysis.	3PL services had positive impact on business performance.
5.	Subrahmanya (2017)	Reviewed empirical literature and personal interview was conducted to understand the entrepreneurial ecosystem in the cities of Hyderabad and Bangalore.	Similarities and differences in the entrepreneurial environment of Bangalore and Hyderabad was found and tabulated.
6.	Manikkandan and Karthikeyan (2016)	Reviewed literature and discussed the startup environment in India on logistics.	Problems and opportunities related to the logistics startups were identified.

Key activities depicted that the actions which were taken by the startup to operate the business. Key partnership explored the different partners (customers, suppliers) who support business activities of the startup.

Cost structure provided details about the cost of service provided to the customer which is borne by the startup.

Table-3 tabulated the content of literature on these topics.

The papers available in SCM literature had discussed that the challenges faced by Indian companies were different from the European or American companies. Hence, one can clearly notice that the available research papers addressed the following:

1. The definition of the terminology of supply chain, SCM and various cross-functional relationship of supply chain.
2. Focused on improving the already present supply chain functional domain in the companies by focusing on better coordination and increased technological enhancements.
3. The startup environment in India in different domains and not being any specific to SCM.

So, one can clearly notice that there are research gaps as literature which discussed supply chain startups in Indian environment were not available. Thus, this paper addresses the research gap using secondary sources based on cross case analysis.

RESEARCH GAP AND RESEARCH OBJECTIVES

The study done by Sahay & Mohan (2003) laid emphasized on the strategies to be followed by Indian companies and advocated that its business strategy should be aligned with supply chain strategies. The paper considered, the different established players but did not focus on startups. The article on logistics

Table 3. Literature and methodology review on SCD, SCOR and BMC

S. No.	Authors	Methodology	Findings
1.	Delipinar and Kocaoglu (2016)	Evaluated articles based on the Supply Chain Operations Reference (SCOR) model.	Research gap was found and observations and recommendations were reported.
2.	Lockamy and McCormack (2004)	Literature on SCM were reviewed and survey was done.	Provided a comparative framework for the supply chain practices
3.	Mishra et. al. (2018)	Citation and co-citation analysis was performed.	Trends in supply chain research areas was found out which would help managers to diversify the supply chain performance measures and metrics.
4.	Georgise et. al. (2017)	Secondary research as well as primary research was carried out.	Applicability of SCOR Model in manufacturing sector of developing countries was found out.
5.	Souza (2014)	SCOR model was used and application of analytics in each level of SCOR model was reviewed.	Highlighted the application of supply chain analytics using SCOR model for each level of decision making.
6.	Pineiro et. al. (2017)	Business Model Canvas (BMC) was used to analyze the cases of the startups	Four startups were evaluated based on BMC and the findings indicated that the startup that did not follow the BMC was successful.

and supply chain practices by Shrivastava (2015), talked about influence of contextual factors such as type of industry, firm size and such others on the supply chain practices and logistics practices. This paper however kept a window for discussion about supply chain startups. Another paper on supply chain discussed impact of 3PL services on business performance (Sahay & Mohan, 2006). This paper left a scope for discussion on the role that supply chain startups could play in improving the efficiency of the businesses. One of the paper discussed about the entrepreneurial environment in Bangalore and Hyderabad in a comparative study (Subrahmanya. 2017). However, this paper didn't discuss about supply chain startups present in these regions. Manikkandan and Karthikeyan (2016) discussed about the problems faced by logistics startups. The major gap present is that there is very limited number of literature available on startups in India and still lesser number available for supply chain startups in India. Indian perspective on SCM startups are not there sufficiently. The current scenario in India is that the Indian economy has been growing at the rate of 6.7% per year and new data on economy demonstrated that economy would continue to grow by more than 7% in coming years ("Indian Economy: Overview", 2018). In this growing economy, startups play a major role in creating jobs. Logistics has been given an infrastructure status (Press Trust of India, 2017). and hence supply chain startups would play a major role in this unorganized sector. So, there exists a gap in the research as there is no study on supply chain startups in India. Thus, this paper explores the area of supply chain startups in India and how these startups help in solving the problems of supply chain in Indian scenario by restructuring it. Thus, the authors study Indian supply chain startups using comparative case study analysis.

1. Using comparative case analysis, the authors have studied
   a. Business models of Indian supply chain Startups
   b. Supply chain drivers on which SCM startups are focusing
   c. To assess the SCM startups using SCOR model

RESEARCH METHODOLOGY

Ten cases on Indian supply chain startups were analyzed using cross case synthesis method (Yin, 2000). The scope of this study was supply chain startups in India which were founded in this decade (2010-March 2018) considering various drivers of supply chain. This study focused on such startups which had received at least Pre-series A funding. This technique is specially applied for analysis of multiple cases. The case studies of startups were formulated as a part of this paper. For using the cross-case analysis, the authors created a word table that displayed the data from individual cases according to some uniform framework. The frameworks used in this study were:

1. Supply Chain Driver (Chopra & Meindl, 2013):
2. SCOR Model (Delipinar & Kocaoglu, 2016):
3. Business Model Canvas (Pineiro, Oliveira et. al.,2017):

The steps involved for analyzing the cases were:

1. For Supply Chain Driver Analysis:
    a. The startups were of supply chain domain, so, supply chain drivers were selected for analyzing the cases.
    b. A matrix with supply chain drivers in rows and startups in columns was constructed and based on analysis of cases, they were marked in the matrix.
    c. This matrix provides an insight about the major drivers on which the supply chain startups are focusing.
2. For SCOR Model Analysis:
    a. The matrix with columns Plan, Make, Source, Deliver and Return and with sub-columns as Strategic, Tactical and Operational were formed.
    b. The rows consisted of the names of startups.
    c. Each of the 10 cases were analyzed and the depending upon the focus area of the startups and the level (Strategic, Tactical and Operational) at which they were operating or assisting in the supply chain.
3. For Business Model Canvas analysis: The following steps were followed to analyze the cases using business model canvas. The matrix was formed with columns with all the components of the business model canvas. The rows were formed with the startups. The matrix provided the detailed idea about the business model of each of the startups where each cell contained details about one of the component of the startup. The following were components that were analyzed for startups:
    a. Customer segments were analyzed for startups to know different type of customers the startups target.
    b. Value proposition for the startups were analyzed based on their offering to the customers.
    c. Channels through which startups communicate with the customers were documented.
    d. Customer relationship for the startups connect with its customers to aid.
    e. Revenue streams were analyzed for the startups which gave details about how the startups are generating revenues from the customers.
    f. Resources provided details about the assets of the startups.
    g. Key activities of the startups were analyzed which were carried out by them to run the business.
    h. Key partnership explored the different partners (customers, suppliers) who support business activities of the startup.
    i. Cost Structure provided details about the cost of service provided by the startup.

Secondary Data on SC Startups

The cases have been tabulated in table 4.

DATA ANALYSIS AND FINDINGS

The cross-case analysis in this domain of SCM (Azevedo, Carvalho, Cruz, & Machado,2011) had been conducted for analyzing the cases of the green SCM practices on firms. This paper uses similar analysis for different startup cases based on the supply chain drivers (Chopra & Meindl, 2013). The drivers of supply chain interact with each other. The drivers were of two types: Cross functional and Logistical drivers. The interaction between the drivers decided the efficiency and responsiveness of the supply

Table 4. Indian SCM startup details

Startups	Founder	Background	Business Opportunity	Business Model	Product or Services offered	Funding	Strengths	Challenges
Rivigo	Deepak Garg and Gazal Kalra	Deepak is an alumnus of IIT Kanpur, IIML and worked with McKinsey (Deepak G, 2018). Gazal is a graduate from IIT Delhi and MBA from Stanford University (Gazal, 2018).	Slow-moving traffic (The Indian Pony Express, 2018) resulting in higher costs of movement of goods, High turnaround time, (Press trust of India, 2016) inhumane treatment for the truck drivers (Gooptu,2017).	Customers were charged based on subscription fees and contracts.	Transportation services were provided using relay model (Rizwana, 2016).	Series D by SAIF Partners (Gooptu, 2017)	Operated its own fleet of trucks, uses algorithms to optimize the routes, fuel efficiency, driver productivity (Bhagayathula, n.d)	Present day challenge is related to GOI stringent norms on pollution (Gooptu, 2017).
BlackBuck	Chanakya Hridaya, Rajesh Yabaji and Rama Subramaniam	Chanakya is an alumnus of IIT Kharagpur. He has worked with ITC (Chanakya, 2018) Rajesh also did his graduation from IIT Kharagpur and joined ITC (Rajesh, 2018). Rama was consultant for ITC and was working with Miebach Consulting before joining ITC (Rama, 2018).	Indian Logistics industry was highly unorganized sector with trucks travelling less than half the distance in a day than in developed countries (Medium, n.d). It targeted the inefficiencies using technology.	Transaction fees and subscription-based fees were charged by Blackbuck for using its services (Dasgupta, 2017).	Transportation services were provided to shippers as well as fleet owners.	Series C funding by Sands Capital (Ganguly, 2017)	Direct Procurement channel, Quality Benchmarking, monitoring and transportation analytics use were some of its strength (Sangwan, 2016)	Routing provided using google maps were not taking truck type into account. Also, there is problem of higher cost which was optimized using algorithms and analytics (Sangwan, 2016).
Delhivery	Bhavesh Manglani, Kapil Bharati, Mohit Tandon, Sahil Barua and Suraj Saharan	Bhavesh is an alumnus of IIMC and had worked with Reliance (Bhavesh, 2018) Kapil is an alumnus of IITD and had worked with Sapient (Kapil, 2018). Mohit is an alumnus of IITK and had worked with Bain & Company (Mohit, 2018). Sahil is an alumnus of IIMB (Sahil, 2018). Suraj graduated from IITB and was project manager at UIDAI (Suraj, 2018).	Last mile delivery for products were operated by the e-commerce players and was inefficient (Ekart, n.d) This gap served as a business opportunity for Delhivery.	Service contracts with the customers and pay per shipment were the modes of revenue generation.	Transportation services for last mile delivery and customized transportation services (Menezes, 2017).	Series D funding from Tiger Global Management (Shu, 2015).	Used Data Science and Artificial Intelligence (Mishra, 2016). Also, it had strong network of fulfilment centers (Shrivastava, 2015).	External threats from the competition provided a major challenge (Pani, 2017)
Ninjakart	Kartheeswaran KK, Ashutosh Vikram, Thirukumaran Nagrajan, Sharath Lognathan	Kartheeswaran is an IIMA alumnus and had worked for Taxiforsure (Kartheeswaran, 2018). Ashutosh is an alumnus of IIMK and was associated with Ola (Ashutosh, 2018). Thirukumaran is also an IIMK alumnus and was associated with Taxiforsure (Thirukumaran, 2018). Sharath also graduated from IIMK and had worked with financial inclusion and operations Ltd (Sharath, 2018).	The direct communication gap which existed between the farmers and retailers served as a business opportunity (Ninjacart, 2015).	They charged a fixed fulfillment fees from the retailers.	Marketplace for farmers and retailers (Team YS, 2017)	Series B (Chitral, 2017)	The major strength lied in its data. It had developed a future ready ERP which enabled to incorporate major flexibility (Rao, 2016). The company also has a mobile ERP which helped to reduce paper SCM (Medium, 2017).	They are facing difficulty in tackling the changing of professions by the farmers and their suicides (Vardhan, 2017). The products procured by the Ninjacart were perishable in nature and hence supply chain should be robust to prevent wastage (Vardhan, 2017).

continued on following page

Table 4. Continued

Locus	Nishith Rastogi and Geet Garg	Nishith is an alumnus of BITS Pilani. He had worked for eBay, Amazon (Nishith, 2018). Geet Garg is an alumnus of IIT Kharagpur. He had been associated with Amazon (Geet, 2018).	Scheduling, tracking on-field fleet, was a common problem being faced by several startups in the on-demand and hyperlocal industry (Vignesh,2016). This served as a business gap.	Pay per transaction model was used and some value-added services were charged.	Route optimization for intra-city logistics using optimization software (D'Cunha, 2017).	Series A fund from Exfinity Venture Partners (Singh, 2016).	Route planning and optimization engine takes into consideration real world conditions (Mukherjee, 2016). Locus has a geocoder which solves problems to provide accurate locations.	Unorganized truck ownership and poor infrastructure (Digifire, 2016).
The Porter	Pranav Goel, Vikas Choudhary and Uttam Digga	Pranav Goel had been associated with Cognizant and J P Morgan (Pranav, 2018). Vikas is an alumnus of IIT Kanpur. He was working with Juniper Networks (Vikas, 2018). Uttam Digga was associated with HSBC and J P Morgan (Uttam, 2018).	Unorganized and hence, the utilization rate was low for all the three legs of Logistics (Intercity Logistics, Intracity Logistics, Last Mile Delivery) (Farooqui, 2015).	For each trip a certain amount was charged and was paid by the driver.	Real time update of the vehicle and helped the shipper to get the vehicle (Mahindra partners, 2018). This matches demand with the supply.	Series A fund from Sequoia capital and Kae capital (Vardaan, 2015).	Varied range of vehicle at its disposal and standard process of the booking provided high rate of vehicle utilization (Farooqui, 2015).	The overloading of vehicle from the customer side or the transporter side is a major problem and a safety issue (Das, 2017).
Pharmarack	Pradyumn Singh, Bhavik Parmar and Kushal Bhandari	Pradyumn had worked with firms like Tata Mutual funds, Edelweiss (Pradyumn, 2018). Bhavik had work experience with Capillary technologies (Bhavik, 2018). Kushal had been associated with DSIJ, NIC (Kushal, 2018).	To make supply chain more efficient it provides more visibility to the customers about inventories across geographies (Nair, n.d).	Pay as you go plan and enterprise plan was used to generate revenue.	Software for SCM	Pre-Series A Rs 4.5 crore from Currae Healthtech and Unicorn India Ventures (Choudhury, 2017).	Mobile first strategy focused on mobile customers, flexible software that could be aligned with B2B, Intelligent systems at every level of SCM for better decision-making capacity (Sharma, 2016).	The major challenge was to educate the customer about using the software (Pharmarack, 2018). The other challenge was to handle the expired medicines (Tiwari, 2017).
Blowhorn	Nikhil Shivaprasad and Mithun Srivatsa	Nikhil is an electrical engineer by profession (Nikhil, 2018). Mithun is a mechanical engineer and did his MBA from Cambridge university (Mithun, 2018)	Intra-city logistics had gained prominence due to e-commerce (Jose, 2018) and were unable to provide efficiencies for fixed contracts.	Fixed contracts as well as spot booking for the customers (Blowhorn, 2018)	It provided a platform to the shippers and fleet owners (Shah, 2017). Hence, matching demand with the supply.	Series A fund from the Michael Dell foundation, Draper Associates (Shah, 2017).	They use technology to efficiently deliver goods and maximize the volume of goods in each trip (Fok, 2015).	Tough competition in the market (Owler, n.d)
Box My Space	Pratyush Jalan	Pratyush had done his graduation from Manipal Institute of Technology and Cornell University. He had worked with Microsoft and Qualcomm (Pratyush, 2018).	Huge market potential for storage facility as space is shrinking in cities like Mumbai (Vardhan, 2015).	Monthly storage plans were used to generate revenue from the customers (Vardhan, 2015).	Pick-up and drop-off of items and warehouse facilities (Ghildiyal, 2017).	Pre-series A funding from R. Jayakumar (Gupta, 2017).	The strength lies in their USP of concept of self-storage. The technological assistance helped in fare pricing and transparency in tracking and security of items (Vardhan, 2015).	The major challenge was in marketing this new concept of rental storage (Vardhan, 2015). among masses and to convince them. Competition from other players (Kuriakose, 2015).

continued on following page

Table 4. Continued

Frontal Rain Technologies	Jayaram Srinivasan, Ravi Mandayam and Sreeram P	Jayaram, Ravi and Sreeram were working with SAP (Ghosh, 2015).	The challenges for farmers were mainly pricing, market access and low farm productivity which is the result of lower technological access (Sharma, 2012). This served as a business gap.	They charged a subscription fees for using their software (FrontalRain Technologies, n.d)	Software for SCM	Series A funding from Omnivore Capital (Sainul, 2012).	Provided software to integrate the e-commerce, mobile services which helps in interaction with the customer (Food Supply Chain, n.d)	The major challenge was to keep harvest loss as low as possible (FrontalRain Technologies, n.d)

chain. As per authors study, Table-5 demonstrate the drivers of supply chain on which the supply chain startups have been focusing significantly.

As per Table-5 findings were:

1. Rivigo focused on logistics driver with its network. It focused on businesses like e-commerce and provided vehicles with temperature controlled environment.
2. BlackBuck was an online marketplace platform for freight where shippers and fleet operators could interact with each other. It helped in meeting supply and demand.
3. Delhivery was a third-party logistics service provider which worked into the segment of last mile delivery. It also had its fulfilment centers.
4. Ninjacart was an agri-marketing platform for fruits and vegetables. It enabled farmers to connect directly with the retailers and thus eliminated the middle men.
5. Locus provided a platform to enterprises where they could schedule their on-demand deliveries and scheduled deliveries in an intra-city environment.
6. The Porter was an on-demand logistics marketplace which provided commercial vehicles through bookings via app.
7. Frontal rain technology was a supply chain software making company which offered services to agri-business companies through cloud.

Table 5. Indian SCM startups and SCD (Chopra & Meindl, 2013)

Supply Chain Drivers	Companies									
	Rivigo	BlackBuck	Delhivery	Ninjakart	Locus	The Porter	Frontal Rain Technologies	Pharmarack	Blowhorn	Box My Space
Logistical Drivers										
• Facilities										j
• Inventory										
• Transportation	a	b	c			f			i	
Cross Functional Drivers										
• Information					e		g	h		
• Sourcing				d						
• Pricing										

8. Pharmarack is a healthcare focused product company which designs simple tools to better manage the supply chain.
9 Blowhorn used technology to create an asset light, efficient marketplace for logistics.
10. Box my space was a startup which provided space related solutions to its customers using technology and value addition.

Table-5 depicted that five startups out of the ten considered for the study focused its operation on the transportation driver of SCM. Three of the SCM startups focused on information and IT support for the SCM. These new technologies were on artificial intelligence, IoT which helped in omitting the inefficiencies in the logistical drivers. Less number of startups were into the facility driver which was evident from Table-5. The second analysis of the cases was done using the Supply Chain Operations Reference Model (SCOR). Table-6 depicted the analysis.

One should note that as per the authors, blank spaces indicated that authors had felt that the firm though made an impact on this dimension of supply chain but was not focusing significantly on it. Table-6, depicted the areas of supply chain such as Plan, Source, Make, Deliver and Return. The areas had levels of decision or operations. The supply chain startups were categorized into these levels where they operated significantly. The authors believed that other levels of the area of supply chain were impacted but they were not impacted significantly, thus not reported in this paper.

The findings have been tabulated in Table-7.

The analysis demonstrated that six out of ten startups were working in delivery, and thus supported operational activities and decision making. Two out of ten startups worked in sourcing area and supported tactical decisions and activities. Rest of the startups worked in make area of the SCM and supported tactical decisions and activities.

The third analysis was carried out using business model canvas. The business model canvas depicted the different components and their linkages with each other. It provided the logical context in which the

Table 6. Indian SCM startups and SCOR model (Delipinar & Kocaoglu, 2016)

Startup	SCOR Model														
	Plan			Make			Source			Deliver			Return		
	Strategic	Tactical	Ops.	Strategic	Tactical	Ops.	Strategic	Tactical	Ops.	Strategic	Tactical	Ops.	Strategic	Tactical	Ops.
Rivigo												1			
BlackBuck												2			
Delhivery												3			
Ninjakart								4							
Locus												5			
The Porter												6			
Frontal Rain Technologies								7							
Pharmarack					8										
Blowhorn												9			
Box My Space					10										

Table 7. Indian SCM startups and SCOR model

1	It worked to deliver the operational efficiency to the logistics and to make logistics more human centric.
2	It was an online market platform where both shipper and transporter could engage. It helped in price discovery, route optimization and brought operational efficiency.
3	It was a Logistics player which provided tailormade solutions to the small as well as large business.
4	It provided an online marketplace to the farmers, so that they could sell their products directly to the retailers.
5	It provided on-demand logistics support and optimizes vehicle routes to reduce the cost.
6	It was an on-demand logistics service provider which aggregated the demand and serves through commercial vehicles at its disposal.
7	It provided a cloud based platform to the companies in agribusiness where they could interact with their suppliers and customers.
8	It provided a platform to the drug manufacturer so that it could have a clear visibility of the inventory across geographies which would help in better planning and prevent stock out.
9	It focused on intra-city logistics where its focus was on being asset light and provide maximum efficiency to the clients through technological intervention.
10	It managed the warehouse infrastructure and assisted in order tracking and dispatch through the warehouse at SKU level.

business created value. Table-8 portrayed the different components of the business model populated in columns and startups were populated in rows.

DISCUSSION

Based on the above multi-case analysis one can clearly notice that customer segments could be divided into mainly business (large firms, medium small and micro enterprises) and individual customers such as farmers and retailers. The startups having customer segment as firms were Rivigo, Delhivery and BlackBuck. The startups focusing on local businesses and individuals were Locus, Blowhorn and Porter. The firms having agribusiness and farmers as their customers were Frontal Rain technologies and Ninjacart. Pharmarack and Box my space focused on the pharma supply chain and B2C as well as B2B customers respectively.

The analysis of the startups reveals that they are helping the firms and individuals to restructure their supply chain. The value these startups delivered to their customers were reduced cost, fair pricing and improved efficiency. The transformation of supply chain has three important dimensions- people, technology and information. The channels through which customer interaction was carried out was through online marketplace application. The facilities provided through apps were direct tracking of shipments, online booking of shipments and return shipments were also arranged. Hence, the information flow and the technology helped to provide hassle-free experience to the user.

The revenue models used by these startups were based on Pay per use (Gupta, 2014), Fixed fulfilment rate model, subscription model for software and Monthly plans (Vardhan, 2015).

Most of these startups were asset light and through this these firms minimized the losses. The resources held within these startups were mainly a series of funding, software development team and fleet

Table 8. Business model canvas (Pineiro, Oliveira et. al.,2017)

Startups	*Customer Segments*	*Value Proposition*	*Channels*	*Customer Relationships*	*Revenue Streams*	*Key Resources*	*Key Activities*	*Key Partnership*	*Cost Structure*
Rivigo	Large firms, MSMEs and Individual Clients	Cost Reduction, Efficiency, Reliability and Transparency	Online Booking, Fleet of GPS Enabled Trucks	Automated Services and customized solutions for the customers	Advertising, Usage fees and subscription based fees	Fleet of Trucks, Drivers, Employees, Series of Funding	Transportation Service and customized solutions provider through its relay model	Truck Drivers, OEM Manufacturers, Clients such as large and MSM firms	Fixed Costs related to Trucks and Pit Stops, Variable cost of operation and maintenance of vehicles, Salary of Employees
BlackBuck	Shippers and Fleet Operators	Cost Reduction, route optimization and transparency	Online marketplace for shippers and fleet owners	Automated Services and marketplace for shippers and fleet owner through mobile apps	Transaction commission and subscription fees along with the option of insurance purchase	Fleet owners and shippers, Employees, Technology based resources, Funding	Marketplace for Shippers as well as Fleet owners, provides quality benchmarking and uses transportation analytics	Shippers, Fleet owners, Business partners such as IOCL, Insurance companies	Operating cost of application, salary of employees, cost involved with optimization of truck routes
Delhivery	Large firms, MSMEs, E-commerce and Individual Clients	Last mile delivery and tailormade solution for logistics	Service contract based booking	Web tracking and warehouse services though internet	Service contracts and pay per courier charges	Fleet of Trucks, Drivers, Employees, Series of Funding and warehousing solutions	Last mile delivery and customized transportation services	Truck Drivers, OEM Manufacturers, Clients such as large and MSM firms	Office, manpower, technology expenditure, Fixed cost related to trucks and operational costs
Ninjakart	Farmers and Retailers	Reduced price and more revenue	Online marketplace for farmers and retailers	Directly moving the produce from farm to retailers, connecting the farmers to retailers through mobile app	Fixed fulfilment fees from the Retailers	Fleet of Trucks, Technology driven supply chain, Series of Fundings	Marketplace for farmers and retailers, Educate farmers about pricing and market, transportation of goods from farmers to retailers	Truck Drivers, Farmers, Retailers	Fixed costs related to trucks, operational cost and expenditure on technology
Locus	local companies, enterprises in courier, e-commerce, food delivery, FMCG	Efficiency in logistics using automation and technology	On-demand service for automation in logistics	Web tracking and providing notification for quicker timely deliveries	Pay per transaction model	Route planning and optimization development team, Funding	Optimization for intra-city logistics using automation and geolocation	Intra-city players in e-commerce, FMCG, food delivery	Operational and Fixed costs related to automation and technology
The Porter	local companies, enterprises in courier, e-commerce, individuals	Reducing Inefficiencies and cost savings	Online marketplace for shippers and fleet owners	Web tracking through apps and on-demand supply of trucks through bookings	Commission is charged for each trip and is paid by the driver	Fleet of Truck owners, Mobile application development team, Series of Fundings	Real time tracking of vehicles, availability of vehicles and matching of supply and demand	Vehicle owners, Customers	Operational and Fixed costs related to automation and technology
Frontal Rain Technologies	Small and Large-scale agribusiness firms	High Productivity. Lower Cost and better communication	On-demand software as a service on cloud through web sales.	Automated Services are given to the customers.	Subscription fees for using the software	Software development team and the leadership team, Series of fundings (Funding type A)	Software development for support, training, implementation	Clients in procurement, dispatch, processing, trade including large and small firms	Operational and Fixed costs related to development of the software
Pharmarack	Pharma Value chain starting from Company, C&F, Distributors, Retailers	Revenue growth. Reduction in cost, improved productivity	On-demand software service	Automated Services are given to the customers.	Pay as you go plan as well as enterprise plan are provided to the companies	Software development team and the leadership team, Series of fundings	Software development for managing daily business as well as intelligence system for making informed decision	Customers which includes (Retailers, Distributors, C&F and companies)	Operational and Fixed costs related to the development of the software

continued on following page

Table 8. Continued

Startups	Customer Segments	Value Proposition	Channels	Customer Relationships	Revenue Streams	Key Resources	Key Activities	Key Partnership	Cost Structure
Blowhorn	B2C market for spot market	Reducing Inefficiencies and cost savings	On-demand online marketplace for shippers and fleet owners	Automated services such as mobile apps help in web-tracking and booking for spot requirement	Fixed contract and Spot booking for the services	Fleet of Truck owners, Mobile application development team, Series of Fundings	Aggregation of Demand for transportation of goods in an intra-city environment	Vehicle owners, Customers	Operational and fixed costs related to development of the software and contracting with the fleet owners
Box My Space	B2C as well as B2B market (e-commerce, Food Products)	Decluttering homes, Clear pricing	On-demand warehousing space provider	Automated Services such as tracking the boxes and recalling the boxes	Monthly storage plans for Boxes and Spaces	Warehousing space, Pickup and drop off vehicles, series of fundings	Pick up of items and storage of items in warehouses	Warehouse owners, vehicle owners, Customers	Operational cost of warehouse and pickup and delivery, Costs associated with mobile application

of trucks which were owned by the startup in case of Rivigo. One of the key metrics for supply chain restructuring is people. The unique selling proposition of Rivigo is their relay model. The truck drivers operate in relay which increases efficiency. The startups which focused on transportation drivers were responsible for carrying key activities as customized transportation services and further provided benchmarking services in terms of quality using analytical tools. Startups like Ninjakart educated farmers about the pricing and market working apart from sourcing the produce from the farmers. Startups like Frontal Rain Technologies provided software support for the agribusinesses.

The startups were mostly asset light and these firm partnered with the other firms which provided for the assets. The key partners for these startups included its customers, suppliers or both. For the SCM startup firms focusing on the transportation driver of the partners were truck owners and truck drivers. For enabling the supply chain restructuring, the useful measure would be imparting education. The startups such as Ninjacart enables farmers by providing them education related to market and pricing. Farmers and retailers were the partners for the startup which focused on the agribusiness. The customers were partners for the agribusiness software solution providers such as Frontal Rain Technology. Box my space had warehouse owners as its partners.

The cost structure of the SCM startups could be divided into two categories, fixed costs and variable costs (Wang & Yang, 2001). The operational cost was the variable component (Murray, 2015). The startups which had its own trucks were having higher fixed costs such as Rivigo. The operational cost was also related to the level of automation and technological interventions applied in the firm.

CONCLUSION

Ten Indian SCM startup cases were analyzed using different frameworks using the methodology of cross case analysis (Yin, 2003). The analysis revealed that the prominent drivers (Chopra, 2013) on which the supply chain startups were focusing were transportation and information. The startups were focusing on improving the efficiency and increasing the responsiveness of the supply chain. The business models of these startups were also examined using Business Model Canvas (Pineiro, 2017). The BMC analysis helped us to relate the different components of business models with each other and help us to understand the logic behind creating the customers. The third analysis of the cases was carried out with respect to the area of supply chain on which these startups were focusing. It also revealed that at which level of decision making the startups were helping its customers. This analysis was done using SCOR model (Delipinar & Kocaoglu, 2016). The model based analysis demonstrated that most of the Indian SCM startups helped in operational activities of their customers. There were more number of startups in the area of "Delivery" of the supply chain in SCOR model than in any other area. The startups mentioned in cases focus mostly on improving the efficiency of the firms. These startups work mostly in handling the operations for the firm like in the case of Rivigo, Blackbuck and Delhivery. They help in restructuring the supply chain of the companies by providing the logistics solutions at a lower cost. In India, where the logistics amount to around 14% of the GDP, the role of these startups becomes significant. The startups also focus on the data and technological interventions which help the firms to gather insights. These insights help them to redesign their supply chain. Frontal Rain Technology is one such startup which has helped its customer firms to improve the productivity and better the communication. This flow of information results in better coordination among the functions which earlier used to work in silos, hence, improving the responsiveness of the firm. One of the factors which hinders the cost competitiveness of the Indian farmers is the presence of intermediaries. Indian farmers often have less or no visibility of market pricing hence they get less price for their produce and intermediaries make profit. The startups like Ninjacart helps the farmers by moving their farm produce directly from farm to market using its own fleet. It uses technology to create a marketplace for the farmers which helps them in price discovery and educate them to maximize the output. This agribusiness model has restructured the supply chain by eliminating the middlemen by focusing on the technological interventions. These startups played a significant role in the Indian economy. India was ranked 3rd among all the startup ecosystems (NASSCOM-Zinnov, 2015). The average age of a startup founder was 28 years in India. India also had more than 50% population below the age of 25 years (Basu, BBC, 2004). One could notice that more jobs were needed for this young population as they reached the working age group and the startups would play a significant role in job creation (Tyagi, YourStory, 2016). Therefore, startups in India assume a significant role in her development. Supply chain has been cost center for any company (Backer, 2017). Customer experience has been directly affected by the responsiveness and efficiency of the company (Meulen, *Gartner*, 2017). So, to reduce inefficiency and make supply chain responsive, the technological interventions and innovative business models of startups have assumed importance.

The analysis of supply chain startups was beneficial for managers in more than one way. Supply chain managers should consider two major tradeoffs between two characteristics, efficiency and responsiveness (Chopra & Meindl, 2013). The profit center for any business has been its customers (Drucker, 2002). Customer service had direct impact on a company's brand and reputation (McCall, 2017). Supply chain startups could help firms to get more insights and improve the business while the firm itself could focus on its core competency.

Supply chain startups could also serve as third party for firms and could generate useful insights while engaging in last mile delivery which could be beneficial for firms in business expansion. Supply chain startups such as Frontal Rain technologies focused on information driver. They provided IT support for agribusinesses which helped the managers to generate more visibility of firm products. Thus, study on supply chain startups also provided an insight to the potential business gaps which were being addressed by the startups to make a more efficient and responsive supply chain. Future research work can be carried out using primary research data from startups and analyzing it through other frameworks incorporating financial aspects on SCM also.

REFERENCES

Adams, R., Alexander, A., & Oberg, C. (2014). *Innovation Management Capabilities for Start-Ups and Spin-Offs: A Literature Review*. Academic Press. doi:10.4471/redimat.2013.49

Ashutosh Vikram. (n.d.). In *LinkedIn*. Retrieved 20 April 2018, from https://www.linkedin.com/in/ashutoshvikram/

Azevedo, S. G., Carvalho, H., & Cruz Machado, V. (2011). The influence of green practices on supply chain performance: A case study approach. *Transportation Research Part E, Logistics and Transportation Review*, *47*(6), 850–871. doi:10.1016/j.tre.2011.05.017

Backer, S. A. (2017). *'Supply Chain' is traditionally considered as a 'cost center', how can you turn it into a 'profit center'? - Bayt.com Specialties*. Retrieved 24 April 2018, from https://www.bayt.com/en/specialties/q/357444/supply-chain-is-traditionally-considered-as-a-cost-center-how-can-you-turn-it-into-a-profit-center/

Basu, K. (2007). *India's demographic dividend*. Retrieved 24 April 2018, from http://news.bbc.co.uk/2/hi/south_asia/6911544.stm

Bhavesh Manglani. (n.d.). In *LinkedIn*. Retrieved 20 April 2018, from https://www.linkedin.com/in/bhavesh-manglani-14a3663/

Bhavik Parmar. (n.d.). In *LinkedIn*. Retrieved 20 April 2018, from https://www.linkedin.com/in/bhavik-parmar/

Blackbuck. (n.d.). Retrieved 20 April 2018, from https://www.blackbuck.com/company

Blowhorn! Mini-Trucks on hire in Bengaluru/Hyderabad/Chennai/Mumbai. (n.d.). Retrieved 24 April 2018, from https://blowhorn.com/solutions

BoxMySpace - FAQs | Frequently Asked Questions for Storage Needs. (n.d.). Retrieved 24 April 2018, from http://boxmyspace.com/faq

Capitalist, V. (2017). In *Investopedia*. Retrieved from https://www.investopedia.com/terms/s/startup.asp

Carter, C. R., Rogers, D. S., & Choi, T. Y. (2015). *sec1-further- Toward the theory of the supply chain*. Academic Press.

Chanakya Hridaya. (n.d.). In *LinkedIn*. Retrieved 20 April 2018, from https://www.linkedin.com/in/chanakya-hridaya-44743425/

Chen, I. J., & Paulraj, A. (2004). Understanding supply chain management: Critical research and a theoretical framework. *International Journal of Production Research*, *42*(1), 131–163. doi:10.1080/00207540310001602865

Chitral, R. (2017). *Agri-marketing platform Ninjacart raises $5.5 million - Times of India*. Retrieved 20 April 2018, from https://timesofindia.indiatimes.com/business/india-business/agri-marketing-platform-ninjacart-raises-5-5-million/articleshow/58119275.cms

Chopra, S., & Meindl, P. (2013), Supply Chain Management: Strategy, Planning, and Operations (3rd ed.). Prentice-Hall.

Choudhury, A. (2017). *How this Pune-based startup is automating the pharmaceutical supply chain management*. Retrieved 20 April 2018, from https://yourstory.com/2017/03/pharmarack-technologies-startup/

Community, K. (2017). *What role are Startups playing in the Digital Transformation of SCM?* Retrieved from https://medium.com/@KodiakRating/what-role-are-startups-playing-in-the-digital-transformation-of-supply-chain-management-d617ef2e6e4d

Competitors, B. Revenue and Employees - Owler Company Profile. (n.d.). Retrieved 24 April 2018, from https://www.owler.com/company/blowhorn

D'Cunha, S. (2017). *These Logistics Startups Are Tackling India's Infrastructural Challenges With AI And Big Data*. Retrieved 20 April 2018, from https://www.forbes.com/sites/suparnadutt/2017/11/15/these-logistics-startups-are-tackling-indias-infrastructural-challenges-with-ai-and-big-data/#6068e8eea7cf

Das, M. (2017). *Logistics start-up Porter loses a few customers as it says no to overloading - Business Line*. Retrieved 20 April 2018, from https://www.thehindubusinessline.com/economy/logistics/logistics-startup-porter-loses-a-few-customers-as-it-says-no-to-overloading/article9735224.ece

Dasgupta, M. (2017). *Logistics Startups Trukky, BlackBuck, ThePorter Are Revving Up With Logistics Management Apps*. Retrieved 20 April 2018, from https://medium.com/@MoumitaDasgupta/logistics-startups-trukky-blackbuck-theporter-are-revving-up-with-logistics-management-apps-d21c536a8c48

Deepak Garg. (n.d.). In *LinkedIn*. Retrieved 20 April 2018, from https://www.linkedin.com/in/deepak-garg-4204b439/

Delipinar, G. E., & Kocaoglu, B. (2016). Using SCOR Model to Gain Competitive Advantage: A Literature Review. *Procedia: Social and Behavioral Sciences*, *229*, 398–406. doi:10.1016/j.sbspro.2016.07.150

Drucker, P. (2003). *Managing in Next Society* (1st ed.). Oxford, UK: Butterworth-Heinemann.

Dvorkin, M. (2017). *Startups Create Many Jobs, but They Often Don't Last | St. Louis Fed*. Retrieved 19 April 2018, from https://www.stlouisfed.org/publications/regional-economist/third-quarter-2017/startups-create-many-jobs-but-they-often-dont-last

Ekart Logistics. (n.d.). Retrieved 20 April 2018, from https://www.ekartlogistics.com/about_us

Ellram, L. M., & Cooper, M. C. (2014). Supply Chain Management: It's All About the Journey, Not the Destination. *The Journal of Supply Chain Management*, *50*(1), 8–20. doi:10.1111/jscm.12043

Farooqui, M. (2015). *Want to shift your goods? Porter is a click away | Business Standard News*. Retrieved 20 April 2018, from http://www.business-standard.com/article/companies/want-to-shift-your-goods-porter-is-a-click-away-115092800008_1.html

Fok, E. (2015). *How ecommerce ventures are using 'milk-run' model to ensure last-mile delivery - The Economic Times*. Retrieved 24 April 2018, from https://economictimes.indiatimes.com/small-biz/startups/how-ecommerce-ventures-are-using-milk-run-model-to-ensure-last-mile-delivery/articleshow/47981225.cms

Freight, M. 'A Seamless Experience' – The BlackBuck Blog – Medium. (n.d.). Retrieved 24 April 2018, from https://medium.com/the-blackbuck-blog/making-freight-a-seamless-experience-156ec172ebe5

FrontalRain Technologies - Software for Agri Businesses | FrontalRain Technologies. (n.d.). Retrieved 24 April 2018, from http://www.frontalrain.com/plans/

Ganguly, P. (2017). *Funding: Trucking marketplace BlackBuck bags $70M from Sands Capital, others, Technology News, ETtech*. Retrieved 20 April 2018, from https://tech.economictimes.indiatimes.com/news/startups/trucking-marketplace-blackbuck-bags-70-m-from-sands-capital-others/57755778

Gazal Kalra. (n.d.). In *LinkedIn*. Retrieved 20 April 2018, from https://www.linkedin.com/in/gazal-kalra-a5b6523/

Geet Garg. (n.d.). In *LinkedIn*. Retrieved 20 April 2018, from https://www.linkedin.com/in/geetgarg/

Georgise, F. B., Wuest, T., & Thoben, K.-D. (2017). SCOR model application in developing countries: Challenges & requirements. *Production Planning and Control*, *28*(1), 17–32. doi:10.1080/09537287.2016.1230790

Ghildiyal, H. (2017). *BoxMySpace – Technology Enabled Warehousing and Logistics*. Retrieved 24 April 2018, from https://blog.boxmyspace.com/

Ghosh, S. (2015). *5 Indian Startups to boost the agriculture of the country - KnowStartup*. Retrieved 24 April 2018, from http://knowstartup.com/2015/07/startups-help-the-agriculture/

Giudice, V., & Lu, W. (2017). *India Seen Topping Global Labor Force In Next Decade, Data Show - Bloomberg*. Retrieved 19 April 2018, from https://www.bloomberg.com/news/articles/2017-08-31/india-seen-topping-global-labor-force-in-next-decade-data-show

Gooptu, B. (2017). *Rivigo: A roadside chat set me on my way for Rivigo moment: Deepak Garg, CEO, Rivigo - The Economic Times*. Retrieved 20 April 2018, from https://economictimes.indiatimes.com/small-biz/startups/features/a-roadside-chat-set-me-on-my-way-for-rivigo-moment-deepak-garg-ceo-rivigo/articleshow/62143469.cms

Göran, S. (2007). *Supply Chain Management versus Sustainable Chain Management*. Academic Press.

Gupta, B. (2017). *Exclusive: BoxMySpace raises pre-Series A funding from clutch of investors*. Retrieved 24 April 2018, from https://www.dealstreetasia.com/stories/exclusive-boxmyspace-raises-pre-series-funding-clutch-investors-79586/

Gupta, H. (2016). *E-startups: Online logistics marketplace Porter set to enter Pune and Ahmedabad - The Financial Express*. Retrieved 24 April 2018, from https://www.financialexpress.com/industry/estartups-online-logistics-marketplace-porter-set-to-enter-pune-and-ahmedabad/473460/

Harland, C. M. (1996). Supply Chain Management: Relationships, Chains and Networks. *British Journal of Management*, *7*(s1), S63–S80. doi:10.1111/j.1467-8551.1996.tb00148.x

Holloway, S. (2015). *Mobile Supply Chain Management Software | Software Research | Crozdesk*. Retrieved 19 April 2018, from https://crozdesk.com/software-research/mobile-supply-chain-management-software

Huppe, B. (2017). *Technology and the 'last mile' - Marketing Tech News*. Retrieved 19 April 2018, from https://www.marketingtechnews.net/news/2017/may/19/technology-and-last-mile/

iMIS - Welcome to the World of iMIS. (n.d.). Retrieved from https://cscmp.org/imis0/CSCMP/Educate/SCM_Definitions_and_Glossary_of_Terms

India loses $65 billion every year due to inefficient supply chain systems. (2010). Retrieved 20 April 2018, from https://www.moneylife.in/article/india-loses-65-billion-every-year-due-to-inefficient-supply-chain-systems/8786.html

Indian Economy: Overview, Market Size, Growth, Development, Statistics...IBEF. (2018). Retrieved 22 April 2018, from https://www.ibef.org/economy/indian-economy-overview

Indian Economy: Overview, Market Size, Growth, Development, Statistics...IBEF. (n.d.). Retrieved from https://www.ibef.org/economy/indian-economy-overview

International Labor Organization. (2017). *World Employment and Social Outlook Report*. Retrieved from: www.ilo.org/wcmsp5/groups/public/---dgreports/---.../wcms_541211.pdf

Interview with Nishith. Co-Founder at Locus – Digifire. (2016). Retrieved 20 April 2018, from https://www.digifire.in/2016/01/12/interview-with-nishith-co-founder-at-locus/

Iqbal, R. (n.d.). *Business week*. Retrieved from: http://bwdisrupt.businessworld.in/article/Rivigo-Disrupting-the-Logistics-Sector-With-Its-Unique-Driver-Relay-Model-and-Cutting-Edge-Technology-/16-08-2016-104469/

Joerss, M. (2016). *How customer demands are reshaping last-mile delivery | McKinsey & Company*. Retrieved 19 April 2018, from https://www.mckinsey.com/industries/travel-transport-and-logistics/our-insights/how-customer-demands-are-reshaping-last-mile-delivery

Jose, J. (2018). *Last mile intra-city logistics: The key to e-commerce customer satisfaction - Re-Tales by Jolly Jose | ET Retail*. Retrieved 26 April 2018, from https://retail.economictimes.indiatimes.com/re-tales/last-mile-intra-city-logistics-the-key-to-e-commerce-customer-satisfaction/2900

Kapil Bharati. (n.d.). In *LinkedIn*. Retrieved 20 April 2018, from https://www.linkedin.com/in/kbhara/

Kartheeswaran, K. K. (n.d.). In *LinkedIn*. Retrieved 20 April 2018, from https://www.linkedin.com/in/kartheeswarankk/

Kuriakose, S. (2015). *Don't box up*. Retrieved 24 April 2018, from http://www.dnaindia.com/mumbai/report-don-t-box-up-2056875

Kushal Bhandari. (n.d.). In *LinkedIn*. Retrieved 20 April 2018, from https://www.linkedin.com/in/kushal-bhandari-8518b51/

LeMay, S., Helms, M. M., Kimball, B., & McMahon, D. (2017). Supply chain management: The elusive concept and definition. *International Journal of Logistics Management*, *28*(4), 1425–1453. doi:10.1108/IJLM-10-2016-0232

Lockamy, A. III, & McCormack, K. (2004). Linking SCOR planning practices to supply chain performance. *International Journal of Operations & Production Management*, *24*(12), 1192–1218. doi:10.1108/01443570410569010

Locus.sh. Overview. (n.d.). In *LinkedIn*. Retrieved 20 April 2018, from https://www.linkedin.com/company/locus-sh/?originalSubdomain=in

Lummus, R. R., Krumwiede, D. W., & Vokurka, R. J. (2001). The relationship of logistics to supply chain management: Developing a common industry definition. *Industrial Management & Data Systems*, *101*(8), 426–432. doi:10.1108/02635570110406730

Mahindra Partners - Our Business. (n.d.). Retrieved 20 April 2018, from http://www.mahindrapartners.com/porter.html

Manikkandan, R., & Karthikeyan, P. (2016). A Study on Challenges Faced by Startups in Indian Logistics Sector. *Imperial Journal of Interdisciplinary Research*, *2*(11), 312–315. Retrieved from http://www.onlinejournal.in/IJIRV2I11/060.pdf

McCall, K. (2017). *Customer Experiences Impact Brand Reputation | Rival IQ*. Retrieved 24 April 2018, from https://www.rivaliq.com/blog/customer-experiences-business-reputation/

Menezes, R. (2017). *Delhivery losses 4 times higher than before; What's causing the money drain? | IndianOnlineSeller.com*. Retrieved 20 April 2018, from http://indianonlineseller.com/2017/01/delhivery-losses-4-times-higher-than-before-whats-causing-the-money-drain/

Min, S., & Mentzer, J. T. (2006). *The role of marketing in supply chain management*. Academic Press. doi:10.1016/S0019-8501(03)00032-4

Ministry of Finance. Government of India, (2016-17), Economic Survey. (n.d.). Available at: http://www.indiabudget.gov.in/survey.asp

Mishra, D., Gunasekaran, A., Papadopoulos, T., & Dubey, R. (n.d.). Supply chain performance measures and metrics: A bibliometric study. *Benchmarking. International Journal (Toronto, Ont.)*. doi:10.1108/BIJ-08-2017-0224

Mishra, P. (2016). *How data is making Delhivery India's first e-logistics unicorn | FactorDaily*. Retrieved 20 April 2018, from https://factordaily.com/logistics-delhivery-data-science/

Mithun Srivatsa. (n.d.). In *LinkedIn*. Retrieved 24 April 2018, from https://www.linkedin.com/in/mithunsrivatsa/

Mohit Tandon. (n.d.). In *LinkedIn*. Retrieved 20 April 2018, from https://www.linkedin.com/in/mohit-tandon-03b9046/

Moody's upgrade Sovereign Credit Rating of India to Baa2 from Baa3. (n.d.). Retrieved from http://pib.nic.in/newsite/PrintRelease.aspx?relid=173609

Mukherjee, S. (2016). *By 2020, we aim to automate all human decisions in logistics: Nishith Rastogi, Locus.sh*. Retrieved 20 April 2018, from https://techseen.com/2016/12/19/nishith-rastogi-locus-sh/

Murray, J. (2017). *How to Create a Business Startup Budget*. Retrieved 24 April 2018, from https://www.thebalancesmb.com/how-to-create-a-business-startup-budget-397500

Nair, L. (n.d.). *'We are trying to implement total automation across the supply chain' - BPD*. Retrieved 20 April 2018, from http://www.expressbpd.com/pharma/market-pharma/we-are-trying-to-implement-total-automation-across-the-supply-chain/384209/

NASSCOM. (2015). *Start-up India – Momentous Rise of the Indian Start-up Ecosystem*. Author.

NASSCOM-Zinnov. (2015). *Startup India Report*. Retrieved from http://www.nasscom.in/knowledge-center/publications/tech-start-ups-india-bright-future

Nikhil Shivaprasad. (n.d.). In *LinkedIn*. Retrieved 24 April 2018, from https://www.linkedin.com/in/nikhil-shivaprasad-1a2b6a8/

NinjaCart – India's largest Agri Marketing Platform. (n.d.). Retrieved 20 April 2018, from http://ninjacart.in/

Nishith Rastogi. (n.d.). In *LinkedIn*. Retrieved 20 April 2018, from https://www.linkedin.com/in/nishithrastogi/

Pani, P. (2017). *Logistics firm Delhivery's losses increase four-fold - Business Line*. Retrieved 26 April 2018, from https://www.thehindubusinessline.com/companies/logistics-firm-delhiverys-losses-increase-fourfold/article9455476.ece

Pharmarack | Crunchbase. (n.d.). Retrieved 20 April 2018, from https://www.crunchbase.com/organization/pharmarack

Pounder, P. (2013). A Review of Supply Chain Management and Its Main External Influential Factors in the global market economy Supply Chain. *Supply Chain Forum, 14*(3), 42–50. 10.13140/2.1.3787.3289

Pradyumn Singh. (n.d.). In *LinkedIn*. Retrieved 20 April 2018, from https://www.linkedin.com/in/pradyumn/

Pranav Goel. (n.d.). In *LinkedIn*. Retrieved 20 April 2018, from https://www.linkedin.com/in/pranav-goel-5570b138/

Pratyush Jalan. (n.d.). In *LinkedIn*. Retrieved 24 April 2018, from https://www.linkedin.com/in/pratyushjalan/

Press Trust of India. (2016). *Logistics firm Rivigo to treble truck fleet to 3,000 unit, banks on driver relay system*. Retrieved 20 April 2018, from https://yourstory.com/2016/05/logistics-firm-rivigo-banks-driver-relay-system/

Press Trust of India. (2018). *Infrastructure Status: Logistics sector gets infrastructure status - The Economic Times*. Retrieved 22 April 2018, from https://economictimes.indiatimes.com/news/economy/policy/logistics-sector-gets-infrastructure-status/articleshow/61724575.cms

Rajesh Yabaji. (n.d.). In *LinkedIn*. Retrieved 20 April 2018, from https://www.linkedin.com/in/rajesh-yabaji-302347a/

Ramasubramanian, B. (n.d.). In *LinkedIn*. Retrieved 20 April 2018, from https://www.linkedin.com/in/ramasubramanian-b-2a2b99/

Rao, M. (2016). *Ninjacart wants to make India's farmers tech savvy*. Retrieved 20 April 2018, from https://www.techinasia.com/ninjacart-data-tech-farms

Rivigo is helping the Indian truck-driving industry out of a jam - The Indian pony express. (2017). Retrieved 20 April 2018, from https://www.economist.com/news/business/21729811-its-pit-stops-and-relay-system-could-elevate-low-status-truck-drivers-rivigo-helping

Sahay, B. S., Gupta, J. N. D., & Mohan, R. (2006). Managing supply chains for competitiveness: The Indian scenario. *Supply Chain Management*, *11*(1), 15–24. doi:10.1108/13598540610642439

Sahay, B. S., & Mohan, R. (2003). Supply chain management practices in Indian industry. *International Journal of Physical Distribution & Logistics Management*, *33*(7), 582–606. doi:10.1108/09600030310499277

Sahay, B. S., & Mohan, R. (2006). 3PL practices: An Indian perspective. *International Journal of Physical Distribution & Logistics Management*, *36*(9), 666–689. doi:10.1108/09600030610710845

Sahil Barua. (n.d.). In *LinkedIn*. Retrieved 20 April 2018, from https://www.linkedin.com/in/sahil-barua-58a4096/

Sainul, K. (2012). *Agri-tech startup FrontalRain raises Rs 5Cr from Omnivore Capital | Techcircle*. Retrieved 24 April 2018, from http://techcircle.vccircle.com/2012/10/03/agri-tech-startup-frontalrain-raises-rs-5cr-from-omnivore-capital/

Sangwan, S. (2016). *BlackBuck an Online Marketplace for Logistics Transactions Helping Customers Move Full Truck Loads Between Cities - BW Disrupt*. Retrieved 20 April 2018, from http://bwdisrupt.businessworld.in/article/BlackBuck-An-Online-Marketplace-for-Logistics-Transactions-Helping-Customers-Move-Full-Truck-Loads-Between-Cities/03-07-2016-99946/

Schrauf Stefan, B. P. (2016). *Industry 4.0: How digitization makes the supply chain more efficient, agile, and customer-focused*. Retrieved 20 April 2018, from https://www.strategyand.pwc.com/reports/digitization-more-efficient

Shah, B. (2017). *'Disruptive Logistics Startup' Blowhorn raises Rs 25Cr, to expand to 8 cities*. Retrieved 24 April 2018, from https://yourstory.com/2017/03/logistics-startup-blowhorn-raises-rs-25cr/

Sharath Loganathan. (n.d.). In *LinkedIn*. Retrieved 20 April 2018, from https://www.linkedin.com/in/sharathloganathan/

Sharma, D. (2016). *Exclusive: SaaS startup Pharmarack raises pre-Series A funding | Techcircle*. Retrieved 20 April 2018, from http://techcircle.vccircle.com/2016/09/22/exclusive-saas-startup-pharmarack-raises-pre-series-a-funding/

Sharma, S. (2012). *Bangalore based agri-tech venture FrontalRain Technologies raises INR 5 Crore from Omnivore Capital*. Retrieved 24 April 2018, from https://yourstory.com/2012/10/bangalore-based-agri-tech-venture-frontalrain-technologies-raises-inr-5-crore-from-omnivore-capital/

Shrivastava, A. (2015). *Delhivery to add 3 new lines of business to boost revenue, carve distinct identity - The Economic Times.* Retrieved 20 April 2018, from https://economictimes.indiatimes.com/small-biz/startups/delhivery-to-add-3-new-lines-of-business-to-boost-revenue-carve-distinct-identity/articleshow/50304533.cms?utm_source=contentofinterest&utm_medium=text&utm_campaign=cppst

Shu, C. (2015). *Indian E-commerce Logistics Startup Delhivery Raises $85M Series D | TechCrunch.* Retrieved 20 April 2018, from https://techcrunch.com/2015/05/06/delhivery-seriesd/

Singh, A. (2016). *Exfinity leads $2.75M Series A funding round in logistics startup Locus – VCCircle.* Retrieved 20 April 2018, from https://www.vccircle.com/logistics-startup-locus-raises-275m-series-exfinity-blume-and-others/

Singh, R. K. (2011). *Developing the framework for coordination in supply chain of SMEs.* Academic Press. doi:10.1108/14637151111149456

Singh, V. (2015). *Mumbai Based The Porter, A Startup By IITians Gets INR 3 Cr. To Make Intracity Goods Movement A Breeze - Inc42 Media.* Retrieved 20 April 2018, from https://inc42.com/buzz/mumbai-based-the-porter-a-startup-by-iitians-gets-inr-3-cr-to-make-intracity-goods-movement-a-breeze/

Souza, G. C. (2014). Supply chain analytics. *Business Horizons, 57*(5), 595–605. doi:10.1016/j.bushor.2014.06.004

Srivastava, S. (2006). Logistics and supply chain practices in India. *The Journal of Business Perspective, 10*(3).

Start Up -Definition changes. (2017). Press Information Bureau. Retrieved from http://pib.nic.in/newsite/PrintRelease.aspx?relid=162140

Start-up Report - Momentous Rise of the Indian Start-up Ecosystem | NASSCOM. (n.d.). Retrieved 19 April 2018, from http://www.nasscom.in/knowledge-center/publications/start-report-momentous-rise-indian-start-ecosystem

Startup. (2017). In *Merriam Webster's dictionary.* Retrieved from https://www.merriam-webster.com/dictionary/start-up

Subrahmanya, M. H. B. (2017). Comparing the Entrepreneurial Ecosystems for Technology Startups in Bangalore and Hyderabad, India. *Technology Innovation Management Review, 7*(7), 47–62. doi:10.22215/timreview/1090

Suraj Saharan. (n.d.). In *LinkedIn.* Retrieved 20 April 2018, from https://www.linkedin.com/in/suraj-saharan-94b3383/

Thirukumaran Nagarajan. (n.d.). In *LinkedIn.* Retrieved 20 April 2018, from https://www.linkedin.com/in/thirukumaran-nagarajan-51870242/

Tiwari, A. (2017). *We can fix unavailability of medicines: Pradyumn Singh.* Retrieved 24 April 2018, from http://www.dnaindia.com/business/interview-we-can-fix-unavailability-of-medicines-pradyumn-singh-2299529

Tyagi, S. (2016). *Are more startups really good for economic growth?* Retrieved 24 April 2018, from https://yourstory.com/2016/06/startups-economic-growth/

Uttam Digga. (n.d.). In *LinkedIn*. Retrieved 20 April 2018, from https://www.linkedin.com/in/uttamdigga/

van der Meulen, R. (2018). *How Your Supply Chain Can Improve the Customer Experience - Smarter with Gartner*. Retrieved 24 April 2018, from https://www.gartner.com/smarterwithgartner/how-your-supply-chain-can-improve-the-customer-experience/

Vanga, P. (2017). *Try this five-step networking guide to scale and develop your startup*. Retrieved 19 April 2018, from https://yourstory.com/2017/11/five-step-networking-guide-scale-develop-startup/

Vardaan. (2015). *Mumbai-Based Logistics Startup The Porter Raises $5.5 Mn Funding Led By Sequoia Capital*. Retrieved 20 April 2018, from https://www.indianweb2.com/2015/06/25/mumbai-based-logistics-startup-the-porter-raises-5-5-mn-funding-led-by-sequoia-capital/

Vignesh, J. (2016). *Logistics startup Locus is helping ease problems for e-comm and delivery cos, Technology News, ETtech*. Retrieved 20 April 2018, from https://tech.economictimes.indiatimes.com/news/startups/logistics-startup-locus-is-helping-ease-problems-for-e-comm-and-delivery-cos/54727998

Vikas Choudhary. (n.d.). In *LinkedIn*. Retrieved 20 April 2018, from https://www.linkedin.com/in/vikas-choudhary-8bb75315/

Wang, X. H., & Yang, B. Z. (2001). Content Articles in Economics Fixed and Sunk Costs Revisited. *Journal of Economic Education*, *32*(2), 178–185. doi:10.1080/00220480109595183

What role are Startups playing in the Digital Transformation of Supply Chain Management? (2017). Retrieved 19 April 2018, from https://medium.com/@KodiakRating/what-role-are-startups-playing-in-the-digital-transformation-of-supply-chain-management-d617ef2e6e4d

Yin, R. K. (2003). *Case study research: Design and methods*. Thousand Oaks, CA: Sage Publications.

Compilation of References

Abdouli, M., & Hammami, S. (2017). Investigating the causality links between environmental quality, foreign direct investment and economic growth in MENA countries. *International Business Review*, *26*(2), 264–278. doi:10.1016/j.ibusrev.2016.07.004

Abreu, M., Ferreira, C., Barata, L., & Escária, V. (2007). *Economia Monetária e Financeira*. Lisbon: Escolar Editora.

ACRA. (2017). *ACRA Financial Stress Index* (ACRA FSI RU). Retrieved from https://www.acra-ratings.ru/research/index

Adams, R., Alexander, A., & Oberg, C. (2014). *Innovation Management Capabilities for Start-Ups and Spin-Offs: A Literature Review*. Academic Press. doi:10.4471/redimat.2013.49

Adler, N. (1997). International Dimensions of Organizational Behavior (3rd ed.). Cincinnati, OH: South-Western College Publishing.

AEP. (2014). *Compro o que é nosso*. Retrieved February 7, 2015, from http://www.compronosso.pt/index.php?option=com_content&task=view&id=2&Itemid=2

Agénor, P. R., Kharroubi, E., Gambacorta, L., Lombardo, G., & Pereira da Siva, L. A. (2017), *The International Dimensions of Macroprudential Policies, Bank for International Settlements*. BIS Working Papers, N°. 643, June.

Agur, C. (2018). Re-imagining the Indian state: External forces and the transformation of telecommunications policy, 1947–present. *Global Media and Communication*, *14*(1), 65–83. doi:10.1177/1742766518759794

Ahokangas, P. (1998). *Internationalisation and resources: an analysis of processes in Nordic SMEs*. Academic Press.

Ajzen, I. (1988). *Attitudes, personality, and behavior*. Milton Keynes, UK: Open University Press.

Akkermans, H., & Van Helden, K. (2002). Vicious and virtuous cycles in ERP implementation: A case study of interrelations between critical success factors. *European Journal of Information Systems*, *11*(1), 35–46. doi:10.1057/palgrave.ejis.3000418

Alexander, N., & Quinn, B. (2002). International retail divestment. *International Journal of Retail & Distribution Management*, *30*(2), 112–125. doi:10.1108/09590550210418137

Aliouche, E. H., & Schlentrich, U. (2011). A model of optimal international market expansion: The case of US hotel chains expansion into China. In M. Tuunanen, J. Windsperger, G. Cliquet, & G. Hendrikse (Eds.), *New Developments in the Theory of Networks. Franchising, Alliances and Cooperatives* (pp. 135–154). Heidelberg, Germany: Physica. doi:10.1007/978-3-7908-2615-9_9

Allan, S., & Clanni, M. (2012). *Middle managers: Their critical and growing role in M&A transactions, About Towers Watson*. Retrieved January 20, 2018 from https://www.towerswatson.com/

Allen, R. S., Helms, M. M., Takeda, M. B., White, C. S., & White, C. (2006). A Comparison of Competitive Strategies in Japan and the United States. *S.A.M. Advanced Management Journal, 71*(1), 24–34.

Almeida, C. Q., Alves, H. M. B., & Miguel, R. A. L. (2011). *A Imagem das Marcas Portuguesas de Vestuário Image of the Portuguese Fashion Brands. Vida Económica*. Lisboa: Vida Económica.

Altuntas, M., Rauch, J., & Wende, S. (2016). Strategic group performance and dynamics under different economic conditions. *The Geneva Papers on Risk and Insurance. Issues and Practice, 41*(2), 325–347. doi:10.1057/gpp.2015.28

Ambrosini, V., & Bowman, C. (2009). What are dynamic capabilities and are they a useful construct in strategic management? *International Journal of Management Reviews, 11*(1), 29–49. doi:10.1111/j.1468-2370.2008.00251.x

Amel, D. F., & Rhoades, S. A. (1988). Strategic groups in banking. *The Review of Economics and Statistics, 70*(4), 685–689. doi:10.2307/1935834

Amiti, M., & Wei, S. J. (2009). Service offshoring and productivity: Evidence from the US. *World Economy, 32*(2), 203–220. doi:10.1111/j.1467-9701.2008.01149.x

Amit, R., & Schoemaker, P. (1993). Strategic assets and organizational rent. *Strategic Management Journal, 14*(1), 33–46. doi:10.1002mj.4250140105

Andersen, O. (1993). On the Internationalization Process of Firms: A Critical Analysis. *Journal of International Business Studies, 24*(2), 209–231. doi:10.1057/palgrave.jibs.8490230

Anderson, B. S., & Eshima, Y. (2013). The influence of firm age and intangible resources on the relationship between entrepreneurial orientation and firm growth among Japanese SMEs. *Journal of Business Venturing, 28*(3), 413–429. doi:10.1016/j.jbusvent.2011.10.001

Ansoff, H. I. (1988). *New Corporate Strategy*. New York: Wiley.

Ansoff, I. (1965). *Corporate Strategy*. New York: McGraw Hill.

Antila, E. M., & Kakkonen, A. (2008). Factors affecting the role of HR managers in international mergers and acquisitions: A multiple case study. *Personnel Review, 37*(3), 280–299. doi:10.1108/00483480810862279

Antweiler, W., Copeland, B. R., & Taylor, M. S. (2001). Is free trade good for the environment? *The American Economic Review, 91*(4), 877–908. doi:10.1257/aer.91.4.877

Appelbaum, S. H., Lefrancois, F., Tonna, R., & Shapiro, B. T. (2007). Mergers 101 (part one): Training managers for communications and leadership challenges. *Industrial and Commercial Training, 39*(3), 128–136. doi:10.1108/00197850710742225

Appelbaum, S. H., Roberts, J., & Shapiro, B. T. (2013). Cultural strategies in M&As: Investigating ten case studies. *Journal of Executive Education, 8*(1), 3. Retrieved from https://digitalcommons.kennesaw.edu/jee/vol8/iss1/3

Araújo, L. (2011). Organização, Sistemas e Métodos e As Tecnologias de Gestão Organizacional - Vol. 1. Atlas.

Araújo, L. (2014). Gestão de Pessoas - Estratégias e Integração Organizacional. Atlas.

Ardichvili, A., Cardozo, R., & Souray, R. (2003). A theory of entrepreneurial opportunity identification and development. *Journal of Business Venturing, 18*(1), 105–123. doi:10.1016/S0883-9026(01)00068-4

Arend, R. (2003). Revisiting the logical and research considerations of competitive advantage. *Strategic Management Journal, 24*(3), 279–284. doi:10.1002mj.285

Arendt, H. (1998). *The Human Condition*. Chicago: University of Chicago. doi:10.7208/chicago/9780226924571.001.0001

Arlbjørn, J. S., & Mikkelsen, O. S. (2014). Backshoring manufacturing: Notes on an important but under-researched theme. *Journal of Purchasing and Supply Management, 20*(1), 60–62. doi:10.1016/j.pursup.2014.02.003

Arlbjørn, J. S., Mikkelsen, O. S., Schlichter, J., & Thoms, L. (2013). *Danske producenters udflytning og hjemtagning af produktion*. Kolding.

Armenakis, A. A., Harris, S. G., & Mossholder, K. W. (1993). Creating readiness for organizational change. *Human Relations, 46*(6), 681–703. doi:10.1177/001872679304600601

Aron, R., Clemons, E. K., & Reddi, S. (2005). Just Right Outsourcing: Understanding and Managing Risk Introduction : objectives of this paper. *International Conference on System Sciences*, 1–10. 10.1109/HICSS.2005.368

Arvidsson, I., Magnusson, A., & Nilsson, K. (2014). *Reshoring, a trend in Sweden?* Umea School of Business and Economics.

Asakawa, K., Ito, K., Rose, E. L., & Westney, D. E. (2013). Internationalization in Japan's service industries. *Asia Pacific Journal of Management, 30*(4), 1155–1168. doi:10.100710490-012-9325-5

Ashutosh Vikram. (n.d.). In *LinkedIn*. Retrieved 20 April 2018, from https://www.linkedin.com/in/ashutoshvikram/

Associação Portuguesa de Bancos (APB). (2008). Annual Statistical Bulletins, 44.

Associação Portuguesa de Bancos (APB). (2009). Annual Statistical Bulletins, 45.

Associação Portuguesa de Bancos (APB). (2010). Annual Statistical Bulletins, 46.

Atici, C. (2009). Carbon emissions in Central and Eastern Europe: Environmental Kuznets curve and implications for sustainable development. *Sustainable Development, 17*(3), 155–160. doi:10.1002d.372

ATP. (2014). *Plano Estratégico Têxtil 2020 – Projetar o Desenvolvimento da Fileira Têxtil e Vestuário até 2020*. V. N. de Famalicão: ATP.

Azevedo, S. G., Carvalho, H., & Cruz Machado, V. (2011). The influence of green practices on supply chain performance: A case study approach. *Transportation Research Part E, Logistics and Transportation Review, 47*(6), 850–871. doi:10.1016/j.tre.2011.05.017

Azofra, V., & De La Fuente, J. M. (1987). El Comportamiento estratégico de la banca española durante el período 1975–1985: Una aproximación. *Anales de Estudios Económicos y Empresariales, 2*, 35–54.

Baaij, M., Bosch, F., & Volberda, H. (n.d.). The international relocation of corporate centres - Are corporate centres sticky? European Management Journal, 22(2), 141–149.

Backer, S. A. (2017). *'Supply Chain' is traditionally considered as a 'cost center', how can you turn it into a 'profit center'? - Bayt.com Specialties*. Retrieved 24 April 2018, from https://www.bayt.com/en/specialties/q/357444/supply-chain-is-traditionally-considered-as-a-cost-center-how-can-you-turn-it-into-a-profit-center/

Bagley, C., & Hunter, B. (1992). Restructuring, constructivism, and technology: Forging a new relationship. *Educational Technology, 32*(7), 22–27.

Bailey, D., & De Propris, L. (2014). Manufacturing reshoring and its limits: The UK automotive case. *Cambridge Journal of Regions, Economy and Society, 7*(3), 379–395. doi:10.1093/cjres/rsu019

Bainbridge, S. M. (2011). Dodd Frank: Quark Federal Corporate Governance Round II. *Minnesota Law Review, 95*, 1779–1821.

Baird, I. S., Sudharshan, D., & Thomas, H. (1988). Addressing temporal change in strategic group analysis: A three-mode factor analysis approach. *Journal of Management, 14*(3), 425–439. doi:10.1177/014920638801400306

Bakar, L. J. A., & Ahmad, H. (2010). Assessing the relationship between firm resources and product innovation performance: A resource-based view. *Business Process Management, 16*(3), 420–435. doi:10.1108/14637151011049430

Bals, L., Daum, A., & Tate, W. (2015). From Offshoring to Rightshoring: Focus on the Backshoring Phenomenon. *AIB Insights, 15*(4), 3–8.

Baltagi, B. H. (1995). *Econometric analysis of panel data*. John Wiley & Sons.

Bandeira, R. (2009). *Fatores de Decisão de Terceirização Logística: Análise baseada na percepção dos executivos*. Universidade Federal Do Rio Grande do Sul. Retrieved from http://hdl.handle.net/10183/17636

Bank for International Settlements (1995). 65th Annual Report, 1994–1995.

Bank for International Settlements. (2017). *Understanding Globalisation*. BIS Annual Economic Report, Bank for International Settlements. Accessed in December 05, 2018 on https://www.bis.org/publ/arpdf/ar2017e6.htm

Bank of Portugal. (2016). *White Paper on the Regulation and Supervision of the Financial System*. Bank of Portugal, Governor's Office, Lisbon, Portugal.

Bank of Russia. (2014). Corporate Governance Code. *Bulletin of The Bank of Russia, 40*(1518), 15.

Bank of Russia. (2017). *External sector statistics*. Retrieved from http://www.cbr.ru/statistics/?PrtId=svs

Bargeron, L., Smith, J., & Lehn, K. (2012). *Corporate culture and M&A activity*. Working paper.

Barker, V., & Duheim, I. (1997). Strategic Change in the Turnaround Process. Theory and Empirical Evidence. *Strategic Management Journal, 18*(1), 13–38. doi:10.1002/(SICI)1097-0266(199701)18:1<13::AID-SMJ843>3.0.CO;2-X

Barney, J. (1991). Firm Resources and Sustained Competitive Advantage. *Journal of Management, 17*(1), 99–120. doi:10.1177/014920639101700108

Barney, J. (1995). Looking inside for competitive advantage. *The Academy of Management Perspectives, 9*(4), 49–61. doi:10.5465/ame.1995.9512032192

Barney, J. (2001). Resource-based theories of competitive advantage: A ten-year retrospective on the resource-based view. *Journal of Management, 27*(6), 643–650. doi:10.1177/014920630102700602

Barney, J. B., & Hoskisson, R. E. (1990). Strategic groups: Untested assertions and research proposals. *Managerial and Decision Economics, 11*(3), 187–198. doi:10.1002/mde.4090110306

Barratt, M., Choi, T. Y., & Li, M. (2011). Qualitative case studies in operations management: Trends, research outcomes, and future research implications. *Journal of Operations Management, 29*(4), 329–342. doi:10.1016/j.jom.2010.06.002

Barreto, I. (2010). Dynamic Capabilities: A Review of Past Research and an Agenda for the Future. *Journal of Management, 36*(1), 256–280. doi:10.1177/0149206309350776

Barth, J. R., Brumbugh, R. D., & Wilcox, J. A. (2000, Spring). The Repeal of Glass- Steagall and the Advent of Broad Banking. *The Journal of Economic Perspectives, 14*(2), 191–204. doi:10.1257/jep.14.2.191

Basu, K. (2007). *India's demographic dividend.* Retrieved 24 April 2018, from http://news.bbc.co.uk/2/hi/south_asia/6911544.stm

Bauer, M. W., & Gaskell, G. (2000). *Qualitative researching with text, image and sound: a practical handbook.* London: Sage publications. doi:10.4135/9781849209731

BBC News. (2002, October 16). *Enron auditor fined $500,000.* Retrieved from http://news.bbc.co.uk/2/hi/business/2334761.stm

Bebchuk, L. A., & Weisbach, M. S. (2009). *The state of Corporate Governance research.* NBER. Working Paper No. 15537.

Beck, T., & Demirguc-Kunt, A. (2009). *Financial institutions and markets across countries and over time-data and analysis.* The World Bank. doi:10.1596/1813-9450-4943

Beck, T., Demirgüç-Kunt, A., & Levine, R. (2010). Financial institutions and markets across countries and over time: The updated financial development and structure database. *The World Bank Economic Review, 24*(1), 77–92. doi:10.1093/wber/lhp016

Beckwith, N. E., Kassarjian, H. H., & Lehmann, D. R. (1978). Halo Effects in Marketing Research: Review and Prognosis. *Advances in Consumer Research. Association for Consumer Research (U. S.), 5*, 465–467.

Behnt, R. (1983). The fundamentals of Cutback Management. In R. Zeckhauser & D. Leebaert (Eds.), *What role for government: lessons from policy research.* Duke University Press.

Belderbos, R., & Zou, J. (2006). Foreign investment, divestment and relocation by Japanies electronics firms in East Asia. *Asian Economic Journal, 20*(1), 1–27. doi:10.1111/j.1467-8381.2006.00222.x

Bell, T. E. (1990). From monopoly to competition: Long-term research is vulnerable. *IEEE Spectrum, 27*(10), 46–50. doi:10.1109/6.58476

Benito, G. (1997). Divestment of foreign production operations. *Applied Economics, 29*(10), 1365–1377. doi:10.1080/00036849700000027

Benito, G. R. G. (2005). Divestment and international business strategy. *Journal of Economic Geography, 5*(2), 235–251. doi:10.1093/jnlecg/lbh041

Benito, G. R. G., & Welch, L. (1997). De-internationalization. *Management International Review, 37*, 7–25.

Benston, G. (1990). *The Separation of Commercial and Investment Banking: The Glass-Steagall Act Revisited and Reconsidered.* Oxford, UK: Oxford University Press. doi:10.1007/978-1-349-11280-7

Berezinets, I. V., Ilyina, Y. B., & Fakhritdinov, D. N. (2014). Corporate conflicts and financial performance of companies. *Bulletin of St. Petersburg University., 2*, 100–135.

Berger, A. N., Demsetz, R. S., & Strahan, P. E. (1999, February). The Consolidation of the Financial Services Industry: Causes, Consequences and Implications for the Future. *Journal of Banking & Finance, 23*(2–4), 135–194. doi:10.1016/S0378-4266(98)00125-3

Berger, A. N., Kashyap, A. K., Scalise, J. M., Gertler, M., & Friedman, B. M. (1995). The transformation of the U.S. Banking Industry: What a long strange trip it's been. *Brookings Papers on Economic Activity, 2*(2), 55–201. doi:10.2307/2534612

Berger, P., & Luckmann, T. (1966). *The Social Construction of Reality: A Treatise of Sociology of Knowledge.* New York: Doubleday.

Bergh, D. D., & Lawless, M. W. (1998). Portfolio Restructuring and Limits to Hierarchical Governance: The Effects of Environmental Uncertainty and Diversification Strategy. *Organization Science*, *9*(1), 87–102. doi:10.1287/orsc.9.1.87

Bernstorff, V. (2003). Influenciar a escolha dos profissionais de outra empresa para realizar tarefas para a sua organização garante o sucesso da terceirização da tecnologia da Informação? *EnANPAD*.

Berry, J. W. (1997). Immigration, acculturation, and adaptation. *Applied Psychology*, *46*, 5–30.

Bhavesh Manglani. (n.d.). In *LinkedIn*. Retrieved 20 April 2018, from https://www.linkedin.com/in/bhavesh-manglani-14a3663/

Bhavik Parmar. (n.d.). In *LinkedIn*. Retrieved 20 April 2018, from https://www.linkedin.com/in/bhavikparmar/

Bibault, D. (1982). *Corporate Turnaround: How Managers Turn Losers into Winners*. New York: McGraw-Hill.

Bibeualt, D. (1999). *Corporate Turnaround*. Washington, DC: Beard.

Bijlsma-Frankema, K. (2001). On managing cultural integration and cultural change processes in mergers and acquisitions. *Journal of European Industrial Training, 25*(2/3/4), 192-207.

Blackbuck. (n.d.). Retrieved 20 April 2018, from https://www.blackbuck.com/company

Blowhorn! Mini-Trucks on hire in Bengaluru/Hyderabad/Chennai/Mumbai. (n.d.). Retrieved 24 April 2018, from https://blowhorn.com/solutions

Boddewyn, J. J. (1979). Foreign divestment: Magnitude and factors. *Journal of International Business Studies, 10*(1), 21–27. doi:10.1057/palgrave.jibs.8490786

Boddewyn, J. J. (1983). Foreign direct divestment theory: Is it the reverse of FDI theory? *Weltwirtschaftliches Archiv, 119*(2), 345–355. doi:10.1007/BF02706431

Bofinger, P. (2001). *Monetary Policy, Goals, Institutions, Strategies, and Instruments* (1st ed.). New York: Oxford University Press.

Bonaccorsi, A. (1992). On the relationship between firm size and export intensity. *Journal of International Business Studies*, *23*(4), 605–635. doi:10.1057/palgrave.jibs.8490280

Bortolotti, B., D'Souza, J., Fantini, M., & Megginson, W. L. (2002). Privatization and the sources of performance improvement in the global telecommunications industry. *Telecommunications Policy*, *26*(5-6), 243–268. doi:10.1016/S0308-5961(02)00013-7

Bossche, P. Van den, Gupta, P., Gutierrez, H., & Gupta, A. (2014, January). Solving the Reshoring Dilemma. *Supply Chain Management Review*, 26–33.

Bottini, N., Ernst, C., & Luelbker, M. (2007). *Offshoring and the labour market : What are the issues*. Economic and Labour Market Paper.

Bouchard, P. J., & Pellet, L. (2002). *Getting You Shift Together. Making Sense of Organization Culture Change*. CCI Press.

Bougon, M. (1983). In G. Morgan (Ed.), Uncovering cognitive maps: The selfQ technique,Beyond method: Strategies for social research (pp. 112–144). Academic Press.

Bourdieu, P. (2000). *Les Estructures Sociales de L'economie*. Paris: De Seuil.

Bouwman, C. S. (2013). The Role of Corporate Culture in Mergers & Acquisitions. In E. Perrault (Ed.), *Mergers and Acquisitions: Practices, Performance and Perspectives*. Hauppauge: NOVA Science Publishers.

Bowman, C., & Ambrosini, V. (2003). How the Resource based and the Dynamic Capability Views of the Firm Inform Corporate level Strategy. *British Journal of Management*, *14*(4), 289–303. doi:10.1111/j.1467-8551.2003.00380.x

BoxMySpace - FAQs | Frequently Asked Questions for Storage Needs. (n.d.). Retrieved 24 April 2018, from http://boxmyspace.com/faq

Boyatzis, R. E. (1998). *Transforming qualitative information: Thematic analysis and code development*. Sage Publications, Inc.

Boyd, C., Tuckey, M., & Winefield, A. (2014). Perceived effects organizational downsizing and staff cuts on the stress experience: The role of resources. *Stress and Health*, *30*(1), 53–64. doi:10.1002mi.2495 PMID:23868509

Boyer, K. K., & Lewis, M. W. (2002). Competitive Priorities: Investigating the need for trade-offs in operations strategy. *Production and Operations Management*, *11*(1), 9–20. doi:10.1111/j.1937-5956.2002.tb00181.x

Bradley, F. (2005). *International marketing strategy*. Pearson Education.

Bruce, R. R. (1989). Restructuring the telecom sector in developing countries: Some new options for policymakers. *IEEE Technology and Society Magazine*, *8*(4), 16–20. doi:10.1109/44.44528

Bruno, V., & Shin, H. S. (2015). Cross-Border Banking and Global Liquidity. *The Review of Economic Studies*, *82*(2), 535–564. doi:10.1093/restud/rdu042

Buckley, P. J., & Casson, M. (2011). Marketing and the multinational: Extending internalisation theory. *Journal of the Academy of Marketing Science*, *39*(4), 492–508. doi:10.100711747-010-0243-0

Buckley, P. J., & Casson, M. C. (1976). *The Future of the Multinational Enterprise*. London: The Macmillan press. doi:10.1007/978-1-349-02899-3

Buckley, P. J., Doh, J. P., & Benischke, M. H. (2017). Towards a renaissance in international business research? Big questions, grand challenges, and the future of IB scholarship. *Journal of International Business Studies*, *48*(9), 1045–1064. doi:10.105741267-017-0102-z

Buckley, P. J., Pass, C. L., & Prescott, K. (1992). The internationalization of service firms: A comparison with the manufacturing sector. *Scandinavian International Business Review*, *1*(1), 39–56. doi:10.1016/0962-9262(92)90035-5

Buckley, P., & Casson, M. (1976). *The future of the multinational corporation*. London: Macmillan.

Buono, A. F., & Bowditch, J. L. (1989). *The Human Side of Mergers and Acquisitions*. San Francisco: Jossey-Bass.

Buono, A. F., & Bowditch, J. L. (2003). *The Human Side of Mergers and Acquisitions; Managing Collisions Between People, Cultures, and Organizations* (1st ed.). Reprinted by Beard Books, Washington D.C. U.S.A.

Bureau Van Dijk. (n.d.). *Sabi - Spain and Portugal financial company information and business intelligence - BvD*. Retrieved March 4, 2018, from https://www.bvdinfo.com/en-us/our-products/company-information/national-products/sabi

Burt, S., Coe, N. M., & Davies, K. (2019). A tactical retreat? Conceptualising the dynamics of European grocery retail divestment from East Asia. *International Business Review*, *28*(1), 177–189. doi:10.1016/j.ibusrev.2018.05.010

Cabral, J. E. O., Coelho, A. F. M., Coelho, F. J. F., & Costa, M. (2015). Capabilities, innovation, and overall performance in brazilian export firms. *RAM. Revista de Administração Mackenzie*, *16*(3), 76–108. doi:10.1590/1678-69712015/administracao.v16n3p76-108

Cameron, K. (1994). Strategic for successful organizational downsizing. *Human Resource Management, 33*(2), 189–201. doi:10.1002/hrm.3930330204

Canham, S., & Hamilton, R. T. (2013). SME internationalisation: Offshoring, "backshoring", or staying at home in New Zealand. *Strategic Outsourcing, 6*(3), 277–291. doi:10.1108/SO-06-2013-0011

Cano, J. E. G., & Oliva, E. J. D. (2008). Grupos estratégicos en la banca colombiana: análisis estático y dinámico. *Innovar: Revista de Ciencias Administrativas y Sociales, 18*,(32),195–226.

Cantwell, J., Dunning, J. H., & Lundan, S. M. (2010). An evolutionary approach to understanding international business activity: The co-evolution of MNEs and the institutional environment. *Journal of International Business Studies, 41*(4), 567–586. doi:10.1057/jibs.2009.95

Cantwell, J., Dunning, J. H., & Lundan, S. M. (2015). An evolutionary approach to understanding international business activity: The co-evolution of MNEs and the institutional environment. In J. Cantwell (Ed.), *The eclectic paradigm* (pp. 192–223). London: Palgrave Macmillan UK. doi:10.1007/978-1-137-54471-1_8

Capaldo, A. (2007). Network structure innovation: The leveraging of dual network as a distinctive relational capability. *The Journal of Strategic Management, 28*(6), 585–608. doi:10.1002mj.621

Capitalist, V. (2017). In *Investopedia*. Retrieved from https://www.investopedia.com/terms/s/startup.asp

Carleton, J. R. (1996). *Cultural Due Diligence*. Vector Group, Inc.

Carleton, J. R., & Lineberry, C. S. (2004). *Achieving Post-Merger Success – A Stakeholder's Guide to Cultural Due Diligence, Assessment, and Integration*. San Francisco: Pfeiffer, an Imprint of John Wiley & Sons.

Carmel, E., & Abbott, P. (2007). Distance Matters. *Communications of the ACM, 50*(10), 139–178.

Carson, R. T. (2010). The environmental Kuznets curve: Seeking empirical regularity and theoretical structure. *Review of Environmental Economics and Policy, 4*(1), 3–23. doi:10.1093/reep/rep021

Carter, C. R., Rogers, D. S., & Choi, T. Y. (2015). *sec1-further- Toward the theory of the supply chain*. Academic Press.

Carter, S., & Greer, C. (2013). Strategic leadership: Values, styles, and organizational performance. *Journal of Leadership & Organizational Studies, 20*(4), 375–393. doi:10.1177/1548051812471724

Cartwright, S., & Cooper, C. L. (1996). *Managing Mergers, Acquisitions & Strategic Alliances*. Oxford, UK: Butterworth Heinemann, Inc.

Cartwright, S., & Schoenberg, R. (2006). Thirty years of mergers and acquisitions research: Recent advances and future opportunities. *British Journal of Management, 17*(S1), 1–5. doi:10.1111/j.1467-8551.2006.00475.x

Cascio, W. (2010). *Employment Downsizing and its Alternatives: Strategies for Long-term Success*. Alexandria, VA: Society for Human Resources Management.

Cascio, W., & Wynn, P. (2004). Managing a downsizing process. *Human Resource Management, 43*(4), 425–436. doi:10.1002/hrm.20034

Casey, S. R., & Hamilton, R. T. (2014). Export performance of small firms from small countries: The case of New Zealand. *Journal of International Entrepreneurship, 12*(3), 254–269. doi:10.100710843-014-0126-4

Cassell, C., & Symon, G. (2004). *Essential guide to qualitative methods in organizational research*. London: Sage Publications Inc. doi:10.4135/9781446280119

Caves, R., & Porter, M. E. (1977). From entry barriers to mobility barriers. *The Quarterly Journal of Economics*, *91*(2), 241–261. doi:10.2307/1885416

Cavusgil, T., & Zou, S. (1994). Marketing strategy-performance relationship: An investigation of the empirical link in export market ventures. *Journal of Marketing*, *58*(1), 1–21. doi:10.1177/002224299405800101

Ceccagnoli, M. (2009). Appropriability, preemption, and firm performance. *Strategic Management Journal*, *30*(1), 81–98. doi:10.1002mj.723

Ceccarelli, M. A., Maddaloni, A., & Peydro, J. L. (2013). Heterogeneous Transmission Mechanism: Monetary Policy and Financial Fragility in the Eurozone. *Economic Policy*, *28*(75), 459–512. doi:10.1111/1468-0327.12015

Cecchetti, S. (2006). *Money, Banking and Financial Markets* (2nd ed.). McGraw-Hill.

Chadwick, C., Hunter, L., & Walson, S. (2014). Effects of downsizing practices on the performance of hospitals. *Journal of Strategic Management*, *25*(5), 405–427. doi:10.1002mj.383

Chanakya Hridaya. (n.d.). In *LinkedIn*. Retrieved 20 April 2018, from https://www.linkedin.com/in/chanakya-hridaya-44743425/

Chanchai, T., Abebe, M., & Li, Z. (2013) A Temporal Approach to Successful Turnaround in Declining Firms. *Academy of Management Annual Meeting Proceedings*, *2013*(1).

Chandler, A. D. (1962). Strategy and Structure. *Business History Review*. doi:10.15347/wjm/2014.010

Chang, S. J., & Singh, H. (1999). The impact of modes of entry and resource fit on modes of exit by multibusiness firms. *Strategic Management Journal*, *20*(11), 1019–1035. doi:10.1002/(SICI)1097-0266(199911)20:11<1019::AID-SMJ66>3.0.CO;2-9

Chan-Olmsted, S., & Jamison, M. (2001). Rivalry through alliances: Competitive strategy in the global telecommunications market. *European Management Journal*, *19*(3), 317–331. doi:10.1016/S0263-2373(01)00028-7

Chatterjee, S., Lubatkin, M., Schweiger, D., & Weber, Y. (1992). Cultural differences and shareholder value in related mergers: Linking equity and human capital. *Strategic Management Journal*, *13*(5), 319–334. doi:10.1002mj.4250130502

Cheng, Y., Farooq, S., & Johansen, J. (2015). International manufacturing network: Past, present, and future. *International Journal of Operations & Production Management*, *35*(3), 392–429. doi:10.1108/IJOPM-03-2013-0146

Chen, I. J., & Paulraj, A. (2004). Understanding supply chain management: Critical research and a theoretical framework. *International Journal of Production Research*, *42*(1), 131–163. doi:10.1080/00207540310001602865

Chen, M. J., & Miller, D. (2012). Competitive dynamics: Themes, trends, and a prospective research platform. *The Academy of Management Annals*, *6*(1), 135–210. doi:10.5465/19416520.2012.660762

Cherchiglia, M. (2004). *Terceirização do trabalho nos serviços de saúde: alguns aspectos conceituais, legais e pragmáticos*. CADRHU.

Chetty, S. K. (1999). Dimensions of Internationalisation of Manufacturing Firms in the Apparel Industry. *European Journal of Marketing*, *33*(1/2), 121–142. doi:10.1108/03090569910249201

Chetty, S., & Blankenburg Holm, D. (2000). Internationalisation of small to medium-sized manufacturing firms: A network approach. *International Business Review*, *9*(1), 77–93. doi:10.1016/S0969-5931(99)00030-X

Chetty, S., & Campbelt-Hunt, C. (2004). A Strategic Approach to Internationalization: A Traditional Versus a "Born-Global" Approach. *Journal of International Marketing*, *12*(1), 57–81. doi:10.1509/jimk.12.1.57.25651

Chitral, R. (2017). *Agri-marketing platform Ninjacart raises $5.5 million - Times of India*. Retrieved 20 April 2018, from https://timesofindia.indiatimes.com/business/india-business/agri-marketing-platform-ninjacart-raises-5-5-million/articleshow/58119275.cms

Chopra, S., & Meindl, P. (2013), Supply Chain Management: Strategy, Planning, and Operations (3rd ed.). Prentice-Hall.

Choudhury, A. (2017). *How this Pune-based startup is automating the pharmaceutical supply chain management*. Retrieved 20 April 2018, from https://yourstory.com/2017/03/pharmarack-technologies-startup/

Christofferson, S. A., McNish, R. S., & Sias, D. L. (2004). Where mergers go wrong? *McKinsey Quarterly*. Retrieved May 24, 2018 from https://www.mckinsey.com/business-functions/strategy-and-corporate-finance/our-insights/where-mergers-go-wrong

Clark, G. L., & Wrigley, N. (1997). Exit, the firm and sunk costs: Reconceptualizing the corporate geography of divestment and plant closure. *Progress in Human Geography*, *21*(3), 338–358. doi:10.1191/030913297674898950

Claver-Cortés, E., Molina, J. F., & Pereira-Moliner, J. (2006). Strategic groups in the hospitality industry: Intergroup and intragroup performance differences in Alicante, Spain. *Tourism Management*, *27*(6), 1101–1116. doi:10.1016/j.tourman.2005.11.006

Claver-Cortés, E., Molina, J. F., & Tarí, J. J. (2003). Strategic groups and firm performance: The case of Spanish house-building firms. *Construction Management and Economics*, *21*(4), 369–377. doi:10.1080/0144619032000111250

Claver-Cortés, E., Pereira-Moliner, J., & Molina-Azorín, J. (2009). Strategic groups and performance in the Spanish hotel sector. *Service Industries Journal*, *29*(7), 943–961. doi:10.1080/02642060902749567

Coase, R. (2012). The nature of the firm. In The Economic Nature of the Firm: A Reader (3rd ed.). Academic Press. doi:10.1007/978-3-642-27922-5_22

Coe, N. M., Lee, Y. S., & Wood, S. (2017). Conceptualising contemporary retail divestment: Tesco's departure from South Korea. *Environment & Planning A*, *49*(12), 2739–2761. doi:10.1177/0308518X17733265

Cogburn, D. L. (2017). From NWICO to Global eCommerce: Telecommunications Restructuring and the GII. In Transnational Advocacy Networks in the Information Society (pp. 53-92). Palgrave Macmillan.

Cogburn, D. L. (1998). Globalization and state autonomy in the information age: Telecommunications sector restructuring in South Africa. *Journal of International Affairs*, *51*(2), 583–604.

Cohen, J. A. (2005). *Intangible Assets: Valuation and Economic Benefit*. Hoboken, NJ: Wiley.

Cohen, W., & Levinthal, D. (1990). Absorptive Capacity: A New Perspective on Learning and Innovation. *Administrative Science Quarterly*, *35*(1), 128. doi:10.2307/2393553

Cole, M. A. (2004). Trade, the pollution haven hypothesis and the environmental Kuznets curve: Examining the linkages. *Ecological Economics: The Journal of the International Society for Ecological Economics*, *48*(1), 71–81. doi:10.1016/j.ecolecon.2003.09.007

Cole, M. A. (2006). Does trade liberalization increase national energy use? *Economics Letters*, *92*(1), 108–112. doi:10.1016/j.econlet.2006.01.018

Colotla, I., Shi, Y., & Gregory, M. J. (2003). Operation and performance of international manufacturing networks. *International Journal of Operations & Production Management*, *23*(10), 1184–1206. doi:10.1108/01443570310496625

Community, K. (2017). *What role are Startups playing in the Digital Transformation of SCM?* Retrieved from https://medium.com/@KodiakRating/what-role-are-startups-playing-in-the-digital-transformation-of-supply-chain-management-d617ef2e6e4d

Competitors, B. Revenue and Employees - Owler Company Profile. (n.d.). Retrieved 24 April 2018, from https://www.owler.com/company/blowhorn

Conner Partners. (2010). *Corporate culture and its impact on strategic change.* White Papers. Retrieved February 22, 2018 from http://www.connerpartners.com/thought-leadership/white-papers

Connington, J. (2017). Mapped: the world's cheapest stock markets. *Telegraph.* Retrieved from http://www.telegraph.co.uk/investing/shares/worlds-cheapest-markets-2017/

Contractor, F. J., Kumar, V., Kundu, S. K., & Pedersen, T. (2010). Reconceptualizing the firm in a world of outsourcing and offshoring: The organizational and geographical relocation of high-value company functions. *Journal of Management Studies, 47*(December), 1417–1433. doi:10.1111/j.1467-6486.2010.00945.x

Contractor, F. J., Kundu, S. K., & Hsu, C.-C. (2003). A three-stage theory of international expansion: The link between multinationality and performance in the service sector. *Journal of International Business Studies, 34*(1), 5–18. doi:10.1057/palgrave.jibs.8400003

Cooke-Davies, T. (2002). The "real" success factors on projects. *International Journal of Project Management, 20*(3), 185–190. doi:10.1016/S0263-7863(01)00067-9

Cool, K. (1985). *Strategic group formation and strategic group shifts: a longitudinal analysis of the U.S. Pharmaceutical* (Unpublished doctoral dissertation). Purdue University.

Cool, K., & Dierickx, I. (1993). Rivalry, strategic groups and firm profitability. *Strategic Management Journal, 14*(1), 47–59. doi:10.1002mj.4250140106

Cool, K., & Schendel, D. (1987). Strategic group formation & performance: The case of the U.S. pharmaceutical industry, 1963–1982. *Management Science, 33*(9), 1102–1124. doi:10.1287/mnsc.33.9.1102

Cool, K., & Schendel, D. (1988). Performance differences among strategic group members. *Strategic Management Journal, 9*(3), 207–223. doi:10.1002mj.4250090302

Copeland, B. R., & Scott Taylor, M. (2013). *Trade and the environment: Theory and evidence.* Princeton University Press.

Corsetti, G., Pesenti, P., & Roubini, N. (1999). What Caused the Asian currency and financial crisis? *Japan and the World Economy, 11*(3), 305–373. doi:10.1016/S0922-1425(99)00019-5

Cortes, A., & Rosell, J. (n.d.). *Parmalat scandal.* Retrieved from https://prezi.com/8xmxofrc2tcw/copy-of-parmalat-scandal/

Cortina, C. (2015). *The role of organizational culture in mergers and acquisitions.* Retrieved January 20, 2018 from https://www.linkedin.com/pulse/role-organizational-culture-mergers-acquisitions-cecilia-cortina/

Cottrill, K. (2014). *Reshoring: New Day, False Dawn, or Something Else?* Retrieved January 24, 2015, from https://ctl.mit.edu/news/reshoring-new-day-false-dawn-or-something-else

Coviello, N. E., & Martin, K. A.-M. (1999). Internationalization of Service SMEs: An Integrated Perspective from the Engineering Consulting Sector. *Journal of International Marketing.*

Coviello, N. (2015). Re-thinking research on born globals. *Journal of International Business Studies, 46*(1), 17–26. doi:10.1057/jibs.2014.59

Coviello, N., & Munro, H. (1997). Network relationships and the internationalisation process of small software firms. *International Business Review*, *6*(4), 361–386. doi:10.1016/S0969-5931(97)00010-3

Crémer, J. (1993). Corporate culture and shared knowledge. *Industrial and Corporate Change*, *3*(3), 351–386. doi:10.1093/icc/2.3.351

Cretin, F., Dieudonné, S., & Bouacha, S. (2015). M&A activity: Where are we in the cycle? *Alternative Investment Analyst Review,* 38-44.

Crick, D. (2004). U.K. SMEs' decision to discontinue exporting: An exploratory investigation into practices within the clothing industry. *Journal of Business Venturing*, *19*(4), 561–587. doi:10.1016/S0883-9026(03)00032-6

Crick, D., & Spence, M. (2005). The internationalisation of 'high performing' UK high-tech SMEs: A study of planned and unplanned strategies. *International Business Review*, *14*(2), 167–185. doi:10.1016/j.ibusrev.2004.04.007

Cuervo-Cazurra, A., Narula, R., & Un, C. A. (2015). Internationalization motives: Sell more, buy better, upgrade and escape. *Multinational Business Review*, *23*(1), 25–35. doi:10.1108/MBR-02-2015-0009

Currie, W. L., & Willcocks, L. P. (1998). Analysing four types of IT sourcing decisions in the context of scale, client/supplier interdependency and risk mitigation. *Information Systems Journal*, *8*(2), 119–143. doi:10.1046/j.1365-2575.1998.00030.x

Cyert, R. M., & March, J. G. (1963). *A behavioral theory of the firm.* Retrieved from https://books.google.pt/books/about/A_Behavioral_Theory_of_the_Firm.html?id=9PydngEACAAJ&source=kp_cover&redir_esc=y

Czarnecki, C., & Dietze, C. (2017). Understanding today's Telecommunications Industry. In *Reference Architecture for the Telecommunications Industry* (pp. 17–54). Cham: Springer. doi:10.1007/978-3-319-46757-3_2

D'Cunha, S. (2017). *These Logistics Startups Are Tackling India's Infrastructural Challenges With AI And Big Data.* Retrieved 20 April 2018, from https://www.forbes.com/sites/suparnadutt/2017/11/15/these-logistics-startups-are-tackling-indias-infrastructural-challenges-with-ai-and-big-data/#6068e8eea7cf

da Silva, P. M. F., & Moreira, A. C. (2019). The Evolution of Corporate Divestment: Towards a New Research Paradigm? In *Handbook of Research on Contemporary Approaches in Management and Organizational Strategy* (pp. 292–316). IGI Global. doi:10.4018/978-1-5225-6301-3.ch015

Dachs, B., & Kinkel, S. (2013). Backshoring of production activities in European manufacturing – Evidence from a large-scale survey. In *20th International Annual EurOMA Conference* (pp. 7–12). Dublin, Ireland: Academic Press.

Dachs, B., Ebersberger, B., Kinkel, S., & Waser, B. R. (2006). *Offshoring of production – a European perspective. European Manufacturing Survey.* Retrieved from http://www.isi.fraunhofer.de/isi-en/i/projekte/fems.php

Damanpour, F., Szabat, K. A., & Evan, W. M. (1989). The relationship between types of innovation and organizational performance. *Journal of Management Studies*, *26*(6), 587–601. doi:10.1111/j.1467-6486.1989.tb00746.x

Dangayach, G., & Deshmukh, S. (2001). Manufacturing strategy: Literature review and some issues. *International Journal (Toronto, Ont.)*, *21*(7), 884–932.

Daniels, J. D., Radebaugh, L. H., & Sullivan, D. P. (2014). *International business: Environments and operations.* Addison-Wesley.

Das, M. (2017). *Logistics start-up Porter loses a few customers as it says no to overloading - Business Line.* Retrieved 20 April 2018, from https://www.thehindubusinessline.com/economy/logistics/logistics-startup-porter-loses-a-few-customers-as-it-says-no-to-overloading/article9735224.ece

Dasgupta, M. (2017). *Logistics Startups Trukky, BlackBuck, ThePorter Are Revving Up With Logistics Management Apps*. Retrieved 20 April 2018, from https://medium.com/@MoumitaDasgupta/logistics-startups-trukky-blackbuck-theporter-are-revving-up-with-logistics-management-apps-d21c536a8c48

Dass, P. (2000). Relationship of Firm Size, Initial Diversification, and Internationalization with Strategic Change. *Journal of Business Research*, *48*(2), 135–146. doi:10.1016/S0148-2963(98)00097-6

Davies, A., Kim, S., & Abboud, L. (2014). Battle for control destroyed $35-billion Omnicom-Publicis merger. *Reuters*. Retrieved February 3, 2018 from https://www.reuters.com/article/us-omnicom-group-publicis-groupe/battle-for-control-destroyed-35-billion-omnicom-publicis-merger-idUSBREA4713R20140509

Davis, F. D. (1989). Perceived Usefulness, Perceived Ease of Use, and User Acceptance of Information Technology. *Management Information Systems Quarterly*, *13*(3), 319–340. doi:10.2307/249008

Day, G. S., Reibstein, D. J., & Gunther, R. (1999). *A Dinâmica da Estratégia Competitiva*. São Paulo: Editora Campus.

Deardorff, A. V. (n.d.). "Social cost". *Deardorffs' Glossary of International Economics*. Retrieved from http://www-personal.umich.edu/~alandear/glossary/s.html#SocialCost

Decree-Law nº 298/92, of 31st of December. Diário da República, Nº 301 — 1.ª series –A — Ministry of Finance.

Deepak Garg. (n.d.). In *LinkedIn*. Retrieved 20 April 2018, from https://www.linkedin.com/in/deepak-garg-4204b439/

Delipinar, G. E., & Kocaoglu, B. (2016). Using SCOR Model to Gain Competitive Advantage: A Literature Review. *Procedia: Social and Behavioral Sciences*, *229*, 398–406. doi:10.1016/j.sbspro.2016.07.150

Deloitte. (2012). *The reshoring of America - How can we take advantage of it?* Samson Bélair/Deloitte & Touche.

Deloitte. (2017). *Safeguarding M&A deal value: Managing culture clash*. Retrieved March 3, 2018 from https://www2.deloitte.com/content/dam/Deloitte/us/Documents/mergers-acqisitions/us-ma-safeguarding-m-and-a-deal-value-managing-culture-clash.pdf

Denscombe, M. (2010). *The Good Research Guide: For Small-Scale Social Research Projects: For small-scale social research projects*. Leicester, UK: McGraw-Hill.

Denzin, N. (1978). The logic of naturalistic inquiry. New York: Sociological Book.

Desai, M. A., Foley, C. F., & Hines, J. R. Jr. (2006). Capital controls, liberalizations, and foreign direct investment. *Review of Financial Studies*, *19*(4), 1433–1464. doi:10.1093/rfs/hhj041

DeSarbo, W. S., Grewal, R., & Wang, R. (2009). Dynamic strategic groups: Deriving spatial evolutionary paths. *Strategic Management Journal*, *30*(13), 1420–1439. doi:10.1002mj.788

Dess, G. G., & Davis, P. S. (1984). Porter's (1980) Generic strategies as determinants of strategic group membership and organizational performance. *Academy of Management Journal*, *27*, 467–488.

Dhanaraj, C., & Beamish, P. W. (2003). A Resource-Based Approach to the Study of Export Performance. *Journal of Small Business Management*, *41*(3), 242–261. doi:10.1111/1540-627X.00080

Di Giorgio, G., & Di Noia, C. (2008). *Designing a Regulatory and Supervisory Framework for Integrated Financial Markets* (Discussion Paper). Working Paper LUISS Guido Carli.

Di Mauro, C., Fratocchi, L., Orzes, G., & Sartor, M. (2018). Offshoring and backshoring: A multiple case study analysis. *Journal of Purchasing and Supply Management*, *24*(2), 108–134. doi:10.1016/j.pursup.2017.07.003

Dibbern, J. (2003). *The Sourcing Of Application Software Services: Empirical Evidence Of Cultural, Industry And Functional Differences (Information Age Economy).* Physica-Verlag.

Dibbern, J., Goles, T., Hirschheim, R., & Jayatilaka, B. (2004). Information systems outsourcing: A survey and analysis of the literature. *The Data Base for Advances in Information Systems, 35*(4), 6–102. doi:10.1145/1035233.1035236

Didier, T., & Schumkler, S. L. (2014). *Financial Development in Asia: Beyond Aggregate Indicators.* Policy Research Working Paper, Paper 6761, The World Bank.

Dikmen, I., Birgonul, T., & Budayan, C. (2009). Strategic group analysis in the construction industry. *Journal of Construction Engineering and Management, 135*(4), 288–297. doi:10.1061/(ASCE)0733-9364(2009)135:4(288)

DiMaggio, P. J., & Powell, W. W. (2000). The iron cage revisited institutional isomorphism and collective rationality in organizational fields. *Advances in Strategic Management, 17*, 143–166. doi:10.1016/S0742-3322(00)17011-1

Dinda, S. (2004). Environmental Kuznets curve hypothesis: A survey. *Ecological Economics: The Journal of the International Society for Ecological Economics, 49*(4), 431–455. doi:10.1016/j.ecolecon.2004.02.011

Dinnie, K. (2003). Country-of-Origin 1965-2004: A Literature Review. *Journal of Customer Behaviour, 3*(2), 165–213. doi:10.1362/1475392041829537

Distler, J., Fernández-Seara, J., Gottstein, H., Haemmerle, V., Rasch, S., & Rohrhofer, S. (2014). *Apparel at a Crossroads - The End of Low-Cost-Country Sourcing.* Academic Press.

Dominguez, N. (2016). Risk-seeking behaviours in SMEs' internationalization. In The Changing Global Economy and Its Impact on International Entrepreneurship. Academic Press.

dos Santos, T. (2001). *O Sistema Financeiro e a Globalização – A Regulação do Sistema Financeiro.* CMVM. Retrieved from www.cmvm.pt

Drucker, P. (2003). *Managing in Next Society* (1st ed.). Oxford, UK: Butterworth-Heinemann.

Dubois, F. L., Toyne, B., & Oliff, M. D. (1993). International Manufacturing Strategies of U.S. Multinationals: A conceptual framework based on a four-industry study. *Journal of International Business Studies*, 307–333.

Duhaime, I., & Grant, J. (1984). Factors Influencing Divestment Decision-making: Evidence from a Field Study. *Strategic Management Journal, 5*(4), 301–318. doi:10.1002mj.4250050402

Dunning, J. H. (1980). Towards an eclectic theory of international production: Some empirical tests. *Journal of International Business Studies, 11*(1), 9–31. doi:10.1057/palgrave.jibs.8490593

Dunning, J. H. (1988). The eclectic paradigm of international production: A restatement and some possible extensions. *Journal of International Business Studies, 19*(1), 1–31. doi:10.1057/palgrave.jibs.8490372

Dunning, J. H. (1993). *The Globalization of Business.* London: Routledge.

Dunning, J. H. (1998). Location Enterprise : The Multinational Neglected Factor? *Journal of International Business Studies*, 45–66. doi:10.1057/palgrave.jibs.8490024

Dunning, J. H. (2000). The eclectic paradigm as an envelope for economic and business theories of MNE activity. *International Business Review, 9*(2), 163–190. doi:10.1016/S0969-5931(99)00035-9

Dunning, J. H. (2009). Explaining changing patterns of international production. In defense of the eclectic theory. *Oxford Bulletin of Economics and Statistics, 41*(4), 269–295. doi:10.1111/j.1468-0084.1979.mp41004003.x

Duriau, V. J., Reger, R. K., & Pfarrer, M. D. (2007). A Content Analysis of the Content Analysis Literature in Organization Studies: Research Themes, Data Sources, and Methodological Refinements. *Organizational Research Methods*, *10*(1), 5–34. doi:10.1177/1094428106289252

Dvorkin, M. (2017). *Startups Create Many Jobs, but They Often Don't Last | St. Louis Fed*. Retrieved 19 April 2018, from https://www.stlouisfed.org/publications/regional-economist/third-quarter-2017/startups-create-many-jobs-but-they-often-dont-last

Dyer, J. H., & Singh, H. (1998). The Impacts of Customer Interaction and Social Capital on New Service Development Performance. *Academy of Management Review*, *23*(4), 660–679. doi:10.5465/amr.1998.1255632

Easterby-Smith, M., Lyles, M. A., & Peteraf, M. A. (2009). Dynamic Capabilities: Current Debates and Future Directions. *British Journal of Management*, *20*(1), S1–S8. doi:10.1111/j.1467-8551.2008.00609.x

Ebbes, P., Grewal, R., & DeSarbo, W. S. (2010). Modeling strategic group dynamics: A hidden Markov approach. *Quantitative Marketing and Economics*, *8*(2), 241–274. doi:10.100711129-010-9081-0

Edwards, F., & Mishkin, F. S. (1995). The Decline of Traditional Banking: Implications for financial stability and regulatory policy. *Federal Reserve Bank of New York Economic Policy Review*, *1*(3), 27–45.

Eisenhardt, K. M. (1989). Building Theories from Case Study Research. *Academy of Management Review*, *14*(4), 532–550. doi:10.5465/amr.1989.4308385

Eisenhardt, K. M., & Graebner, M. E. (2007). Theory Building From Cases: Opportunities and Challenges. *Academy of Management Journal*, *50*(1), 25–32. doi:10.5465/amj.2007.24160888

Eisenhardt, K. M., & Martin, J. A. (2000). Dynamic capabilities: What are they? *Strategic Management Journal*, *21*(10–11), 1105–1121. doi:10.1002/1097-0266(200010/11)21:10/11<1105::AID-SMJ133>3.0.CO;2-E

Ekart Logistics. (n.d.). Retrieved 20 April 2018, from https://www.ekartlogistics.com/about_us

Elango, B. (1998). An empirical examination of the influence of industry and firm drivers on the rate of internationalization by firms. *Journal of International Management*, *4*(3), 201–221. doi:10.1016/S1075-4253(98)00011-8

Elango, B., & Sethi, S. P. (2007). An Exploration of the Relationship between Country of Origin (COE) and the Internationalization-Performance Paradigm. *Management International Review*, *47*(3), 369–392. doi:10.100711575-007-0021-5

Ellram, L. M. (2013). Offshoring, Reshoring and the Manufacturing Location Decision. *The Journal of Supply Chain Management*, *49*(2), 1–3.

Ellram, L. M. (2013). Offshoring, reshoring and the manufacturing location decisions. *The Journal of Supply Chain Management*, *49*(2), 3–5. doi:10.1111/jscm.12023

Ellram, L. M., & Cooper, M. C. (2014). Supply Chain Management: It's All About the Journey, Not the Destination. *The Journal of Supply Chain Management*, *50*(1), 8–20. doi:10.1111/jscm.12043

Ellram, L. M., Tate, W. L., & Petersen, K. J. (2013). Offshoring and Reshoring: An update on the manufacturing local decision. *The Journal of Supply Chain Management*, *49*(2), 14–22. doi:10.1111/jscm.12019

Engwall, L., & Wallenstal, M. (1988). Tit for tat in small steps: The internationalization of Swedish banks. *Scandinavian Journal of Management*, *4*(3/4), 147–155. doi:10.1016/0956-5221(88)90006-1

Enriques, L., & Volpin, P. (2007). Corporate Governance Reforms in Continental Europe. *The Journal of Economic Perspectives*, *21*(1), 117–140. doi:10.1257/jep.21.1.117

Epure, M., Kerstens, K., & Prior, D. (2011). Bank productivity and performance groups: A decomposition approach based upon the Luenberger productivity indicator. *European Journal of Operational Research, 211*(3), 630–641. doi:10.1016/j.ejor.2011.01.041

Erber, G., & Sayed-Ahmed, A. (2005). Offshore outsourcing. A global shift in the present IT Industry. *Inter Economics, 40*(2), 100–112. doi:10.100710272-005-0141-8

Erickson, G. M., Johansson, J. K., & Chao, P. (1984). Image Variables in Multi-Attribute Product Evaluations: Country-of-Origin Effects. *The Journal of Consumer Research, 11*(2), 694–699. doi:10.1086/209005

Ernst and Young. (2015). *Investment climate in Russia -Foreign investor perception.* Retrieved from https://www.ey.com/Publication/

Erramilli, M. K., & Rao, C. P. (1993). Service Firms' International Entry-Mode Choice: A Modified Transaction-Cost Analysis Approach. *Journal of Marketing, 57*(3), 19.

Eskeland, G. S., & Harrison, A. E. (2003). Moving to greener pastures? Multinationals and the pollution haven hypothesis. *Journal of Development Economics, 70*(1), 1–23. doi:10.1016/S0304-3878(02)00084-6

Espitia, M. A., Polo, Y., & Salas, V. (1991). Grupos estratégicos y resultados en el sector bancario español. *Información Comercial Española, 690*, 189–212.

Etemad, H. (2004). Internationalisation of small and medium-sized enterprises: A grounded theoretical framework and an overview. *Canadian Journal of Administrative Sciences, 21*(1), 1–21. doi:10.1111/j.1936-4490.2004.tb00319.x

EUR-Lex. (2003). *Definition of micro, small and medium-sized enterprises.* Retrieved from https://eur-lex.europa.eu/eli/reco/2003/361/oj

European Central Bank (ECB). (2014). *Guide to Banking Supervision.* ECB Banking Supervision.

European Commission. (2003). *Observatory of European SMEs 2003.* Luxembourg: Author.

European Commission. (2013). *Applying Behavioral Sciences to EU Policy-making.* JRC Scientific and Policy Reports, EUR 26033.

European Union. (2013). *European Union Capital Requirements Directive IV, 575/2013.* European Parliament.

Eurostat. (2018). *Statistics on small and medium-sized enterprises.* Retrieved November 27, 2018, from https://ec.europa.eu/eurostat/statistics-explained/index.php/Statistics_on_small_and_medium-sized_enterprises

Fadeeva, A., Burmistrov, S., Balashov, A., Podobedova, L., & Dzyadko, T. (2017). *The court charged RUR 136 billion from Sistema in favor of Rosneft.* RBC. Retrieved from http://www.rbc.ru/business/23/08/2017/59703cc89a794716007986d7

Fakhrutdinova, E., Kolesnikova, J., & Yurieva, O. K. (2014). Current trends of realization of the intellectual capital and problems of intellectual migration. *Procedia Economics and Finance, 14*(1), 326–332.

Farooqui, M. (2015). *Want to shift your goods? Porter is a click away | Business Standard News.* Retrieved 20 April 2018, from http://www.business-standard.com/article/companies/want-to-shift-your-goods-porter-is-a-click-away-115092800008_1.html

Farzipoor Saen, R. (2011). International market selection using advanced data envelopment analysis. *IMA Journal of Management Mathematics, 22*(4), 371–386. doi:10.1093/imaman/dpr011

FCT. (2014). *Estratégia Nacional de Investigação e inovação para uma especialização inteligente 2014-2020 – Diagnóstico de Apoio às Jornadas de Reflexão Estratégica.* Retrieved from https://www.fct.pt/esp_inteligente/docs/TIC_ENEI_Lisboa.pdf

Federal State Statistics Service. (2017). *Business Confidence Index.* Retrieved from http://www.gks.ru/free_doc/new_site/metod/prom/met_pred-uver.htm

Federwoski, R. (2007). Routines in a turnaround - What are they good for. *International conference on corporate routines: Empirical Research and Conceptual Foundations.*

Ferdows, K. (1989). Mapping international factory networks. In K. Ferdows (Ed.), *Mapping International Manufacturing*. New York: North Holland.

Ferdows, K. (1997). Made in the World: The Global Spread of Production. *Production and Operations Management, 6*(2), 102–109. doi:10.1111/j.1937-5956.1997.tb00418.x

Ferguson, T. D., & Ketchen, D. Jr. (1999). Organizational configuration and performance: The role of statistical power in extant research. *Strategic Management Journal, 20*(4), 385–395. doi:10.1002/(SICI)1097-0266(199904)20:4<385::AID-SMJ24>3.0.CO;2-X

Fernández-Olmos, M., & Díez-Vial, I. (2015). Intangible resources, export channel and performance: Is there any fit? *Journal of Business Economics and Management, 16*(5), 1013–1033. doi:10.3846/16111699.2012.726928

Ferrari, M. (2018). The structure and dynamics of the CEO's "small world" of Stakeholders: An application to the industrial downsizing. *Technological Forecasting and Social Change, 140*, 147–159. doi:10.1016/j.techfore.2018.04.006

Fiegenbaum, A., & Thomas, H. (1990). Strategic Groups and Performance: The U.S. Insurance Industry, 1970–84. *Strategic Management Journal, 11*(3), 197–215. doi:10.1002mj.4250110303

Financial Stability Board's (FSB). (2014). Guidance on Supervision Interaction with Financial Institutions on Risk Culture: A Framework for Assessing Risk Culture. Financial Stability Board.

Finch, D., McDonald, S., & Staple, J. (2013). Reputational interdependence: An examination of category reputation in higher education. *Journal of Marketing for Higher Education, 23*(1), 34–61. doi:10.1080/08841241.2013.810184

Fine, C. (2013). Intelli-Sourcing to Replace Offshoring as Supply Chain Transparency Increases. *The Journal of Supply Chain Management, 49*(2), 6–7. doi:10.1111/jscm.12018

Finn, S. (2015). *WVU Researchers Help Bust Volkswagen for Pollution Violations.* WVPublic. Retrieved from http://wvpublic.org/post/wvu-researchers-help-bust-volkswagen-pollution-violations

Fishbein, M., & Ajzen, I. (1975). *Belief, Attitude, intention and behaviour. Belief, Attitude, Intention, and Behavior: An Introduction to Theory and Research.* doi:10.1016/j.ecolecon.2004.07.008

Fisher, C. M. (2010). *Researching and writing a dissertation: an essential guide for business students.* Harlow, UK: Pearson Education.

Flanagan, J., & O'Shaughnessy, K. (2005). The effect of layoffs on firm reputation. *Journal of Management, 31*(3), 445–463. doi:10.1177/0149206304272186

Flavián, C., Haberberg, A., & Polo, Y. (2002). Food retailing strategies in the European Union. A comparative analysis in the UK and Spain. *Journal of Retailing and Consumer Services, 9*(3), 125–138. doi:10.1016/S0969-6989(01)00011-X

Flores-Márquez, S., Rodríguez-Monroy, C., & Flores-Gutiérrez, J. (2015). Identificación y evolución de los grupos estratégicos de la industria bancaria Venezolana. *Interciencia, 40*(3), 165–171.

Foerstl, K., Kirchoff, J. F., & Bals, L. (2016). Reshoring and insourcing: Drivers and future research directions. *International Journal of Physical Distribution & Logistics Management*, *46*(5), 492–515. doi:10.1108/IJPDLM-02-2015-0045

Fok, E. (2015). *How ecommerce ventures are using 'milk-run' model to ensure last-mile delivery - The Economic Times.* Retrieved 24 April 2018, from https://economictimes.indiatimes.com/small-biz/startups/how-ecommerce-ventures-are-using-milk-run-model-to-ensure-last-mile-delivery/articleshow/47981225.cms

Foresight. (2013). *The Future of Manufacturing: A new Era of opportunity and challenge for the UK.* London: Author.

Fornell, C., & Larcker, D. F. (1981). Evaluating Structural Equation Models with Unobservable Variables and Measurement Error. *JMR, Journal of Marketing Research*, *18*(1), 39–50. doi:10.1177/002224378101800104

Foroohar, R. (2013). *How "Made in the USA" is Making a Comeback.* Retrieved from http://business.time.com/2013/04/11/how-made-in-the-usa-is-making-a-comeback/

Frank Prevos. (2013). *Backshoring of Dutch Manufacturing Firms.* Amsterdam Business School, University of Amsterdam.

Frankel, J. A., & Rose, A. K. (2005). Is trade good or bad for the environment? Sorting out the causality. *The Review of Economics and Statistics*, *87*(1), 85–91. doi:10.1162/0034653053327577

Fratocchi, L., & Silva, S. C. L. da C. e. (2018). Manufacturing Back-Shoring and Direct Brand Creation in the Footwear Industry. In P. Thorvald & K. Case (Eds.), Avances in Manufacturing Technology XXXII (pp. 461–466). doi:10.3233/978-1-61499-902-7-461

Fratocchi, L., Ancarani, A., Barbieri, P., Di Mauro, C., Nassimbeni, G., & Sartor, M. (2016). Motivations of manufacturing reshoring: an interpretative framework. *International Journal of Physical Distribution & Logistics Management, 46*(2), 153–176.

Fratocchi, L., Ancarani, A., Barbieri, P., Di Mauro, C., Nassimbeni, G., Sartor, M., … Zanoni, A. (2015). Manufacturing Back-Reshoring as a Nonlinear Internationalization Process. Academic Press.

Fratocchi, L., Ancarani, A., Barbieri, P., Di Mauro, C., Nassimbeni, G., Sartor, M., … Zanoni, A. (2015). Manufacturing Back-Reshoring as a Nonlinear Internationalization Process. In Progress in International Business Research (pp. 365–403). Emerald Group Publishing Limited. doi:10.1108/S1745-886220150000010011

Fratocchi, L., Equizi, S., Nassimbeni, G., Sartor, M., Ancarani, A., Di Mauro, C., … Vignoli, M. (2013). Manufacturing Back-shoring: Theoretical Conceptualization and Empirical Evidence. In *15th Conference of the International Academy of Management and Business* (pp. 1–10). Retrieved from http://beachvolleyball.guidedbees.com/~ruben/EDSI/papers/dimauro_manufacturing.pdf

Fratocchi, L., Ancarani, A., Barbieri, P., Di Mauro, C., Nassimbeni, G., Sartor, M., ... Zanoni, A. (2016). Motivations of manufacturing reshoring: An interpretative framework. *International Journal of Physical Distribution & Logistics Management*, *46*(2), 98–127. doi:10.1108/IJPDLM-06-2014-0131

Fratocchi, L., Di Mauro, C., Barbieri, P., Nassimbeni, G., & Zanoni, A. (2014). When Manufacturing Moves Back: Concepts and Questions. *Journal of Purchasing and Supply Management*, *20*(1), 54–59. doi:10.1016/j.pursup.2014.01.004

Frazer Winsted, K., & Patterson, P. G. (1998). Internationalization of services: The service exporting decision. *Journal of Services Marketing*, *12*(4), 294–311. doi:10.1108/08876049810226964

Freeman, R. (1984). *Strategic Management: A Stakeholder Approach.* Boston: Pitman.

Freeman, R., & McVea. (2001). *Strategic management; a stalkholder approach.* Pitman.

Freeman, S., Deligonul, S., & Cavusgil, T. (2013). Strategic re-structuring by born-globals using outward and inward-oriented activity. *International Marketing Review, 30*(2), 156–182. doi:10.1108/02651331311314574

Freight, M. 'A Seamless Experience' – The BlackBuck Blog – Medium. (n.d.). Retrieved 24 April 2018, from https://medium.com/the-blackbuck-blog/making-freight-a-seamless-experience-156ec172ebe5

Freitas, J. A. (1998). *Determinantes do desinvestimento em Portugal*. GEPE - Ministério da Economia.

From, J., & Eliassen, K. A. (Eds.). (2007). *The privatisation of European telecommunications*. Ashgate Publishing, Limited.

FrontalRain Technologies - Software for Agri Businesses I FrontalRain Technologies. (n.d.). Retrieved 24 April 2018, from http://www.frontalrain.com/plans/

Fuchs, M., & Köstner, M. (2016). Antecedents and consequences of firm's export marketing strategy: An empirical study of Austrian SMEs (a contingency perspective). *Management Research Review, 39*(3), 329–355. doi:10.1108/MRR-07-2014-0158

Fukuyama, T. (2017). *Workplace culture should be measured, just like sales or ROI. Uber's issues should have leadership everywhere asking, "How healthy is our culture?"* Retrieved February 3, 2018 from https://www.recode.net/2017/4/18/15327848/workplace-culturemeasurement-metrics-healthy-uber

Galeotti, M., Lanza, A., & Pauli, F. (2006). Reassessing the environmental Kuznets curve for CO2 emissions: A robustness exercise. *Ecological Economics: The Journal of the International Society for Ecological Economics, 57*(1), 152–163. doi:10.1016/j.ecolecon.2005.03.031

Galeotti, M., Manera, M., & Lanza, A. (2009). On the robustness of robustness checks of the environmental Kuznets curve hypothesis. *Environmental and Resource Economics, 42*(4), 551–574. doi:10.100710640-008-9224-x

Galphin, T. J., & Herndon, M. (2000). *The Complete Guide to Mergers and Acquisitions-Process Tools to Support M&A Integration at Every Level*. San Francisco: Jossey-Bass Publishers Inc.

Ganguly, P. (2017). *Funding: Trucking marketplace BlackBuck bags $70M from Sands Capital, others, Technology News, ETtech*. Retrieved 20 April 2018, from https://tech.economictimes.indiatimes.com/news/startups/trucking-marketplace-blackbuck-bags-70-m-from-sands-capital-others/57755778

Gankema, H. G. J., Snuif, H. R., & Zwart, P. S. (2000). The internationalization process of small and medium-sized enterprises: An evaluation of stage theory. *Journal of Small Business Management, 38*(4), 15.

Gao, X. (2018). *Measuring the Generalized Global Industry Relocation*. Academic Press.

Gary, M. S., & Wood, R. E. (2011). Mental models, decision rules, and performance heterogeneity. *Strategic Management Journal, 32*(6), 569–594. doi:10.1002mj.899

Gazal Kalra. (n.d.). In *LinkedIn*. Retrieved 20 April 2018, from https://www.linkedin.com/in/gazal-kalra-a5b6523/

Geet Garg. (n.d.). In *LinkedIn*. Retrieved 20 April 2018, from https://www.linkedin.com/in/geetgarg/

Georgise, F. B., Wuest, T., & Thoben, K.-D. (2017). SCOR model application in developing countries: Challenges & requirements. *Production Planning and Control, 28*(1), 17–32. doi:10.1080/09537287.2016.1230790

Gewald, H., Wüllenweber, K., & Weitzel, T. (2006). The influence of perceived risks on banking managers' intention to outsource business processes-a study of the German banking and finance industry. *Journal of Electronic Commerce Research, 7*(2), 78–97.

Ghauri, P. N., & Yamin, M. (2009). Revisiting the impact of multinational enterprises on economic development. *Journal of World Business*, *44*(2), 105–107. doi:10.1016/j.jwb.2008.05.010

Ghildiyal, H. (2017). *BoxMySpace – Technology Enabled Warehousing and Logistics*. Retrieved 24 April 2018, from https://blog.boxmyspace.com/

Ghosh, S. (2015). *5 Indian Startups to boost the agriculture of the country - KnowStartup*. Retrieved 24 April 2018, from http://knowstartup.com/2015/07/startups-help-the-agriculture/

Giddens, A. (1984). *The Constitution of Society, Outline of the Theory of Structuration*. Cambridge, UK: Polity.

Giessner, S. R., Viki, G. T., Otten, S., Terry, D. J., & Täuber, S. (2006). The challenge of merging: Merger patterns, premerger status, and merger support. *Personality and Social Psychology Bulletin*, *32*(3), 339–352. doi:10.1177/0146167205282151 PMID:16455861

Giudice, V., & Lu, W. (2017). *India Seen Topping Global Labor Force In Next Decade, Data Show - Bloomberg*. Retrieved 19 April 2018, from https://www.bloomberg.com/news/articles/2017-08-31/india-seen-topping-global-labor-force-in-next-decade-data-show

Glaser, B., & Strauss, A. (1967). *The discovery of Grounded Theory*. London. *Weidenfeld and Nicholson*, *24*(25), 288–304.

Gleich, R., Kierans, G., & Hasselbach, T. (2010). Value in Due Diligence: Contemporary Strategies for Merger and Acquisition Success. Farnham, UK: Gower.

Gnizy, I., & Shoham, A. (2014). Explicating the Reverse Internationalization Processes of Firms. *Journal of Global Marketing*, *27*(4), 262–283. doi:10.1080/08911762.2014.917755

Goffman, E. (1959). *The Presentation of Self in Everyday Life*. Garden City, NY: Doubleday.

Goleman, D. (1998). *Working with Emotional Intelligence*. New York: Bantam.

Goleman, D. (2000). Leadership that gets results. *Harvard Business Review*, *78*(2), 78–89.

Goles, T., & Chin, W. W. (2005). Information Systems Outsourcing Relationship Factors: Detailed Conceptualization and Initial Evidence. *The Data Base for Advances in Information Systems*, *36*(4), 47–67. doi:10.1145/1104004.1104009

Gomes, E., Weber, Y., Brown, C., & Tarba, S. Y. (2011). *Mergers, Acquisitions, and Strategic Alliances: Understanding the Process*. Melbourne: Macmillan International Higher Education.

Goo, K. Rao, & Nam. (2009). The Role of Service Level Agreements in Relational Management of Information Technology Outsourcing: An Empirical Study. *Management Information Systems Quarterly*. doi:10.2307/20650281

Gooptu, B. (2017). *Rivigo: A roadside chat set me on my way for Rivigo moment: Deepak Garg, CEO, Rivigo - The Economic Times*. Retrieved 20 April 2018, from https://economictimes.indiatimes.com/small-biz/startups/features/a-roadside-chat-set-me-on-my-way-for-rivigo-moment-deepak-garg-ceo-rivigo/articleshow/62143469.cms

Göran, S. (2007). *Supply Chain Management versus Sustainable Chain Management*. Academic Press.

Graaff, J. de V. (1987). "Social cost". *The New Palgrave: A Dictionary of Economics*, *4*, 393-395.

Graham, S. (1999). Global grids of glass: On global cities, telecommunications and planetary urban networks. *Urban Studies (Edinburgh, Scotland)*, *36*(5-6), 929–949. doi:10.1080/0042098993286

Grant, R. M. (1998). *Contemporary strategy analysis: concepts, techniques, applications*. Malden, MA: Blackwell.

Gray, J. V., Skowronski, K., Esenduran, G., & Rungtusanatham, M. J. (2013). The Reshoring Phenomnon: What supply chain academics ought to know and should do. *The Journal of Supply Chain Management, 49*(2), 27–33. doi:10.1111/jscm.12012

Griffith, D. A., Cavusgil, S. T., & Xu, S. (2008). Emerging themes in international business research. *Journal of International Business Studies, 39*(7), 1220–1235. doi:10.1057/palgrave.jibs.8400412

Grossman, G. M., & Krueger, A. B. (1995). Economic growth and the environment. *The Quarterly Journal of Economics, 110*(2), 353–377. doi:10.2307/2118443

Grotberg, E. (2003). *Resilience for Today*. Westport, CT: Praeger.

Groysberg, B., Lee, J., Price, J., & Cheng, J. Y. (2018, January). *The leader's guide to corporate culture. Harvard Business Review.*

Guedes, J. F. (2015). Maximizing return on investment without increasing project risks - Near-shoring as a key practice on a business transformation programme: Case study on a training project for a global consumer goods company. *2015 10th Iberian Conference on Information Systems and Technologies, CISTI 2015.* 10.1109/CISTI.2015.7170387

Gugin. (2013). *Cultural due diligence: Identifying your cultural DNA*. Retrieved February 8, 2018 from www.gugin.com

Gupta, B. (2017). *Exclusive: BoxMySpace raises pre-Series A funding from clutch of investors*. Retrieved 24 April 2018, from https://www.dealstreetasia.com/stories/exclusive-boxmyspace-raises-pre-series-funding-clutch-investors-79586/

Gupta, H. (2016). *E-startups: Online logistics marketplace Porter set to enter Pune and Ahmedabad - The Financial Express*. Retrieved 24 April 2018, from https://www.financialexpress.com/industry/estartups-online-logistics-marketplace-porter-set-to-enter-pune-and-ahmedabad/473460/

Gusakov, V. (2017). Key Trends of the Russian Share Market. *Moscow Exchange*. Retrieved from http://www.oecd.moex.com/s624

Habeck, M. M., Kroger, F., & Tram, M. R. (2000). *After the Merger: Seven Strategies for Successful Post-Merger Integration*. Harlow: Pearson Education.

Hadjikhani, A. (2015). A Note on the Criticisms Against the Internationalization Process Model. In *Knowledge, Networks and Power* (pp. 64–87). London: Palgrave Macmillan. doi:10.1057/9781137508829_3

Hahn, E. D., Bunyaratavej, K., & Doh, J. P. (2011). Impacts of Risk and Service Type on Nearshore and Offshore Investment Location Decisions. *Management International Review, 51*(3), 357–380. doi:10.100711575-011-0078-z

Hahn, W., & Powers, T. L. (2010). Strategic plan quality, implementation capability, and firm performance. *Academy of Strategic Management Journal, 9*(1), 63–82.

Hair, J., Hult, G. T. M., Ringle, C. M., & Sarstedt, M. (2013). *A primer on Partial least Squares Structural Equation Modeling (PLS-SEM)*. SAGE Publications, Inc.

Håkansson, H., & Snehota, I. (2006). No business is an island" 17 years later. *Scandinavian Journal of Management, 22*(3), 271–274. doi:10.1016/j.scaman.2006.08.001

Håkonsson, D., Eskildsen, E., Argote, L., Mønster, D., Burton, R., & Obel, B. (2015). Exploration versus exploitation: Emotions and performance as antecedents and consequences of team decisions. *Strategic Management Journal, 37*, 935–1001.

Halaj, G., & Zochowski, D. (2009). Strategic groups and banks' performance. *Financial Theory and Practice, 33*(2), 153–186.

Hallen, L. (1992). *Infrastructural networks in international business*. Företagsekonomiska Institutionen vid Uppsala Universitet.

Hambrick, D., & Schecter, S. (1983). Turnaround Strategy for mature industrial-product Business Units. *Academy of Management Journal*, *26*(2), 231–248.

Hamel, G., & Prahalad, C. K. (1994). *Competing for the Future*. Boston: Harvard Business School Press.

Hamel, G., & Valikangas, L. (2003, September). The Quest for resilience. *Harvard Business Review*, 52–63. PMID:12964393

Hamilton, R., & Chow, Y. (1993). Why Managers Divest: Evidence from New Zealand's largest companies. *Strategic Management Journal*, *14*(6), 479–484. doi:10.1002mj.4250140606

Hammer, M., & Champy, J. (1993). Reengineering the Corporation. New York: Academic Press.

Han, c. M., & Qualls, W. J. (1985). Country-Of-Origin Effects and Their Impact Upon Consumers' Perception of Quality. *Historical Perspective in Consumer Research: Natitional and International Perspectives*, 162–167.

Haq, S., Raza, M., Zia, A., & Khan, M. N. A. (2011). Issues in Global Software Development: A Critical Review. *Journal of Software Engineering and Applications*, *04*(10), 590–595. doi:10.4236/jsea.2011.410069

Harland, C. M. (1996). Supply Chain Management: Relationships, Chains and Networks. *British Journal of Management*, *7*(s1), S63–S80. doi:10.1111/j.1467-8551.1996.tb00148.x

Harrigan, K. (2012). *A Turnaround Strategy Framework. Columbia Casework*. New York: Columbia University.

Harrison, S., & Farrell, P. (2007). Communication flow in mergers and acquisitions. *The Third Scottish Conference for Postgraduate*, 191-201.

Haspeslagh, P. C., & Jemison, D. B. (1991). *Managing Acquisitions: Creating Value through Corporate Renewal*. New York: The Free Press.

Hatten, K. J. (1974). *Strategic models in the brewing industries* (Unpublished doctoral dissertation). Purdue University.

Hatten, K. J., & Hatten, M. L. (1987). Strategic groups, asymmetrical barriers & contestability. *Strategic Management Journal*, *8*(4), 329–342. doi:10.1002mj.4250080404

Hawkesby, C. (2000, July). The Institutional Structure of Financial Supervision: A Cost benefit Analysis. *The Journal of International Banking Regulation*, 36-54.

Hayes, R. H., & Wheelwright, S. C. (1984). *Restoring our competitive edge: Competing through manufacturing*. New York: Wiley.

Hayes, S. L., Spence, A. M., & Marks, D. V. P. (1983). *Competition in the investment banking industry*. Harvard University Press Cambridge.

Hecksher, E., & Ohlin, B. (1933). *Interregional and international trade*. Cambridge, MA: Harvard UniversityPress.

He, J. (2006). Pollution haven hypothesis and environmental impacts of foreign direct investment: The case of industrial emission of sulfur dioxide (SO2) in Chinese provinces. *Ecological Economics: The Journal of the International Society for Ecological Economics*, *60*(1), 228–245. doi:10.1016/j.ecolecon.2005.12.008

Hennart, J.-F. (1991). The Transaction Costs Theory of Joint Ventures: An Empirical Study of Japanese Subsidiaries in the United States. *Management Science*, *37*(4), 483–497. doi:10.1287/mnsc.37.4.483

Hennart, J.-F., Kim, D.-J., & Zwng, M. (1998). The Impact of Joint Venture status on the Longevity of Japanese Stakes in US Manufacturing Affiliates. *Organization Science*, *9*(3), 382–395. doi:10.1287/orsc.9.3.382

Herndon, M. (2017). *Caution ahead - Cultural flashpoints*. Retrieved February, 25, 2018 from https://www.mapartners.net/insights/caution-ahead-cultural-flashpoints

Herring, R. J., & Carmassi, J. (2008). The Structure of Cross Sector Financial Supervision, *Financial Markets. Institutions and Instruments*, *17*(1), 51–76. doi:10.1111/j.1468-0416.2007.00132.x

Hervás, J. L., Dalmau, J. I., & Albors, J. (2006). 1972–2005: En la cuarta década de la investigación sobre grupos estratégicos ¿Qué hemos aprendido? *Investigaciones Europeas de Dirección y Economía de la Empresa*, *12*(1), 167–205.

He, S., Fallon, G., Khan, Z., Lew, Y. K., Kim, K. H., & Wei, P. (2017). Towards a new wave in internationalization of innovation? The rise of China's innovative MNEs, strategic coupling, and global economic organization. *Canadian Journal of Administrative Sciences*, *34*(4), 343–355. doi:10.1002/cjas.1444

Hessels, J., & Parker, S. C. (2013). Constraints, internationalisation and growth: A cross-country analysis of European SMEs. *Journal of World Business*, *48*(1), 137–148. doi:10.1016/j.jwb.2012.06.014

Hewitt, A. (2011). *Culture integration in M&A- survey findings*. Retrieved April 9, 2018 from www.aon.com/attachments/thoughtleadership/M_A_Survey

He, X., & Wei, Y. (2011). Linking market orientation to international market selection and international performance. *International Business Review*, *20*(5), 535–546. doi:10.1016/j.ibusrev.2010.10.003

He, X., & Yao, X. (2017). Foreign direct investments and the environmental Kuznets curve: New evidence from Chinese provinces. *Emerging Markets Finance & Trade*, *53*(1), 12–25. doi:10.1080/1540496X.2016.1138813

Hill, M. (2014). Cautionary Tales From The Enron Of American Churches. *Forbes*. Retrieved from https://www.forbes.com/sites/robasghar/2014/09/16/mars-hill-cautionary-tales-from-the-enron-of-american-churches/#15d4a249583a

Hill, C. W. L. (2007). *International Business: Competing in the global marketplace* (6th ed.). New York, NY: McGraw-Hill/Irwin.

Hill, T. J. (1994). Teaching Manufacturing Strategy. *International Journal of Operations & Production Management*, *6*(3), 10–20. doi:10.1108/eb054762

Hitt, M., Bierman, L., Shimizu, K., & Kochhar, R. (2001). Direct and moderating effects of human capital on strategy and performance in professional service firms: A resource-based perspective. *Academy of Management Journal*, *44*(1), 13–28.

Hofer, C. (1980). Turnaround strategies. Analytical concepts. *The Journal of Business Strategy*, *1*(1), 19–31. doi:10.1108/eb038886

Hofstede, G. (n.d.). *Compare countries - Hofstede Insights*. Retrieved December 29, 2018, from https://www.hofstede-insights.com/product/compare-countries/

Hofstede, G. (1983). The Cultural Relativity of Organizational Practices and Theories. *Journal of International Business Studies*, *14*(2), 75–89. doi:10.1057/palgrave.jibs.8490867

Holloway, S. (2015). *Mobile Supply Chain Management Software | Software Research | Crozdesk*. Retrieved 19 April 2018, from https://crozdesk.com/software-research/mobile-supply-chain-management-software

Holm, U., & Pedersen, T. (2000). *In The Emergence and Impact of MNC Centres of Excellence – A Subsidiary Perspective*. London: Macmillan.

Hong, Y. (2017). Pivot to Internet Plus: Molding China's Digital Economy for Economic Restructuring? Hudson, H. E. (1991). Telecommunications in Africa the role of the ITU. *Telecommunications Policy, 15*(4), 343–350.

Hsu, D. H., & Ziedonis, R. H. (2013). Resources as Dual Sources of Advantage: Implications for Valuing Entrepreneurial-Firm Patents. *Strategic Management Journal, 34*(7), 761–781. doi:10.1002mj.2037

Huang, W. H., Chao, S. L., & Chang, C. C. (2017). Assessment of differences in efficiency across strategic groups in the container shipping context: A data envelopment analysis. *International Journal of Shipping and Transport Logistics, 9*(6), 651–672. doi:10.1504/IJSTL.2017.086934

Hughes, K. (2005). *IT Fundamentals*. Croydon: Tertiary Press.

Hung, R., Yang, B., Lien, B., McLean, G. N., & Kuo, Y.-M. (2010). Dynamic capability: Impact of process alignment and organizational learning culture on performance. *Journal of World Business, 45*(3), 285–294. doi:10.1016/j.jwb.2009.09.003

Hunt, M. (1972). *Competition in the Major Home Appliance Industry, 1960–1970* (Unpublished doctoral dissertation). Harvard University.

Huppe, B. (2017). *Technology and the 'last mile' - Marketing Tech News*. Retrieved 19 April 2018, from https://www.marketingtechnews.net/news/2017/may/19/technology-and-last-mile/

Hutchinson, K., Alexander, N., Quinn, B., & Doherty, A. M. (2007). Internationalization Motives and Facilitating Factors: Qualitative Evidence from Smaller Specialist Retailers. *Journal of International Marketing, 15*(3), 96–122. doi:10.1509/jimk.15.3.96

Hutzel, T., & Lippert, D. (2014). *Bringing Jobs Back to the USA. CRC Press*. doi:10.1201/b17056

iMIS - Welcome to the World of iMIS. (n.d.). Retrieved from https://cscmp.org/imis0/CSCMP/Educate/SCM_Definitions_and_Glossary_of_Terms

India loses $65 billion every year due to inefficient supply chain systems. (2010). Retrieved 20 April 2018, from https://www.moneylife.in/article/india-loses-65-billion-every-year-due-to-inefficient-supply-chain-systems/8786.html

Indian Economy: Overview, Market Size, Growth, Development, Statistics...IBEF. (2018). Retrieved 22 April 2018, from https://www.ibef.org/economy/indian-economy-overview

Indian Economy: Overview, Market Size, Growth, Development, Statistics...IBEF. (n.d.). Retrieved from https://www.ibef.org/economy/indian-economy-overview

Initiative, R. (2015). *Reshoring Initiative - Bringing Manufacturing Back Home*. Retrieved January 31, 2015, from http://www.reshorenow.org/what-is-reshoring/

InovaRia. A. (2011). *Análise do Comportamento das Empresas Portuguesas de Tecnologias de Informação e Eletrónica face à Internacionalização*. Retrieved from http://anetie.pt/wp-content/uploads/2017/09/Estudo_Internacionalização_ANETIE.pdf

InovaRia; Sociedade Portuguesa de Inovação. (2014). *Estudo Prospetivo do setor TICE*. Retrieved from http://www.pofc.qren.pt/ResourcesUser/2013/Publicacoes/Setor_TICE_EstudoPropectivo.pdf

Interfax. (2010, July 16). *Corporate Wars: NLMK vs Maksimov*. Retrieved from http://www.interfax.ru/business/145521

Interfax. (2010, October 21). *Finest hour Minority*. Retrieved from https://www.interfax.ru/business/161222

International Labor Organization. (2017). *World Employment and Social Outlook Report*. Retrieved from: www.ilo.org/wcmsp5/groups/public/---dgreports/---.../wcms_541211.pdf

International Transparency. (2014). *Corruption Perceptions Index 2014-results*. Author.

Interview with Nishith. Co-Founder at Locus – Digifire. (2016). Retrieved 20 April 2018, from https://www.digifire.in/2016/01/12/interview-with-nishith-co-founder-at-locus/

Ioannidou, V. P. (2005). Does Monetary Policy Affect the Central Bank's Role in Bank Supervision? *Journal of Financial Intermediation*, *14*(1), 58–85. doi:10.1016/j.jfi.2004.04.002

Iqbal, R. (n.d.). *Business week*. Retrieved from: http://bwdisrupt.businessworld.in/article/Rivigo-Disrupting-the-Logistics-Sector-With-Its-Unique-Driver-Relay-Model-and-Cutting-Edge-Technology-/16-08-2016-104469/

Isey, K. (2016). *Culture strategy in M&A: Context is everything*. Retrieved March 22, 2018 from https://www.linkedin.com/pulse/culture-strategy-ma-where-context-everything-karen-isely

Ivancevich, J., Schweiger, D., & Power, F. (1987). Executive action for managing human resources before and after acquisition. *The Academy of Management Executive*, *1*(2), 127–138.

Jansen, J. J. P., Van Den Bosch, F. J., & Volberda, H. W. (2005). Managing Potential and Realized Absorptive Capacity: How Do Organizational Antecedents Matter? *Academy of Management Journal*, *48*(6), 999–1015. doi:10.5465/amj.2005.19573106

Javalgi, R. G., & Martin, C. L. (2007). Internationalization of services: Identifying the building-blocks for future research. *Journal of Services Marketing*, *21*(6), 391–397. doi:10.1108/08876040710818886

Javidan, M., & House, R. J. (2002). Leadership and cultures around the world: Findings from GLOBE: An introduction to the special issue. *Journal of World Business*, *37*(1), 1–2. doi:10.1016/S1090-9516(01)00068-2

Jayawardhena, C., & Foley, P. (2000). Changes in the banking sector – the case of Internet banking in the UK. *Internet Research*, *10*(1), 19–31. doi:10.1108/10662240010312048

Jegers, M. (1989). On the detection of strategic groups and the relation between their occurrence and industry profitability. *Rivista Internazionale di Scienze Economiche e Commerciali*, *36*(6), 497–511.

Jensen, M. C., & Meckling, W. H. (1976). Theory of the Firm: Managerial Behavior: Agency Costs and Ownership Structure. *Journal of Financial Economics*, *3*(4), 305–360. doi:10.1016/0304-405X(76)90026-X

Jiang, L., Zhou, H.-F., Bai, L., & Zhou, P. (2018). Does foreign direct investment drive environmental degradation in China? An empirical study based on air quality index from a spatial perspective. *Journal of Cleaner Production*, *176*, 864–872. doi:10.1016/j.jclepro.2017.12.048

Jin, D. Y. (2005). The telecom crisis and beyond: Restructuring of the global telecommunications system. *Gazette (Leiden, Netherlands)*, *67*(3), 289–304. doi:10.1177/0016549205052232

Jin, D. Y. (2008). Neoliberal restructuring of the global communication system: Mergers and acquisitions. *Media Culture & Society*, *30*(3), 357–373. doi:10.1177/0163443708088792

Joerss, M. (2016). *How customer demands are reshaping last-mile delivery | McKinsey & Company*. Retrieved 19 April 2018, from https://www.mckinsey.com/industries/travel-transport-and-logistics/our-insights/how-customer-demands-are-reshaping-last-mile-delivery

Johanson, J., & Mattsson, L. (1988). Internationalization in industrial systems — a network approach. In P. J. Buckley & P. N. Ghauri (Eds.), *The internationalization of the firm: a reader* (pp. 303–321). London: Academic Press.

Johanson, J., & Mattsson, L. G. (1988). *Internatianalisation in Industrial Systems-A Network Approach. Strategies in Global Competition*. Croom Helm.

Johanson, J., & Mattsson, L.-G. (2015). Internationalisation in Industrial Systems — A Network Approach. In *Knowledge, Networks and Power* (pp. 111–132). London: Palgrave Macmillan UK. doi:10.1057/9781137508829_5

Johanson, J., & Vahlne, J.-E. (1977). The Internationalization Process of the Firm—A model of knowledge development and increasing foreign market commitments. *Journal of International Business Studies*, *8*(1), 23–32. doi:10.1057/palgrave.jibs.8490676

Johanson, J., & Vahlne, J.-E. (1990). The mechanism of internationalisation. *International Marketing Review*, *7*(4). doi:10.1108/02651339010137414

Johanson, J., & Vahlne, J.-E. (2003). Business relationship learning and commitment in the internationalization process. *Journal of International Entrepreneurship*, *1*(1), 83–101. doi:10.1023/A:1023219207042

Johanson, J., & Vahlne, J.-E. (2009). The Uppsala internationalization process model revisited—From liability of foreignness to liability of "Outsidership". *Journal of International Business Studies*, *40*(9), 1411–1431. doi:10.1057/jibs.2009.24

Johanson, J., & Wiedersheim-Paul, F. (1975). The internationalization of the firm—Four swedish cases. *Journal of Management Studies*, *12*(3), 305–323. doi:10.1111/j.1467-6486.1975.tb00514.x

Jose, J. (2018). *Last mile intra-city logistics: The key to e-commerce customer satisfaction - Re-Tales by Jolly Jose | ET Retail*. Retrieved 26 April 2018, from https://retail.economictimes.indiatimes.com/re-tales/last-mile-intra-city-logistics-the-key-to-e-commerce-customer-satisfaction/2900

Josiassen, A., Lukas, B., & Whitwell, G. J. (2008). Country-of-origin contingencies: Competing perspectives on product familiarity and product involvement. *International Marketing Review*, *25*(4), 423–440. doi:10.1108/02651330810887477

Kabanoff, B., & Brown, S. (2008). Knowledge structures of prospectors, analyzers, and defenders: Content, structure, stability, and performance. *Strategic Management Journal*, *29*(2), 149–171. doi:10.1002mj.644

Kaika, D., & Zervas, E. (2013). The environmental Kuznets curve (EKC) theory — Part A: Concept, causes and the CO2 emissions case. *Energy Policy*, *62*, 1392–1402. doi:10.1016/j.enpol.2013.07.131

Kakabadse, N., & Kakabadse, A. (2000). Critical Review--Outsourcing: A Paradigm Shift. *Journal of Management Development*, *19*(8), 668–728. doi:10.1108/02621710010377508

Kalaf & Bomtempo, J. V. (1999). Grupos Estratégicos, Competição baseada em Recursos e a Operacionalização da Estratégia. XXIII encontro nacional da ANPAD, Foz do Iguaçu. Anais...Foz do Iguaçu.

Kale, S., & Arditi, D. (2003). Differentiation, conformity, & construction firm performance. *Journal of Management Engineering*, *19*(2), 52–59. doi:10.1061/(ASCE)0742-597X(2003)19:2(52)

Kanter, R. (2004). *Confidence*. Random House.

Kapil Bharati. (n.d.). In *LinkedIn*. Retrieved 20 April 2018, from https://www.linkedin.com/in/kbhara/

Karakaya, F. (2000). Market exit and barriers to exit: Theory and practice. *Psychology and Marketing*, *17*(8), 651–668. doi:10.1002/1520-6793(200008)17:8<651::AID-MAR1>3.0.CO;2-K

Kartheeswaran, K. K. (n.d.). In *LinkedIn*. Retrieved 20 April 2018, from https://www.linkedin.com/in/kartheeswarankk/

Kaufmann, D., Kraay, A., & Mastruzzi, M. (2013). *The Worldwide Governance Indicators (WGI) project*. World Bank.

Kayo, E. K. (2002). *A estrutura de capital e o risco das empresas tangível e intangível-intensivas: uma contribuição ao estudo da valoração de empresas*. Tese (Doutorado em Administração). FEA/USP.

Kearsley, A., & Riddel, M. (2010). A further inquiry into the pollution haven hypothesis and the environmental Kuznets curve. *Ecological Economics: The Journal of the International Society for Ecological Economics*, *69*(4), 905–919. doi:10.1016/j.ecolecon.2009.11.014

Kershis, O., & Gosh, A. (2017). *Reputation of the country and business: many people - one strategy.* Reputation Capital Group blog. Retrieved from https://reputationcapital.blog/2017/10/reputacija-strany-i-biznesa-mnogo-lic-odna-strategija

Kershis, O., & Gosh, A. (2017). *World leaders in corporate reputation – 2017.* Reputation Capital Group. Retrieved from https://reputationcapital.blog/2017/04/lidery-korporativnoj-reputacii-2017-ana

Ketchen, D. Jr, & Shook, C. (1996). The application of cluster analysis in strategic management research: An analysis and critique. *Strategic Management Journal*, *17*(6), 441–458. doi:10.1002/(SICI)1097-0266(199606)17:6<441::AID-SMJ819>3.0.CO;2-G

Keupp, M., & Gassmann, O. (2009). The past and the future of international entrepreneurship: A review and suggestions for developing the field. *Journal of Management*, *35*(3), 600–633. doi:10.1177/0149206308330558

Khan, A. (2018). *A Behavioral Approach to Financial Supervision, Regulation, and Central Banking.* IMF Working Papers, WP / 18 / 178. International Monetary Fund.

Khandwalla, N. (1998). *Effective Turnaround of Sick Enterprises (Indian Experience): Text and Cases.* London: Commonwealth secretariat.

Khanna, V., & Zyla, R. (2010). *Survey Says.* IFC. Retrieved from https://www.ifc.org/wps/wcm/connect/dbfd8b004afe7d-69bcb6bdb94e6f4d75/IFC_EMI_Survey_web.pdf?MOD=AJPERES

Kiesler, S., & Cummings, J. N. (2002). What do we know about proximity and distance in work groups? A legacy of research. In *Distributed work* (Vol. 1, pp. 57–80). Boston, MA: MIT Press; doi:10.1161/HYPERTENSIONAHA.107.103572

Kim, M. H., & Adilov, N. (2012). The lesser of two evils: An empirical investigation of foreign direct investment-pollution trade-off. *Applied Economics*, *44*(20), 2597–2606. doi:10.1080/00036846.2011.566187

Kim, S., & Kim, J. (2014). Integration strategy, transformational leadership and organizational commitment in Korea's corporate split-offs. *Procedia: Social and Behavioral Sciences*, *109*, 1353–1364. doi:10.1016/j.sbspro.2013.12.637

Kim, W., & Mauborgne, R. (2005). *Blue Ocean Strategy*. Boston: Harvard Business Press.

Kinkel, S., & Montalvo, C. (2014). Setting the scene: Global value chains, re-shoring activities, global innovation networks, and their impact on global innovation platforms. In *6CP Conference* (pp. 1–28). Hertogenbosch.

Kinkel, S. (2012). Trends in production relocation and backshoring activities: Changing patterns in the course of the global economic crisis. *International Journal of Operations & Production Management*, *32*(6), 696–720. doi:10.1108/01443571211230934

Kinkel, S. (2014). Future and impact of backshoring-Some conclusions from 15 years of research on German practices. *Journal of Purchasing and Supply Management*, *20*(1), 63–65. doi:10.1016/j.pursup.2014.01.005

Kinkel, S., Lay, G., & Maloca, S. (2007). Development, motives and employment effects of manufacturing offshoring of German SMEs. *International Journal of Entrepreneurship and Small Business*, *4*(3), 256. doi:10.1504/IJESB.2007.013251

Kinkel, S., & Maloca, S. (2009). Drivers and antecedents of manufacturing offshoring and backshoring-A German perspective. *Journal of Purchasing and Supply Management*, *15*(3), 154–165. doi:10.1016/j.pursup.2009.05.007

Knight, G. A., & Cavusgil, S. T. (2004). Innovation, organizational capabilities, and the born-global firm. *Journal of International Business Studies*, *35*(2), 124–141. doi:10.1057/palgrave.jibs.8400071

Knilans, G. (2009). Mergers and acquisitions: Best practices for successful integration. *Employment Relations Today, 35*(4), 39–46. doi:10.1002/ert.20224

Kogut, B., & Chang, S. J. (1996). Platform investments and volatile exchange rates: Direct investment in the US by Japanese electronic companies. *The Review of Economics and Statistics, 78*(2), 221–231. doi:10.2307/2109924

Kohn, J. W., & McGinnis, M. A. (1997). Logistics strategy: A longitudinal study. *Journal of Business Logistics.*

Kontinen, T., & Ojala, A. (2010). The internationalisation of family businesses: A review of extant research. *Journal of Family Business Strategy, 1*(2), 97–107. doi:10.1016/j.jfbs.2010.04.001

Kotabe, M., & Ketkar, S. (2009). Exit Strategies. In M. Kotabe & K. Helsen (Eds.), *The Sage Handbook of International Marketing*. London: Sage Publications.

Kozul-Wright, R., & Fortunato, P. (2012). International trade and carbon emissions. *European Journal of Development Research, 24*(4), 509–529. doi:10.1057/ejdr.2012.15

KPMG. (2016). *U.S. executives on M&A: Full speed ahead in 2016.* Retrieved April 27, 2018 from https://assets.kpmg.com/content/dam/kpmg/pdf/.../us-jnet-2016-issue2-article1-EN.pdf

Kroll, M. M. (2008). *M&A beyond borders: Opportunities and risks.* Retrieved April 5, 2018 from https://www.insurancejournal.com/news/international/2008/04/15/89131.htm

Kuivalainen, O., Sundqvist, S., Saarenketo, S., & McNaughton, R. (2012). Internationalisation patterns of small and medium-sized enterprises. *International Marketing Review, 29*(5), 448–465. doi:10.1108/02651331211260331

Kumar, V., Stam, A., & Joachimsthaler, E. A. (1994). An Interactive Multicriteria Approach to Identifying Potential Foreign Markets. *Journal of International Marketing.*

Kuriakose, S. (2015). *Don't box up.* Retrieved 24 April 2018, from http://www.dnaindia.com/mumbai/report-don-t-box-up-2056875

Kushal Bhandari. (n.d.). In *LinkedIn.* Retrieved 20 April 2018, from https://www.linkedin.com/in/kushal-bhandari-8518b51/

Kwan, S. H., & Laderman, E. S. (1999). On the Portfolio Effects of Financial Convergence – A Review of the Literature, *Economic Review. Federal Reserve Bank of San Francisco., 2*, 18–31.

Lacity, M. C., & Willcocks, L. (2001). Global Information Technology Outsourcing: In Search of Business Advantage. New York: John Wiley & Sons, Inc.

Lacity, M. C., Khan, S., Yan, A., & Willcocks, L. P. (2010). A review of the IT outsourcing empirical literature and future research directions. *Journal of Information Technology, 25*(4), 395–433. doi:10.1057/jit.2010.21

Lacity, M., & Hirschheim, R. A. (1993). *Information Systems Outsourcing: Myths, Metaphors and Realities.* Wiley Series in Information Systems.

Laeser, A. (2014). *Managing Culture Clashes in M&A's.* Hamburg: Anchor Academic Publishing.

Lahidji, B., & Tucker, W. (2014). The Case for Re-shoring Manufacturing Jobs. XXVI Convegno annuale di Sinergie, Manifattura: quale futuro? doi:10.7433/SRECP.2014.29

Lal, D., Pitt, D. C., & Beloucif, A. (2001). Restructuring in European telecommunications: Modelling the evolving market. *European Business Review, 13*(3), 152–158. doi:10.1108/09555340110391266

Lämsä, A-M., & Hautala, T. (2005). Organisaatiokäyttäymisen perusteet. *Edita,* 189-190.

Lane, P. (2012). The European Sovereign Debt Crisis. *The Journal of Economic Perspectives*, *26*(3), 49–68. doi:10.1257/jep.26.3.49

Larsson, R., & Lubatkin, M. (2001). Achieving acculturation in mergers and acquisitions: An international case study. *Human Relations*, *54*(12), 1573–1607. doi:10.1177/00187267015412002

Lawless, M. W., & Tegarden, L. F. (1991). Test of performance similarity among strategic group members in conforming and non-conforming industry structures. *Journal of Management Studies*, *2*, 656–664.

Lazear, E. P. (1995). Corporate Culture and Diffusion of Values in Trends. In Business Organization: Do Participation and Cooperation Increase Competitiveness. Tubingen.

Leask, G. (2004). *Strategic groups & the resource based view: Natural complements enhancing our understanding of the competitive process.* Working paper, Ashton Univ., Birmingham, UK.

Leask, G., & Parker, D. (2007). Strategic groups, competitive groups and performance within the U.K. pharmaceutical industry: Improving our understanding of competitive process. *Strategic Management Journal*, *28*(7), 723–745. doi:10.1002mj.603

Leask, G., & Parnell, J. A. (2005). Integrating strategic groups and the resource based perspective: Understanding the competitive process. *European Management Journal*, *23*(4), 458–470. doi:10.1016/j.emj.2005.06.003

Lechner, C., & Gudmundsson, S. V. (2014). Entrepreneurial orientation, firm strategy and small firm performance. *International Small Business Journal*, *32*(1), 36–60. doi:10.1177/0266242612455034

Lee, H., Kelley, D., Lee, J., & Lee, S. (2012). SME Survival: The impact of internationalization, technology resources and alliances. *Journal of Small Business Management*, *50*(1), 1–19. doi:10.1111/j.1540-627X.2011.00341.x

Lee, S., Adair, W. L., & Seo, S. J. (2013). Cultural perspective taking in cross-cultural negotiation. *Group Decision and Negotiation*, *22*(3), 389–405. doi:10.100710726-011-9272-4

LeMay, S., Helms, M. M., Kimball, B., & McMahon, D. (2017). Supply chain management: The elusive concept and definition. *International Journal of Logistics Management*, *28*(4), 1425–1453. doi:10.1108/IJLM-10-2016-0232

Leonard-Barton, D. (1992). Core capabilities or core rigidities: A paradox in managing new product development. *Strategic Management Journal*, *13*(S1), 111–125. doi:10.1002mj.4250131009

Leuz, C., Lins, K. V., & Warnock, F. E. (2009). *Do Foreigners Invest Less in Poorly Governed Firms?* NBER, 2-5.

Levi-Faur, D. (1998). The Competition State as a Neomercantilist State: Understanding the restructuring of national and global telecommunications. *Journal of Socio-Economics*, *27*(6), 665–685. doi:10.1016/S1053-5357(99)80002-X

Lewin, A. Y., & Peeters, C. (2006). Offshoring Work: Business Hype or the Onset of Fundamental Transformation? *Long Range Planning*, *39*(3), 221–239. doi:10.1016/j.lrp.2006.07.009

Lewis, A., & McKone, D. (2016). *So many M&A deals fail because companies overlook this simple strategy.* Retrieved May 25, 2018 from https://hbr.org/2016/05/so-many-ma-deals-fail-because-companies-overlook-this-simple-strategy

Lewis, D. (2017). China's Global Internet Ambitions: Finding Roots in ASEAN. *Institute of Chinese Studies: Occasional Paper, 14*.

Lewis, M. (2013). *Made in the USA, Again: 3 Firms Bringing Jobs Home.* Retrieved from http://www.dailyfinance.com/2013/08/30/made-in-the-usa-again-companies-reshoring-jobs/

Lewis, M. K., & Mizen, P. D. (2000). *Monetary Economics.* Oxford University Press.

Liao, W. C. (2012). Inshoring: The geographic fragmentation of production and inequality. *Journal of Urban Economics*, *72*(1), 1–16. doi:10.1016/j.jue.2012.01.001

Li, J. (2008). Asymmetric interactions between foreign and domestic banks: Effects on market entry. *Strategic Management Journal*, *29*(8), 873–893. doi:10.1002mj.693

Lindegren, C. J., Balino, J. T., Enoch, C., Gulde, A. M., Quintyn, M., & Teo, L. (1999). *Financial Sector Crisis and Restructuring Lessons from Asia.* IMF Occasional Paper, N° 188. International Monetary Fund.

Lindqvist, M. (1997). Infant multinationals: internationalisation of small technology-based firms. In *Technology, innovation and enterprise* (pp. 303–324). Springer. doi:10.1007/978-1-349-25770-6_10

Liu, H., & Kim, H. (2018). Ecological footprint, foreign direct investment, and gross domestic production: Evidence of Belt & Road initiative countries. *Sustainability: Science Practice and Policy*, *10*(10), 3527. doi:10.3390u10103527

Li, Z. (2018). Telecommunication 4.0: Opportunities and Challenges. In *Telecommunication 4.0* (pp. 107–133). Singapore: Springer. doi:10.1007/978-981-10-6301-5_6

Lockamy, A. III, & McCormack, K. (2004). Linking SCOR planning practices to supply chain performance. *International Journal of Operations & Production Management*, *24*(12), 1192–1218. doi:10.1108/01443570410569010

Locus.sh. Overview. (n.d.). In *LinkedIn.* Retrieved 20 April 2018, from https://www.linkedin.com/company/locus-sh/?originalSubdomain=in

Lopez, S., Chambel, M., & Diaz-Valdez, A. (2018). Job insecurity, procedural justice and downsizing survivors affects. *International Journal of Human Resource Management.* doi:10.1080/09585192.2018.1482939

Love, C. K. (2000). Mergers and Acquisition: The role of HRM Success. *IRC Press-Current Issues Series,* 1-16.

Love, E., & Kraatz, M. (2009). Character, conformity or the bottom line? How and why downsizing affected corporate reputation. *Academy of Management Journal*, *52*(2), 314–335. doi:10.5465/amj.2009.37308247

Lovelock, C., & Wirtz, J. (2007). *Services Marketing: People, Technology, Strategy. Upper Sadle River.* Pearson Prentice Hall.

Lozano-Vivas, A., & Pastor, J. T. (2010). Do performance and environmental conditions act as barriers for crossborder banking in Europe? *Omega*, *38*(5), 275–282. doi:10.1016/j.omega.2009.05.002

Lubatkin, M. (1983). Mergers and the performance of the acquiring firm. *Academy of Management Review*, *8*(2), 218–225.

Lubatkin, M., Schweiger, D., & Weber, Y. (1999). Top management turnover in related M&A's: An additional test of the theory of relative standing. *Journal of Management*, *25*(1), 55–73.

Lu, J. W., & Beamish, P. W. (2002). The Internationalization and Growth of SMEs. *ASAC*, *2002*, 86–96.

Lummus, R. R., Krumwiede, D. W., & Vokurka, R. J. (2001). The relationship of logistics to supply chain management: Developing a common industry definition. *Industrial Management & Data Systems*, *101*(8), 426–432. doi:10.1108/02635570110406730

Luostarinen, R. (1979). *Internationalization of the firm: an empirical study of the internationalization of firms with small and open domestic markets with special emphasis on lateral rigidity as a behavioral characteristic in strategic decision-making* (Vol. 30). Academic Press.

Luostarinen, R. (1979). *Internationalization of the firm: an empirical study of the internationalization of firms with small and open domestic markets with special emphasis on lateral rigidity as a behavioral characteristic in strategic decision-making* (Vol. 30). Helsinki School of Economics.

Ma, H. (2000). Competitive advantage and firm performance. *Journal of Global Competitiveness*, *10*(2), 15–32. doi:10.1108/eb046396

Mahindra Partners - Our Business. (n.d.). Retrieved 20 April 2018, from http://www.mahindrapartners.com/porter.html

Makadok, R. (2001). Toward a synthesis of the resource-based and dynamic-capability views of rent creation. *Strategic Management Journal*, *22*(5), 387–401. doi:10.1002mj.158

Manikkandan, R., & Karthikeyan, P. (2016). A Study on Challenges Faced by Startups in Indian Logistics Sector. *Imperial Journal of Interdisciplinary Research, 2*(11), 312–315. Retrieved from http://www.onlinejournal.in/IJIRV2I11/060.pdf

Mani, M., & Wheeler, D. (1998). In search of pollution havens? Dirty industry in the world economy, 1960 to 1995. *Journal of Environment & Development*, *7*(3), 215–247. doi:10.1177/107049659800700302

Mariotti, S., & Piscitello, L. (1997). Divestment as fa ilure or part of a restructuring strategy: evidence from the italian MNEs. *Proceedings of the 23rd Conference of EIBA*.

Markides, C. (2000). Cross talk: Strategy and management: Constantinos Markides discusses strategic innovation, an interview by Peter Mang. *European Management Journal*, *18*(4), 357–366.

Marks, M. L., & Mirvis, P. H. (1985). Merger syndrome: Stress and uncertainty. *Mergers & Acquisitions,* 50-55.

Marks, M. L. (1997). Consulting in mergers and acquisitions. *Journal of Organizational Change Management*, *10*(3), 261–280.

Marks, M. L. (1999). Adding cultural fit to your diligence checklist. *Mergers & Acquisitions: The Dealermaker's Journal*, *34*(3), 14–24.

Marks, M. L., & Mirvis, P. H. (1992). Rebuilding after the merger: Dealing with "survival sickness.". *Organizational Dynamics*, *21*(2), 18–32. doi:10.1016/0090-2616(92)90061-Q

Marks, M. L., & Mirvis, P. H. (2001). Making merger and acquisitions work: Strategic and psychological preparation. *The Academy of Management Executive*, *15*(2), 35–47.

Markus, M. L. (1983). Power, politics, and MIS implementation. *Communications of the ACM*, *26*(6), 430–444. doi:10.1145/358141.358148

Márquez, S. L. F., & Gutiérrez, J. O. F. (2012). Strategic groups: Their influence on the performance of the Venezuelan banking industry and its relationship with the geographic coverage. *Dirección y Organización*, *47*, 41–61.

Marr, B., & Roos, G. (2005). A strategy perspective on intellectual capital. In *Perspectives on intelectual capital* (pp. 28–52). New York: Routledge. doi:10.1016/B978-0-7506-7799-8.50007-3

Martinez, J. I., & Jarillo, J. C. (1989, Fall). The evolution of research on coordination mechanisms in multinational corporations. *Journal of International Business Studies*, *20*(3), 489–514. doi:10.1057/palgrave.jibs.8490370

Martínez-Mora, C., & Merino, F. (2014). Offshoring in the Spanish footwear industry: A return journey? *Journal of Purchasing and Supply Management*, *20*(4), 225–237. doi:10.1016/j.pursup.2014.07.001

Martínez, R. (1992). *Grupos Estratégicos en el Sector de Cajas de Ahorro Espanolas*. Madrid: Caja de Ahorros de Madrid.

Martins, T. S., Cruz, J. A., Kato, H. T., Silva, W. V., & Silva, E. D. (2010). Análise de grupos estratégicos e desempenho na indústria de bancos comerciais no Brasil. *RCO – Revista de Contabilidade e Organizações – FEA–RP/USP, 4*(9), 100–125.

Marucheck, A., Pannesi, R., & Anderson, C. (1990). An Exploratory Study of the Manufacturing Strategy Process in Practice. *Journal of Operations Management, 9*(1), 101–123. doi:10.1016/0272-6963(90)90148-7

Mascarenhas, B. (1989). Strategic group dynamics. *Strategic Management Journal, 32*(2), 333–352.

Mascarenhas, B., & Aaker, D. (1989). Mobility barriers and strategic groups. *Strategic Management Journal, 10*(5), 475–485. doi:10.1002mj.4250100506

Masciandaro, D., & Quityn, M. (2013). The Evolution of Financial Supervision: The Continuing Search for the Holy Grail. In *50 Years of Money and Finance: Lessons and Challenges*. SUERF - The European Money and Finance Forum.

Masciandaro, D. (2007). Divide et Impera. Financial Supervision Unification and Central Bank Fragmentation Effect. *European Journal of Political Economy, 23*(2), 285–315. doi:10.1016/j.ejpoleco.2006.02.001

Masciandaro, D. (2008). Unification in Financial Sector Supervision: The Trade Off between Central Bank and Single Authority. *Journal of Financial Regulation and Compliance, 12*(2), 151–169. doi:10.1108/13581980410810768

Más-Ruíz, F. J. (1999). Dynamic analysis of competition in marketing: Strategic groups in Spanish banking. *International Journal of Bank Marketing, 17*(5), 233–250. doi:10.1108/02652329910292710

Más-Ruíz, F. J., Nicolau-Gonzálbez, J. L., & Ruiz-Moreno, F. (2005). Asymmetric rivalry between strategic groups: Response, speed of response and ex ante vs. ex post competitive interaction in the Spanish bank deposit market. *Strategic Management Journal, 26*(8), 713–745. doi:10.1002mj.471

Más-Ruiz, F. J., Ruiz-Conde, E., & Calderón-Martínez, A. (2018). Strategic group influence on entry mode choices in foreign markets. *International Business Review, 27*(6), 1259–1269. doi:10.1016/j.ibusrev.2018.05.007

Más-Ruíz, F. J., Ruíz, F. M., & Martínez, A. L. (2014). Asymmetric rivalry within and between strategic groups. *Strategic Management Journal, 35*(3), 419–439. doi:10.1002mj.2102

Más-Ruíz, F. J., & Ruíz-Moreno, F. (2011). Rivalry within strategic groups and consequences for performance: The firm-size effects. *Strategic Management Journal, 32*(12), 1286–1308. doi:10.1002mj.936

Más-Ruíz, F. J., & Sala, J. C. (1992). Identificación de grupos estratégicos en las cajas de ahorros españolas. *Revista Europea de Dirección e Economía de la Empresa, 1*(3), 9–28.

Más-Ruíz, F. J., & Sala, J. C. (1993). Análisis de la competencia en las cajas de ahorros: Grupos Estratégicos. *ESIC Market, 79*, 143–167.

Mata, J., & Portugal, P. (1997). The Exit Mode of Foreign Entrants: The Impact of Entry and Post-Entry Strategies. Paper delivered at the 6º Encontro de Economia Industrial, Lisbon, Portugal.

Mata, J., & Portugal, P. (2000). Closure and Divestiture by Foreign entrants: The impact of entry and post-entry strategies. *Strategic Management Journal, 21*(5), 549–562. doi:10.1002/(SICI)1097-0266(200005)21:5<549::AID-SMJ94>3.0.CO;2-F

Matthyssens, P., & Pauwels, P. (2000). Uncovering international market-exit processes: A comparative case study. *Psychology and Marketing, 17*(8), 697–719. doi:10.1002/1520-6793(200008)17:8<697::AID-MAR3>3.0.CO;2-T

Maudos, J., & Pastor, J. M. (2003). Cost and profit efficiency in the Spanish banking sector (1985–1996): A nonparametric approach. *Applied Financial Economics, 13*(1), 1–12. doi:10.1080/09603100110086087

Mayor, M. G., Davo, N. B., & Hera, M. L. (2012). Technological innovation as a determining factor on national competitiveness. *Revista de Economía Mundial*, *31*, 137–166.

McCall, K. (2017). *Customer Experiences Impact Brand Reputation | Rival IQ*. Retrieved 24 April 2018, from https://www.rivaliq.com/blog/customer-experiences-business-reputation/

McDougall, P. P., & Oviatt, B. M. (2000). International entrepreneurship: The intersection of two research paths. *Academy of Management Journal*, *43*(5), 902–906.

McFarlan, F. W., & Nolan, R. L. (1995). How to manage an IT outsourcing alliance? *Sloan Management Review*. doi:10.1016/0024-6301(95)91610-5

McGee, J., & Thomas, H. (1986). Strategic groups: Theory, research and taxonomy. *Strategic Management Journal*, *7*(2), 141–160. doi:10.1002mj.4250070204

McGrath, R. G. (1999). Falling forward: Real options reasoning and entrepreneurial failure. *Academy of Management Review*, *24*(1), 13–30. doi:10.5465/amr.1999.1580438

McIvor, R. (2010). Global Services Outsourcing. In *Global Services Outsourcing* (pp. 1–6). Cambridge, UK: Cambridge University Press; doi:10.1017/CBO9780511844911.001

Mcivor, R. (2013). Understanding the manufacturing location decision: The case for the transaction cost and capability perspectives. *The Journal of Supply Chain Management*, *49*(2), 23–26. doi:10.1111/jscm.12010

McNamara, G., Luce, R. A., & Tompson, G. H. (2002). Examining the effect of complexity in strategic group knowledge structures on firm performance. *Strategic Management Journal*, *23*(2), 153–170. doi:10.1002mj.211

Mefford, R. N. (2010). Offshoring, lean production and a sustainable global supply chain. *European Journal of International Management*, *4*(3), 303–315. doi:10.1504/EJIM.2010.033006

Mehra, A. (1996). Resource and market based determinants of performance in the U.S. banking industry. *Strategic Management Journal*, *17*(4), 307–322. doi:10.1002/(SICI)1097-0266(199604)17:4<307::AID-SMJ820>3.0.CO;2-2

Meijboom, B., & Vos, B. (1997). International manufacturing and location decisions: Balancing configuration and co-ordination aspects. *International Journal of Operations & Production Management*, *17*(8), 790–805. doi:10.1108/01443579710175565

Mellahi, K. (2003). The de-internationalization process: A case study of Marks and Spencer. In C. Wheeler, F. McDonald, & I. Greaves (Eds) Internationalization (pp. 150–162). The Academy of International Business. doi:10.1057/9780230514638_10

Menezes, R. (2017). *Delhivery losses 4 times higher than before; What's causing the money drain? | IndianOnlineSeller.com*. Retrieved 20 April 2018, from http://indianonlineseller.com/2017/01/delhivery-losses-4-times-higher-than-before-whats-causing-the-money-drain/

Menon, A., Bharadwaj, S., Adidam, P. T., & Edison, S. W. (1999). Antecedents and consequences of marketing strategy making: A model and a test. *Journal of Marketing*, *63*(April), 18–40. doi:10.1177/002224299906300202

Merriam, S. B. (1998). *Qualitative research and case study applications in education. Revised and expanded from: Case study research in education.* San Francisco, CA: Jossey-Bass Publishers.

Miles, M. B., & Huberman, A. M. (1994). *Qualitative Data Analysis: an expanded sourcebook* (2nd ed.). Academic Press.

Miller, F. (2015). Addressing culture differences in M&A. *The Wall Street Journal*. Retrieved January 12, 2018 from http://deloitte.wsj.com/cio/2015/06/18/addressing-culture-differences-in-ma/

Miller, D. (1986, November). Common syndromes of business fail. *Business Horizons*, 43–53.

Mills, J., Platts, K., & Gregory, M. (1995). A framework for the design of manufacturing strategy processes: A contingency approach. *International Journal of Operations & Production Management*, *15*(4), 17–49. doi:10.1108/01443579510083596

Miltenburg, J. (2009). Setting manufacturing strategy for a company's international manufacturing network. *International Journal of Production Research, 47*, 6179–6203.

Miltenburg, J. (2005). *Manufacturing Strategy: How to formulate and implement a winning plan* (2nd ed.). New York: Productivity Press. doi:10.4324/9781482278392

Min, S., & Mentzer, J. T. (2006). *The role of marketing in supply chain management*. Academic Press. doi:10.1016/S0019-8501(03)00032-4

Ministry of Finance. Government of India, (2016-17), Economic Survey. (n.d.). Available at: http://www.indiabudget.gov.in/survey.asp

Mirvis, P. H., & Marks, M. L. (1992). *Managing the Merger. Making It Work*. Prentice Hall.

Mishkin, F. S. (2001). Prudential Supervision: Why Is It Important and What are the Issues? In Prudential Supervision: What Works and What Doesn't. University of Chicago Press.

Mishkin, F. S. (1999). Lessons from the Asian Crisis. *Journal of International Money and Finance*, *18*(4), 709–723. doi:10.1016/S0261-5606(99)00020-0

Mishkin, F. S. (2017). *The Economics of Money, Banking and Financial Markets* (12th ed.). Pearson.

Mishra, P. (2016). *How data is making Delhivery India's first e-logistics unicorn | FactorDaily*. Retrieved 20 April 2018, from https://factordaily.com/logistics-delhivery-data-science/

Mishra, D., Gunasekaran, A., Papadopoulos, T., & Dubey, R. (n.d.). Supply chain performance measures and metrics: A bibliometric study. *Benchmarking. International Journal (Toronto, Ont.)*. doi:10.1108/BIJ-08-2017-0224

Mitchell, W. (1994). The dynamics of evolving markets: The effects of business sales and age on dissolutions and divestitures. *Administrative Science Quarterly*, *39*(4), 575–602. doi:10.2307/2393772

Mithun Srivatsa. (n.d.). In *LinkedIn*. Retrieved 24 April 2018, from https://www.linkedin.com/in/mithunsrivatsa/

Mitra, S., & Webster, S. (2008). Competition in remanufacturing and the effects of government subsidies. *International Journal of Production Economics*, *111*(2), 287–298. doi:10.1016/j.ijpe.2007.02.042

Mohanty, S. (2012). *Strategic changes in the telecommunications sector: Europe vs. India* (Master's thesis). Universidade de Aveiro.

Mohanty, S., & Moreira, A. C. (2014). Sustainability in global telecommunications. *IEEE Potentials*, *33*(5), 29–34. doi:10.1109/MPOT.2013.2292540

Mohanty, S., Moreira, A. C., & Nobre, H. (2013). Marketing Challenges for the Emerging Services of Big Data Technologies and Solutions. *International Conference on Big Data Management and Cloud Computing*.

Mohanty, S., & Routray, S. K. (2017). CE-Driven Trends in Global Communications: Strategic sectors for economic growth and development. *IEEE Consumer Electronics Magazine*, *6*(1), 61–65. doi:10.1109/MCE.2016.2614420

Mohit Tandon. (n.d.). In *LinkedIn*. Retrieved 20 April 2018, from https://www.linkedin.com/in/mohit-tandon-03b9046/

Möller, K. (2006). Role of competences in creating customer value: A value-creation logic approach. *Industrial Marketing Management, 35*(8), 913–924. doi:10.1016/j.indmarman.2006.04.005

Molloy, J. C., Chadwick, C., Ployhart, R. E., & Golden, S. J. (2011). Making Intangibles "Tangible" in Tests of Resource-Based Theory: A Multidisciplinary Construct Validation Approach. *Journal of Management, 37*(5), 1496–1518. doi:10.1177/0149206310394185

Monteiro, A., Soares, A. M., & Rua, O. L. (2017). Entrepreneurial orientation and export performance: The mediating effect of organisational resources and dynamic capabilities. *Journal of International Business and Entrepreneurship Development, 10*(1), 3–19. doi:10.1504/JIBED.2017.082749

Moody's upgrade Sovereign Credit Rating of India to Baa2 from Baa3. (n.d.). Retrieved from http://pib.nic.in/newsite/PrintRelease.aspx?relid=173609

Morgan, J. P. (2013). *Investor Opinions of Russian Companies.* Depositary Receipts Group. Retrieved from https://www.jpmorgan.com/jpmpdf/1320635528566.pdf

Morgan, N., Kaleka, A., & Katsikeas, C. S. (2004). Antecedents of Export Venture Performance : A Theoretical Model. *Journal of Marketing, 68*(1), 90–108. doi:10.1509/jmkg.68.1.90.24028

Morgan, N., Vorhies, D. W., & Schlegelmilch, B. B. (2006). Resource–performance relationships in industrial export ventures: The role of resource inimitability and substitutability. *Industrial Marketing Management, 35*(5), 621–633. doi:10.1016/j.indmarman.2005.05.018

Morgan, P. I., & Ogbonna, E. (2008). Sub-cultural dynamics in transformation: A multi-perspective study of healthcare professionals. *Human Relations, 6*(1), 39–65. doi:10.1177/0018726707085945

Morosini, P., Shane, S., & Singh, H. (1998). National cultural distance and cross border acquisition performance. *Journal of International Business Studies, 29*(1), 137–158. doi:10.1057/palgrave.jibs.8490029

Morrison, S. (2015). *Culture assessments for mergers and acquisitions.* Retrieved January 12, 2018 from https://talent-management360.com/culture-assessments-for-mergers-and-acquisitions/

Mozzini, S. (2011). *Fatores de decisão de terceirização em tecnologia da informação.* Universidade Federal do Rio Grande do Sul.

MSCI. (2017). *MSCI Russia index.* Retrieved from http://www.msci.com/

Mugurusi, G., & de Boer, L. (2014). Conceptualising the production offshoring organisation using the viable systems model (VSM). *Strategic Outsourcing, 7*(3), 275–298. doi:10.1108/SO-10-2014-0026

Mukherjee, S. (2016). *By 2020, we aim to automate all human decisions in logistics: Nishith Rastogi, Locus.sh.* Retrieved 20 April 2018, from https://techseen.com/2016/12/19/nishith-rastogi-locus-sh/

Mukherji, P., Sorescu, A., Prabhu, J. C., & Chandy, R. K. (2011). Behemoths at the gate: How incumbents take on acquisitive entrants (and why some do better than others). *Journal of Marketing, 75*(5), 53–70. doi:10.1509/jmkg.75.5.53

Murray, J. (2017). *How to Create a Business Startup Budget.* Retrieved 24 April 2018, from https://www.thebalancesmb.com/how-to-create-a-business-startup-budget-397500

Murrow, J., Johson, R., & Busenitz, L. (2004). The effects of cost and assets retrenchment on Firm Performance: The Overlooked Role of Firm's Competitive Environment. *Journal of Management, 30*(2), 198–208.

Musso, F., & Francioni, B. (2014). International strategy for SMEs: Criteria for foreign markets and entry modes selection. *Journal of Small Business and Enterprise Development, 21*(2), 301–312. doi:10.1108/JSBED-10-2013-0149

Muthoni, E. (2012). *Effects of Organization Culture on Strategy Implementation in Commercial Banks in Kenya* (Dissertation). University of Nairobi.

Nag, R., Hambrick, D., & Chen, M. (2007). What is strategic management, really? Inductive derivation of a consensus definition of the field. *Strategic Management Journal, 955*, 935–955.

Nahavandi, A., & Malekzadeh, A. (1988). Acculturation in mergers and acquisitions. *Academy of Management Review, 13*(1), 79–90. doi:10.5465/amr.1988.4306790

Nair, L. (n.d.). *'We are trying to implement total automation across the supply chain' - BPD.* Retrieved 20 April 2018, from http://www.expressbpd.com/pharma/market-pharma/we-are-trying-to-implement-total-automation-across-the-supply-chain/384209/

Nair, A., & Kotha, S. (2001). Does group membership matter? Evidence from the Japanese steel industry. *Strategic Management Journal, 22*(3), 221–235. doi:10.1002mj.154

Naisbitt, J., & Abundene, P. (1985). *Reinventing the corporation.* Megatrends.

Naitove, M. H. (2013). *"Reshoring" is not a myth.* Retrieved from http://www.ptonline.com/articles/reshoring-is-not-a-myth

Narula, R., & Driffield, N. (2012). Does FDI cause development? The ambiguity of the evidence and why it matters. *European Journal of Development Research, 24*(1), 1–7. doi:10.1057/ejdr.2011.51

NASSCOM. (2015). *Start-up India – Momentous Rise of the Indian Start-up Ecosystem.* Author.

NASSCOM-Zinnov. (2015). *Startup India Report.* Retrieved from http://www.nasscom.in/knowledge-center/publications/tech-start-ups-india-bright-future

Neumayer, E. (2001). Trade liberalisation, economic growth and the environment. *Journal of Environmental Policy and Planning, 3*(3), 245–254. doi:10.1002/jepp.73

Newbert, S. (2007). Empirical research on the resource-based view of the firm: An assessment and suggestions for future research. *Strategic Management Journal, 146*(2), 121–146. doi:10.1002mj.573

Newbert, S. (2008). Value, rareness, competitive advantage and performance: A conceptual level empirical investigation of the resource-based view of the firm. *Strategic Management Journal, 29*(1), 745–768. doi:10.1002mj.686

Newman, C., Rand, J., Talbot, T., & Tarp, F. (2015). Technology transfers, foreign investment and productivity spillovers. *European Economic Review, 76*, 168–187. doi:10.1016/j.euroecorev.2015.02.005

Newman, H. H. (1978). Strategic groups and the structure-performance relationship. *The Review of Economics and Statistics, 60*(3), 417–427. doi:10.2307/1924167

Nguyen, H., & Kleiner, B. (2003). The effective management of mergers. *Leadership and Organization Development Journal, 24*(8), 447–445. doi:10.1108/01437730310505876

Nicolau-Gonzálbez, J. L., & Ruiz-Moreno, F. (2014). Who performs a stronger response to whom? Detecting individual competitive actions and reactions. *Review of Managerial Science, 8*(3), 385–403. doi:10.100711846-013-0109-1

Nieto, M. J., & Rodríguez, A. (2011). Offshoring of RD: Looking abroad to improve innovation performance. *Journal of International Business Studies, 42*(3), 345–361. doi:10.1057/jibs.2010.59

Nikhil Shivaprasad. (n.d.). In *LinkedIn.* Retrieved 24 April 2018, from https://www.linkedin.com/in/nikhil-shivaprasad-1a2b6a8/

NinjaCart – India's largest Agri Marketing Platform. (n.d.). Retrieved 20 April 2018, from http://ninjacart.in/

Nishith Rastogi. (n.d.). In *LinkedIn.* Retrieved 20 April 2018, from https://www.linkedin.com/in/nishithrastogi/

NLMK. (n.d.). *The official position of NLMK.* Retrieved from http://maxi-group.nlmk.ru/

Noailly, J., & Ryfisch, D. (2015). Multinational firms and the internationalization of green R&D: A review of the evidence and policy implications. *Energy Policy, 83*, 218–228. doi:10.1016/j.enpol.2015.03.002

Norton, R., & Kaplan, D. (2008). *Execution Premium.* Barcelona: Deusto.

Norton, R., & Rees, J. (1979). The product cycle and the spatial decentralization of American manufacturing. *Regional Studies, 13*(2), 141–151. doi:10.1080/09595237900185121

O'Neill, H. (1986). An analysis of %Turnaround in Commercial Bank. *Journal of Management Studies, 23*(2), 165–188. doi:10.1111/j.1467-6486.1986.tb00418.x

O'Reilly, C. A., & Chatman, J. A. (1996). Culture as social control: Corporations, cults, and commitment. In B. M. Staw & L. L. Cummings (Eds.), Research in organizational behavior: An annual series of analytical essays and critical reviews (pp. 157-200). Elsevier Science/JAI Press.

O'Shannassy, T. (2008). Sustainable competitive advantage or temporary competitive advantage: Improving understanding of an important strategy construct. *Journal of Strategy and Management, 1*(2), 168–180. doi:10.1108/17554250810926357

OECD. (2009). *Top Barriers and Drivers to SME Internationalisation.* Retrieved from http://strathprints.strath.ac.uk/15845/

OECD. (2012), Sustainability in Impact Assessment: A Review of Impact Assessment System in Selected OECD Countries and the European Commission. Organisation for Economic Co-operation and Development.

OECD. (2017). *Meeting of the OECD Council at Ministerial Level.* Retrieved from https://www.oecd.org/mcm/documents/C-MIN-2017-8-EN.pdf

Okpara, J. (2009). Entrepreneurial orientation and export performance: Evidence from an emerging economy. *Int. Rev. Bus. Res. Papers, 5*(6), 195–211.

Omri, A., & Kahouli, B. (2014). Causal relationships between energy consumption, foreign direct investment and economic growth: Fresh evidence from dynamic simultaneous-equations models. *Energy Policy, 67*, 913–922. doi:10.1016/j.enpol.2013.11.067

Onkelinx, J., Manolova, T. S., & Edelman, L. F. (2016). The Consequences of De-Internationalization: Empirical Evidence from Belgium. In Global Entrepreneurship: Past, Present & Future (pp. 45-66). Emerald Group Publishing Limited. doi:10.1108/S1571-502720160000029006

Onkelinx, J., & Sleuwaegen, L. (2008). *Internationalisation of SMEs.* Leuven, Belgium: Flanders DC Studies.

Onyango, W. P. (2014). Effects of organization culture on change management: A case of the vocational training centre for the blind and deaf sikri. *European Journal of Business and Management, 6*(34), 204–214.

Osipov, I. (2011, February 9). The case of the missing billions. *Forbes.* Retrieved from http://www.forbes.ru/ekonomika-opinion/lyudi/63116-delo-o-propavshih-milliardah

Oster, S. M. (1982). Intraindustry structure & the ease of strategic change. *The Review of Economics and Statistics, 64*(3), 376–383. doi:10.2307/1925935

Otterspeer, W. (2016). *The impact of cultural differences on the performance of mergers and acquisitions* (Dissertation). Radboud University Nijmegen.

Oviatt, B. M., & McDougall, P. P. (1994). Toward a theory of international new ventures. *Journal of International Business Studies*, *25*(1), 45–64. doi:10.1057/palgrave.jibs.8490193

Pablo, A. L. (1994). Determinants of acquisition integration level - a decision- making perspective. *Academy of Management Journal*, *37*(4), 803–836.

Padmanabhan, P. (1993). The impact of European divestment announcements on shareholder wealth: Evidence from the UK. *Journal of Multinational Financial Management*, *2*(3/4), 185–208.

Palthe, J., & Kossek, E. L. (2003). Subcultures and employment modes: Translating HR strategy into practice. *Journal of Organizational Change Management*, *16*(3), 287–308. doi:10.1108/09534810310475532

Palugod, N., & Palugod, P. (2011). Global Trends in Offshoring and Outsourcing. *International Journal of Business and Social Science*, *2*(16), 13–19.

Pandit, N. (2000). Some recommendation to improved research in corporate turnaround. *M@n@gement*, *3*(2), 31-56.

Pandit, N. R. (1996). The creation of theory: A recent application of the grounded theory method. *Qualitative Report*, *2*(4), 1–15.

Pani, P. (2017). *Logistics firm Delhivery's losses increase four-fold - Business Line*. Retrieved 26 April 2018, from https://www.thehindubusinessline.com/companies/logistics-firm-delhiverys-losses-increase-fourfold/article9455476.ece

Panibratov, A., & Brown, T. (2018a). Mitigating divestment stigma: A legitimation perspective. *Kybernetes*, *47*(5), 920–936. doi:10.1108/K-12-2017-0470

Panibratov, A., & Brown, T. (2018b). Foreign divestments from Russia: An exploration of the mediating factors. *Strategic Change*, *27*(4), 359–367. doi:10.1002/jsc.2208

Papadakis, V. (2007). Growth through mergers and acquisitions: How it won't be a loser's game. *Business Strategy Series*, *8*(1), 43–50. doi:10.1108/17515630710686879

Papadopoulos, N., & Martín Martín, O. (2011). International market selection and segmentation: Perspectives and challenges. *International Marketing Review*, *28*(2), 132–149. doi:10.1108/02651331111122632

Papirian, G. (2010). BP in Russia: The conflict in TNK-BP and ways to resolve it. *Journal of Economic Policy*, *1*, 184–203.

Paradi, J. C., Zhu, H., & Edelstein, B. (2012). Identifying managerial groups in a large Canadian bank branch network with a DEA approach. *European Journal of Operational Research*, *219*(1), 178–187. doi:10.1016/j.ejor.2011.12.022

Parnell, J. A. (2011). Strategic capabilities, competitive strategy, and performance among retailers in Argentina, Peru and the United States. *Management Decision*, *49*(1), 130–155. doi:10.1108/00251741111094482

Passmore, S. W. (1985). *Strategic groups and the profitability of banking*. Research Paper nº 8501. Federal Reserve Bank of New York.

Pätäri, S., Puumalainen, K., Jantunen, A., & Sandstrüm, J. (2011). The interface of the energy and forest sectors—Potential players in the bioenergy business. *International Journal of Production Economics*, *131*(1), 322–332. doi:10.1016/j.ijpe.2009.08.015

Patch, A., & Mylander, M. (2010). *Gesundeheit! Bringing good health to you, the medical system, and society through physician, service, complementary therapies, humor and joy*. Rochester, VT: Healing Arts Press.

Patton, G. R. (1976). *A Simultaneous Equation Model of Corporate Strategy: The Case of the U.S. Brewing Industry* (Doctoral Thesis). Purdue University.

Patton, M. Q. (1990). *Qualitative evaluation and research methods* (2nd ed.). Thousand Oaks, CA: Sage Publications, Inc.

Pauwels, P., & Matthyssens, P. (1999). A strategy process perspective on export withdrawal. *Journal of International Marketing*, *7*(3), 10–37. doi:10.1177/1069031X9900700304

Pauwels, P., & Matthyssens, P. (2004). Strategic flexibility in export expansion: Growing through withdrawal. *International Marketing Review*, *21*(4/5), 496–510. doi:10.1108/02651330410547162

Pearce, J. II, & Robbins, K. (1993). Toward an Improved Theory and Research of Business Turnaround. *Journal of Management*, *19*(3), 613–636. doi:10.1177/014920639301900306

Pearson, J., Pitfield, D., & Ryley, T. (2015). Intangible resources of competitive advantage: Analysis of 49 Asian airlines across three business models. *Journal of Air Transport Management*, *47*, 179–189. doi:10.1016/j.jairtraman.2015.06.002

Pedersen, T., Devinney, T. M., Tihanyi, L., & Camuffo, A. (Eds.). (2017). *Breaking up the global value chain: opportunities and consequences*. Emerald Group Publishing. doi:10.1108/S1571-5027201730

Pedriali, M. (2004). Business Process Outsourcing: uma importante ferramenta estratégica da terceirização. Anais do Congresso Brasileiro de Custos-ABC.

Pellet, L. (2011). *M&A 2011 style*. The cultural fit factor. Retrieved March 11, 2018 from http://chiefexecutive.net/ma-2011-style-the-cultural-fit-factor/

Pennings, E., & Sleuwaegen, L. (2000, May). International relocation: Firm and industry determinants. *Economics Letters*, *67*(2), 179–186. doi:10.1016/S0165-1765(99)00269-4

Penrose, E. (1959). *The theory of the growth of the firm*. Oxford, UK: Oxford University Press.

Penrose, E. T. (1959). *The Theory of the Growth of the Firm*. New York: John Wiley.

Pereira, E. T. (2019). Economia Monetária. *Sílabo Editora. (forthcoming)*

Peteraf, M. (1993). The cornerstones of competitive advantage: A resource-based view. *Strategic Management Journal*, *14*(3), 179–191. doi:10.1002mj.4250140303

Peteraf, M., & Barney, J. (2003). Unravelling the resource-based tangle. *Managerial and Decision Economics*, *24*(1), 309–323. doi:10.1002/mde.1126

Petrick, J. F. (2004). The roles of quality, value and satisfaction in predicting cruise passengers' behavioral intentions. *Journal of Travel Research*, *42*(4), 397–407. doi:10.1177/0047287504263037

Pfeffer, J. (1981). *Power in organizations*. Pitman Pub. Retrieved from https://books.google.pt/books?id=pSe3AAAAIAAJ

Pfeffer, J. (1982). *Organizations and organization theory*. Pitman. Retrieved from https://books.google.pt/books?id=xy1VAAAAMAAJ

Pharmarack | Crunchbase. (n.d.). Retrieved 20 April 2018, from https://www.crunchbase.com/organization/pharmarack

Piercy, N., Kaleka, A., & Katsikeas, C. (1998). Sources of competitive advantage in high performing exporting companies. *Journal of World Business*, *33*(4), 378–393. doi:10.1016/S1090-9516(99)80081-9

Pinkse, J., & Kolk, A. (2012). Multinational enterprises and climate change: Exploring institutional failures and embeddedness. *Journal of International Business Studies*, *43*(3), 332–341. doi:10.1057/jibs.2011.56

Pla-Barber, J., & León-Darder, F. (2004). La internacionalización de la industria hotelera española. Formas de entrada y factores determinantes. *Papeles de Economía Española*, *102*(102), 193–206.

Platform. (2017). Conflicts in the fuel and energy complex as an indicator of the investment climate. *Key Corporate Conflicts in Russia, 1*, 25-28.

Platts, K. W., Mills, J. F., Bourne, M. C., Neely, A. D., Richards, A. H., & Gregory, M. (1998). Testing manufacturing strategy formulation processes. *International Journal of Production Economics, 56–57*, 517–523. doi:10.1016/S0925-5273(97)00134-5

Plumer, B. (2013). *Is U.S. manufacturing making a comeback - or is it just a hype?* Retrieved from http://www.washingtonpost.com/blogs/wonkblog/wp/2013/05/01/is-u-s-manufacturing-set-for-a-comeback-or-is-it-all-hype/

Podsakoff, P. M., MacKenzie, S. B., Lee, J. Y., & Podsakoff, N. P. (2003). Common method biases in behavioral research: A critical review of the literature and recommended remedies. *The Journal of Applied Psychology, 88*(5), 879–903. doi:10.1037/0021-9010.88.5.879 PMID:14516251

Porac, J. F., Thomas, H., & Baden-Fuller, C. (2011). Competitive Groups as Cognitive Communities: The Case of Scottish Knitwear Manufacturers Revisited. *Journal of Management Studies, 48*(3), 646–664. doi:10.1111/j.1467-6486.2010.00988.x

Porter, M. (1973). *Consumer behaviour, retailer power, and manufacturer strategy in consumer goods industry* (Unpublished doctoral dissertation). Universidade de Harvard.

Porter, M. E., & Linde, C. van der. (1995). Toward a new conception of the environment-competitiveness relationship. *The Journal of Economic Perspectives: A Journal of the American Economic Association, 9*(4), 97-118.

Porter, M. (1976, Winter). Please note location of nearest exit: Exit barriers and planning. *California Management Review, 19*(2), 21–33. doi:10.2307/41164693

Porter, M. (1979). The Structure within industries and companies' performance. *The Review of Economics and Statistics, 61*(1), 214–227. doi:10.2307/1924589

Porter, M. (1980). *Competitive Strategy*. New York: The Free Press.

Porter, M. (1980). The contributions of industrial organization to strategic management. *Academy of Management Review, 6*(4), 609–620.

Porter, M. (1985). *The Competitive Advantage: Creating and Sustaining Superior Performance*. Free Press.

Porter, M. E. (1986). Changing patterns of international competition. *California Management Review, XXVIII*(2), 9–40. doi:10.2307/41165182

Porter, M. E. (1994). The Role of Location in Competition. *International Journal of the Economics of Business, 1*(1), 35–40. doi:10.1080/758540496

Porter, M. E. (1998). Clusters and the new economics of competition. *Harvard Business Review*. doi:10.1042/BJ20111451 PMID:10187248

Pounder, P. (2013). A Review of Supply Chain Management and Its Main External Influential Factors in the global market economy Supply Chain. *Supply Chain Forum, 14*(3), 42–50. 10.13140/2.1.3787.3289

Prado, E. P. V. (2009). Terceirização de Serviço de TIC: Uma avaliação sob o ponto de vista do fornecedor. *Revista Eletrônica de Administração, 15*(3), 653–678.

Pradyumn Singh. (n.d.). In *LinkedIn*. Retrieved 20 April 2018, from https://www.linkedin.com/in/pradyumn/

Pranav Goel. (n.d.). In *LinkedIn*. Retrieved 20 April 2018, from https://www.linkedin.com/in/pranav-goel-5570b138/

Pratyush Jalan. (n.d.). In *LinkedIn*. Retrieved 24 April 2018, from https://www.linkedin.com/in/pratyushjalan/

Press Trust of India. (2016). *Logistics firm Rivigo to treble truck fleet to 3,000 unit, banks on driver relay system.* Retrieved 20 April 2018, from https://yourstory.com/2016/05/logistics-firm-rivigo-banks-driver-relay-system/

Press Trust of India. (2018). *Infrastructure Status: Logistics sector gets infrastructure status - The Economic Times.* Retrieved 22 April 2018, from https://economictimes.indiatimes.com/news/economy/policy/logistics-sector-gets-infrastructure-status/articleshow/61724575.cms

Procher, V. D., & Engel, D. (2018). The investment-divestment relationship: Resource shifts and intersubsidiary competition within MNEs. *International Business Review, 27*(3), 528–542. doi:10.1016/j.ibusrev.2017.10.004

Putrevu, S., & Lord, K. R. (1994). Comparative and Noncomparative Advertising : Attitudinal Effects under Cognitive and Affective Involvement Conditions. *Journal of Advertising, 23*(2), 77–90. doi:10.1080/00913367.1994.10673443

PwC Report. (2017). *Making M&A successful post-merger integration survey.* Retrieved March 12, 2018 from https://www.pwc.com/us/en/services/deals/library/ma-integration-survey.html

Quinn, J. B. (1999). Strategic Outsourcing : Leveraging Knowledge Capabilities. *MIT Sloan Management Review.* doi:10.1074/jbc.M608048200

Quinn, J. B., & Mccann, J. E. (1980). Strategies for Change : Logical Incrementalism. *Academy of Management Review.* doi:10.2307/257320

Rajan, H. C. (2010). *Double-layered acculturation in cross-border mergers &acquisitions: Examining the role of national culture.* The 11th International Conference on HRD Research and Practice Across Europe.

Rajesh Yabaji. (n.d.). In *LinkedIn.* Retrieved 20 April 2018, from https://www.linkedin.com/in/rajesh-yabaji-302347a/

Ramasubramanian, B. (n.d.). In *LinkedIn.* Retrieved 20 April 2018, from https://www.linkedin.com/in/ramasubramanian-b-2a2b99/

Ramnath, S., Javali, A., Narang, B., Mishra, P., & Routray, S. K. (2017). IoT based localization and tracking. In *IoT and Application (ICIOT), 2017 International Conference on* (pp. 1-4). IEEE. 10.1109/ICIOTA.2017.8073629

Ramsler, M. (1982). *Strategic groups and foreign market entry in global banking competition* (Unpublished doctoral dissertation). Harvard University, Cambridge, MA.

Rao, M. (2016). *Ninjacart wants to make India's farmers tech savvy.* Retrieved 20 April 2018, from https://www.techinasia.com/ninjacart-data-tech-farms

Rao, T. R., & Naidu, G. M. (1993). Are the stages of internationalization empirically supportable? *Journal of Global Marketing, 6*(1–2), 147–170. doi:10.1300/J042v06n01_08

Rasheed, H. (2002) Grow or Retrenchment Strategy Choice for Declining Entrepreneurial Firms: The Effect of Performance and Resources. *Journal of Business and Enterpreunership.*

Rawls, J. (2001). *Justice as Fairness.* Boston: Harvard.

RBC. (2004, January 20). *"Parmalat case": arrests continue.* Retrieved from http://www.rbc.ru/economics/20/01/2004/5703c0a49a7947dde8e075c8

RBC. (2008, July 16). *TNK-BP will split in two.* Retrieved from http://rbcdaily.ru/industry/562949979036495

Reed-Lajoux, A., & Elson, C. (2010). *The Art of M&A: Due Diligence: Navigating Critical Steps and Uncovering Crucial Data.* Maidenhead, UK: McGraw-Hill.

Reeves, M., & Deimler, M. (2011). *Adaptability: The New Competitive Advantage.* Boston: Harvard Business Press.

Regalado, A. (2013). *Made in America, Again*. Retrieved from http://www.technologyreview.com/news/509326/made-in-america-again/

Reger, R., & Huff, A. S. (1993). Strategic groups: A cognitive perspective. *Strategic Management Journal, 14*(2), 103–124. doi:10.1002mj.4250140203

Reiljan, E. (2004). *De-Internationalization motives: A Theoretical Framework*. Retrieved from http://www. mattimar.ee/publikatsioonid/ettevottemajandus/2004/11_Reiljan.pdf

Reiljan, E. (2004). *Reasons for de-internationalization: an analysis of Estonian manufacturing companies*. Universitas Tartuensis.

Rennie, M. W. (1993). Born Global. *The McKinsey Quarterly*, (4): 45–53.

Rennie, M. W. (1993). Born Global. *The McKinsey Quarterly, 4*, 45–53.

Research, P. (2012). *2012 Survey Results: Made in the USA Matters to Shoppers*. Academic Press.

Rhee, M., & Mehra, S. (2006). Aligning operations, marketing, and competitive strategies to enhance performance: An empirical test in the retail banking industry. *Omega, 34*(5), 505–515. doi:10.1016/j.omega.2005.01.017

Ria. (2010, August 27). *Putin said that Shareholder conflict damages Norilsk Nickel*. Retrieved from https://ria.ru/economy/20100827/269597280.html

Ribau, C. P., Moreira, A. C., & Raposo, M. (2018). SME internationalization research: mapping the state of the art. *Canadian Journal of Administrative Sciences/Revue Canadienne Des Sciences de l'Administration, 35*(2), 280–303.

Ribau, C. P., Moreira, A. C., & Raposo, M. (2018a). Categorising the internationalisation of SMEs with social network analysis. *International Journal of Entrepreneurship and Small Business, 35*(1), 57–80. doi:10.1504/IJESB.2018.094264

Ribau, C. P., Moreira, A. C., & Raposo, M. (2018b). SME internationalization research: Mapping the state of the art. *Canadian Journal of Administrative Sciences, 35*(2), 280–303. doi:10.1002/cjas.1419

Ribau, C., Moreira, A. C., & Raposo, M. (2015). Internationalisation of the firm theories: A schematic synthesis. *International Journal of Business and Globalisation, 15*(4), 528–554. doi:10.1504/IJBG.2015.072535

Ribes, A. (2001). *Modelo antropológico para humanizar las organizaciones. Papeles de ética, Economía y Dirección, n 6*. Universidad de Valencia.

Rivigo is helping the Indian truck-driving industry out of a jam - The Indian pony express. (2017). Retrieved 20 April 2018, from https://www.economist.com/news/business/21729811-its-pit-stops-and-relay-system-could-elevate-low-status-truck-drivers-rivigo-helping

Rodríguez, A. (2002). Determining factors in entry choice for international expansion. The case of the Spanish hotel industry. *Tourism Management, 23*(6), 597–607. doi:10.1016/S0261-5177(02)00024-9

Rodríguez, A., & Nieto, M. J. (2012). The internationalization of knowledge-intensive business services: The effect of collaboration and the mediating role of innovation. *Service Industries Journal, 32*(7), 1057–1075. doi:10.1080/02642069.2012.662493

Roe, M. J. (2003). *Political Determinants of Corporate Governance: Political Context, Corporate Impact* (No. 451). Economics and Business Discussion Paper Series.

Rosenbloom, A. H. (2002). Due Diligence for Global Deal Making: The Definitive Guide to Cross-Border Mergers and Acquisitions, Joint Ventures, Financings, and Strategic Alliances. Princeton: Bloomberg Press.

Roth, K. P., & Diamantopoulos, A. (2008). *Advancing the Country Image Construct* (No. 12288). Academic Press.

Rothaermel, F. T., Kotha, S., & Steensma, H. K. (2006). International market entry by U.S. internet firms: An empirical analysis of country risk, national culture, and market size. *Journal of Management*, *32*(1), 56–82. doi:10.1177/0149206305277793

Roth, K. (1995). Managing international interdependence: CEO characteristics in a resource-based framework. *Academy of Management Journal*, *38*(1), 200–231.

Rotting, D., Reus, T., & Tarba, S. Y. (2014). The Impact of Culture on Mergers and Acquisitions: A Third of a Century of Research. In C. L. Cooper & S. Finkelstein (Eds.), *Advances in Mergers and Acquisitions (Advances in Mergers and Acquisitions. Emerald Group Publishing Limited.*

Rouleau, L., & Balogun, J. (2011). Middle managers, strategic sensemaking, and discursive competence. *Journal of Management Studies*, *48*(5), 953–983. doi:10.1111/j.1467-6486.2010.00941.x

Rousseau, D. M. (2000). Assessing Organizational Culture: The case for Multiple Methods. In B. Schneider (Ed.), *Organizational climate and culture*. San Francisco: Jossey-Bass.

Routray, S. K., & Sharmila, K. P. (2016a). 4.5 G: A milestone along the road to 5G. In *Information Communication and Embedded Systems (ICICES), 2016 International Conference on* (pp. 1-6). IEEE.

Routray, S. K., & Sharmila, K. P. (2016b). Green initiatives in 5G. In *Advances in Electrical, Electronics, Information, Communication and Bio-Informatics (AEEICB), 2016 2nd International Conference on* (pp. 617-621). IEEE.

Routray, S. K., & Sharmila, K. P. (2017). Green initiatives in IoT. In *Advances in Electrical, Electronics, Information, Communication and Bio-Informatics (AEEICB), 2017 Third International Conference on* (pp. 454-457). IEEE. 10.1109/AEEICB.2017.7972353

Routray, S. K. (2014). The changing trends of optical communication. *IEEE Potentials*, *33*(1), 28–33. doi:10.1109/MPOT.2013.2279908

Roy, S. (2017). *ETFs With The Lowest Valuations*. ETF. Retrieved from http://www.etf.com/sections/features-and-news/etfs-lowest-valuations?nopaging=1

Rubashkina, Y., Galeotti, M., & Verdolini, E. (2015). Environmental regulation and competitiveness: Empirical evidence on the Porter hypothesis from European manufacturing sectors. *Energy Policy*, *83*, 288–300. doi:10.1016/j.enpol.2015.02.014

Rugman, A. M. (2010). Reconciling internalization theory and the eclectic paradigm. *Multinational Business Review*, *18*(2), 1–12. doi:10.1108/1525383X201000007

Ruíz-Moreno, F., Ladrón-de-Guevara, A., & Más-Ruíz, F. J. (2010). Development of a model of price competition in the Spanish loans market. *International Journal of Bank Marketing*, *28*(6), 479–496. doi:10.1108/02652321011077715

Rumelt, R. (2003). *What in the world is competitive advantage*. Working Paper No. 2003-105. University of Califórnia. Los Angeles: The Anderson School.

Ruzzier, M., Hisrich, R. D., & Antoncic, B. (2006). SME internationalization research: Past, present, and future. *Journal of Small Business and Enterprise Development*, *13*(4), 476–497. doi:10.1108/14626000610705705

Sahay, B. S., Gupta, J. N. D., & Mohan, R. (2006). Managing supply chains for competitiveness: The Indian scenario. *Supply Chain Management*, *11*(1), 15–24. doi:10.1108/13598540610642439

Sahay, B. S., & Mohan, R. (2003). Supply chain management practices in Indian industry. *International Journal of Physical Distribution & Logistics Management*, *33*(7), 582–606. doi:10.1108/09600030310499277

Sahay, B. S., & Mohan, R. (2006). 3PL practices: An Indian perspective. *International Journal of Physical Distribution & Logistics Management, 36*(9), 666–689. doi:10.1108/09600030610710845

Sahil Barua. (n.d.). In *LinkedIn.* Retrieved 20 April 2018, from https://www.linkedin.com/in/sahil-barua-58a4096/

Sainul, K. (2012). *Agri-tech startup FrontalRain raises Rs 5Cr from Omnivore Capital | Techcircle.* Retrieved 24 April 2018, from http://techcircle.vccircle.com/2012/10/03/agri-tech-startup-frontalrain-raises-rs-5cr-from-omnivore-capital/

Sakai, K. (2002). *Global Industrial Restructuring.* OECD Online Library.

Sakarya, S., Eckman, M., & Hyllegard, K. H. (2007). Market selection for international expansion. *International Marketing Review, 24*(2), 208–238. doi:10.1108/02651330710741820

Samiee, S., Shimp, T. A., & Sharma, S. (2005). Brand origin recognition accuracy: Its antecedents and consumers' cognitive limitations. *Journal of International Business Studies, 36*(4), 379–397. doi:10.1057/palgrave.jibs.8400145

Sangwan, S. (2016). *BlackBuck an Online Marketplace for Logistics Transactions Helping Customers Move Full Truck Loads Between Cities - BW Disrupt.* Retrieved 20 April 2018, from http://bwdisrupt.businessworld.in/article/BlackBuck-An-Online-Marketplace-for-Logistics-Transactions-Helping-Customers-Move-Full-Truck-Loads-Between-Cities/03-07-2016-99946/

Santana, M., Valle, R., & Galan, J. (2018). Sources of decline, Turnaround Strategy, and HR Strategies and Practices: The Case of Iberia Airlines. *Economic and Industrial Democracy.* doi:10.1177/0143831X18772356

Santo, R. D. (2013). *The impact of human factors on M&A performance, and the importance of careful culture and knowledge integration* (Dissertation). Alaidos University of Applied Sciences Switzerland.

Santos, F. C. (2000). Integration of human resource management and competitive priorities of manufacturing strategy. *International Journal of Operations & Production Management, 20*(5), 610–628. doi:10.1108/01443570010318986

Sapienza, H. J., Autio, E., George, G., & Zahra, S. A. (2006). A capabilities perspective on the effects internationalization on firm survival and growth. *Academy of Management Review, 31*(4), 914–933. doi:10.5465/amr.2006.22527465

Sapolsky, H. M., Crane, R. J., Neuman, W. R., & Noam, E. M. (2018). *The Telecommunications Revolution: Past, Present and Future.* London: Routledge. doi:10.4324/9781351115704

Sarasvathy, S. D. (2001). Causation and effectuation: Toward a theoretical shift from economic inevitability to entrepreneurial contingency. *Academy of Management Review, 26*(2), 243–288. doi:10.5465/amr.2001.4378020

Sarstedt, M., Ringle, C. M., Smith, D., Reams, R., & Hair, J. F. Jr. (2014). Partial least squares structural equation modeling (PLS-SEM): A useful tool for family business researchers. *Journal of Family Business Strategy, 5*(1), 105–115. doi:10.1016/j.jfbs.2014.01.002

Savelyev, S., & Bazhenov, A. (2018). Corporate disputes in arbitration courts. Statistics. *Corporate Lawyer, 10*, 4–5.

Sayem, A., Feldmann, A., & Ortega-Mier, M. (2018). Coordination in International Manufacturing: The Role of Competitive Priorities and the Focus of Globally Dispersed Facilities. *Sustainability, 10*(5), 1314. doi:10.3390u10051314

Sayem, A., Feldmann, A., & Ortega-mier, M. (2019). Investigating the influence of network-manufacturing capabilities to the phenomenon of reshoring: An insight from three case studies. *BRQ Business Research Quarterly, 22*(1), 68–82. doi:10.1016/j.brq.2018.07.001

Scannell, N. J., Safdari, C., & Newton, J. (2003). An extended application of Factor Analysis in establishing peer groups among banks in Armenia. *Journal of Academy of Business and Economics, 1*(1).

Schein, E. H. (1980). *Organizational Psychology*. Prentice-Hall.

Schein, E. H. (1985). *Organizational Culture and Leadership*. San Francisco, CA: Jossey-Boss.

Schmitt, G. (1994). *Turnaround*. Buenos Aires: Atlántida.

Schneck, O. (2007). *Cultural due diligence. Warum Unternehmensübernahmen scheitern*. Kredit & Ratingpraxis.

Schneider, B. (2006). Resiliencia: Cómo Construir Empresas en Contextos de Inestabilidad. Bogotá: Norma.

Schneider, S., & Sunyaev, A. (2016). Determinant Factors of Cloud-Sourcing Decisions: Reflecting on the IT Outsourcing Literature in the Era of Cloud Computing. *Journal of Information Technology*, *31*(1), 1–31. doi:10.1057/jit.2014.25

Schonberger, R. (1986). *World Class Manufacturing*. New York: The Free Press.

Schrauf Stefan, B. P. (2016). *Industry 4.0: How digitization makes the supply chain more efficient, agile, and customer-focused*. Retrieved 20 April 2018, from https://www.strategyand.pwc.com/reports/digitization-more-efficient

Schreyögg, J., & Von Reitzenstein, C. (2008). Strategic groups & performance differences among academic medical centers. *Health Care Management Review*, *33*(3), 225–233. doi:10.1097/01.HMR.0000324908.42143.1fPMID:18580302

Schueffel, P., Baldegger, R., & Amann, W. (2014). Behavioral patterns in born-again global firms: Towards a conceptual framework of the internationalization activities of mature SMEs. *Multinational Business Review*, *22*(4), 418–441. doi:10.1108/MBR-06-2014-0029

Schumpeter. (2013). *Manufacturing - The factory of the future*. Retrieved from http://www.economist.com/blogs/schumpeter/2013/10/manufacturing

Schutt, R. K. (2014). *Investigating the social world: The process and practice of research*. London: Sage Publications.

Schwab, K. (2016). *The Global Competitiveness Report 2016–2017*. World Economic Forum.

Schwab, K. (2017). *The Global Competitiveness Report 2017–2018*. World Economic Forum.

Schwab, K., & Sala-i-Martin, X. (2015). *World Economic Forum's Global Competitiveness Report, 2014-2015*. Academic Press.

Schwartz, J., Cremer, A., Thomasson, E., & Thomas, S. (2015, October 4). *Volkswagen to hold extraordinary board meeting on Wednesday: sources*. Thomson Reuters. Retrieved from http://www.reuters.com/article/us-volkswagen-emissions/volkswagen-to-hold-extraordinary-board-meeting-on-wednesday-sources-idUSKCN0RY0P020151004

Schweiger, D. M., Ivancevich, J. M., & Power, F. R. (1987). Executive actions for managing human resources before and after acquisition. *The Academy of Management Executive*, *1*, 127–138.

Schweizer, R., Vahlne, J.-E., & Johanson, J. (2010). Internationalization as an entrepreneurial process. *Journal of International Entrepreneurship*, *8*(4), 343–370. doi:10.100710843-010-0064-8

Scott, T., Mannion, R., Davies, H., & Marshall, M. (2003). The quantitative measurement of organizational culture in health care: A review of the available instruments. *Health Services Research*, *38*(3), 923–945. doi:10.1111/1475-6773.00154 PMID:12822919

Selden, T. M., & Song, D. (1994). Environmental quality and development: Is there a Kuznets curve for air pollution emissions? *Journal of Environmental Economics and Management*, *27*(2), 147–162. doi:10.1006/jeem.1994.1031

Senge, P. (1990). *The Fifth Discipline: The Art and Practice of the Organizational Learning*. New York: Doubleday.

Seo, M. G., & Sharon, H. N. (2005). Understanding the human side of merger and acquisition: An integrative framework. *The Journal of Applied Behavioral Science*, *41*(4), 422–443. doi:10.1177/0021886305281902

Serrano-Cinca, C. (1998). From Financial Information to Strategic Groups: A Self–organizing Neural Network Approach. *Journal of Forecasting*, *17*(5-6), 415–428. doi:10.1002/(SICI)1099-131X(1998090)17:5/6<415::AID-FOR705>3.0.CO;2-X

Shah, B. (2017). *'Disruptive Logistics Startup' Blowhorn raises Rs 25Cr, to expand to 8 cities*. Retrieved 24 April 2018, from https://yourstory.com/2017/03/logistics-startup-blowhorn-raises-rs-25cr/

Shao, Y. (2017). Does FDI affect carbon intensity? New evidence from dynamic panel analysis. *International Journal of Climate Change Strategies and Management*, *34*, 27–43.

Sharath Loganathan. (n.d.). In *LinkedIn*. Retrieved 20 April 2018, from https://www.linkedin.com/in/sharathloganathan/

Sharma, D. (2016). *Exclusive: SaaS startup Pharmarack raises pre-Series A funding | Techcircle*. Retrieved 20 April 2018, from http://techcircle.vccircle.com/2016/09/22/exclusive-saas-startup-pharmarack-raises-pre-series-a-funding/

Sharma, L., Javali, A., Nyamangoudar, R., Priya, R., Mishra, P., & Routray, S. K. (2017). An update on location based services: Current state and future prospects. In *Computing Methodologies and Communication (ICCMC), 2017 International Conference on* (pp. 220-224). IEEE.

Sharma, S. (2012). *Bangalore based agri-tech venture FrontalRain Technologies raises INR 5 Crore from Omnivore Capital*. Retrieved 24 April 2018, from https://yourstory.com/2012/10/bangalore-based-agri-tech-venture-frontalrain-technologies-raises-inr-5-crore-from-omnivore-capital/

Shi, W., Markoczy, L., & Dess, G. G. (2009). The role of middle management in the strategy process: Group affiliation, structural holes, and tertius iungens. *Journal of Management*, *35*(6), 1453–1480. doi:10.1177/0149206309346338

Shi, Y., & Gregory, M. (1998). International manufacturing networks— To develop global competitive capabilities. *Journal of Operations Management*, *16*(2-3), 195–214. doi:10.1016/S0272-6963(97)00038-7

Shrivastava, A. (2015). *Delhivery to add 3 new lines of business to boost revenue, carve distinct identity - The Economic Times*. Retrieved 20 April 2018, from https://economictimes.indiatimes.com/small-biz/startups/delhivery-to-add-3-new-lines-of-business-to-boost-revenue-carve-distinct-identity/articleshow/50304533.cms?utm_source=contentofinterest&utm_medium=text&utm_campaign=cppst

Shu, C. (2015). *Indian E-commerce Logistics Startup Delhivery Raises $85M Series D | TechCrunch*. Retrieved 20 April 2018, from https://techcrunch.com/2015/05/06/delhivery-seriesd/

Sigalas, C. (2015). Competitive advantage: The known unknown concept. *Management Decision*, *53*(9), 2004–2016. doi:10.1108/MD-05-2015-0185

Sigalas, C., & Pekka Economou, V. (2013). Revisiting the concept of competitive advantage: Problems and fallacies arising from its conceptualization. *Journal of Strategy and Management*, *6*(1), 61–80. doi:10.1108/17554251311296567

Silva, P., & Moreira, A. (2019). The evolution of corporate divestment: Towards a new research paradigm? In C. Dogru (Ed.), *Handbook of Research on Contemporary Approaches in Management and Organizational Strategy* (pp. 292–316). Hershey, PA: IGI Global.

Silva, S. C., & Silva, M. F. (2012). Failure is a stepping stone for success. *International Review on Public and Nonprofit Marketing*, *9*(2), 153–179. doi:10.100712208-012-0084-2

Simões, V. C. (1992). European Integration and the pattern of FDI inflow in Portugal. In Multinational Investment in Modern Europe (pp. 256-297). Academic Press.

Simões, V. C., Biscaya, R., & Nevado, P. (2001). Subsidiary Decision-Making Autonomy: Competences, Integration and Local Responsiveness. In Network Knowledge in International Business. Academic Press.

Simões, V., & Nevado, P. (2000). MNE centres of excellence and acquisitions: long evolutionary paths or capturing opportunities. *MESIAS Project.*

Simões, V. C. (1987). Capital extranjero y empleo: Comparación del comportamiento de las mayores empresas industriales. *Información Comercial Española*, *643*, 121–132.

Simões, V. C. (1997). *Estratégias de internacionalização das empresas portuguesas (ICEP–Inves).* Lisboa: ICEP.

Singh, A. (2016). *Exfinity leads $2.75M Series A funding round in logistics startup Locus – VCCircle.* Retrieved 20 April 2018, from https://www.vccircle.com/logistics-startup-locus-raises-275m-series-exfinity-blume-and-others/

Singh, R. K. (2011). *Developing the framework for coordination in supply chain of SMEs.* Academic Press. doi:10.1108/14637151111149456

Singh, V. (2015). *Mumbai Based The Porter, A Startup By IITians Gets INR 3 Cr. To Make Intracity Goods Movement A Breeze - Inc42 Media.* Retrieved 20 April 2018, from https://inc42.com/buzz/mumbai-based-the-porter-a-startup-by-iitians-gets-inr-3-cr-to-make-intracity-goods-movement-a-breeze/

Sinkey, Jr. (1992). *Commercial Bank Financial Management in the Financial Services Industry.* New York: Macmillan Publishing Company.

Sirkin, H. L., Zinser, M., & Hohner, D. (2011). *Made in America.* Again - Why Manufacturing Will Return to the U.S.

Siza, R. (2014). *Novas sanções europeias contra a Rússia entram em vigor esta sexta-feira.* Retrieved from http://www.publico.pt/mundo/noticia/novas-sancoes-europeias-contra-a-russia-entram-em-vigor-esta-sextafeira-1669404

Skinner, C. (1964). Management of International Production. *Harvard Business Review*, *42*(5), 125–136.

Skinner, C. (1969). Manufacturing: Missing link in Corporate Strategy. *Harvard Business Review*, *3*, 163–145.

Skoenberg, R., Collier, N., & Bowman, C. (2013). Strategy for business turnaround and recovery: A review and synthesis. *European Business Review*, *25*(3), 243–262. doi:10.1108/09555341311314799

Smith, A. (1776). *An inquiry into the wealth of nations.* London: Strahan and Cadell.

Smith, K. G., Grimm, C. M., Young, G., & Wally, S. (1997). Strategic groups and rivalrous firm behavior: Towards a reconciliation. *Strategic Management Journal*, *18*(2), 149–157. doi:10.1002/(SICI)1097-0266(199702)18:2<149::AID-SMJ854>3.0.CO;2-O

Smollan, R. K., & Sayers, J. S. (2009). Organizational culture, organizational change and emotions: A qualitative study. *Journal of Change Management*, *9*(4), 435–457. doi:10.1080/14697010903360632

Socconini, L. (2013). Lean Company. Bogotá: Norma.

Soto, J. H. (2012). *Money, Bank Credit and Economic Cycles* (3rd ed.). Ludwig Von Mises Institute.

Sousa, C. M. P., Martínez-López, F. J., & Coelho, F. (2008). The determinants of export performance: A review of the research in the literature between 1998 and 2005. *International Journal of Management Reviews*, *10*(4), 343–374. doi:10.1111/j.1468-2370.2008.00232.x

Sousa, C., & Tan, Q. (2015). Exit from a Foreign Market: Do poor performance, strategic fit, cultural distance, and international experience matter? *Journal of International Marketing*, *23*(4), 84–104. doi:10.1509/jim.15.0003

South, S. (1981). Competitive advantage: The cornerstone of strategic thinking. *The Journal of Business Strategy*, *1*(4), 15–25. doi:10.1108/eb038908

Souza, G. C. (2014). Supply chain analytics. *Business Horizons*, *57*(5), 595–605. doi:10.1016/j.bushor.2014.06.004

Spoljarik, M., & Másdottir, H. K. (2016). *Merger Failure within the Integration Process & the Contributing Extent of Human Resources* (Dissertation). School of Economics & Management, Lund University.

Srivastava, S. (2006). Logistics and supply chain practices in India. *The Journal of Business Perspective, 10*(3).

Staake, T., Thiesse, F., & Fleisch, E. (2012). Business strategies in the counterfeit market. *Journal of Business Research*, *65*(5), 658–665. doi:10.1016/j.jbusres.2011.03.008

Stagliano, D. (1994). The ITU's role in the restructuring revolution. *IEEE Communications Magazine*, *32*(11), 48–49. doi:10.1109/35.330226

Standard & Poor's. (n.d.). *S&P Global Ratings.* Retrieved from https://www.standardandpoors.com/

Stanisauskaite, V., & Kock, S. (2016). The dynamic development of international entrepreneurial networks. In The Changing Global Economy and Its Impact on International Entrepreneurship. Academic Press. doi:10.4337/9781783479849.00012

Star Capital. (2017). *Global Stock Market Valuation Ratios.* Retrieved from http://www.starcapital.de/research/stock-marketvaluation

Start Up -Definition changes. (2017). Press Information Bureau. Retrieved from http://pib.nic.in/newsite/PrintRelease.aspx?relid=162140

Start-up Report - Momentous Rise of the Indian Start-up Ecosystem | NASSCOM. (n.d.). Retrieved 19 April 2018, from http://www.nasscom.in/knowledge-center/publications/start-report-momentous-rise-indian-start-ecosystem

Startup. (2017). In *Merriam Webster's dictionary.* Retrieved from https://www.merriam-webster.com/dictionary/start-up

Stepanov, S., & Gabdrakhmanov, S. (2011). *Corporate conflicts in modern Russia and abroad.* National Board of Corporate Governance.

Stern, D. I. (2004). The rise and fall of the environmental Kuznets curve. *World Development*, *32*(8), 1419–1439. doi:10.1016/j.worlddev.2004.03.004

Stern, N., & Stern, N. H. (2015). *Why are we waiting? The logic, urgency, and promise of tackling climate change.* MIT Press.

Stouraitis, V., Harris, M., Harun, M., & Kyritsis, M. (2017). Motivators of SME initial export choice and the European Union regional effect in manufacturing. *International Journal of Entrepreneurial Behaviour & Research*, *23*(1), 35–55. doi:10.1108/IJEBR-05-2015-0120

Strauss, A., & Corbin, J. (1990). *Basics of qualitative research: Grounded theory procedures and techniques.* Sage Publications.

Strom, M., & Levy, M. (2013). Going beyond reshoring to right-shoring. PwC.

Stuart, I., McCutcheon, D., Handfield, R., McLachlin, R., & Samson, D. (2002). Effective case research in operations management: A process perspective. *Journal of Operations Management*, *20*(5), 419–433. doi:10.1016/S0272-6963(02)00022-0

Subrahmanya, M. H. B. (2017). Comparing the Entrepreneurial Ecosystems for Technology Startups in Bangalore and Hyderabad, India. *Technology Innovation Management Review*, *7*(7), 47–62. doi:10.22215/timreview/1090

Sudharshan, D., Thomas, H., & Fiegenbaum, A. (1991). Assessing mobility barriers in dynamic strategic groups analysis. *Journal of Management Studies*, *28*(5), 429–438. doi:10.1111/j.1467-6486.1991.tb00762.x

Suraj Saharan. (n.d.). In *LinkedIn*. Retrieved 20 April 2018, from https://www.linkedin.com/in/suraj-saharan-94b3383/

Surdu, I., Mellahi, K., & Glaister, K. W. (2018). Once bitten, not necessarily shy? Determinants of foreign market re-entry commitment strategies. *Journal of International Business Studies*, 1–30.

Surdu, I., Mellahi, K., Glaister, K. W., & Nardella, G. (2018). Why wait? Organizational learning, institutional quality and the speed of foreign market re-entry after initial entry and exit. *Journal of World Business*, *53*(6), 911–929. doi:10.1016/j.jwb.2018.07.008

Suri, V., & Chapman, D. (1998). Economic growth, trade and energy: Implications for the environmental Kuznets curve. *Ecological Economics: The Journal of the International Society for Ecological Economics*, *25*(2), 195–208. doi:10.1016/S0921-8009(97)00180-8

Sussking, A., Moore, O., & Katmar, K. (2018). *Organization Downsizing: How Communication Networks Connect with the Employee Performance*. Retrieved from https://scholarship.sha.cornell.edu/chrpubs/255

Suzuki, N. (1985). *The Cross National Comparison of Turnaround Strategies The USA and Japan*. Academic Management Proceeding.

Tang, M., & Thomas, H. (1992). The concept of strategic groups: Theoretical construct or analytical convenience. *Managerial and Decision Economics*, *13*(4), 323–329. doi:10.1002/mde.4090130407

Tate, W. L. (2014). Offshoring and reshoring: U.S. insights and research challenges. *Journal of Purchasing and Supply Management*, *20*(1), 66–68. doi:10.1016/j.pursup.2014.01.007

Tate, W. L., Ellram, L. M., Schoenherr, T., & Petersen, K. J. (2014). Global competitive conditions driving the manufacturing location decision. *Business Horizons*, *57*(3), 381–390. doi:10.1016/j.bushor.2013.12.010

Taylor, J. B. (1993). Discretion versus policy rules in practice. Carnegie-Rochester Conference Series on Public Policy, 39(1), 195-214. doi:10.1016/0167-2231(93)90009-L

Teece, D. (2011). Dynamic capabilities. Oxford, UK: Oxford.

Teece, D. J. (2007). Explicating dynamic capabilities : The nature and microfoundations of (sustainable) enterprise performance. *Strategic Management Journal*, *1350*(13), 1319–1350. doi:10.1002mj.640

Teece, D., Pisano, G., & Shuen, A. (1997). Dynamic capabilities and strategic management. *Strategic Management Journal*, *18*(7), 509–533. doi:10.1002/(SICI)1097-0266(199708)18:7<509::AID-SMJ882>3.0.CO;2-Z

Teerikangas, S., Very, P., & Pisano, V. (2011). Integration manager's value-capturing roles and acquisition performance. *Human Resource Management*, *50*(5), 651–683. doi:10.1002/hrm.20453

Tenbglad, S. (2018). Organizational resilience: Theoretical Framework. In S. Tenbglad & M. Oudhuis (Eds.), *The Resilience Framework: Work, Organization and Employment*. Singapore: Springer.

The Reality of IT Outsourcing in 2018 - ITChronicles. (2018). Retrieved January 5, 2019, from https://www.itchronicles.com/practices/the-reality-of-it-outsourcing-in-2018/

Thelen, S. T., Yoo, B., & Magnini, V. P. (2011). An examination of consumer sentiment toward offshored services. *Journal of the Academy of Marketing Science*, *39*(2), 270–289. doi:10.100711747-010-0192-7

Thirukumaran Nagarajan. (n.d.). In *LinkedIn*. Retrieved 20 April 2018, from https://www.linkedin.com/in/thirukumaran-nagarajan-51870242/

Thomas, H., & Carroll, Ch. (1994). Theoretical and empirical links between strategic groups, cognitive communities, and networks of interacting firms. In H. Daems & H. Thomas (Eds.), Strategic groups, strategic moves and performance (pp. 7–29). Oxford, UK: Pergamon.

Thomas, H., & Venkatraman, N. (1988). Research on Strategic Groups: Progress and Prognosis. *Journal of Management Studies*, *25*(6), 537–555. doi:10.1111/j.1467-6486.1988.tb00046.x

Tiwari, A. (2017). *We can fix unavailability of medicines: Pradyumn Singh*. Retrieved 24 April 2018, from http://www.dnaindia.com/business/interview-we-can-fix-unavailability-of-medicines-pradyumn-singh-2299529

Torneden, R. L., & Boddewyn, J. J. (1974). Foreign divestment: Too many mistakes. *The Columbia Journal of World Business*.

Tortosa-Ausina, E. (2002). Financial costs, operating costs, and specialization of Spanish banking firms as distribution dynamics. *Applied Economics*, *34*(17), 2165–2176. doi:10.1080/00036840210138400

Trąpczyński, P. (2016). De-internationalisation: A review of empirical studies and implications for international business research. *Baltic Journal of Management*, *11*(4), 350–379. doi:10.1108/BJM-08-2015-0153

Tsai, W., Su, K. H., & Chen, M. J. (2011). Seeing through the eyes of a rival: Competitor acumen based on rival-centric perceptions. *Academy of Management Journal*, *54*(4), 761–778. doi:10.5465/amj.2011.64870138

Tseng, N.-H. (2011). *Made (again) in the USA: The return of American manufacturing*. Retrieved from http://finance.fortune.cnn.com/2011/06/29/return-of-american-manufacturing/

Turcan, R. (2011). De-internationalization: A conceptualization. AIB-UK & Ireland Chapter Conference "International Business: New Challenges, New Forms, New Practices."

Turcan, R. (2013). The Philosophy of Turning Points: A Case of De-Internationalization. In T. M. Devinney, T. Pedersen, & L. Tihanyi (Eds.), Philosophy of Science and Meta-Knowledge in International Business and Management (pp. 219–235). Emerald Group Publishing Limited. doi:10.1108/S1571-5027(2013)0000026014

Turcan, R. V. (2017). *De-internationalization: Evolution of the Concept*. Paper presented at McGill International Entrepreneurship Conference: Speed, Diversity, Complexity in International Entrepreneurship, Galway, Ireland.

Turcan, R. (2003). De-internationalization and the small firm. In *Internationalization* (pp. 208–222). London: Palgrave Macmillan. doi:10.1057/9780230514638_13

Tyagi, S. (2016). *Are more startups really good for economic growth?* Retrieved 24 April 2018, from https://yourstory.com/2016/06/startups-economic-growth/

Tywoniak, S., Galvin, P., & Davies, J. (2007). New Institutional Economics' Contribution to Strategic Groups Analysis. *Managerial and Decision Economics*, *28*(3), 213–228. doi:10.1002/mde.1323

Ulset, S. (2007). Restructuring diversified telecom operators. *Telecommunications Policy*, *31*(3-4), 209–229. doi:10.1016/j.telpol.2007.01.006

UNCTAD. (2016). Annex III: G20 Guiding Principles for Global Investment Policymaking. *Investment Policy*, 1–2.

UNCTAD. (2018). *World Investment Report – 2018*. Retrieved from https://unctad.org/en/PublicationsLibrary/wir2018_en.pdf

United Nations Conference on Trade and Development. (2018). *World Investment Report 2018*. Author.

Uttam Digga. (n.d.). In *LinkedIn*. Retrieved 20 April 2018, from https://www.linkedin.com/in/uttamdigga/

Vaara, E. (2003). Post-acquisition integration as sense-making: Glimpses of ambiguity, confusion, hypocrisy, and politicization. *Journal of Management Studies*, *40*(4), 859–894. doi:10.1111/1467-6486.00363

Vachani, S. (1997). Economic Liberalization's Effect on Sources of Competitive Advantage of Different Companies: The Case Groups of India. *International Business Review*, *6*(2), 165–184. doi:10.1016/S0969-5931(96)00044-3

Vale, M. (2001). *Desinvestimento: Caracterização e Literatura de Referência*. DivesT project.

Vallerand, R. J., Deshaies, P., Cuerrier, J. P., Pelletier, L. G., & Mongeau, C. (1992). Ajzen and Fishbein's Theory of Reasoned Action as Applied to Moral Behavior: A Confirmatory Analysis. *Journal of Personality and Social Psychology*, *62*(1), 98–109. doi:10.1037/0022-3514.62.1.98

van der Meulen, R. (2018). *How Your Supply Chain Can Improve the Customer Experience - Smarter with Gartner*. Retrieved 24 April 2018, from https://www.gartner.com/smarterwithgartner/how-your-supply-chain-can-improve-the-customer-experience/

Van Knippenberg, D., Van Knippenberg, B., Monden, L., & Lima, F. (2002). Organizational identification after a merger: A social identity perspective. *British Journal of Social Psychology*, *41*(2), 233–252. doi:10.1348/014466602760060228 PMID:12133226

Vanga, P. (2017). *Try this five-step networking guide to scale and develop your startup*. Retrieved 19 April 2018, from https://yourstory.com/2017/11/five-step-networking-guide-scale-develop-startup/

Vardaan. (2015). *Mumbai-Based Logistics Startup The Porter Raises $5.5 Mn Funding Led By Sequoia Capital*. Retrieved 20 April 2018, from https://www.indianweb2.com/2015/06/25/mumbai-based-logistics-startup-the-porter-raises-5-5-mn-funding-led-by-sequoia-capital/

Vermeulen, F., & Barkema, H. (2001). Learning through acquisitions. *Academy of Management Journal*, *44*, 457–176.

Vernon, R. (1966). Product Life-Cycle Theory. *The Quarterly Journal of Economics*.

Very, P., Lubatkin, M., & Calori, R. A. (1996). Cross-national assessment of acculturative stress in recent European mergers. *International Studies of Management & Organization*, *26*(1), 59–86. doi:10.1080/00208825.1996.11656674

Vesti Finance. (2017, May 5). *The lawsuit of Rosneft crashed shares of Sistema by 25%*. Retrieved from http://www.vestifinance.ru/articles/84936

Veugelers, R. (2013). *Manufacturing Europe's future* (Vol. 21). Bruegel Blueprint Series.

Vignesh, J. (2016). *Logistics startup Locus is helping ease problems for e-comm and delivery cos, Technology News, ETtech*. Retrieved 20 April 2018, from https://tech.economictimes.indiatimes.com/news/startups/logistics-startup-locus-is-helping-ease-problems-for-e-comm-and-delivery-cos/54727998

Vikas Choudhary. (n.d.). In *LinkedIn*. Retrieved 20 April 2018, from https://www.linkedin.com/in/vikas-choudhary-8bb75315/

Vissak, T. (2006). *Re-internationalization: A conceptual framework and some evidence from Estonia*. Retrieved from https://www.impgroup.org/uploads/papers/5805.pdf

Vissak, T., & Francioni, B. (2013). Serial nonlinear internationalization in practice: A case study. *International Business Review, 22*(6), 951–962. doi:10.1016/j.ibusrev.2013.01.010

Vogel, D., & Kagan, R. A. (2004). *Dynamics of regulatory change: How globalization affects national regulatory policies.* University of California Press.

Volberda, H. (1997). Building a Flexible Organization for Fast-moving Markets. *Long Range Planning, 2*(30), 169–183. doi:10.1016/S0024-6301(96)00110-0

Voss, C., Tsikriktsis, N., & Frohlich, M. (2002). Case research in operations management. *International Journal of Operations & Production Management, 22*(2), 195–219. doi:10.1108/01443570210414329

Wadhwa, V. (2012). *The End of Chinese Manufacturing and Rebirth of U.S. Industry.* Retrieved from http://www.forbes.com/sites/singularity/2012/07/23/the-end-of-chinese-manufacturing-and-rebirth-of-u-s-industry/

Wang, C., & Ahmed, P. K. (2007). Dynamic capabilities: A review and research agenda. *International Journal of Management Reviews, 9*(1), 31–51. doi:10.1111/j.1468-2370.2007.00201.x

Wang, X. H., & Yang, B. Z. (2001). Content Articles in Economics Fixed and Sunk Costs Revisited. *Journal of Economic Education, 32*(2), 178–185. doi:10.1080/00220480109595183

Wan, W. P., Chen, H. S., & Yiu, D. W. (2015). Organizational image, identity, and international divestment: A theoretical examination. *Global Strategy Journal, 5*(3), 205–222. doi:10.1002/gsj.1101

Ward, P. T., McCreery, J. K., Ritzman, L. P., & Sharma, D. (1998). Competitive Priorities in Operations Management. *Decision Sciences, 29*(4), 1035–1046. doi:10.1111/j.1540-5915.1998.tb00886.x

Warter, I., & Warter, L. (2014). *Latest trends in mergers and acquisitions research. the new pattern of globalization.* Buletinul Instititilui Politehnic Din Iasi, Publicat de, Universitatea Tecnica, Gheorgehe Asachi din Iasi, Tomul LX (LXIV), Fasc.2 Sectia Constructii De Maasini.

Warter, I., & Warter, L. (2015). Intercultural negotiation in mergers and acquisitions. the integration of the cultural dimension into the negotiation domain. BULETINUL INSTITUTULUI POLITEHNIC DIN IASI Publicat de Universitatea Tehnică „Gheorghe Asachi" din Iasi, Tomul LXI (LXV). *Fasc., 1*, 2015.

Warter, I., & Warter, L. (2017). Cultural due diligence in M&A: Importance of soft risks factors. *Annals of Spiru Haret University. Economic Series, 2*, 38–61.

Watiez, J. (2000). Flexibilité et adaptation de l'organisation á l'environnement: La flexibilité en tanque réponse a l'asymétrie intra et intra entreprise. *Finance Contrôle Stratégie, 5*(1), 217-254.

Watts, H. (1991). Plant Closures in Urban Areas: Towards a Local Policy Response. *Urban Studies (Edinburgh, Scotland), 28*(5), 803–817. doi:10.1080/00420989120080941

Watts, H., & Stafford, H. (1986). Plant Closure and the multiplan firm: Some conceptual issues. *Progress in Human Geography, 10*(2), 206–227. doi:10.1177/030913258601000203

Weber, Y. (1996). Corporate cultural fit and performance in mergers and acquisitions. *Human Relations, 40*(9), 1181–1202. doi:10.1177/001872679604900903

Weber, Y., & Menipaz, E. (2003). Measuring cultural fit in mergers and acquisitions. *International Journal Business Performance Management, 5*(1), 54–72. doi:10.1504/IJBPM.2003.002100

Weber, Y., & Pliskin, N. (1996). The effects of information systems integration and organizational culture on a firm's effectiveness. *Information & Management, 30*(2), 81–90. doi:10.1016/0378-7206(95)00046-1

Weber, Y., & Schweiger, D. M. (1992). Top management culture conflict in mergers and acquisitions: A lesson from anthropology. *International Journal of Conflict Management, 3*(4), 1–17. doi:10.1108/eb022716

Welch, C. L., & Welch, L. S. (2009). *Re-internationalisation: Exploration and conceptualisation.* Academic Press.

Welch, C., & Welch, L. (2009). Re-internationalisation: Exploration and conceptualisation. *International Business Review, 18*(6), 567–577. doi:10.1016/j.ibusrev.2009.07.003

Welch, L., & Luostarinen, R. (1988). Internationalization: Evolution of a concept. *Journal of General Management, 14*(2), 34–55. doi:10.1177/030630708801400203

Welch, L., & Wiedersheim-Paul, F. (1980). Initial exports–a marketing failure? *Journal of Management Studies, 17*(3), 333–344. doi:10.1111/j.1467-6486.1980.tb00407.x

Wellenius, B., & Stern, P. A. (Eds.). (1994). *Implementing reforms in the telecommunications sector: Lessons from experience.* The World Bank. doi:10.1596/0-8213-2606-6

Wernerfelt, B. (1984). A resource-based view of the firm. *Strategic Management Journal, 5*(2), 171–180. doi:10.1002mj.4250050207

What role are Startups playing in the Digital Transformation of Supply Chain Management? (2017). Retrieved 19 April 2018, from https://medium.com/@KodiakRating/what-role-are-startups-playing-in-the-digital-transformation-of-supply-chain-management-d617ef2e6e4d

Whitelock, J. (2002). Theories of internationalisation and their impact on market entry. *International Marketing Review, 19*(4), 342–347. doi:10.1108/02651330210435654

Wilkinson, S., Gregory, M., & Arnold, P. (2015). Reshoring manufacturing- Time To Seize the Opportunity. EY Building a Better Working World, 1–24.

Willcocks, L. P., Lacity, M. C., & Sauer, C. (2017). *Outsourcing and offshoring business services.* Springer. doi:10.1007/978-3-319-52651-5

Williamson, O. E. (1985). *The Economic Institutions of Capitalism: Firms, Markets, Relational Contracting.* Free Press. Retrieved from https://books.google.pt/books?id=lj-6AAAAIAAJ

Williamson, O. E. (1975). *Markets and hierarchies: analysis and antitrust implications: a study in the economics of internal organization.* The Free Press. doi:10.2139srn.1496220

Williamson, O. E. (1981). The Economics of Organization: The Transaction Cost Approach. *American Journal of Sociology, 87*(3), 548–577. doi:10.1086/227496

Williamson, O. E. (1985). *The Economic Institutions of Capitalism.* New York: Free Press; doi:10.2307/2392889

Williamson, O. E. (2008). Outsourcing: Transaction cost economics and supply chain management. *The Journal of Supply Chain Management, 44*(2), 5–16. doi:10.1111/j.1745-493X.2008.00051.x

Willianson, O. E. (1975). Markets and hierarchies: analysis and antitrust implications. New York: Academic Press.

Wood, V. R., & Robertson, K. R. (1997). Strategic orientation and export success: An empirical study. *International Marketing Review, 4*(6), 424–444. doi:10.1108/02651339710192975

World Bank. (2015). *Mind, Society, and Behavioral. World Development Report.* Washington, DC: The World Bank.

World Bank. (2017). *Doing Business.* Retrieved from http://www.doingbusiness.org/

World Economic Forum. (2017). *Global Competitiveness Index.* Retrieved from https://www.weforum.org/

Wu, L.-Y., & Wang, C.-J. (2007). Transforming resources to improve performance of technology-based firms: A Taiwanese empirical study. *Journal of Engineering and Technology Management, 24*(3), 251–261. doi:10.1016/j.jengtecman.2007.05.002

WWF. (2012). *Living Planet Report 2012*. WWF.

Xiao, L., & Cao, H. (2017). Organizational Resilience: The theoretical model and Research Implication. *IYM Conference 04021*. 10.1051/itmconf/20171204021

Yadav, V., & Gupta, R. K. (2008). A paradigmatic and methodological review of research in outsourcing. *Journal of Information Technology Research, 1*(4), 41–61. doi:10.4018/jitr.2008100104

Yildirim, E. (2014). Energy use, CO2 emission and foreign direct investment: Is there any inconsistence between causal relations? *Frontiers of Energy and Power Engineering in China, 8*(3), 269–278.

Yin, R. (1994). *Case study research: Design and methods* (2nd ed.). Newbury Park, CA: Sage.

Yin, R. K. (1994). *Case Study Research: Design and Methods* (2nd ed.). Thousand Oaks, CA: Sage Publications.

Yin, R. K. (2009). *Case study research: design and methods* (4th ed.). Sage Publications.

Yoshino, M., & Rangan, S. (1995). *Strategic Alliances: An Entrepreneurial Approach to Globalization*. Boston, MA: Harvard Business School Press.

Young, S., Hamill, J., Wheeler, C., & Davis, J. R. (1989). *International market entry and development: Strategies and management*. Englewood Cliffs, NJ: Prentice-Hall.

Yu, H. (2017). Networking China: The Digital Transformation of the Chinese Economy. *The China Quarterly, University of Illinois Press, 231*, 817–819.

Zahra, S., & Garvis, D. (2000). International corporate entrepreneurship and firm performance: The moderating effect of international environmental hostility. *Journal of Business Venturing, 15*(5-6), 469–492. doi:10.1016/S0883-9026(99)00036-1

Zahra, S., & George, G. (2002). Absorptive capacity: A review, reconceptualization, and extension. *Academy of Management Review, 27*(2), 185–203. doi:10.5465/amr.2002.6587995

Zeng, S. X., Xie, X. M., & Tam, C. M. (2010). Relationship between cooperation networks and innovation performance of SMEs. *Technovation, 30*(3), 181–194. doi:10.1016/j.technovation.2009.08.003

Zhang, C., & Zhou, X. (2016). Does foreign direct investment lead to lower CO2 emissions? Evidence from a regional analysis in China. *Renewable & Sustainable Energy Reviews, 58*, 943–951. doi:10.1016/j.rser.2015.12.226

Zhulz, A., & Johann, S. (2018). Downsizing and the Fragility of Corporate Reputation: An Analysis of Impact on contextual factors. *Scandinavian Journal of Management, 34*(1), 40–50. doi:10.1016/j.scaman.2017.11.004

Zlobin, A. (2017). The second scandal in two years: Volkswagen, BMW and Daimler were accused of cartel collusion. *Forbes*. Retrieved from http://www.forbes.ru/kompanii/348439-vtoroy-skandal-za-dva-goda-volkswagen-bmw-i-daimler-obvinili-v-kartelnom-sgovore

Zollo, M., & Meier, D. (2008). What is M&A performance? *The Academy of Management Perspectives, 22*(3), 55–77. doi:10.5465/amp.2008.34587995

Zorzini, M., Stevenson, M., & Hendry, L. (2011). *A contingency-based approach to internationalization: a multi-case study analysis in Argentina.* LUMS Working Papers.

Zugravu-Soilita, N. (2015). How does foreign direct investment affect pollution? Toward a better understanding of the direct and conditional effects. *Environmental and Resource Economics*, *66*(2), 293–338. doi:10.100710640-015-9950-9

Zúñiga-Vicente, J. Á., Fuente-Sabaté, J. M., & González, I. S. (2004a). Dynamics of the strategic group membership-performance linkage in rapidly changing environments. *Journal of Business Research*, *57*(12), 1378–1390. doi:10.1016/S0148-2963(03)00071-7

Zúñiga-Vicente, J. Á., Fuente-Sabaté, J. M., & Rodríguez-Puerta, J. (2004b). A study of industry evolution in the face of major environmental disturbances: Group and firm strategic behaviour of Spanish banks, 1983–1997. *British Journal of Management*, *15*(3), 219–245. doi:10.1111/j.1467-8551.2004.00416.x

Zyglidopoulos, S. (2005). The impact of downsizing on corporate reputation. *British Journal of Management*, *16*(3), 253–259. doi:10.1111/j.1467-8551.2005.00460.x

About the Contributors

Antonio C. Moreira obtained a Bachelor's degree in Electrical Engineering and a Master's degree in Management, both from the University of Porto, Portugal. He received his PhD in Management from UMIST-University of Manchester Institute of Science and Technology, England. He has a solid international background in industry leveraged working for a multinational company in Germany as well as in Portugal. He has also been involved in consultancy projects and in research activities. He is Associate Professor at the Department of Economics, Management, Industrial Engineering, and Tourism, University of Aveiro, Portugal, where he headed the Bachelor and Master Degrees in Management for five years. He is member of GOVCOPP research unit.

Pedro Silva obtained a Bachelor's degree and a Master's degree in Management from the University of Aveiro, Portugal. He received his PhD in Marketing and Strategy also from the University of Aveiro, Portugal. He has working experience in a multinational company and has been involved in several consultancy projects and in research activities.

* * *

João Bento is an Assistant Professor at the Department of Economics, Management, Industrial Engineering and Tourism (DEGEIT) in the University of Aveiro, Portugal. He has a bachelor degree from Université Catholique de Louvain, Belgium, and a master's degree from Universidade de Coimbra, Portugal. He received a Ph.D. in Economics from the University of Reading, United Kingdom. He is a member of the Competitiveness, Innovation and Sustainability Research Group in the Research Unit on Governance, Competitiveness and Public Policy (GOVCOPP). His research interests are in the empirical analysis of the relationship between foreign direct investment and sustainability. He has been an invited lecturer at Green Energy Management Summer School (GEM) University of Milano-Bicocca, Italy.

Som Sekhar Bhattacharyya is a Strategic Management faculty at National Institute of Industrial Engineering (NITIE), Mumbai, India. He has Bachelor of Technology (B.Tech) in Mining Engineering from Indian Institute of Technology , ISM, Dhanbad, India. He has done his Fellow Programme in Management (FPM) in the functional specialization of Strategic Management from Management Development Institute (MDI) Gurgaon, India. He has research interest in 'Strategic Management', 'Strategic leadership', 'Strategic Corporate Social Responsibility' and 'Qualitative business research'. He has published many research papers and teaching cases in international journals of repute. For his research he has been awarded with Emerald Literati Awards for Excellence: Outstanding Paper Award – 2011 and

Emerald Literati Awards for Excellence: Highly Commended Paper Award – 2014. For his teaching, he has received various awards like NITIE best teacher award 2014 and Business School Award for Best Professor in Strategic Management in India in 2014.

Arnaldo Coelho holds a Master degree from the Institute of Business Administration at the University of Poitiers and a PhD in Business Administration from the University of Barcelona. He is a professor at the Faculty of Economics of the University of Coimbra since 1987 and coordinates different courses in the Business Management area. He is a Researcher at CEBER - Center for Business and Economics Research. He is a researcher in the Marketing field, with emphasis on Relationship Marketing and Branding, Corporate Social Responsibility and Human Resources Management and has publications in several international indexed journals such as the Journal of Business Research, the European Journal of Marketing, the International Journal of Human Resources Management, among others. He acts, as well, as a business consultant in the fields of marketing and strategy.

Andreas Feldmann is an Assistant Professor at the Royal Institute of Technology in Stockholm, doing research in global operations, supply chain management and sustainable supply chains. He has been published in journals such as Production Planning and Control, International Journal of Production Economics, International Journal of Operations and Production Management and Journal of Cleaner Production.

Hugo Rafael Oliveira Gadim was born in Aveiro, Portugal. He has a bachelor's degree in Commerce at the School of Technology and Management of Águeda, University of Aveiro, Portugal. In 2016 he finished his Master's Degree in Management - specialization in Marketing and International Business, also at the University of Aveiro where he studied De-internationalization of SMEs. He is professionally involved in the area of Logistics, where he works for a company focused on the development, manufacturing and commercialization of the different exhaust system components (manifolds, catalytic converters, diesel particulate filters and silencers) for carmakers.

Asli Goksoy is a professor of Management at American University of Bulgaria. She holds an MBA from Pace University and a Ph.D. degree in Organizational Behavior from Marmara University. Her current areas of interest are organizational change, resistance to change, merger and acquisition management and corporate culture.

Mikhail Kuznetsov is Director, System Transformation Center, Moscow State University. More than 15 years of experience in investment and management consulting, working in one of the largest financial development institutions - IFC, World Bank Group. More than 10 years of experience in the Board of Directors in huge and middle-sized companies in finance, energetic, transport, food sectors. Founder of the National Association of Corporate Directors (more than 400 participants, 25 cities). Member of the Expert Committee on Corporate Governance under Federal Agency for State Property Management, Central Bank of the Russian Federation. Phd, MBA lector at RANEPA (Russian Presidential Academy of National Economy and Public Administration under the President of the Russian Federation), and MSU (Lomonosov Moscow State University), author of 3 books and more than 30 articles about corporate governance and strategic management.

Orlando Manuel Lima Rua is an Adjunct Professor of Management at the Porto School of Accounting and Administration (ISCAP) of the Polytechnic of Porto (Portugal). Researcher at Center for Organisational and Social Studies of Polytechnic of Porto (CEOS.PP), Management Applied Research Unit (UNIAG/APNOR) and Research Center in Business Sciences (NECE/UBI).

Konstantin Lukoyanov, Ph. D. Attorney-at-Law, Partner at Chernyshov, Lukoyanov & Partners Law Offices. Dr Lukoyanov educated from St. Petersburg State University, Faculty of Law (PhD) and Cambridge University, Faculty of Law (LLM). Konstantin Lukoyanov is a professional director (member of Association of Independent Directors), attorney-at-law (member of StPetersburg Bar, ABA, IBA). Dr Lukoyanov is one of the leading experts in corporate disputes, arbitration and litigation practice in Russia with 20 years of extensive experience in that field, in particular in Oil&Gas and Telecom sectors. He was the long-standing head of the litigation team at Egorov, Puginsky, Afanasiev & Partners (EPAM) and for over three years - head of Dispute Resolution practice at Linklaters Russia and CIS.

Pedro Macedo was a statistician in EDP Gas Distribution, a natural gas supply company from EDP Group, and is currently an assistant professor in Department of Mathematics at University of Aveiro and a member of CIDMA – Center for Research & Development in Mathematics and Applications.

Paolo Maranzano is a PhD student in Statistics at University of Milano-Bicocca (DISMEQ - Department of Statistics and Quantitative Methods), Italy. He has a bachelor degree in Economics at University of Bergamo, Italy. He also has a master degree in Statistics & Economics from University of Milano-Bicocca, Italy. His research interests are environmental economics and time series analysis. He has been a visiting researcher at the University of Aveiro, Portugal.

Raquel Meneses holds a Ph.D. in Business Science from the University of Porto, where she teaches in the area of strategy and international marketing. She researches in the same area, attending international conferences and having several book chapters and papers published in scientific peer reviews journals.

Adriana Miranda is a purchase manager at Ramada Steel. She holds a Master´s degree in Management.

Sasmita Mohanty is a PhD scholar in the Department of Economics, Mnagement, and Industrial Engineering of University of Aveiro, Aveiro, Portugal. She earned her B.A. and M.A. degrees in economics from Ravenshaw University, Cuttack, India, in 2006, and 2008, respectively. She earned her master's degree in management from the University of Aveiro, Portugal, in 2012. Her areas of interest are: strategic management, telecommunications management, economics and marketing.

Jorge H. Mota is a Ph.D. student in Management, specialization in Finance at the School of Economics and Management of the University of Porto, Portugal; was an exchange visiting Phd student / research fellow at the University of Oklahoma Price College of Business, Oklahoma, USA; holds a MSc degree in Accounting and Auditing from the University of Aveiro, Portugal; and holds an undergraduate degree in Economics from the Lusíada University of Porto. Jorge is an Assistant Professor of Management – Finance at the Department of Economics, Management, Industrial Engineering, and Tourism (DEGEIT), University of Aveiro, Portugal, where he holds teaching positions at undergraduate and MSc levels. Research interests include corporate finance and management control.

Miguel Ortega-Mier is a Professor at Universidad Politecnica de Madrid (UPM), Spain. His research interests are in the areas of operations research, operations management, and simulation. He has publications in several journals, such as Advances in Production Management Systems, Production and Operations Management Society, International Journal of Manufacturing Technology and Management, International Journal of Heavy Vehicle Design, Managing Complexity, are the few.

Maria Nikishova is Head of Corporate Governance practice in the Center for Corporate Development "TopCompetence". Head of the annual research "The National Corporate Governance Index" in Russia. Author and editor in chief of the media on corporate governance Corpshark.ru. Postgraduate student of the Financial University under the Government of the Russian Federation. Ms. Nikishova specializes in corporate governance, digital business transformation and IT Governance.

Elisabeth T. Pereira is Assistant Professor at the Department of Economics, Management, Industrial Engineering and Tourism, at the University of Aveiro (Portugal). She is full researcher in the Research Unit GOVCOPP. She holds a MSc on Economics (University of Coimbra) and a PhD in Business and Economics Competitiveness (University of Aveiro). She teaches at the undergraduate and graduate levels, namely Monetary Economics, Macroeconomics, Economic Applied Studies, and Economics of SMEs. She has been visiting professor in some European Universities. She has been supervisor of national and international M.Sc., PhD and PostDoc PhD theses. She is author of several dozen articles published in international scientific journals indexed, books, book chapters and institutional reports. She is also reviewer of national and international journals. She is involved in several national and international projects, as coordinator and researcher. She has been involved as coordinator and lecturer in several international summer schools, as well as chair and member of scientific committees on international conferences.

Hélder Pinho holds an MSc in Economics and Business Administration from the University of Porto. He has been attending some international conferences, presenting his research works.

José Carlos Martins Rodrigues Pinho (Ph.D., Warwick University) is an Associate Professor of Marketing at School of Economics and Management, University of Minho, Gualtar Campus, 4710-057, Braga, Portugal (e-mail: jcpinho@eeg.uminho.pt); José Carlos Pinho counts a vast number of publications in peer reviewed journals including Journal of World Business, International Marketing Review, European Journal of Marketing, International Journal of Tourism Research, Journal of International Entrepreneurship, European Business Review, among others. He has also been actively involved in a number of International Projects, published in a number of International Conference Proceedings, served as reviewer for a number of international conferences and journals and has served as Chair, Track Chair and Co-Chair for International Conferences.

Daniel Ferreira Polónia is an Invited Assistant Professor at the Department of Economy, Management, Industrial Engineering and Tourism of the Universidade de Aveiro in Portugal. He is also a researcher with the Governance, Competitiveness and Public Policies (GovCoPP) Research Unit of the same University. He holds a PhD in Electrical Engineering and a bachelor's degree in Electronic Engineering. His research interests are in the area of healthcare management and innovation.

Albérico Manuel Fernandes Travassos Rosário is a PhD marketing and Strategy, University of Aveiro, Department of Economics, Management, Industrial Engineering, and Tourism University of Aveiro, Portugal. He is member of GOVCOPP research unit.

Ahmed Sayem is a Professor in the Industrial and Production Engineering Department. He holds a Master of Science Degree in Management, Economics and Industrial Engineering from Politecnico di Milano, Italy. He obtained the PhD in Industrial Management with "excellent" grade. As a researcher, Sayem read his PhD at Universidad Politécnica de Madrid, Spain, under the Program "European Doctorate in Industrial Management (EDIM)". As part of his PhD program he has attended two well-known universities –Universidad Politécnica de Madrid, Spain and KTH- Royal Institute of Technology, Stockholm, Sweden. Ahmed Sayem has worked with management of international manufacturing and the phenomenon of reshoring. In doing so, he has collaborated with numerous multinational companies originated from Sweden and Spain. In particular, his interests concern three key activities in this context: management of resources, knowledge development, and qualitative research. Articles documenting his research in aforementioned areas have been published in journal, such as BRQ Business Research Quarterly, Sustainability, etc. His current lines of inquire concerns the coordination structures of international manufacturing networks, as well as sustainability issues of supply chain management. Furthermore, Dr. Sayem engages in research concerning productivity and market dynamics.

Susana Silva holds a PhD in Marketing from the University College de Dublin – Ireland. She is a professor at Católica Porto Business School, where she is also research member of the Research Centre in Management and Economics. She is the author of several books and book chapters published in Portugal, UK, USA and Brazil. She has been presenting papers in international conferences in Marketing and International Business fields. She publishes in international journals in the same fields. She has been visiting professor at several universities in Europe, Brazil and China. She is currently visiting researcher at Wrocław University of Economics, Poland.

Ana Maria Soares is an Assistant Professor of Marketing and Strategic Management at the School of Economics and Management, University of Minho, Portugal. She conducts research in international marketing and strategy and international consumer behaviour. Her papers have been published in Journal of Business Research, International Journal of Consumer Studies, Studies in Higher Education, The International Journal of Cross-Cultural Management and Journal of Research in Interactive Marketing among others.

Valeria Solovyova specializes in research projects in corporate governance and sustainable development, analysis of companies. Ms Solovyova has experience of participation in projects to assess the performance of the board of directors; to evaluate the performance of the State Development Institutes, companies with state participation; Russian and international benchmarking projects. Analyst of annual research "The National Corporate Governance Index" in Russia.

Miguel Torres is Senior Research Fellow at the Leeds University Business School, University of Leeds, UK. Marie Skłodowska-Curie Research Fellow between 2015 and 2017. In parallel to his academic career, since 2015 he was appointed as a licensed insolvency practitioner authorised to take insolvency appointments in Portugal and in 2017, and also appointed as Tax Arbitrator in the CAAD for the resolution of disputes, particularly in the context of international commercial transactions. The focus of his research is International Business Policy (IBP), building upon my earlier PhD research on the mechanisms through which public incentives interact with firms behaviour, and the modelling of the effects of internationalisation promotion incentives.

Index

www.ingramcontent.com/pod-product-compliance
Lightning Source LLC
La Vergne TN
LVHW062113300926
849161LV00010B/2452

* 9 7 8 1 5 2 2 5 8 9 0 6 8 *